IMPORTANT

HERE IS YOUR REGISTRATION CODE TO ACCESS MCGRA
PREMIUM CONTENT AND MCGRAW-HILL ONLINE RESOUR

For key premium online resources you need THIS CODE to gain access. Once the code is entered, you will be able to use the web resources for the length of your course.

D0902958

Access is provided only if you have purchased a new book.

If the registration code is missing from this book, the registration screen on our website, and within your WebCT or Blackboard course will tell you how to obtain your new code. Your registration code can be used only once to establish access. It is not transferable.

To gain access to these online resources

1. USE your web browser to go to: **www.mhhe.com/rickabaugh**

2. CLICK on "First Time User"

3. ENTER the Registration Code printed on the tear-off bookmark on the right

4. After you have entered your registration code, click on "Register"

5. FOLLOW the instructions to setup your personal UserID and Password

6. WRITE your UserID and Password down for future reference. Keep it in a safe place.

If your course is using WebCT or Blackboard, you'll be able to use this code to access the McGraw-Hill content within your instructor's online course.

To gain access to the McGraw-Hill content in your instructor's WebCT or Blackboard course simply log into the course with the user ID and Password provided by your instructor. Enter the registration code exactly as it appears to the right when prompted by the system. You will only need to use this code the first time you click on McGraw-Hill content.

These instructions are specifically for student access. Instructors are not required to register via the above instructions.

The McGraw-Hill Companies

Mc Graw Hill **Higher Education**

Thank you, and welcome to your McGraw-Hill Online Resources.

978-0-07-319719-7
0-07-319719-X t/a
Rickabaugh: Sex and Gender:
Student Projects and Exercises, 1/e

REGISTRATION CODE
REGISTRATION CODE

Registration Codes N

The McGraw-Hill Companies

Mc Graw Hill **Higher Education**

TRANSFORMATIONS

Women, Gender, and Psychology

FIRST EDITION

Mary Crawford

University of Connecticut

Boston   Burr Ridge, IL   Dubuque, IA   Madison, WI   New York   San Francisco   St. Louis
Bangkok   Bogotá   Caracas   Kuala Lumpur   Lisbon   London   Madrid   Mexico City
Milan   Montreal   New Delhi   Santiago   Seoul   Singapore   Sydney   Taipei   Toronto

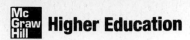

TRANSFORMATIONS: WOMEN, GENDER, AND PSYCHOLOGY
Published by McGraw-Hill, a business unit of The McGraw-Hill Companies, Inc.,
1221 Avenue of the Americas, New York, NY, 10020. Copyright © 2006 by
The McGraw-Hill Companies, Inc. All rights reserved. No part of this publication may
be reproduced or distributed in any form or by any means, or stored in a database or
retrieval system, without the prior written consent of The McGraw-Hill Companies, Inc.,
including, but not limited to, in any network or other electronic storage or transmission,
or broadcast for distance learning.
Some ancillaries, including electronic and print components, may not be available to
customers outside the United States.

This book is printed on acid-free paper.

    4 5 6 7 8 9 0 FGR/FGR 0 9 8

ISBN-13: 978-0-07-292077-2
ISBN-10: 0-07-292077-7

Editor in Chief: *Emily Barrosse*
Executive Editor: *Michael J. Sugarman*
Marketing Manager: *Melissa Caughlin*
Developmental Editor: *Kirsten Stoller*
Managing Editor: *Jean Dal Porto*
Project Manager: *Ruth Smith*
Text and Cover Designer: *Marianna Kinigakis*
Cover Credit: *A Love Song © 1985 by Sara Steele, All Rights Reserved.*
Art Editor: *Katherine McNab*
Production Supervisor: *Tandra Jorgensen*
Media Project Manager: *Alexander Rohrs*
Photo Research Coodinator: *Natalia C. Peschiera*
Photo Researcher: *Christine Pullo*
Senior Media Producer: *Stephanie George*
Permissions Editor: *Marty Granahan*
Composition: *10/12 Janson by Cenveo*
Printing: *Black, 45 #New Era Matte, Quebecor World Fairfield*

Credits: The credits section for this book begins on page C-1 and is considered an extension of the
copyright page.

Library of Congress Cataloging-in-Publication Data

Crawford, Mary (Mary E.)
    Transformations : women, gender, and psychology / Mary Crawford.— 1st ed.
      p. cm.
    Includes bibliographical references and index.
    ISBN 0-07-292077-7 (softcover : alk. paper)
    1. Women—Psychology. 2. Gender identity. 3. Feminist psychology. 4. Sex role. 5. Sex
differences (Psychology) 6. Social change. I. Title.
  HQ1206.C733 2006
  155.3'33—dc22

                          2004063175

The Internet addresses listed in the text were accurate at the time of publication. The inclusion of a Web site
does not indicate an endorsement by the authors of McGraw-Hill, and McGraw-Hill does not guarantee the
accuracy of the information presented at these sites.
www.mhhe.com

To Roger
Dhanyabaad

About the Author

∾

MARY CRAWFORD is professor of psychology and former director of the Women's Studies Program at the University of Connecticut. She has taught the psychology of women and gender for 30 years. As a faculty member at West Chester University of Pennsylvania, she earned the Trustees' Award for Lifetime Achievement for her research and teaching on women and gender. She has also held the Jane W. Irwin Chair in Women's Studies at Hamilton College, served as distinguished visiting teacher/scholar at the College of New Jersey, and directed the graduate program in women's studies at the University of South Carolina. Professor Crawford received her PhD in experimental psychology from the University of Delaware. She is a consulting editor for *Sex Roles*, an associate editor of *Feminism and Psychology*, and a Fellow of both the American Psychological Association and the American Psychological Society. Mary Crawford has spoken and written about women's issues for audiences as diverse as the British Psychological Society, the Swedish Research Council, and the Oprah Winfrey Show. Books she has authored or edited include *Gender and Thought: Psychological Perspectives* (1989); *Talking Difference: On Gender and Language* (1995); *Gender Differences in Human Cognition* (1997); *Coming into Her Own: Educational Success in Girls and Women* (1999); *Innovative Methods for Feminist Psychological Research* (1999); *Practicing Perfection: Memory and Piano Performance* (2002) and, with Rhoda Unger, a widely used text and reader, *Women and Gender: A Feminist Psychology* (4th ed., 2004) and *In Our Own Words* (2nd ed., 2001). For the academic year 2004–2005, Dr. Crawford was awarded a Fulbright Senior Scholar research grant for work on reducing trafficking of girls and young women in Nepal.

Contents

❧

Chapter 10   Mothering   311

Preface

∾

Transformations. Do you find this title intriguing? I chose it because I hoped to explore many kinds of transformations in this book.

First, and most obvious, are the developmental transformations of a woman's life. Each of us progresses in turn from gender-innocent infant to gender-socialized child, from girl to woman, and from young woman to old woman. The process of developing a gender identity and a sexual identity can be transformative. Think, too, of the transformation from sexual inexperience to sexual agency, and the shift in identity that happens as one becomes a working adult or retires from paid work. Motherhood is a profound transformation of self, roles, and behavior. And too often, girls and women are forced to transform themselves from victim of violence to survivor. Being a woman is not a static condition, but rather a dynamic, ever-shifting social construction.

A second meaning of my title reflects the transformation that made this book, and others like it, possible. Only a few short years ago, women were routinely omitted from psychology textbooks, research on women was scarce, much of the existing research was negatively biased, and women themselves encountered resistance to becoming psychologists and engaging in research and practice. Today, the psychology of women and gender is a flourishing part of psychological research and practice. The new perspectives of feminist psychology have changed research, practice, and theory in every area of psychology. Division 35 is one of the largest of APA. Women now earn the majority of professional degrees in psychology. And over half of all psychology departments offer undergraduate courses in women and gender. The change, which came about after a great deal of activism and struggle, has been astonishingly successful. When I taught my first course on the psychology of women in 1975, I had the "choice" of only one textbook, a psychoanalytically oriented volume that focused on women's intrapsychic conflicts and deficiencies. Today, there are so many that one might even ask, Why another new book on the psychology of women and gender?

I believe there are good reasons for a fresh approach. This is not my first textbook on the topic. *Women and Gender: A Feminist Psychology* (coauthored with Rhoda Unger, and also published by McGraw-Hill) is now in its fourth edition and continues to earn positive responses from teachers and students. I've been teaching undergraduate and graduate courses on women and gender for 30 years now.

Although I didn't consciously realize it when I chose the title, now that the book is finished, I think that it represents another kind of transformation: the gradual change in my thinking over time about how best to integrate this now-huge field of study for instructors and make it accessible for students. The success of *Women and Gender* has been very gratifying, but it also meant that Rhoda and I were invested in keeping a format that worked very well for many users. At the same time, my own conceptualization of the field was changing, and I wanted to try a new approach. The result of this disciplinary (and personal) transformation is this book, a new synthesis of the psychology of women and gender.

Gender: A Social System Linked to Status and Power

Transformations presents a broad, comprehensive theoretical framework for understanding how the lives of all people, but particularly the lives of girls and women, are shaped by gender. Rather than conceiving gender as a collection of individual traits or attributes, this book presents gender as a *social system* that is used to categorize people and is linked to power and status.

The gender system is analyzed throughout the book at three levels: sociocultural, interpersonal, and individual. Because conceptualizing gender as a social system is important from the start, the second chapter of the book is devoted to gender, status, and power. This chapter explains the gender system and how it works at each of the three levels, and demonstrates how the levels are linked by analyzing violence against girls and women.

As Chapter 2 explains, at the sociocultural level men have more institutional and public power; and, therefore, political, religious, and normative power is concentrated largely in the hands of men. Of course, all men are not equally privileged, nor are all women equally disadvantaged. The gender system interacts with systems based on race/ethnicity, social class, heterosexuality, and other dimensions of difference. An understanding of the gender system at this level provides a context for the other levels and reduces the tendency to think of gender as mere sex differences.

At the second level of the gender system, gender is created, performed, and perpetuated in social interaction—what social constructionists call *doing gender*. I explore this topic not just as the social display of differences, but also as the social display of status and power. Gender-linked behaviors such as interrupting, smiling, and the effects of tokenism all reflect and perpetuate women's subordinate status.

The gender system operates at the individual level as women internalize their subordinate social status. Well-documented psychological phenomena such as denial of personal discrimination, lack of entitlement, and gendered psychological disorders such as depression can be related to internalized subordination. In summary, by conceptualizing gender as a social system operating at three levels, my goal is to provide students with an analytical tool for understanding how gender affects all our lives in both public and private domains.

I have also initiated other conceptual and organizational innovations in *Transformations:*

The Issue of Violence toward Girls and Women Is Incorporated into Every Chapter

For decades, I have been teaching the topic of violence as a separate unit within my courses. Increasingly, I have found this unsatisfactory. Although it may have been a viable teaching strategy 20 years ago, today we know much more about the different kinds of violence against girls and women. Gender violence is related to patriarchy, and I introduce this connection very early in the text (Chapter 2). However, the specific types of violence are very different. Lumping them into a single chapter obscures their different predictors, effects, and social contexts—which we know a great deal more about today than was known 20 years ago.

A second reason for integrating the topic of violence into every chapter is its effect on student learning. Teaching about violence by using a brief, intense focus can be depressing and overwhelming to students. It can induce defensive denial and accusations that the instructor is engaging in male-bashing. This book offers a fresh approach to the topic by introducing violence against girls and women as a systemic problem of power in Chapter 2, then discussing each type of violence where it is most relevant. Child sexual abuse and sexual harassment in schools are covered in the chapter on childhood and adolescence; workplace sexual harassment, in the chapter on work and achievement; relationship violence, in chapters on relationships and marriage; and so on. Thus, each type is placed in its immediate social context *and* connected to a larger analysis.

Embodiment Is Theorized as a Determinant of Experience

Increasingly, feminist theorists and researchers are focusing on women's experience in their bodies as a determinant of the psychology of women and gender. New work on women's bodily objectification addresses not only the social consequences of inhabiting an objectified body, but also the affective, cognitive, and behavioral consequences to women of their own objectification: shame, anxiety, loss of peak experience, sexual dysfunction, and so on. This book features a core chapter, "In a Woman's Body," that brings these recent theoretical and empirical developments into focus.

This innovation originated in a discussion with Britain Scott, who attended a Division-35-sponsored workshop on teaching the psychology of women where I was a speaker. Britain's insights were so important to my thinking that I asked her to write Chapter 7 for this book. In addition to the phenomena linked with objectification, Britain's superb chapter also addresses recent work on the psychological aspects of women's embodied experience—work that is on the increase. For example, Britain's chapter addresses the contradictions between femininity and physical activity; femininity, heterosexuality, and the female athlete; and the benefits of embodied experience for girls and women. Moreover, I have integrated the topics of objectification and embodiment throughout the book, in sections on the impact of stereotypes (Chapter 3); bodily configuration and gender identity (Chapters 5 and 6); the bodily changes of puberty (Chapter 6); attractiveness, disability and sexuality (Chapter 8); others' reactions to pregnant women (Chapter 10); and living in an aging body (Chapter 12).

Women's Health Is Comprehensively Covered

Women's health is a burgeoning area of research. However, some texts cover this important topic more or less as a list of sex differences in various disorders and diseases. This book integrates health issues into every chapter. Moreover, a broad conception of health is used, including wellness, fitness, and optimal adjustment. Integrating health issues into each chapter allows for discussing each health-related topic within its social context. For example, the health effects of the second-class status of women and people of color are discussed in the context of patriarchal power (Chapter 2). The movement for ethical health care for intersex people is discussed in Chapter 5. Fitness, sport, and adventure are integrated into Chapters 7 and 12. Risky sexual behavior is covered in the context of sexuality and sexual scripts (Chapter 8); reproductive rights and woman-centered childbirth are set in the context of motherhood (Chapter 10).

Women's psychological health and well-being are comprehensively addressed in Chapter 13, contributed by Britain Scott. Rejecting an approach that merely catalogs sex differences in psychological disorders, Britain provides a thought-provoking analysis of the social construction of female madness. After showing how women have been institutionalized, medicated, and placated by traditional therapy, Britain offers a positive alternative in discussing feminist therapy and how it is valuable to diverse women.

Women's Diversity Is a Core Value and Topic

Throughout the book, women of color in the U.S. context and women around the world are presented as centrally important in feminist theory and research. This starts in Chapter 1, where black feminist perspectives are introduced and gender is compared to other systems of social classification such as race and ethnicity, and continues in Chapter 2 with extended discussion of how systems of oppression are linked and mutually reinforcing. Chapter 4, "The Meaning of Difference," focuses on the social dimensions that define difference and cause some groups to be evaluated as less worthy than others. Having set the theoretical framework for integrating diversity, each chapter for the remainder of the book incorporates the experiences of women of diverse sexualities, ethnicities, nationalities, and ages. Cross-cultural perspectives are incorporated both for their intrinsic value and for what they can reveal about the social construction of gender.

Historical Perspectives Enrich Student Learning

In a field that is growing exponentially, it is tempting to focus entirely on recent research. However, historical perspectives can aid student understanding in many ways. A look back at the treatment of women in the past can offer the clarity of hindsight to students who may have trouble seeing the gender problems in their own era. Moreover, historical analysis can show how some problematic characterizations of women recur over time. In this book, I often present a classic study in detail before introducing current work on a topic. Moreover, this book offers rich historical accounts of such topics as the women's movement and the history of women in psychology (Chapter 1); the Victorian belief in women's intellectual inferiority (Chapter 4); changes in stereotypes over time (Chapter 3); the concept of sexual orientation and the destigmatization of homosexuality (Chapters 5 and 9); and women, madness, institutionalization, and the psychiatric establishment (Chapter 13).

Comprehensive and Positive Coverage of Older Women

Chapter 12 focuses on the second half—topics on midlife and elderly women. In writing this chapter I drew on the most recent research on aging and incorporated the latest data on health issues, such as hormone replacement therapy and heart disease. I also explore the social role changes associated with aging, both positive and negative. Women's work lives are an important part of this chapter, with discussions of the consequences of the wage gap and retirement. In keeping with the book's earlier emphasis on embodiment, a section of this chapter is devoted to life in an aging woman's body. For example, fitness and wellness are an increasing feature of middle and later life for many women, yet rarely mentioned in textbooks. I discuss research showing the benefits of continued physical activity in middle and later life. Older women's sexuality, too, is rarely discussed; here, the stigmatization of older women's sexuality—and women's resistance to it—is a focus of attention. These are dimensions on which older women resist the cultural message that aging is only decay and decline. Perhaps this too is part of my own transformation; as I grow older, it is more and more important to me that psychology textbooks include positive aspects of women's aging. Although most student readers are far from midlife, I believe that they will find this chapter engaging and thought-provoking.

Spotlight on the Gendering of Emotion and Emotionality

Emotional research is burgeoning. Emotion is, of course, strongly gender-linked in many ways. Emotionality is a core aspect of feminine gender stereotypes; children are socialized differently for emotional expressiveness; and social actors express emotion according to display rules that are defined by gender and culture. This area is given new prominence in the text, both empirically and for its theoretical significance. Chapter 4 critically explores the social construction of emotional expressiveness and the social construction of women as the (over)emotional sex. Building on this foundation, later chapters discuss emotionality as a critical part of gender role socialization and emotion in relationships throughout life.

A Positive Message of Change

In my years of teaching the psychology of women and gender, I've seen students react to the course material in diverse and sometimes disturbing ways. Studying the psychology of women and gender can be a rewarding experience. However, learning about sexism, oppression, and the difficulty of changing the gender system can also be overwhelming. I have found that, even though most social science research focuses on problems, it is crucial to offer students a focus on solutions as well. In other words, it is important that students learn not only what is wrong about the gender system, but also what is happening to change it.

Feminist activism has brought about tremendous social changes within the lifetimes of most of us. Therefore, this book does more than focus on injustice and inequality. Every chapter ends with a major section titled Making a Difference that focuses on the social changes that have been achieved and are continuing. In keeping with the organizing theoretical framework of the book, social changes at the societal/cultural level, interpersonal level, and individual levels are presented and evaluated. Transforming psychology, and transforming the world, toward being more woman-friendly and less oppressive is an ongoing process. A central message of this book, and one that closes each chapter, is that every student can be a part of this transformation.

A Student-Friendly Text

As a teacher, I care very much about engaging students' interest and holding their attention. *Transformations* is readable, lively, and easy to follow. The student-friendliness of this text is achieved by a selective focus on research. I make no attempt to emulate the style of a *Psychological Review* article that describes every study ever done on a topic! Rather, I make selective use of *classic* studies that first demonstrated an important phenomenon, as well as the most *current* results and theories. I explain meta-analysis early in the text in a student-friendly way, and, wherever meta-analyses are available to organize large research literatures, I cite and discuss them. When describing individual studies, I report the methods and results in enough detail so that students can see *how* the researcher reached her conclusions.

In my own classroom teaching, I often use humor to diffuse tension, encourage dialogue on sensitive topics, and counter resistance to feminist knowledge. In this book, I incorporate that emphasis with a generous sprinkling of cartoons, boxed features, visual aids, and photographs that liven the pages. Finally, each chapter ends with Exploring Further, which offers not only scholarly research resources but also popular movies and books that illustrate the chapter's themes.

In my own teaching, I also use *In Our Own Words: Writings from Women's Lives* (McGraw-Hill, 2001), a reader I developed with Rhoda Unger specifically to connect the psychological research and theory in textbooks with the voices and experiences of diverse girls and women. *In Our Own Words* is a collection of short (2 to 20 pages) essays, each with a distinctive personal voice. Some are humorous (Gloria Steinem's "If Men Could Menstruate"), some are poignant (Judith Ortiz Cofer's "The Story of My Body"), and all are memorable.

In Our Own Words is organized into five sections: Making Our Voices Heard; The Making of a Woman: Bodies, Power, and Society; Making Meaning; Making a Living: Women, Work, and Achievement; and Making a Difference. A section of five to seven readings and their associated two-page introduction can be read along with a textbook chapter. For example, the section on Bodies, Power, and Society nicely complements Chapter 7 of my text, Britain Scott's "In a Woman's Body." Another way to use the reader is to ask students to write brief reaction papers on selections of their choice, connecting them to research and theory in the textbook. *In Our Own Words* provides a stimulus for student interest and class discussion and an experiential counterpoint to research.

The forthcoming *Transformations* Instructor's Manual will be a comprehensive resource containing test items (multiple choice, short answer, and essay), current video listings, classroom demonstrations and other techniques for stimulating active involvement, suggestions for using worldwide Web resources, and much more. Contact your McGraw-Hill representative for further information about supplements that accompany this text.

Acknowledgments

Writing a textbook, on top of an already full schedule of teaching, research, and family life, is a daunting task. I could not have done it without the support of a host of family, friends, and colleagues.

I am grateful to Britain Scott for contributing her two wonderful chapters (Chapters 7 and 13) as well as the section on pornogrpahy in Chapter 3. Britain's is a fresh new voice and her expertise adds a great deal to this work. Working with Britain, I soon came to appreciate not only her expertise but also her cheerfulness, her attention to lively writing, her passion for the issues, and, not least, her ability to meet deadlines under pressure.

Michelle Kaufman, a graduate student in social psychology at the University of Connecticut, contributed hundreds of hours of reference checking; fact-finding; and preparation of tables, figures, and text boxes. Michelle, I thank you for helping to keep me (relatively) sane! Student intern Meghan Deveau contributed valuable background research and literature searches, as well as wrote several text boxes. Roxanne Donovan, PhD, a former UConn clinical graduate student, now an assistant professor at the University of Massachusetts Boston; and Jessica Lord, clinical graduate student at UConn, each contributed a text box. Working with these strong and capable young women gives me renewed hope that the feminist transformation of society will continue.

I am grateful for the wider network of support that makes my work possible— a collegial and friendly faculty and administration here at the University of Connecticut, and friends and family who put up with the absent-minded crankiness of a writer in the throes of a project.

Special thanks go to my editor at McGraw-Hill, Kirsten Stoller, who has been a positive presence every step of the way, as well as Michael Sugarman, Executive Editor; Ruth Smith, Project Manager; Marianna Kinigakis, Designer; Natalia Peschiera, Photo Research Coordinator, and Katherine McNab, Art Editor. I would also like to acknowledge Kathy Field, whose editorial suggestions helped shape the book. I thank, too, the prepublication reviewers who generously provided me with feedback on all or parts of the manuscript: Veanne N. Anderson, *Indiana State University*; Carole R. Beal, *University of Massachusetts at Amherst*; Joan C. Chrisler, *Connecticut College*; MaryBeth Hartshorn, *Diablo Valley College*; Mary L. Meiners, *San Diego Miramar College*; Charisse Nixon, *Penn State Erie*; Samantha Swindell, *Washington State University*; and Angela Walker, *Quinnipiac University*. They helped me write more clearly and directly, pointed out overlooked sources, and gave me the encouragement I needed during this long process.

Finally, I wish to acknowledge, as I do in every book I write, my life partner Roger Chaffin. Roger has his own full schedule of teaching and research, yet he always manages to be there when I need support. This past year has been one of many changes in our lives, but our relationship, grounded in equality and mutual respect, is a constant I know I can count on. Thank you, Roger.

Mary Crawford
University of Connecticut
October 2004

PART 1

Introduction

CHAPTER 1

Paving the Way

- **Beginnings**
  How Did the Psychology of Women Get Started?
  Psychology and the Women's Movement
  Voices from the Margins: A History
- **What Is Feminism?**
  Feminism Has Many Meanings
  Is There a Simple Definition?
- **Methods and Values in Psychological Research**
  Toward Gender-Fair Research
  Feminist Values in Research
- **About This Book**
- **A Personal Reflection**
- **Exploring Further**

$\mathcal{C}$onsider the following facts and events from the past decade:

- After more than 200 years of U.S. democracy, only 13 percent of U.S. senators, 14 percent of members of Congress, and 10 percent of state governors are women.
- In the United States, women earn about 80 cents for every dollar earned by men.
- The United Nations estimates that 100 million women worldwide are missing from the population—dead because, as females, they were unwanted.
- One in four U.S. college students believes that the activities of married women should be limited to home and family (down from one in two in 1970).
- Women have been heads of state in 23 countries around the world, yet in others they lack basic human rights such as voting and going to school.
- Women in the United States are far more likely than men to suffer from serious depression and eating disorders.
- Less than 5 percent of the artists in New York's Metropolitan Museum collections are women, but 85 percent of the nude paintings are of females.

What do these facts and events have in common? They demonstrate that equality has not yet been achieved. Although some things have changed for the better, a worldwide wage gap, underrepresentation of women in positions of status and power, and significant problems of violence against girls and women persist. Gender, sexuality, and power are at the core of social controversies around the world.

Beginnings

We are living in an era in which nothing about women, sexuality, and gender seems certain. Entering this arena of change, a new branch of psychology has developed research and theory about women and gender. The new branch is a form of ***critical psychology***—it questions and challenges the moral, political, and scientific claims of psychology and tries to influence the direction of the field as a whole (Fox & Prilleltensky, 1997). It is usually called ***feminist psychology,*** the ***psychology of women,*** or the ***psychology of gender*** (Russo & Dumont, 1997). Those who use the term *feminist psychology* tend to emphasize theoretical connections to women's studies. Those who use *psychology of women* tend to focus on women's lives and experiences as the subject matter. Those who use *psychology of gender* tend to focus on the social and biological processes that create gender differences. This book includes all these perspectives and uses all three terms. There is a lot to learn about this exciting new field, and an open-minded, inclusive approach fosters exploration.

How Did the Psychology of Women Get Started?

As the women's movement of the late 1960s made women and gender a central social concern, the field of psychology began to examine the bias that had characterized its knowledge about women. The more closely psychologists began to look at the ways psychology had thought about women, the more problems they saw. They began to realize that women had been left out of many studies. Even worse, theories were constructed from a male-as-norm viewpoint, and women's behavior was explained as a deviation from the male standard. Often, stereotypes of women were unquestioned or considered to be an accurate portrayal of women's behavior. Good psychological adjustment for women was defined in terms of fitting into gender norms—marrying, having babies, and *not* being too independent or ambitious. When women behaved differently from men, the differences were likely to be attributed to biology, instead of social influences (Crawford & Marecek, 1989; Kahn & Jean, 1983; Unger, 1979b).

These problems, though not universal, were very widespread. Psychologists began to realize that most psychological knowledge about women and gender was **androcentric,** or male centered. They began to rethink psychological concepts and methods and to produce new research with women as the focus of study. Moreover, they began to study topics of importance and concern to women and to develop ways of analyzing social relations between women and men. As a result, psychology developed new ways of thinking about women, expanded its research methods, and developed new approaches to therapy and counseling.

Women within psychology were a very important force for change. They published many books and articles showing how psychology was misrepresenting women and how it needed to change. One of the first was Naomi Weisstein (1968), who declared that psychology had nothing to say about what women are really like, what they need, and what they want because psychology did not know. Another was Phyllis Chesler, whose book *Women and Madness* (1972) claimed that psychology and psychiatry were used to control women.

Here are a few more examples of the strong critical voices of women who helped develop the new feminist psychology:

Carolyn Sherif, 1964: "Ignorance about women pervades academic disciplines in higher education, where the requirements for the degree seldom include thoughtful inquiry into the status of women, as part of the total human condition." (cited in Sherif, 1979, p. 93)

Mary Parlee, 1975: "The academic discipline (of psychology) . . . has distorted facts, omitted problems, and perpetuated pseudoscientific data relevant to women." (p. 124)

Kathleen Grady, 1981: "The promise of science cannot be realized if . . . certain questions are never asked, or they are asked of the wrong people and in the wrong way, or they are not published because they do not fit accepted theories." (p. 629)

Michelle Fine, 1985: "Women who represent racial and ethnic minorities, working-class and poor women, and disabled women and lesbians, need to be involved in [psychological] research. The lives of these women need to be integrated into this literature. . . ." (p. 178)

The growth of feminist psychology can be charted through many statistics. Before 1968, almost no psychology departments offered courses in the psychology of women or gender; today, over half of psychology departments offer these courses. Psychology of women courses are often connected to women's studies programs, which began about 1970. In 2002, the National Women's Studies Association reported 736 women's studies programs in the United States. In 1974, there was not a single journal article on women and achievement; in 1993, there were 161. Similar growth has occurred in the number of articles on many other topics, including rape and sexual assault, sexual harassment, and feminist therapy (Worell, 1996). In fact, the new field soon developed its own journals, focusing on the psychology of women or gender: for example, *Sex Roles*, which began publishing in 1975; *Psychology of Women Quarterly*, published since 1977; and *Feminism & Psychology*, published since 1991.

The psychology of women and gender is rich and varied. Virtually every area of psychology has been affected by its critical analysis (Crawford & Marecek, 1989; Wilkinson, 1997a, 1997b). This book is an invitation to explore the knowledge and to participate in the ongoing debates of feminist psychology.

Psychology and the Women's Movement

The emergence of interest in women and gender took place in a social context marked by changing roles for women and the growth of a feminist social movement in the late 1960s. Questioning psychology's representation of women was part of the general questioning of women's place that was led by women's liberation activists.

The First Wave

The women's movement of the late 1960s was not the first. A previous women's rights movement had reached its peak more than a hundred years earlier with the Seneca Falls Declaration of 1848, which rejected the doctrine of female inferiority then taught by academics and clergy (Harris, 1984). However, this *first wave* of the women's movement lost momentum in the 1920s, after women had won the vote, because women believed that voting would lead to political, social, and economic equality. Psychology's interest in sex differences and gender waned.

The Second Wave

With the rebirth of the women's movement in the 1960s, researchers again became interested in the study of women and gender. Women psychologists and men who supported their goals also began to work toward improved status for women within the field of psychology. Feminist activism made a big difference for women of this era, who had been openly discriminated against (Unger, 1998; 2001). Psychologist Carolyn Sherif remembered it this way:

> To me, the atmosphere created by the women's movement was like breathing fresh air after years of gasping for breath. . . . I did not become a significantly better social psychologist between 1969 and 1972, but I surely was treated as a better social psychologist. (Sherif, 1983, p. 280)

Activists—mostly graduate students and newcomers to psychology—formed the Association for Women in Psychology (AWP) in 1969. At about the same time, others—mostly older, more established psychologists—lobbied the American Psychological Association (APA) to form a Division of the Psychology of Women (Unger, 1998; 2001). This Division 35 was officially approved in 1973. Divisions on ethnic minority psychology and gay/lesbian issues were established later, with the support of Division 35. Progress in incorporating women has also occurred among Canadian psychologists (Parlee, 1985) and the British Psychological Society, where there is now a Psychology of Women Section (Wilkinson, 1997a).

These organizational changes have acknowledged the presence of diverse women in psychology and helped enhance their professional identity (Scarborough & Furumoto, 1987). And none too soon—women now earn 67 percent of PhDs awarded in psychology, and ethnic minorities earn 19 percent (Bailey, 2004).

The Third Wave

AWP continues to thrive as an activist organization with no formal ties to the psychological establishment, holding annual conferences that welcome students. Division 35, now named the Society for the Psychology of Women, has become one of the larger divisions of APA, with about 3,000 members. Feminist theory and activism continue to develop as younger women follow up on the gains made by the second wave.

Today, the third wave of the women's movement tackles some of the unfinished business of the first two waves, such as ensuring reproductive freedom, ending violence against girls and women, and integrating women into politics, through groups such as the Third Wave Foundation. But third-wave groups such as the Riot Grrrls have their own agenda, too, speaking out to reclaim girl culture, assert women's place in rock and pop music, and proclaim the joys of women's sexuality. Though the issues and the voices have changed, third-wave feminism is clearly connected to its foremothers' visions (Baumgardner & Richards, 2000).

Voices from the Margins: A History

Until recently, the power to define and pursue knowledge has been largely in the hands of men. Men controlled the institutions of knowledge, and even if women acquired expertise, they did not always acquire legitimacy or respect. History is full of stories about learned women whose work was attributed to their fathers, their brothers, their teachers, or "anonymous."

One illustration of how a woman could have outstanding expertise and yet be denied legitimacy is the story of Mary Calkins (1863–1930), who attended Harvard University during the latter part of the 19th century. Because Harvard was an all-male university, she was permitted to take courses only if she sat behind a curtain or was tutored individually. Despite completing an impressive PhD dissertation, she was denied a PhD from Harvard because she was a woman. Nevertheless, Calkins taught for many years at Wellesley College, established an experimental laboratory there, and made important contributions to psychology. She was the first woman president of both the American Psychological Association and the American Philosophical Association. In 1927, toward the end of her life, a group of distinguished psychologists and philosophers, all Harvard degree holders, wrote to the president of Harvard requesting that Calkins be awarded the degree that she had earned. Their request was refused (Scarborough & Furumoto, 1987).

Although Mary Calkins triumphed personally, her life illustrates the way even outstanding women may be marginalized. For example, she taught during her entire life at a women's college where she did not have doctoral students of her own. Under these conditions, her theories and research projects did not receive the continuity of investigation they deserved. Similar stories have been uncovered about other early feminist psychologists (Scarborough & Furumoto, 1987). If a woman scientist does not have the power to have her research and theories taken seriously and passed on to the next generation, she is being denied true equality.

By the early 1900s, women had begun to gain access to higher education in the United States and Europe. Some of the first scientifically trained women devoted much research effort to challenging accepted wisdom about the extent and nature of sex differences. Helen Thompson Wooley conducted the first experimental laboratory study of sex differences in mental traits. In interpreting her results, she stressed the overall similarity of women's and men's performance. She also was openly critical of the antiwoman prejudices held by some male scientists, remarking daringly in a 1910 *Psychological Bulletin* article: "There is perhaps no field aspiring to be scientific where flagrant personal bias, logic martyred in the cause of supporting a prejudice, unfounded assertions, and even sentimental rot and drivel, have run riot to such an extent as here" (Wooley, 1910, p. 340).

The work of a few early women psychologists opened the way for critical research to replace unexamined assumptions about women's so-called natural limitations (Rosenberg, 1982). Determined to demonstrate women's capacity to contribute to modern science on an equal basis with men, they chose to measure sex differences in order to challenge beliefs about women's limitations. In a sense, their research interests were dictated by questions chosen by others. Faced with the necessity of proving their very right to do research, these women labored to refute hypotheses that they did not find credible (Unger, 1979a). Moreover, they worked in a social context that denied them opportunities because of their sex and forced them to make cruel choices between work and family relationships (Scarborough & Furumoto, 1987). Their story is one,

> in many ways, of failure—of women restricted by simple prejudice to the periphery of academe, who never had access to the professional chairs of the major universities, who never commanded the funds to direct large-scale research, who never trained the graduate students who might have spread their influence, and who, by the 1920s, no longer had the galvanizing support of a woman's movement to give political effect to their ideas. (Rosenberg, 1982, p. xxi)

The challenges to psychology to develop knowledge about all humanity have been present throughout psychology's history (Guthrie, 1976). However, the efforts of women and minorities remained voices from the margins until recently. The existence of AWP, Division 35, women's studies programs, and dozens of feminist journals makes it unlikely that interest in the psychology of women and gender will fade away as it did in the 1920s. Because this new psychology clearly has developed in a social context of feminism, it is important to look closely at the relationship between the two.

What Is Feminism?

The writer Rebecca West noted in 1913: "I myself have never been able to find out precisely what feminism is: I only know that people call me a feminist whenever I express sentiments that differentiate me from a doormat" (quoted in Kramarae & Treichler, 1985, p. 160). Nearly a hundred years later, it seems that feminism and the women's movement are still controversial and difficult to define (see Figure 1.1). Exactly what is feminism and what does it mean to call oneself a feminist?

Feminism Has Many Meanings

Contemporary feminist theory has many variants (Tong, 1998). Each can be thought of as a different lens through which to view the experiences of women, and, like different lenses, each is useful for focusing on particular phenomena.

What are the most influential feminist theoretical perspectives? In the United States, they include liberal, radical, socialist, womanist (woman of color), and cultural feminism. Belief in these different branches of feminism has been defined, reliably measured, and shown to predict people's behavior (Henley et al., 1998). Let's look briefly at each perspective.

Socialist feminism emphasizes that there are many kinds of divisions between groups of people that can lead to oppression. Socialist feminists believe that acts of discrimination based on social class, race, and gender are equally wrong. Moreover, it views these forms of discrimination as inseparable: Differential treatment according to one's sex, race, or social class reinforce each other, so that, for example, a poor woman of color is triply disadvantaged. This book presents many examples of relationships among different kinds of disadvantage, from teen mothers (Chapter 10) to social class differences in gender-role learning during childhood and adolescence (Chapter 6).

Woman-of-color feminism, or *womanism,* began with criticism of the white women's movement for excluding women of color and issues important to them: poverty, racism, and needs such as jobs, health care, good schools, and safe neighborhoods for all people. Asian American, Hispanic, and African American women and men who are activists often choose to join forces with each other to fight racism and classism, even though the women are aware of their oppression as women (Chow, 1996). In general, womanists do not see men of color as their oppressors but as brothers who suffer the effects of racism just as women of color do. People who adopt this feminist perspective often point out the strengths and positive values of minority communities, such as the multigenerational support and closeness emphasized by African American families (Chapter 10).

Radical feminism emphasizes male control and domination of women throughout history. This perspective views the control of women by men as the first and most fundamental form of oppression: Women as a group are oppressed, not by

FIGURE 1.1
Sisterhood is complicated!

Source: Copyright © Lynda Barry. First printed in *Newsweek,* 1994. Courtesy Darhansoff, Verrill, Feldman Literary Agents.

their biology or their social class, but by men as a group. According to radical feminists, oppression on the basis of being a woman is one thing all women have in common. Radical feminist theory has fostered much research on violence against women and on sexuality, seeking to understand the sources and consequences of males' greater power (Chapter 2).

Liberal feminism is familiar to most people because it relies on deeply held American beliefs about equality—an orientation that connects it to political liberalism. From this perspective, a feminist is a person who believes that women are entitled to full legal and social equality with men and who favors changes in laws, customs, and values to achieve the goal of equality. The liberal feminist perspective has fostered research on such topics as how people react to others when they violate gender norms (Chapter 2), how children are socialized to accept gender roles (Chapters 4 and 6), and sex discrimination in employment (Chapter 11). It emphasizes the similarities between men and women, maintaining that given equal environments and opportunities, they will behave similarly.

Cultural feminism emphasizes differences between women and men. This perspective stresses that qualities characteristic of women have been devalued and should be honored and respected in society. Cultural feminism has been useful in understanding the importance of unpaid work contributed by women, such as child care (Chapter 11). It is often used in discussing gender differences in values and social behaviors—for example, the apparent tendency for women to be more nurturing and caring than men.

Feminism is increasingly becoming a worldwide social movement. ***Global feminism*** focuses on how prejudice and discrimination against women are related across cultures, and how they are connected to neocolonialism and global capitalism. Issues of special concern to global feminists include sweatshop labor conditions, unequal access to health care and education, and forced prostitution. An important part of global feminism is the recognition that Western feminists do not have all the answers for women from other cultures. For example, in some societies women are strongly pressured to undergo genital cutting (Chapter 8) or required to veil their faces and bodies in public. Though Western women may criticize these practices, it is important to remember that Western society also restricts women's bodily freedom and integrity through practices like sexual harassment in public places and pressure to seek the perfect body through dieting and cosmetic surgery (hooks, 2000). Strategies for change work best if they come from within each culture, rather than being imposed from outside.

The diversity of frameworks and values in feminist thought may seem confusing, but it is also healthy and productive. The lenses of different feminist perspectives can be used to develop and compare diverse viewpoints on women's experiences. This book draws on a variety of feminist perspectives, using each as a lens to help clarify particular topics, and sometimes comparing several feminist perspectives on an issue. However, within psychology, liberal feminism and cultural feminism have generated more debate and research than any other views. Therefore, Chapter 4 is devoted to contrasting liberal and cultural feminist perspectives on the question, Just how different are women and men?

Is There a Simple Definition?

Because of the plurality of definitions and viewpoints, it is perhaps more appropriate to speak of feminism*s* than feminism. However, feminist perspectives share two important themes. First, feminism values women as important and worthwhile human beings. Second, feminism recognizes the need for social change if women are to lead secure and satisfying lives. Perhaps the simplest definition of a ***feminist*** is an individual who holds these basic beliefs: that women are valuable and that social change to benefit women is needed. The core social change that feminists advocate is an end to all forms of domination, those of men over women and those among women (Kimball, 1995). Therefore, perhaps the simplest definition of *feminism* is one proposed by bell hooks (1984): It is a movement to end sexism and sexist oppression. (The definition and implications of sexism are explored more fully in Chapter 2 of this book.) Broad definitions allow feminists to work for political change together, while recognizing that ideas about how to reach their goals may differ.

Can men be feminists? Certainly! Men can hold the values we have described as feminist; they can value women as worthwhile human beings and work for social change to reduce sexism and sex discrimination. Some men who share these values call themselves feminists. Others prefer the label *profeminist,* believing that this term acknowledges women's leadership of the feminist movement and expresses their understanding that women and men have different experiences of gender.

Feminist perspectives in general can be contrasted to *conservatism* (Henley et al., 1998). Conservatives seek to keep gender arrangements as they have been in much of the recent past, with males holding more public power and status and

FIGURE 1.2
The Southern Baptist sect made the news by urging a return to female submission.

Source: Copyright © 1998 Dan Wasserman. Tribune Media Services, Inc. All rights reserved.

women being more or less defined by their sexuality and their roles as wives and mothers. The conservative view has usually been justified on the grounds of biology or religion. The biological justification states that gender-related behaviors are determined by innate and unchangeable biological differences far more than by social conditions. Therefore, women should not be encouraged to try to do things that go against their nature. For example, if women are biologically destined to be more nurturing due to the fact that they are the sex that gives birth, it is unnatural and wrong for women to limit their childbearing or take on jobs that do not involve nurturing others. The religious justification (often combined with the biological justification) is that a supreme being ordains female submission and subordination. For example, some religions teach that women must be obedient to their husbands; others forbid contraception or grant the right to divorce only to men (see Figure 1.2). Over the past 30 years, attitudes toward women have grown less conservative and more liberal. Women have been more liberal than men all along, but this gender difference has decreased as men's attitudes have moved in the direction of women's (Twenge, 1997). However, more subtle forms of prejudice against women have emerged (see Chapter 2).

The history of women in psychology teaches us that psychologists are not immune to such prejudice. The attitudes that permeate a culture also seep into scientific research. One important goal of feminist psychology is to challenge hidden biases in research and thus to foster better research on women and gender.

Methods and Values in Psychological Research

Scientific research is often represented as a purely objective process in which a neutral, disinterested scientist investigates and reveals the secrets of nature. However, psychology has sometimes been anything but neutral in explaining the behavior of women. Interest in the psychology of women has led psychologists to identify specific methodological flaws in traditional research on women.

Toward Gender-Fair Research

Let's look briefly at the research process. The researcher starts by generating a question to be answered by gathering information systematically. The question may originate in a theory, a personal experience, or an observation; or it may be raised by previous research. The next step is to develop a systematic strategy for answering the question—often called *designing the research.* In the design stage, a method is selected, such as experiment, survey, or case study. Research participants are chosen, materials such as questionnaires or laboratory setups are devised, and ways to measure the behaviors in question are decided on.

Next, the data are collected and analyzed so that patterns of results become clear. Statistical techniques are usually used for this task. The researcher then interprets the meaning of his or her results and draws conclusions from them. If reviewers and journal editors judge the research to be well conducted and important, the results are published in a scientific journal where they can influence future research and theory. Some research makes its way from journals into textbooks, influencing teachers and students as well as other researchers. Some even gets reported in the mass media, opening the possibility that it may influence millions of readers' and viewers' beliefs.

Biases can enter into the research process at any stage. In describing a few common types of bias at each stage, I will focus on gender-related examples. However, the principles of gender-fair research also apply to eliminating biases related to such characteristics as race/ethnicity, social class, or sexual orientation (Denmark, Russo, Frieze, & Sechzer, 1988).

Question Formulation

The process of creating research questions is perhaps the most neglected and undervalued part of the scientific enterprise. Textbooks and research courses say very little about where hypotheses come from or how to decide if a question is worth studying (Wallston & Grady, 1985). It is not surprising, then, that unexamined personal biases and androcentric theories often lead to biased research questions. Gender stereotypes related to the topic can bias the question and therefore the outcome of the study.

For example, many studies of leadership have defined it in terms of dominance, aggression, and other stereotypically male attributes. A more inclusive definition of leadership might include the ability to negotiate, to be considerate of others, and to help others resolve conflicts without confrontation (Denmark et al., 1988). Another example of bias in question formulation is found in the large amount of research on mothers who work outside the home. Much of it focuses on the question of whether the mothers' work endangers their children's psychological welfare. There is much less research on whether fathers' work endangers their children's welfare or on whether mothers' employment might benefit mothers or children (Hare-Mustin & Marecek, 1990).

Designing Research

In the design phase of research, one important aspect is deciding how to measure the behaviors under study. If the measures are biased, the results will be, too. An extreme example of a biased measure comes from a study of women's sexuality. Participants were asked to describe their roles in sexual intercourse by choosing one of the following responses: passive, responsive, resistant, aggressive, deviant, or other. The outcome of this research might have been very different if women had also been allowed to choose from alternatives such as active, initiating, playful, and joyous (Bart, 1971; Wallston & Grady, 1985).

Another aspect of the design phase is the choice of a comparison group. The results and conclusions of a study can be very different depending on which groups are chosen for comparison with each other. For example, one group of researchers was involved in an ongoing study of aging among a selected group of college-educated professional men. When they decided to add a sample of women, the biomedical scientists on the research team suggested that they should add the sisters of the men already in the study. Because they had the same parents, these two groups would be similar in physiological characteristics. The social scientists on the research team, however, suggested that the appropriate sample would be college-educated professional women who were similar in social status. Although one choice is not necessarily right and the other wrong, the choice is conceptually important. The conclusions reached about gender differences in aging might be very different depending on which group of women was chosen, and the group chosen depends on assumptions about what kind of explanations (physiological or social) are most important (Parlee, 1981).

Choice of research participants is subject to many possible biases. Since the 1940s, psychology has come to rely more and more on college student samples, creating biases of age, social class, and developmental stage (Sears, 1986). Moreover, males have been more likely to be studied than females, perhaps because topics were gender-linked in the minds of researchers and so-called male topics were considered more important (Wallston & Grady, 1985).

The proportion of male-only studies has decreased since the 1970s (Gannon, Luchetta, Rhodes, Pardie, & Segrist, 1992). However, subtler kinds of sex bias persist. Nearly 30 percent of psychological journal articles still do not report the gender of the participants. When researchers use an all-female sample, they are more likely to state it in the article's title, to discuss their reasons for studying women, and to point out that their results cannot be generalized to men (Ader & Johnson, 1994). It seems that psychologists feel it is important to indicate the limitations of an all-female sample, but they see nothing remarkable about an all-male sample—males are still the norm.

Other types of bias also persist. Research on ethnic minority people of both sexes is scarce except when they are seen as creating social problems (Reid & Kelly, 1994). There is abundant research on teen pregnancy among African American women, for example, but little research on their leadership, creativity, or coping skills for dealing with racism. Poor and working-class women, too, have been virtually ignored (Bing & Reid, 1996; Reid, 1993).

Many well-known psychologists, both female and male, have pointed out that psychology, supposedly the science of human behavior, is in danger of becoming a science of the behavior of college sophomores, and white male college sophomores at that. Feminist psychology, with its valuing of women as worthy subjects of research and its recognition of the diversity of social groupings, is providing an important corrective to this type of bias.

Analyzing Data: A Focus on Differences

Psychologists have come to rely on statistical tests in data analysis. Over the past 30 years, both the number of articles using statistics and the number of statistical tests per article have increased. Statistics can be a useful tool, but they also can lead to many conceptual difficulties in research on sex and gender (Wallston & Grady, 1985).

Statistical models lead to a focus on differences rather than similarities. The logic of statistical analysis involves comparing two groups to see if the average difference between them is statistically significant. Unfortunately, it is not easy to make meaningful statements about similarities using statistical reasoning.

It is also unfortunate that statisticians chose the term *significant* to describe the outcome of a set of mathematical operations. As used by most people, the word means "important," but as used by statisticians it means only that the obtained difference between two groups is unlikely to be due to mere chance. A statistically significant difference does not necessarily have any practical or social significance (Favreau, 1997). The meaning and interpretation of difference will be discussed in more detail in Chapter 4.

Interpreting and Publishing Research Results

Psychology's focus on group differences affects the ways that results are interpreted and conveyed to others. One type of interpretation bias occurs when gender differences in performing a specific task are interpreted as evidence of a more general difference. For example, because special samples of highly gifted junior-high boys score higher on SAT math tests than similar samples of girls, some psychologists have argued that males in general have a biological superiority in math ability.

Another kind of interpretation bias occurs when the performance style more typical of girls or women is given a negative label. For example, girls get better grades in school in virtually every subject, but no one interprets this to mean that females are biologically superior in intelligence. Instead, girls' academic achievement is discounted; they are said to get good grades by being nice or compliant.

Biased interpretations of gender differences lead to thinking of men and women as two totally separate categories. But it is simply not true that "men are from Mars; women from Venus." On many traits and behaviors, men and women are more alike than different. Even when a statistically significant difference is found, there is always considerable overlap between the two groups (see Chapter 4).

Problems of interpretation are compounded by publication biases. Because of reliance on the logic of statistical analysis, studies that report differences between women and men are more likely to be published than those that report similarities. Moreover, the editorial boards of most journals still are predominately made up of white men, who may perhaps see topics relevant to women and ethnic minorities as less important than topics relevant to people more like themselves (Denmark et al., 1988). Until feminist psychology was formed, there was very little psychological research on pregnancy and mothering, women's leadership, violence against women, or gender issues in therapy.

Bias continues after publication. The media notice some findings, but others are overlooked. Television and the popular press often actively publicize the latest discoveries about gender differences. Of course, some of these differences may not be very important, and others may not hold up in future research; but the public is less likely to hear about that because gender similarities are not news (Crawford, 1989).

In summary, research is a human activity, and the biases held by those who do research can affect any stage of the process. As more diverse people become psychologists, they are bringing new values, beliefs, and research questions. They also may question and challenge the biases in others' research. Feminist psychologists have led the way by demonstrating gender bias in psychological research and showing how it can be reduced.

Gender-fair research is not value-free; that is, gender-fair research practices do not eliminate value judgments from the research process. Androcentric research is based on the value judgment that men and their concerns are more important and worthy of study than women and their concerns. In contrast, gender-fair research is based on the value judgment that women and men and their concerns are of equal worth and importance (Eichler, 1988).

Feminist Values in Research

Although feminist psychologists have been critical of psychology, they remain committed to it, expressing feminist values in their work (Grossman et al., 1997). What are some of these values?

Empirical Research Is a Worthwhile Activity

Although feminist psychologists recognize that science is far from perfect, they value its methods. Scientific methods are the most systematic way yet devised to answer questions about the natural and social world. Rather than abandon those methods or endlessly debate whether there is one perfect feminist way to do research, they go about their work using a rich variety of methods, theories, and approaches. Good research on women and gender is necessary and important (Peplau & Conrad, 1989; Unger, 2001; Worell, 1996).

Research Methods Must Be Critically Examined

Feminist theorists have pointed out that methods are not neutral tools; the choice of method always shapes and constrains what can be found (Crawford & Kimmel, 1999; Marecek, 1989; Unger, 1983). For example, what is the best way to study female sexuality—by measuring physiological changes during arousal and orgasm or by interviewing women about their subjective experiences of arousal and orgasm? The two methods might produce very different discoveries about female sexuality (Tiefer, 1989).

Traditionally, experimentation has been the most respected psychological method. Psychologists like to do experiments because they can control for many outside factors that could affect results and because they can show causation (changing X causes a change in Y). However, experimental methods have been criticized for at least two reasons. First, in an experiment, the researcher creates an artificial environment and manipulates the experience of the participants. However, behavior in the laboratory may not be representative of behavior in other situations (Sherif, 1979). Second, experiments are inherently hierarchical, with "the powerful, all-knowing researchers instructing, observing, recording, and sometimes deceiving the subjects" (Peplau & Conrad, 1989). The inequality of the experimental situation may be particularly acute when the researcher is male and the person being studied is female (McHugh, Koeske, & Frieze, 1986).

On the other hand, many important advances in understanding women and gender have come about because of experimental results. For example, experimental research has clarified the nature and functioning of stereotypes about women (see Chapter 3). Although psychology has perhaps used the experimental method too much and too unreflectively, it should not be rejected. Just as any research method can be used in biased ways, all methods can be used toward the goal of understanding women and gender. When a large variety of methods are used, results based on different approaches can be compared with each other, and a richer and more complete picture of women's lives will emerge.

Both Women and Men Can Conduct Feminist Research

Most feminist researchers in psychology are women. The membership of APA's Division 35 is more than 90 percent female, and "women have taken the lead in investigating topics relevant to women's lives and in developing new concepts and theories to explain women's experiences" (Peplau & Conrad, 1989, p. 391). However, it is important not to equate female with feminist and male with nonfeminist. Women who are psychologists work in every area from physiological and learning to industrial and clinical psychology. Women psychologists may or may not personally identify as feminists, and even when they do, they may not bring a feminist perspective to their research. Also, male psychologists can identify as feminist. Men can and do conduct research on women and gender, and many conduct research on male gender roles. Of course, all psychologists—male and female, feminist and nonfeminist—should, at a minimum, conduct their research in gender-fair ways and work to eliminate gender bias from their professional practices and behaviors.

Science Can Never Be Fully Objective or Value-Neutral

Science is done by human beings, all of whom bring their own perspectives to their work, based on their personal backgrounds. Personal experience sensitizes people to different aspects of problems (Unger, 1983). Because the values of dominant groups in a society are normative, they are not always recognized as values. When others—women and minorities, for example—question the assumptions of the dominant group, the underlying values are made more visible.

One of the most important insights of feminism is that research and the creation of knowledge do not occur in a social vacuum. Rather, each research project or theory is situated in a particular period in history and a particular social context. The psychology of women and gender is not unique in being affected by social currents such as feminism, conservatism, and liberalism. All of psychology is affected. Moreover, psychology in turn affects social issues and social policy through providing ways to interpret human behavior. Because psychology is a cultural institution, doing psychological research is inevitably a political act (Crawford & Marecek, 1989).

Although the effects of values on the scientific process are inevitable, they need not be negative for women. I believe that psychology should admit its values and acknowledge that they are part of the research process (Crawford & Marecek, 1989). An awareness of the politics of science can help feminist psychologists use science to foster social change and improve women's lives (Peplau & Conrad, 1989).

Social, Historical, and Political Forces Shape Human Behavior

Because feminists believe that gender equality is possible, although it has not yet been achieved, they are sensitive to the ways that social contexts and forces shape people's behavior and limit human potential. Feminist psychologists try to understand not only the effects of gender, but also the effects of other systems of social classification such as race, social class, and sexual orientation. They tend to be skeptical that psychology will ever discover universal laws of behavior. Rather, they prefer to try to clarify the ways that sociocultural forces, as well as biological and psychological ones, affect behavior.

Feminist psychologists respect the diversity of women and recognize that it is important to study varied groups. For example, U.S. women generally have lower self-esteem than men, but this is not true of African American women. Such differences can show how women's psychology is affected by their social and cultural backgrounds, not just their biology.

About This Book

This book draws on the work of hundreds of psychologists, both women and men, who have contributed to the ongoing process of revising—and transforming—psychology. It also draws on the work of feminist theorists and researchers in other disciplines, including philosophy, history, anthropology, sociology, political science, and cultural studies. This book, then, provides both a critique of androcentric knowledge about women and an introduction to the groundbreaking research that has emerged from this new field.

As you read the chapters that follow, you will see that certain threads run through them. Three of these threads in particular are important to highlight at the start. First, *women have not yet achieved full equality with men.* There are persistent differences in power and social standing that shape women's lives. In many cultures and time periods, women have been socially defined as unequals and treated as second-class citizens. Sometimes the inequalities are glaring—such as denying women the right to vote, own property, use public spaces, or make decisions about their own bodies. Other times the inequalities are more subtle—such as being subjected to everyday sexist hassles or being paid less at work. Everywhere, power differences are implicated in the shocking worldwide prevalence of violence against girls and women. Gender, power, and social status are so important that they are the focus of Chapter 2. The causes and effects of various kinds of violence against girls and women are discussed as part of every chapter.

A second thread that runs throughout this book concerns *differences and similarities.* Women and men are not complete opposites of each other. Rather, there is a great deal of overlap in the psychology of women and men. Gender differences are important, but we should also think about gender similarities. When gender differences do occur, we should ask where they come from and how they connect to differences in power and social position.

Another kind of difference is differences among women. Women are not all alike, and we should not assume that all women necessarily have much in common with each other simply because they are women. A woman who is wealthy and privileged may, for example, have as much in common with wealthy and privileged men as she has with poor women. African American and Latina women share with the men of their ethnic groups—and not with white women—the experiences of racism. Lesbians share the experience of being in a sexual minority with bisexuals and gay men, not with heterosexual women. Dimensions such as age and (dis)ability are relevant, too. The viewpoints and concerns of older women and disabled women are not necessarily the same as those of young, able-bodied women. Studies of different groups of women can help us to understand how biological, social, and cultural factors interact to influence behavior.

Yet creating a psychology of all women is not an easy task. If women of color are studied only in comparison to a mythical generic (white, privileged-status) woman, researchers are implicitly making white women the norm, just as previous generations of psychologists made men the norm (Greene & Sanchez-Hucles, 1997; Yoder & Kahn, 1992). Understanding women of color on their own terms increases our understanding of all women and the complexity of their differences. Women of color and white women may both encounter sexism, but in very different ways.

In writing this book, I have tried to respect and express the diversity of women's (and men's) experiences. Over the years, I have noticed that feminist psychologists often use metaphors of gender as a lens or prism through which to view the social structure (Bem, 1993; Crawford & Marecek, 1989; Unger, 1990). Viewing psychological and social phenomena through the lens of gender allows us to see aspects of social reality that are otherwise obscured. However, like any lens, gender can reveal only some features of the social landscape. Lenses such as race, class, and age reveal other equally important features. Feminist psychologists do not wish to copy the limitations of androcentric psychology by replacing "male as norm" with "white-middle-class-heterosexual female as norm." Throughout your study of this book, I invite you to consider what women have in common as women, how their experiences may or may not differ from those of men, and also how women differ from each other.

A third thread that runs throughout this book is that *psychology can contribute to social change*. Traditionally, psychologists have focused on changing individuals. They have developed techniques to change attitudes, increase insight and self-understanding, teach new behavioral skills, and reduce or eliminate self-defeating thinking and behaviors. They have applied these techniques in a variety of educational and therapeutic settings. In this book, there are many examples of how feminist psychology has adapted and used these techniques.

However, research on women and gender indicates that there are limits to the power of individual change. Many of the problems that confront women are the result of social structures and practices that put women at a disadvantage and interfere with their living happy, productive lives. Social-structural problems cannot be solved solely through individual changes in attitudes and behavior; rather, the social institutions that permit the devaluation and victimization of women must also be changed. Therefore, throughout this book I discuss the implications of psychological research for changing institutions such as traditional marriage, language use, child rearing, the workplace, and the media. Every chapter ends with a section called *Making a Difference*, which showcases how individuals and groups are changing society toward a more feminist ideal.

A Personal Reflection

Because I believe that personal values shape how a researcher approaches his or her topic, I would like to share with you a little about myself and the experiences and values that shaped the writing of this book.

I started out as a psychologist in the field of learning theory. I was taught that to be a good scientist I must separate my personal or social concerns from my scientific problem solving. My dissertation was an analysis of species-specific reactions in rats and their effects on classical and operant conditioning. I enjoyed doing research. It was exciting to learn how to design a good study, do statistical tests, and write an article for publication. Learning theory is one of the oldest branches of psychology; methods and theories were highly developed, and I could learn how to do it all from well-established experts. My mentor and dissertation advisor was a good scientist and a kind man who treated me with respect. He understood that as a single mom with two young children I was juggling a lot of competing demands, yet he encouraged me to become the best researcher I could.

However, soon after I completed my PhD research, my feelings about being a psychologist began to change. More and more, my research seemed like a series of intellectual puzzles that had no connection to the rest of my life. In the lab, I studied abstract theories of conditioning, accepting the assumption that the principles were similar for rats and humans. In the "real world," I became involved in feminist activism and began to see things I had never noticed before. I saw sex discrimination in my university and knew women who struggled to hold their families together in poverty. Trying to build a new egalitarian marriage and bring up my children in nonsexist ways made me much more aware of social pressures to conform to traditional gender roles. I began to ask myself why I was doing a kind of psychology that had so little to say about the world as I knew it. I turned to the study of women and gender in order to make my personal and intellectual life congruent and to begin using my skills as a psychologist on behalf of social change.

Today, I still value my early research for teaching me how to go about scientific inquiry systematically and responsibly, but I have changed my views about what the important questions in psychology are and which theoretical frameworks have the most potential. I chose to develop a new specialization, the study of women and gender, and I have been doing research in this area since 1975. I write this book in the hope that it will contribute in some small way to the creation of a new, transformed psychology, by introducing the psychology of women to the next generation of students (and future psychologists).

A study of 51 distinguished feminist psychologists suggests that my experience of professional and personal change through feminism is not unusual. Asked to describe their experience of feminism, these psychologists indicated that, to them, feminism meant valuing women and their experiences, a concern with equality of power, the need for change and activism, and the idea of gender as a social construct. Their focus on women and gender in their research and teaching was part of a feminism whose meaning was "much more than the dictionary would suggest . . . a lived, conscious, changing experience." Researcher Ellen Kimmel noted the transformative power of feminist thought among her research participants and in her own life: "Feminism (whatever it is and all that it is) transformed my life by connecting it to my work and gathering the disparate parts of myself into a whole" (Kimmel, 1989, p. 145).

I have taught the psychology of women to graduate and undergraduate students for nearly 30 years. My students have differed in their racial and ethnic backgrounds, age, life experience, and sexual orientation. Their personal beliefs and values about feminism, women, and gender varied a great deal. In short, my students have been a diverse group of people. I have welcomed that diversity, and in this book I try to reflect what I have learned from it. Whatever your own background, I welcome you, my newest student, to the study of women and gender. I hope that it will make a difference for you.

I anticipate that you, like many of my students before you, will experience growth in at least some of the following areas as a result of your studies:

- *Critical Thinking Skills.* By studying the psychology of women, you can learn to evaluate psychological research critically and become a more astute, perceptive observer of human behavior.
- *Knowledge and Understanding about Social Inequities.* The focus is on the gender system, sexism, and sex discrimination. However, gender always interacts with other systems of domination such as racism and heterosexism.
- *Empathy for Women.* You may come to appreciate the experiences and viewpoints of your mother, your sisters, and your women friends better. In addition, women students may experience a heightened sense of sisterhood with all women.
- *Desire to Work toward Social Change That Benefits Women—and a Commitment to Do So.* Psychological research and knowledge only matters when it is used.
- *The Ability to See the Larger Context of Women's Lives.* The psychology of women is linked to their place in society and culture.
- *The Understanding That "Women" Is a Complex Category.* Women are a diverse group and must be studied in the context of their lives.

Many of my students in the past have told me that their first course in women and gender raised as many questions as it answered and was at times challenging, even upsetting. From these students I learned that I cannot promise my future students any easy answers. Acquiring knowledge is an ongoing process, for professional researchers as well as for college students.

Feminist psychology and feminism in general seem to be at the point of trying to piece together the individual parts of a quilt. The overall pattern of the quilt that we want to create is still emerging. No one knows what a feminist psychology will look like. . . . We are beginning to piece the separate parts together—to explore the kinds of stitching to use in connecting the pieces and how to place the separate pieces into the pattern. But we have not stopped questioning the process of quilting itself. (Gentry, 1989, pp. 5–6)

Perhaps most important, the quilt is already useful, and the conversations around the margins are vibrant.

Exploring Further

Dicker, Rory, & Piepmeier, Alison (Eds.). (2003). *Catching a wave: Reclaiming feminism for the 21st century.* Boston: Northeastern University Press.
Feminism is alive and well in this collection of essays organized to reflect the process of consciousness-raising. This exciting book points the way toward developing feminist knowledge and activism for the 21st century by building on the past but also recognizing today's realities.

hooks, bell (2000). *Feminism is for everybody: Passionate politics.* Cambridge, MA: South End Press.
An African American feminist writes about the development of feminist thought and its impact on diverse women.

Crawford, Mary, & Unger, Rhoda. (2001). *In our own words: Writings from women's lives* (2nd ed.). New York: McGraw-Hill.
A collection of diverse voices. A mother whose daughter was stalked and murdered, an Asian American woman on the politics of cosmetic surgery, feminist Gloria Steinem's "If Men Could Menstruate"—and many more.

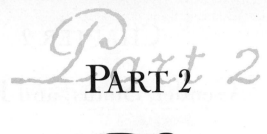

PART 2

Gender in Social Context

CHAPTER 2

Gender, Status, and Power

❦

If combat means living in a ditch, females have biological problems staying in a
ditch for 30 days because they get infections and they don't have upper body
strength. . . . On the other hand, men are basically little piglets. You drop them
in the ditch, they roll around in it, it doesn't matter.

*—Former Speaker of the U.S. House of Representatives, Newt Gingrich,
on women in the military*

I think everyone has to work at being a man or a woman. Transgendered people
are probably more aware of doing the work, that's all.

—Transgender activist Kate Bornstein

As far as I'm concerned, being any gender at all is a drag.

—Rock artist Patti Smith

These three speakers seem to have very clear ideas about men, women, and gender. Yet their words reflect contradictory notions about the meanings of these concepts. Gingrich believes that women have biological limitations that make them
unfit for military duty, although men's "piglet" qualities do not seem to be a problem. In contrast, Patti Smith and Kate Bornstein view gender almost as a choice,
like a costume that one can choose to wear—or not.

Sorting out the multiple and conflicting meanings of biological sex, femininity,
masculinity, and the social roles related to them has not been an easy task for psychologists. In this chapter we separate sex from gender and look at how gender is
related to status and power.

What Is Gender?

Researchers who study the psychology of women distinguish between the concepts
of sex and gender, a distinction that was first made in the late 1970s (Unger, 1979b).
Sex was defined as biological differences in genetic composition and reproductive
anatomy and function. Human infants are labeled as one sex or the other, female
or male, at birth, based on the appearance of their genitals. It sounds like a simple
and straightforward matter, though in fact it can be surprisingly complex (see Chapter 5).

Gender, in contrast to sex, was originally defined as "those characteristics and
traits socioculturally considered appropriate to males and females," the traits that
make up masculinity and femininity (Unger, 1979b, p. 1085). All known societies
recognize biological differentiation and use it as the basis for social distinctions. In
our own society, the process of creating gendered human beings starts at birth.
When a baby is born, the presence of a vagina or penis represents sex—but the pink
or blue blanket that soon enfolds the baby represents gender. The blanket serves as
a cue that this infant is to be treated as a boy or girl, not as a generic human being,
from the start.

According to these definitions, sex is to gender as nature is to nurture. That is,
sex pertains to what is biological or natural, while gender pertains to what is learned

or cultural. The sex/gender distinction was important because it enabled psychologists to separate conceptually the social aspects of gender from the biology of sex, and opened the ways to scientific study of such topics as how children are socialized to conform to their society's gender rules. Distinguishing sex from gender was a very important step in recognizing that biology is not destiny—that many of the apparent differences between women and men might be societally imposed rather than natural or inevitable.

However, the sex/gender distinction made at that time was soon seen to be limited. First, it sets up sex and gender as a nature/nurture dichotomy. Most psychologists now acknowledge that nature and nurture are so intertwined in human psychology that it is often impossible to determine the exact contribution of each. Another problem is that viewing gender as a set of stable, socialized traits does not capture the dynamic, interactive ways that people act out their own gender roles and respond to others according to their gender (Deaux & Major, 1987; Crawford, 1995). The trait view of gender also fails to recognize that gender is a culturally shared system through which societies organize relations between males and females (Bem, 1993), or that it marks social power and status (Henley, 1977; Crawford, 1995). A broader concept of gender was needed.

In this book, I take a dynamic approach, defining **gender** as *a classification system that influences access to power and resources and shapes the relations among women and men.* All known human societies make social distinctions based on gender.

Gender distinctions occur at many levels in society. Their influence is so pervasive that, like fish in water, we may be unaware that they surround us. Gender-related processes influence behavior, thoughts, and feelings in individuals; they affect interactions among individuals; and they help determine the structure of social institutions. The processes by which differences are created and power is allocated can be understood by considering how gender is played out at three levels: societal, interpersonal, and individual. In this chapter, I describe how gender distinctions are created and maintained at these three levels and how the levels are linked. Throughout the book, I will return to these levels of analysis to help illuminate how gender works.

Gender Shapes Societies and Cultures

Most societies are *hierarchical*—they have one or more dominant groups and other subordinate groups. The dominant group has more of whatever that society values, whether it be cattle, land, the opportunity to get a good education, or high-paying jobs. In other words, the dominant group has more **power**—defined as the ability to control the outcomes of others by providing or withholding resources—and higher **status**—defined as social standing that elicits respect (Keltner, Gruenfeld, & Anderson, 2003). Societies can organize hierarchies in terms of a wide variety of arbitrary distinctions—tribe, caste, skin color, religion—and these vary from one society to another. Gender, however, is used universally. To a greater or lesser degree, most modern societies are *patriarchal,* a word that literally means "ruled by the fathers." Patriarchal social systems allocate more power and higher status to men.

Gender and Power

The power conferred by gender is pervasive and multidimensional. For example:

- By and large, men make the laws that everyone must obey. According to the United Nations, in the year 2002, women accounted for only about 14 percent of members of national parliaments and congresses worldwide.
- Organized religion is a powerful influence in maintaining patriarchy. The Jewish, Islamic, and Christian traditions all view the deity as masculine, prescribe subservient roles for women, and limit women's participation and influence within the religious establishment (Galliano, 2003). Cross-culturally, greater religiosity is linked with hostility toward women and opposition to gender equality (Harville & Rienzi, 2000).
- Men have more control over public discourse. On television and radio, women are relatively invisible as voices of authority. For example, only 5 percent of U.S. radio talk show hosts are women (Flanders, 1997). Cross-culturally, stereotypical and demeaning images of women prevail in advertising and the mass media (see Chapter 3).
- According to the United Nations, men have more wealth and more leisure time in virtually every society. Much of the work women do is unpaid (child care, subsistence farming, and housework). When they work for pay, women earn less than men for similar or equivalent tasks (see Chapter 11). Therefore, women have less wealth despite working longer hours than men.
- Women have less access to education than men do. In developing countries, more boys are sent to school, while girls are kept at home to care for younger siblings and do housework. Worldwide, literacy rates are lower for women (Galliano, 2003). In some developed countries, girls and women are legally entitled to education; however, many studies show that boys and men get more attention from teachers and are more often allowed to dominate class time (Ditsch, 1999).
- Men have more political and military power in most societies. In the United States, 84 percent of police officers and 86 percent of the military (including 98 percent of the highest-ranking officers) are men. There is no modern society in which women, as a group, control the political practices or the means of warfare (Sidanius & Pratto, 1999).

Justifying Gender Inequality

Not only do dominant groups have more power in many domains, but they use a variety of tactics to hold on to their power and maintain inequity among groups (Sidanius & Pratto, 1999). *Legitimizing myths* are attitudes, values, and beliefs that serve to justify hierarchical social practices. Many of the legitimizing myths of patriarchy emphasize that women are fundamentally different from men. They may be seen as evil and treacherous (in need of control), or incompetent (in need of restriction for their own good). They may be regarded as helpless, overemotional, and fragile (in need of protection), or pure and self-sacrificing (to be put on a pedestal). Such myths are deeply embedded in culture (see Chapter 3). For example, the archetype of women as evil and treacherous recurs in religion (witch hunts, Eve), fairy tales (wicked stepmothers), personality stereotypes (women are seen as gossipy, catty) and myths about rape (the belief that women frequently make false accusations in order to trap men). Legitimizing myths are often so widely accepted that they seem to reflect undeniable truth.

Prejudice is a negative attitude or feeling toward a person because of his or her membership in a particular social group. The negative attitudes and feelings could include disdain, hatred, or simply feeling uncomfortable around the devalued group. Prejudice often involves the belief that unequal treatment for the devalued group is acceptable. Prejudice on the basis of sex or gender is termed *sexism.* For example, the belief that education is less important for girls than for boys is sexist. However, sexism is often more subtle and complicated than in this example; we return to sexist prejudice later in this chapter. A related prejudice is *heterosexism,* or negative attitudes and beliefs about lesbian, gay, and bisexual people.

Discrimination involves treating people unfairly because of their membership in a particular group. A teacher who pays more attention to the boys in class or a committee that preferentially awards scholarships to male students is engaging in *sex discrimination.* Many studies have found that sex discrimination is common, for example, in employment (Crosby, Iyer, Clayton, & Downing, 2003).

A widespread and systematic pattern of prejudice and discrimination is sometimes termed *oppression.* For example, from 1996 to 2002, the Taliban government oppressed women and girls in Afghanistan by denying them basic human rights such as health care, education, freedom of movement, and a voice in public affairs. Today, women are still denied these basic human rights in many parts of the world.

In addition to gender, other ranking systems, such as race, class, age, and sexuality, also influence social power and can be the basis of prejudice, discrimination, and oppression. Like white women, people of color often face discrimination in employment (Crosby et al., 2003). Feminist research and theory emphasize that these systems are connected—they operate simultaneously in social institutions and everyday interactions, often outside awareness (Weber, 1998). Being white, male, middle or upper class, and heterosexual confers advantages that often are taken for granted by those who have them (Rosenblum & Travis, 1996).

Gender Shapes Social Interactions

Gender affects interactions among people in everyday life. Here we look at how people notice gender and how status and power are conveyed through gender cues.

The Cognitive Impact of Gender

Think of the last time you bought coffee or a snack. Quickly, try to describe the person who waited on you by listing his or her most important characteristics. Try to give the best eyewitness testimony you can.

What characteristics did you list first? People were asked to do a similar task—describe the person who had just sold them a subway token—in a study meant to show that gender is an important category in interpersonal interaction (Grady,

1977). Gender was indeed important. Participants always mentioned that the token seller was a woman; in fact, it was the first or second characteristic listed by every single participant. In this study, the token seller happened to be not only female but also African American. Statistically, mentioning race first would provide more information—*female* rules out only half the population, while *African American* rules out about 85 percent. But people do not categorize along statistical lines. Some categories are more salient or noticeable than others—and gender is one of the most salient of all. Many other studies have shown that people over-rely on gender as a cognitive category. For example, when research participants watch a video of a discussion group, and later mistakenly mix people up in trying to remember who said or did what, they are more likely to confuse two people of the same gender than two of the same age, race, or even the same name (Fiske, Haslam, & Fiske, 1991).

Gender is so important that when gender cues are ambiguous, people engage in cognitive puzzle-solving to figure out the correct gender (see Figure 2.1). Try reading the following story (adapted from John & Sussman, 1989, p. 264). After each segment, state whether you think each of the two characters is female or male:

FIGURE 2.1

Remember the character Pat on *Saturday Night Live*? In creating Pat, the SNL writers played with the kind of gender cues we usually take for granted (hairstyle, clothing, name) and set viewers guessing about how to read the cues.

The scene is a singles bar where some people are dancing, and others are sitting around socializing or drinking at the bar. Chris walks purposefully toward Pat and begins a conversation. After a few minutes, Chris asks Pat to dance. Pat agrees . . .

Chris's sex?

Pat's sex?

As they start to dance, Pat says to Chris, *"You're a good dancer. I don't come across many people who dance this well."*

"Thank you," says Chris with a slightly embarrassed smile. *"I think you dance well too."*

"What do you do for a living?" asks Pat.

"I'm a high school teacher," answers Chris. *"And you?"*

"I'm a research technician," says Pat, *"but I'm thinking of getting into computers."*

As the music ends, Pat says, *"You are a very interesting person. I'd like us to talk some more . . . why don't we sit over here?"*

Chris's sex?

Pat's sex?

Chris orders more drinks, and they continue to talk. *"I'd like to get to know you better."*

Pat replies, *"I find you exciting too, but I'm not sure I'm able to handle too much familiarity now. I'm really interested in my career. . . ."*

Chris's sex?

Pat's sex?

"I understand," says Chris, *"but I'd really like to see more of you."*

"I'm going to think about it," says Pat. *"Why don't we stop off at my place for coffee and. . . ."*

Chris's sex?

Pat's sex?

When research participants tried this task, they changed the gender of the two characters from one scenario to the next, as the gender cues shifted (John & Sussman, 1989). They tried to make sense of the interaction by deciding who was male and who was female according to gender-typed behavior—even though this meant they had to "re-sex" Chris and Pat as they went along! Did you do the same? Apparently, it is cognitively easier to change Pat's and Chris's sex than to recognize that they might engage in gender-inconsistent behaviors. Interestingly, not one participant thought that both characters might be men, or that they both might be women.

By creating experimental situations in which gender cues are ambiguous, psychologists have demonstrated how much we ordinarily rely on such cues. In real life, however, the cues are usually far from ambiguous, and most people are adept at responding to them. The cognitive salience of gender leads to treating women and men as members of a group rather than as individuals.

People tend to perceive their own social group more positively than other groups—a tendency termed the ***intergroup bias effect.*** They also tend to characterize outgroup members as being all alike and having similar qualities, the ***outgroup homogeneity effect.*** We can see these tendencies in action by eavesdropping on a study where women and men talked about each other.

In this study, college students in same-sex pairs were asked to discuss American men and American women for 5 minutes each (Harasty, 1997). In these open-ended discussions, participants generalized more when talking about the gender outgroup than when talking about their own gender group. In other words, male pairs made more comments of the "women are all like that" variety, and female pairs made more "men are all alike" comments. When talking about people of their own gender, they were more specific and less likely to generalize about the entire gender group. The most general comments tended to be negative, suggesting that outgroup members are not only viewed as all alike but not quite as good as the ingroup.

When people evaluate outgroups, they treat high-status and low-status outgroups differently. When college students were asked to rate 17 social groups on various traits, their responses tended to cluster into two types of outgroups: those who were competent but not likable and those who were incompetent but likable. Low-status groups such as Latinos, housewives, and people with mental retardation or physical disability were judged likable but incompetent. High-status groups, which included rich people, feminists, and businesswomen, were judged as competent but dislikable. These results suggest that people are threatened by high-status outgroups and defend themselves by believing that members of such groups are unfriendly, uncaring, and not likable (Fiske, Xu, Cuddy, & Glick, 1999). The 2001 movie *I Am Sam* illustrates how the media use these categories (see Figure 2.2).

Intergroup bias and perceived outgroup homogeneity can lead to particular forms of prejudice and discrimination. Low-status outgroups may be treated with *paternalistic prejudice*—they are seen as needing to be guided and taken care of for

FIGURE 2.2
Outgroups often are stereotypically portrayed in the movies. In *I Am Sam*, a mentally retarded father (Sean Penn) was portrayed as lovable, pure of heart, and devoted to his daughter, but lacking the cognitive skills to care for her—in other words, likable but incompetent. His high-powered female attorney (Michelle Pfeiffer), on the other hand, was portrayed as rude, selfish, and driven, as well as neglectful of her own child—competent but not likable (until she learns life's big lessons from Sam).

their own good by the dominant group. High-status outgroups may be regarded with *envious prejudice*—grudging acknowledgment of their competence along with dislike.

Intergroup biases can lead to characterizing an entire group by the actions of one member. For example, a person may say, "I worked for a woman once and she was impossible. Never again." Using gender as a cue to status, and casting women employers as the outgroup, this individual is treating them as completely homogeneous; if one woman is a difficult boss, all women must be. Male employers are the higher-status ingroup, so a difficult male employer is likely to be seen as an individual. Even after more than one experience with a male bully or tyrant in the office, it is rare to hear people say they would never again work for a man.

Gender as a Presentation of Self

Not only do we respond to others on the basis of gender, but we strive to present ourselves as gendered beings. We turn now to exploring how people perform the gender that is assigned to them.

Imagine that you are deciding what to wear for a job interview. You want the job and expect that the interviewer will be an important man. Now imagine that you find out that the interviewer has very traditional—even sexist—attitudes toward women. When college women were put in this situation as research participants, they changed their style according to their expectations about the interviewer. When they expected to meet a sexist man, they wore more makeup and accessories than when they expected to meet a nonsexist man. Although the interviewer knew nothing about their expectations and behaved similarly to all, the women made less eye contact with the "sexist" man and gave more conventional responses to his questions about their plans for marriage and children (von Baeyer, Sherk, & Zanna, 1981). This is an example of *self-presentation*, or acting out a self in response to the expectations of others.

Both women and men tailor their self-presentation to the audience. In a classic study, female college students were given a description of a male student who was either desirable or undesirable as a potential date and who was characterized as having traditional or more modern values. When the women thought they would have the opportunity to meet the man, they changed their descriptions of themselves to fit the man's traditional or modern values—but only if he was attractive (Zanna & Pack, 1975). A later study showed that male students do exactly the same thing when they think they will have a chance to meet an attractive woman (Morier & Seroy, 1994).

Self-presentation is a strategic choice. For example, women may not label themselves as feminists or express feminist opinions in public or in mixed-gender groups because of the undesirable connotations. Men, in contrast, may express liberal views in public or in mixed-gender groups, but more sexist views around other men. In one study, the men followed just this pattern, endorsing more positive and "politically correct" attitudes about feminism when they thought their attitudes would be more public. The women in the study, however, did not tailor their views to the audience (Rosell & Hartman, 2001). In another study, in which real-life conversation among friends was recorded, a woman talked about gender stereo-types in subtly different ways when with her female peers than when in a mixed-sex group. With women she directly referred to the disadvantages stereotyping causes for women; with men, she talked about the disadvantages of stereotypes for society in general (Stapleton, 2001). Which behaviors reflect the real attitudes of the peo-ple in these studies? Perhaps the reality is constructed by—and changes with—the situation.

Self-presentation strategies make sense because they may have a positive influ-ence on others. Clearly, people's behavior influences how others respond to them. People's actions may even produce the very behaviors they expected from others. This is illustrated by a classic study that involved deceiving people about their in-teraction partner. Pairs of college women and men had telephone conversations. Unbeknownst to the women, the men had been provided with photographs of ran-dom women, some attractive and some unattractive. Thus, each man thought he was conversing with either an attractive or an unattractive woman, but the actual person he talked to was not the one in the photo he saw. Next, independent judges listened to the women's part of the conversation and rated each woman on her per-sonality. Women who had been labeled as attractive were rated as friendlier, more sociable, and more likable than those who had been labeled as unattractive. What was happening here? Apparently, the men treated the women differently in subtle ways, so the conversation brought out the best in those who were treated like at-tractive women (Snyder, Tanke, & Berscheid, 1977). This kind of influence is most likely to occur when people are relying on minimal information about another per-son—such as initial encounters (Valentine, Blankenship, Cooper, & Sullins, 2001).

These studies show that gender can become a ***self-fulfilling prophecy.*** In other words, expectations can make the expected events come true. The earliest studies on self-fulfilling prophecies showed that they can have powerful and lasting effects. When a teacher was led to believe that a particular child was gifted, the child's IQ score went up, even though that child had been randomly selected (Rosenthal & Jacobson, 1968). Apparently, the teachers' beliefs led them to unwittingly treat the "gifted" children in ways that fostered their intellectual growth.

"Doing Gender"

With these dynamic processes in mind, gender can be viewed as a social perfor-mance: Like actors in a play, people enact "man" or "woman." With themselves and others as the audience, they actively create and construct their gender (See Fig-ure 2.3). From this perspective, gender is not something people *have*, like brown eyes or curly hair, but something that people *do* (West & Zimmerman, 1987). In this ongoing performance, "being a woman" is created by social consensus:

> There is no such thing as "being a woman" outside the various practices that define womanhood for my culture—practices ranging from the sort of work I do to my sexual preferences to the clothes I wear to the way I use language. (Cameron, 1996, p. 46)

The performance of gender is sometimes quite conscious and planned. Have you ever seen the TV and print ads for 900-lines that promise conversations with

FIGURE 2.3

Gender as a performance. The same woman, Linda Green, is shown in both photos. On the right, Ms. Green is dressed for her job as a Las Vegas dancer. On the left, she is less concerned with "doing gender."

"Hot babes!" and "Sexy, horny women!"? One researcher interviewed a group of phone-sex workers employed on these lines (Hall, 1995). The sex workers reported that they consciously strove to create themselves as the fantasy women that their clients desired. Because phone sex does not allow for visual cues to contribute to self-presentation, the sex workers created the sexy "babes" of male fantasy entirely through their language. As sellers of a commodity, the workers were aware of what kind of women's language is marketable as sexy: feminine or flowery words, suggestive comments, and a dynamic intonation pattern (breathy, excited, varied in pitch, lilting).

This study illustrates that people cooperate in producing gender (Marecek, Crawford, & Popp, 2004). To the male callers, the fantasy woman constructed entirely through language was presumably satisfying. Callers paid well for the service, and many requested the same worker on repeat calls. The sex workers reported that they liked their jobs because they earned good money and had low overhead (they did not need expensive clothing and they could work from home). One even said that she often washed the dishes while talking to a caller. Strikingly, one of the most successful phone-sex workers was a man who impersonated a woman. Clearly, this man was adept at performing femininity.

Of course, gender performances are not limited to femininity and not always enacted consciously. Indeed, femininity has meaning only in contrast to masculinity. The gender system requires that men "do" being a man as much as women "do" being a woman. In a study of male college students' conversation while watching a basketball game on TV, the students bragged about their sexual exploits with women and gossiped about other men, especially those they did not like, whom they denigrated as "gay," "artsy-fartsy fags," and "homos." In their talk, these young men displayed their heterosexuality and distanced themselves from other men who were supposedly less masculine. This kind of talk "is not only *about* masculinity, it is a sustained performance *of* masculinity" (Cameron, 1997, p. 59).

"Doing gender" is not just a matter of creating and displaying differences. Remember that gender is linked to power and status. When women and men are "doing gender," they are also "doing status" and women in particular are "doing subordination." In other words, the gender category "male" is socially and cognitively linked with greater prestige, prominence, and value than the gender category "female" (Cohen, Berger, & Zeldich, 1972; Ridgeway, 1992).

It is important to remember that "doing gender" usually takes place without reflection or conscious awareness. Unlike phone-sex workers or Vegas dancers, most people are not consciously striving to produce a gendered persona. Instead, like the women who shaped their own behavior to meet what they thought were the expectations of an interviewer, or the men who disparaged "fags" in the studies described earlier, most people do gender without thinking consciously about the process. However, women's subordinate status is created and maintained as people do gender in everyday interaction. Let's look at how this can happen.

Talking Down, Ordering Around, and Silencing

Members of subordinate groups may be treated disrespectfully in everyday conversation. Dominant group members may use particular ways of talking or kinds of talk to assert and maintain their status, especially when the person they are talking to wants or expects to be seen as an equal (Ruscher, 2001).

The most basic kind of conversational disrespect is not allowing the other person to be heard at all by interrupting, controlling the topic, and taking up most of the talk time. A great deal of research shows that men use these tactics in conversation with women more than they do with other men and more than women do with each other. For example, a classic study in which researchers listened in on same- and mixed-gender conversations in public places showed that 96 percent of interruptions in male-female conversations were by male speakers. In same-gender pairs, interruptions were about equally divided between the two speakers (Zimmerman & West, 1975). Of course, not all interruptions are hostile. Sometimes a listener jumps in and interrupts out of interest and enthusiasm. These sorts of interruptions are relatively gender-neutral. However, men do more ***intrusive interruptions***—the kind that are active attempts to end the other speaker's turn and take over the conversation. Moreover, men make a larger proportion of intrusive interruptions in unstructured and naturalistic settings than in the lab—settings that more closely resemble everyday interaction (Anderson & Leaper, 1998).

disap(u?)

If a woman does interrupt another speaker, she risks social disapproval—especially if she interrupts a man. When college students heard audiotapes of (carefully matched) same- and mixed-gender interactions, they gave the lowest ratings to a woman who interrupted a man. Both male and female participants saw her as more rude and disrespectful than interrupters in the other pairs. Their judgments reflect the view that men *should* have higher status in conversation. When a woman interrupts a man, she is doing more than just breaking a politeness rule; she is violating the social order that gives more respect to men (LaFrance, 1992).

Despite widespread beliefs that women are more talkative, men have been shown to take more than a fair share of talk time in a variety of settings, including classrooms, business meetings, and informal conversations (Crawford, 1995). In one review of 63 studies done over a 40-year period, 34 studies showed men talking more than women overall, and only two showed women talking more than men (the others showed no differences or had mixed results) (James & Drakich, 1993). The differences were most apparent in relatively formal, task-oriented situations, such as committee meetings, classrooms, and problem-solving groups; in these settings, men talked more in about three-quarters of all studies. However, even in ordinary social conversation, over 37 percent of studies showed men talking more than women, and only 6 percent (one study) showed women talking more than men. These results suggest that context does make a difference: Men dominate talk more in contexts where there is more at stake in terms of asserting one's status and getting one's own way.

People are so accustomed to men's control of talk time that they may not even notice it, let alone perceive it as unfair. One feminist researcher described her own informal attempts to examine perceptions of conversational fairness (Spender, 1980). She unobtrusively made audiotapes of 16 ordinary conversations between male and female college professors in hallways and other public areas. As soon as she had made each tape, she introduced herself to the speakers, asked their permission to count the number of minutes each person had spoken, and then asked each speaker, "Do you think you had a fair share of the conversation?" The majority of the women said yes, although they had actually spoken between 8 percent and 38 percent of the time. The one woman who thought that she had received *more* than her fair share actually spoke for 35 percent of the time.

Conversational dominance can be more subtle than just taking up most of the talk time. For example, imagine that you are teaching someone how to do the wash. Would you be more likely to use direct commands ("Put the whites in one pile") or suggestions ("It's probably best to separate the whites and the colors")? The use of imperative (command) verbs can be a way of talking down, which implies that the learner is not very competent. In an interesting study of gender, status, and language, college students learned how to do the Heimlich maneuver by watching a slide show (Duval & Ruscher, 1994). This task was chosen because it was gender-neutral and unfamiliar to most students. After watching the slide show, participants were asked to explain the Heimlich maneuver to a same- or other-gender individual. The researchers predicted that men would use more direct orders in explaining the technique to women than to other men, because they would presume that women held lower status and less knowledge than themselves. As predicted, men used more imperative verbs when teaching a woman than occurred in any of the other teacher-learner pairs. Of course, being ordered around as though incompetent may create a self-fulfilling prophecy in which the learner comes to think of herself as less capable.

Conversational dominance is an important aspect of doing gender because it so clearly involves women "doing subordination." But is this invariant across race, ethnicity, and cultures? Very little research has been done on this question. However, one study compared African American and European American adolescents in mixed-gender discussion groups. Overall, the African American groups showed more gender equality in conversational style than the European American groups (Filardo, 1996).

Nonverbal Messages

> Tara and Tom are assistant managers at separate branches of a local business. They meet for lunch to talk about ideas for increasing profits. When Tom talks, Tara keeps her eyes on his face and smiles a lot. When Tara talks, Tom gazes out the window. When he wants to jot something down, he borrows Tara's pen without asking. While they talk, Tom leans away from Tara and pulls the papers on the table between them closer to him. When they get up to leave, Tara looks closely at Tom's face to assess whether he has found the meeting useful. Tom touches Tara lightly on the shoulder.

As this example shows, not all communication relies on words. Here we consider how gendered patterns of nonverbal communication convey status and power in North American society. Although Tara and Tom are ostensibly meeting as equal colleagues, their nonverbal communication patterns convey a clear message about who is more powerful and important.

High-status people seem to have more nonverbal privileges and fewer nonverbal obligations. They can take up more space, invade the space of others, and touch them and their possessions. They are less obligated to show their interest and involvement in others' talk. Pioneering research by Nancy Henley led her to propose the theory that when women and men interact, the nonverbal behavior of men is like that of high-status, dominant individuals, and the nonverbal behavior of women is like that of lower-status, submissive individuals (Henley, 1973, 1977). (See Figure 2.4.) This nonverbal dominance not only reflects status differentials, but it performs—and thus perpetuates—them. With Henley's theory in mind, let's look at each of the differences shown by Tom and Tara.

Many studies have found that women smile more than men do in interaction (LaFrance & Hecht, 2000). Smiling is a socially positive activity that conveys emotional expressiveness and shows interest and involvement, but are all those smiles genuine? High- and low-status people may give (and get) different kinds of smiles. When people are interacting with equal- or lower-status others, their smiles are likely to be consistent with the emotions they report. However, when they are interacting with higher-status others, their smiles are less related to their actual positive emotions (Hecht & LaFrance, 1998). In other words, when high-status people smile at others, it is because they are feeling good; when low-status people smile, it

FIGURE 2.4

Which person is higher in status? Cues to status in interaction include patterns of smiling, posture, eye contact, talking, and listening.

may be because they feel a need to please their interaction partner. High-status people probably should not assume that their subordinates are over-joyed or even interested just because they are smiling.

Women, like low-status people, seem to feel an obligation to smile (LaFrance, 2001). If a woman violates that obligation, she may be admonished to "Cheer up" or be asked "What's the matter with you?" One feminist pro-posed a "smile boycott:" For an entire day, try smiling only when you are gen-uinely pleased, and keep a journal about others' reactions. Do you think the re-sults would be different for males and females who decline to smile?

The patterns of looking and speak-ing used by Tom and Tara also reflect status differences. Looking at conversa-tional partners when they are speaking communicates respect and interest. The more power and status a person has, the less they need to offer this kind of re-spect. High-status people look at their subordinates while speaking to them, but tend to look away when it's the subordinate's turn to talk—a pattern termed *visual dominance*. In a study of interaction in mixed-gender pairs, visual dominance was about equal in women and men who had more expertise on the topic than their conversational partners. However, when their expertise was the same as their partner's, men showed more visual dominance than women. In other words, when participants lacked any other cues to status, they relied on gender and enacted the men's dominance in eye contact (Dovidio, Ellyson, Keating, Heltman, & Brown, 1988).

When Tom leaned away from Tara and pulled the papers closer to himself, he was echoing a gendered pattern of distancing behavior documented in research. In one study, college students in same- and mixed-gender pairs were given 10 minutes to build a domino tower (Lott, 1987). When working with a woman, men more often turned their faces or bodies away and put the dominoes closer to themselves than when they worked with another man; women treated men and other women alike. A follow-up study of prime-time TV shows found the same pattern: Men were more likely to move away and separate from women during social interactions (Lott, 1989). This kind of microdiscrimination reflects and reinforces men's higher status.

Probably the most ambiguous nonverbal behavior between Tom and Tara was Tom's parting touch. Did it communicate friendship? Sexual interest? Or "Don't forget that I'm in charge here"? Like many other nonverbal behaviors, touch can communicate either intimacy or dominance. Whether A is caressing or pawing B, being affectionate or invasive, can be hard to determine (Ruscher, 2001). (See Figure 2.5.) Henley suggests that intimacy behaviors can be distinguished from dominance behaviors by whether the recipient welcomes the touch and whether she can comfortably reciprocate it. Men, because of their higher status, are allowed to initiate more touch with women. This gender privilege is most evident in public settings among people who are not intimately connected (Major, Schmidlin, & Williams, 1990).

In a creative field study, college student researchers were trained to unobtrusively observe professors interacting at professional conventions (Hall, 1996). The researchers did not just determine whether men touched women more

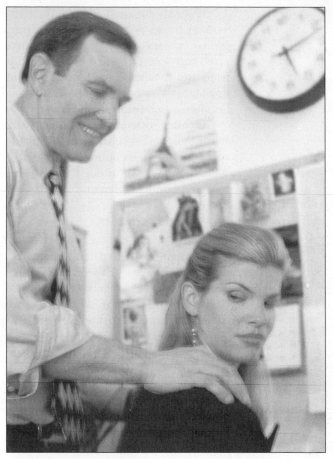

FIGURE 2.5
Touch can be an ambiguous cue. Is this rapport—or sexual harassment?

than vice versa. They coded the kinds of touch that were used: brief touches or more personal pats and hugs, what body parts were touched (hand, arm, shoulder), and the apparent function (greeting, affection, control). Also, they independently assessed each professor's status based on his or her number of publications, the prestige of his or her university, and related measures. There was strong evidence that lower- and higher-status people initiated different kinds of touch. Lower-status people initiated more handshakes, but higher-status people more often touched others' arm or shoulder. It seemed that high-status people were *displaying* status through using more intrusive arm-and-shoulder touch, while lower-status people were trying to *gain* status by politely offering to shake hands. Gender was important, too. When the male and female professor in a pair had equal status, men initiated more touching. In other words, gender itself served as a cue to status when all else was equal, and women were treated like lower-status others.

Cues to dominance don't always work the same way for women and men. If women try to assert dominance through touch, their behavior may be misinterpreted as a sexual move. Or it may evoke negative reactions: When people interacted with low-status and high-status interviewers (undergraduate students wearing jeans and sneakers versus graduate students in business clothes), they did not like low-status women who initiated touch. Status had no effect on liking for men who initiated touch (Storrs & Kleinke, 1990).

all across cultures?

Gender differences in nonverbal behavior are not solely due to power and status. Nonverbal behavior has many functions and varies considerably according to age, ethnicity, and cultures. Nonverbal behavior may also be related to physical size differences. Clearly, though, one function of nonverbal cues is to signal the unequal status of women and men.

Hassles and Stressors

If women are indeed treated as a subordinate group, we would expect that they would often experience hassles that are related to second-class status. Research confirms that these hassles are a part of life for women. When college women and men were asked to keep diaries of sexist incidents and their impact in a series of studies, the women reported an average of one to two such incidents each week, while men reported only about one every two weeks (Swim, Hyers, Cohen, & Ferguson, 2001). Here are a few examples of the experiences reported by women:

Gender role stereotyping: "You're a woman, so fold my laundry."

Demeaning remarks: "I was hanging out with some friends when one guy in the apartment said, "Yo bitch, get me some beer!""

Sexual objectification: Walking home from a party, a woman encountered three men. One complimented her on the belt she was wearing, and another said, "Forget the belt, look at her rack."

Although both women and men sometimes experienced demeaning remarks, the ones directed at women were more personal, whereas the ones aimed at men were more likely to address men in general. For example, one man reported hearing someone say that "men are jerks." Women were far more likely to experience sexually degrading and objectifying remarks (Swim et al., pp. 36–37, 42).

Living with everyday sexism has a negative effect on the well-being of both women and men. In these studies, participants who experienced more sexist hassles reported higher anger, anxiety, and depression, along with lower self-esteem and reduced comfort in social situations. Because women experience significantly more sexist hassles overall than men, the impact on them is greater.

note

Studies using more diverse samples show similar results. When researchers used a detailed survey to measure women's experiences of sexism within the past year and also over the lifetime, they found that such experiences are almost universal—99 percent of the women had experienced a sexist event at least once, and 97 percent within the past year (Klonoff & Landrine, 1995). The most common experiences included being subjected to sexist jokes (94 percent), being treated with a lack of respect (83 percent), being called sexist names, and being sexually harassed (82 percent for each). A majority of the women surveyed (56 percent) said that they had been hit, pushed, or physically threatened because of being a woman. (See Table 2.1).

The sample of more than 600 women in this study was ethnically, racially, and economically diverse. Women of color and white women reported experiencing similar kinds of sexist events; however, women of color reported more sexist

TABLE 2.1   Women's Experiences of Sexism

Percentages are those women who said they had experienced each type of incident *because of being a woman.*

Item	Percent Who Experienced It within Lifetime	Percent Who Experienced It within Past Year
Treated unfairly by		
teachers/professors	53	25
your employer, boss or supervisors	60	32
your co-workers, fellow students, or colleagues	58	37
people in service jobs (store clerks, servers, bartenders, bank tellers, mechanics)	77	62
strangers	73	59
people in helping jobs (doctors, nurses, psychiatrists, case workers, dentists, school counselors, therapists, pediatricians, school principals, gynecologists)	59	40
your boyfriend, husband, or other important man in your life	75	50
Denied a raise, promotion, tenure, good assignment, job, or other such thing at work that you deserved	40	18
People have made inappropriate or unwanted sexual advances to you	82	55
People failed to show you respect	83	62
Been really angry about something sexist that was done to you	76	52
Forced to take drastic steps (filing a grievance/lawsuit, quitting your job, moving away) to deal with a sexist incident	19	9
Been called a sexist name like bitch, cunt, chick, or other names	82	54
Gotten into an argument or a fight about something sexist that was done or said to you or somebody else	66	44
Been made fun of, picked on, pushed, shoved, hit, or threatened with harm	56	29
Heard people making sexist jokes or degrading sexual jokes	94	84

Source: Adapted from Klonoff & Landrine, 1995. Percentages have been rounded to nearest whole number.

experiences overall. Like the college students in the diary studies, these women also experienced psychological costs. The number of sexist experiences reported was related to the overall number of psychological and physical symptoms reported and to specific problems such as depression, premenstrual symptoms, and obsessive-compulsive behaviors. In fact, sexism statistically predicted psychological and physical problems better than other measures of stressful life events alone (Landrine, Klonoff, Gibbs, Manning, & Lund, 1995).

Clearly, being treated like a second-class citizen in everyday interactions is a major source of stress for members of subordinate groups. (For more on societal sources of women's psychological distress, see Chapter 13.) As the authors of these studies noted, sexist events have a greater negative impact than do other life events on women's psychological and physical health because "sexist events are inherently demeaning, degrading, and highly personal; they are attacks upon and negative responses to something essential about the self that cannot be changed: being a woman" (Klonoff & Landrine, 1995, p. 442).

Double Binds

Why do women (and members of other subordinated groups) put up with unequal treatment? Why don't they just start acting like members of the dominant group? Surely, women can tell sexist jokes, order men around, interrupt them, and call them names (see Figure 2.6). Aside from the fact that this kind of equality would create a pretty unpleasant society to live in, there are other reasons.

An important aspect of being part of a subordinated group is that subordinate status creates **double binds,** or "damned-if you-do, damned if-you-don't" situations. If the subordinate group member acts like a member of the dominant group, she is criticized for stepping out of her place and not being a model member of her subordinate group. If she acts like a model subordinate group member, she is criticized for not being as competent as dominant group members. Double binds create no-win situations. For example, a white middle-class mother who works at a high-status career outside the home may be criticized as selfish, neglectful of her children, and cold; one who stays home may be viewed as a dull, uninteresting housewife. The double bind may work differently for a black woman; like the white woman, she may be seen as a bad mother for working outside the home, and also an unmotivated worker if she needs to take time off for her children. Either way, double binds like these do not exist for men; being a good father is seen as compatible with focusing on a job or career for both white and black men.

Studies of everyday social situations have shown that women often face double binds. This occurs partly because dominant behaviors are strongly associated with men. In one study, college students and other young adults were shown a list of dominant and submissive social behaviors and asked to rate how often a typical man or woman would behave that way. The participants reported that dominant acts (setting goals for a group, refusing to back down in an argument) were more likely to be done by a man, and submissive acts (accepting verbal abuse, not complaining when overcharged at the store) were more likely to be done by a woman (McCreary & Rhodes, 2001). Because dominant behaviors are linked in people's belief systems with men, they may be less effective when used by women.

FIGURE 2.6
Perhaps not the best kind of equality . . .

Let's take the example of communication style. In American society, speaking up for oneself, expressing opinions, and being assertive about one's rights are valued—so much so that assertiveness training courses and workshops are a popular type of psychological self-improvement. Many of these workshops are aimed specifically at women. However, when women adopt this new assertive style, they may be judged differently than men who speak the same way. In one study, college students and older adults were asked to read scenarios in which a male or female speaker behaved assertively but respectfully (e.g., politely asking a supervisor not to call him/her kiddo in front of clients). Participants, especially those who were older and male, judged assertive women as equally competent but less likable than assertive men (Crawford, 1988). The double bind is obvious: Women, but not men, have to choose between being unassertive (and letting others dominate them) and being assertive (and risking being disliked).

Other studies also show that so-called masculine speech is less effective for women than for men. Male raters viewed women who spoke in a competent, assertive style as less likable, less influential, and more threatening than men who used the same style—unless they went out of their way to appear warm and friendly (Carli, 2001). In a study of the effects of tentative versus assertive speech, both women and men judged a woman who spoke tentatively as less competent and knowledgeable than a woman who spoke assertively; speech style did not affect judgments about men. This result suggests that speaking more assertively would benefit women. However, male listeners were more influenced by the woman who spoke tentatively, while female listeners were more influenced by the woman who spoke assertively (Carli, 1990).

Gender is an asset for men because masculinity is linked with perceptions of dominance, competence, and normative behavior. Gender is a liability for women because these dominant and masterful characteristics are still not equally valued in women. The ever-present possibility of being devalued, disliked, or discounted for behaving in ways that are acceptable for men means that women must adopt **gender management strategies:** ways of behaving that are aimed at softening a woman's impact, reassuring others that she is not threatening, and displaying niceness as well as (not too much) competence. It isn't easy; behaviors that make women appear more competent (like speaking up about one's own ability) also may make them appear less likable (Rudman & Glick, 1999).

What happens to women who do not play the gender management game? An example is the case of Ann Hopkins, who was denied a partnership in a major corporation despite the fact that she had contributed more billable hours and brought in more earnings than any of the 87 male employees proposed for partner—$25 million in revenue (Fiske, Besoff, Borgida, Deaux, & Heilman, 1991). The reason? Hopkins was told that she lacked "interpersonal skills," ought to go to "charm school," wear makeup and jewelry, have her hair styled, and dress in more "feminine" clothes. Hopkins sued, and a group of eminent psychologists served as expert witnesses on her behalf when the case (*Hopkins v. Price Water House*) went to the U.S. Supreme Court. Fortunately, the Court was not fooled by the excuses given for denying Hopkins her promotion. Ruling in her favor, they specifically pointed out the double bind she had been placed in:

> An employer who objects to aggressiveness in women but whose positions require this trait places women in an intolerable Catch-22: out of a job if they behave aggressively and out of a job if they don't. (as cited in Fiske et al., 1991)

Gender Shapes Individuals

To a greater or lesser extent, women and men come to accept gender distinctions visible at the social structural level and enacted at the interpersonal level as part of the self-concept. They become **gender-typed,** ascribing to themselves the traits, behaviors, and roles normative for people of their sex in their culture. Gender typing is an important part of identity for most people, and the topic has generated a great deal of psychological research. In Chapter 6, I will look in detail at the gender-typing process during childhood and adolescence. Here, in keeping with the theme of power and status, I focus on how women's subordinate status becomes internalized.

People accept much more than the traits designated as masculine or feminine in their culture. They also internalize the ideologies that support the gender system. These ideologies become consensual—they are shared by members of dominant and subordinate groups alike (Sidanius & Pratto, 1999). In other words, members of both the dominant and subordinate groups come to believe the legitimizing myths of the dominant group and develop attitudes that serve to justify its dominance. When members of subordinate groups accept the myths that justify their inequality, the dominant group usually does not need to control them through force or other harsh methods. Instead, subordinates usually control themselves (Foucalt, 1972; Marecek, Crawford, & Popp, 2004).

Identity, Power, and Gender Differences

Do women internalize their devaluation and subordination? Do they accept the legitimizing myths that keep them in their place? Jean Baker Miller (1986) has looked closely at the relationship between power and feminine personality. She proposed that because women are a subordinate group in society, they develop personality characteristics that reflect their subordination and enable them to cope with it.

Dominant groups define acceptable roles for subordinates, which usually involve services that the dominant group members do not want to perform for themselves. Thus, women, minorities, and poor people are relegated to low-status, low-paying jobs that often involve cleaning up the waste products of the dominant group or providing them with personal services. Roles and activities that are preferred are closed to subordinates. Subordinates are said to be unable to fill those roles, and the reasons given by the dominants usually involve subordinates' deficiencies of mind or body. In our society, the status and pay accorded nurses, teachers, homemakers, and child-care workers versus physicians, attorneys, carpenters, and auto mechanics reflect devaluation of "women's work"; and it is easy to find people who believe that women are unsuited for certain prestigious or demanding jobs.

Being a subordinate has psychological consequences, too, according to Miller. Subordinates are encouraged to develop psychological characteristics that are useful and pleasing to the dominant group, and the ideal subordinate is described in terms of these characteristics that

> form a certain familiar cluster: submissiveness, passivity, docility, dependency, lack of initiative, inability to act, to decide, to think, and the like . . . qualities more characteristic of children than adults—immaturity, weakness, and helplessness. If subordinates adopt these characteristics they are considered well-adjusted. (1986, p. 7)

Moreover, women may come to accept the dominant group's untruths about women. According to Miller, there are a great many women who believe, consciously or not, that they are less important than men. People in subordinate social

groups may be the last to recognize their own predicament and may even participate in perpetuating it. Strange as it may seem, "oppression is very much a cooperative game" (Sidanius & Pratto, 1999, p. 43).

Denial of Personal Discrimination

The American legal system is based on the idea of fairness: If you believe you have
been wronged or discriminated against, you have the right to seek justice. Unfortunately, a large research literature in social psychology shows that victims of injustice
often do not recognize that they are being treated unfairly.

It's not that people are blind to discrimination at the group level. If you ask
Latinos or Latinas about racial discrimination in the United States, or ask women
about sex discrimination, or ask gay and lesbian people about heterosexist discrimination, they are very likely to acknowledge that such discrimination does happen.
However, when asked if they have ever *personally* been discriminated against, they
are much less likely to acknowledge that it has happened to them. This discrepancy
is termed **denial of personal discrimination** (Crosby et al., 2003*)*.

Denial of personal discrimination is pervasive. It has been documented in
women, ethnic and linguistic minorities in Canada, as well as many samples of
women, gay and lesbian people, and African Americans in the United States
(Crosby et al., 2003). In the first, now-classic study (Crosby, 1982), a large sample
of employed women and men in the Northeastern United States were asked in detail about their perceptions of the position of working women and about their satisfaction with their own working position. The researcher was surprised to find
that, although the employed women were, by objective measures, victims of salary
discrimination,

> they expressed no more dissatisfaction about their personal situations than did the men.
> The women did, however, recognize the disadvantages faced by working women in gen-
> eral. It seemed as if each woman saw herself as the one lucky exception to the general
> rule of sex discrimination. (Crosby et al., 2003, p. 104)

Of course, it is logically impossible for a group to be subject to discrimination
and for every individual in that group to be exempt from it!

Denial of personal discrimination is probably related to the need to believe in
a just world, where each person gets what he or she deserves (Crosby et al., 2003).
It may also be related to shifting standards of evaluation—people may evaluate a
salary of X dollars a week as merely adequate for a man but very good for a woman,
instead of comparing them equally (Biernat & Kobrynowicz, 1999). And denial of
personal discrimination is related to belief in the legitimizing myths of the dominant group. In other words, the more one accepts ideologies that justify the status
quo of power and status, the less one perceives discrimination. This was tested in a
recent study comparing high-status groups (European Americans and men) with
low-status groups (African Americans, Latino/Latina Americans, and women). The
more that members of low-status groups accepted the belief that America is an open
society where anyone can get ahead if they just work hard enough, the less likely
they were to report that they had experienced discrimination. Next, the researchers
rigged a laboratory situation in which women experienced rejection by a man (not

being offered a desirable job in the experiment) or men experienced the same rejection from a woman. The more a woman believed in the myth of the open society, the less likely she was to believe that her rejection was due to discrimination. In contrast, the more a man believed in the myth, the more likely he was to believe he'd been discriminated against. Thus, believing in upward mobility—the ideology of the dominant group—affects how people interpret whether they have experienced discrimination (Major, Gramzow, McCoy, Levin, Schmader, & Sidanius, 2002).

Denial of personal discrimination has important social consequences. When members of subordinated groups do not have a sense of personal injustice, they may be slow to take action against their own disadvantaged situation. "Protests are not likely if the wronged party has little awareness of being wronged. It is hard to correct a problem if the problem goes unrecognized" (Crosby et al., 2003, p. 103).

How Much Is Your Work Worth? Gender and Entitlement

> You are an employee in an assisted living facility for older adults. Your supervisor is considering offering the residents help with shopping, and asks you to generate some ideas on whether it would be a good idea to encourage online shopping. Because it's an extra project, the supervisor asks you to suggest how much you think you should be paid for the task of writing down your thoughts on this issue.

In an experiment where the situation was similar to our example (Jost, 1997), the women who participated paid themselves 18 percent less and rated their ideas as less original than did the men, despite the fact that independent judges (who did not know the gender of the author) rated the men's and women's work as equally good. Research studies have repeatedly shown that when women and men are asked to specify an appropriate pay rate for their work, women say their work is worth less than men do (Steil, McGann, & Kahn, 2001). They seem not to feel entitled to equality.

Women often justify the lower pay they give themselves by believing that their work is not as good as others' work, but even when they recognize that the quality of their work is equal, they still may pay themselves less (Major, 1994). Like denial of personal discrimination, this is a pervasive phenomenon that deters women from taking action or protesting against their subordinate status. Like denial, it may reflect internalization of the values of the dominant group.

Of course, it is also possible that the men in these studies *over*value their work. And it may be that women's relative lack of entitlement is based on actual experience of lower pay. In one study, college students were asked about their expectations of earnings in the future. The women tended to believe that they deserved less than did the men. However, this gender difference in entitlement disappeared when the researchers controlled for the actual earnings from the students' most recent summer jobs, where the women had earned less than the men on average (Desmarais & Curtis, 1997). Gender differences in entitlement reflect status inequalities, too. When researchers experimentally raised women's status (by telling participants that women were particularly good at the task), the gender difference disappeared—high status women paid themselves as much as men did (Hogue & Yoder, 2003).

Whatever the underlying reasons for denial of personal discrimination and gender differences in entitlement (and there may be several), these lines of research suggest that, as Miller's theory predicts, those who are treated like second-class citizens learn to accept inequality as the norm. When this happens, members of the dominant group may not even have to exercise prejudice and discrimination very often. They can count on members of the subordinate group to do it to themselves.

In later chapters, we look at other gender-related differences that may reflect internalized subordination. Girls may lose self-esteem and confidence in their academic ability, especially in mathematics and science, as they progress through the educational system (Chapter 4) and are more likely to suffer from disturbances of body image, eating disorders, and depression (Chapters 7 and 13). These differences are not natural. They are shaped by differential opportunities and maintained in social interaction. They are the product of the gender system.

Sexist Attitudes

Sexist prejudice is not just a matter of men's disliking women. Sexist attitudes are more complicated than that. Both women and men agree that women are generally nicer and more pleasant than men (Eagly & Mladinic, 1993). Moreover, as noted in Chapter 1, attitudes toward women have changed in a positive direction over past decades (Twenge, 1997). However, sexism persists. Today's sexism is likely to be more subtle and conflicted than the sexism of the past. How is sexism measured in contemporary Western societies and what do these measures reveal about contemporary sexist attitudes?

One version of contemporary sexism, termed *neosexism,* reflects the conflict between egalitarian values and residual negative feelings and beliefs about women (Tougas, Brown, Beaton, & Joly, 1995). For example, people who have neosexist beliefs tend to agree with statements such as, "It is difficult to work for a female boss," and "Women shouldn't push themselves where they are not wanted." Studies of male college students and employees showed that neosexist attitudes predicted opposition to affirmative action in both groups.

A related measure, *modern sexism,* involves beliefs that equality has more or less been achieved and that whatever inequalities may remain are not due to discrimination (Swim, Aiken, Hall, & Hunter, 1995). People who score high on measures of modern sexism see little need for social policies aimed at improving women's status. They do not support women's struggle toward equality because they are somewhat hostile to women's demands and believe that women are no longer discriminated against.

Another important aspect of contemporary sexism aimed at women is that it is *ambivalent*: It involves both hostility and benevolence toward women (Glick & Fiske, 1996). *Hostile sexism* involves the beliefs that women are inferior and that they are threatening to take over men's rightful (dominant) place. Men who score high on hostile sexism agree with statements such as these:

- Women seek to gain power by getting control over men.
- Most women interpret innocent remarks or acts as being sexist.

Benevolent sexism emphasizes that women are special beings to be cherished and protected, as measured by items such as these:

- A good woman should be set on a pedestal by her man.
- Many women have a quality of purity that few men possess.

Men who endorse both kinds of sexism—termed *ambivalent sexists*—seem to have polarized images of women. For example, they acknowledge that "career women" are intelligent and hardworking, but they also believe that they are aggressive, selfish, and cold. The women they feel the most positive about are those in roles that serve men's needs, such as homemakers and "sexy babes" (Glick, Diebold, Bailey-Werner, & Zhu, 1997). Ambivalent sexism is hard to change because the sexist man can easily deny his prejudice. ("But I *love* women; I think they're wonderful and deserve to be treasured!") This paternalism may hinder him and others from recognizing the more hostile aspect of his sexism ("as long as they stay in their place").

Ambivalent sexism has been measured in more than 15,000 men and women in 19 nations (Glick et al., 2000). Both hostile and benevolent sexism were found to be quite common across cultures. In every country studied, men endorsed hostile sexism more than women did, although the gender differences were much larger in some cultures (South Africa, Italy) than in others (England, the Netherlands). (See Figure 2.7.) Surprisingly, though, women endorsed benevolent sexism as much as men did in about half the countries studied—and, in four countries, women scored higher than did men (see Figure 2.8). Patterns of correlations showed that the more sexist a

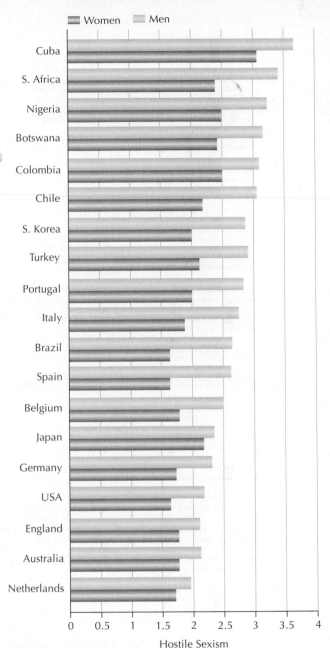

FIGURE 2.7

Hostile sexism across countries.

Note: "Hostile Sexism Across Countries," from "Beyond Prejudice as Simple Antipathy: Hostile and Benevolent Sexism Across Cultures," 2000, P. Glick, et al., *Journal of Personality and Social Psychology*, 79, p. 770. Copyright © 2000 by the American Psychological Association. Reprinted with permission.

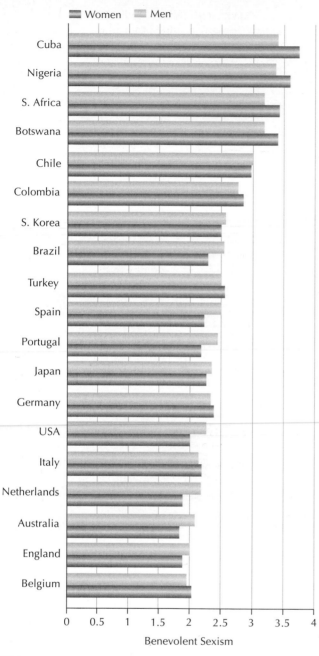

Women   Men

FIGURE 2.8

Benevolent sexism across countries.

Note: From "Beyond Prejudice as Simple Antipathy: Hostile and Benevolent Sexism Across Cultures," 2000, P. Glick, et al., *Journal of Personality and Social Psychology*, 79, p. 770. Copyright © 2000 by the American Psychological Association. Reprinted with permission.

nation's men were, the more women of that nation endorsed benevolent sexism.

Moreover, the differences among cultures in this study were systematically related to women's status and power within each culture. Using measures of gender inequality developed by the United Nations that assessed such factors as women's proportion of seats in parliament, earned income, literacy rates, and life expectancy, the research team found that the more that men in a given country endorsed sexist beliefs, the lower the status of women in that country.

If benevolent sexism reflects a positive view that women should be cherished and protected by men, why is it a problem? Although benevolent sexism seems less harmful than hostile sexism, it still exaggerates the differences between women and men. Moreover, people who are pure, innocent, and worthy of protection are not likely to be thought of as capable leaders. Being put on a pedestal may offer some compensation for the patriarchal status quo; however, life on a pedestal can be quite confining.

Benevolent sexism is correlated with hostile sexism, and the two sustain patriarchy in complementary ways. Hostile sexism punishes women who challenge the status quo, while benevolent sexism rewards those who accept conventional gender norms and power relations (Glick & Fiske, 2001). In cultures where a great many men are hostile sexists, women may cope by believing that if they behave according to the societal rules for good women, they will be protected. "The irony is that women are forced to seek protection from the very group that threatens them, and the greater the threat, the stronger the incentive to accept benevolent sexism's protective ideology" (Glick & Fiske, 2001, p. 113).

Sexist attitudes such as these portray women as *either* competent and autonomous *or* likable and worthy, and they are one source of many double binds like those described earlier. Thus, both hostile and benevolent sexism help perpetuate the higher status and social power of men. Overall, the varieties of sexism all reflect an ideology that is used to justify gender inequality.

Sexism is related to prejudice against other lower-status groups. ***Social dominance orientation (SDO)*** is a general measure of how much an individual supports the domination of so-called inferior groups by superior groups (Sidanius & Pratto, 1999). SDO is relevant to many dimensions of discrimination, including race, religion, sexuality, gender, and nationality. People who are high in SDO tend to agree with statements such as these:

- This country would be better off if inferior groups stayed in their place.
- To get ahead in life, it is sometimes necessary to step on other groups of people.

People who are high in SDO tend to show racial and ethnic prejudice, sexism, heterosexism, acceptance of rape myths, and political conservatism. They tend to support social policies that favor high-status groups and oppose policies that would give more power to lower-status groups. Thus, they are likely to support more spending on prisons and the military, and oppose women's rights, gay and lesbian rights, universal health care, antipoverty programs, and affirmative action. Men and women have been measured on SDO in 45 samples totaling over 19,000 participants in 10 countries. In 39 of these samples, men scored significantly higher on SDO than did women, and in six, they scored about the same; there was not a single sample in which women scored higher than men (Sidanius & Pratto, 1999).

Linking the Levels of Gender: A Summary

Gender has a complex structure of meanings. Feminists initially distinguished it from sex by defining it as the traits and roles considered appropriate for males and females. With this definition, they emphasized that gender is a socialized part of self and identity. Today, the understanding of gender is much broader. We have learned that gender can be conceptualized as:

- a universal system of social classification that accords greater power and status to men.
- a dynamic process of performing what it means to be female or male.
- an aspect of individual identity and attitudes.

When focusing on gender as a social system, we emphasized societal power structures that support patriarchy. When focusing on gender as a self-presentation and a performance, we emphasized the many small, almost invisible, ways that people present themselves as gendered beings and conform to others' gender-based expectations, emphasizing that for women, doing gender also means doing subordination. The performance of gender is usually not a conscious, self-aware choice; rather it is a more or less automatic response to social pressures. When focusing on gender as a socialized aspect of individuals, we saw that both males and females become gender typed—they become more or less acceptable examples of what it means to be a masculine man or a feminine woman in their particular culture, even though for women this may entail demeaning their own gender. Gender becomes part of the self and identity. The three levels of the gender system are linked, reinforcing each other.

There is one important aspect of gender that characterizes all these levels: power. Patriarchy is a system that accords more power and higher social status to men. Gender is expressed differently in different cultures, and the degree of women's subordination varies across time and place, but there are no known cultures where women have more social and political advantages than men. One result of this power imbalance is evident cross-culturally: high rates of violence against girls and women.

brief summary

The Gender System and Violence

Perhaps the clearest demonstration of the worldwide harm done by patriarchal social systems is violence against girls and women. In virtually every culture, some kinds of violence against women are taken for granted. Forced genital surgery or mutilation, sexual harassment, rape, incest, forced marriage, and physical and emotional violence in relationships can be seen as culturally useful ways of controlling girls and women.

Some forms of violence, such as stoning women (but not men) for adultery, may be officially permitted by the state; others represent a kind of unofficial terrorism. Although they are not technically legal, everyone knows they happen, and the government rarely intervenes (Sidanius & Pratto, 1999). For example, in Nepal, India, Thailand, and other developing countries, young girls from rural areas are often sold into sexual slavery. The sex trafficking involves many people: villagers who lie to the girls and their families about jobs in the city; families who may close their eyes to their daughter's fate; brokers who take the girls from the village to the city; brothel owners and pimps who keep them in bondage; customers who buy the use of their bodies. Until recently, the governments of the countries involved did little to intervene.

Research has documented many other examples of the prevalence of gendered violence:

- In studies conducted around the world, one-third of women have been physically assaulted, subjected to coerced sexual activity, and victimized by severe emotional abuse (Heise, Ellsberg, & Gottemmoeller, 1999).
- One-third of all U.S. women report being hit, choked, kicked, or otherwise physically harmed by acquaintances or partners. Fifteen percent—about one in every six—are raped (Gazmarian et al., 2000).
- Over a quarter of U.S. women have experienced sexual abuse during childhood (Gazmarian et al., 2000).
- Rape and other violent acts against women are widespread in war zones and refugee camps throughout the world (Mollica et al., 1993).

- Infanticide—the murder of unwanted infants—has been culturally accepted at various times and places in history. About 9 percent of cultures have practiced sex-biased infanticide. In the majority of these, the unwanted sex was female (Hrdy, 1988).
- Female genital mutilation is a common practice in at least 28 African countries and in some parts of Asia. It involves cutting away the clitoris and lips of the vagina and sometimes sewing together the outer vaginal lips. Its purpose is to control women's sexuality. It is usually performed on girls between the ages of 4 and 12 (Abusharaf, 1998).
- In some countries, over half of all female murder victims are killed by a current or former partner. In the United States, the rate is only slightly lower (42 percent) (Neft & Levine, 1997).

Although not every woman will experience violence directly, the threat of it is an important part of the fabric of life for all women. Gender-linked violence has profound negative effects on women's physical health and psychological well-being. It can lead not only to physical injury, but also to chronic pain, disability, unwanted pregnancy, sexually transmitted diseases, depression, anxiety, elevated suicide risk, substance abuse, and post-traumatic stress syndrome. The inequalities and oppression suffered by women recently led one expert in public health to state, "Being born female is dangerous for your health" (Murphy, 2003, p. 205). According to the World Health Organization, gender-linked forms of violence share an underlying cause: "the lower social status of women and the belief that women are the property of men" (as cited in Murphy, 2003, p. 208).

I will discuss specific types of violence, along with their predictors, social contexts, and aftermath in more detail in later parts of this book. For now, I want to focus on the connections between the gender system and violence.

Violence against girls and women involves all the levels of the gender system (White & Kowalski, 1998). Patriarchy, operating at the sociocultural level, affects the power dynamics of relationships. Ideas and beliefs about the greater value of men, passed down through cultural influences, are part of our social communities. Power dynamics are enacted in interpersonal encounters and become internalized parts of the self. Thus,

> cultural norms governing the use of aggression as a tool of the more powerful to subdue the weaker combine with gender inequalities to create a climate conducive to violence against women. Violence against women is inextricably bound to the social context of male domination and control. The patriarchal view of society gives men a higher value than women. It is taken for granted that men should dominate in politics, economics, and the social world, including family life and interpersonal relationships. This is seen as normal and natural. Violence against women is an assertion of the power and control men have over women. (White, Donat, & Bondurant, 2000, p. 484)

Let's look at one recent example of patriarchal violence against women in our own society to see how these levels are linked. Early in 2003, a major scandal erupted at the U.S. Air Force Academy. Over 50 female cadets and former cadets alleged that they had been sexually assaulted or raped while attending the academy, and that when they tried to report the assaults, the victims were shunned, pressured to keep quiet, or disciplined. None of the perpetrators had been punished.

As the news media publicized the situation, it became apparent that sexual harassment and violence against women were longstanding problems at all the service academies. A 1994 government report had concluded that 50 percent to 75 percent of women at these institutions had experienced sexual harassment at least twice a month. In fact, the Air Force's own annual survey at the academy had revealed problems over the past five years (Lunney, 2003).

How does the violence against women at the Air Force Academy reflect the gender system and the links among its levels? Clearly, at the broadest level, the men who held social and political power at the academy did not enforce its honor code. Instead, they tolerated a climate that was hostile and dangerous for women. At the interpersonal level, the male cadets who harassed and assaulted their classmates abused the status and power they held as men and as upperclassmen. For example, two women testified in a military hearing that an upperclassman lured them to his room in two separate incidents and forced one to fondle him. The women reported that they were afraid to disobey because they are taught that upperclassmen have legitimate authority and may order first-year students to do anything they want. "You don't really question that," a roommate of one of the victims testified. Others reported that if a woman complained or reported an assault, the perpetrator would use his power and influence to have her shunned by other cadets (Crist, 2003). At the individual level, the assaults were traumatizing to the women; being disbelieved or socially shunned for reporting an assault added to the trauma.

How can this kind of violence be stopped? Interventions must encompass all the levels of the gender system. At the individual level, survivors of assault require counseling and medical care. Their recovery is also aided by seeing the perpetrator brought to justice. At the institutional level, the leadership of the academy must be held accountable. (Indeed, several high officials lost their positions because of the scandal.) But others questioned whether a mere change of leaders would change the academy's patriarchal and hierarchical culture, and Congress ordered an independent investigation (Lunney, 2003). In the hostile climate of the academy, everyday interactions between male and female cadets, which are based on gendered power, occur in a hypermasculine context. A new survey conducted in May 2003 documented once again that almost 20 percent of female cadets had experienced sexual assault; fewer than 20 percent of the assaults were ever reported, and among the women who did report the crime, nearly half said they experienced some form of reprisal (Edmonson, 2003). If you were in charge of solving this problem, which level would be your starting point?

Making a Difference

Women's movements around the world and across time have been made up of women and men working to secure equal human rights for all. The first wave of feminist activists included the suffragists who achieved the vote for women in the early 1900s. The second wave, whose activism began in the 1960s, worked on issues such as reproductive rights, workplace equality, sexism in the media, and an end to violence against women. Many younger women identify as third-wave feminists who are defining their own goals for the next round of social change.

Transforming Ourselves

Most women have internalized at least some of the sexist messages of our culture. As documented in this chapter, some doubt their abilities or do not feel entitled to equal treatment. The chapters that follow document that many women feel shame about their bodies, their sexuality, or the normal changes of aging; feel guilt about not being perfect mothers; or blame themselves for having been subjected to rape, incest, or sexual harassment. This self-hatred is fostered by exposure to media images (Chapter 3), gender socialization in childhood and adolescence (Chapter 6), and the experience of having lower status and power in everyday interactions and relationships.

What can women do to change these beliefs and attitudes? In the 1970s, second-wave feminists developed *consciousness-raising (C-R) groups,* in which women met informally to talk about their lives as women. Women who took part in these groups began to see that their problems were not just individual deficiencies but were related to society's devaluation of women. Consciousness-raising groups encouraged social action, leading to such activities as opening shelters for battered women and protesting against sexist advertising. However, as women made some social progress in the 1970s and 1980s, many of these groups became more individually focused and then disappeared altogether (Kahn & Yoder, 1989; Rosenthal, 1984). Nevertheless, many organizations working for social change have incorporated the values and norms of C-R groups into their process.

C-R groups often led to positive changes for the women in them, including an altered worldview, greater awareness of sexism, positive changes in self-image, increased self-acceptance, and increased awareness of anger (Kravetz, 1980). Consciousness-raising became a model for feminist therapy because it offered women an opportunity to share experiences without being treated as patients in need of help and because C-R groups assumed that the environment plays a major role in women's problems and difficulties (Brodsky, 1973). Today, although C-R groups no longer exist, feminist counseling and therapy empower women who want to make changes in their lives (see Chapter 13).

Although relatively few women take part in feminist therapy, many develop political and personal values compatible with feminism in other ways. Some women develop feminist values after having personal experiences with sexism. These negative experiences can lead to transformative moments in which a woman suddenly realizes that she lives in a sexist society and wants to change it, not just for herself but also for other women (Cole, Zucker, & Duncan, 2001).

Still another route to feminist consciousness and activism is education. When students begin to think critically about the gender system, it may lead to a motivation for social justice. The growth of women's studies programs and courses focusing on women and gender may be filling some of the gap left by the disappearance of C-R groups (Cole et al., 2001; Davis, Crawford, & Sebrechts, 1999). Women's studies classes often provide powerful consciousness raising (James, 1999). In one study, taking a single women's studies course led to a decrease in the passive acceptance of sexism, an increase in commitment to feminism, and plans for social activism (Bargad & Hyde, 1991).

Do women's studies courses change men's attitudes? In one study, the attitudes of male students changed in a profeminist direction, but not as much as the attitudes of female students (Steiger, 1981). However, most women's studies classes do not include enough male students to provide an adequate research sample. There is a need for more and better research on how to change men's attitudes toward women, both inside and outside the classroom.

Transforming Interpersonal Relations

As this chapter has shown, gender inequity is reproduced in everyday interactions with others, often outside our awareness. Even the most well-meaning people can respond to others in sexist ways, and sexist patterns of interaction lead to self-fulfilling prophecies. These social processes are largely invisible and taken for granted.

Doing gender can be disrupted when people treat others with respect. One important strategy for change is to become aware of how we often respond to others as members of a category rather than as individuals with unique personalities and experiences. Knowing how power creates double binds for women can help change the categorization processes that create sex discrimination. Psychological research on power and stereotyping was influential in the Supreme Court decision in the *Price Waterhouse v. Ann Hopkins* case, in which Hopkins won the partnership she had earned (Fiske et al., 1991).

When awareness of sexism is raised, small acts of resistance can follow. Writer Gloria Steinem called this kind of resistance "outrageous acts and everyday rebellions" (Steinem, 1983). For example, although not everyone can run for the Senate or aid battered women, each of us can give money or time to those who do. We can unite with others who may be devalued for their differences, working to end racism and heterosexism. Both women and men can support others who work for change; in particular, women can choose to support and mentor each other. The motto of one feminist organization that provides leadership seminars for women is "Lift as you climb."

Doing gender is also disrupted when people refuse to be cooperative or silent in the face of sexism. It isn't easy to speak up when you hear a sexist or racist remark. However, research has shown that such interventions are effective. Confronting prejudice is most likely to change attitudes when the confrontation is nonthreatening in tone and when it comes from someone who is not a member of the target group (Monteith & Czopp, 2003). In other words, white people who speak out against racism, men who speak out against sexism, and straight people who speak out against heterosexism may be particularly likely to be heard—especially if they do it with respect and tact.

Humor can be an effective tool (Crawford, 1995). Not laughing at sexist jokes undermines their aggressiveness. And women can challenge gender-based power plays with their own take-charge humor. When Britain's former Prime Minister Margaret Thatcher received the backhanded compliment from a member of the opposing political party, "May I congratulate you for being the only man on your team?" she responded, "That's one more than you've got on yours" (Barreca, 1991).

Transforming the Structures of Inequality

Transforming gender at the social structural level is linked with the individual and interactional transformations just described. When people are empowered as individuals, they can speak out against injustice, and they can begin to change the institutions, laws, customs, and norms that harm girls and women. The effect is reciprocal, as speaking out leads to increased feelings of self-efficacy and empowerment.

Feminist activists of the 1970s achieved many important goals, and third-wave feminist activists are building on them. There are examples throughout this book. However, social change is not easy; attempts to change power relations almost always provoke backlash. Certainly, there has been a strong backlash against each wave of feminist activism throughout history. Today, the backlash ranges from repeated media claims that "feminism is dead" to the murder of people connected with women's health clinics. Moreover, change does not always result in progress. Feminist activists worked for no-fault divorce laws, only to find that they worsened the economic consequences of divorce for women (see Chapter 9). When more women entered the workforce, one result was the second shift of paid work followed each day by child care and housework (Chapter 11). When Title IX legislated equality in sports opportunity in schools and colleges, the number of coaching positions for women's sports rose—but men took 75 percent of the new jobs. Attempts to change society must be reevaluated periodically to judge whether they have had their intended effects and also whether they have had unanticipated negative effects. Fortunately, social science research can help find the answers.

As feminism becomes a more global movement, the issues of women in other cultures become more visible. Many societies do not allow women to have access to basic human rights such as freedom of movement, education, and a voice in government. Feminist activist groups have intervened in such human rights violations as the sexual slavery trade that takes Asian girls as young as nine to brothels in India, Thailand, and other countries. They have founded organizations to rescue these girls and provide them with education and medical care. Moreover, they speak up about the pervasive devaluing of females that underlies the slave trade in girls. Other activists are working on issues such as sweatshop labor in Asian countries, female genital surgery in African countries, and rape as a tactic of war around the world. Yet global feminism may bring troubling questions of who is entitled to define a problem and whose viewpoint should determine what constitutes a solution. For example, Western feminists may be appalled by compulsory female genital surgery, but the women who perpetuate it may see themselves as protecting their daughters from social ostracism (Chapter 8). Whose viewpoint should prevail?

New women's issues, reflecting the differences in women's positions in diverse cultures, continue to emerge. The Internet is a powerful tool for connecting activists around the world and creating dialogue among diverse groups of women. For example, organizations such as Feminist Majority and Women Leaders Online/Women Organizing for Change draw attention to human rights abuses and provide information on how women can make their voices heard in protest.

Many societies now guarantee women equal rights under the law. Some have recognized the need to remedy existing imbalances in political power by mandating women's participation in government. For example, in Norway, a fixed proportion of political candidates from major parties *must* be women. The United States has a much less activist approach to integrating women into positions of political and social power. However, the Supreme Court recently ruled in support of affirmative action plans that seek to monitor fairness in access to education and employment (Crosby, 2004). As long as women are paid less than men for similar work, or are denied opportunities to get ahead through education, equality cannot be achieved.

An end to patriarchal inequality is still a vision for the future, and not yet a reality. The global feminist vision is one of a just and caring society "that will give not only to men but also to women, bread and roses, poetry and power" (Alindogan-Medina, 2001, p. 57).

Exploring Further

∾

Crawford, Mary, & Popp, Danielle (Eds.). "Body politics: Power, sex, and nonverbal communication:" A reappraisal. *Feminism & Psychology, 12,* 291–338.
Twenty-five years after Nancy Henley's pioneering research on gender, power, and nonverbal behavior, feminist scholars write about its impact on their own work and its lasting significance to psychology. A weave of past, present, and future feminist research.

Far from Heaven. (2002).
This gripping film set in the 1950s shows how sexism, racism, and heterosexism can interact in the lives of ordinary people. A white woman (Julianne Moore) wants only to be a wife and mother, but the tortured life of her closeted gay husband (Dennis Quaid) and her friendship with a Black man (Dennis Haysbert) inflame the prejudices of their neighbors, with tragic consequences for all.

Naples, Nancy A., (Ed.). (1997). *Community activism and feminist politics.* London: Routledge.
This exciting collection shows how women are working to curtail the impact of racism, sexism, heterosexism, and violence in their communities through local organizing and community activism.

CHAPTER 3

Images of Women

∾

- **Words Can Never Hurt Me?**
  Language about Women and Men
  Language about Violence

- **Worth a Thousand Words: Media Images**
  Representing Women and Men
  Face-ism and Sexualization
  Diversity and the Media
  Invisible Women
  Do Sexist Images Matter?

- **Language, Imagery, and Stereotypes about Women and Men**
  The Content of Gender Stereotypes
  Sexuality Stereotypes
  Race and Social Class Stereotypes
  Cross-Cultural Similarities and Differences in Gender Stereotypes
  Are Stereotypes Accurate?

- **The Impact of Stereotypes**
  Stereotypes, the Self, and Stereotype Threat
  Stereotypes, Status, and Power
  Stereotypes and Sexist Behavior
  Stereotypes Are Hard to Change

- **The Problem of Pornography**
  What Is "Pornography"?
  Pornography Is Pervasive
  Stereotypes in Pornography
  Pornography as Violence against Women

- **Making a Difference**
  Transforming Language
  Alternative Images
  How *Not* to Stereotype
  Education and Activism

- **Exploring Further**

- Miss Marple, writer Agatha Christie's elderly, mild-mannered detective, often finds out "whodunnit" before anyone even notices that she is investigating the crime—because nobody thinks that a "little old lady" could be an ace detective.
- In the film *Legally Blonde*, Elle (Reese Witherspoon) has to work harder than all the other students at Harvard Law. She's smart enough, but she's also blonde and pretty. Stereotyped as a dumb blonde, she gets little respect.
- Charlene, who loves sports cars, finally has enough money to buy one. When she goes into the auto showroom, one salesperson asks if the car is for her boyfriend, and another asks if she knows how to drive a stick shift.

These examples illustrate the power of cultural beliefs about women. Whether we like it or not, we may be affected by societally prevalent views of women (and men). This chapter analyzes how cultural messages about gender are represented in language and visual images, as well as in beliefs about groups of people.

Words Can Never Hurt Me?

When people use language to communicate with others, they make choices that are not only practical but also political. The term *linguistic sexism* refers to inequitable treatment of women and gender issues that is built into the language. Feminists have worked to draw attention to sexist language and to change it (Crawford, 2001).

Language about Women and Men

In the 1970s, a great deal of research was aimed at uncovering linguistic sexism of various kinds. This early research found that language patterns sometimes trivialized women, with gender-marked terms such as *steward* and *stewardess*. Other terms sexualized and devalued women. There were far more negative sexual terms in English for women than for men, and words referring to women tended to acquire more negative meanings over time (Schultz, 1975). (See Box 3.1.) Linguistic sexism also marked both women and men who deviated from expected occupations and roles with terms such as *career woman* and *male nurse*.

Some of these practices have changed, but the transition to nonsexist language is not complete. For example, *stewardess* has been replaced by the gender-neutral *flight attendant*, but women's sports teams are still the Bronco-ettes or the Lady Lions. One college has Lady Rams, which doesn't even make anatomical sense! Let's look at still other varieties of linguistic sexism.

Mrs. Man

Language traditionally marked women as the possessions or property of men. Until recently, a woman's marital status was marked by the use of either *Mrs.* or *Miss*; *Mr.*, the corresponding title for men, was neutral with respect to marital status. When feminists proposed *Ms.* as a parallel term to *Mr.*, they were accused of being dangerous radicals bent on mutilating the English language (Crawford, Stark, &

BOX 3.1 ❧ "He Is. . . . She Is. . . .": Linguistic Inequality

Consider the following pairs of terms.

Term for Male	Term for Female
Lord	Lady
Sir	Madam
King	Queen
Master	Mistress
Dog	Bitch

Terms used for women often become lower in status over time. *Lord* and *lady* started out as equivalent terms. Today only God and some English nobility are referred to as Lord, but any woman can be addressed as "Hey, lady."

Terms for women also pick up negative sexual connotations over time. *Sir, king,* and *master* are terms of respect, but their formerly parallel terms have taken on new meanings. A mistress is a sexual partner, a madam may be a prostitute or female pimp, and queen is a derogatory term for a gay man.

Even animal terms are not exempt from linguistic sexism. A dog is "man's" best friend—but a bitch is friend to no one!

Renner, 1998). Women who used *Ms.* were seen as more masculine and less likable than women who stuck to the traditional titles (Dion, 1987).

The practice of women's taking their husband's name upon marriage is a heritage of patriarchy. The majority of women still follow this custom, and choosing to keep one's own name is controversial because of its symbolic meaning. Consider these contrasting opinions of women on whether a woman should take her husband's name upon marriage:

- When I got married, it seemed a bit late in life to get used to a new last name, as I'd had mine for 35 years. I also frankly couldn't see what choosing to share your life with someone had to do with changing your name.

- I feel desperately sorry for all those young women who will never know the joy and/or soaring pride of taking their new husband's name.

- When my husband and I decided to give our daughter my last name, it seemed like a sensible plan. . . . Little did we know how controversial our decision would be. Routinely, people assume that my daughter is not my husband's—and when it is explained, they look at us in utter shock. They ask my husband, "Didn't you want your kid to have your name?" and say to me, "Your husband must be a really nice guy" . . . The idea that a man would give up the privilege of "passing down his name" is virtually unthinkable; the assumption that women will give up this privilege unquestioned. . . . (Henry, 1998, p. E6)

Babes, Chicks, Ho's and Bitches

In everyday talk, people use vivid and often derogatory terms to describe outgroup members. These terms usually focus on alleged physical and social differences between ingroup and outgroup members. For example, many terms for women describe them by appearance or body parts, from the relatively mild *skirt* and *tail* to *gash, piece of ass,* and *cunt.* Slang also refers to women as animals, food, and aspects of nature: Think of *chick*, *fox*, and *old hen*; *honey* and *peach*; *brown sugar* and *cherry blossoms*. These metaphors imply that women are to be tamed or consumed by men.

Slang referring to women is much more likely to have sexual meaning than slang referring to men (Crawford & Popp, 2003). When students were asked to list slang terms for both sexes, 50 percent of the terms for women were sexual in connotation, compared to 23 percent of the terms for men (Grossman & Tucker, 1997). The most common terms for women were *chick*, *bitch*, *babe*, and *slut*; for men, they were *guy*, *dude*, *boy*, and *stud*. As these examples show, the terms for women are not only more sexual, but more negative.

He/Man Language

In many languages, the word for *man* is used to refer to humans in general—in Spanish, it's *hombre*; in French, *homme*; in Italian, *uomo*. In English, this supposedly generic use of *man* was long commonplace in academic as well as everyday language (as in "a history of man," "the rights of man," "the working man," "the man in the street," "the rational man"). In addition, unlike many languages, English does not have a gender-neutral singular pronoun, so speakers must choose either *he* or *she*. Traditionally, forms of *he* were used to refer to both males and females.

Unfortunately, these supposedly generic masculine terms are not really generic at all. A great deal of research has shown that when people read *he*, *his*, and *man*, they think of men, not people in general (Henley, 1989). Moreover, this interpretation affects their behavior. When male and female college students read an essay titled "The Psychologist and His Work," which used *he* throughout to refer to psychologists, the women in the group later remembered the facts in the essay more poorly than when they had read the same essay in a gender-inclusive (*he or she*) version—despite the fact that they could not remember which form they'd read. The differential language had no effects on memory among the male students (Crawford & English, 1984).

Studies of the sexist imagery and memory evoked by "generic" masculine language provided an impetus for language reform. Feminists advocated replacing *man* and its many compounds (*policeman*, *chairman*) with gender-inclusive terms (*humanity*, *people*, *police officer*, *chairperson*, *chair*). Feminists also advocated alternatives to use of the pseudogeneric *he* and *his*, such as using *he or she*, *his or her*, or alternating the pronouns. Despite the resistance these efforts produced, they led to some lasting changes in English usage.

However, there may be a cognitive bias that goes beyond language. Even when they hear gender-neutral terms, people may still assume a male is the subject. This ***people = male bias*** has been shown in several studies (Merritt & Kok, 1995; Silviera, 1980). For example, in one study, when participants read a set of gender-neutral instructions and were then asked to describe a (sex-unspecified) character, they produced three times as many spontaneous descriptions of males as females (Hamilton, 1991).

There is even an ***animal = male bias***. When children in three age groups and adults were shown stuffed toys (a dog, a deer, a mouse, etc.) and asked to tell stories about them, both children and adults showed a very strong bias toward using masculine pronouns and believing the animals were males. For example, 100 percent of

3- to 10-year-old children and 100 percent of adults used *he* to refer to a teddy bear. Preschool-aged children used *he* to refer to a dog (100 percent), a mouse (95 percent), a deer (87 percent), a snail (94 percent), and a butterfly (88 percent). Only cats were seen as (sometimes) female, mostly by girls. Even when the experimenters tried to disrupt the bias by using feminine pronouns to introduce the animals ("Here is a panda bear. She's eating bamboo now, but she had fish for breakfast"), 100 percent of the children still used masculine pronouns in their own stories (Lambdin, Greer, Jibotian, Wood, & Hamilton, 2003). It seems that from an early age, children are learning that males are the norm and females should be linguistically invisible.

Language about Violence

Although men are most often treated as though they stand for all of humanity, there is one place where men are rendered linguistically invisible: when they have committed violence against women. Consider the following sentences:

1. In the United States, a man rapes a woman every six minutes.
2. In the United States, a woman is raped by a man every six minutes.
3. In the United States, a woman is raped every six minutes.

Do the meanings of these sentences differ? Feminist theorists have claimed that in talking and writing about rape and other kinds of violence against women, people overuse the passive voice, as in sentence 2. Further, they argue that relying on passive verbs, especially with the actor deleted, as in sentence 3, deflects attention from the perpetrator of violence.

The tendency to deflect attention from the perpetrator is particularly striking in the mass media. In one analysis of real-life talk, the researcher examined how participants in a public radio educational program on date rape talked about male rapists and the females they raped (Crawford, 1995). Here are some of the phrases they used:

> Alcohol . . . can permit men to do things they ordinarily wouldn't do.
>
> It definitely is rape season . . . it happens to the young freshmen because they are very unaware.
>
> (Date rape) did happen a bit.
>
> (The young woman) in this sort of drinking fraternity house sort of situation that gets raped . . .

In these phrases, rape is just something that happens, never a behavior chosen and enacted by a man against a woman's will. Even when men "do things," it's really alcohol that deserves the blame; men's choices to drink do not enter into the picture.

Other groups of researchers have tested the hypotheses that news reports use the passive voice in reporting violence against women, and that this leads readers to be more accepting of such violence. When they classified over 1,500 examples of verb use in print media, Nancy Henley and her colleagues found that for both rape and murder, reporters used the passive voice more often than they did for stories about nonviolent crime or noncrime topics. The research team then asked whether verb use matters. To do this, they asked college students to read news reports of rape, robbery, and murder and rate how much harm was done to the victim, how responsible the victim and perpetrator were for the crime, and how acceptable such crimes are. The news reports were identical except for the use of active or passive verb forms. Both male and female participants thought that violence against women was more acceptable after reading the passive-voice stories. Males, but not females, also thought the victim had suffered less harm and the perpetrator was less responsible (Henley, Miller, & Beazley, 1995).

The tendency to focus on the victims rather than the perpetrators of violence against women is widespread. An analysis of articles about wife abuse in U.S. women's magazines over nearly three decades (1970s to late 1990s) showed that there was virtually no discussion of the male abuser or the social context of greater

FIGURE 3.1a
This photo of Ivan Pavlov and colleagues in his lab appeared in an introductory psychology textbook used by hundreds of thousands of psychology students.

male power. Instead, the articles were constructed as an individual woman recounting "my problem and how I solved it" (Berns, 1999). Only 4 of 111 articles focused any attention on the perpetrator, and only one suggested that some men may need to change their attitudes and behaviors toward women. In another study, newspaper articles that used terms such as *the abusive relationship* instead of directly stating that a man had beaten his wife led people to place less responsibility on the perpetrator (Lamb & Keon, 1995).

Taking the emphasis away from the perpetrator's acts makes it harder to perceive him as responsible for his behavior. Instead, the focus is on the woman, and the reader may think, "What did she do to bring on this attack?" (Ruscher, 2001). Terms like *domestic violence*, *spousal abuse*, and *abusive relationships* may function to hide the fact that most serious violence and harm in relationships are committed by men against women. Passive and indirect language about violence against women may be used without sexist intentions, but it can still have sexist effects.

Worth a Thousand Words: Media Images

Every day, each of us is exposed to hundred of images of women and men, most of them from the mass media: television, newspapers, magazines, movies, comics, video games, billboards, and the Internet. Most of the time, we pay little attention

FIGURE 3.1b
Unfortunately, some of Pavlov's colleagues were erased from the historical record. This is the original, complete photo. How might this selective elimination of women in the history of psychology affect students' attitudes and beliefs about women scientists?

to these images—they are just part of daily life, relegated to the background. However, media images play to our deepest needs while they create a distorted reality. Let's look more closely at media representations of women compared to those of men.

Representing Women and Men

In general, women are under-represented in the mass media. About 51 percent of the population is female. However, females appear in various types of media less often than males. For example, one study of prime-time TV shows revealed nearly 2½ times as many male as female characters (Gerbner, 1997). Although women do most of the purchasing of goods, they are underrepresented in prime-time network commercials for all types of goods except health and beauty products. In a recent tally, women were 46.4 percent of the primary characters in TV network commercials, up exactly .4 percent from the 1980s (Ganahl, Prinsen, & Netzley, 2003).

No form of media is immune to the under-representation bias. (See Figures 3.1a and 3.1b.) Women and girls are even underrepresented in the comics, where men and boys appear more often as both primary and secondary characters. One study looked at comic strips over a 54-year-time period, finding that they have become more inclusive of women and nonwhite families over time, but boys are still the featured children (LaRossa, Jaret, Gadgil, & Wynn, 2001). Even the animated cartoon figures that appear in ads are predominantly male. Little creatures such as the Keebler elves and the Energizer bunny are cute and easy to remember, but why aren't any of them female? Perhaps this biased imagery is one source of the people = male and animal = male linguistic biases discussed earlier. Similar patterns of underrepresentation have been shown when other cultures have been studied, such as Kenya (Mwangi, 1996), Portugal (Neto & Pinto, 1998), and Japan, where the ratio of males to females on TV is 2:1 (Suzuki, 1995).

Sheer numbers may be the least of the problems in mass media's depictions of women. Media images portray women and men quite differently in personality attributes. In movie roles, men are more likely than women to be aggressive and dominant; women are more likely than men to be passive and relatively powerless (Haskell, 1997). In popular comic strips such as *Blondie* and *Dennis the Menace*, girls and women have become more active characters over the years but are still less active than boys and men (Brabant & Mooney, 1986, 1997). When researchers analyzed the portrayal of women and men in 1,600 commercials shown on popular TV shows, both the white and African American male characters were more aggressive and active and gave more orders than female characters did. The white female characters, but not the African American ones, were more passive and emotional than the male characters (Coltrane & Messineo, 2000).

The media also show women and men in different settings and occupations. For example, one study examined nearly 8,000 illustrations of men in magazines aimed at women, men, and general readers. In male-oriented magazines, men were almost always shown in work and occupational roles, almost never as husbands or fathers. Images of men as members of families and caretakers of children showed up only in women's magazines (Vigorito & Curry, 1998). Women's work, in contrast, is downplayed. Although the majority of women today are employed outside the home, TV ads and magazine illustrations are less likely to show women than men at their jobs (Coltrane & Adams, 1997) and more likely to show women than men at home (Coltrane & Messineo, 2000). One of the few realistic aspects of the media's images of women is that they are more likely than men to be shown doing housework—even in the Sunday comics (Brabant & Mooney, 1997).

These differential gender portrayals occur cross-culturally. In India, for example, TV ads portray women almost exclusively in contexts of choosing products that transform them into better housekeepers and mothers (Roy, 1998). Single women are shown in European clothing outside the home, whereas married women are shown in the home, wearing traditional saris. In a study of Japanese TV ads, five character types emerged. Three of the types—housewife, young woman, and young celebrity—were female, while the other two—older people and middle-aged worker bee—were predominantly male. In Japan, just as in the United States, most women work outside the home, yet the worker bee was marked as a man. In the ads, "men go to the office no matter how sick they are . . . they do not go home after work. Instead they have an alcoholic session with their colleagues or attend receptions" (Arima, 2003, p. 88).

Face-ism and Sexualization

Some differences in how the media represent men and women are less obvious than others. Although most people do not notice, the composition of visual images of men and women is quite different. This phenomenon has been termed *face-ism* (Archer, Iritani, Kimes, & Barrios, 1983). Face-ism is measured by comparing the relative size of the head and body and expressing it as a proportion.

As Figure 3.2 illustrates, the facial prominence in published images is usually higher for men. In a study of more than 1,700 photos from magazines and newspapers, the average index for men was .65, and for women only .45. In other words,

FIGURE 3.2

Face-ism in the sports news. These photos of male and female athletes appeared on the same page in *Sports Illustrated on Campus*, a magazine aimed at college students. Despite the fact that wrestling is a body contact sport and track and field is not, the men are represented by a facial closeup and the woman by a full body shot in which her crotch is almost as prominent as her head.

Source: Sports Illustrated on Campus (April 29, 2004), 5.

two-thirds of a typical photo image of a man featured the man's face, while less than half of a typical image of a woman featured her face (Archer, et al., 1983).

How prevalent is face-ism? The research team went on to look at photos published in 11 different countries and found similar results—more facial prominence for men. They also examined paintings in art museums, finding that face-ism occurred in paintings from the 17th century onward and has increased over time (Archer et al., 1983). Face-ism favoring men even occurred in women's magazines like *Good Housekeeping* and the feminist magazine *Ms.* (Nigro, Hill, Gelbein, & Clark, 1988). In a study of news magazines, the face-ism index favored not only men over women but also European American over African American people; Black women had the lowest face-ism index of all (Zuckerman & Kieffer, 1994). Although systematic research on face-ism was done mostly in the 1980s, it is still very easy to find examples of face-ism in politics and news reporting, as well as in advertising and fine art.

Why should we care about face-ism? It can have subtle but very real effects on how individuals are evaluated by others. We tend to associate a person's individuality, personality, and intelligence with his or her face more than with the body. When students were asked to rate the same people shown in different photos, they rated an individual higher on dominance, ambition and intelligence, as well as attractiveness, when the photo had a higher face-ism index (Archer et al., 1983; Zuckerman & Kieffer, 1994). In other words, seeing more of a person's face, and less of his or her body, in visual images leads us to think of that person as more outstanding in character and ability. The widespread tendency to show more of men's faces and women's bodies may function without our awareness to focus attention on men's character—and women's physical characteristics (see Figure 3.3).

Depicting women as bodies is not limited to the subtlety of facism. Studies from around the world show a strong tendency to sexualize portrayals of women in more blatant ways as well. Overall, one of every four white women characters in U.S. television commercials is shown dressed or posed in a sexually provocative way, compared with one in 10 Black women and one in 14 men (Coltrane & Messineo, 2000). In magazine ads, more and more women are being shown partially undressed or completely nude, even when revealing the body has nothing to do with using the product (Kong, 1997; Plous & Neptune, 1997). Music videos, which are very popular with young teens, are a particularly sexist form of popular culture. In these videos, men are most often aggressive and sexually dominant, whereas women are the most often sexually compliant objects of men's actions (Sommers-Flanagan, Sommers-Flanagan, & Davis, 1993). Words and images combine, especially in some forms of rap music, to derogate women as *ho's* and *bitches*; images of rape and sexual degradation are common. Popular music, particularly rock and

FIGURE 3.3   Face-ism and Bodies
Face-ism has very real effects, and is prevalent everywhere in advertising. These two recent billboards clearly show a focus on the body for the woman and the face for the man.

rap, is an industry dominated by men, who remain the great majority of managers, performing artists, DJs, journalists, and producers. In this context, it is difficult for the voice of a woman artist to be heard unless she plays by the men's rules (see Box 3.2).

Diversity and the Media

Most of the research on media images has focused on white middle-class characters, probably because most of the images available for analysis depict this group. In a large-scale study of nearly 2,500 characters in TV ads, for example, only 257 were African American, 50 were Asian American, and 29 were Latinos/Latinas (Coltrane & Messineo, 2000). On TV programs, people of color are shown mainly in situation comedies (Wilson & Gutierrez, 1995). Latinos/Latinas, who are about 12 percent of the U.S. population, are virtually invisible in TV programming. In the movies, they are usually in supporting, even demeaning, roles. For example,

---

BOX 3.2 ∽ Ani and the Politics of Music

Ani DiFranco sings to the beat of a different drum. Her music, which she began writing at the age of 15, can be categorized as punk folk music. Ani started playing in local bars in Buffalo before moving to New York City to pursue her music career. Unlike other hopeful musicians, Ani rejected offers from major record labels and chose to build her own company, Righteous Babe Records, in order to have more power and control in making her music. She is the writer, producer, vocalist, musician, and publisher of her meaningful music that deals with topics ranging from war to gender, sexuality, and love. Ani tours the United States, playing at colleges, theaters, and other local venues. People are attracted to Ani's music because of its acoustic sound, poetic lyrics, and powerful messages. During the 1990s, Ani released 13 solo albums with one debuting in the Top 100, which is a feat for an independent release. Despite her success as an independent artist and entrepreneur, Ani wants to be known not for her money, but for her music. Ani wrote in a letter to *Ms.* magazine that she and her company are "people who incorporate and coordinate politics, art and media every day into a people-friendly, sub-corporate, woman-informed, queer-happy small business that puts music before rock stardom and ideology before profit."

Sources: www.righteousbabe.com; www.onherown.net; contributed by Meghan Deveau.

Lupe Ontiveros, who played Carmen in the hit movie *Real Women Have Curves*, has made over 40 films, but still remains largely unknown because she often has played maids and housekeepers (Lewis, 2002).

Images of African American women are biased in racist as well as sexist ways. These images cast black women into types such as the Mammy, the Jezebel, and the Matriarch (West, 2004). The prototype of the Mammy goes back to *Gone with the Wind*, in which Mammy was a happy slave whose huge breasts and perpetual smile symbolized her role as nurturer, while her dark complexion, bandana-covered hair, broad features, and fat body marked her as asexual. Aunt Jemima, a Mammy symbol for over a century, finally lost her bandana in the 1990s (West, 2004). Originally, Aunt Jemima spoke in a caricature of slave dialect: "Honey, . . . Yo know how de men folks and de young folks all loves my tasty pancakes" (West, 2004, p. 240). Today's Pinesol lady may not wear a slave's bandana but she is still calling people Honey and mopping the floor with a smile. (See Figure 3.4.)

The Jezebel represents a stereotype of black women's sexuality. During slavery, white slave owners and traders brutalized African women by raping them, forcing them to bear children who would be sold away from them, and forbidding them to

FIGURE 3.4   Stereotypes in Media Images
Many media images are bias in racial ways with the use of images that are very stereotypical. This ad for a cleaning product is reminiscent of the Mammy stereotype.

FIGURE 3.5

marry African men. There was a conscious attempt to destroy black families. The victims were blamed, and the oppression justified, by portraying black women as immoral, seductive, and promiscuous. Today, the Jezebel is represented in music videos, rap music, advertising, and pornography as the "ho." One way the so-called wild nature of black women's sexuality is symbolized is that black women are far more likely than white women to be shown in magazine ads wearing animal print fabrics (Plous & Neptune, 1997). (See Figure 3.5.)

The Matriarch is portrayed as domineering, aggressive, strong, and unfeminine. This image, too probably originated in slavery, when black women were forced to do heavy labor alongside black men, and it served both to justify their oppression and to separate them from the image of white Southern women, which was one of passivity, frailty, and domesticity. The Matriarch is often portrayed as a hostile tongue-lashing nag who drives men away and bullies everyone else (West, 2004). Today, the Matriarch is the black woman with attitude and anger, like the character of Bernadine (Angela Bassett) in the movie *Waiting to Exhale*, who gets revenge on her husband by setting fire to his expensive clothes and car. Like the Mammy and the Jezebel, the Matriarch image may be a distortion and exaggeration of coping strategies that enabled black women to survive centuries of oppression (West, 2004).

Invisible Women

Who is left out of the media representations of women? A short answer might be "Any woman who is not young, rich, thin, white, stereotypically feminine, and sexually available!" Let's look at some of the women who remain underrepresented or invisible.

Older Women

If a Martian observer were to estimate the U.S. population demographics from TV, he or she might think that some mysterious virus had killed off all the human females over the age of 40. Older women are among the least visible groups in the mass media. TV newscasters can have gray hair and wrinkled brows only if they are male. Studies from the 1970s to the present show that the majority of female characters in commercials are under the age of 35. One study compared the actual proportion of people over the age of 51 in the U.S. population with the representation of characters in a large sample of prime-time commercials. Although people over the age of 51 are 27 percent of the population, they accounted for only 18 percent of the characters in the commercials. And despite the fact that the ratio of females to males increases with age (i.e., there are increasingly more women in older age groups because women live longer on average), two-thirds of the older characters were men (Ganahl, Prinsen, & Netzley, 2003).

Bigger Women

The media ideal for women is an extremely thin one. It has become more extreme and less attainable over time. The published body measurements of Playboy centerfold models and Miss America contestants have shrunk over the past 40 years (Spitzer, Henderson, & Zivian, 1999). At the same time, the actual body size of adult Americans has gotten heavier. The latest version of the ideal woman is not only extremely thin but also large-breasted—a size 4 in the hips, 2 in the waist, and 10 in the bust (Harrison, 2003). Of course, this figure type rarely occurs in nature. Nor can it be achieved by dieting—it must be created through surgical intervention. (Idealized beauty images in the media are discussed more extensively in Chapter 7.)

When a token overweight woman is portrayed, she is rarely allowed to be like other women. Her weight defines her, making her unlovable. For example, the character of Ellenor Frutt on *The Practice* was so needy and vulnerable that she dated a psychopath who attacked her with a butcher knife. As an overweight woman, she was portrayed as unappealing to normal men (Mintz, 2003). On *Friends*, the character Monica was shown in repeated flashbacks about being overweight and rejected in high school. In an analysis of TV sitcoms, male characters directed more positive comments toward thinner female characters, and more negative ones to heavier characters (Fouts & Burggraf, 2000). The great majority of the negative comments to heavier women were followed by laugh-track laughter, reinforcing the idea that it is socially acceptable to ridicule overweight women.

Poor Women

Another group unlikely to appear on your TV screen is poor women. Almost all the characters on prime-time TV are middle-class or wealthy. On afternoon talk shows, working-class women are shown as being out of control, belligerent, and victims of dysfunctional families. In the print media, newspapers and magazines feature poor women (particularly women of color) in stories about welfare reform, but not in stories about other issues. Few women are called on to comment on issues of poverty, although the majority of poor people in the United States are women and children. In one analysis of major media coverage of welfare reform, 77 percent of the experts used as sources were male (Flanders, 1997). The majority of poor and low-income women who struggle to work and care for families under difficult

"IN THE NEXT HALF HOUR, MY WEALTHY WHITE
CONSERVATIVE MALE FRIENDS AND I WILL DISCUSS
THE ANNOYINGLY PERSISTENT BLACK UNDER-
CLASS, AND WHY WOMEN GET SO EMOTIONAL
ABOUT ABORTION."

FIGURE 3.6

Source: Copyright © Kirk Anderson/www.kirktoons.com.

conditions are not considered worthy of airtime (Bullock et al., 2001). (See Figure 3.6.)

Athletic Women

The mass media seem to construe sports and athletics as a men-only club. For example, during the Olympic year of 1996, women made the cover of *Sports Illustrated* only 4 times in 53 issues. Television coverage of women's sports is dismal—less than 10 percent of total sports coverage (Hall, 2004; Koivula, 1999), and newspaper coverage has ranged from 3.5 percent to 11 percent in recent studies (Hall, 2004). Like the music industry, the sports industry is dominated by men—for example, only 3 percent of sports journalists and 20 percent of TV sportscasters are women (Hall, 2004).

The audience for women's sports is increasing, and some changes have taken place (Hall, 2004). In the 1990s, compared to the 1980s, national coverage of women's sports increased, and descriptions of the athletes were more positive. A few women are now getting the lucrative endorsement contracts usually offered to male athletes: Venus and Serena Williams (Reebok) and Martina Navratilova (Subaru) are notable examples. However, we are still a long way from equal respect and visibility for female and male athletes. More on the portrayal of women athletes in the media can be found in Chapter 7.

Voices of Authority

Women are relatively invisible in the media as responsible citizens and experts. The news media focus on the actions, opinions, and expertise of men much more than women. For example, women are asked for commentary on the front pages of newspapers only about 25 percent of the time (Hernandez, 1994), and only 5 percent of talk-show hosts on radio are women (Flanders, 1997). In television commercials, women may gush about the microwave snack food or the toilet bowl cleaner, but the authoritative voice directing the viewer to "Buy it now!" is usually not a woman's voice. Studies in many countries—the United States, Australia, Denmark, France, and Portugal—show that 70 to 90 percent of these voiceovers in TV commercials are male (Bartsch, Burnett, Diller, & Rankin-Williams, 2000; Furnham & Mak, 1999; Neto & Pinto, 1998).

The media's overreliance on the expertise of men may result in biased reporting. Consider the *New York Times* coverage of the controversy over breast implants and their effects on women's health. In writing 21 articles on the issue, one journalist consulted 83 sources—only two of whom were women (both had undergone surgical removal of a breast). Of the 81 male sources consulted, there were 33 physicians and surgeons, 20 executives of implant manufacturing companies, and 17 FDA officials. These experts made many stereotypical claims about why women want and need breast implants, but these claims were not backed up by scientific data. The researcher who did this study (Darling-Wolf, 1997) argued that the "voices of authority" used in the newspaper's reporting largely reflected the position of the breast implant manufacturers and plastic surgeons.

Even when women's voices are heard in the media, they are likely to be presented in a context that focuses on their appearance, clothes, marital status, and bodies rather than their words and ideas—a practice that has been documented since the 1970s (Foreit et al., 1980). This kind of bias makes it more difficult for women to be taken seriously. For example, in a 2003 article about a political appearance by Senator Hillary Clinton (Keller, 2003), the women who turned out to support Clinton were described in trivializing terms: "a fortysomething from Newton with suspiciously jet-black hair who's risking perspiration stains on her cashmere sweater," "a well-tailored woman in her fifties," "a middle-aged woman wearing expensive glasses," "a fortyish black woman." In contrast, men were described as experts ("Former Labor Secretary Robert Reich") or by occupation ("healthcare worker Andy Johnson"). Their age, race, and fashion preferences were not considered relevant. Collectively, Clinton's supporters were referred to as "the chevre and Chardonnay sisterhood," and one was quoted as saying that Clinton has "beautiful skin, and let me tell you, that's important to women." In other words, Senator Clinton's supporters were portrayed as ditzy middle-aged women, not serious and politically informed voters.

Even when women have the authority to be heard, they may be judged more by their appearance than their performance. When Boston TV anchorwoman Natalie Jacobson appeared on the evening news with her usually smoothly groomed hair in a looser wind-blown style, the station was flooded with complaining calls from viewers. The station president, other newscasters, and an official station spokeswoman each offered commentary on the "beach hair crisis," all the while insisting that their primary concern was not Jacobson's appearance but "the content and quality of the newscast" ("Hair-raising experience," 2003).

Do Sexist Images Matter?

Despite the fact that people in Western society consume a daily diet of sexist images, there has been remarkably little research on the effects of repeated exposure to these images (Davies, Spencer, Quinn, & Gerhardstein, 2002). Still, some effects have been documented.

Watching a great deal of television is related to having more sexist attitudes. Compared to light viewers, heavy TV viewers have more sexist views about what careers and professions are best for women, and lower estimates of women's abilities than men's abilities (Gerbner, Gross, Morgan, & Signorielli, 1993). This research was correlational and cannot determine whether watching TV causes viewers to become more sexist, or whether more sexist people watch more TV in the first place. A review of experimental studies, however, showed that presenting participants with biased media images increased their acceptance of gender-biased beliefs (Herrett-Skjellum & Allen, 1996). In these studies, the change in beliefs can be directly attributed to the experimental presentation of sexist images. In other words, sexist media images *do* matter—they foster sexist beliefs and attitudes.

Language, Imagery, and Stereotypes about Women and Men

Widely held beliefs about members of a social group are termed ***stereotypes*** (von Hippel, Sekaquaptewa, & Vargas, 1995). Stereotypes can be thought of as theories that people carry around in their heads about how members of a particular group think, look, and behave and how these attributes are linked. An individual may be unaware that he or she holds stereotypical beliefs or behaves in accordance with them. Still, the network of associations around a group forms a ***schema,*** or mental network, that guides people as they experience the world around them (von Hippel et al., 1995). For a particular schema to be stereotypical, most or all of the content of the schema must be similar to others' schemas for the same group. For example, Charlotte may believe that short people are more likely to be grumpy, but this belief is idiosyncratic, not stereotypical. On the other hand, if Charlotte believes that women are more likely than men to become emotional in a crisis, her belief is shared by many others. ***Gender stereotypes*** are networks or schemas of related beliefs that reflect the common wisdom about women and men.

Stereotyping is not an all-or-none matter; three limitations are especially noteworthy. First, people do not say (unless forced to choose) that women and men are complete opposites; instead, they think that, women and men differ *on average,* and they allow for overlap. Second, although many or most individuals in a social group may hold a particular stereotype, others may not. Third, people may or may not apply their stereotype to members of the target group at any particular time. Typically, stereotypes have the biggest influence when you are registering a first impression of a stranger or thinking generally about a category of people (Deaux & Lewis, 1984).

In sum, stereotypical beliefs are probabilistic. Most of the students at University X, for example, may believe that female cheerleaders are airheads and male football players are typical jocks, but a minority may disagree. And even among those who hold the stereotype, there may be differences in how important it is to their judgments about a particular cheerleader or football player. Those who actually know a member of these groups are more likely to judge them as individuals. On the whole, though, people operate as though stereotypes are widely shared and use them in communicating with others (Ruscher, 2001). As a result, a quip about a ditzy cheerleader or a slow-witted jock is easily understood at University X and may often go unchallenged.

The Content of Gender Stereotypes

In general, people believe that women and men differ on a number of dimensions, including personality, behaviors, occupations, and physical characteristics.

Physical Stereotypes

I will discuss physical characteristics first because more than any other component of stereotypes, they activate the other components. The special role of physical characteristics was shown in a classic study in which participants read about a hypothetical woman or man. The target person was described using one component of gender stereotypes: either personality traits, gender-role behavior, occupation, or physical characteristics. Then the participants were asked to judge the probability that the target would have other stereotypical characteristics. When targets were described as having stereotypically feminine physical characteristics, such as daintiness, softness, and gracefulness, participants were very certain that they would also have feminine personalities, occupations, and gender-typed behaviors. Parallel judgments were made about men: When they were described as tall, strong, and sturdy, participants were very sure they would also have stereotypically masculine personalities, gender-role behaviors, and jobs. If the initial descriptions focused on traits, occupations, or behaviors, participants were not nearly as certain that they could tell what the target would be like on the other dimensions. (Deaux & Lewis, 1984).

Physical appearance conveys a package of stereotypical expectations. It is particularly important because information about physical appearance is the first thing we perceive when we meet someone. In fact, this information is conveyed within one-tenth of a second (Locher, Unger, Sociedade, & Wahl 1993).

Personality Traits

When people are asked to respond to lists of traits by choosing whether each trait is more characteristic of a woman or a man, or by rating the typicality of each for women and men, they attribute such traits as independent, competitive, decisive, active, self-confident, dominant, competent, unemotional, and ambitious more to men. In contrast, they attribute traits such as warm, gentle, understanding, nurturing, helpful, aware of others' feelings, expressive, emotional, and sensitive more to women. The traits considered characteristic of men are **instrumental** and **agentic:** They describe a person who is active and effective. The traits considered characteristic of women are **affective** and **communal:** They describe a person who is concerned with feelings and other people. The instrumental-affective (or agentic/communal) dimension of gender stereotypes was first found more than 30 years ago (Broverman, Vogel, Broverman, Clarkson, & Rosendrantz 1972) and is still found today (Spence & Buckner, 2000). It is personified in classic TV pairs like Dharma and Greg.

Role Stereotypes

Many behaviors and social roles are stereotyped as more typical of women or men. This aspect of stereotyping becomes evident when people are asked to think of particular *types* of women and men. In the first study of gender subtypes (Deaux, Winton, Crowley, & Lewis, 1985), people easily generated these categories. For women, the types included the housewife/mother, who was believed to be self-sacrificing, focused on her family, and nurturing. The housewife/mother subtype is closest to the more general stereotype of women, suggesting that a "real women" is one who plays the roles of wife and mother. Another type, the sexy woman, was described less in terms of personality and more in terms of physical characteristics: having a good body, long hair, nail polish, and so on. (The lack of overlap between these two also suggests that moms are never sexy, and sexy women are never moms—a point we'll take up in Chapter 10.) Another type was the athletic woman, described in terms of physical characteristics (muscular, strong) as well as traits (aggressive, masculine). Finally, participants nominated a career woman type, seen as smart, hardworking, organized, and not very feminine.

Corresponding categories for men included blue-collar, athletic, macho, and businessman. Although the characteristics attributed to each type differed, all of the male types were seen as masculine—blue-collar men were described as hardworking; macho men as hairy-chested—and none were seen as having any feminine traits or behaviors. In contrast, some of the female types were seen as more feminine than others (e.g., housewives versus career women). Beliefs about these subtypes of women and men were as strongly held as beliefs about women and men in general.

More recent studies have shown similar results: People still differentiate between housewife/mothers and career women, and the housewife type remains closest in attributes to the generic female or typical woman. Men are strongly differentiated from women, and beliefs about subtypes are as strong as overall gender stereotypes (Eckes, 1994).

Occupational Stereotypes

We've already seen that some general occupational categories are stereotyped as belonging to men (blue-collar worker) and others to women (housewife). Are there more specific occupational gender stereotypes? This question, first asked in a 1975 study, was assessed again more than 20 years later (Beggs & Doolittle, 1993). When women and men were asked to classify each of 129 occupations as masculine, neutral, or feminine, 124 of them were classified the same way as they had been in

1975. Manicurist had the most extreme feminine rating, and miner, the most extreme masculine one. The stereotypes were not impervious to changes in reality. During this period, women actually increased as a proportion of the workforce in many jobs; the great majority of these jobs were rated less masculine in the 1990s than in 1975. However, only one (sales manager) went from masculine to neutral.

Sexuality Stereotypes

Gender and sexuality are closely linked in most people's cognitive schemas. Gay, lesbian, bisexual, and transgendered people pose a problem for gender stereotypes because these stereotypes are implicitly heterosexual. Often, people solve this problem by putting lesbians into the male/masculine schema and gay men into the female/feminine one. This is particularly true for physical characteristics, which are key to overall stereotyping. For example, early researchers of sexuality claimed to find "long clitorises, narrow hips, small breasts, and deep voices" in lesbians (Kitzinger 2001). Even today, one of the most prevalent stereotypes about lesbians is that they are all "butch" or mannish in appearance (Eliason, Donelan, & Randall, 1992).

Likewise, gay men are stereotyped as effeminate and obsessed with girly pursuits such as fashion and decor in such TV shows as *Queer Eye for the Straight Guy*. Same-sex relationships are stereotyped as playing out heterosexual roles in reverse, with one partner the femme and one the butch. (Lesbian relationships are much more varied than the stereotypes suggest—see Chapter 8.)

Women who are particularly strong, either in personality traits or physical skills, are most likely to be stereotyped as lesbians, a cognitive trick that helps maintain the stereotype of heterosexual women as the weaker sex as well as the mannish lesbian stereotype. For example, two longstanding and still prevalent myths about women in sport are "Sports make girls masculine" and "Only lesbians play sports" (Hall, 2004). Of course, some female athletes are lesbians—and so are some female doctors, teachers, nurses, and attorneys. The majority of women in all these occupations are heterosexual. "Clearly, any correlation made between athleticism and sexual orientation is misleading" (Hall, 2004, p. 67).

Both in and outside the realm of athletics, sexuality stereotypes may be a means of keeping women subordinated, because those who are strong, independent, assertive, and outspoken in their feminist beliefs are most likely to be labeled lesbian (Hall, 2004). As long as the label *lesbian* carries a social stigma, it can be used as a weapon against all women.

Race and Social Class Stereotypes

Most psychological studies of gender stereotypes have asked participants about "typical" women and men. A big problem with this approach is that participants (who are most often college students) may equate *typical* with white and middle-class. This only becomes apparent when researchers specifically ask about race or class. For example, when researchers asked college students to list traits for American women and Black women, there was no overlap in the top-ranked traits.

Typical American women were seen as intelligent, materialistic, and sensitive (similar to stereotypes of white women), whereas typical black women were seen as loud, talkative, and aggressive (Weitz & Gordon, 1993). When students were asked to describe societal stereotypes of white, black, middle-class, and lower-class women, they described white women as more dependent, emotional and passive than black women. Again, white women resembled the "typical" women of earlier studies that did not ask about race. Also, lower-class women, compared to middle-class women, were stereotyped as more dirty, hostile, inconsiderate, and irresponsible (Landrine, 1985).

Stereotypes about race and gender may interact for African American women. In one recent study, white college students rated a fictional character's speech and also generated sample dialogue for the character. This method allowed an indirect assessment of stereotypes about the characters' race and sex. Black target characters (both female and male) were rated as more direct and emotional and less socially appropriate than white ones were. Female characters (both black and white) were rated as less direct and more emotional than men were. The dialogues that students created were less grammatical and more profane for black speakers than for white speakers (Popp, Donovan, Crawford, Peele, & Marsh 2003). Thus, race and gender stereotypes held contradictions for African American women. As African Americans, they were perceived as loud, talkative, aggressive, and socially inappropriate. As women, they were perceived as sensitive, emotional, and indirect.

So far we have talked about research comparing only African American and white targets. Are gender stereotypes linked to race/ethnicity stereotypes in other groups? The evidence is limited, because few studies have been done, but the answer seems to be that gender and ethnicity do interact in stereotypical beliefs. When a multiethnic group of college students were asked to list adjectives that described men and women of different ethnic groups, they agreed on the characteristics shown in Table 3.1. You can see from the table that the characteristics they came up with are a combination of traits, physical characteristics, and role behaviors. Some gender stereotypes were represented in all groups. For example, women, whether Mexican, Asian, African, or Anglo in origin, were all believed to be pleasant and friendly. Although the men in various groups did not share specific traits, all were seen as having some instrumental or agentic characteristics such as being achievement oriented or hardworking. Equally interesting, however, are the perceived differences across ethnic and gender groupings. Overall, stereotypes of African Americans and Mexican Americans were more negative than stereotypes of Asian and Anglo Americans. Although participants were not asked about social class stereotypes in this study, they spontaneously associated Mexican Americans with lower-class people (Niemann et al, 1994).

Cross-Cultural Similarities and Differences in Gender Stereotypes

When gender stereotypes held in different nations and cultures have been compared, remarkable similarity has been found. For example, several multination studies showed that agentic/instrumental traits (forceful, independent, adventurous) were associated with men and communal/affective traits (sentimental, submissive,

TABLE 3.1   Gender and Ethnic Stereotypes

Participants in this study were asked to list the first 10 adjectives that came to mind when they thought of members of each group. Here are the traits they listed most often.

Anglo-American Males	*Anglo-American Females*
Intelligent	Attractive
Egotistical	Intelligent
Upper class	Egotistical
Pleasant/friendly	Pleasant/friendly
Racist	Blond/light hair
Achievement oriented	Sociable/socially active

African American Males	*African American Females*
Athletic	Speak loudly
Antagonistic	Dark skin
Dark skin	Antagonistic
Muscular appearance	Athletic
Criminal activities	Pleasant/friendly
Speak loudly	Unmannerly
	Sociable/socially active

Asian American Males	*Asian American Females*
Intelligent	Intelligent
Short	Speak softly
Achievement oriented	Pleasant/friendly
Speak softly	Short
Hard workers	

Mexican American Males	*Mexican American Females*
Lower class	Black/brown/dark hair
Hard workers	Attractive
Antagonistic	Pleasant/friendly
Dark skin	Dark skin
Noncollege education	Lower class
Pleasant/friendly	Overweight
Black/brown/dark hair	Baby makers
Ambitionless	Family oriented

Source: Adapted from Niemann, Jennings, Leilani, Richard, Baxter, & Sullivan, 1994.

such equality = enmeshment?

agreeable) were associated with women in virtually every nation studied (Best, 2001; Williams & Best, 1990). This apparent uniformity suggests that gender stereotypes of agency and communality are universal. However, there are other explanations. First, cross-cultural studies typically rely on college student samples, which may be exposed to Western cultural influences and which do not represent their countries' population as a whole. Second, cross-cultural studies have measured only trait stereotypes. Perhaps there is more variability in other components of gender stereotypes—physical attributes, social roles, and so on. Until there is more cross-cultural research, this is an open question.

Another open question is the relationship between trait stereotypes and social roles within and across cultures. In England, for example, girls were playing so-called masculine sports such as field hockey long before these sports were accept-able for girls in the United States. In many African countries, women do the heavy work of subsistence farming. How are these activities reconciled with stereotypes of feminine frailty? It is interesting that many countries with more restrictive gender stereotypes than our own have chosen women as heads of state—Bangladesh, India, Ireland, Pakistan, Poland, and Turkey are examples—while in the United States a female president still seems to be a vision for the distant future.

Are Stereotypes Accurate?

Stereotypic judgments are the end result of a series of steps in cognitive processing. First, the perceiver (let's call her Carmen) must sample from a social category. In forming a belief about Asian American women, Carmen would think of those she has encountered. Second, Carmen must encode the information into long-term memory. Then, later, she must retrieve the information from memory and estimate what proportion of it confirms or disconfirms a stereotypic interpretation. Finally, Carmen uses this estimate to make a stereotypical (or unique) judgment. Of course, all this happens very quickly and automatically (Ottati & Lee, 1995).

There is plenty of evidence for bias at every step of this process. Carmen's sam-ple is likely to be biased in unknown ways—it is not a random sample of the popu-lation. If all Carmen's Asian American friends are college students, she is likely to confirm the stereotype of achievement orientation through *sampling bias*. Second, she is likely to engage in *selective encoding* and *selective retrieval*—without being aware of it, Carmen may enter into memory and later recall stereotype-congruent examples better than stereotype-incongruent ones. For example, she may reach a judgment that all Asian American women are achievement oriented because she did not notice (or noticed but later did not recall) meeting several Asian American women who were not. Stereotypes can be inaccurate as a cumulative result of all these biases.

On the other hand, stereotypes may, to some extent, reflect the social world; and some may hold a kernel of truth. If your stereotypical image of a secretary is fe-male, and a computer scientist is male, you are more accurate than not, because these occupations are in fact very gender segregated. We saw earlier that occupa-tional stereotypes had changed somewhat as women's actual distribution in the workforce changed. In order for stereotypes to function as effective cognitive short-cuts, they need to be at least somewhat anchored in reality (Ottati & Lee, 1995).

However, it is not always clear what counts as reality. What criteria should be used to defend or refute stereotypical judgments is always open to debate, and often the debater's position depends on his or her social and political agenda. More important than arguing over whether stereotypes are accurate is to recognize that even when they are somewhat accurate as an overall group judgment, they may be very inaccurate when making judgments about individuals, and they can cause harm:

> It *matters* when stereotypes are misused. It matters when an employer hires a man rather than a woman for a given job because he believes that men are inherently more suited for it. It matters when girls are told that they should take English rather than mathematics in high school. It matters when a Black family is excluded from the possibility of owning a house in a nice neighborhood because a real estate agent believes that they will have too many children and not take care of the property. In this sense, the critical issues of stereotyping go beyond the question of whether the perceiver, on average, is accurate in his or her perceptions, to the potential negative outcomes. . . . (Stangor, 1995)

Even when stereotypes contain a kernel of truth, they are *never* true of every group member. Unfortunately, because they are by definition widely shared, the harmful potential for stereotypes of gender, race, sexuality and class is immense. We turn now to the impact of stereotypes.

The Impact of Stereotypes

Stereotypes matter! Here we look at several ways in which stereotypes have very real effects: They become part of the self-schema and may cause stereotype threat and create harmful self-fulfilling prophecies; they reinforce differences in status and power; and they prime sexist behavior and lead to discrimination.

Stereotypes, the Self, and Stereotype Threat

Because gender is such an important dimension in perceiving and evaluating others, the gender schema becomes part of the self-schema. In other words, females and males may come to believe that the attributes of their gender stereotypes are true expressions of their identity.

Research offers both good news and not-so-good news about today's self-schemas. The good news is that, compared to earlier generations, today's college women see themselves as more instrumental. They endorse traits such as "acts like a leader," "self-reliant," and "assertive," just as much as college men do. However, men still rate themselves higher on about 40 percent of instrumental traits. Thus, the gender gap in instrumentality is narrowing, but not yet closed. The not-so-good news is that women and men still see themselves as very different in expressiveness. Virtually every expressive trait—kind, emotional, understanding, warm, gentle, tender, and so on—still is endorsed significantly more by women than by men (Spence & Buckner, 2000). Thus, gender stereotypes are still being internalized as part of the self. Although the stereotypes are internalized somewhat differently than in the past, the change is not equal for women and men. Women are seeing themselves as more instrumental, but men are not seeing themselves as more expressive.

When people know that there is a negative stereotype about their group's abilities, the pressure caused by their fear of confirming the stereotype can interfere

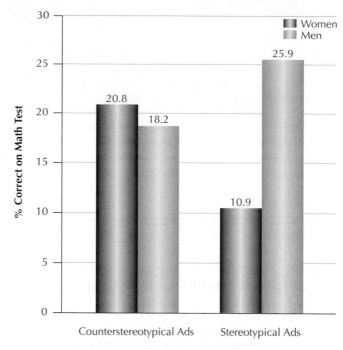

**FIGURE 3.7   The Impact of Stereotype Threat on Women's Math
Performance**

In this study, female and male college students were selected on the basis of having
good math attitudes and achievement. The students then saw television commercials.
Some of these commercials were gender-stereotypical (a woman bouncing on her
bed with joy over a skin product, or drooling with pleasure over a brownie mix);
others were counterstereotypical (a woman speaking knowledgeably about health
care issues). All students then took a difficult math test. Although none of the ads had
anything to do with math, viewing the stereotypical commercials caused the women's
subsequent math performance to drop quite noticeably because women became
anxious about fulfilling the stereotype. Men's performance was not affected, probably
because sexist stereotypes of women were not personally relevant to them.

Source: "The Impact of Stereotype Threat on Women's Math Performance," 2002, adapted
from P. G. Davies, S. J. Spencer, D. M. Quinn & R. Gerhardstein, 2002, "Consuming Images:
How Television Commercials that Elicit Stereotype Threat Can Restrain Women Academically
and Professionally," *Personality and Social Psychology Bulletin*, 28, pp. 1615–1628. Reprinted by
permission of Sage Publications, Inc.

with their performance—a phenomenon called ***stereotype threat.*** (See Figure 3.7
for the results of one study of stereotype threat.) Because stereotypical images of
women are so common, women may experience stereotype threat all too often, with
detrimental effects on their self-confidence and performance. Unfortunately, their
impaired performance may then confirm stereotypes about them, leading to a
vicious cycle. If Aisha performs below par on a math test because she is aware of the
stereotype that women are inferior in mathematics, her instructor and classmates

gain (apparent) evidence that the stereotype is accurate. Thus, stereotypes may create their own truth by acting as self-fulfilling prophecies.

In addition, stereotypes may generate self-fulfilling prophecies because they often depict not only a consensus about the way things are but also the way they should be. Gender stereotypes are particularly dangerous in this respect. Although racial and ethnic stereotypes are thought to characterize particular groups, they are not seen as rules for behavior. For example, Alex may stereotype African Americans as loud and Mexican Americans as lazy, but he does not think they *should* be that way. However, gender stereotypes often prescribe how the ideal woman or man should think, look, and behave. Thus, a woman who does not want to have children not only violates the stereotype that women are nurturing but may be judged to be an inadequate woman; a man who is not dominant or ambitious may be seen as not a real man. There is strong pressure for women to act feminine and men to act masculine in male-female relationships, and both women and men report that they do tend to play by the rules (Sherman & Spence, 1997).

Stereotypes, Status, and Power

In general, people with more power engage in stereotyping of people with less power (Fiske, 1993; Keltner et al., 2003). Powerful people pay more attention than less powerful people to stereotype-consistent information and less attention to information that might disrupt their stereotypical beliefs. Although both these tendencies contribute to maintaining imbalances, they make sense cognitively and socially. Powerful people may seek to confirm beliefs that work for them. And they do not need to pay much attention to the individual differences among the powerless, because their well-being does not depend on it. For example, a worker must pay more attention to the moods and demands of the boss than the boss must pay to the worker's, because the boss controls important outcomes for the worker.

Group-based power differences also increase the tendency to stereotype. Recall that people who are higher in social power (men compared to women, European American compared to African American) tend to be higher in social dominance orientation, or SDO (see Chapter 2). In turn, SDO predicts the tendency to stereotype others—with higher SDO scores linked to more stereotyping.

Stereotypes and Sexist Behavior

Another harmful effect of stereotypes is that they can prime sexist behavior. To illustrate this, I will describe an award-winning study grounded in real-world sex discrimination.

In the early 1990s, women workers at the Stroh's brewery in Minnesota sued the company over sexual harassment in the workplace. The attorney representing the women introduced Stroh's infamous "Swedish Bikini Team" beer commercials as evidence that Stroh's tolerated a hostile workplace; that is, her argument was that any company that produces such sexist and objectifying commercials is sending a clear message to its employees about how to regard women. The case settled out of court, but graduate student Laurie Rudman was inspired to investigate how commercials that portray women as sex objects affect male viewers. Using a computer-timed word-recognition task, Rudman and her colleague Gene Borgida found that men who had watched sex-object commercials were quicker to recognize words associated with the sex-object female stereotype (e.g., bimbo) than were men who had viewed commercials that did not portray women as sex objects. Moreover, when they were asked to interview a female job applicant, these men rated her as less competent, remembered fewer details from her resumé, and remembered more about her appearance. In other words, activation of the stereotype distorted men's perceptions of the female applicant and affected their behavior toward her (Rudman & Borgida, 1995).

Stereotypes Are Hard to Change

Gender stereotypes have been studied for over 35 years. During that time, there have been enormous changes in gender-related attitudes and behaviors. For example, attitudes towards women's rights in education and employment have become more liberal, many more women now work outside the home, and many women have entered professions once reserved for men (Spence & Buckner, 2000). However, gender stereotypes have changed remarkably little. Various studies measured gender stereotypes as early as the 1950s, and later studies compared these to stereotypes in the 1970s and 1990s (Lueptow, Garovich, & Lueptow, 1995; Werner & LaRussa, 1985). In these studies, the majority of traits believed to characterize women and men in the 1950s were still thought to apply decades later. However, some negative stereotypes about women had dropped out. Women had become nicer, but no more likely to be seen as competent.

In a recent study, a sample of U.S. college students was asked to rate the typical male and female college student on instrumental traits (such as active, self-reliant, and decisive) and expressive traits (such as devoted to others, warm, and emotional) that were first measured in the early 1970s (Spence & Buckner, 2000). The results were quite clear: On virtually every instrumental trait, both male and female students agreed that the typical male is higher, and on virtually every expressive trait, they agreed that the typical female is higher. At least on these trait measures, gender stereotypes had changed very little since the early 1970s.

If social reality is changing, why are stereotypes relatively static? People tend to hang on to their stereotypical beliefs even when they are challenged by new or incongruent information (von Hippel et al., 1995).

We may be reluctant to abandon some stereotypes because they help us feel good about ourselves. Jokes and stories about women who are lousy drivers or gay men who are effeminate may serve to make others feel superior. And since everybody knows that women or gay men are "all like that," stereotypes serve to make the ingroup members feel more cohesive and in tune with each other. When someone tells a fag, JAP, or dumb blonde joke, the ingroup gets to feel superior to the outgroup and any outgroup members who hear the joke get a dose of prejudice (Ruscher, 2001).

Stereotypes also persist because they are useful cognitive shortcuts, helping us to allocate cognitive processing time efficiently and get through the day with a minimum of mental effort. Stereotypical thinking helps keep us from getting bogged down as we navigate a complex social world. There is a lot of evidence consistent with this view of stereotyping. For example, people rely on stereotypes more when they are least alert—"morning people" stereotype more at night, and "night people" do it more in the morning. And most people rely on stereotypes more when they are under time pressure or overloaded with incoming information (von Hippel et al., 1995).

One reason stereotypes survive is that they influence the amount and kind of information that the individual takes in (Von Hippel et al., 1995). When you have a well-developed schema, you tend to encode information that is congruent with the schema, then to stop encoding. You do not perceive the incongruent information that is all around you. Recall the example of Carmen, who engaged in selective encoding to hold on to her stereotype of Asian Americans. As another example, imagine a group of four women and four men working together on a job site. One of the four women in the group is more talkative than average. If other group members hold the stereotypical belief that women talk or gossip a lot, they may pick up on her talkativeness and notice it. But perhaps the other three women say very little, and on balance more of the talking is done by the four men (a normative pattern discussed in Chapter 2). Because the silent women are stereotype-incongruent, their behavior is less likely to be encoded into memory and used to form judgments.

Stereotypes about gay, bisexual, and lesbian people may be even more resistant to change than male-female stereotypes because sexuality is not immediately visible or identifiable. People may interact with gays and lesbians quite often without realizing it. Thus, gay or lesbian people who do not match the stereotypes (the lesbian who wears dresses or does flower arranging, the gay man who drives an SUV or plays football) may not be recognized as such (Garnets, 2004).

Another cognitive mechanism that helps stereotypes persist in the face of incongruent information is the formation of subtypes. If Trisha, who believes that women love children, meets a woman who is focused on her career and has no interest in becoming a mother, she may protect her stereotype by putting the woman into a "career woman" subtype. Career women are unfeminine, Trisha may decide, but real women still love children.

The media may contribute to stereotype maintenance by providing exceptions to the rule that are so extreme that they encourage the perceiver to form a new subtype rather than assimilate the exemplar to the group (Ruscher, 2001). When the media trumpet a female mountain climber or racecar driver, readers and viewers may not change their overall view of women at all, because they perceive the examples as not representing the group as a whole. Exemplars who violate stereotypes in more modest ways actually influence stereotypical beliefs more: The female math teacher, the African American law school graduate, or the somewhat graceful lesbian may slip past the cognitive barriers to stereotype change.

Does all this mean that stereotyping and its negative consequences are inevitable? No. People can make conscious decisions to pay attention to their automatic stereotyping and to combat their natural tendency to judge others stereotypically (Devine & Monteith, 1999).

The Problem of Pornography

Probably the most controversial of all the depictions of women are those found in pornography. Many women are ignorant of the amount of misogynist and violent content in pornography, but these words and images are an integral part of male sexual socialization in our culture and affect many women's lives in ways they do not realize.

What Is "Pornography"?

When most people hear the word *pornography*, they think of photographs or films of people who are nude or engaged in sex (e.g., Lottes, Weinberg, & Weller, 1993). Some people believe that whether an image is pornographic depends upon the perspective of the beholder: What some consider pornographic, others consider artistic; what some consider morally objectionable or sexist, others defend as free speech (e.g., Senn, 1993; Cowan, 1992).

It may seem difficult to pin down exactly what is pornography and what isn't, but many scholars concur that different types of sexual images can be distinguished in terms of their potential psychological impacts and social consequences. Social psychological experiments demonstrate that the sexual explicitness of the material does not matter nearly so much as whether the sex is presented in a violent or degrading context. Sexually violent or degrading images, explicit or not, desensitize male viewers to violence against women, increase men's belief in rape myths, and lower men's support for sexual equality (e.g., Linz, Donnerstein, & Penrod, 1987). Several scholars therefore suggest that the term *pornography* should be reserved for material that combines sexual themes with violence, dehumanization, degradation, or abuse, whereas material that is merely sexually arousing without these other themes might best be called *erotica* (e.g., Steinem, 1980; Russell, 1993; Scott, 2003). In most pornography, *women* are the ones subject to the violence, dehumanization, degradation, and abuse.

Pornography Is Pervasive

Since 1990, pornographic images of women have become *much* more available to all citizens in the United States, male and female, adults and children. The themes in pornography are not new, but the widespread production and distribution of pornographic images is.

Playboy publisher Hugh Hefner launched his magazine in 1953 with a nude centerfold of Marilyn Monroe, casting some legitimacy on "adult" entertainment for the first time in the United States. The first pornographic film to receive mainstream attention was *Deep Throat*, released in 1972, and the first adult video was released just over 25 years ago (Adult Video News, 2002). According to recent news reports, the production and distribution of pornography in the United States is now a $10-billion-a-year industry, making it bigger business than the NFL, the NBA, and Major League Baseball combined. Much of the distribution of adult content is done by large companies such as AOL Time Warner, DirecTV, and the communications company Comcast (ABC News, 2003; CBS News 60 minutes, 2003).

The tremendous growth in the industry during the 1990s was due primarily to the popularity of adult videos, the availability of subscription cable television, and the proliferation of porn sites on the Internet. According to the founder of *Adult*

Video News, more than 11,000 adult videos are now produced annually in the United States (as compared to 400 Hollywood films) (Rich, 2001). Estimates of the number of pornography pages currently on the Internet range upwards of 260 million. A Kaiser Family Foundation (2001) study surveyed 15- to 17-year-olds and found that 95 percent of those who had ever gone online had "accidentally" encountered pornography.

As the pornography industry has flourished, it has had a tangible influence on U.S. popular culture. Pornography has been mainstreamed in unprecedented ways. Advertisers use themes from porn to sell mundane objects such as wristwatches and jeans (see Figure 3.8), and porn stars are being recruited to hawk products such as athletic shoes. References to porn and appearances by porn stars are increasingly common on prime-time television and in Hollywood films (Farrell, 2003). The PornStar line of clothing and accessories does a multimillion dollar international business. As noted earlier, pornographic themes and depictions of women run through many, if not most, music videos (Jhally, 1995). Adult in-room movies are available in many popular U.S. hotel chains, including Hilton, Marriott, Hyatt, Sheraton, and Holiday Inn, accounting for almost 70 percent of in-room profits (CBS News 60 Minutes, 2003). Tourist brochures in these hotel rooms commonly

FIGURE 3.8   Mainstreaming of Pornography
Porn star Jenna Jameson appeared in a series of advertisements for Pony footwear in the spring of 2003.

BOX 3.3 ∽ Pornographic Images of Women with Disabilities

Most sexually oriented images, whether porno-graphic or merely erotic, are similar to other media images of women in that they rarely include women who are not young, stereotypically attrac-tive, or able bodied. Viewers who are interested in a wider variety of women can find them easily on the Internet on Web sites dedicated to specific categories of women that deviate from the porno-graphic prototype; examples include hirsute women, obese women, mature women, women with unusually large or small breasts, and so on.

Self-labeled disability devotees can find plenty of pornographic images presenting women with visi-ble disabilities as the ultimate passive, dependent, and compliant sex objects (Elman, 2001). These images are controversial among disability activists because at the same time that they can be con-sidered exploitative and are typically framed as fetishistic, they also are seen by some as progressive in that they acknowledge the sexuality of women with disabilities (Aguilera, 2000; Waxman-Fiduccia, 1999).

include ads for gentlemen's clubs—strip establishments that frequently offer perks to attract businessmen such as hotel pickup service and five-star menus (Powell, 2003). Evidence of the mainstreaming of pornography is abundant.

Stereotypes in Pornography

The primary female stereotype in pornography is "woman as sex object," and this includes subtypes such as "naughty housewives," "sexy secretaries," and "barely le-gal teens." Diversity among women is represented, too, via racist subtypes (Cowan & Campbell, 1994; Mayall & Russell, 1993). For example, African American women are frequently portrayed as sexual slaves or animal-like savages (Collins, 1997). Asian women are often shown in bondage or being tortured. Anti-Semitic pornography portrays women as concentration camp victims in publications such as *Swastika Snatch* (Russell, 1993).

Pornography also contains stereotypes about women's sexuality. Women are frequently portrayed as masochistic, deriving pleasure from their own pain or hu-miliation. Women's sexual orientation is represented as fluid in images of "lesbian" sex between ostensibly heterosexual women who are missing a man (more informa-tion on faux lesbianism can be found in Chapter 7). Paradoxically, sexually explicit materials in general often challenge the stereotype that women are passive or disin-terested in sex (e.g., Strossen, 1996).

Pornography as Violence against Women

Pornographic violence against women can be found in many forms of mainstream entertainment as described above, and often there is a mocking or boastful tone to the material. For example, in a popular late-1990s computer game, *Duke Nukem 3D*, nude women tied to posts (by aliens) are frequently caught in the cross-fire between the player and his enemies. According to one reviewer of the game,

> Everywhere you go in Duke Nukem there are scantily clad women. Posters for porn movies and sex shows line the walls, porno mags lie around on tables and couches. Start the projector in the movie theater and you get a show! Pressing the action button near some women (or even just some statues of women) causes them to open their blouses and give you a quick peek. . . . (Ferris, 1996)

More recently, an amateur videographer filmed nude women being hunted in the desert by camouflage-clad men wielding paintball guns. He made the video called "Hunting for Bambi," available on his Web site, which featured several pages touting sexual violence against women. The front page reassured viewers it "is not a scam!" and described the video,

> More shocking than anything you've ever seen before. . . . Women are being hunted down like animals and shot with paintball guns. . . . When it comes to **hunting women** if you can think of it we probably show it. Women are **screaming** with fear as our Team Bambi hunters track them down and blast them with paintball guns. . . . [emphasis in original]

The Wall Mounts page on the Web site displayed photos of women's nude torsos taxidermied like animal trophies. At the time of this writing, the Web site is still up and the video is now available from mainstream outlets including Best Buy and Amazon.com.

Pornographic images are of particular concern not just because they portray sexual violence but also because of the ways that the creation and use of pornography are intimately linked to actual violence against women.

Violence in the Making of Pornography

Although today even amateurs can alter photographs or fabricate images, this is a recent technological development. Many of the blatantly violent pornographic images of women from recent years past are not merely images but are *documentation* of actual sexual violence or humiliation. Women in these pictures may have volunteered for such treatment in exchange for money or other rewards, but according to first-hand accounts, some may have been coerced. Linda Lovelace, the star of the porn movie *Deep Throat*, reported in her autobiography that she was forced by her husband at gunpoint to make the film and that the bruises visible on her body in the film were the result of beatings (Lovelace & McGrady, 1980). Lovelace's claims have been widely disputed by porn industry insiders, but it is very difficult to believe that images of women being burned by cigarettes, slashed with knives, forcibly penetrated by objects such as vacuum cleaner hoses, covered in excrement, and so on, were produced with their eager consent (Russell, 1993).

Pornography as a Script for Sexual Violence

Women involved in the making of porn are not the only ones hurt by it. We know from experimental research that pornography has at least temporary negative effects on men's attitudes and behaviors toward women. For practical and ethical reasons, experimental research cannot establish the relationship between pornography and violence against women in the real world. Some correlational studies have involved interviewing battered women regarding the use of porn by their abusers and the role of pornography in episodes of abuse.

Cole (1987) found that 57 percent of the battered women she interviewed reported that their partners used pornography, and 53 percent described the porn as related to their batterers' use of sexual force against them. Sommers and Check (1987) interviewed 44 battered women and 32 women from a mature university population and found that the battered women reported significantly more use of porn by their partners than did the university sample. Thirty-nine percent of the battered women (compared to 3 percent of the other women) described how their batterers had tried to force them to do something seen in pornography. Cramer and McFarlane (1994) surveyed 87 women who were filing battery charges against their male partners. Forty percent of the women reported that their batterers used pornography, and use was significantly associated with these women being asked or forced to participate in violent sex.

In a study on the sexual abuse of prostitutes, Silbert and Pines (1984) had not planned to study pornography, but were confronted with the subject when 24 percent of their study participants implicated pornography in their open-ended accounts of rape. One rape survivor recalled her attacker saying, "I know all about you bitches, you're no different; you're like all of them. I seen it in all the movies. You love being beaten" (p. 864). At public hearings regarding an antipornography ordinance drafted at the University of Minnesota law school in 1983 (MacKinnon & Dworkin, 1997), one former prostitute described how she and others in her trade "were forced constantly to enact specific scenes that men had witnessed in pornography" (p. 116). She recounted how one prostitute she knew was told by a client holding a picture of a beaten woman, "I want you to look like that. I want you to hurt" (p. 118).

We cannot conclude from accounts like these that pornography causes male violence against women, but it is clear that pornography is associated with sexual violence and that it can provide sexually arousing behavioral scripts for men with aggressive impulses. Pornography is used for masturbation; men who masturbate to pornography may be conditioning their bodies to pleasurably respond to violence against women (e.g., Seto, Maric, & Barbaree, 2001; Reed, 1994). In an interview the night before he was executed in 1989, serial rapist and murderer Ted Bundy described his "addiction" to pornography:

> I grew up in a wonderful home with two dedicated and loving parents . . . As a young boy of 12 or 13, I encountered, outside the home . . . softcore pornography . . . I want to emphasize this. The most damaging kind of pornography—and I'm talking from hard, real, personal experience—is that that involves violence and sexual violence. The wedding of those two forces—as I know only too well—brings about behavior that is too terrible to describe . . . Before we go any further, it is important to me that people believe what I'm saying. I'm not blaming pornography. I'm not saying it caused me to go out and do certain things. I take full responsibility for all the things that I've done. That's not the question here. The issue is how this kind of literature contributed and helped mold and shape the kinds of violent behavior . . . Once you become addicted to it, and I look at this as a kind of addiction, you look for more potent, more explicit, more graphic kinds of material. . . . until you reach the point where the pornography only

goes so far—that jumping off point where you begin to think maybe actually doing it will give you that which is just beyond reading about it and looking at it . . . I'm no social scientist, . . . but I've lived in prison for a long time now, and I've met a lot of men who were motivated to commit violence. Without exception, every one of them was deeply involved in pornography—deeply consumed by the addiction. (Focus on the Family, 1989)

Among all the popular media images of women in our culture, pornographic ones are potentially the most damaging.

Making a Difference

Verbal and visual representations of women are everywhere in our culture, and they can be powerful agents in fostering sexist beliefs, discriminatory behavior, and even violence against women. Feminists view these representations as an important opportunity for education and work toward societal change. Here we look at some of their efforts.

Transforming Language

Feminists from many cultures and societies have taken action to change linguistic sexism through *feminist language reform:* efforts to eliminate gender bias in the structure, content, and usage of language and to provide nonsexist alternatives (Pauwels, 1998). Feminist language reform has modified old language and also created new language (Crawford, 2001).

One of the biggest successes in feminist language reform has been the adoption of nonsexist language guidelines. By the mid-1970s, major educational publishers and professional organizations (such as APA and National Council of Teachers of English) had adopted guidelines for nonsexist language. In 1975, the U.S. Department of Labor eliminated gender bias in occupational titles. Changes were not limited to English-speaking societies; government agencies adopted nonsexist language in Germany, Italy, France, Spain, and other countries (Pauwels, 1998).

Guidelines to nonsexist language led to noticeable and important changes. Occupational titles and terms are now almost always gender-neutral—*letter carrier* has replaced mailman, and chairperson is an everyday word. There has been a dramatic drop in the use of pseudogeneric masculine terms in magazines and newspapers in all the countries studied (Pauwels, 1998). Politicians are usually very careful to refer to citizens as "he or she" and troops as "our men and women in uniform." (An exception is former President George H. W. Bush, who justified the invasion of Panama by saying, "We cannot tolerate attacks on the wife of an American citizen." The woman in question was herself an American citizen!) (Cameron, 1995).

However, nonsexist language guidelines did not address more subtle aspects of linguistic sexism such as use of the passive voice to hide male agency or the people = male bias. Nor did they address the blatant sexism of referring to women in terms of animals, appearance, and sexualized body parts. In 2003, a cover story in

New York magazine on successful women executives still asked whether men would want to go to bed with these "chicks."

Feminists have also provided new words for new times by adding many terms to the English language. Some coinages, such as *herstory*, were aimed at making people think twice about hidden sexism. Others named aspects of women's experience that had been culturally invisible. The writer Gloria Steinem perhaps best expressed the importance of naming and the influence of feminist activism on language when she said, "We have terms like sexual harassment and battered women. A few years ago, they were just called 'life.'" (Steinem, 1983, p. 149).

Lesbian, gay, bisexual, and transgender activists, too, have taken over the power to name. Gay activists coined *heterosexism*, *homophobia*, and *biphobia*. Rejecting the psychiatric label *homosexual*, they adopted *gay*, and made *LGBT* a convenient shorthand term for diverse sexualities. Formerly derogatory epithets such as *queer* and *dyke* are being reclaimed as positive badges of identity (Marecek et al., 2004).

Despite resistance and backlash (consider the new term *feminazi*), efforts to change language are ongoing. They are important because "language is more than just talk. In using language, we create our social reality. By changing language, we can contribute to changing that reality" (Crawford, 2001, p. 244).

Alternative Images

Not all mass media portrayals of women are stereotypical. Some TV shows become popular by reversing the stereotypes—think of *Xena: Warrior Princess* and *Buffy the Vampire Slayer*. Although the female characters on Buffy are perhaps overly concerned with their looks, they also are tough, independent, active, and strong—quite capable of saving the world. The characters are complex and ambivalent (Byers, 2003).

Dr. Kerry Weaver on ER is another female TV character who is presented as a complex developing person. Over several seasons of the show, Dr. Weaver has matured from being overly bossy and rule directed to being a highly competent physician who cares about her colleagues and patients. She has struggled to understand and accept her lesbian sexuality. Weaver is also an exception to the general invisibility of people with disabilities on TV. Her need for a crutch is not explained or remarked upon in the scripts, thus integrating her disability as a part (but not the most important part) of her identity (Mintz, 2003).

Individuals are providing alternatives to sexist portrayals in many media. In rock music, bands such as Pearl Jam, Hole, and Fugal infuse a feminist sensibility into their music and their self-presentation and refuse to cooperate with sexist representations. As Eddie Vetter of Pearl Jam said,

> I quit my last band over a conflict over a song. . . . I just refused to sing it. It seemed like it was from the perspective of a bunch of guys standing around watching a woman go by. It also used words like "baby" and "sweetie." . . . that's not how I would express myself, so I quit. (Schippers, 2003, p. 288)

Feminist voices are heard in hip-hop culture, too—Queen Latifa's *Ladies First* video shows black female leaders like Sojourner Truth and depicts Black Power symbols. Although many feminists are enraged about the woman-hating and violence of much rap music, some point out that hip-hop culture is a powerful force worldwide and ask, "What would happen if we could harness the power that rap music has to make people dance and make them work toward change in women's lives?" (Pough, 2003, p. 238).

Young feminists are increasingly using Web sites and 'zines to publish their own words and images. Adolescent girls often use their personal Web sites to explore their ideal and possible selves; on their personal pages, girls keep diaries, write their biographies, and share their sexual feelings. Although generations of girls have kept diaries, Web pages are different because they are open to a very large audience (Stern, 2002). However, girls who have access and technological skills to create and maintain a Web site are still a mostly white and socioeconomically privileged minority.

'Zinesters are a global, somewhat underground community, and they often satirize conventional images of femininity (Harad, 2003). Feminist 'zines such as *Bust* (www.bust.com) are smart and funny alternatives to the mainstream media.

How Not *to Stereotype*

It isn't easy to change or eliminate stereotypes. Because they are part of the cognitive process of categorization, they are relatively automatic, and they are activated without awareness. However, psychological research has shown how to reduce the likelihood that stereotypes will be used.

First, people rely less on stereotypes when they are trying to be accurate in their judgments of others. For example, in one study, participants were provided with both stereotypical and nonstereotypical information about another individual and instructed to convey their impression to another person. Participants conveyed more balanced information when they were in situations that stressed the importance of accuracy (Ruscher & Duval, 1998). Instead of disregarding nonstereotypical information that was provided to them, they included it in their accounts.

There is also evidence that nonprejudiced people can suppress or override their stereotypes (von Hippel et al., 1995). In other words, virtually everyone is aware of stereotypes such as the mammy, bimbo, and housewife; the words and images of our culture routinely activate these stereotypes. Prejudiced people—those who score high on the measures of sexism and racism described in Chapter 2—are likely to rely on such stereotypes when they are automatically activated; the stereotypes affect their judgments and behavior. Less prejudiced people stop and think about the stereotypes and replace them with more accurate information, so they are less likely to respond to others as stereotypes and more likely to respond to them as individuals. *Not* stereotyping requires paying attention and making a conscious choice, but it can be done.

Education and Activism

Many feminist activists have worked to raise awareness of the harm done by stereotypical words, images, and beliefs and to provide positive alternatives. Those who wish to get involved in education and activism against stereotyping can find information and action groups through groups such as Media Watch (www.mediawatch.org), Fairness and Accuracy in Reporting (www.fair.org), and About Face (www.about-face.org). Activist educator Jean Kilbourne (www.jeankilbourne.com) has become a familiar presence on college campuses through her videos documenting sexism in advertising (see Box 3.4). Despite a long history of feminist activism on cultural images of women, the need for change is as great as ever.

BOX 3.4 ∾ Jean Kilbourne: Media Activist

"No one in the world has done more to improve the image of women in the media than Jean Kilbourne."[1] Kilbourne is an educator and an

activist through her work on women's depiction in the media. She began by lecturing to college students on how advertisers misuse images of women to sell products by showing them as sexual objects and setting unrealistic beauty standards. From her powerful lectures came one of the most popular educational films of all time, *Killing Us Softly: Advertising's Image of Women*. This film and its sequels, *Still Killing Us Softly* and *Killing Us Softly 3*, along with Kilbourne's writings, *Can't Buy My Love: How Advertising Changes the Way We Think and Feel*, have raised awareness of media sexism in generations of students. Because of the depth of her research and the relevance of her work, Kilbourne has served as an advisor to two former surgeons generals and is on the board for the Women's Action Alliance and the Media Education Foundation. Kilbourne's activism is especially exemplary because its message is spread through various media including books, newspapers, films, and television. Her work spans audiences from government officials to college students. Her research has transcended the scholarly or purely academic realm and has become a form of educational activism. By recognizing the damage that advertising has done to women, Kilbourne is working to remedy it not only by speaking out, but also by trying to make society take responsibility for its attitudes towards women that are reflected in advertisements.

[1]Elaine LeGaro, Chair of the Women's Committee of the American Federation of Television and Radio Artists.

Source: http://www.jeankilbourne.com/. Contributed by Meghan Deveau.

Exploring Further

Rabbit Proof Fence. (2002).
In 1931, three aboriginal girls were abducted from their home in the Australian outback by government officers and sent to state schools to become domestic servants. This true story recounts how they escaped and walked 1,500 miles home. An antidote to stereotypes of female passivity.

Bennett, M., & Dickerson, V.D. (Eds.). (2000). *Recovering the black female body: Self-representations by African American women*. New Brunswick, NJ: Rutgers University Press.
Essays and personal accounts about images of black women in literature and mass media, and how black women are defining their own visions of self.

Flanders, Laura. (1997). *Real majority, media minority*. Monroe, Maine: Common Courage Press.
The author, a journalist and host of the nationally syndicated radio program *Counterspin*, gathers a decade's worth of her essays and interviews. Bias in media coverage of working people's issues, violence against women, poor people, welfare, sexuality, women's health, and politics is amply documented and exposed.

CHAPTER 4

The Meanings of Difference

$\mathcal{M}$ost people believe that women and men differ in many important ways. As one pop-psych best seller puts it, "Men are from Mars; women are from Venus." However, I recently saw a T-shirt that proclaimed, "Men are from Earth. Women are from Earth. Deal with it!"

Certainly, the verbal and visual stereotypes discussed in Chapter 2 present women and men in dramatically different ways. But what are the real differences between boys and girls or women and men in traits, abilities, and behaviors? Often, students of psychology want the facts and just the facts, and they expect the science of psychology to be able to provide those facts. However, the study of group differences is not just a matter of establishing facts, because differences that show up in psychological research are open to debate about their origins, meaning, and importance.

The Politics of Difference and Similarity

Some differences between groups do not matter very much in Western society. Almost no one divides the social world into people with freckles and those without, or people who can wiggle their ears and those who cannot. Other differences, like the ones in Figure 4.1, matter very much. These differences have social and political consequences; they represent dimensions of privilege versus disadvantage (Morgan, 1996). For each dimension, there is clearly a good and a bad end. In the case of gender, what is male and masculine is valued more highly than what is female and feminine.

In feminist theory and political movements, there have long been two ways of thinking about gender-related differences (Kimball, 1995), grounded in liberal and cultural feminism respectively (see Chapter 1). The *similarities tradition* claims that women and men are very much alike in intelligence, personality, abilities, and goals. This tradition stems from liberal feminism and is used to argue for equality of the sexes. After all, if men and women are far more alike than different, shouldn't they be treated equally?

The *differences tradition* claims that there are fundamental differences between women and men that should be recognized and honored. This tradition, stemming from cultural feminism, is used to argue that society should give more recognition to the activities, traits, and values of women. After all, if taking care of other people and relationships (traditionally viewed as feminine characteristics) were rewarded as much as dominance and personal ambition (traditionally viewed as masculine characteristics), wouldn't the world be a better place?

Both these ways of thinking have been used to generate research and to form political strategies. Debates about which approach is better have gone on for a long time. In this book I explore both traditions, looking at important research from each. The goal is not to decide which tradition is better. Rather, I hope you will decide that there is value in both—that "double visions are theoretically and politically richer and more flexible than visions based on a single tradition" (Kimball, 1995, p. 2).

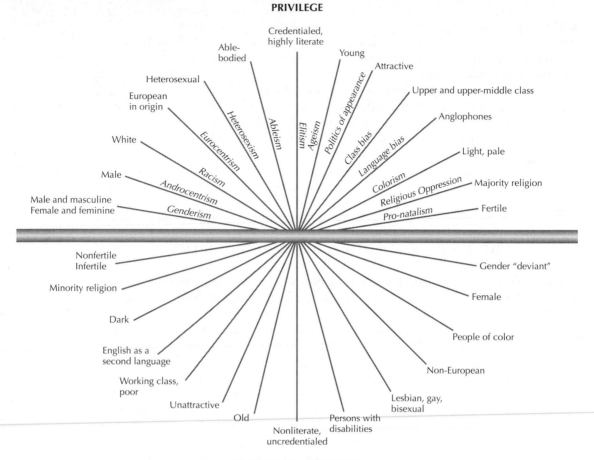

FIGURE 4.1

Intersecting dimensions of privilege and oppression.

Source: From Ann Diller, *The Gender Questions in Education: Theory, Pedagogy and Politics.* Copyright © 1996 by Westview Press, a member of Perseus Books, L.L.C. Reprinted by permission.

Because claims about group differences may be politically and socially controversial, there has been a lack of agreement in *defining* difference, problems in *measuring* difference, and issues of *values and interpretation* in understanding results. Let's examine these controversies in more detail.

Defining Difference and Similarity

Determining the facts about gender differences sounds relatively easy: A psychologist measures a group of women and a group of men for a trait or ability and computes the average difference between the groups. There is a long tradition of this

FIGURE 4.2

Calvin learns how women and men are different.

Source: Calvin and Hobbes Copyright © 1990 Watterson. Distributed by Universal Press Syndicate. Reprinted with permission. All rights reserved.

kind of research. Between 1967 and 2002, *Psychological Abstracts*, which lists published journal articles in psychology, indexed 50,393 articles on human sex or gender differences!

You might think that with all these studies some definitive answers would emerge. However, the meaning of *difference* can be very ambiguous. Suppose you were at a party where you overheard someone explain why there are more men than women judges in the United States by saying, "Let's face it; women just don't reason like men. When it comes to reasoning ability, they just don't have what it takes." Your first reaction might be that this is just an outdated stereotype (see Figure 4.2). Your second reaction might be to ask yourself what evidence could be brought to bear on this claim.

The speaker has asserted that there is a gender-related difference in reasoning, a cognitive ability. Before we examine the evidence, let's consider what he or she might have meant. One interpretation is that all men and no women have the ability to reason—in other words, that reasoning ability is dichotomous by sex. If the entire population of men and women could be measured on a perfectly valid and reliable test of reasoning ability, the two sexes would form two nonoverlapping distributions, with the distribution for women being lower. This hypothetical situation is shown in Figure 4.3a. *But despite a hundred years of research on gender-related differences, no one has ever discovered a psychological trait or cognitive ability on which men and women are completely different.*

Because it would be ridiculous to argue that women are categorically inferior in this way, the speaker probably means something else when talking about *difference.* Perhaps he means that there is a ***mean difference*** (i.e., an average difference), such that the mean for women is slightly lower (Figure 4.3b) or very much lower (Figure 4.3c) than the mean for men. However, an average difference doesn't tell us very much by itself. Sets of distributions can have the same differences in means but large differences in ***variability,*** defined as the range or spread of scores. Figure 4.3d shows males more variable than females and Figure 4.3e shows females more

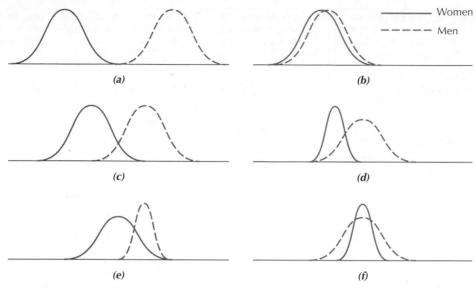

FIGURE 4.3

Some possible distributions of reasoning ability in females and males.

Source: Unger, R. & Crawford, M. (1996).

variable than males. Looking at the areas in which males' and females' distributions do not overlap in each set shows that the meaning of difference is different for each. That is, the proportion of women who score below the lowest-scoring men and the proportion of men who score above the highest-scoring women differ greatly from one set of hypothetical distributions to the next.

Moreover, these are not the only possible population distributions. Women and men could be equal on average, but one sex could be more variable, as shown in Figure 4.3f; here, the area where females and males overlap is larger than those where they do not.

Most research on gender-related differences reports a mean difference between a sample of women and a sample of men, with statistical tests to determine whether the difference is ***statistically significant*** (unlikely to have occurred by chance). As noted in Chapter 1, the concept of statistical significance is not the same as the ordinary meaning of *significant*. A difference may be statistically significant yet be trivially small and useless in predicting differential behavior in other situations. In other words, statistical significance is not the same as importance.

How large does a statistically significant difference have to be before we are justified in labeling men and women more different than similar? Should the importance of a difference be judged in terms of average scores, in terms of the variability for each gender, or in how much the distributions for women and men overlap? And how do we compare the results of several studies of the same trait or ability when the results vary? How many studies are sufficient to settle a question? How consistent must the results be? Is it important to measure the trait or ability in people of different age groups, social classes, ethnic groups, and cultures—or is it safe to assume that what is true for North American college students is true for all people? The answers to these questions involve value judgments about the meaning of difference.

Measuring Differences

Suppose a psychologist wanted to test the claim that there is a gender difference in reasoning ability. She might compare a sample of women and a sample of men on a standard test of reasoning, matching the two groups on any other factors that might affect reasoning ability, such as years of education. She would compare the average scores of her two groups with an appropriate statistical test to determine whether the difference she obtained was likely to have occurred by chance.

The logic of experimental design and hypothesis testing leads psychologists to put more weight on findings of difference than on findings of similarity. Statistical tests allow psychologists to be fairly confident that when a difference is judged to exist, the conclusion is an accurate one. But when a difference is not found, psychologists cannot know for certain that there is no difference in the population; the result could be just a failure of this experiment to detect the difference. They may conclude that they should try again, not that the hypothesis about a difference was wrong. Relying on similar logic, as discussed in Chapter 1, professional journals are less likely to publish articles that report similarities between women and men than they are to publish reports of differences. The possibility of overemphasizing differences is a built-in limitation of hypothesis testing. Furthermore, problems in research design were common in the past (Deaux, 1984; Maccoby & Jacklin, 1974; Parlee, 1981), and some researchers have charged that many reported gender differences are distorted or exaggerated (Grady, 1981).

Research Flaws

What are some of the flaws in difference research? Some studies have measured behaviors of only one sex and erroneously drawn conclusions about differences between the sexes—for example, measuring the relationship between hormonal levels and mood only in women and concluding that only women show such relationships. Of course, it is impossible to demonstrate a gender difference (or similarity) if only one group is studied (Jacklin, 1981). Other flaws include researchers' tendency to overgeneralize from limited samples to all women and men and to conclude that a gender-related difference is due to innate or biological factors when such factors have not been measured.

Examples of these mistakes are easy to find. The eminent psychologist Harry Harlow, who studied behavior in primates, found evidence that male rhesus monkeys are more aggressive than females. The problem with his research arose when he used this evidence to explain the behavior of boys and girls in biological terms:

> There is reason to believe that genetic variables condition similar differences in human primates. The gentle and relatively passive behavior of most little girls is a useful maternal attribute, and the more aggressive behavior of most little boys is useful preparation for the paternal function of protection. (1971, p. 6)

When Harlow's own research showed that female monkeys reared in abnormal environments were much more aggressive than those reared normally, he still was not convinced of the importance of environmental influences. Instead, he ignored the implications of his own data and resorted to stereotypes:

> Negative feedback, however, quickly suppresses this aggression. Females win their way into male hearts and minds through passive resistance and social sophistication. In our society females usually attempt to combine love and marriage with social security. . . . Young males prefer action and young females prefer active attention. (1971, pp. 90–91)

Not only had Harlow failed to study biological factors in aggression, but he hadn't even studied girls and boys. Instead, he generalized from his research on rhesus monkeys!

Confounding

One of the most persistent sources of bias in gender-difference research is the difficulty of separating gender from all the other factors it is related to in our society (Jacklin, 1981). The interaction of gender with other factors leads to *confounding*, in which the effects of two or more variables are mixed, and it becomes impossible to decide which variable is causing experimental effects.

For example, suppose we were matching participants for our imaginary experiment on reasoning ability. We would certainly not choose to compare a male sample with college degrees to a female sample of high school graduates, because this would confound gender and educational level. Obviously, the different backgrounds and experience of the two groups could account for differences in reasoning ability. But even when a researcher attempts to measure comparable men and women, it is often hard to decide what characteristics should be matched. Suppose researchers compared female and male college students. Although a sample of male and female college students can be matched on level of formal education, the women and men may have very different backgrounds in mathematics, science, and the liberal arts and may be concentrated in different majors. These differences may be irrelevant to some research questions but crucial to others.

Meta-Analysis: A Useful Tool

Many psychologists believe that a technique called *meta-analysis* can resolve some of the issues of definition and measurement in research on gender differences. Basically, meta-analysis uses quantitative methods to summarize the results of research done by different people at different times (Hedges & Becker, 1986). It allows researchers to integrate the results of many studies on a single topic and to assess the magnitude and consistency of difference effects statistically (Hyde & Linn, 1986).

In doing a meta-analysis, the investigator first identifies all relevant studies on a topic. The next step is to summarize the results of each study in a common unit of measurement. There are different degrees of statistical significance, and the results of some studies may be stronger than others. In meta-analysis, studies can be distinguished from one another in terms of the magnitude of the gender-related difference. Finally, meta-analysis allows researchers to group studies by subcategory and thereby assess the influence of variables other than gender. For example, if a researcher did a meta-analysis of studies on gender and reasoning ability, she might categorize the studies according to the type of task used or whether there was time pressure in the situation. Perhaps the gender difference only occurs when the task is male oriented or when there is time pressure. A variable that interacts with another variable to change its effect is called a ***moderator variable.***

Many psychologists, especially those who work within the similarities tradition, see meta-analysis as a useful technique for studying gender differences (Eagly, 1987; Hyde & Linn, 1986). It helps researchers interpret data from large numbers of studies and allows them to estimate the size of a gender-related difference. It simplifies the study of other variables that interact with gender—which is important because there almost always are other factors involved (Hyde & Linn, 1986).

But meta-analysis cannot wholly compensate for the biases in the original studies or ensure objective interpretation (Unger & Crawford, 1989). Reviewers must still decide which studies are relevant and whether several measures of the same construct (such as different tests of reasoning ability) are measuring the same thing. Moreover, there could be an overlooked source of bias common to all the studies in a meta-analysis, which could lead to an overall conclusion that is biased (Hedges & Becker, 1986). If all the tests of reasoning ability used in research happened to use problems and examples more familiar to men, for example, a false gender difference might show up in a meta-analysis.

No statistical technique can resolve all problems of interpreting differences. Meta-analysis can show which variables moderate the occurrence of gender differences, but it does not allow conclusions about the *causes* of the differences. Moreover, there is still room for disagreement about how big a difference must be to count as an important one. The meaning of observed differences is still at issue because it is human beings who make meaning out of numbers.

Interpreting Results: Values and Ideology in Research

It is not always easy to see the values and assumptions underlying interpretations of data about gender. Students learn that science is value-free and that scientists are objective, impartial seekers of truth. But values and beliefs related to gender have affected research throughout the history of science (Gould, 1981; Harding, 1986). A brief review of the history of the scientific study of some gender issues will help clarify the interconnections between values and practice.

Throughout most of Western history, the intellectual and moral inferiority of women was seen as self-evident. The first systematic empirical research on women conducted by scientists of the late 19th century took women's inferiority as a given and was aimed at uncovering its biological determinants (Gould, 1980; Hyde & Linn, 1986; Russett, 1989; Shields, 1975). In an era of agitation over women's rights, members of the dominant social group needed to document the inferiority of other groups in order to defend the status quo. "You are women and hence different," was the message conveyed. "Your differences disqualify you for the worldly roles you seem, most unwisely, to wish to assume" (Russett, 1989, p. 23). Sometimes the scientists' antifeminist bias was expressed directly; one British anthropologist presented a so-called scientific paper denouncing the "superficial, flat-chested, thin-voiced Amazons, who are pouring forth sickening prate about the tyranny of men and the slavery of women" (cited in Russett, 1989, p. 27).

The Female Brain: Different and Inferior

Then (as well as now), sexism, racism, and class bias were often intertwined; and the brain often was the battle site (Bleier, 1986; Winston, 2003). First, researchers asserted that the inferiority of women and people of color was due to their smaller brains. One prominent scientist asserted that many women's brains were closer in size to those of gorillas than to the brains of men (cited in Gould, 1981). Similarly, scientists measured cranial size in skulls representing various "races" and concluded that the races could be ranked on a scale of cranial capacity (and, hence, intelligence) with darker people such as Africans at the bottom, Asians intermediate, and white European men at the top. The brain-size hypothesis foundered when it occurred to scientists that, by this criterion, elephants and hippos should be much more intelligent than people. They then turned to the ratio of brain size to body weight as a measure of intellectual capacity. Little more was heard of this measure when it was discovered that women fared better than men by it.

Giving up on gross differences such as brain size, scientists turned to examining supposed differences in specific regions of the brain. When it was believed that the frontal lobe was the repository of the highest mental powers, the male frontal lobe was seen as larger and better developed. However, when the parietal lobe came to be seen as more important, a bit of historical revisionism occurred. Women were now seen as having similar frontal lobes but smaller parietal lobes than men (Shields, 1975).

When size differences in brain regions proved impossible to document, the debate shifted to the variability hypothesis. It was asserted that men, as a group, are more variable—in other words, that although men and women may be similar on average, there are more men at the extremes of human behavior. Variability was viewed as an advantageous characteristic that enabled species to evolve adaptively. The variability hypothesis was used to explain why there were so many more highly intelligent men than women. Only men could achieve the heights of genius. (The prediction of greater incidence of mental deficiency among males was virtually ignored.)

The Female Mind: Different and Deficient

The history is similar for another type of research, the measurement of human abilities, which began in the 19th century with Sir Francis Galton's studies of physical variation and motor skills (cited in Hyde & Linn, 1986). Galton measured height, grip strength, and reaction time because he thought they reflected mental ability. When physical abilities failed to correlate with intellectual functioning, the mental testing movement was born. When tests of mental ability failed to demonstrate male intellectual superiority, scientists returned to the variability hypothesis to explain how apparent similarity reflected underlying difference, claiming that men and women might be equal on average, but only men appeared at the upper end of the distribution of mental ability (Hyde & Linn, 1986; Shields, 1982).

Some of the first generation of women who became psychologists worked to dispute these claims. For example, Leta Hollingworth and Helen Montague examined the hospital records of 2,000 newborn infants to test the variability hypothesis. Others examined gender-related differences in emotionality and intelligence (Wooley, 1910). Few differences were found. However, widespread beliefs about innate gender differences in mental abilities persisted. Today, the search for biological differences underlying intellectual functioning continues.

The Lessons of History

The history of attempts to find biologically based sex differences illustrates some important points about the study of group differences. Much of this history shows haphazard testing for a wide variety of differences. Of course, the number of possible group differences is infinite, and demonstrating the existence of one or many gives no information about their causes. Moreover, the so-called truth discovered by science is historically and contextually limited. It is easy to see how the racist and sexist prejudices of past eras led researchers to search for justifications of the inferiority of women and people of color. It is less easy to see how personal values affect the work of contemporary scientists, but such influences surely exist. Although people could be grouped in any number of ways, in practice only a few—such as race and gender—are usually chosen. There seem to be no "separate but equal" classification schemes available. The traits attributed to women and minorities are less socially desirable than the traits attributed to men. Because white men remain the norm by which others are judged, and because this dominant group is mostly in charge of producing and interpreting scientific research, science is easily enlisted in support of the social status quo.

How can we begin to make sense of the differences between women and men? One approach is to analyze these differences in terms of the gender system—to consider how they are produced and maintained at the sociocultural, interactional and individual levels. To make this task easier, I will focus on two areas where differences have been clearly documented and shown to be socially (as well as statistically) significant: mathematics performance and emotionality.

Gendering Cognition: "Girls Can't Do Math"

The general pattern in cognitive skills is one of gender similarity (Halpern, 1992; Maccoby & Jacklin, 1974). However, math ability and achievement is one of a very few areas where research shows consistent gender differences. In this section we look at ongoing controversies about these differences in mathematics performance.

There are two widely used ways to measure math ability and achievement: school achievement and performance on standardized tests such as the SAT-M. On standardized tests, boys come out ahead. In school achievement, girls come out ahead. From elementary school through college, girls and young women of all ethnic groups get better grades than boys and young men, even in areas in which the boys score higher in ability tests. Girls are less likely to repeat a grade, get assigned to special education classes, or get in trouble over their behavior or schoolwork; and they are more likely to take honors and AP classes, make the honor roll, and be elected to a class office (Coley, 2001; Hyde & Kling, 2001). Their higher academic achievement is rarely interpreted to mean that girls are more intelligent. Rather, it is argued that girls may get their higher grades by being quiet and neat, following directions, and trying hard to please their teachers. This may be an example of devaluing the characteristics of a subordinated group.

Girls' performance on standardized math tests is better than boys' in the elementary school years; in high school they perform equally or slightly less well than boys (Hyde & Kling, 2001). Just a short time ago, in the 1940s to 1960s, the differences in favor of boys were much larger. Today, the similarities outweigh the differences, and there is a lot of overlap between the distributions of males' and females' scores.

There is, however, a well-documented difference favoring males in *advanced* mathematics performance. Every year, over 1 million high school students take the Scholastic Assessment Test, or SAT. For the past 30 years, boys have scored consistently higher on the math portion of the SAT than girls. In national math talent searches using the SAT and similar tests, far more boys than girls are identified as gifted, and the gifted boys score higher than the gifted girls (Benbow & Stanley, 1980; Hyde & McKinley, 1997). The gender gap in math scores occurs within every ethnic group tested (White, Black, Hispanic, and Asian American), and it also occurs on the GRE test, which is used for admissions to graduate school (Coley, 2001).

What a puzzle for psychological research to unravel! Girls start out liking math and believing that girls are better at it than boys (Boswell, 1985). They do better than boys on standardized tests in math and get better grades. Yet by the time they are in high school, they score lower on advanced math. As you might expect, the development of this difference cannot be attributed to just one or two causes.

What Factors Influence Mathematics Performance?

Many interacting factors may be responsible for gender differences in math performance. These include confidence in one's math abilities and opportunities to learn math. They also include stereotypes about math as a male domain. Some researchers view the differences as reflecting biologically based differences in ability.

Gender in the Classroom

In the past, the single biggest influence on math performance was that girls took fewer math courses (Chipman & Thomas, 1985). Fortunately, college-bound girls now are just as likely as their male counterparts to take four years of math. The exception is Hispanic girls, who still take somewhat less high school math than Hispanic boys (Coley, 2001).

Even when they take the same courses, however, boys and girls may experience different worlds in the classroom. At all grade levels, a few males often dominate classroom interaction while other students are silent and ignored (Eccles, 1989) (see Figure 4.4). Gender interacts with race: White males get the most attention from

Doonesbury

BY GARRY TRUDEAU

FIGURE 4.4

Sexism in the classroom.

Source: Doonesbury Copyright © 1992 G. B. Trudeau. Distributed by Universal Press Syndicate. Reprinted with permission. All rights reserved.

teachers, followed by minority males and white females; minority females get the least attention of any group. And this discrimination takes a toll: Girls of all ethnic backgrounds, but particularly African American girls, become less active, assertive, and visible in class as they move through the elementary grades (Sadker & Sadker, 1994).

Sexism in the classroom may be benevolent (Hyde & Kling, 2001). Teachers may protect the feelings of girls by not calling on them for difficult questions or by praising their appearance, not their performance. Sexism can also be hostile. For example, girls experience sexual harassment from their peers and teachers more often than boys and fear it more (AAUW Educational Foundation, 2001). Sexism and its effects are evident in the voices of young women interviewed by Myra Sadker and David Sadker:

> In my science class the teacher never calls on me, and I feel like I don't exist. The other night I had a dream that I vanished.

> I have a teacher who calls me "airhead" and "ditz." I used to think I was smart, but now I don't know. Maybe I'm not. What if he's right? The more he treats me like an airhead, the more I think maybe I am. (Sadker & Sadker, 1994, p. 135)

Low Confidence, Low Self-Expectations

Girls' lower confidence about their math abilities is a consistent finding in many studies, although meta-analysis shows that the difference is not large (Hyde, Fennema, Ryan, Frost, & Hopp, 1990). By the time they are in junior high, girls are losing their early confidence that they can do math as well as or better than boys, and their change in attitude is independent of their actual performance (see Figure 4.5). Although their grades remain better than boys' grades, girls rate themselves lower in math ability, consider their math courses harder, and are less sure that they will succeed in future math courses (Eccles et al., 1985). For adolescent

FoxTrot   by Bill Amend

FIGURE 4.5

Math performance depends on the situation!

girls, self-esteem is linked more to confidence in their physical attractiveness to boys than it is to confidence in their academic ability (Eccles et al., 2000).

Parents of girls probably play a part in these attitude changes. Parents tend to attribute a daughter's success in math to hard work and effort and a son's success to talent. They view math as more difficult for daughters and more important for sons. Research in both Germany (Tiedemann, 2000) and the United States (Eccles, 1989) shows that parents' sterotypical beliefs about gender differences predict children's later beliefs about their math abilities. Boys learn that they have natural talent in an important area, and girls learn that hard work cannot entirely make up for their lack of ability!

Math as a Male Domain

Close your eyes and visualize a mathematician. Chances are your image is of a cerebral-looking man with glasses and an intense but absentminded air—an Einstein, perhaps. Early research showed strong stereotypes that math was for men, and nerdy men at that. When elementary and senior high school students were asked about their perceptions of people in math-related careers such as science, engineering, and physics, they described white-coated loners, isolated in laboratories, with no time for family or friends (Boswell, 1979). Not surprisingly, female mathematicians were stereotyped as unattractive, masculine, cold, socially awkward, and overly intellectual (Boswell, 1985).

The gender deviance of math for girls is heightened by a lack of role models and positive images. Beyond junior high, math and science teachers are predominantly men. Very few girls learn about great women mathematicians like Emmy Noether, who provided the mathematical basis for important aspects of Einstein's relativity theory (Crawford, 1981). Few young girls or boys have opportunities for personal contact with women who are mathematicians and scientists.

In the past, it was thought that the belief that math is for men was held largely by girls and women, and that it deterred them from choosing math courses and math-related activities. However, a meta-analysis of math attitudes has shown that *males* hold this belief much more strongly than females do (Hyde et al., 1990). This finding suggests that gender-related influences on math choices work at the interactional and social structural levels at least as much as at the individual level. In other words, we can no longer conclude that women exclude themselves from math and science because they believe that math is not for them. Rather, their underrepresentation in these fields may be at least partly due to others' beliefs that math is not for women. Such beliefs can create self-fulfilling prophecies (Chapter 2), because boys and men may behave in ways that put subtle pressure on the girls and women they interact with.

Stereotype Threat

One way that beliefs about gender and math ability may have an effect is through stereotype threat. As discussed in Chapter 3, when people know that there is a negative stereotype about their group's abilities, the pressure caused by their fear of confirming the stereotype can interfere with their performance. Stereotype threat can affect anyone. When researchers evoked stereotype threat in white male college students by invoking the stereotype that Asians are better at math, their performance on a difficult math test dropped in comparison to a nonthreatened control group—even though these students were highly competent in math (Aronson, Lustina, Good, Keough, Steele, & Brown, 1999).

Stereotype threat clearly works its damage on the performance of women in math. When college students were given a tough math test after being told that men and women typically do equally well on it, the women and men achieved similar scores. Another group of students took the same test after being told that significant gender differences were expected. In this group, the men outperformed the women. A third group was given the test with no mention of gender similarities or differences (similar to an SAT testing situation). In this group, the men also outperformed the women (Spencer, Steele, & Quinn, 1999).

These results suggest that the gender gap in math performance is at least partly due to stereotype-influenced beliefs and expectations. When people believe that men will do better than women on a math test (either because they're led to by the experimenter or because they have learned this belief elsewhere), they tend to produce the expected results. However, when the stereotype of female inferiority is explicitly challenged, women perform as well as men.

Taking a test in the presence of men may activate stereotype threat for women. In one study, students were tested on difficult math problems in small groups composed of all men, all women, or different male/female combinations. When tested with other women, women got 70 percent of the items correct. When the group was one-third male, their scores dropped to 64 percent; and when they were outnumbered by men, they got only 58 percent correct. Group composition had no effect on the men's performance (Inzlicht & Ben-Zeev, 2000). It seems that being in the minority hinders women's performance by increasing anxiety and stereotype threat. When stereotype threat is activated, it interferes with the ability to generate good problem-solving strategies (Quinn & Spencer, 2001).

Stereotype threat may occur quite often for women in male-dominated areas of study. For example, female college students in math, science, and engineering report higher levels of stereotype threat than those in the arts, education, and social science and are more likely to consider changing their major (Steele, James, & Barnett, 2002). Women who pursue math and science careers are in the minority for most of their working lives, and stereotype threat may be an ongoing problem for them.

What happens when gender and ethnicity both foster negative stereotypes? In a study of 120 Latino/Latina and white college students, ethnicity-based stereotype threat reduced math performance for Latinos and Latinas, and gender-based stereotype threat reduced performance for Latinas and white women. In other words, Latinas were disadvantaged by both gender-based and ethnic-based stereotype threat (Gonzales, Blanton, & Williams, 2002).

Ethnic and gender stereotypes sometimes contradict each other. Asian women, for example, may be stereotyped at different times as not good at math (because they are female) and good at math (because math ability is stereotypically attributed to Asians). To see how these contradictory stereotypes affected math performance among Asian American women, researchers manipulated the salience of gender or ethnic identity by having one group fill out a questionnaire about gender and another a questionnaire about ethnicity before taking a math test. A control group filled out a general questionnaire that did not reference ethnicity or gender. As predicted, women in the ethnicity-primed group did best on the math test; those in the control group did next best; and those in the gender-primed group did worst (Shih, Pittinsky, & Ambady, 1999).

Biological Perspectives

Some psychologists believe that differences in math achievement reflect biological influences. Gender differences, especially in advanced mathematical reasoning, may be in part determined by genetic contributions, hormonal influences, or differences in brain structure (Benbow, 1988; Geary, 1996). So far, however, no one has been able to specify exactly what the biological differences are or how they might work to produce performance differences. The existence of a sex-linked gene for math ability has been ruled out (Sherman & Fennema, 1978). But possible connections between biological influences and intellectual performance continue to be explored.

Overgeneralization and a rush to biologize results are unfortunately frequent in research on gender-related differences. For example, recall that boys are much more likely than girls to be identified as gifted in national math talent searches. Based on this evidence, two prominent researchers concluded that "sex differences in achievement and in attitude toward mathematics result from superior male mathematical ability" (Benbow & Stanley, 1980, p. 1264). Although they had not investigated biological causes in any way, the researchers suggested that biology was at the root of the difference because environmental factors were equated: Their (junior high) boys and girls had taken the same number of math courses. But as two mathematics professors swiftly pointed out, environmental factors had not been ruled out:

> Anyone who thinks that seventh-graders are free from environmental influences can hardly be living in the real world. While the formal training of all students may be

essentially the same, the issues of who helps with mathematics, of what sort of toys and games children are exposed to, of what the expectations of parents and teachers are, and of a multitude of other factors cannot lightly be set aside. (Schafer & Gray, 1981, p. 231)

Indeed, biological and cultural influences can rarely be separated. Even among boys and girls identified as gifted in math and science, the majority do not pursue math and science careers. Among those who do, the influences that shape their choices seem to be similar. In one study, male and female graduate students in math and science who possessed so-called world-class talent had similar test scores and grades to young people selected in giftedness tests. The world-class grad students were distinguished from the other young people by strong scientific interests and values and exceptional persistence in pursuing their goals. Gender differences were minimal on these attributes (Lubinksi, Benbow, Shea, Eftelchari, Sanjani, & Halvorson, 2001). Clearly, ability alone does not determine intellectual growth and career choice.

Ironically, media emphasis on biological explanations may contribute to the sociocultural causes of math deficits in girls and women. When Benbow and Stanley's (1980) article speculating about biological factors in math achievement was published in the prestigious journal *Science*, it was seized on by the media and reported in highly misleading stories (see Figure 4.6). An interesting field study compared the attitudes of parents who had heard about the article with those who had not (Eccles & Jacobs, 1986). (Because Eccles's research on math attitudes and performance was under way at the time, she had a sample of parents whose attitudes toward their daughters' abilities she had already measured.) Reading about so-called scientific evidence for a math gene favoring boys led mothers of daughters to lower their estimates of their daughters' abilities. We have already noted the important effects of parents' beliefs on their children's self-assessments.

Social Implications of Gendered Cognition

We are all so used to living in a gendered world that it is hard for us to appreciate the pervasiveness of gender differentiation (see Chapter 6). We grow up being given gender-typed toys: dolls and play jewelry for girls; microscopes, building sets, and computers for boys. We are told that boys are better at math, science, and reasoning. Because U.S. society tries so hard to make girls and boys different, it is surprising that cognitive differences are not larger and more general than they are. Research from other societies shows that gender differences are not universal—for example, there is no difference in math skills between high school girls and boys in China (Huang, 1993).

One implication of the gender gap in math performance in the United States is that our society needs to pay more attention to the intellectual development of girls. One way to help young girls develop their cognitive abilities is to provide them with computers and so-called boys' toys. "We may be shortchanging the intellectual development of girls by providing them with only traditional sex stereotyped toys" (Halpern, 1992, p. 215). Another strategy is to offer educational environments that optimize chances for girls and young women to do well in math and science.

Do Males Have a Math Gene?

Can girls do math as well as boys? All sorts of recent tests have shown that they cannot. Most educators and feminists

tude Test normally given to high-school seniors. In the results on the math portion of the SAT—there was no appreciable dif-

Newsweek, Dec. 15, 1980

The Gender Factor in Math

A new study says males may be naturally abler than females

Until about the seventh grade, boys and girls do equally well at math. In early high school, when the emphasis

Julian C. Stanley of Johns Hopkins University, males inherently have more mathematical ability than females.

Time, Dec. 15, 1980

Male superiority

Are boys born superior to girls in mathematical ability? The answer is probably Yes, say Camilla Persson Benbow and Julian C. Stanley, researchers in the department of psychology at the Johns

The Chronicle of
Higher Education,
December, 1980

Are Boys Better At Math?

New York Times,
Dec. 7, 1980

BOYS HAVE SUPERIOR MATH ABILITY, STUDY SAYS

Boys are inherently better at math than girls, according to an eight-year study of 10,000 gifted students. Coun-

Education U.S.A.,
Dec. 15, 1980

SEX + MATH = ?

Why do boys traditionally do better than girls in math? Many say it's because boys are encouraged to pursue

Family Weekly,
Jan. 25, 1981

Study suggests boys may be better at math

WASHINGTON (UPI) — Two psychologists said Friday boys are better than girls in math reasoning, and they urged educators to accept the fact that something more than social factors is re-

Ann Arbor News,
Dec. 6, 1980

FIGURE 4.6

Media messages: Biased reporting of a gender-based difference.

Source: From "Media Messages: Biased Reporting of a Gender-Based Difference," 1986, Eccles & Jacobs, "Social Forces Shape Math Attitudes and Performance," *Signs*, 11, pp. 367–389. University of Chicago Press. Reprinted by permission.

Research shows that educational programs that are good for girls are good for boys, too (Davis, Crawford, & Sebrechts, 1999). Figure 4.7 shows one attempt to increase girls' interest in science careers.

A second implication of the math gap is that our society's emphasis on standardized tests may be misplaced. The purpose of standardized tests like the SAT is to predict performance in college. But although women score lower on these tests, they get better grades than men in college. The tests thus underpredict women's performance (Rosser, 1987; Stricker, Rock, & Burton, 1992). This *female underprediction effect* compromises women's right to equal education under the law (Hyde & Kling, 2001). Testing activists have charged that a test that underpredicts the performance of more than half the people who take it should be considered consumer fraud (Rosser, 1987, 1992).

The consequences of the underprediction effect are serious (Hyde & Kling, 2001). Nearly all four-year colleges and universities use test scores in admissions decisions. Because women's college grades are higher than their test scores predict, some women are rejected in favor of male applicants who will do less well in college. Moreover, women lose out on millions of dollars in financial aid because more than 750 organizations use test scores in awarding scholarships (Sadker & Sadker, 1994). Girls also lose out on opportunities to participate in special programs for the gifted. Finally, an individual's test scores affect her self-confidence and her future academic goals (Rosser, 1992; Sadker & Sadker, 1994).

At least one testing specialist maintains that standardized tests are deeply androcentric:

> Excluded are whole areas of human achievement that contribute to success in school and work. . . . Such characteristics and skills as intuition, motivation, self-understanding, conscientiousness, creativity, cooperativeness, supportiveness of others, sensitivity, nurturance, ability to create a pleasant environment, and ability to communicate verbally and nonverbally are excluded from standardized tests. Content that is not tested is judged less valuable than that included on tests. (Teitelbaum, 1989, p. 330)

Although standardized tests are supposed to be objective, they are written by subjective human beings who reflect the values of their society. Furthermore, test takers bring to the test different feelings about themselves and the test and thus interpret items differently. There is no such thing as a value-free test (Teitelbaum, 1989). Because many important decisions are made on the basis of testing in our society, more research is needed on the tests themselves and how they produce similarities and differences among groups. And other criteria besides test scores should be taken into account for college admissions and scholarships.

Finally, beliefs about women's alleged inability to do mathematical and scientific thinking foster the continued exclusion of women and ethnic minorities from prestigious and rewarding careers in science and engineering. Despite gains for women in other areas, math, computer science, and engineering are still among the most male-dominated careers. In most of the world, women—both white and women of color—are still far more likely to be found doing the support work of science as technicians and assistants than being in charge of a research program (Kimball, 1995).

HIGH SCHOOL CHEMISTRY LED HER TO A LIFE OF CRIME.

As Director of the Delaware State Police Crime Lab, forensic microscopist Julie Willey catches murderers, rapists and thieves by analyzing hair and fiber specimens. It's a job she has today because, in high school, she didn't think it was uncool to take chemistry.

There's a whole world of interesting jobs in science out there. Find out how you can turn your daughter on to them.

Call 1-800-WCC-4-GIRLS. Or visit us on the Internet at http://www.academic.org.

EXPECT THE BEST FROM A GIRL.
THAT'S WHAT YOU'LL GET.

Women's College Coalition

FIGURE 4.7

Source: Women's College Coalition.

Women who persevere in scientific careers face prejudice and discrimination. Although they may start out with jobs similar to those of their male peers, a gap appears and widens as time goes on. Research (reviewed by Kimball, 1995) shows that women scientists typically earn about 25 percent less than men and are twice as likely to be out of a job. These differences are not due to the women's publishing less or taking time out to have children or other individual factors. Rather, they seem to reflect built-in structural biases in the scientific professions. The higher the level, the fewer women. Only about 2.5 percent of Nobel Prize for Science winners and 3 percent of members of the prestigious U.S. National Academy of Sciences are women.

Researchers in the similarities tradition have tried to demonstrate that, given the same opportunities, women can do math and science as well as men. By questioning the size of cognitive differences and examining how they are socially produced, feminist researchers have made a contribution toward equality. Yet equality has not been achieved, although women, particularly white women, have made some very real gains. The belief persists that math and science are male domains; women of color continue to be extremely underrepresented in science; and discrimination against women persists.

Recently, women scientists at the Massachusetts Institute of Technology (MIT) worked together to end gender discrimination at their institution. At MIT's School of Science, there were 197 tenured men and only 15 tenured women. The 15 women, all of whom suspected that discrimination was taking place, demanded an investigation, which showed that they had been given less lab space and lower salaries than their male colleagues and had been excluded from positions of power. In response, MIT raised the women's salaries an average of 20 percent, equalized retirement benefits, and pledged a 40 percent increase in female faculty (Zernike, 1999). The success of the MIT women scientists shows that discrimination can be confronted and successfully challenged through persistence, courage, and collective action.

Gendering Emotion: "Boys Don't Cry"

Who are more emotional—women or men? Chances are the answer that pops into your mind is "women!" When most of us think of emotion, gendered images come to mind—a woman who cries over the slightest upset, or blushes with embarrassment. Let's look more closely at gender and the experience and expression of emotion.

Emotional Stereotypes

The belief that women are more emotional than men are has been documented for as long as stereotypes have been measured (Broverman et al., 1972; Plant, Hyde, Keltner, & Devine, 2000; Shields, 2002). It is widely held not only in the United States but in many other countries (Williams & Best, 1990). Not only are women stereotyped as the emotional sex, but particular emotions are attributed to women.

TABLE 4.1   Emotional Stereotypes for American Males and Females

Male Emotions	Female Emotions	Gender Neutral Emotions
Anger	Awe	Amusement
Contempt	Disgust	Interest
Pride	Distress	Jealousy
	Embarrassment	
	Fear	
	Guilt	
	Happiness	
	Love	
	Sadness	
	Shame	
	Shyness	
	Surprise	
	Sympathy	

Source: Adapted from Plant, A. E., Hyde, J. S., Keltner, D., & Devine, P. G. (2000). The gender stereotyping of emotions. *Psychology of Women Quarterly, 24,* 81–92.

Table 4.1 shows the emotion stereotypes of a sample of U.S. college students and working adults. Notice that a far greater number of emotions, both positive and negative, are attributed to women. Only three emotions—anger, contempt, and pride—are thought to be more characteristic of men.

Very few studies have examined whether the emotional stereotype is applied equally to all women. In one such study, college students rated white women as significantly more emotional than black women (Landrine, 1985). In another, when participants were asked about the communication style of African American and European American women and men, they viewed women's speech as more emotional, and African Americans' speech as more offensive, impolite, and socially inappropriate (Popp et al., 2003). These stereotypes place African American women in a classic double bind: If their gender is salient in a particular situation, their talk may be perceived as overemotional; if their race is salient, the same way of talking may be perceived as aggressive and rude.

A closer look at the stereotype of women as the emotional sex reveals that it depends on a peculiar definition of emotion. Emotional displays by men are often not labeled as emotionality. In fact, it is easy to think of many images of men expressing strong emotions: a tennis star throwing a tantrum on the court, a football team hugging each other ecstatically after a touchdown, a man beating his wife in rage. But when people think of women as the emotional sex, it seems they are thinking of those emotions that women are allowed to express, such as sadness, love, surprise, and fear. The stereotype of women as the emotional sex is maintained in part by excluding anger from the everyday definition of emotion (Shields, 2002). A woman who cries when the dog dies may be seen as emotional, but a man who kicks the dog may not be.

Are there gender differences in emotionality that support the stereotype that women are more emotional than men? In studies done in the United States, women and men show consistent differences in expressing their own emotions and recognizing the emotions expressed by others. In spoken and written talk, women use more emotion words than men do (Brody & Hall, 2000). When asked about their emotional experiences, women report more intense emotions (both happy and sad) than men do—and the more they believe in emotion stereotypes, the more they report intense emotions for themselves (Grossman & Wood, 1993). They are more aware of their own and others' emotional states than men are (Barrett, Lane, Sechrest, & Schwartz, 2000). Women are also somewhat more skilled at recognizing emotions expressed by others—termed *decoding ability* (Hall, Carter, & Hogan, 2000).

Like other gender-related differences, there is more overlap and similarity than difference between the emotionality of women and men as a group. To understand the similarities and the differences, let's look at ways in which emotionality and its meaning are socially constructed at the sociocultural, interpersonal, and individual levels.

Culture, Ethnicity, and Emotionality

Expressing Emotion

Ever since Darwin (1872), psychology has emphasized the study of how emotions are expressed. Cross-cultural studies can help us understand similarities and differences in emotional expression. Early studies showed that people from different cultures could usually identify the emotions depicted in posed photographs, leading psychologists to theorize that emotional expression is a biological universal with an evolutionary basis. However, a recent meta-analysis shows that people are somewhat better at recognizing emotions when they are expressed by a member of their own culture than when they are expressed by a member of a different cultural group (Elfenbein & Ambady, 2003).

Although the expression of emotions may be a biological universal, different cultures teach different techniques for channeling emotional expression. Every culture has *display rules* that govern which emotions may be expressed, under what circumstances, and how. For example, in some cultures people are expected to shriek, wail, and cry loudly at funerals. If there are not enough family members to provide a suitably loud chorus, professional mourners may be hired to do the job. In other cultures, people are expected to show respect for the dead by quiet, emotionally subdued expressions of grief.

A society's display rules often incorporate gender stereotypes. In the United States, women are expected to smile more than men, and some women undergo medical procedures such as collagen injections in the lips and tooth bleaching to increase the display value of their smiles. In Japan, however, a wide, tooth-baring smile is considered impolite for a woman; and a woman may hide her smile behind her hand (see Figure 4.8).

Do emotion display rules vary for different ethnic groups within our own society? One way to find out is to ask people of different ethnicities about how men and women are expected to experience various emotions. When members of four

FIGURE 4.8
Cross-cultural differences in smiling.

American ethnic groups (African Americans, Asian Americans, European Americans, and Hispanics) were asked this question, many differences emerged (Durik et al., 2002). Recall that among white European American participants, anger and pride are stereotyped as much more suitable for men. Among African Americans, both these emotions were stereotyped as equally suitable for women and men. When asked about the positive emotion of love, European Americans and African Americans were similar to each other: Both thought that women express love much more than men do. Asian Americans, however, differentiated less between women and men and, overall, reported less expression of love. Among all ethnic groups, respondents expected women to express more guilt and embarrassment than they expected from men. These patterns of differences and similarities across ethnic groups show that the rules for expressing emotions are learned within specific cultural contexts.

Experiencing Emotion

Cultural differences also affect the experience of emotion. For example, college students in Japan reported feeling generally happier when they were experiencing emotions tied to interconnections, such as friendly feelings toward another. American college students, on the other hand, were happier when experiencing emotions tied to separateness, such as pride in an achievement (Kitayama, Markus, & Kurokawa, 2000).

These findings have been linked to a broader differences between two types of cultures: Some cultures encourage the development of an ***independent self***, whereas others foster an ***interdependent self*** (Markus & Kitayama, 1991). The United States and Western Europe hold up the independent ideal: Each individual is seen as unique, and the task of each individual is to fulfill his or her potential and become an autonomous person. Much of the rest of the world has a very different ideal: Individuals are seen as connected in a web of relationships, and their task is to maintain those connections by fitting in, staying in their proper place, and building reciprocal relationships with others. As one South African woman of color put it,

> There is no word for "identity" in any of the African languages. . . . In English the word "identity" implies a singular, individual subject with clear ego boundaries. In Africa . . . ask a person who he or she is, a name will quickly be followed by a qualifier, a communal term that will indicate ethnic or clan origins. To this day, African bureaucracies use forms that require the applicant (for a passport, a driving license (etc.) . . . to specify "tribe." (Mama, 2002, p. 7)

Cultural differences in the sense of self are illustrated in contrasting proverbs from the United States and Japan:

> *The squeaky wheel gets the grease.* (United States)
> *The nail that sticks up gets hammered down.* (Japan)

Most of the research on gender and emotions has been conducted in Western countries that place a premium on independence. Interestingly, gender differences in feeling as well as in expressing emotion are much smaller in collectivist countries than in individualistic ones. In collectivist cultures, both women and men are allowed to feel and express emotion; in individualistic ones, women are assigned the task of compensating for the emotional deficits of the other half of the population (Fischer & Manstead, 2000).

Emotionality and Social Interaction

Learning the Emotional Rules

Children learn their culture's rules for displaying emotion at an early age. In our own society, one important influence is "emotion talk" from parents. Many studies have shown that parents are more likely to talk about people and emotions with their daughters than with their sons. Moreover, they talk to daughters and sons about different emotions. In one study of children between the ages of 2½ and 3, 21 percent of mothers discussed anger with a son during a half-hour conversation, whereas not a single mother discussed anger with a daughter. Mothers also used more positive emotion words (e.g., happy) with girls (Fivush, 1989). Other studies show that both mothers and fathers are much more likely to discuss fear and sadness with a daughter than with a son (Fivush, Brotman, Buckner, & Goodman, 2000; Fivush & Buckner, 2000). This differential attention to girls' and boys' emotions soon has its effects: By the time they are 3 to 4 years old, girls are more likely than boys to bring emotion talk into a conversation—especially talk about sad experiences (Fivush & Buckner, 2000).

As children begin to talk about and attend to emotion in gendered ways, the social environment shapes different consequences for girls and boys. In a study of preschoolers, girls who expressed anger (but not those who expressed sadness or distress) were likely to be rejected by their peers, while boys who expressed anger tended to be popular with their peers (Walter & LaFreneire, 2000). And girls learn early to hide their negative feelings because their emotional expressions are supposed to be nice. For example, think about how you would act if someone gave you a gift you didn't like. Most adults have learned the rule that, in this situation, you should pretend to be happy. When researchers presented first- and third-grade children with disappointing gifts, the girls showed more positive and less negative emotion than the boys, indicating that they had already internalized this rule and were better than the boys at masking their true feelings (Davis, 1995).

Children learn not only the display rules but also *feeling rules* (Shields, 2002). That is, they learn what it means to experience an emotion, what others expect them to feel, and how they are supposed to recognize emotions in others. All these lessons are deeply gendered. "Emotion education includes not only 'because you are a boy, feel/show X,' but also "feel/show X in order to become a boy" (Shields, 2002, p. 91). For example, a study of white suburban teenage boys showed that they valued teasing and bullying because their identity was connected to suppressing emotional reactions. Hostile interactions with others gave them practice in "sucking it up" and "taking it like a man" (Oransky & Marecek, 2002). For both boys and girls, doing emotions appropriately becomes an important part of doing gender, of performing one's identity as a boy or girl.

Through a Gender Lens

Beliefs about the different emotionality of males and females may influence perceptions of others' emotions. Classic studies have shown that observers who are asked to judge the emotions of babies and young children from videotapes rely on gender as a cue. When told that the child they are viewing is a male, they perceive more anger than when told they are viewing a female (Shields, 2002).

The influence of gender on perceptions of emotions occurs for adults, too. In one study, participants viewed photos of women's and men's faces displaying specific emotions (Plant et al., 2000). Some photos clearly portrayed anger, others clearly portrayed sadness, and still others showed a more ambiguous blend of anger and sadness. When people looked at the slides, what they saw depended on whether a woman or a man was displaying the emotion. Even though the actors in the photos had identical expressions, participants saw men's blended expressions as angrier than women's, and women's blended expressions as sadder than men's. Moreover, participants used the same gender lens even when the expressions quite clearly represented a single emotion. They rated women's anger as less angry than men's anger and saw sadness where there was none in women's angry expressions. In another study, participants saw photos from a standardized set that portrayed clear, intense emotions. Again, participants perceived the angry male as showing more anger than the angry female; the angry female, but not the male, was seen as fearful (Algoe, Buswell, & DeLamater, 2000).

These studies show that gender stereotypes of emotion are powerful enough to lead people to misperceive others' feelings, even when they are quite clearly expressed. They also imply that, for women, anger is truly the forbidden emotion. An angry woman is so disturbing and unacceptable that people refuse to see anger in a woman's clearly angry expression and instead choose to see sadness or fear.

Do gender expectations about emotion lead to self-fulfilling prophecies? In one intriguing study, researchers manipulated the gender expectations to find out (Grossman & Wood, 1993). Male and female participants viewed slides designed to elicit negative emotions. Half the participants were given no special information about emotions, whereas the other half were told that research has shown a positive link between emotional responsiveness and mental health. In the first condition, in which gender expectations were presumably operating as usual, women gave more intense emotional responses than men did. However, in the second condition, in which gender expectations were replaced by mental health expectations, men's responses were as emotional as women's were. This study suggests that gendered emotions are not the result of internalized patterns (the individual level) as much as they are due to pressures to conform to emotion stereotypes at the interactional level.

Emotion Internalized

In contrast to the view that women and men merely display different emotions because it is socially appropriate, the differences tradition has developed a psychodynamic approach to understanding gender and emotion. This approach maintains that women and men come to experience emotion differently at the personal level through processes that take place very early in life. In other words, gendered emotionality is constructed not only at the social and cultural level but also by early experiences and unconscious fantasy, so that gendered emotionality becomes a deeply internalized part of the self. To explore this process, I turn to a feminist psychoanalytic theory that proposes that the crucial events underlying the development of gender identity and subsequent gender differences in nurturing, emotional empathy, and connectedness to others occur in the first two years of life (Chodorow, 1978, 1979, 1995).

Developing a Relational Self

According to Nancy Chodorow (and other psychoanalytic theorists) the infant has no self—it cannot distinguish between itself and its caretaker (usually the mother). Because the infant is helpless, it is psychologically merged with the mother as she meets its every need. Infants must go through a gradual process of differentiation in which they come to perceive boundaries between themselves and their primary love object (see Figure 4.9).

Developing a self is not automatic or invariable. It requires psychological and cognitive maturation (such as the ability to understand that objects exist independently of the child's presence). Most important, the self develops *in relation to the*

FIGURE 4.9

An infant's sense of self develops in relationship with a caring adult.

primary caretaker. As the mother leaves and returns, meets (or fails to meet) the infant's needs, asserts her own needs, and interacts with other people, the infant comes to perceive her as separate, to make a me/not me distinction. "Differentiation occurs in relationship, separateness is defined relationally: 'I' am 'not you'" (Chodorow, 1979, p. 67).

Developing a separate sense of self is an essential task for every human infant. What does this process have to do with the development of gender differences? Because most child care is done by women, female infants experience a caretaker who is like them in a very fundamental way. They can define themselves in terms of that similarity; they move from "I and you are one" to "I am like you." Their distinction between self and other (me and not-me) is overlapping and fluid, built on their primary sense of oneness with the mother.

Girls grow up with a sense of similarity to and continuity with their mother and a sense of connection to others in general. Boys, however, must learn the more difficult lesson that their gender identity is not-female, or not-mother. Because mother has been the first object of love, and because fathers are likely to be less involved with their infants, boys develop an identity based on defining themselves in opposition to all that is feminine: Femininity becomes negative and masculinity positive.

These gender differences in identity have important consequences. Boys who define masculinity as the opposite of femininity grow into men who devalue women and believe in the superiority of whatever qualities they define as masculine. They deny and repress their needs for closeness and connection with others, which reduces their ability to be emotionally connected and expressive and leads them to be satisfied with less intimacy.

Women, on the other hand, tend to define themselves in terms of their relationships with others and to feel a need for human connectedness. Their greater relational needs lead them to be more expressive of their own feelings, more attuned to others' emotions, and more concerned with caring for others.

The cycle is repeated as another generation of boys and girls defines gender in relation to female caretakers. In each generation, women become the experts in developing and expressing the emotional intimacy that is required in close relationships. According to this perspective, masculine-feminine identities and roles are not biologically determined but are reproduced in every generation by social arrangements.

Relationality and Mothering

Women's experiences as mothers are central to this theory. Because women's relational needs cannot be entirely satisfied by a man (especially one preoccupied with separateness and independence!), they satisfy their needs for connectedness in other relationships, particularly in the mother-infant bond. (For other perspectives on why women choose to have children, see Chapter 10.) Thus, mothering is the source of not only gendered personalities but also the division of labor in society, in which women do more caretaking than men do. The theory does not devalue mothering or other relationships or suggest that women should try to be more like men. Mothering is viewed as a positive goal for women, one that satisfies important needs. Yet the theory does not claim that mothering is instinctive or inherent in women's nature. If men nurtured and cared for young children, they too would develop relationship skills, emotional expressiveness, and a sense of connection; and these qualities would be socially reproduced in their sons.

Limitations of Relational Theory

There are some limitations to this approach. First, it assumes that children are all brought up in nuclear families and does not ask how development might differ in other kinds of families. Cross-culturally and historically, a nuclear family pattern is the exception, not the rule. Chodorow acknowledges that there are cross-cultural differences in child care, but she believes that these differences affect only the details and not the basic process of forming a self.

Another kind of diversity not addressed by Chodorow's theory is sexual orientation. Obviously, not all women are heterosexual. Because the theory claims that women have greater relational needs than men, it implies that women might tend to turn toward each other for friendship, connectedness, and sexual/affectional bonds, rather than to less satisfying relationships with men. Chodorow, however, glosses over this implication of her theory and views heterosexuality as the only normal outcome of feminine development (Rich, 1980).

Chodorow's psychodynamic theory attempts to explain why so many women seem to focus on feelings and relationships (including mothering) and are willing to sacrifice other aspects of their lives to do so, and why so many men resist involvement in relationships and fathering. It explains these differences in terms of psychosocial processes that create gender-specific unconscious needs. Despite criticisms, this intriguing theory has stimulated research and scholarship (Heenan, 2002).

Gendering Emotion: A Summary

The social construction of females as the emotional sex occurs in many ways. Cultures differ in their rules for displaying and feeling emotion, but most societies have rules that are gender linked. Emotionality is one of the core characteristics of feminine stereotypes cross-culturally. In our own society, this stereotype is maintained in part by defining emotionality more in terms of the emotions attributed to women than the emotions attributed to men. Stereotypes influence perceptions, so identical behavior by a woman or a man may be seen as expressing different emotions. Moreover, stereotypes open the way for self-fulfilling prophecies. People expect women to be more emotional; therefore, they may treat them in ways that encourage emotional displays. According to the differences tradition, however, gender differences in emotional connection to others are also internalized. These differences are part of the structure of the self, and society should value and celebrate women's empathy and emotional expressiveness.

Social Implications of Gendered Emotionality

Gender differences in emotionality are not politically or socially neutral. Instead, they are linked to power and status; and they affect the roles, occupations and opportunities considered appropriate for women and men.

Emotion, Status, and Power

Expressing emotion is linked to status and power as well as to gender. Emotionality may be taken as a sign of weakness if the emotions expressed are sadness, grief, or fear. However, other emotions are reserved for the powerful. People recognize this social fact and expect different emotions from high- and low-status people in the same situations. For example, when college students read scenarios about employees receiving positive performance evaluations, they believed that a low-status employee should feel more appreciation, whereas a high-status employee should feel more pride. When the scenario described a negative evaluation, participants expected that the low-status employee should feel sad or guilty, whereas the high-status employee should feel angry (Tiedens, Ellsworth, & Mesquita, 2000). Notice that the emotions expected of high-status people—anger and pride—are identical to the ones expected of European American men (Plant et al., 2000). The right to display anger is one kind of social power.

Another link between emotionality, status, and power is related to the roles and occupations considered to fit women and men. A person who shows fear and sadness is unlikely to be thought of as a potential leader in government, business, or the military. A person who shows anger, contempt, and pride is unlikely to be thought of as a potential full-time parent, teacher, or nurse.

In all the studies I have described, there is much more overlap than difference in women's and men's emotionality—just as there is in other gender-linked differences. Unfortunately, emotionality remains a core part of feminine stereotypes. As other gender categories are challenged and changed, emotion may become more and more important in differentiating men from women. "In an era where neither masculine work nor masculine clothing unambiguously define gender as difference, emotion is one of the few remaining contested areas . . . in which drawing a line between masculine/manly and feminine still works" (Shields, 2002, p. 136).

There is no reason to think that a person cannot be emotionally expressive and also rational, yet the traits seem polarized in the minds of perceivers, with rational man and emotional woman on opposite sides of the divide. Historically, women's presumed emotionality was used to justify their exclusion from education and career opportunities. Earlier in this chapter, I described how Victorian scientists considered women's reasoning ability to be lesser than men's. They also considered women's emotions to be more delicate, sensitive, and unstable. Therefore, they reasoned, women had better be confined to the home, where their out-of-control emotions could be directed at (presumably trivial) domestic affairs. If women were allowed to take part in public life, their weaker reasoning capacities might be "swamped by the power of emotion" (Shields, 2002, p. 72). Some of the founders of American psychology shared this view. As late as 1936, Lewis Terman claimed that, compared to men, women were more tender, sympathetic, and loving, but also more timid, fearful, jealous, and suspicious. Luckily, women's submissiveness, docility, and lack of adventurousness tended to keep them out of trouble, according to Terman (cited in Shields, 2002).

Echoes of this age-old prejudice reappeared quite recently when women attempted to gain admission to two all-male colleges, the Virginia Military Academy (VMT) and South Carolina's Citadel. These prestigious universities serve as openings to the social networks that control political and economic power in the South. Both offer military-type training. Although taxpayer-funded, they continued to deny admission to women into the 1990s. When their discriminatory admissions policies were challenged, VMI and the Citadel claimed that women were unsuited for the military life because of their feminine natures—although women had long since been integrated into the U.S. military academies at West Point and Annapolis. In testimony to the U.S. Supreme Court, attorneys for VMI claimed psychological research had proven that

> [w]omen are physically weaker; that they are more emotional and cannot take stress as well as men; that they are less motivated by aggressiveness and suffer from fear of failure; and that more than a hundred physiological differences contribute to a "natural hierarchy" in which women cannot compete with men. (*United States of America v. Commonwealth of Virginia*, 1994, p. 4)

In response, a large group of feminist psychologists (a group I was part of) testified in a friend-of-the-court brief that the VMI witnesses had misrepresented and misused the psychological research on gender differences. In ruling against VMI's discriminatory policy, the Court stated that generalizations about women's natures, even if they may apply to some women, do not justify denying equal opportunity to all.

Emotions and Relationship Conflict

Because women are perceived to be the experts at emotion, they may be expected to be in charge not only of their own expressions of feelings, but others' as well (see Figure 4.10). Stereotypes about the emotionally inexpressive male suggest that men need to be coaxed into recognizing and expressing their feelings and that it is women's job to do so. Moreover, women are expected to be responsible for keeping a relationship smooth and free of conflict. Because of these expectations, romantic

FIGURE 4.10

Source: Copyright © The New Yorker Collection, 1995, Tom Cheney, from cartoonbank.com. All
rights reserved.

relationships can become destructive traps for women who put their commitment
to the partner and the relationship ahead of their own needs (White, Donat, &
Bondurant, 2001). (See Chapter 8.)

Married women may be expected to take on the role of emotion manager not
only for their spouses but also for their children and to mediate among spouse, children, and other family members. Being responsible for everyone else's feelings can
be a full-time job and a major source of stress. Women's relational work is discussed
more fully in Chapter 11.

Men in our culture are likely to learn that expressing anger is an acceptable and
effective means of controlling others. Societal acceptance of men's anger and aggression puts heterosexual women at risk of violence from their relationship partners. Men who are violent in dating relationships and those who are violent in
marital relationships share similarities in background and attitudes, including the
belief that violence between intimates is acceptable (White et al., 2001). (For more
on relationship violence, see Chapters 8 and 9.)

If women's relational orientation and emotional skills and men's need for
autonomy and control are a deep part of feminine and masculine personalities,
how can gender roles ever change? According to the theory, these differences are

reproduced in every generation because they are learned in a child's relationship with the primary caretaker, usually a woman. If men were more involved in the care of infants and young children, these aspects of personality might change—but paradoxically, the theory claims that men are poorly equipped for this job because of their relative lack of relational orientation. Of course, men's emotional inexpressiveness and withdrawal may serve to preserve status and power differentials that benefit men. Refusing to recognize the feelings of a partner or a child may be a means of control, and refusing to participate in child care may be a privilege of the more powerful. And as long as women are primarily responsible for maintaining emotional connection through taking care of others, their opportunities in work, achievement, and public life will be curtailed; and they will continue to be at risk for destructive and violent relationships.

false ideologies

Making a Difference

Claims about sex differences have often been used to justify keeping women in their place. Even today, hypotheses about female inferiority and claims of new gender-linked psychological differences keep turning up. Gender differences are the socially constructed product of a system that creates categories of difference and dominance. Because gender is a system of social classification that operates at the sociocultural, interactional, and individual levels, changing the social consequences of gender difference can take place at all those levels.

add to begining of ¶

The Individual Level: Thinking Critically

This chapter has focused on two areas in which gender-linked differences have been demonstrated in research: math performance and emotionality. However, it is important to remember that there are many more areas of thinking, reasoning, personality, and behavior that consistently show *no* gender-linked differences. Thus, one important part of thinking critically about gender and difference is to recognize that differences occur against a background of overall similarity, and there are far more areas of similarity than areas of difference.

Moreover, there is much more variability *within* each sex than *between* the sexes on every cognitive skill, ability, or personality trait tested. Therefore, it is impossible to predict much about a person's behavior by gender alone, even in an area where overall gender-linked differences exist. For example, recall the VMI admissions decision. It may be true that, on average, more men than women are interested in military-style education and prepared to undergo it. However, it is much harder to predict the performance of an individual woman or man. Will Taisha do better than Howard at VMI? That depends not only on his or her gender, but also on fitness, intelligence, and determination. Group differences are not very good predictors of individual behavior.

Solution:

As we have seen, there is debate among feminist theorists over whether gender differences in relational orientation and emotionality are deep aspects of personality or merely displays produced by social demands. It is clear that at least some gender-linked differences are *experienced* as part of the self (Chodorow, 1995), and just as clear that some vary from moment to moment according to social circumstances. For example, women's math performance can be affected by stereotype threat, and women's and men's emotional expressiveness can be affected by experimenter-imposed beliefs about its meaning.

At the individual level, each of us can try to think about gender-linked differences in all their complexity, resisting the urge to treat women and men as opposites. Even though it is tempting to think that "men are from Mars; women are from Venus," women and men are much more similar than different. Thinking critically and responsibly about alleged gender differences can help foster social change on behalf of equality.

The Interactional Level: Difference and Discrimination

We have seen that gender-linked differences are important to the social definition of masculinity and femininity. Therefore, even when women and men behave in similar ways, they may be seen as different. For example, recall the women scientists at MIT who were treated as though they were not as capable or valuable as their male colleagues, although their scientific work was similar. Emotional displays, too, may be judged differently depending on whether the emotion is coming from a woman or a man. Gender-biased perceptions of behavior create ample opportunities for self-fulfilling prophecies. Being aware of this possibility, and guarding against it, helps insure gender equity in evaluations of others.

Even if a gender-linked difference can be reliably demonstrated, it does not justify group discrimination. Suppose you are a parent who is told that your daughter should probably not apply for an AP math class because, in the past, girls in this class have had a higher failure rate than boys. Clearly, you would insist that your daughter be evaluated as an individual, not as a gender category. If her grades, motivation, and skills qualify her for AP math, her gender is unimportant. One solution to gender discrimination, then, is to assess people as individuals. However, this is sometimes impossible. If 2,000 people are applying to an elite college that can only take 300, admissions officers feel they must rely on test scores. For this reason, it is very important to ensure that the measures are fair.

Activist organizations such as FairTest (www.fairtest.org) work to curtail the misuse of standardized testing and foster testing that is both fair and educationally sound. For example, after FairTest filed a complaint with the Office of Civil Rights over gender bias in the National Merit Scholarship competition, the test was changed, and the proportion of semifinalists who were female increased significantly.

The Sociocultural Level: Creating Opportunities for Equality

When gender differences in cognitive abilities and personality traits emerge, they are almost always preceded by differences in social environments and experiences. Comparisons of different ethnic and social groups within and across cultures suggest that diversity in cognitive skills and personality is strongly related to sociocultural factors. The similarities tradition argues that these differences would diminish or disappear with equal opportunity and gender-fair environments. Thus, psychologists and educators have created programs to equalize opportunity for girls and women in math and science.

One example is Calculating the Possibilities, a summer program for high school juniors and seniors funded by the National Science Foundation (Pierce & Kite, 1999). Girls were selected for this program based on grades, interest in science and previous course work. For four weeks, the girls lived on a college campus. During this time, they visited corporations where they interacted with female scientists in pharmaceutics, engineering, medicine, and other areas. They met with career counselors who helped them explore their interests and goals. Moreover, each girl worked with a mentor on research projects in chemistry, biology, and other fields. Other activities included guest speakers and pen pal e-mail mentoring from women scientists. Asked what they liked about the program, the young women were very positive:

> Everything! This was the best learning experience! I learned about researching science and that it is fun and interesting. I learned women have a place in this world and a right to work for it.

> The visits have shown me that women still have a long way to go to be equal. I liked working with the mentors. Their experiences and stories have been very helpful in ways that are impossible to describe. It shows scientists can be real people. (Pierce & Kite, 1999, p. 190)

Very few high school or college students receive the personalized science teaching and mentoring of a program like this. A society that cares about equal opportunity needs to make such programs more available.

The similarities tradition, grounded in liberal feminism, has provided the impetus for special programs in math and science for girls. It is hard to imagine the federal government's sponsoring programs to equalize emotional expressiveness, relational orientation, and empathy. According to the differences tradition, these are so-called feminine characteristics less valued by society. Researchers in the differences tradition argue that women and their characteristic activities should be reappraised (Jordan, Kaplan, Miller, Stiver, & Surrey, 1991). Women have been assigned the task of fostering others' development and taking care of others. Yet neither they nor society as a whole have been encouraged to value these interactions and activities, which may be underpaid on the job (see Chapter 11) and taken for granted at home (see Chapter 10).

Psychology and its theories have failed women by devaluing their strengths, according to researchers in the differences tradition. Many psychological theories of human development focus on *autonomy* as the end point. That is, the ideal adult is seen as one whose sense of self is entirely separate from others and who is independent and self-reliant. Close relationships (e.g., the infant-mother relationship) are characterized negatively in terms of dependency and lack of a differentiated self. But very few people are truly autonomous, and when individuals appear to be so, it is usually because many other people are quietly helping them. The idea that psychological development is a process of separating from others may be an illusion fostered by dominant men. Perhaps instead of the John Wayne/Clint Eastwood ideal of the autonomous man, theories of human development should stress human connection and caring. From this perspective, the criteria for human development should include the ability to engage in relationships that empower others and one-self; empathy, not autonomy, becomes the ideal (Jordan et al., 1991).

Can Similarities and Differences Be Reconciled?

Researchers in both the similarities and the differences traditions have recognized that sociocultural aspects of gender govern access to resources; for example, social forces work to keep women out of careers in math and science, and to overvalue the attributes of dominant groups in society. Both traditions also recognize that gender can become internalized—as when women come to think of themselves as bad at math and good at understanding others' feelings. The similarities tradition encourages a focus on equity for girls and women in family, work, and educational settings. The differences tradition suggests that women's characteristics are strengths, not weaknesses.

Individual feminists may feel an affinity for either the differences or the similarities tradition (Hare-Mustin & Marecek, 1990). And a particular kind of research may be useful for a specific political goal. But both traditions have an important place in feminist theory. Whether we are making comparisons by gender, culture, or some other category, similarities *and* differences can be shown; and they both have strengths and limitations (Kimball, 2001). Becoming familiar with both traditions can help address a very important question: How is the gender system made invisible so that socially produced gender seems inevitable, natural, and freely chosen?

Exploring Further

Shields, Stephanie. (2002). *Speaking from the heart: Gender and the social meaning of emotion.* Cambridge, UK: Cambridge University Press.
  This important book explores how emotion is played out in the movies, on the sports page and the athletic field, and in our public and private lives. It offers new ways to think about how emotion is represented and experienced.

Winston, Andrew (Ed.). (2003). *Defining difference: Race and racism in the history of psychology.* Washington D.C.: American Psychological Association.
  Like gender, race is a system of social classification linked to power and dominance. Throughout psychology's history, there have been both proponents and opponents of racist theories and research. This book critically examines psychology's past, looking at how the concept of race was defined, research on racial differences in intelligence, and activism by antiracist psychologists.

PART 3

Gender and Development

CHAPTER 5

Sex, Gender, and Bodies

- **How Does Sex Develop?**
  Sexual Differentiation during Fetal Development
  Variations in Fetal Development
- **Sex, Gender Identity, and Gender Typing**
  Growing Up with Turner's Syndrome
  Androgen Insensitivity and Identity
  The Impact of CAH
  Transsexualism
- **Sex and Sexual Orientation**
  Is There a Gay Gene?
  Hormones and Sexual Orientation
- **Sex as a Social Construction**
  Constructing Two Sexes
  Constructing Transsexualism
- **Beyond the Binary**
  More Than Two Sexes
  The Transgender Movement
- **Making a Difference**
  Transforming Society: Equality for Sexual Minorities
  Transforming Ourselves: Accepting Biological and Social Diversity
- **Exploring Further**

"*I*t's a girl!" or "It's a boy!" At birth, a child's sex is announced to the world. It is the first label attached to this new person by parents and society, and it will have profound importance throughout the child's life. Why? What does it mean to be male or female?

In our society, three assumptions about sex are so fundamental that most people have perhaps never thought about them (Kessler & McKenna, 1978). The key assumptions are these:

- There are two, and only two, sexes; thus, sex is a binary category.
- Sex exists as a biological fact independently of anyone's beliefs about it.
- Sex and gender naturally go together.

According to the first two assumptions, bodies always fall into two clear, natural categories, based on the same biological facts. The third assumption is that gender follows naturally from sex. In other words, once a child's sex is recognized at birth, the process of becoming gendered should follow a predictable course. A female baby should come to know that she is a girl, accept her female sex as a core part of her identity, act like a girl, and grow into a heterosexual woman. Likewise, a male baby should grow up unambiguously masculine in his identity, interests, roles, and sexuality. From these assumptions follow the entire gender system (Chapter 2), which claims that women and men are opposites, prescribes different roles and opportunities for the two sexes, and awards more power and status to men.

Are these three assumptions valid? Biological sex and its relationship to psychological gender turn out to be surprisingly complex and unpredictable—not at all a neat binary system in which sex and gender are always congruent. This chapter explores sex and its complex relationships with gender and sexual orientation, beginning with the question of how sex develops.

How Does Sex Develop?

Sex is usually defined as two reproductive forms within a species. The female and the male of the species have specialized structures, organs, and hormones that result in different roles in reproduction. Thus, sex involves much more than just being born with a penis and scrotum or a clitoris and vagina. No one characteristic defines sex. Sex involves a cluster of biological attributes—including genetic, hormonal, and anatomical components—that develop gradually before birth. Let's look at how sex is formed during prenatal development—a process called *sexual differentiation.*

Sexual Differentiation during Fetal Development

Each human being has a set of 46 chromosomes in each cell of the body. Each of us inherits these 23 chromosome pairs, one of each pair from the mother and the other from the father. Of these, 22 pairs are *autosomes,* and one pair is composed of the *sex chromosomes,* called the X and Y chromosomes. The X chromosome is similar in size to the autosomes, but the Y chromosome is much smaller; it contains fewer than 50 genes, compared with 1,000 to 2,000 on the X chromosome (Wizemann & Pardue, 2001).

Genetically, a female is defined as a person who has two X chromosomes, and a male is defined as one who has an X and a Y chromosome. The newly conceived embryo inherits one X chromosome from the mother and either an X chromosome or a Y chromosome from the father. Therefore, genetic sex is determined at the moment of conception.

During the first month or so after conception, there is no visible indication of the fetus's sex. The fetus has no internal or external sex organs, only embryonic structures from which these will later develop. For example, the fetus has a structure that will become *either* a clitoris or a penis, depending on whether it follows a male or female developmental pathway (Fausto-Sterling, 2000). However, the fetus does not remain in this unisex state for long. Genes on the sex chromosomes, particularly on the Y chromosome, soon initiate sexual differentiation.

Starting at about the sixth week of pregnancy, a gene called the *sex-differentiation region of the Y chromosome (SRY)* causes the embryonic sex glands, or *gonads,* to grow and develop into *testes,* the pair of male sex glands that much later (starting at puberty) will produce sperm (Sinclair et al., 1990). Of course, only genetically male fetuses develop testes because only they have a Y chromosome.

Once the testes are formed, they produce several steroid hormones collectively known as *androgens.* In turn, these androgens shape the development of a typical male body. The androgen *testosterone* causes the internal structures of male sexual anatomy to develop, such as the tubes that will later transport sperm from the testes. *Dihydrotestosterone* causes the penis to grow and the testicles to form. *Mullerian duct inhibiting hormone (MIH)* prevents the internal embryonic structures from developing into female organs such as a uterus.

When all these hormones are activated at the right times and in the right sequence during prenatal development, the fetus develops male sexual and reproductive anatomy. By the 12th to 14th week of the mother's pregnancy, the process is complete. The fetus is male—genetically, hormonally, and anatomically.

How does sex develop in female fetuses? Much less is known about this process, probably because in the past many reproductive biologists were more concerned with male development and considered females to be the default pathway. In other words, when there is no Y chromosome to stimulate androgen production, the fetus develops as a female. This approach represents females as the product of an absence or lack—as the sex that just happens when there is no Y chromosome. Because of this view, there has been little research on the processes underlying female development until quite recently (Fausto-Sterling, 2000).

There may be parallel or similar processes taking place in male and female development. The X chromosome probably contains several genes that cause sexual differentiation (Fausto-Sterling, 2000). In the female fetus, the gonads develop into *ovaries,* the pair of female sex glands that contain eggs and at puberty produces a group of steroid hormones called *estrogens.* However, estrogens do not function in the fetal development of females exactly the same way that androgens do in male fetal development. The female structures of vagina, labia, and clitoris develop largely before the ovaries are formed, so their development cannot be due to estrogens. Instead, estrogens may be important later in fetal development—but the processes are not yet fully understood (Fitch & Dennenberg, 1998).

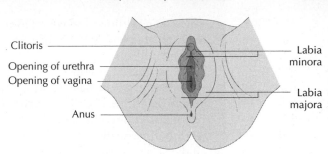

Just as in males, the process of sexual differentiation in females is complete by the 12th to 14th week of the mother's pregnancy. The genetically female fetus has the internal structures (uterus, ovaries, and Fallopian tubes) and external anatomy (vagina, clitoris, labia) of a female. (See Figure 5.1.)

FIGURE 5.1

Female External Sexual Anatomy at Birth.

Source: Courtesy of the Texas Department of State Health Services, Newborn Screening Program.

Thus, sexual differentiation involves coordinated processes influenced by both genetic and hormonal factors. Once the internal structures and external anatomy of sex are established, the sex hormones (androgens and estrogens) are not produced in quantity again until puberty. At that time, the ovaries or testes, along with other glands, produce the hormonal surges that lead to the development of a sexually mature adult body. Females and males both produce androgen and estrogen, but in greatly different amounts, throughout much of the adult lifespan.

Variations in Fetal Development

In the great majority of cases, all the components of biological sex are congruent with each other. An XY fetus develops testes, produces androgens, and develops a penis and testicles. An XX fetus develops a vagina and clitoris, ovaries, and a uterus. Based on the appearance of its genitals at birth, the infant is given the sex label female or male (its *assigned sex*) and raised as either a girl or a boy.

However, about 1.7 percent of babies vary in some way from the biological norm of two distinct sexes (Fausto-Sterling, 2000). In other words, the components of biological sex are not entirely congruent for these individuals. To put this percentage of the population in perspective, sexual variations occur twice as often as albinism, about as often as cystic fibrosis, and about half as often as Down syndrome (Kessler, 2002). *Intersexuality* is a collective term for a number of specific variations on the theme of biological sex; people with any of these variations are referred to as *intersexed.*

Intersexuality has been recorded in many cultures and historical eras. People who did not fit either sex category often became sources of social controversy, and their cases have come down to us through historical records:

- In 1843, the right of a Connecticut resident named Levi Suydam to vote in a local election was contested by town officials because he was "more female than male," and only men had the right to vote. They brought in a physician who examined Suydam and, seeing a penis and testicles, he declared him male;

Suydam was allowed to vote. However, the physician later found that Suydam menstruated and had a vagina. It is not recorded whether Suydam's vote was cancelled.

- Thomas(ine) Hall joined the Colonial Army as a male at the age of 22, after growing up as a female. After military service s/he took up women's clothing again and earned a living sewing lace. Virginia court records show that Thomas/Thomasine went to court claiming to be both a woman and a man, with both a small penis and an underdeveloped vagina. After some indecision and confusion, the court ruled that Thomas(ine) was indeed both a woman and a man and must wear men's clothing plus an apron.

- In Italy, in 1601, after a blacksmith and soldier named Daniel Burghammer gave birth to a baby, he confessed to being "half male and half female." The church called the child a miracle, but granted his wife a divorce because Burghammer did not fit the definition of a husband.

Biologist Ann Fausto-Sterling (2000), who provided these historical examples, points out that making a clear distinction between male and female has been central to law, religion, and politics in many cultures. Those who didn't fit in sometimes were forced to choose male or female and stick with the choice; if they could not or would not, they were punished.

Some intersex variations are visible—the person's genitals or other aspects of their appearance are anomalous. Others, such as chromosome irregularities, may not result in any overtly noticeable bodily differences. What variations on the theme of biological sex occur, and do they affect behavior?

XYY Males: Born Criminals?

Some people have a genetic composition of XYY, or even XYYY. Because the Y chromosome and associated hormone production lead to male sexual differentiation, these people look pretty much like other men, except that they are taller than average (usually over six feet in height). Unless they had a specific reason for having a genetic test done, most men with this condition would be unaware of it.

Does an extra Y chromosome affect behavior? Early studies showed that XYY men were overrepresented in prison populations. Based on this evidence, many people began to believe that the biology of XYY men determined their criminality. The belief was reinforced when the media (falsely) claimed that one notorious mass murderer was an XYY male and therefore "born to kill."

The evidence about XYY males and violent behavior turned out to be quite different from the media hype. A large, well-controlled study was conducted comparing XYY men to genetically typical men and to men with another chromosomal irregularity—XXY, or *Klinefelter's syndrome*. Klinefelter's syndrome causes men to have a less masculine physique and appearance (small penis and testicles, enlarged breasts, little body hair, and a high-pitched voice). The researchers predicted that, compared to the XY men, the undermasculine XXY men would have an exceptionally low rate of criminality, whereas the overmasculine XYY men would have an exceptionally high rate and would be particularly likely to have committed violent crimes (Witkin et al., 1976).

The results were a surprise. Contrary to prediction, a man's chromosomal composition was not directly related to his criminal record. What did predict criminality? Lower intelligence and educational level were associated with crime, and both XXY and XYY men were disadvantaged on these factors compared to XY men. As for violence, there was no relationship with chromosomal status. Less-intelligent people, including some of the men with chromosomal irregularities, were most often in prison for nonviolent crimes like burglary. In other words, the simplistic notion that an extra Y chromosome causes men to be violent criminals was not supported. Rather, some chromosomal irregularities may affect intelligence, which in turn may be linked to lowered opportunities for education and greater likelihood of imprisonment.

The furor over so-called killer chromosomes illustrates the dangers of simplistic thinking about biological determinism. For example, because of the alleged link between the extra Y chromosome and violence, it was proposed that newborn males be subjected to mass testing for extra chromosomes. At least one TV crime drama ran a plot line about an angelic-looking but monstrous XYY little boy. Mass testing for chromosomal status could have stigmatized all those found to have chromosomal irregularities. In turn, stigma could lead to the kind of differential treatment that creates self-fulfilling prophecies. How might a boy's life be shaped by others' beliefs that he was born to kill?

Androgen Insensitivity

Maria Patiño, Spain's top female hurdler, was on her way to the Olympic Stadium in 1988 to start her first race, when she was barred from competition for failing the sex test. Patiño looked like a woman and believed she was a woman "in the eyes of medicine, God, and most of all in my own eyes." However, the test (mandatory only for female athletes) had shown that Patiño's cells contained Y chromosomes, and examinations revealed that she had no uterus or ovaries, but did have testes. Patiño was publicly humiliated by the press. After devoting her life to her sport, she was stripped of all her titles and medals, deprived of her athletic scholarship, and forbidden to compete in the future. Her boyfriend left her (Fausto-Sterling, 2000, pp. 1–2).

Maria Patiño had discovered, in an exceptionally cruel and public way, that she had an anomaly termed *complete androgen insensitivity syndrome (CAIS)*. Her genetic composition was XY, but her body was completely unable to process androgens. Therefore, the androgens that had been produced by her testes during fetal differentiation did not prompt the development of male reproductive structures. Externally, she looked like any other woman; her testes were hidden in the folds of her labia. When she reached puberty, her testes and other glands had produced enough estrogens that she developed the breasts and body curves of a typical woman.

Maria Patiño spent thousand of dollars in medical consultations, then challenged the International Olympic Committee's policy of sex testing. Eventually, she was allowed to rejoin the Spanish Olympic Team (Fausto-Sterling, 2000). However, other Olympic athletes have not had such happy endings to their sex disputes with the International Olympic Committee (IOC). At the 1996 Atlanta Olympics, 3,387 women were tested, and eight were found to have androgen insensitivity or other intersex conditions. They were barred from competition and instructed to feign injury so that no one would know the real reason for their leaving the games. It was not until the 2000 Summer games in Sydney, Australia, that the IOC discontinued sex testing for women on a trial basis ("Gender verification suspended," 2000).

The Missing X

About once in every 3,000 births an individual is born with an XO chromosomal composition—instead of a second X or a Y, there is a missing sex chromosome, an anomaly called *Turner's syndrome* (Fausto-Sterling, 2000). The fetus with this condition lacks androgens and estrogens (other than those produced by the mother's body) during development. As a result, the fetus does not develop complete internal reproductive structures. Externally, however, people with Turner's syndrome look like normal females, with a vagina, clitoris, and labia (recall that female genitals develop in the absence of androgens). Girls with Turner's syndrome are short in stature, and they may have cognitive deficits in spatial visualization tasks, such as map reading and mental rotation of objects. These deficits are not directly related to the sex chromosomes or hormones, and their exact cause is still unclear (Collaer & Hines, 1995).

In the strictly genetic definition of sex, people with Turner's syndrome are neither male (XY) nor female (XX). However, because their external genitals are female, they are invariably labeled females and raised as girls. When they reach the age of puberty, girls with Turner's syndrome are given estrogens to stimulate the development of breasts and an adult woman's body shape. Like CAIS women, those with Turner's syndrome may be given vague half-explanations for their infertility and their need for supplemental hormones.

Ambiguous Bodies

Because XY people with complete androgen insensitivity and XO people with Turner's syndrome look like females, they are treated like females and raised accordingly. In contrast, some intersex conditions result in bodies that are visibly ambiguous: The external genitals may be some combination of penis-like and vagina-like structures, and the internal glands and organs may be intersexed as well. Historically, people with sexually ambiguous bodies were called *hermaphrodites,* after the Greek god and goddess Hermes and Aphrodite, who according to myth produced a child with all the attributes of both its father and mother (Fausto-Sterling, 2000).

Sexually ambiguous bodies may result from a number of genetic, hormonal, and environmental influences. For example, people with *partial androgen insensitivity (PAIS)* may have an external sex organ that could be classified as either a large clitoris or a small penis. Internally, they have male testes, but instead of being located in a (male) scrotal sac, the testes may be located in the abdomen or in the labia.

One of the most common conditions producing a sexually ambiguous body is *congenital adrenal hyperplasia (CAH),* a genetically inherited malfunction of one or more of the enzymes needed to make the steroid hormone cortisol

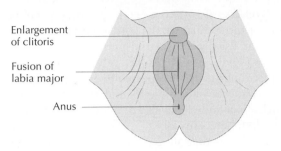

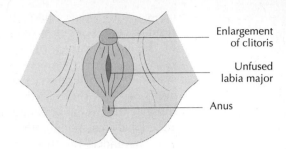

FIGURE 5.2

Ambiguous genitalia of female infants due to CAH.

Source: Courtesy of the Texas Department of State Health Services, Newborn Screening Program.

(Fausto-Sterling, 2000; Hines, 2004). This hormone deficiency causes over-production of other hormones by the mother's body, which act as androgens on the developing fetus. When the condition is discovered at birth, the androgen over-production is stopped (with cortisone). Similar conditions have occurred when pregnant women were prescribed hormones to prevent miscarriage, which had an-drogenic effects on the fetus.

As we have learned, androgens are responsible for the formation of male re-productive structures and anatomy. Female (XX) fetuses with CAH and related dis-orders develop female internal structures—the uterus, ovaries, and fallopian tubes. However, at birth their external genitals may look like those of infant males or may be ambiguous. The clitoris may be enlarged and capable of erection. The labia may fuse (grow together) so that the vagina is hidden and the infant appears to have a male scrotum (see Figure 5.2).

Occasionally, genetic females with CAH have genitals that are so male-appearing that they are labeled male at birth and raised as boys. In one study, for example, this had occurred in about 6 percent of cases (Zucker, 2001). Today, the condition is usually recognized at birth, at least in developed countries, and CAH infants are assigned as females. As infants or toddlers, their unusual genitals are sur-gically changed to a more typical female appearance.

The occurrence of intersex conditions demonstrates that two of the three key assumptions about sex are not universally true. The great majority of human beings do have one of two distinct bodily forms, female or male, along with a correspond-ing genetic composition and hormonal history. However, some do not. We turn now to the third assumption: that sex and gender naturally go together.

Sex, Gender Identity, and Gender Typing

For most people, the genetic, hormonal, and anatomical aspects of sex are congru-ent. At birth, their assigned sex fits these components. As they emerge from infancy, they go on to develop a ***core gender identity***, a fundamental sense of belonging to one sex or the other. Almost always, a child develops a core gender identity that corresponds to his or her biological sex. For most children, the core identity is learned by the age of three. Once formed, it is usually considered permanent (Zucker, 2001). The child then becomes gender typed, adhering to the rules of the gender system of his or her own culture. For example, girls are expected to engage in whatever behaviors their culture defines as appropriate for girls and to refrain from those defined as out of bounds for girls. Each individual also develops an erotic and affectional attraction to others, most often heterosexual.

The underlying theoretical assumption is that all the components of sex and gender *should* fit together (see Figure 5.3). A genetic female should not only have a core gender identity as female but should also be a girly girl, preferring feminine toys and pastimes; and later she should become a heterosexual woman. Echoing the gender stereotypes discussed in Chapter 3, the assumption is that physical attributes, traits, and behaviors are all tightly linked. If they are not, the person is not

"You've been charged with driving under the influence of testosterone."

FIGURE 5.3

developing normally. Whether a man or woman is gender typed and heterosexual is taken as evidence for his or her essential maleness or femaleness (Fausto-Sterling, 2000; Kessler, 2002).

Is gender identity predicted by an individual's chromosomal makeup, prenatal hormones, external genitals, assigned sex, or some combination of these and other factors? Researchers have addressed this question by studying gender in intersexed people. The medical literature often refers to these people as experiments of nature that allow scientists to examine the effects of biological irregularities that they could not ethically induce. (Of course, it would be unethical to do experimental studies of factors influencing human sexual differentiation.) But it is important to recognize

Box 5.1 ∾ As a Woman with Turner's Syndrome

As a woman with Turner Syndrome, I have faced some interesting and unique challenges. Turner Syndrome (TS) is a genetic disorder that affects the sex chromosome pair. There is a wide range of functioning within the TS population, characterized by a variety of physical, neuropsychological and psychosocial difficulties. As someone living with the disorder, I have had to struggle with some important questions that have helped me to grow both personally and professionally.

The specific challenges I have faced have changed and developed as I have matured. Having the short stature commonly associated with TS, I remember being twelve years old and wanting so badly to reach five feet. After three years on growth hormone, my interest in height waned and I began asking doctors how I could look more like my girlfriends who were developing breasts, curves, and a "grownup" look. Now that I am entering the professional world, I find myself aware of presenting myself in an age-appropriate manner despite my younger appearance. As an adult woman searching for a partner to share my life with, I wondered how and when it was appropriate to share the details regarding my infertility with a significant other: What does it mean to me? What might it mean to my partner? Will I find someone who will understand? I have been lucky enough to find a wonderful man who *does* understand. We are happily married and plan to adopt children in the future.

The questions and experiences I have struggled with have made me a better person. As I train to be a child psychologist, I know that my personal experience makes me more insightful and compassionate when working with families. I am also very proud to be a woman with TS who can provide support and resources to others living with the disorder. As I frequently tell others with TS: although we do not have control over the fact that we have a disorder, we do have control over our attitude and the lessons we learn from our experiences. In this way, I view TS as a great opportunity to grow and help others in the process. That perspective has made all the difference!

Please contact the Turner Syndrome Society of the United States at 1-800-365-9944 or www.turner-syndrome-us.org for more information.

Contributed by Jessica Lord, University of Connecticut.

that intersexed people are *people* first and foremost. Like other people, they have personal identities, friends and families, sexual desire and intimate relationships, achievement goals, and dreams for their future. Although they do not fit the gender categories allowed by society, they have to live in a gender-divided world.

When individuals' biological sex is a variant, what happens to their gender? There is a great deal of research attempting to determine which (if any) aspects of biological sex are responsible for one's core gender identity and gender typing.

Growing Up with Turner's Syndrome

It is clear that one does not need two X chromosomes to develop a core gender identity as female. Despite their chromosomal differences from the norm, individuals with Turner's syndrome are assigned as females and develop a core gender identity as female. Girls with Turner's syndrome are similar to other girls in their interests and activities; older studies suggest that they may even be more gender typed than the average girl (Money and Ehrhardt, 1972).

Although Turner's syndrome does not cause problems with gender identity and gender typing, it may cause other developmental problems. For example, the very short stature of girls with this syndrome, and their lack of the hormones that induce puberty, may lead to problems of social adjustment. They and their families may have to make decisions about taking growth hormones in childhood as well as estrogens to stimulate puberty. There is a need for health care practitioners to be sensitive to the psychosocial development of girls who have Turner's syndrome. (See Box 5.1.)

Androgen Insensitivity and Identity

Complete androgen insensitivity is a fairly rare condition, occurring in fewer than 1 in every 100,000 births. Because of their female appearance at birth, most people with CAIS have been classified as female and raised as girls. These girls usually have no trouble establishing a core gender identity as female. Because the child looks and acts like a normal girl, she is treated like a girl, and her gender identity is congruent with her assigned sex.

Neither the girl with CAIS nor her family may be aware of her condition during her childhood. However, when she reaches the age of puberty, her family may seek medical attention because she does not begin to menstruate. At that point, she may be given vague explanations that do not reveal her XY status. Even her parents may not know the truth about her XY chromosomes. Like Olympic athlete Maria Patiño, most individuals with CAIS grow up certain of their female sex.

Like girls with Turner's syndrome, girls with CAIS are born with external genitals that look female, and they are assigned a sex in accordance with the genitals. Therefore, they develop a core gender identity that matches their genitals and assigned sex. Girls with Turner's syndrome or CAIS may never learn of their intersex conditions if they are given selective information by their physicians and family. Problems, if any, occur when the intersex condition and the core gender identity are brought into conflict.

The Impact of CAH

A great deal of research has focused on girls with CAH because researchers believed that they could provide evidence about the effect of androgens on core gender identity and gender typing. Certainly, the exposure to androgens during fetal development influenced these girls' bodies. Do the androgens also affect their identity, interests, and abilities?

Girls affected by CAH almost invariably develop a core gender identity as females. In other words, neither the exposure to androgens nor the families' reactions to their ambiguous genitals at birth disrupt gender identity: CAH girls think of themselves as females and are comfortable with their female identity (Fausto-Sterling, 2000; Zucker, 2001). In the rare cases in which CAH girls have been raised as boys, they apparently developed a male gender identity because their assigned sex fit their genitals and they were socialized as boys (Zucker, 2001).

Do girls with CAH act more like boys in their play patterns and other aspects of gender typing? Dozens of studies have been done in this area. Usually, CAH-affected girls are compared with their non-CAH sisters or other female family members; sometimes they are compared with boys. The general pattern that emerges is that they are somewhat more active, more likely to be tomboys, and play with boys' toys more than other girls do (Zucker, 2001). However, they are not more aggressive or domineering than other girls are (Collaer & Hines, 1995). And they play with girls' toys more than boys do (Berenbaum & Hines, 1992).

This area of research is quite controversial. Critics point out that factors other than prenatal hormonal exposure could be responsible for the behavioral differences between girls with CAH and other girls (or boys). First, it is quite likely that parents and other adults may react differently to a daughter who is born with a penis than to her more typical sister or brother. Second, the high activity level of CAH girls could be a side effect of medications such as cortisone (Zucker, 2001), and this in turn could affect preferences for toys and play patterns. (Boys' toys usually support more active play than girls' toys.) As we learned in Chapter 4, the issues of defining and measuring gender differences are complex; searching for the *causes* of observed differences adds another layer of complexity. In this area, different experts have reviewed the same studies and reached opposite conclusions. Either "the results provide little support for a role for prenatal hormones in the production of gender differences" (Fausto-Sterling, 2000, p. 75) or prenatal exposure to androgens "masculinizes" many domains of behavior (Zucker, 2001, p. 110).

In summary, gender identity in intersexed children seems to be largely dependent on social factors. Being assigned as a female and brought up as a female usually outweigh biological inconsistencies in the components of sex, particularly when the external appearance is clearly female. However, this does not mean that gender identity and gender typing are unrelated to biological sex. Some girls with CAH develop in less gender-typed ways than unaffected girls; whether this is due to prenatal hormones, physical appearance differences, social factors, or some combination of these and other factors is still unknown. Some intersexed people may have problems with gender identity that have not yet been documented because of the secrecy surrounding these conditions. What the research does tell us is that there is not a simple, direct relationship between sex and psychological gender. Instead, the relationships are complex, multidetermined, and still somewhat mysterious.

Transsexualism

James Morris had a full and adventurous life. After serving in the British military as a war correspondent, he became a successful journalist, married, and fathered five children. Morris was a reporter on the British expedition to Mount Everest in 1953 that culminated in the first successful ascent.

Although Morris had an enviable life, he felt that something was very wrong. From earliest childhood he believed that he was meant to be a woman, not a man. After much introspection and conflict, Morris began a 10-year process of transitioning to being a woman. After years of hormone treatments, he underwent sex change surgery: His penis and testicles were removed, and an artificial vagina was constructed. Morris and his/her wife were divorced, but remained emotionally close, bonded by friendship and their mutual love for their children. Jan Morris continued her successful career as a writer and now has more than 30 books to her credit.

Morris's book *Conundrum* (1974) articulates one person's struggle with having been "born in the wrong body." After changing sex, this formerly athletic and adventurous man described his pleasure in the ordinary rituals of femininity: wearing makeup and soft clothes, engaging in small talk with neighbor women, being helped with small tasks such as parallel parking or opening a bottle of wine. Becoming a woman made Morris acutely aware of how women and men are treated differently. She writes that "addressed every day of my life as an inferior, involuntarily, month by month, I accepted the condition" (p. 149). However, she felt that the benefits—being helped, flattered, and treated more kindly—outweighed the costs.

Jan Morris is certain that she found her true self as a woman. Even the ordeals of hormonal and surgical treatments seemed a small price to pay for having her sex congruent with her gender: "I would have gone through the whole cycle ten times over, if the alternative had been a return to ambiguity or disguise" (p. 145). She describes her transsexual journey as "thirty-five years as a male . . . , ten in between, and the rest of my life as me" (p. 146).

Gender Identity Disorder

Morris's account reflects a traditional and still prevalent view that a person whose biological sex does not fit his or her core gender identity has a psychological disorder. *Gender identity disorder* is an official psychiatric category for those individuals who experience a disjunction between their assigned sex and their core gender identity (American Psychiatric Association, 1994, 2000). The APA defines this disorder as a strong and persistent desire to be the other sex or belief that one is really the other sex (American Psychiatric Association, 2000). About one in 30,000 men and one in 100,000 women apply for sex change surgery; however, the number of people who fit the criteria for gender identity disorder may be considerably higher, since not all those who meet the diagnostic criteria choose to have surgery. Like James/Jan Morris, many transsexuals report feeling trapped in the wrong body. Many say that they were aware of their sex/gender conflict from early childhood, but took a long time to articulate it and act on it.

Individuals with gender identity disorder are not physically intersexed. Almost always, their genetic sex, hormonal history, and reproductive anatomy form an unambiguous biological sex as female or male. Their childhoods are typically unremarkable except for their growing sense that they are different from other children and that their assigned sex is a mistake. Some individuals struggle to conform to their assigned sex and accept the corresponding gender roles, while for others, the contradictions become impossible to live with, and they elect to change their appearance and behavior to fit what they believe is their true sex.

Changing Sex

The transition from one sex to the other usually takes place over a long period of time. A woman may change her sex appearance with cosmetic alterations such as binding the breasts and getting a man's haircut. A man may wear makeup and women's clothes and strap his penis between his legs. Some transsexuals use hormonal supplements: estrogens to grow feminine breasts and reduce body hair on a male, or androgens to build muscle bulk and deepen the voice of a female. Others undergo sex-change surgery. (See Figure 5.4.) The transsexual person must adjust

FIGURE 5.4
Female-to-male transsexual Matt Kailey, shown here before and after his transition, is the author of *Just Add Hormones: An Insider's Guide to the Transsexual Experience*, and leads workshops and seminars on gender identity issues. www.mattkailey.com

Source: www.mattkailey.com.

to a changing body, learn new ways of behaving, and accommodate to others' reactions to the changed body and behavior (Bolin, 1996). As we learned in Chapter 2, innumerable small differences in verbal and nonverbal behavior mark gender in social interaction. For example, a man who becomes a woman must not only dress like a woman; he should also walk, sit, talk, flirt, sip coffee, and throw a ball like a woman. To pass as a woman, s/he should have feminine interests and activities. And s/he must learn how to respond when treated like a woman.

Not all transsexuals go as far as having sex-change surgery. It is quite possible to pass as the other sex without surgery, because in daily interactions we rely on social cues, not genitals, to judge someone's sex (Kessler & McKenna, 1978). Passing is much more a matter of fulfilling others' social expectations for a woman or a man than of having male or female genitals. Some researchers estimate that two-thirds of those who are living as the other sex on a full-time basis have not had sex-change surgery.

Clinical records of sex change surgeries show that there are more male-to-female (MTF) than female-to-male (FTM) transsexuals. However, these records may underestimate the number of FTM transsexuals. Surgery to construct a penis is more complicated and often less successful than surgery to remove one. Because it is relatively simple for a woman to don men's clothes and change her body contours with testosterone injections, and relatively difficult to construct a passable penis, FTMs may be more likely than MTFs to pass without undergoing surgery (Devor, 1997). Another possible reason for the apparently greater number of MTFs is that the rules for masculinity are more restrictive than the rules for femininity. A woman who wears pants, cuts her hair short, and plays rugby is hardly controversial; but a man who wears dresses, uses makeup, and asks to have the door held open for him would likely experience severe social sanctions. Therefore, men whose gender is atypical for men in their society may be quicker than atypical women to turn to surgery.

Many cases of sex-change surgery have made headlines in the media. When the prominent economist Donald McCloskey became Deirdre McCloskey, her story was recounted in the *Chronicle of Higher Education* (Wilson, 1996) and in a moving interview on National Public Radio. McCloskey mourned the loss of her marriage and the alienation from her children, but nevertheless felt that she had made the right choice, indeed the only choice, for her psychological well-being. Concert pianist David Buechner's sex change and subsequent stage debut as Sara Buechner were covered by the *New York Times* (Jacobs, 1998). Stories like these engage our sympathy. It must be very difficult to live one's life feeling trapped in the wrong body, and even more difficult to undergo the process of sex change.

Sex and Sexual Orientation

It may seem obvious, but one of the biggest differences between women and men is that the great majority of men are attracted to women, and the great majority of women are attracted to men. **Sexual orientation** is a multidimensional concept involving erotic attraction, affectional relationships, sexual behavior, erotic fantasies, and emotional attachments. The gender of one's sex partners is only one component and not always the most important one. Often, the various components are inconsistent within a given person (Hoburg, Konik, Crawford, & Williams, 2004; Rothblum, 2000). Moreover, a person's sexual orientation may change over time. Despite the complexity of defining it, researchers have looked for genetic and hormonal influences on sexual orientation.

Is There a Gay Gene?

Several studies have shown that same-sex sexual orientation runs in families. In other words, gay, lesbian, and bisexual people tend to have a higher-than-average number of gay, lesbian, or bisexual people among their relatives. These studies suggest that either particular family environments or genetic factors could increase the likelihood of gay, lesbian, or bisexual orientation, but cannot distinguish between the two kinds of factors. Recently, some researchers have turned to *twin studies* to help separate the influences of genetics and environment. These studies compare *monozygotic (MZ)* or identical twins with *dizygotic (DZ)* or fraternal twins. MZ twins are genetically identical, whereas DZ twins are only as genetically alike as any other siblings are. If MZ twins share the same sexual orientation more often than DZ twins do, it suggests that there is some genetic contribution to sexual orientation (Hines, 2004).

Studies of male twins provide evidence consistent with a genetic influence. For example, in one study, 66 percent of the MZ co-twins of gay men were also gay, compared with 30 percent of the DZ co-twins (Whitam, Diamond, & Martin, 1993). This study also found one set of MZ triplets who all were gay. Of course, MZ twins may be treated more similarly than DZ twins because they look exactly alike and may have very similar temperaments. A better way to separate heredity from environment requires studying twins who were reared apart (e.g., by being adopted at birth into different families). As you might expect, gay men with a twin adopted into a different family are rather rare, and only a few cases have been studied. These cases, too, suggest that male MZ twins are more likely than male DZ twins to share a gay sexual orientation (Hines, 2004).

For females, however, the story is different. Some twin studies show the same pattern as the studies with men—female MZ twins are more similar in sexual orientation than female DZ twins are. However, others show little or no relationship between genetic similarity and lesbian or bisexual orientation. In the rare cases of female MZ twins reared apart, none of the pairs studied have shared a lesbian or bisexual orientation (Hines, 2004).

There is still much to be learned about genetic contributions to sexual orientation. Certainly, there is no single gay gene that determines whether a person becomes gay, straight, or bisexual. If there is a genetic predisposition, it appears to be stronger in men than in women. Little is known about how such a genetic predisposition might work. Is there a group of genes that codes directly for a particular sexual orientation? Do genes influence sexual orientation indirectly, perhaps by predisposing to personality traits or interests that influence sexual orientation? Or do genes influence prenatal hormones in some way that relates to sexual orientation?

In summary, the evidence for a genetic component to sexual orientation is preliminary. Even for males, where the evidence is strongest, there is also strong evidence for nongenetic factors: across all studies, more than half of the co-twins of gay men are not gay (Hines, 2004). For females, the picture is even less clear, and whether there is a genetic component to the sexual orientation of females is still an open question.

Hormones and Sexual Orientation

Recall that XX and XY fetuses experience very different exposure to gonadal hormones during fetal development. Male fetuses are exposed to high levels of androgens, whereas female fetuses are not. Do fetal androgens play a role in the later development of sexual attraction to women? One way to study the effects of fetal hormonal exposure on later sexual orientation is to assess the sexual orientation of people whose intra-uterine hormonal exposure was atypical.

Individuals with partial androgen insensitivity syndrome (PAIS) are XY males who effectively receive little androgen during fetal development and therefore develop ambiguous genitalia. Depending on the appearance of the genitals at birth, the individual may be assigned as either a male or a female, and the genitals are surgically altered to fit the assigned sex. Regardless of which sex they are brought up as, individuals with PAIS usually develop a heterosexual orientation—in other words, those brought up as girls become attracted to males, and those brought up as boys become attracted to females. In these cases, it is clear that a normal dose of fetal androgens was not necessary for the individual to develop a sexual orientation toward females. Despite their similar hormonal histories, the individuals raised as boys and those raised as girls developed different sexual orientations, illustrating "a surprising degree of flexibility in human psychosexual development" (Hines, 2004, p. 92).

Other researchers have asked whether an excess of androgens during fetal development could predispose a female to become attracted to women. To answer this question, they have looked at the sexual orientation of women with a history of CAH, which causes exposure to fetal androgens. (Recall that CAH also causes intersexed male-appearing genitals that are surgically altered in infancy.)

The majority of CAH women identify as heterosexual. However, when they are compared to their non-CAH sisters or other female family members, some differences have emerged. For example, the CAH-affected women in one study reported greater same-sex desire and a history of more frequent lesbian experiences (Dittmann, Kappes, & Kappes, 1992). In another study, they reported fewer heterosexual experiences (Collaer & Hines, 1995). Taken together, various studies suggest that CAH women are more likely to have lesbian orientation, fantasies, or experience—and less likely to have heterosexual orientation, fantasies, or experience—than unaffected comparison groups.

Critics point out that these studies lacked a common definition of sexual orientation. Some studies measured fantasies, others measured same-sex experiences, and still others asked about long-term relationships. As discussed earlier, sexual orientation is a multidimensional concept. When studies do not agree on its definition and measurement, it is difficult to combine and compare them. Moreover, many CAH-affected women have had genital surgery, which may affect their ability to experience sexual pleasure and their comfort in intimate situations with men. What is clear is that prenatal hormones do not fully determine sexual orientation, because the majority of women with prenatal exposure to androgens identify as heterosexual.

Sex as a Social Construction

The presence of intersex bodies challenges the fundamental assumption that everyone is either male or female and that this is an "irreducible fact" (Kessler & McKenna, 1978, p. vii). The presence of naturally occurring variations in biological sex also challenges the assumption that gender follows naturally from sex. If sex is not a distinct binary system, why does gender have to follow a binary pattern of masculinity/femininity?

According to some feminist theorists, sex is a *social construction,* which means that the assumptions underlying our commonsense beliefs about sex and gender are the products of a specific culture, not universal or fixed truths about nature (Marecek et al., 2004). In other words, sex is a belief system rather than a fact (Crawford, 2000). However, in every culture, the belief system about sex seems perfectly natural to members of that culture. In our own society, most people firmly believe that sex is a biological dichotomy. It is hard to recognize that what is taken as fact might be the product of social negotiation and cultural consensus.

Even the label "It's a girl!" or "It's a boy" given at birth is a social construction. As we have seen, this classification is usually based on the appearance of the external genitals—but genitalia are only one aspect of biological sex. Choosing to use genital appearance, and not other determinants of sex, is the product of a social consensus. And sex classification is the crucial first step in creating gender. "It is *because* we have already classified someone as male or female that all the other gender attributions we might use—masculine, feminine, lesbian, gay, transsexual— make sense" (Crawford, 2000, p. 8). The concepts of core gender identity and sexual orientation, for example, presume that each infant *is* male or female *before* these psychological processes begin.

Questions of how we become gendered are interesting and important, of course. But even more important is the question of how the social reality of two, and only two, sexes is constructed in the first place (Golden, 2000). Here we look at the process of making social decisions that *create* two sexes by exploring the medical treatment of people who are intersexed or transsexual. These treatments spark heated debate because they involve tailoring unruly bodies to fit the only two sex categories that are culturally permissible.

Constructing Two Sexes

For many years, the standard treatment for intersex conditions began with assigning a child the label of male or female as soon as possible after birth. This was followed by medical and surgical interventions designed to alter the genitals to look more "normal." These surgeries were often done before the child was old enough to consent to them. Often, parents were not given the exact diagnosis. As intersexed children grew older, they were rarely told the truth about their condition. Instead, their medical records were sealed. Here, we consider the social implications of each step in this process.

When physicians recognize that an intersexed child has been born, they attempt to decide what they term the ***optimal gender*** for the child. By this they mean, Which sex will the child fit best? The criteria for best fit are flexible. Physicians must consider whether such children have reproductive potential as a male or female, whether they will be able to function sexually as a male or female, and whether they can be made to look like a typical male or female. If the child is old enough to have formed a core gender identity before the condition is diagnosed, this also must be taken into account.

As you can imagine, deciding a child's optimal gender is a complex matter involving both medical criteria and social norms. Some critics have suggested that the criteria may be applied in sexist ways: For those children who are assigned as females, reproductive capability is given more weight, and for those assigned as males, sexual function is given more weight (Fausto-Sterling, 2000; Kessler, 1998, 2002). In other words, for males, the ability to have an erection and engage in heterosexual sex is the primary criterion, but for females it is the potential for motherhood, not sexual pleasure.

Although medical professionals use the concept of optimal gender among themselves, they consider the indeterminacy of the child's actual sex too unsettling a concept for parents. Critics claim that in treating intersex children and counseling their families, the medical profession uses a gender doublespeak whereby they deliberately hide the intersex status. Instead of saying that the infant is a mixture of female and male and that they are deciding on an optimal gender, they tell the family that they know the "true" sex and will "correct" the "incomplete development" (Fausto-Sterling, 2000; Kessler, 1998). Even when physicians perform major surgery on intersex children (e.g., removing the testes from CAIS girls), they consider it best not to be too candid. As one group of medical researchers wrote:

> An intersex child assigned to become a girl . . . should understand any surgery she has undergone not as an operation that changed her into a girl, but as a procedure that removed parts that didn't belong to her as a girl . . . (although the gland removed is a functioning testis) in the patient's own formulation it is best regarded as an imperfect organ . . . not suited to life as a female, and hence removed. (Cited in Fausto-Sterling, 2000, p. 65)

Why do physicians conceal the truth about intersex from patients and their families? Traditionally, they have believed that the child's core gender identity might be compromised and that this would lead to psychological conflict and poor adjustment. This reflects the assumptions that there must be only two sexes and that gender identity and gender typing must follow biological sex. Although physicians know that some infants do not fit the pattern, they have felt obligated to pretend that the sex/gender binary is universal.

The social construction of two sexes has resulted in withholding personal medical information from intersex people. In one case, an androgen-insensitive child had surgery to remove sex glands when she was too young to consent or understand the procedure. After puberty, doctors explained her need for estrogen pills and her infertility by telling her that her ovaries had not been normal and her uterus had not developed. Of course, this child, a genetic male, never had either a uterus or ovaries (Kessler, 1990). What would happen to this person's trust in her physicians and her family, and to her gender identity, if she found out the truth?

In constructing unambiguous genitals for intersexed infants, the medical profession enforces a standard that allows no overlap between male and female genitals. (See Figure 5.5.) For an intersexed child to be considered a functional girl, she must have a clitoris that is smaller than the smallest permissible penis for a boy. If her clitoris is "too big," it will be surgically "downsized" (Fausto-Sterling, 2000, p. 60). In the past, surgeons often removed the clitoris of intersexed girls entirely. Today, clitoral reduction surgery is performed. Despite considerable natural variability in clitoral size at birth, physicians often rely on their personal impressions or opinions about the appropriate size and appearance of this organ. Suzanne Kessler (1998; 2002) has compiled a list of the adjectives used in the medical literature to describe clitorises that were perceived as needing surgical reduction. The list includes *defective, deformed, obtrusive, offending, troublesome,* and *disfiguring.* Clearly, these are value judgments. It is the physician, and not necessarily the child, her parents, or her future sex partners, who is troubled by a clitoris that is "too big."

Some intersexed individuals have genital surgery several times during the first few years of life, followed by more surgery after puberty (Fausto-Sterling, 2000). Female-assigned children may face repeated surgeries to construct a vagina. Following surgery, instruments must be inserted into the vagina daily by the parents in order to keep the new structure open. A male-assigned child may have genital surgery in order to repair or construct an acceptable penis. The medical literature reports hundreds of techniques for this task, along with techniques to repair the unsatisfactory results of previous surgeries. The costs of genital surgery include visible scarring, loss of sexual sensation, and loss of the ability to reach orgasm. Interviews with adult intersexed

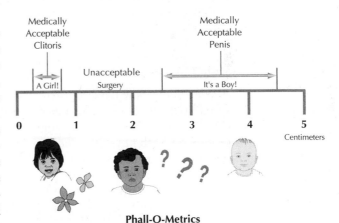

Phall-O-Metrics

FIGURE 5.5

Phall-o-Metrics. The ruler numbers indicate centimeters (not to scale).

Source: A. Fausto-Sterling, *Sexing the Body: Gender Politics and the Construction of Sexuality.* Copyright © 2000 by Basic Books, a member of the Perseus Books Group. Reprinted by permission of Basic Books, a member of Perseus Books, L.L.C.

people, as well as medical data on the results of genital surgery, have shown that poor overall appearance and dissatisfaction with the results are common (Kessler, 2002; Hines, 2004).

The medical interventions aimed at intersexed children also have other costs. Because they may not have access to their medical records, the affected individuals may not know about medical conditions that could compromise their health. Moreover, due to repeated experiences of surgery and the suspicion that they are being deceived, some intersexed people distrust the medical profession to the extent that they fail to get help for other conditions, causing overall health to degenerate (Kessler, 2002).

Physicians and other professionals who treat intersexed patients are faced with difficult decisions involving not only medical criteria, but also ethical and social dilemmas. Their problems of diagnosis and treatment are increased because there is very little information available on the outcome of previous decisions in similar cases. Most patients are not followed up over long periods to see how their sex assignment has worked out for them. Also, it is impossible to know how a person with the same condition might have fared if assigned to the other sex. Unfortunately, life-altering decisions may be made with little evidence about whether they have proved to be good decisions for others in past cases (Kessler, 2002).

The medical management of intersex conditions shows that sex is not just a biological given. Its meaning is negotiated through social decision making. In any social negotiations, members of dominant groups have more power to define reality. In this case, the medical profession has had more power to define the sex of intersex individuals than the intersex people themselves or their families have had. The consequences for intersex people have sometimes been tragic because they have been subjected to life-altering medical treatments without informed consent. A different but equally complex set of issues comes up when fully informed and consenting adults choose to change their sex.

Constructing Transsexualism

Transsexual people have engaged in a long struggle to have their condition recognized by the medical profession. Their demands for legal recognition and medical care have forced society to recognize and name their problem, and to help them change sex both physically and socially. However, not everyone believes that labeling cross-sex gender identity as a psychiatric disorder and providing the option of sex change is entirely a positive change. Some argue that this recognition has had the paradoxical consequence of reinforcing the idea that there are and can be two and only two sexes and that gender must conform to one or the other. "By requesting surgery to make their bodies match their gender, transsexuals enacted the logical extreme of the medical profession's philosophy that within an individual's body, sex and gender must conform" (Fausto-Sterling, 2000, p. 107). Their dilemmas of identity may be a result of our binary system of sex and gender. If you do not feel like a man, then you *must* be a woman—there is no other choice available.

But, given the social construction of sex as a binary system, what other options have transsexuals had? If they wanted to obtain surgery, it was necessary to present themselves within the binary framework (Fausto-Sterling, 2000). Their only alternative was to adopt as closely as possible the physiology, appearance, and roles of the other sex. For example, the more feminine a man acted, the more likely it was that he would be ruled eligible for surgery. In order to convince the medical authorities of his "true" sex, he had to be the best, most stereotypical example of a woman that he could manage. Before undergoing surgery, MTF transsexuals have been required to divorce their wives because lesbian marriage has been illegal (Bolin, 1996). Even if the two long-term partners could adjust to the sex change, society will no longer allow their marriage. Thus, transsexuals have participated in the social construction of sex and gender by changing their bodies to be a better fit to the system that allows only two categories and insists that gender must conform to sex.

Jan Morris, who felt that her transsexualism was both biological and spiritual, wondered whether transsexualism would still occur in a society that did not enforce gender differences. "Would my conflict have been so bitter if I had been born now, when the gender line is so much less rigid? If society had allowed me to live in the gender I preferred, would I have bothered to change sex?" (p. 172).

In summary, the medical treatment of intersex and transsexualism provides evidence that sex is a process of social consensus and social enforcement, not a natural biological dichotomy. Constructing two and only two sexes through surgical intervention may be done with the best of intentions, but it also may reinforce the belief that these two categories are the only natural and acceptable ones (Golden, 2000). However, there are other ways to categorize the human body and psyche.

Beyond the Binary

For those of us brought up within a binary system of sex and gender, it may be difficult to think outside the boxes. However, in some cultures, the idea that people come in more than two sexes is commonplace. In other words, these cultures have women, men, and others (Williams, 1987). In our own culture, as well, some people are beginning to challenge the idea that one must choose between only two sex or gender categories. We turn now to these steps beyond the binary.

More Than Two Sexes

Societies that have a third-sex category are found in many parts of the world. These categories contrast with our own society's binary categories of female/male, masculine/feminine, or gay/straight. They are neither, both, and all of the above. The social roles and social positions of third-sex people vary across cultures. Let's look at a few examples.

Third Sexes across Cultures

In India about half a million people identify as *hijras* (Nanda, 1990) or *Aravanis* (Mahalingam, 2003). Hijras and Aravanis represent a third-sex category and have an ambiguous social position, being sometimes revered and sometimes persecuted.

Hijras take female names and wear women's clothes, but they set themselves apart from women by being much more sexually overt in their behavior. Unlike proper Indian women, they wear heavy makeup, joke about sex, and wear their hair loose. One's genitals do not determine being a hijra. Some hijras have male genitalia, some were born biologically male but chose to be castrated, and still others were born with intersexed genitals. Within their society, hijras are not considered to be women because they cannot bear children; they are not considered to be men because they do not function sexually as men. Hijras form a northern Indian sect that is considered to incorporate the divine powers of the goddess; they sing and dance at weddings and birth celebrations, and traditionally are asked to bless newborn babies (Nanda, 1990).

In southern India, hijras are known as Aravanis. Like their counterparts in north Indian society, they dress as women and may use hormones or surgery to effect a sex change. However, they are not merely trying to mimic true women; rather, "gender-bending is central to their identity," and they "pride themselves on being 'superwomen,'" a third gender that both enacts femininity and flouts it (Mahalingam, 2003, p. 491).

In Thailand, there are third-sex people called **kathoeys** (Herdt, 1997). Kathoeys have male genitalia but wear women's clothes. Like hijras, they do not try to pass as proper women; instead, they "behave and dress in dramatic, loud, brash ways that violate the norms of femininity in Thai culture" (Marecek et al., 2004, p. 207).

In the South Pacific, Samoans call the third sex *fa'afine,* which translates as "in the way of a woman" (see Figure 5.6). Typically, fa'afine are biological males who dress as women and take up women's characteristic tasks such as caretaking and teaching. They are highly valued as dancers and entertainers and are usually treated with respect. However, although they are treated like women in social interactions, they are clearly differentiated from biological women. A popular nickname for the fa'afine is "50/50s," because they can be both masculine and feminine. Like men, they are allowed to tell bawdy jokes, engage in dirty dancing, and play baseball; like women,

FIGURE 5.6

they are allowed to be artistic and concerned with fashion and appearance (Fraser, 2002).

Anthropologists and historians studying North American Indian cultures have found that more than 150 of these societies have (or had in the past) a third-sex category that the anthropologists term the ***berdache*** and Native Americans themselves sometimes term ***two-spirit people*** (Wilson, 1996). The exact characteristics allowed to berdaches have varied widely across different Native American cultures and across time (Fausto-Sterling, 2000). Most often, berdaches were biological males who wear women's clothes and take up some of the roles and tasks of women. However, they could also adopt men's customs and clothing, switch back and forth, or combine the two (Roscoe, 1996). Thus, their gender was changeable and not always congruent with their sexual anatomy. Berdaches were often seen as particularly creative and artistic.

A category known as ***pledged virgin*** is unusual because it is a third-sex category for women. This category exists in areas of the Balkans (the former Yugoslavia) (Gremaux, 1996). A pledged virgin takes over a man's roles when there is no man available—for example, when all the male children in a family die before adulthood. A pledged virgin is no longer thought of as a woman. S/he wears men's clothes, does heavy work, and even serves as a man in the military. Unlike other third-sex categories, pledged virgins do not engage in sexual activity.

Third-Sex Categories and the Gender System

In their respective cultures, third-sex people are not considered to be gay. Berdaches are expected to have sex with supposedly heterosexual men, not with women or with each other. Fa'afafine, too, have sex with supposedly heterosexual men, often initiating young men and giving them practice sexual experience prior to their becoming sexually active with women. Because the fa'afafine are seen as women, this is not considered to be gay sex. In other words, sex is defined as a social role rather than as a particular anatomy. Third-sex people may be accepted in cultures where homosexuality is strongly tabooed, such as India and Samoa. As one Samoan said, "We can have a fa'afafine singing in the church choir and the preacher will . . . preach how un-Godly it is to be gay" (Fraser, 2002, p. 74).

Across cultures, there are more opportunities for biological males than for biological females to opt for a third category. As we have seen, hijras, Aravanis, katheoys, and fa'afafine all are biological males (or, more rarely, intersexed). The pledged virgin category is unusual; few societies allow women to move to a third-sex role. Some Native American societies that had male berdaches also permitted biological females to become berdaches by taking up some of the clothing and tasks of men, but these societies were in the minority (Roscoe, 1996).

Why are third-sex categories more often available to males than to females? Beliefs about sex and gender may hold the answer. One unique study asked 100 Aravanis about their beliefs regarding the possibility of sex change (Mahalingam, 2003). The Aravanis thought that gender role transgressions were equally acceptable for girls and boys. For example, they saw nothing wrong with a boy who wanted to wear flowers in his hair or a girl who wanted to do carpentry. However, when asked whether a girl could *become* a boy, or vice versa, they were virtually unanimous in agreeing that only a boy could change sex, by dressing like the other sex, having surgery, or performing a religious ceremony. In other words, they saw *male* sex as changeable and fluid, but *female* sex as immune to change. The only way they thought a girl might become a boy was through reincarnation.

Of course, all the Aravanis were themselves biological males who had changed sex. They were also Hindus, whose religion emphasizes goddess worship and represents female identity as primordial, strong, and powerful. Thus, the irreducible facts of sex and gender for the Aravanis were influenced by their culture, religion, and social position and are quite different from our own irreducible facts.

In summary, the various third-sex categories around the world challenge more than the assumption that sex is a binary category. Societies that include a third sex may view sex and sexual orientation as changeable depending on the social situation (Roscoe, 1996). These views contrast with our own society's belief that sex and sexual orientation are biologically fixed and permanent.

The Transgender Movement

Transsexuals in our own society have challenged the permanence of sex. However, transsexuals could be viewed as buttressing the idea that sex must be binary, that people are either male or female. When transsexual adults such as Jan Morris and Deirdre McCloskey describe their identities as opposite to their biological sex and change their bodies to fit the opposite sex category, they may reinforce the idea that there are only two possibilities. Many transsexuals think of themselves as suffering from gender identity disorder because their body and their gender are in conflict—they are trapped in the wrong body (Golden, 2000; Tiefer, 2000). However, others whose core gender identity does not fit their physical body have begun to analyze their situation differently.

The ***transgender movement*** is an increasingly visible and vocal movement for the social acceptance of more than two sex categories (Marecek et al., 2004). Within the transgender movement, some people permanently adopt a transgender identity that is neither female nor male. They do not see themselves as in transition from one sex to another. Instead, they see themselves and others like them as a third-sex category. For example, transgender activist Kate Bornstein describes herself as a gender outlaw and has said, "I am not a man—about that much I am very clear, and I've come to the conclusion that I'm probably not a woman either" (Bornstein, 1994). Or they may view sex and gender as continuous, like sliding scales on which a person can place him/herself at any point. Some transgender people take up life as the other sex while keeping their biologically given bodies intact—they are men with vaginas and women with penises. Others have sex-change surgery but keep their prior sexual orientation—so a heterosexual man who becomes a woman also becomes a lesbian (Bolin, 1996; Fausto-Sterling, 2000).

Rather than trying to pass as the other sex or become the other sex, some transgender activists wish to "make their crossing visible, to pose it as a counter to the dominant account that there are only two sexes" (Marecek et al., 2004, p. 207).

Some transgender activists claim that their lives reveal the social construction of sex, and thus their perspectives are crucial to feminist social change.

As we learned in Chapter 3, changing language can be a way of raising consciousness and drawing attention to a social or political issue. Transgender activists have adopted new pronouns; Leslie Feinberg (1996), for example, identifies as a he-she. Some have appropriated older terms or proposed new terms for alternative sex categories, including androgyny, butch, femme, hermaphrodite, drag king, she-male, he-she, boy-dyke, girlfag, and many others (Stryker, 1998, p. 148).

The transgender movement is a "radical re-visioning of sex and gender" (Fausto-Sterling, 2000, p. 107). Indeed, it can be seen as "guerilla warfare against dominant constructions of sex, gender and sexuality" (Marecek et al., 2004, p. 207).

What would happen to the gender system if the "irreducible fact" of sex were discarded? Would the acceptance of transgender imply that our current concepts of sex and gender would disappear entirely? Fausto-Sterling (2000) suggests that it would not erase these categories, but would allow us to focus more on variability and less on conformity. If our society were to develop more inclusive definitions of sex and gender, it would become more like the other societies I've discussed that have allowed some people to be neither male nor female, but "other." It would also open up alternatives to the surgical "correction" of intersexed people. If the stigma of having an ambiguously sexed body were diminished, some people with unusual bodies might choose to keep them and enjoy them as is.

But merely recognizing variability or allowing a third-sex category does not guarantee that the gender system will change. As we learned in Chapter 2, the gender system is not just a matter of individual beliefs; it is a system of social classification that governs access to power. If sexual variability were recognized and accepted, laws and customs that regulate marriage and sexual behavior would have to change, too.

Making a Difference

Transforming Society: Equality for Sexual Minorities

The medical treatment of intersexed people is increasingly being questioned. Some intersexed individuals and their advocates characterize the standard medical management of intersex as a form of child abuse. One activist made these comparisons:

> Like other incest survivors, intersex children are physically and sexually violated by those we trust the most, those same people who claim to have our best interest at heart. Like other incest survivors, intersex children are told not to ask questions or tell anyone else about our experiences. Like other incest survivors, intersex children learn that there is something wrong with who we are, and made to feel ashamed and guilty. And, like other incest survivors, many intersex people are starting to break the silence. (Koyama, 2002)

Cheryl Chase is one activist who has done a great deal to break the silence. Chase's history was not unusual for an intersexed person in our society. Born with ambiguous sex glands but the internal organs of a female, she was assigned as a boy at birth because she had a large clitoris, and raised as a boy for the first 1½ years of her life. However, she was then reassigned as a girl. Her clitoris was surgically removed. Her parents took their physician's advice and eliminated all evidence of her past as a boy. Her name was changed, her clothes were replaced, and her baby pictures destroyed (Fausto-Sterling, 2000).

Chase's intersex history was kept secret from her. When she had to have further surgery as a teen, she was told that it was a hernia operation. It was not until much later in life that she entered therapy for severe depression and began to piece together the facts. Cheryl Chase realized that many of the difficulties she had experienced in growing up and her lack of sexual fulfillment were due to her treatment and the stigma attached to her intersex condition by the medical profession and thus by her family. In 1993, Cheryl Chase founded the Intersex Society of North America, a nonprofit organization "dedicated to ending shame, secrecy and unwanted genital surgeries on children born with intersex conditions or atypical reproductive anatomies" (www.isna.org). ISNA advocates for open, honest disclosure about intersex conditions and provides support for intersex children and their families.

Transgender and intersex activists point out that people whose genitals do not match their gender may suffer grave consequences from a society that cannot tolerate them. In one court case, a jury awarded a mother nearly $3 million in damages after the death of her son. Paramedics had stopped treating the son, who was cross-dressed, when they discovered his male genitals (cited in Fausto-Sterling, 2000, p. 110). The 1999 film *Boys Don't Cry* dramatizes the true story of Teena Brandon, whose male gender identity did not match her female body. (See Figure 5.7.) Teena succeeded in passing as a male, Brandon Teena, for a time, but when her gender-crossing was discovered, she was brutally raped and murdered.

At a more mundane level, virtually every form of identification (drivers' licenses, passports, medical records) requires that the person check M or F. Which box applies to those who have

FIGURE 5.7
Hilary Swank as Teena/Brandon in the 1999 film *Boys Don't Cry*.

the genitals of one sex and the appearance, mannerisms, and gender identity of the other—or who feel that neither applies? Transgender and intersex people may experience legal difficulties if their apparent sex does not match their official sex. In several cases, their marriages have been annulled.

Transgender and intersex activists argue that given the risk of discrimination and violence, transgender and intersex people need legal protections, such as the International Bill of Gender Rights proposed by transgender activists. (See Box 5.2.) Some transgender activists also propose changes in how we use sex categories in everyday life. For example, Leslie Feinberg suggests that sex labels should be removed not only from passports and drivers' licenses, but also from birth certificates,

---

BOX 5.2   ❧   An International Bill of Gender Rights

The International Bill of Gender Rights (IBGR) was first drafted and adopted at the International Conference on Transgender Law and Employment Policy (ICTLEP) in August 1993. Below are some of the rights included in the document.

The Right to Define Gender Identity

All human beings have the right to define their own gender identity regardless of chromosomal sex, genitalia, assigned birth sex, or initial gender role; and further, no individual shall be denied Human or Civil Rights by virtue of a self-defined gender identity which is not in accord with chromosomal sex, genitalia, assigned birth sex, or initial gender role.

The Right to Free Expression of Gender Identity

All human beings have the right to free expression of their self-defined gender identity; and further, no individual shall be denied Human or Civil Rights by virtue of the expression of a self-defined gender identity.

The Right to Control and Change One's Own Body

Individuals shall not be denied the right to change their bodies as a means of expressing a self-defined gender identity; and further, individuals shall not be denied Human or Civil Rights on the basis that they have changed their bodies cosmetically, chemically, or surgically, or desire to do so as a means of expressing a self-defined gender identity.

The Right to Sexual Expression

No individual's Human or Civil Rights shall be denied on the basis of sexual orientation; and further, no individual shall be denied Human or Civil Rights for expression of a self-defined gender identity through sexual acts between consenting adults.

The Right to Form Committed, Loving Relationships and Enter Into Marital Contracts

Individuals shall not be denied the right to form committed, loving relationships with one another or to enter into marital contracts by virtue of their own or their partner's chromosomal sex, genitalia, assigned birth sex, or initial gender role, or on the basis of their expression of a self-defined gender identity.

The Right to Conceive, Bear, or Adopt Children

The Right to Nurture and Have Custody of Children and to Exercise Parental Capacity

Individuals shall not be denied the right to conceive, bear, or adopt children, nor to nurture and have custody of children, nor to exercise parental capacity with respect to children, natural or adopted, on the basis of their own, their partner's, or their children's chromosomal sex, genitalia, assigned birth sex, or initial gender role, or by virtue of a self-defined gender identity or the expression thereof.

Source: Adapted from Feinberg, L. (1996), pp. 171–175.

allowing each individual to define her or his own sex when ready (Feinberg, 1996). Although a sex label may *seem* necessary for identification purposes, there are many other attributes that are more visible (height, eye color) and more definitive (DNA, fingerprints) (Fausto-Sterling, 2000).

Transforming Ourselves: Accepting Biological and Social Diversity

The contents of this chapter make many students very uncomfortable. The most disturbing idea of all may be the idea that sex is a social construction. Suzanne Kessler and Wendy McKenna (1978), authors of a pioneering book on the social construction of sex, called the belief in two biological sexes an "incorrigible proposition"—in other words, a belief that is deeply held and stubbornly resistant to change. However, they maintain that as long as "female" and "male" are seen as "external, objective, dichotomous, physical facts," sex and gender will be a basis for discrimination and oppression. "Unless and until gender, in all of its manifestations *including the physical*, is seen as a social construction, action that will radically change our incorrigible propositions cannot occur" (1978, p. 164). Kessler and McKenna urged that "people must be confronted with the reality of other possibilities, as well as the possibility of other realities." In this chapter, I have attempted to explore both realities and possibilities, encouraging you to begin to think of sex as not just female and male, but neither, both, and all of the above.

Exploring Further

Crawford, Mary (Ed.). (2000). *A reappraisal of gender: An ethnomethodological approach. Feminism & Psychology, 10,* 7–72.
   Twenty-five years after Kessler and McKenna wrote their landmark book on sex as a social construction, it is still controversial. In this special journal feature, commentators (including a feminist sexologist, sex/gender researchers, and transgender activists) discuss its impact and implications for the future, and Kessler and McKenna offer their response.

Fausto-Sterling, Anne. (2000). *Sexing the body: Gender politics and the construction of sexuality.* New York: Basic Books.
   Very few people can claim expertise in reproductive biology, feminist theory, *and* the history of science. Fausto-Sterling is the exception. In this richly detailed book, she shows how cultural assumptions create biological realities.

Boys Don't Cry. (1999).
   Hilary Swank won critics' praise in this film for her portrayal of Teena Brandon, who was raped and murdered for gender transgression. Enforcing sex and gender conformity in spite of individual difference and diversity can have tragic consequences.

CHAPTER 6

Gendered Identities:
Childhood and Adolescence

"*A*s the twig is bent, so the tree will grow." This proverb reflects the belief that what children learn in their early years shapes them for their entire lives. One of the most important tasks of children in all cultures is to learn what it means to be a woman or a man in their society. Moreover, every child is expected to put this knowledge into practice.

Becoming gendered is a process whereby people learn to fit in to the gender system. It takes place in a context of greater male power and status—the sociocultural level of the gender system. It is conveyed in everyday interactions in families, schools, and playgrounds, often in subtle and unnoticed ways—the interactional level of the system. Finally, gender becomes a part of the self for both boys and girls—the individual level of the gender system. As childhood progresses into adolescence, gendered identities and behaviors take on new importance, initiating a lifelong presentation of oneself as a man or a woman.

Theories of Gender Development

Some approaches to gender development stress how the environment shapes children's learning and behavior. Others stress cognitive factors within the child. The differences between these theories are relative, not absolute. Most developmental psychologists recognize that becoming gendered is a result of biological, cognitive, and social factors interacting with each other.

Social Learning Theory

Almost everyone can remember childhood events that taught what a good girl or boy should—or shouldn't—do. Perhaps we were expected to do gender-specific household chores—boys may take out the trash, while girls set the table for dinner. We may have been encouraged to follow a same-gender example: "Susan doesn't talk back to *her* mother. . . ." When asked to explain how and why adult men and women seem so different from each other, students frequently remember events like these and express the idea that "we've all been conditioned by society." This way of thinking about gender is consistent with ***social learning theory,*** an approach that emphasizes how children learn gendered behavior from their environment (Mischel, 1966, 1970).

Learning through Reinforcement

Social learning theory draws its principles from experimental research on learning (Bandura & Walters, 1963). According to the theory, people learn their characteristic behavior patterns mainly through the process of ***reinforcement.*** Behavior that is followed by desirable consequences is reinforced and is more likely to occur in the future. If a behavior is never reinforced, it will eventually disappear.

Reinforcement of gender-linked behaviors is not always direct and obvious. Parents do not usually follow their little girl around feeding her candy when she picks up a doll and frowning at her when she picks up a toy bulldozer! But behavior shaping can be quite effective without being especially noticeable. If Dad merely glances up from his computer with a warm smile when little Debbie is coloring quietly in her coloring book but stays absorbed in his work when she builds a block tower, she will, according to social learning theory, be more likely to color than to build towers in the future. The newly learned behavior may generalize to other situations—Debbie may begin to prefer coloring books to blocks at nursery school as well as at home. The lesson may also be quite broad—Debbie may learn that, in general, quiet play is nicer than active play.

Learning gender-typed behavior is made easier when parents set up the environment in such a way that some activities are much more likely to occur (and thus be reinforced) than others. If a boy's room is filled with sports equipment and furnished in bright colors and sturdy furniture that can take a beating, he is probably more likely to engage in rough-and-tumble play than is his sister, whose room is done in pink-and-white ruffles and furnished with a dressing table. (See Figure 6.1.) Parents may then notice and reinforce the difference with approving comments about how "Boys will be boys," and "She's a real little lady."

According to social learning theory, the effects of reinforcement occur whether or not the adult is deliberately attempting to influence behavior. An adult need not *intend* to teach a lesson about gender for her or his behavior to serve as a reinforcer for a child. Parents, teachers, grandparents, and other adults may sincerely believe that they treat boys and girls similarly while they actually are reinforcing very different behaviors.

FIGURE 6.1
When parents provide gender-differentiated environments—frills for girls, action for boys—they foster gender-differentiated play.

Learning through Imitation and Observation

FIGURE 6.2
Children learn by imitating adults.

Social learning theory proposes that, in addition to reinforcement, people learn by observing others and imitating their behavior. *Imitation*—copying someone else's behavior—seems to be spontaneous in young children. They imitate mannerisms and postures. One 2-year-old girl, who was cared for by a woman who wore a leg brace as a result of childhood polio, developed a style of walking that dragged one leg in imitation of her caretaker, and learned to walk more normally only when another adult also joined her day care setting. Children also imitate language, as many a parent has found to her dismay when a swear word used in an unguarded moment is repeated by her toddler. And they imitate all sorts of other behaviors. A young boy shaves with a play razor while his father does the real thing; a young girl plays with her dolls as her mother feeds the new baby. Imitation is often expressed in play, as children drive to the store, play house or play school. (See Figure 6.2.)

Observational learning occurs through watching others' behavior, even though it may not always be expressed in immediate imitation, but instead is stored for later use. A boy might observe that his father spends a lot of time watching sports on TV and later develop the same interests. A small girl may observe her mother's shopping for clothes, planning new outfits, applying makeup, doing her hair, and dieting to lose weight. She learns through these observations that attractiveness is a very important dimension for women, although she might not express that knowledge very much until adolescence.

A classic study by Albert Bandura (1965) illustrates the operation of both reinforcement and imitation in learning to be aggressive. In Bandura's study, children were shown one of three films. In all the films, an adult behaved aggressively by hitting and kicking a large toy clown. In one film, the adult was rewarded; in another, the adult was punished; and in the third, no specific consequences followed the aggression. The children were then given the opportunity to play with the toy clown. Just as social learning theory would predict, children imitated the behavior most when it had been reinforced; that is, children who had seen the first film were more aggressive than those who had seen either of the other films. Overall, boys were more aggressive than girls.

In the next part of the experiment, children were offered small treats for performing as many of the adult model's aggressive behaviors as they could remember. Here, all children were more aggressive; and girls were, overall, nearly as aggressive as boys. Bandura's experiment shows that children do imitate adult models even when the children are not directly reinforced for doing so. In particular, they imitate models that are themselves reinforced. Furthermore, children may learn a behavior through observation but show no particular evidence of that learning until the behavior is reinforced—like the girls in the second part of the experiment.

Learning Gender

Social learning theory explains gender identity and gender typing as the result of moment-to-moment, day-to-day interactions between the developing child and the immediate social environment—mother, father, and other caretakers; the media; school; and playmates. It assumes that what a child learns about femininity and masculinity will vary according to his or her social class, ethnic group, and family composition—indeed, any and all social and environmental factors.

When gender-typed behavior is particularly visible, it is readily learned. Most preschool children see their mothers in largely gender-typed roles simply because mothers are more likely to be responsible for housework and child care, activities that a child can observe often and directly. If only women are seen cleaning house and changing diapers, both boys and girls may acquire the knowledge that these tasks are women's work. When mothers and fathers go to their jobs outside the home, the child does not observe their work directly. Of course, even if a child's home environment is relatively gender-neutral, she or he usually has plenty of opportunities to see gender-stereotypical behavior in the media.

Although social learning theory emphasizes environmental influences on gender-typing, cognitive factors also play a role (Bussey & Bandura, 2004). Once children know that there are two gender categories and have developed a core gender identity, they pay more attention to same-gender models than to other-gender models. The likelihood that a child will imitate the behavior of same-gender adults depends on what proportion of same-gender adults display the behavior. In other words, a preschool-aged girl who sees one TV show about a woman who races sports cars may or may not play with toy cars. However, if the same girl sees dozens of stories and commercials on TV featuring women who take care of babies and children, she is very likely to model this behavior by playing with dolls. The more gender-typical a behavior is, the more likely a child will imitate it.

Social learning theory implies that we can reduce gender typing in children. Parents, schools, and the media could choose to reinforce and model more adventurous, instrumental behavior for girls and more nurturing, cooperative behavior for boys. Implicit in the theory is the idea that gender typing can be lessened or even eliminated if we as a society and as individuals choose to do so.

Cognitive Theories

- Neil, age 6, has liked to draw ever since he could pick up a crayon. His drawings have earned him lots of attention and praise from his preschool teachers, and the refrigerator at home is covered with them. His parents are proud of his talent and even took him to meet a real artist in his studio. They are amazed when Neil suddenly loses interest in drawing, saying that art is for girls.

- Rosa, age 3½, goes to a female pediatrician for her regular checkups and has an aunt who is a physician. Therefore, her parents are astounded to hear her announce to a playmate, "Girls can't be doctors! Girls are nurses, and doctors are boys!"

These behaviors are hard to explain using social learning theory. How did Neil and Rosa become gender typed when it seems that *non*stereotypical beliefs and attitudes were being reinforced and modeled for them? One answer to this question is offered by cognitive developmental and gender schema theories of gender development. These two cognitive theories offer the intriguing idea that children willingly socialize themselves to be masculine or feminine (Martin & Ruble, 2004).

Cognitive Developmental Theory

This approach to gender development began by building on the research of Jean Piaget, who observed that young children think in ways that are qualitatively different from older children and adults (Kohlberg, 1966). Piaget believed that children move through a fixed series of stages in their cognitive development, and there are concepts they cannot grasp until they have reached the appropriate cognitive stage. Children's predictable errors in thinking indicate that they have different, less mature ways of thinking than adults—less sophisticated modes of cognitive organization. Regardless of what stage they have reached, however, children actively strive to interpret and make sense of the world around them. According to the cognitive developmental approach, gender identity and gender typing are the outcome of children's active structuring of their physical and social world.

Children understand some things about the concepts of sex and gender long before others. A 2- or 3-year-old child can answer correctly when asked if he or she is a boy or a girl. However, the child may believe that people can change sex by changing their hairstyles or clothing. (At age 2½, one of my children maintained stubbornly that the real difference between boys and girls was that only girls wear barrettes!) The child may believe that boys can grow up to be mommies, as the following conversation between two young boys shows:

> JOHNNY (age 4½): I'm going to be an airplane builder when I grow up.
> JIMMY (age 4): When I grow up, I'll be a mommy.
> JOHNNY: No, you can't be a mommy. You have to be a daddy.
> JIMMY: No, I'm going to be a mommy.
> JOHNNY: No, you're not a girl, you can't be a mommy.
> JIMMY: Yes, I can.
> (Kohlberg, 1966, p. 95)

This conversation illustrates that children's understanding of gender is concrete and limited. Johnny, who is slightly older, understands **gender constancy**—he knows that gender is permanent—while Jimmy does not. By the age of 6 or 7, almost all children understand gender constancy. According to cognitive developmental theory, this is a result of cognitive maturation.

Once children know that they are, and always will be, one sex or the other, they turn to the task of matching the cultural expectations for people of their sex. Children come to value behaviors, objects, and attitudes that are consistent with their sex label. Girls want to do girl things such as wear dresses. Boys, too, behave as though they are thinking, "I am a boy: therefore I want to do boy things; therefore the opportunity to do boy things (and to gain approval for doing them) is rewarding" (Kohlberg, 1966, p. 89). Children exaggerate gender roles, with boys proclaiming anything remotely associated with girls as yucky and girls avoiding boys activities like the plague. This exaggeration may be due to children's need to keep gender categories cognitively distinct (Maccoby, 1980).

External rewards and punishments for gender-typed behavior are relatively unimportant, according to this theory. Rather than being passively influenced by whatever reinforcers the social environment sends their way, children actively try to fit their beliefs, values, and behaviors to their sex (see Figure 6.3). In their search to become the best possible girl (or boy), children rely on reinforcers only as a guide to how well they are doing.

FIGURE 6.3

As predicted by cognitive developmental theory, girls often seek out feminine activities and roles.

As girls become aware of the categories of masculinity and femininity, they may also recognize the status advantages of men. How then do girls come to value their devalued role enough to want to follow it? In fact, some do not—for example, many girls are "tomboys" throughout middle childhood (Hyde, Rosenberg, & Behrman, 1977). However, most girls eventually do adopt feminine ways. They may find some aspects of femininity (such as nurturance) more appealing than some aspects of masculinity (such as aggression). Moreover, adult women have more power than girls, and that may provide a reason to identify with them. However, the cognitive developmental approach does not provide a complete answer to the question of how girls come to adopt an orientation that is associated with low power and status.

Like social learning theory, cognitive developmental theory has generated a great deal of research. This research supports the idea that children's understanding of gender is related to their cognitive maturity. However, research does not support the idea that children become gender typed only after they acquire an understanding of gender constancy. On the contrary, children show a preference for gender-typed objects and activities by the age of 3 (Maccoby, 1998), while they do not fully understand gender constancy until several years later.

Gender Schema Theory

A more recent cognitive approach downplays developmental stages in favor of a focus on the cognitive structures that comprise a child's knowledge about gender. As discussed in Chapter 3, a schema is a network of mental associations. According to schema theory, it is difficult or impossible to understand information when you cannot connect it to a schema or when you unintentionally connect it to the wrong schema (Crawford & Chaffin, 1986). However, when incoming information fits a preexisting schema, it is readily noticed, stored, and remembered. (See Box 6.1 and try it for yourself before looking at the answers in Box 6.2.)

Gender schema theory uses this cognitive approach to explain gender typing. Like other schemas, the gender schema is used by the individual as an aid to thinking and understanding (Bem, 1981). According to gender schema theory, the gender schema is learned very early, and it guides the individual in becoming gender typed. As children learn the contents of their society's gender schema, they learn

---

BOX 6.1 ～ Schematic Processing: A Do-It-Yourself Demonstration and a Riddle

1. Read the following paragraph and then, without looking back at it, try to recall as much of it as possible. Write down every idea you remember from the paragraph.

The procedure is actually quite simple. First, you arrange things into different groups. Of course, one pile may be sufficient, depending on how much there is to do. If you have to go somewhere else due to lack of facilities, that is the next step; otherwise you are pretty well set. It is important not to overdo things. That is, it is better to do too few things at once than too many. In the short run this may not seem important, but complications can easily arise. A mistake can be expensive as well. At first the whole procedure will seem complicated. Soon, however, it will become just another facet of life. It is difficult to foresee any end to the necessity for this task in the immediate future, but then one never can tell. After the procedure is completed, one arranges the materials into different groups again. Then they can be put into their appropriate places. Eventually they will be used once more and the whole cycle will then have to be repeated. However, that is part of life.

Many students find that understanding and remembering this paragraph are very difficult. For an explanation, see Box 6.2.

2. Try to solve this riddle—and ask a few friends.

A big Indian and a little Indian are sitting on a log. The big Indian points to the little Indian and says, "That Indian is my son." The little Indian points to the big Indian and says, "That Indian is not my father." Both are telling the truth. How is this possible?

For the answer, see Box 6.2

Source: From J. D. Bransford & M. K. Johnson, 1972, "Contextual Prerequisites for Understanding: Some Investigations of Comprehension and Recall," *Journal of Verbal Learning and Verbal Behavior,* 11, p. 722. Copyright © 1972 by Elsevier. Reprinted with permission.

which attributes are linked to their own sex and hence to themselves. Gender schema theory conceives of gender typing as a readiness to organize the world in terms of gender and to process information in terms of gender associations. This is more than just learning how boys and girls are ranked on each dimension—that boys are supposed to be stronger than girls, for example—but also that the dimension of strength is more important in evaluating boys (Bem, 1981).

In other words, an important difference between people who are highly gender typed and those who are not is that gender-typed people have a well-developed gender schema and rely on it spontaneously in making sense of the world—they are *gender-schematic.* Less gender-typed people have less-developed gender schemas and rely more on other schemas—they are *gender-aschematic.* The difference is a matter of degree, because everyone in our society has developed some sort of schema for gender.

Gender schemas lead to selective attention and selective memory. In one experiment, 5- and 6-year-old children saw pictures of boys and girls doing stereotype-consistent activities (such as a boy playing with a truck) and stereotype-inconsistent ones (such as a girl using a hammer). A week later, when the children's

---

BOX 6.2   ∾   Schematic Processing: Answers and Explanations

....

1. Why is it so difficult to make sense of the paragraph in Box 6.1? The words are ordinary and the sentence structure is simple. Yet most people find it frustrating to read and difficult to remember the ideas in the paragraph for even a short time. The reason is that comprehension and memory depend on the activation of a schema. This paragraph does not activate any particular schema for most people, and thus it is vague, ambiguous, and difficult to understand.

   The title for the paragraph is "Washing Clothes." If you now look back at it, you will find that you read it with a new understanding and your memory for the ideas will be much better. The clothes-washing schema provides the structure that interrelates and explains all of the previously obscure details. Without the schema, the individual sentences are straightforward, but their relationship cannot be grasped.

2. The answer to the riddle is that the big Indian is the little Indian's mother.

   Why is this riddle difficult for many people to solve? Even the most ordinary sentences require the reader to go beyond the information

given and use her own stores of information about the world—her schemas. For most North Americans, the schema for "Indian" is based on stereotypes from movies and stories about the Wild West. Therefore we automatically think "male" when we think "Indian." Because the schema activated by "Indian" assumes "male," the schema is not much help in solving the riddle (Crawford & Chaffin, 1986).

Puzzles like this can help us understand aspects of our schemas that we are normally unaware of in everyday comprehension. If you had been asked directly "Can the word *Indian* refer to a female?" you would no doubt answer yes. Yet if you found this riddle difficult, it is because your mental representation of "Indian" is primarily male. (Incidentally, does this riddle help you see why Native-American people prefer not to be called Indians?)

Source: From J. D. Bransford & M. K. Johnson, 1972, "Contextual Prerequisites for Understanding: Some Investigations of Comprehension and Recall," *Journal of Verbal Learning and Verbal Behavior,* 11, p. 722. Copyright © 1972 by Elsevier. Reprinted with permission.

memory for the pictures was tested, they tended to misremember the stereotype-inconsistent pictures—for example, they thought they had seen a boy using a hammer (Martin & Halverson, 1983). This study suggests that as early as the age of 5, children have gender schemas and use them to filter information as they categorize the world around them. By this age, they already believe that certain occupations are for men and others are for women; and when asked what they would like to be when they grow up, they are likely to choose an occupation that is stereotyped for their gender (Helwig, 1998).

However, gender schema theory suggests that children *can* be brought up in ways that minimize the development of a gender schema and thus bypass gender-stereotyped thinking and behavior. If others around them paid less attention to gender stereotypes, children would not automatically categorize by gender, any more than they automatically categorize in terms of eye color. If they were taught to use the concept of sex to refer to anatomical differences, they would not assimilate irrelevant dimensions to the gender schema. They would differentiate male and female in sexuality and reproduction, but all other aspects of behavior would remain gender-neutral (Bem, 1983).

In summary, social learning and cognitive theories emphasize different influences on children's gender development. Social learning theory maintains that children are shaped by the people and environments they encounter in everyday life. Cognitive theories emphasize that the child's mind is actively trying to comprehend and categorize gender information. Cognitive developmental theory proposes that this occurs in distinct stages, whereas gender schema theory emphasizes the gradual development of a complex mental network about gender and its assimilation to the self. No single theory has all the answers. Rather, social forces interact with cognitive factors in gender development (Powlishta, Sen, Serbin, Poulin-Dubois, & Eichstedt, 2001). In what follows, we will look in detail at gender influences in children's lives, showing how social and cognitive factors interact to produce adults who fit in to the gender system.

Gender in the Child's Daily Life

When a child is born, the words "It's a boy!" or "It's a girl!" are usually the first words used to describe the child. Almost immediately, the infant is viewed differently and treated differently depending on its sex, in accord with the gender beliefs of adults. At first, parents and family are the strongest influence on gender. As the child grows, peers become more important. Environmental influences support social influences, as clothes, toys, books, movies, and TV provide highly gendered messages. The child's own concept of gender interacts with all these influences, as he or she forms cognitive schemas and progresses to more cognitively mature ways of thinking about gender. These influences—from adults, other children, the media, the physical environment, and the child's own cognitive development—construct gender at the interactional level. They are all important in shaping adults who fit into their society's gender system, and we will look at each in more detail.

Parental Influences

As soon as a woman announces that she is pregnant, others begin to speculate—will it be a boy or a girl? Throughout history, there were many superstitious methods of guessing the future baby's sex. If the mother "carries high," it is a boy; if she "carries low," it's a girl. If the fetus is active, moving, and kicking a lot, it must be a boy. If the mother is sick during pregnancy, it's a girl. In much of this folk wisdom, the symbolically more negative characteristic of a pair (low/high, sick/healthy) was used to predict a girl. The birth of a girl is an occasion for shame and disappointment in many traditional cultures.

Boys: The Preferred Sex

The preference for sons is so extreme in some cultures that *female infanticide* has been practiced. In ancient Greece, infant girls were sometimes left on a mountainside to die of exposure or be eaten by wild animals (Rouselle, 2001). Sex-based infanticide has been documented in about 9 percent of cultures, and girls are most often the vulnerable sex (Hrdy, 1988). Although no society today officially approves of female infanticide, there are persistent reports from areas where girls are particularly devalued that it still takes place. For example, in rural China, far more births of boys than girls are recorded. In the southern Indian state of Tamil Nadu, an increase in female infanticide recently prompted the government to promise bonuses to parents if their daughters survived childhood (Miller, 2001).

Selecting boys for survival occurs in other ways, too. There is strong evidence that *female-selective abortion*—aborting healthy fetuses only because they are female—is widely practiced in Asian countries, including Korea, China, India, Taiwan, and Pakistan. For example, almost immediately after fetal sex-determination techniques became available in Indian cities, social workers reported huge imbalances in the gender ratio of aborted fetuses; one study of 8,000 abortions showed that 7,997 were female fetuses (Hrdy, 1988). Some Asian immigrant groups in the United States and Canada may practice female-selective abortion as well (Miller, 2001).

Experts estimate that in the past two decades, millions of healthy female fetuses have been aborted in Asian countries alone (Miller, 2001). The problem seems to be most acute in societies such as India and Korea where there is increasing prosperity (allowing women to pay for fetal sex tests and medical abortions), coupled with strong traditional ideas about the greater worth of sons (Dugger, 2001; "India's Religious leaders," 2001).

Female infanticide, female-selective abortion, and neglect and starvation of girls in early infancy are affecting the gender ratio in many countries. In China, for example, officials predict a shortage of some 40 to 60 million women over the next decade and say that the gender imbalance is already causing violent competition for wives among men (Baculinao, 2004). Demographers, women's groups, medical associations, and religious leaders have united to condemn female feticide and infanticide ("India's Religious Leaders," 2001).

The reasons for son preference are related to patriarchy. The more patriarchal a society is, the more that males control economic, political, and social power, and the more the ideology of gender supports their domination. In some traditional Asian cultures, females tend to be economically dependent on fathers and husbands and to have lower social status, and they are considered impure or polluting. Because of dowry systems that require a bride's family to provide large sums of money and costly possessions to the groom's family, the birth of a daughter is an economic disaster. Moreover, tradition holds that only a son can provide for his parents in their old age. All these factors combine to influence both women and men to prefer sons (Miller, 2001).

Are boys the preferred sex in Western society? In our society, people often say that they just want a healthy baby and the baby's sex is irrelevant, adding that they would like to have both boys and girls to complete their family. However, there are other indicators that boys are still valued more than girls, especially by men. For example, in Gallup Polls (that measure the attitudes of large representative samples of U.S. adults), overall preference for a boy has remained virtually unchanged over 60 years of polling (Leonhardt, 2003). Men in particular prefer boys by a large margin (45 percent versus 19 percent; the remainder express no preference).

Further intriguing evidence suggesting a preference for boys comes from divorce statistics showing that married couples with sons are less likely to get divorced than married couples with daughters are. Based on the huge samples provided by U.S. census data, researchers have shown that the higher divorce rate for families with daughters has existed at least since the 1940s. It is found in every region of the country, regardless of family size, racial/ethnic group, and educational level. Families with both boys and girls are intermediate in divorce rate. Overall, the more girls a family has, the more likely the parents will divorce (Leonhardt, 2003). While the difference is quite small in magnitude, its persistence over time and the fact that it occurs in diverse ethnic and social class groups suggest that it reflects something important about the relative value of girls and boys. The statistical data are open to many interpretations (remember that correlations don't reveal why two variables are linked). However, some social scientists have suggested that fathers' preference for sons may contribute to dissatisfaction and less involvement in family life when they have only daughters, and "almost certainly plays a role in creating the divorce gap" (Leonhardt, 2003, p. 4).

Parents: Not Gender-Neutral

From the first minutes of a baby's life, its parents are forming impressions of this new little person. Do parents perceive their babies in gender-stereotyped ways? In one study, mothers and fathers rated their newborn sons as stronger, as well as less delicate, feminine, and fine featured than did parents of newborn daughters. However, when asked to provide their own descriptions of the baby, the parents used language that did not differ according to the baby's sex (Karraker, Vogel, & Lake, 1995). This study suggests that gender stereotyping of infants can be primed—in this case, by providing a list of gender-stereotyped characteristics. Of course, our society provides many ways to prime gender stereotypes about infants—see Box 6.3. When they were asked the same questions a week later, mothers in this study no longer stereotyped their infants, but fathers still did (Karraker et al., 1995). The mothers in this sample may have decreased their tendency to stereotype because

BOX 6.3   ⧢   Gender Stereotyping Starts Early

....

"It's a boy!"
"It's a girl!"

A study conducted by Judith Bridges (1993) of the visual images and verbal messages in birth congratulations cards sampled 61 cards announcing the birth of a girl and 61 announcing the birth of a boy from 18 stores in 4 different municipalities in Hartford, Connecticut. Content analysis of the cards revealed stereotypical differences between boy and girl cards. Visual images on boy cards included more physical activity, such as action toys and active babies, than that of girl cards. Girl cards included more verbal messages of expressiveness, including sweetness and sharing. Surprisingly, boy cards presented a message of happiness for the parents and/or the baby more than girl cards.

Even though this study was conducted over a decade ago, birth congratulations cards still tend to portray gender stereotyping. When I checked out a name-brand greeting card store in 2004, I found that most of the cards portrayed girl and boy babies as very different from each other. For example, two of the cards on display depicted the new baby as a teddy bear, but the messages were quite different. The girl teddy bear baby was asleep in a cradle, tucked under a pink blanket. The boy teddy bear baby was holding a baseball and bat and had a big, wide-eyed smile. The verse on the girl's card referred to her sweetness, whereas the boy's verse called him a "star." What activities and traits do the two cards imply that parents can expect from their children? How might these expectations create self-fulfilling prophecies?

Contributed by Michelle R. Kaufman, University of Connecticut.

they got to know their babies as individuals, whereas the fathers, who had less contact with the infants, did not. Many other studies of infants and young children show that fathers view their children in gender-stereotyped ways more than mothers do. Although fathers may stereotype more, they spend much less time overall with infants and young children; mothers therefore have more opportunity to convey their gender schemas to their offspring (Tenenbaum & Leaper, 2002).

Differences in parental behavior may provide important models for children to observe and imitate. One of the most important ways parents socialize babies and young children is by talking to them. From the time they are toddlers, girls and boys get different kinds and amounts of talk about emotion, contributing to gender differences in emotionality (Chapter 4). Overall, mothers talk more to children than fathers do, and their talk is more supportive and emotion focused, while fathers' talk is more directive and informative (Leaper, Anderson, & Sanders, 1998). These differences in parental behavior are congruent with gender stereotypes of expressiveness for females and instrumentality for males. Mothers also talk more and use more supportive speech to their daughters in particular. This pattern is consistent with socializing girls toward connectedness and communality.

Parents also play with their sons and daughters differently during the preschool years. They do more pretending and fantasy play with girls, and fathers, in particular, do more rough and tumble, physical, and pretend-aggression play with boys (Lindsey, Mize, & Pettit, 1997: Lindsey & Mize, 2001). In a meta-analysis of over 150 North American studies, fathers were more likely than mothers to encourage their children toward gender-typed play and activities (Lytton & Romney, 1991).

It is clear that children pick up the messages their parents send. In one study of four-year-olds, almost half of the boys said that they could not play with girls' toys because their fathers would think they were bad (Raag & Rackliff, 1998). In a recent meta-analysis, parents' attitudes about their own masculinity/femininity as well as their gender-stereotyped attitudes about others significantly predicted their children's gender-related beliefs and attitudes. The more traditional the parent's gender ideology, the more gender typed their children were. Interestingly, the effect was stronger for mothers (Tenenbaum & Leaper, 2002). Thus, the gender schemas of children, which are applied both to themselves and to others, are formed partly through exposure to their parents' gender schemas.

But before you conclude that parents are entirely responsible for turning out typically gender-typed girls and boys, it is important to remember two points. First, meta-analyses show that the areas in which parents treat their children similarly are more numerous than the areas in which they treat them differently (Lytton & Romney, 1991). Second, parental treatment of children may be influenced by the children's own characteristics. Parents may talk more to girls because girls on average are more responsive to talk. They may play more rough and scary games with boys because boys enjoy them more. The child's characteristics probably interact with the parents' beliefs about gender to influence parents' differential treatment of sons and daughters. Finally, there are plenty of other influences over which parents have little control.

Peer Influences

From an early age, children choose to play with same-gender friends—a pattern called *gender segregation*. This preference emerges around the age of 2, when girls start to orient more toward playing with other girls; boys' preference for other boys develops about a year later (Powlishta et al., 2001). Gender segregation increases steadily during the preschool years. By age 4½, about 90 percent of a child's social playtime is with same-gender others (Martin & Fabes, 2001). It occurs not only in our own society but also in others (Maccoby, 1998).

Adults do not usually initiate or encourage gender segregation. Why then do children self-segregate by gender? One theory is that children choose others with compatible play styles. According to this explanation, boys on average have a higher activity level than girls (a difference that may have a biological basis) and may prefer to play with others who are as active as they are. Girls may be more verbally and socially advanced and prefer to play with others who are as good at sharing and communicating as they are (Moller & Serbin, 1996). In other words, girls would rather play with other girls because they think boys are pushy, obnoxious, and always get their way (Shields, 2002).

Another reason for gender segregation, consistent with cognitive developmental theory, may be the child's desire to fit the gender roles their culture prescribes. In one study, preschool and early elementary school children believed that others would approve of them more if they played with same-gender friends (Martin, Fabes, Evans, & Wyman, 1999).

When children are observed playing alone, the play style of boys is similar to the play style of girls (Maccoby, 1998). When they play in groups, however, their play styles diverge and become increasingly gender typed (Martin & Fabes, 2001). Boys' play in gender-segregated groups involves more competition, confrontation, and risk-taking; girls' play in their groups involves more negotiation, cooperation, talking about oneself, and contact with adults (Maccoby, 1998). The more territorial and physical a game is, the more likely it is that elementary school children will segregate while playing it (Kelle, 2000). In other words, gender differences in play are shaped by the peer context.

Gendered play in turn affects friendship styles. By the time they are in fourth or fifth grade, girls' friendships are organized around confiding in each other and talking about others, whereas boys' friendships are more often organized around sports and other activities. These different friendship styles continue into adulthood. The playgroups of childhood are an important step in creating each new generation of gender-typed adults (Maccoby, 1998).

Gender-segregated play is not just a matter of difference; however, it is also a matter of status. Boys, in particular, create ingroup solidarity and derogate the outgroup (girls). For example, boys taunt other boys who do not conform to group norms by calling them faggot (Thorne & Luria, 1986) or sissy (Edwards, Knoche, & Kumru, 2001). They also reinforce gender segregation by teasing and making jokes about romantic attraction. If Tory is a low-status, unpopular girl, boys may tease another boy by accusing him of liking her and saying that he will get "cooties" from her. Girls rarely tease other girls for being tomboys or accuse boys of having cooties. When a girl picks a fight, she may be called mean, but she is not accused of being like a boy (Shields, 2002). Usually, boys are the ones who patrol the boundaries between groups by encouraging opposition between boys and girls, defining cross-gender contact in terms of sex and pollution, and scapegoating some girls as untouchables (Thorne & Luria, 1986). For girls like Tory, who may be unpopular because she is poor, overweight, or shy, hostile teasing from high-status boys may make school into a nightmare (Keltner, Capps, Kring, Young, & Heerey, 2001).

Because boys learn competitive, dominance-oriented play styles, and girls learn more cooperative styles, girls are at a big disadvantage in mixed-gender groups. The tactics they use to gain power and influence with other girls (persuasion and negotiation) simply do not work with boys. In one early study, children were allowed to play with a movie-viewing toy in groups of four (two boys and two girls). Only one child at a time could see the movie. In this situation, boys ended up with three times as much viewing time as girls (Charlesworth & LaFreniere, 1983). Similar patterns may occur when children have to share computers in a classroom or compete for a teacher's attention (see Chapter 4). Thus, the tactics boys learn in all-boy groups help them achieve dominance in many different kinds of interactions.

However, we should not conclude that girls are not competitive or not interested in status. The difference seems to be that girls' self-structured play teaches them interpersonal skills, which they prefer to use over overt physical aggression, whether they are competing or cooperating. When girls want to be aggressive and dominant, they may engage in *relational aggression*—hostile acts that attempt to damage another's close relationships or social standing (Crick & Rose, 2000). In other words, a girl may spread a rumor about another girl, give her the silent treatment, or say "I won't be your friend if you don't do it my way!" Relational aggression can be just as harmful as physical aggression.

Traditionally, psychologists have claimed that there is a consistent gender difference in aggression, with boys being more aggressive than girls from early childhood (Maccoby & Jacklin, 1974). This difference largely disappears when relational aggression is taken into account (Crick & Rose, 2000). The gender difference may have been the result of an androcentric definition of aggression, a kind of research bias discussed in Chapters 1 and 4.

Gender segregation and the resulting differences in interaction style are not absolute or inevitable. In an observational study of elementary school children on their playgrounds, there was a great deal of variety in play. Unsegregated and nonstereotypical play actually occurred quite often. The strictest segregation was among the most popular and socially visible students; others quietly went their own way, often violating the rules of gender segregation (Thorne, 1993). Cross-gender friendships do occur, though they may be kept out of sight. I remember a middle-school friendship with a boy who, like me, was obsessed with chemistry experiments. We never talked at school, but on Saturdays we happily burned holes in our parents' carpets as we tried to mix potions that could eat through any substance. Our friendship was underground, but it was important to both of us.

Gendered Environments

Though girls and boys grow up together, their environments foster different activities, values, and beliefs. Here we look at just one of many aspects of the environment: the toys children play with.

When I was 8, I really wanted a chemistry set. I asked for it for my birthday, but got a Cinderella watch instead. I liked the watch but I still wanted a chemistry set. I put it on my Christmas list, but Santa failed me. Finally, on my ninth birthday, my wish was granted and my career in chemical catastrophes began. I was not surprised, years later, to come across a study showing that children were more likely to get an item on their Christmas list if it was gender-stereotypical than if it was not (Etaugh & Liss, 1992). My parents weren't being mean; they just thought in terms of gender schemas when providing me with toys. And they weren't alone. Studies conducted from the 1970s into the 1990s show that boys and girls as young as 5 months old are provided with different toys, such as more vehicles for boys and more dolls for girls (Pomerleau et al., 1990; Rheingold & Cook, 1975).Gender typing in toys is not due only to parents' influence. From an early age, children themselves express strong preferences for gender-typed toys. By the time they are 1½ years old, boys typically prefer trucks to dolls and girls typically prefer the opposite.

Gendered toy preferences continue to increase during the preschool and elementary school years (Powlishta et al., 2001). Both boys and girls continue to play with gender-neutral toys. It is only the "opposite-gender" toys that they avoid—and boys do this more than girls do. Children develop activity preferences, too, based on their toys. When elementary school children were asked to list the activities they did with their friends, girls mentioned outdoor games, playing house, and playing with dolls; boys mentioned playing ball, playing war, and playing with cars (Etaugh & Liss, 1992).

These gender-typed patterns are reinforced by blatantly stereotypical marketing aimed at children. Large retailers like Toys "R" Us clearly distinguish boys' aisles, with brightly colored action figures, tanks, trucks, and guns, from girls' aisles, with pastel-colored crafts, dolls, toy appliances, and makeup kits (Bannon, 2000). Children are steered away from gender neutrality by the way the store is structured. It seems that no toy or activity is exempt from having gender imposed on it. (See Box 6.4.) Even with an undeniably gender-neutral toy, such as a bicycle, manufacturers create two versions—a pink flower-trimmed bike with a wicker basket for girls, and a black heavy-duty BMX version for boys. Distinctions like these may foster the development of extended gender schemas in young children. It's as though the adults in their lives are telling them, "Gender is the most important category in the world—even your bike has to have one!"

Media Influences

The books children read, the TV shows they watch, and the video games they play are all powerful sources of gender socialization. Starting in the 1970s, feminists drew attention to gender stereotyping in children's readers and storybooks. Several studies from the 1970s to the early 1990s showed that boys and men more often were represented as independent, active, competent, and aggressive, whereas girls and women more often were shown as passive, helpless, nurturing, or dependent. Overall, males appeared much more often than females as the main character of a book (Evans & Davies, 2000; Gooden & Gooden, 2001).

Since then, gender stereotyping has declined but not disappeared. A study of 83 children's books selected by the American Library Association and published from 1995 to 1999 showed that about half of the main characters were female, a big improvement from the past. However, males (both people and animals) were more often shown in illustrations. Men were shown in a much greater variety of roles and occupations than women, but they were rarely shown taking care of children, and no man was ever shown doing household chores. Most of the women still were shown in traditional roles such as mother, grandmother, and washerwoman, although a few were shown in occupations such as doctor and chef (Gooden & Gooden, 2001). A content analysis of first- to fifth-grade readers from the same time period showed that male characters were significantly more likely to be aggressive, argumentative, and competitive, whereas female characters were more likely to be affectionate, emotionally expressive, passive, and tender (Evans & Davies, 2000). With educational materials like these, it is not surprising that children absorb gender stereotypes at an early age.

BOX 6.4 ⁓ Dracula and the Princess

Halloween is a time for fantasy, when children can dress up and pretend to be just about anything or anybody. However, even the fantasy play of Halloween is gender stereotyped. In a study by Nelson (2000), the researcher analyzed 469 costumes and sewing patterns for Halloween. Less than 10 percent of children's costumes were gender neutral. Girls' costumes tended to depict princesses, beauty queens, and other examples of traditional femininity, such as a Colonial Belle, Blushing Bride, or Pretty Mermaid. Boys' costumes were also stereotypical, depicting characters who battle opponents, such as Bronco Rider, Dick Tracy, or Hercules. Boys' costumes were more likely to portray famous villains, such as Captain Hook, Wolfman, or Frankenstein.

In costumes depicting death, there was an especially large difference in gender stereotypes. Boy's costumes included Dracula, a devil, and the Grim Reaper, accessorized with blood, body parts, or weapons. The few villainous costumes for girls emphasized their erotic nature—Sexy Devil or Bewitched—or their harmless charm—Little Skull Girl or Pretty Little Witch.

Although Halloween costumes may seem like harmless fun, they are another example of the way in which gender stereotypes are transmitted to children and gender roles are acted out in play.

Unfortunately, most children spend a lot more time watching TV and playing video games than they spend with their reader or library book. The typical child watches TV approximately 38 hours each week. Even young children (ages 2 to 7) get in about 25 viewing hours each week (Rideout, Foehr, Roberts, & Brodie, 1999). In fact, children spend more time with entertainment media than they do with any other activity except school and sleeping, and many children watch TV for more hours each week than they spend in school (Anderson et al., 2003). A meta-analysis showed that the more a child watches TV, the more likely he or she is to have gender-stereotyped beliefs (Herrett-Skjellum & Allen, 1996). This is not surprising—we learned in Chapter 3 that television programs and commercials present extremely stereotyped images of women and men.

Even when they are watching the Saturday morning cartoons, children are getting a dose of sexism. Male cartoon characters are more numerous, more visible, and more active than female characters. They talk more, interrupt more, get involved in aggressive acts more often, and show more ingenuity in getting out of trouble (Thompson & Zerbinos, 1995).

FIGURE 6.4

Barbie is everywhere. These little girls are playing outside their house in Kathmandu, Nepal.

Video games may surpass all other media in sexism. In one analysis of popular Nintendo and Saga Genesis games, there were no female characters at all in 41 percent of the games (Dietz, 1998). However, it may be better when women are absent, since when they did appear it was usually as sex objects, helpless victims, or targets of aggression. Only 15 percent of the games had female action heroes, whereas 28 percent showed females solely as sex objects.

Violent video games are popular with boys, but Barbie dolls and all the media products connected with them are more popular with girls (see Figure 6.4). For example, Barbie Fashion Designer is a top-selling software game, and a video of Barbie as a ballet dancer in *The Nutcracker* sold 3.5 million copies, spurring toymaker Mattel to introduce a *Barbie in Swan Lake* video, in which an animated Barbie will swoon over the handsome prince (Gladstone, 2003).

Should we be concerned about children's exposure to gender stereotypes? According to cognitive developmental and gender schema theories, children are actively seeking the meaning of being a boy or a girl, and the lessons they learn from the media get attached to their own gender schemas and to their sense of self. According to social learning theory, the more often children see models of gendered behavior, the more likely they are to imitate it and store it up for later use. All these theories suggest that children who are bombarded with gender stereotypes in their toys, TV shows, and games are likely to make these messages part of their own identity and to expect that this is how women and men should look and behave in real life. Barbie, for example, gives girls an everyday model of extremely unrealistic body shape. If Barbie were a full-sized woman, she would have a 42-inch bust, 18-inch waist, and 33-inch hips (Gray & Phillips, 1998). The odds of a real woman having the same proportions as Barbie are 1 in 100,000. (Ken is considerably more realistic—the odds of a man having his proportions are about 1 in 50) (Norton, Olds, Olive, & Dank, 1996).

Children's exposure to violence in the media is a particular cause for concern (see Figure 6.5). The majority of TV programs and video games contain violence, and the violent acts are usually portrayed as trivial, justified, or funny. By the time a U.S. child finishes elementary school, he or she has seen more than 100,000 acts of violence on TV, including 8,000 murders. Thirty years of research have definitively shown that exposure to media violence is related to an increase in aggressive emotions, thoughts, and behavior in children and adolescents (Anderson et al., 2003). Media violence desensitizes people to real violence and at the same time builds schemas of the world as a dangerous, scary place where a person must be aggressive in order to survive (Larson, 2003).

Violent media messages are more often aimed at boys than at girls. For example, violent programming tends to use male lead characters—think of Batman,

FIGURE 6.5

Spiderman, and X-Men—increasing the imitation potential for boys (Anderson et al., 2003). Commercials echo the programming themes. In a recent study, 37 percent of commercials during weekday afternoon and Saturday morning children's programming depicted an aggressive act. The most aggressive commercials were those with only White children and those that showed boys and girls together. White boys, in particular, were shown being verbally and physically aggressive, from making sarcastic remarks to twisting someone's arm on a playground and shooting goo at people (Larson, 2003).

Video games are the newest technology for teaching children to be aggressive. Over 85 percent of popular video games in the United States and Japan contain some violent content. Many psychologists are concerned that video games have an even greater potential for fostering violence than other forms of media because the child actively participates in the game's violence. Meta-analyses have shown that exposure to violent video games is related to increases in aggressive thoughts, beliefs, attitudes, emotions, and behavior and decreases in socially positive behavior such as helping others (Anderson et al., 2003).

Ethnicity, Social Class, and Gender Typing

A child's socialization is affected not only by gender but also by other factors such as ethnicity and social class, and these may be intertwined. Parents' attitudes about gender are often based on their ethnic group's cultural heritage. For example, Asian American families may retain the tradition that women should be nurturing and home oriented and that men should be strong and stoic, but also family oriented; and these ideals are still passed on to Asian American children (Bronstein, in press).

When a sample of Latinas aged 20 to 45 were asked in in-depth interviews what their parents taught them about how girls and boys *should* behave, the majority recalled traditional role expectations. Their brothers were granted more freedom, while the girls were expected to help with housework, learn to cook, and behave properly. A second, larger sample of Latino/Latina college students supported these findings and showed that gender socialization messages were usually conveyed by the same-gender parent: Fathers taught boys what was expected of them, and mothers taught girls (Raffaeli & Ontai, 2004).

In African American families, extended-family relatives and neighbors are often very involved in children's lives, forming an extended community of discipline and guidance that may reflect a heritage of African tribal life (Bronstein, in press). In general, studies suggest that African American children are less likely to rely on gender-stereotypical thinking than European American children are (Leaper, 2000). For example, by age 6, most European American boys have learned that only girls like babies, and they show little interest when invited to play with an infant. However, at age 10, African American boys are still equally as responsive as girls are to the infant (Reid & Trotter, 1993).

Just over half of all African American children are raised by a single-parent mother who works outside the home. Therefore, African American children are likely to see many models of women as both providers and caretakers, which may be particularly important for girls. Several studies show that African American girls and women do less gender stereotyping and hold less stereotypical attitudes than their European American counterparts and less than African American boys and men. When African Americans are compared with European Americans from single-mother homes, the differences are smaller. Thus, these ethnic group differences may be due to growing up in different kinds of family structures (Leaper, 2000).

Social class differences in African American households may also create different gender-socialization patterns. In a recent interview study of a class-diverse group of African American parents, there was very strong support for gender equality. Parents stressed that they had high educational goals for both boys and girls, and they expected both their sons and daughters to learn independence and equality of roles. As one mother said,

> I will definitely teach my son that men and women are equal; he is not the head of anybody. His wife will always have input and say-so in whatever is going on in their lives. And he needs to know that . . . when we were growing up, boys washed dishes, boys cooked; girls washed dishes, girls cooked. My mother taught us pretty equally to do everything, just in case you were on your own you wouldn't have to depend on somebody. (Hill, 2002, p. 497)

However, some of the families studied were newly arrived in the middle class—they had come from poor families or were less educated than others in the sample. These parents gave more mixed messages to their children. For example, one mother said that she wanted her daughter to be a warrior for racial justice, and also that she wanted her to be respectable, sit properly, avoid being loud, and act like a lady. Fathers in this group were more likely to be worried that their sons would become homosexual if they were not taught traditional masculinity. This study suggests that African American parents' support for gender equality in child raising depends on how secure they feel in their middle-class status; more secure families were more able to take the risk of raising gender-flexible children (Hill, 2002).

Vulnerabilities of Childhood

Childhood is not always a time of toys and books, safety and security, and imitating Mom and Dad. Because they are small and dependent on others, children are vulnerable to victimization and exploitation by adults. It is unfortunately true that some children learn far too young "the major lesson of patriarchy: The more powerful control the less powerful" (White, Donat, & Bondurant, 2001). Here we look at one kind of gender-linked exploitation: childhood sexual abuse. We also examine poverty, a pervasive cause of developmental problems for boys and girls alike.

Childhood Sexual Abuse

A significant minority of children experience **childhood sexual abuse,** defined as coercive sexual interaction between a child and an adult. Girls are more likely to be abused than boys, according to phone surveys of randomized national samples

(White et al., 2001). In one such sample of adults, 27 percent of women and 16 percent of men reported that they had experienced sexual abuse as children; in another sample of young people aged 10 to 16, 15 percent of girls and 6 percent of boys reported a history of abuse.

Tragically, children, and particularly girls, are most often abused by someone they know and trust. For example, family members and acquaintances are responsible for almost 90 percent of child rapes. Older relatives, brothers, and the child's own father or stepfather are the leading abusers of girls within the family (Laumann, Gagnon, Michael, & Michaels, 1994).

Who is most at risk for child sexual abuse? Any child can be abused, and there seem to be few differences in rates of abuse among various ethnic and racial groups. Rather, there are particular kinds of families that provide a context in which abuse is likely. Abusive families are most often emotionally distant and unaffectionate. They tend to be strongly patriarchal: Father is the head of the household, Mother is subservient, and children are taught to obey without question. Finally, they are families with a lot of conflict among family members (White et al., 2001).

Before the abuse starts, the perpetrator may gradually earn the child's love and trust by treating her as special. The perpetrator may buy her toys, tuck her in at night, or take her out for treats. He may increase his inappropriate contact gradually, so that the child may not realize the behavior is sexually directed until it is well established. After each abusive episode, he may apologize and promise it will never happen again. However, the loving, apologetic behavior gives way to another period of building the child's trust, and then to more sexual transgressions, in a cycle of abuse. Because the abuser has power and authority over the child and may even live in the same home, the child may feel overwhelmed and alone, with nowhere to turn to for help. Living in a patriarchal, authoritarian family, the victim of childhood sexual abuse may be emotionally neglected and afraid to question the power and authority of adults. Under these conditions, the perpetrator may succeed in convincing the child that their relationship is a special, loving secret, rather than the crime and betrayal of trust that it is (White et al., 2001).

Sexual abuse may negatively affect any aspect of the child's emotional, cognitive, and social development (Kendall-Tackett, 2001). For example, the child may show supposedly irrational emotions such as fear of the dark, of going to bed at night, or of being alone. Later, she or he may experience depression and withdrawal. Behavioral responses include problems in school, bedwetting, nightmares, and, later, running away from home or becoming sexually active at an early age. Survivors of abuse are at increased risk for suicide.

A study of survivors who managed to function well as adults showed that these women had developed coping strategies that kept them from giving in psychologically to the abuse. They dreamed about the future and immersed themselves in school achievements or creative activities such as writing in order to cope with their pain (diPalma, 1994). Despite attempts to develop coping strategies, the majority of adult women who have survived childhood abuse say that it significantly affected their entire lives (Laumann et al., 1994).

Not all sexual abuse of children is family based. There is a global sex trade in children. In Southeast Asia alone, UNICEF estimates that 1 million children are trafficked into commercial sex work each year (Meier, 2000). (See Box 6.5.) This

BOX 6.5   ∽   Lek: The Story of a Child Prostitute

Lek grew up in a slum near a tourist resort area in Thailand. Her story, documented by anthropologist Heather Montgomery, is one of exploitation from a very early age:

Lek was introduced to commercial sex at the age of three by Ta, her eight-year-old neighbour . . . She was taken by Ta to meet James, a British businessman. Lek . . . remembers watching as Ta was paid to masturbate him. A few weeks later Lek did the same and continued to do so until she began, at the age of six, to have intercourse with him. In return for this, James gave money to Lek's family . . . She has been a prostitute ever since, averaging around twenty men a year, although her most regular source of income is still James. She refuses to call him a client or a customer, referring to him instead as a boyfriend. She also refuses to see him as an exploiter; she says "he is so good to me, how can you say he's bad?"

When I met her, Lek was twelve and pregnant by another of her foreign customers. She gave birth prematurely . . . to a daughter . . . Lek debated putting the child into an orphanage, but eventually decided against it, returning to prostitution as a means of supporting the child. There was no money in the family for the medical expenses of the birth, and so she turned to her cousin Nuk's client, a sixty-year-old Australian called Paul, for help. Paul paid all her medical expenses, and in return she traded sex after she gave birth. Six weeks after the birth, she was back at work as a prostitute . . .

Source: From H. Montgomery, 2001, *Modern Babylon*, p. 80. New York: Berghahn Books. Reprint permission obtained via the Copyright Clearance Center.

---

sex trafficking takes many forms. In Thailand, children in urban slums near resort areas may be prostituted to Western tourists who are pedophiles (Montgomery, 2001). In Nepal, rural girls may be lured or sold to traffickers who take them to nearby countries to work in brothels, where they are held as prisoners (Poudel & Carryer, 2000; UNIFEM, 1998). The HIV/AIDS epidemic has increased the market value of very young girls, as men seek virginal sex partners to avoid acquiring HIV and other sexually transmitted diseases.

Trafficking of children takes place in a larger context of extreme poverty, gender inequality, and limited choices that makes families vulnerable. In Thailand, for example, some parents allow their children to be sexually abused because the only survival alternative is for the child to work 12-hour days of picking through garbage and trash in dumps (Montgomery, 2001). In Nepal, rural poverty and lack of educational opportunities make escape to a city seem desirable even when it involves prostitution (Poudel & Carryer, 2000).

Trafficking is a grave violation of the fundamental human rights of women and girls. There are many testimonies from survivors and their advocates about the misery, pain, and degradation of forced prostitution (ABC/Nepal, 1996; O'Dea, 1993). Even when girls are rescued, returning home is difficult, because those associated with the sex trade are stigmatized. A girl or woman who is even suspected of such an association may be considered ruined, unmarriageable, and without family status.

Children and Poverty

The United States is a wealthy nation, and the poverty that exists in the midst of this wealth is often invisible. However, more than 35 million Americans live below the poverty line, including over 14 million children (Arnold & Doctoroff, 2003). Poor children face many obstacles to healthy development, both in their social environments and their physical environments.

Children from low-income families are exposed to more violence at home and in their neighborhoods and schools than those from middle-income families. They are more likely to experience parents' divorce, family breakup, and foster care (Evans, 2004). Poverty makes it difficult or impossible for parents to provide for their children's needs. Poor parents are more likely than middle-class parents to be working two or more jobs and working late hours; so they have less time to read to children, help with homework, take them to the library, or supervise their play. They often lack basic resources such as a reliable car, health insurance, and decent child care. Moreover, poverty is strongly linked to depression in parents, leading to less-consistent and effective parenting (Belle, 2004). From infancy onward, poor children are exposed to more punishment and less positive parental interaction than are middle-income children.

Poverty has a "devastating negative effect on academic achievement" for both girls and boys (Arnold & Doctoroff, 2003, p. 518). Poor children receive less cognitive stimulation and enrichment than wealthier children do. They are much less likely to have a computer or Internet access at home, and their schools cannot fill the gap because they are likely to have less-qualified teachers, outdated facilities, and few educational materials (Evans, 2004).

Childhood poverty is not gender-equal in its effects. Because boys are more likely to act out and cause trouble for others, their poverty-related problems may receive more attention, and more programs are designed to help them. The poverty-related problems that are more likely to afflict girls, such as underachievement, depression, and poor mental health, are less often noticed and treated (Arnold & Doctoroff, 2003).

The physical environment of poverty includes higher exposure to toxins such as lead poisoning and air pollution, along with crowded and inadequate housing. For example, poor children are over four times as likely to have high levels of lead in their blood, 3.6 times more likely to live in houses infested with rodents, and 2.7 times more likely not to have enough heat in the winter, compared with other children. Multiple stressors in the social and physical environment have a cumulative effect on poor children (Evans, 2004).

I have focused on poor children in our own nation, but childhood poverty is a worldwide problem. In poor and developing countries, many children lack safe drinking water and basic sanitation. Their housing is particularly inadequate and may be located in flood zones, toxic waste areas, or other undesirable locations (Evans, 2004). They may not go to school at all. Girls, in particular, may be kept at home to do household work, denying them the education that could help lift them out of poverty. In most parts of the developing world, there is a gender gap in literacy, with fewer girls than boys learning to read and write (UNESCO, 2000).

Leaving Childhood Behind: Puberty and Adolescence

When does a child become an adult? ***Puberty*** is a series of physiological events that changes a child into a person capable of reproducing. However, there is much more to being an adult than the capability to reproduce. The period after puberty and before adulthood, termed ***adolescence,*** is the time that a society allocates for young people to mature and grow into their adult roles. The adolescent must negotiate sexuality, independence, and identity while being not yet an adult.

The biological changes of puberty and the social meanings of adolescence are closely intertwined, because the biological changes take place in a cultural context that defines their meaning. For adolescent boys, the maturing body signifies an increase in status and power. As boys grow taller and more muscular, they are given more freedom. For girls, the maturing body signifies a more mixed status. It is wonderful to become a woman, and some girls eagerly await their first period and first bra. On the other hand, girls may not be granted more freedom—in fact, their independence may be curtailed. In this section, I discuss the physical changes of puberty and their social meaning.

Changing Bodies

Puberty begins with a rise in hormonal production that gradually causes the body to mature. For girls, the first external sign may be a ***growth spurt*** or the development of ***secondary sex characteristics***—breasts and body hair. (See Figure 6.6.) The growth spurt is not just a gain in height, but also a gain in body fat. This increase is necessary and normal. In order for a girl to begin menstruating, she must reach a critical level of body fat (Frisch, 1983). Healthy adult women have up to twice as much body fat as healthy adult men (Warren, 1983). However, developing womanly curves conflicts with societal norms for extreme thinness at the same time it makes girls' sexuality visible to all. Many girls dislike the attention paid to their changing bodies:

"I think I'll be more relaxed once my secondary sex characteristics kick in."

FIGURE 6.6

I remember when I was in 6th grade and this boy called me "stuffy," in other words he was accusing me of stuffing my bra, because . . . I was developing very early as a 6th grader and I didn't like my body at all . . . my boobs were just so big that, I mean, I am still busty and I mean, they are huge and I was a small person and they got in my way . . . and I really hated them . . . I just remember feeling that I was going to grow up and the only thing that I would be good for was something like a Playboy bunny . . . I guess that maybe that's why I felt so angry about my period because I associated it with these feelings about my boobs. (Lee, 2003, p. 89)

Although gaining weight and adding body fat are a normal part of becoming sexually mature for females, girls may interpret this normal process as becoming fat. During adolescence, there is a dramatic increase in girls' concern about their weight (Smolak & Striegel-Moore, 2001). In one national survey, 60 percent of high school girls said they were trying to lose weight (Phillips, 1998). In a study of factors that predict body dissatisfaction, the most important were not only actually being over-weight but also perceived pressure from others to be thin, belief in a thin-is-better ideal, and lack of social support (Stice & Whitenton, 2002).

White girls, in particular, tend to tie their self-esteem to their weight, whereas African American girls tend to be more satisfied with their bodies (Tashakkori, 1993). For example, 40 percent of a large sample of African American girls, and only 9 percent of White girls, said that they felt attractive (Phillips, 1998). Although body dissatisfaction was more prevalent among the White girls, it was present in every ethnic group studied.

The preoccupation with weight can have serious health consequences. For ex-ample, girls may start smoking and using diet pills in futile attempts to eliminate body fat (Phillips, 1998). Some girls develop eating disorders—a topic that will be discussed in Chapter 13.

The onset of menstruation—termed *menarche*—is the most visible and dra-matic sign of puberty. Menarche occurs at about 12½ years of age on average. Euro-pean American girls reach menarche several months later than African American and Latina girls, and earlier than Asian American girls; these ethnic differences may be related to average body weight. However, there is a great deal of variability in its timing. Some girls reach menarche as early as age 8 (O'Sullivan, Graber, & Brooks-Gunn, 2001).

Virtually every woman remembers the day she got her first period:

So I was 10 years old and didn't understand any of it. In fact I misunderstood most of it. What I remember about it from the book was that somehow the menstrual blood came out on the outside of your lower abdomen somehow like it seeped through your skin! . . . So I told my mother and it was like 'oh,' she did seem rather pleased but it wasn't like the kind of pleased where if I got a really good grade or . . . the solo in the school play . . . She pulls out the Kotex kit and that is when I begin to connect, this is what it is, it doesn't come out of your stomach! (Lee, 2003, p. 93)

When it came, I was a high school exchange student in Europe, staying with the family of a friend. I felt like I was out of control, that something was happening to me that I couldn't stop. I bled terribly all over the sheets and was horribly embarrassed telling my friend's aunt (especially since I didn't know the right words, menstruation is hardly one of the common vocabulary words you have to learn). . . . I felt like it was all happening to someone else, not me, like I was watching myself in a movie and now was this sexual being. (Lee, 2003, p. 87)

I saw blood on my underwear and it was like I just sat on the toilet . . . and I am like "mom." She comes in and she was like, "What? Well honey, congratulations, you are a little lady now." I am like, "Say what?!!"(Lee, 2003, p. 93)

FIGURE 6.7

Source: Stone Soup Copyright © 2004 Jan Eliot. Distributed by Universal Press Syndicate. Reprinted with permission. All rights reserved.

Girls receive both positive and negative messages about this aspect of becoming a woman (see Figure 6.7). Menstruation is associated with disgust, shame, and secrecy in our society as well as in many others (Reame, 2001). (See Box 6.6.) In one study of U.S. college students, about two-thirds said that they knew nothing about their own mothers' menstrual experiences, and their mothers reacted negatively when told about the girls' first period (Costos, Ackerman, & Paradis, 2002). For many years, menstrual products were banned from TV and radio, and magazine ads were so vague it was hard to tell what was being advertised. Even today, when advertising of menstrual products such as tampons and pads is more open and positive, there is an underlying message that menstruation must be kept invisible and secret (Merskin, 1999; Simes & Berg, 2001).

Menstruating women are still stigmatized. In one creative study, college students saw a woman "accidentally" drop either a hair clip or a tampon in front of them. Students were then asked about their attitudes toward the woman, although they did not know that their responses had anything to do with the incident. When the woman had dropped the tampon, participants (both male and female) rated her as less likable and competent and sat further away from her than when she had dropped the hair clip (Roberts, Goldenberg, Power, & Pyszczysnski, 2002). The mixed messages of "You're a young woman now," "You will be disgraced and humiliated if anyone discovers that you are having your period," and "Menstruating women are to be avoided" may leave girls wondering what is so wonderful about becoming a woman.

Gender Intensification

Beginning in early adolescence, girls' freedom to violate gender norms becomes more restricted. Many young girls are tomboys: They like boys' toys, sports, and active games. In a recent three-generational study of college students, their mothers, and their grandmothers, a two-thirds majority said they had been tomboys during childhood. They also said that they stopped being tomboys at some point, and

---

| BOX 6.6 ∾ | Call It Anything, but Don't Call It Menstruation |

Societies generate *euphemisms* to disguise or soften the meaning of taboo topics. Menstruation has generated many euphemisms. Which of these have you heard and which are new to you?

I've got the painters in. (Australia)

Monthlies (Australia)

Mary is visiting. (Belgium)

I'm putting a cork in the bottle. (Brazil)

I have my moon. (Canada)

Blowjob time (England)

On the blob (England)

Lingonberry days (Finland)

Japanese week (Germany)

Monthly tax (Germany)

Cranberry woman (Germany)

Casual leave (India)

Out of doors (India)

Aunty Mary (Ireland)

Little Miss Strawberry (Japan)

Ketchup (Japan)

The tomato soup overcooked. (Netherlands)

Mrs. Noodles (New Zealand)

Doing time (Nigeria)

I have the red label in the old typewriter. (Portugal)

Aunt Bertha (Scotland)

My aunt parked her red Porsche outside. (South Africa)

Wearing the red beret (Vietnam)

The curse (U.S.)

The plague (U.S.)

Aunt Flow (U.S.)

Riding the cotton pony (U.S.)

On the rag (U.S.)

My redheaded friend (U.S.)

Source: Museum of Menstruation & Women's Health (www.mum.org). Contributed by Michelle R. Kaufman, University of Connecticut.

---

the average age reported was 12.6 years, almost exactly the age the average girl reaches puberty. However, it was not the physical changes of puberty that caused these girls to give up their tomboy ways. Although they still liked active, adventurous play, they reported that they quit doing these things because of social pressure to be feminine (Morgan, 1998).

The shift from tomboy to young lady illustrates the process of **gender intensification,** or increased pressure to conform to gender roles beginning in early adolescence. By the time they are 11 or 12 years of age, girls start to get more messages from parents, other adults, and peers to act feminine and to stake their self-esteem on being attractive.

As you might expect, the timing of puberty affects the timing of these messages. The earlier a girl matures, the earlier she is subject to gender intensification. On the one hand, early maturity may make a girl more popular with boys. Early-maturing girls date more than late-maturing girls and are more likely to get involved with boyfriends in middle school and junior high (Brooks-Gunn, 1988). On the other hand, early-maturing girls may experience a more stressful adolescence. For example, they get lower grades and score lower on achievement tests than late-maturing girls (Simmons & Blyth, 1987). They engage in more risky behaviors such as smoking, drinking, and early sexual intercourse; and they have higher rates of depression and eating disorders than late-maturing girls (Ge, Conger, & Elder, 2001; Stice, Presnell, & Bearman, 2001).

These timing effects may occur because early-maturing girls tend to become part of an older, more experienced peer group involved in adult activities that they imitate. Pressures can come from adults, too, who expect a physically mature girl to behave like an adult woman—as discussed in Chapter 3, physical characteristics are particularly important in triggering gender stereotypes. However, a 12-year-old girl with the body of a woman is still a 12-year-old girl emotionally, cognitively, and in her life experience.

Vulnerabilities of Adolescence

The transition from childhood to adulthood has traditionally been thought of as a time of increasing self-confidence and competence. However, for some girls adolescence is a time of *decreasing* self-confidence and self-esteem as they learn that speaking out and being themselves leads to trouble (Brown, 1998).

Self-Silencing and Self-Esteem

Interviews with adolescent girls during the middle-school and junior high years showed that many stifled their own feelings and thoughts in an effort to fit in and be seen as a nice girl, a phenomenon termed **self-silencing** (Brown & Gilligan, 1992). The girls in this study were from privileged backgrounds and attended a private school. However, they are not the only ones to experience self-silencing. In another study, girls from diverse racial and ethnic backgrounds were asked to complete the sentence, "What gets me into trouble is _____." More than half the girls answered "my mouth" or "my big mouth" (Taylor, Gilligan, & Sullivan, 1995).

Self-silencing and loss of confidence may occur among adolescent girls because they come up against a "wall of 'shoulds' in which approval is associated with their silence" (Brown, 1998). The pressure to conform to an idealized femininity in which good girls are never angry or oppositional leads girls to doubt the truth of their own knowledge and feelings and to feel less positive about themselves.

Self-esteem refers to a person's overall level of positive regard and self-respect. It is measured by asking people to agree or disagree with statements such as "I feel good about myself and who I am." Do adolescent girls suffer from low self-esteem? Recent meta-analyses of hundreds of studies of self-esteem in children and adults of all ages showed that boys and men scored higher than girls and women. This difference emerges at adolescence, but is not very large (Kling, Hyde, Showers, & Buswell, 1999; Major, Barr, Zubek, & Babey, 1999). When different ethnic samples were examined separately, the gender self-esteem gap occurred only among European Americans. Self-esteem was also related to social class, with the gender gap largest in economically disadvantaged groups.

In other words, a girl's self-esteem is dependent not only on her gender, but also on other factors that influence her place in society, and adolescence may increase her vulnerability. Low self-esteem is a cause for concern because it is linked to problems with psychological adjustment, physical health, and life satisfaction.

Peer Culture and Harassment

A school principal in Maine reported that a group of girls went to a teacher because the boys were scaring them by saying,

> "You're my girlfriend. And I'm gonna marry you and . . . we're gonna have sex." . . . it got pretty aggressive and real loud and pretty soon there were lots of things coming out from all the boys: "Yeah, we're gonna have sex with you," and "Yeah, we're gonna rape you; we're gonna kill you." And "Yeah, 'cause you're our girlfriend." And then one boy said, "I'm gonna put an engagement ring on you 'cause that's what you do when you love someone, but I'm gonna NAIL it on 'til the blood comes out! (Brown, 1998, p. 104)

These children were 6 and 7 years old. Too young to fully understand the meaning of words like sex and rape, they nevertheless acted out a scenario of masculine dominance: "The boys felt powerful using hostile language they knew would strongly affect the girls; the girls . . . felt uncomfortable, frightened, and angry" (Brown, 1998, p. 105).

A great deal of research shows that gender-related harassment by peers is prevalent in schools and that it intensifies as children reach adolescence. When the American Association of University Women conducted a national survey of students in grades 8 through 11, they found that 83 percent of girls and 79 percent of boys had experienced harassment. This included behaviors such as spreading sexual rumors, making remarks about one's body or sexuality, forced kissing and unwanted touching (AAUW, 2001). White girls reported the most sexual harassment, followed by African American and Latina girls. Although the overall rates were nearly gender-equal, the consequences were not. In this study as well as others, boys tended to view sexualized attention as flattering; they reported that it makes them feel proud of themselves. Girls were much more likely to report that it makes them feel frightened, self-conscious, and embarrassed. As a result, they lose self-confidence and may withdraw from active participation in class and activities.

In another large study of 14- and 15-year-old students in the Netherlands, girls were more than twice as likely as boys to report incidents of unwanted sexual attention at school (Timmerman, 2003). For boys, the most common forms were verbal taunts such as "gay" or "homo." For girls, there was more physical harassment. As one girl reported, "I was pawed and blocked. I was very frightened and helpless. It was a group of boys" (p. 239).

Although sexual harassment can happen to anyone, girls or boys who violate gender norms are most often targets for peer aggression. Those who are believed to be gay or lesbian are targeted with names such as *fag* and *queer* (Boxer, Cook, & Herdt, 1999; Hunter & Mallon, 2000). The term *slut* is freely applied to girls for even the most minor gender transgression, as shown in this incident at a summer camp, when Molly (age 9) got chlorine in her eyes at the pool and walked into the boys' locker room by mistake:

> Many of the boys laughed at her and ridiculed Molly for her mistake. Brian (age 11) said, "She just wanted to look at our private stuff," and Thomas (age 12) called her a "slut." Molly started to cry. (McGuffey & Rich, 1999, p. 622)

In the middle-school years, the boundaries for acceptable behavior are policed by a few "alpha boys," who keep potential gender transgressors in line by name-calling, exclusion, and physical aggression (McGuffey & Rich, 1999). The dominant boys exert influence over both girls and other boys. As girls enter adolescence and become more worried about their appeal to boys, these tactics take on even more power to control and limit their behavior.

A striking feature of peer gender harassment among children and teens is that it often takes place in full view of adults, who may do little to stop it. Often, teachers stand by and watch without comment as sexual teasing and harassment take place (Stein, 1995)—a powerful modeling experience for both boys and girls. Girls may report harassment only to be told, "Boys will be boys." In a particularly horrifying incident, gang rapes of female students were reported at a major Japanese university. In response, a member of parliament said in a public forum, "Boys who commit group rape are in good shape. I think they are rather normal. Whoops, I shouldn't have said that" (French, 2003, p. A4).

Girls may be encouraged to interpret their experiences of gender-related harassment and hostility in terms of heterosexual romance. For example, after the "We're gonna rape you" incident described earlier, 7-year-old Melissa struggled to understand how boys who she thought were her friends could be so hostile. She was comforted when she remembered that her grandfather had told her, "If boys chase you, then that means that they love you." Although Melissa's grandfather probably meant well, it is dubious whether this is a good lesson for Melissa to learn (Brown, 1998, p. 105). For more on the ideology of heterosexual romance and its relationship to violence against girls and women, see Chapter 8.

Unfortunately, teachers may even be the perpetrators of sexual harassment. Students of all ages are legally protected from sexual contact with teachers (Watts, 1996). However, teacher-student sexual harassment is amply documented. A survey of high school students in the Netherlands found that 27 percent of reported unwanted sexual behavior at school was done by a teacher, principal, or other adult authority. The perpetrators were overwhelmingly male; the victims, mostly female. Teacher harassment was more severe and led to more negative psychological consequences than peer harassment (Timmerman, 2003).

The power imbalance between teachers and students leads to underreporting of this kind of violence, because girls are afraid of the consequences. When a 13-year-old Japanese girl brought charges against her 51-year-old teacher for fondling her in a school office, more than 40 teachers signed a petition asking that he should be treated leniently. The girl was rejected by her classmates, and her best friend told her she had ruined the teacher's life. She replied that it had been the other way around (French, 2003).

Making a Difference

Children and adolescents need to be protected and cared for by adults, and they also need respect for their own choices and developmental pathways. Changes at the societal, interpersonal, and individual levels of gender can improve the lives of girls and boys.

Transforming Society: Protecting Children from Abuse

In countries where child prostitution is rampant, governments are beginning to take measures against it. In addition, a large number of nongovernmental organizations have responded to the trafficking problem with innovative programs aimed at preventing future trafficking and redressing the situation of survivors. Efforts so far include antitrafficking legislation; educational programs for those at risk and their communities; rescue, shelter, and medical/psychological care for survivors; and prosecution of traffickers. International organizations dedicated to ending the sex trade in children, and the poverty that fuels it, include Oxfam (www.oxfam.org.uk) and the Asia Foundation (www.asiafoundation.org). For example, the Asia Foundation has initiated village task forces in rural Nepal to plan local ways to reduce trafficking, and also sponsored job training for girls at risk for trafficking and girls rescued from the sex trade.

In the United States, many schools now sponsor programs to teach children that they have the right not to be touched inappropriately and encourage them to tell an adult if someone acts in a sexual way toward them (Wurtele, 2002). However, these programs have limitations because they place the responsibility for prevention largely on the child. As we have seen, abusers play on the cognitive limitations and emotional vulnerability of their child victims, whose minds may become even more traumatized than their bodies. Childhood sexual abuse is a form of exploitation that no child should have to endure.

Transforming Social Interactions

Feminists have maintained that child rearing aimed at producing gender-typed boys and girls is harmful because it closes off possibilities for both. As long as humans are raised to believe that there are certain things they cannot or should not do because of their gender, society is losing potentially unique contributions and individuals are losing potential sources of fulfillment.

Many feminist researchers and parents have explored alternative approaches to bringing up children (Katz, 1996). Considerable research shows that the gender roles modeled by parents and other adults affect children's gender typing. Children who grow up in families where parents share child care and household work are less gender typed in the preschool years than those who grow up in more traditional families (Fagot & Leinbach, 1995). Similarly, those whose mothers work in gender-neutral or male-dominated occupations have less gender-typed interests and beliefs (Barak, Feldman, & Noy, 1991). Parents who are concerned about reducing gender stereotyping in their children can start by paying attention to their own behavior and becoming more flexible (Bem, 1998).

For girls in the vulnerable teen years, the main issues include keeping a healthy identity and self-esteem, becoming comfortable with a woman's body, and expressing sexuality in relationships. We discuss the latter two topics in the chapters that follow. For now, let's look at the factors that help prevent self-silencing and foster healthy self-esteem in adolescent girls.

In one study of a diverse sample, girls were asked what made them feel good about themselves. Athletics topped the list, probably because sports may increase body satisfaction (see Chapter 7). Another important influence was creative self-expression—music, art, or theater. These activities provided opportunities to meet a challenge (a reason especially important to more affluent girls, European American and Asian American girls, and those in urban areas) and also just because they were enjoyable or involved being with friends (most important to girls from rural areas) (Erkut, Fields, Sing, & Marks, 1997).

Providing creative activities may be one route to supporting girls. For example, the ACT NOW! Program sponsors MOVIExperience, a program that provides girls with the tools to make 20-minute movies about their lives (Heitner, 2003). Each girl selects a site, creates a story, and improvises the action for the camera. During the process, girls work collaboratively to express themselves, drawing on their own experiences, dreams, and imagination. According to its sponsors, the program builds self-esteem, helps girls speak out, and fosters cooperation. As one 12-year-old girl said, "I didn't really know who I was. The movie let me express myself. It showed me that a lot of people like me for who I am." More about programs to empower adolescent girls can be found at www.actnow-online.org and in *The Girls Report* (Phillips, 1998).

Another avenue to empowering girls is collective action. In one example, Canadian students in a boarding school participated in group discussions about their bodies and objectification. They then decided collectively to lobby the administration to make changes such as putting tampon dispensers in the girls' bathrooms. Although their victories were small, working together provided an experience of empowerment (Piran, 2001).

Service to others is another experience that helps girls feel good about themselves (Erkut et al., 1997). When more privileged girls help those who are disadvantaged, both groups benefit. In one successful program, students from a women's college served as mentors to inner-city high school students who were mostly from poor Hispanic and immigrant families (Moayedi, 1999). The high school girls visited the college campus, participated in leadership workshops, and learned about college life and career possibilities. Both the college students and the high school girls learned from this experience. As one college mentor said, "My friend Elisabeth has nobody to count on. She came here with nothing in her pockets to start a new life from the bottom. That is why I have learned more from her" (pp. 237–238). As for the high school girls, they reported that before the mentoring program they had never been on a college campus, knew few white people, and had never thought about going to college. As a result of the program, their goals were changed and their options expanded.

Children from disadvantaged backgrounds particularly need mentoring to help them overcome the many deficits induced by poverty. *Big Brothers/Big Sisters* program is a nationwide attempt to foster healthy development in disadvantaged children through mentoring. Involvement in Big Brothers/Big Sisters has been shown to improve older children's grades, academic skills, and relationships with parents and peers (Grossman & Tierney, 1998).

Transforming Ourselves: Resisting Gender

Many educational programs have been designed to reduce gender stereotyping or change gender-related attitudes in children. These programs might include seeing counter-stereotypical examples (a woman scientist) or reading about nurturing boys and achieving girls. Unfortunately, they are usually not very effective (Bigler, 1999). Changes in children's attitudes following the programs are few and short-lived. Their messages may simply be outweighed by the many stereotypical messages children receive about gender at home and from the media. Gender stereotyping is very resistant to change in adults (Chapter 3), and the same is true for children.

On the other hand, girls and boys are not just passive victims of gender socialization. On the contrary, many girls actively resist gender pressures and develop identities in opposition to the norms of femininity. In a study conducted in Israel, girls who continued being tomboys into their adolescent years were less gender typed as adult women (Safir, Rosenmann, & Kloner, 2003).

Understanding how girls resist gender may require close study of their own accounts of their experience. In an extended observational study of girls in a small town in Maine, Brown (1998) reported that working-class girls, in particular, tend to "fight verbally, and physically when necessary, to speak the unspeakable, to be nurturing and also tough and self-protecting," disrupting the boundaries of femininity. They are not the so-called good girls their teachers want, but they may be holding on to their identities in a system that does not understand or value them.

Understanding and supporting girls is a crucial area for feminist research and activism, because girls

> have the potential to contribute alternative visions and voices, but they have to recognize themselves as complete and whole beings, with a range of feelings and thoughts connected to their experiences. Teaching girls how to pinpoint what is causing them anger or pain and how to act on their feelings constructively provides a kind of warrior training for social justice. (Brown, 1998, p. 224)

Exploring Further

Bem, Sandra L. (1998). *An unconventional family.* New Haven: Yale University Press.
A personal memoir by a prominent feminist psychologist about how she and her husband tried to bring up ungendered children. The now-grown children, Emily and Jeremy, have their say, too. This book is controversial—see the review in the journal *Feminism and Psychology.*

Gray, H. M., & Phillips, S. (1998). *Real girl real world: Tools for finding your true self.* Seattle: Seal Press.

A guide to help preteen and adolescent girls deal with gender pressures. This book relies on girls' own voices to address topics such as images and the media, sexualities, body image, and eating disorders; and it provides Web resources for them to learn more.

The Whale Rider. (2003).

Pai (Keisha Castle-Hughes) is a Maori girl who is called to be a chief at a time and place that cannot accept female leaders. Her perseverance, determination, and courage are a model for girls everywhere. Director Niki Caro based this beautiful film on a traditional Maori legend and made it in consultation with tribal leaders.

CHAPTER 7

Chapter contributed by Britain Scott, Ph.D.

In a Woman's Body

> Woman? Very simple, say the fanciers of simple formulas: she is a womb, an
> ovary; she is a female—this word is sufficient to define her. (p. 3) . . . These
> biological considerations are extremely important. In the history of woman they
> play a part of the first rank . . . But I deny that they establish for her a fixed and
> inevitable destiny . . . (pp. 32–33) . . . the body of woman is one of the essential
> elements in her situation in the world. But that body is not enough to define her
> as woman . . . Biology is not enough to give an answer to the question that is
> before us: why is woman the *Other?* (pp. 36–37)
>
> —*Simone de Beauvoir,* The Second Sex *(1952)*

French existential philosopher and feminist Beauvoir's groundbreaking book explored the question of what it means to be a woman in an androcentric world. In the first chapter she recognized that women's bodies are central to their experiences as women; hers was one of the earliest well-known works to consider the role of women's bodies in the social construction of their identities as women. Although she insisted that women's anatomy was not their destiny—for example, just because women can become mothers does not mean they must (she didn't)—she recognized that women's bodies and their reproductive role significantly affect the way women view themselves and the way women are culturally defined. And the way that Beauvoir saw women defined was as the "Other" in contrast to men.

Bodily Objectification of Women

Beauvoir's premise was that in a culture dominated and defined by the subjective experiences of men, women are chronically in the position of the object. Although she was not a psychologist and she was writing in an era not known for its feminist activism, Beauvoir made the insightful observation that women's objectified status in society has much to do with their bodies. A decade and a half later, when women in the United States staged the first recognized public demonstration of feminism's second wave outside the Miss America pageant in Atlantic City, they were protesting bodily objectification of women.

Today, when we say a woman is being *objectified,* we mean that she is being perceived not in terms of her individual personhood, but in a way that dehumanizes her, strips her of her identity, and reduces her to her body, or even just parts of her body. When a woman is referred to as a blonde or a hottie, she is being objectified. When scantily clad women are used to draw attention to a product or service, they are being objectified. When an advertisement features a close-up shot of just a woman's breasts, butt, or lips, objectification is occurring. When a news article prioritizes the physical appearance of a female politician, that politician is being objectified. When a woman uses her hand mirror to better scrutinize and evaluate the backs of her thighs (which she hates), she is objectifying herself.

This chapter discusses theory and research concerning the origins of women's bodily objectification, presentations of women's bodies in popular culture, the paradox between being a feminine object and being a physically active subject, the consequences of objectification for women, and the benefits to women of *embodied* experiences that may allow them to transcend objectification.

Origins of Objectification

A Biological Basis for Objectification?

Some researchers suggest that our tendency to perceive and value women primarily in terms of their appearance is a natural phenomenon stemming from women's role in reproduction. These researchers adopt an ***evolutionary perspective*** to explain human social behavior. They suggest that we inherited many of our behaviors from early human ancestors who lived about 150,000 years ago. Behaviors that helped our ancestors survive were passed on to us through our genes. Of course, as critics of the evolutionary perspective point out, it is impossible for us to truly know what the world was like in the Middle Pleistocene, and so we must be cautious about inferring an evolutionary basis for behaviors observed today. Some feminist scholars have been especially wary of evolutionary theorizing that posits a biological basis for such socially abhorrent and sexist behaviors as rape (Thornhill & Palmer, 2000), wife abuse (Wilson & Daly, 1996), and wife killing (Shackelford, Buss, & Weekes-Shackelford, 2003).

According to David Buss and David Schmitt (1993), the evolutionary explanation for the emphasis on women's attractiveness is tied to reproduction. Biologically, both men's and women's bodies serve important functions in reproduction, but in some ways women's bodies are more important. In many species there is an imbalance in the relative contributions each sex must make to reproduction; in humans, women make the larger investment. Minimally, women must contribute nine months and substantial bodily resources to create a child; add to this the investment of breastfeeding and it is clear that women's role in producing offspring is quite large. Men, minimally, must contribute much, much less to create offspring (a few minutes and a bodily resource that is continually renewed). So ***minimal parental investment*** is dramatically different in women and men.

In addition, women's potential to produce offspring is considerably less than men's. A woman is typically able to produce only one child at a time, whereas it is possible for a man to have several children in the making simultaneously (if he has multiple partners). Women are fertile for only about four decades of their lives, but most men remain fertile throughout their lives. Women's total reproductive potential, then, is extremely limited relative to men's. What is the maximum number of offspring that one woman could produce: somewhere around 20? What is the maximum number one man could produce? Theoretically, his potential is limited only by the number of sexually available, fertile mates he is able to find.

According to Buss and Schmitt (1993), the differences between women's and men's minimal parental investment and reproductive potential mean that the sexes have evolved different mating strategies. When seeking mates, women and men prioritize different qualities. Women look for clues that a potential mate is able and willing to help ensure the survival of her (relatively valuable) offspring (i.e., he has resources and will share them with their children). Men look for indications of sexual availability and fertility.

Sexual availability may be suggested if the woman does not already have a mate or if she communicates sexual interest. Assessment of a woman's fertility is a little trickier. Buss and Schmitt explain,

> The capacity of a woman to bear children is not stamped on her forehead . . . So how could a preference [for fertile women] evolve [when fertility] cannot be directly discerned? . . . The answer lies with those features of women that provide cues that are correlated with fertility . . . age and health. However, age and health, like reproductive capacity, are not qualities that can be observed directly . . . Nevertheless, our ancestral humans did have access to . . . cues that provide probabilistic evidence of a woman's age and health status: (a) features of physical appearance (e.g., full lips, clear skin, smooth skin, clear eyes, lustrous hair, symmetry, good muscle tone, and absence of lesions), (b) observable behavior (e.g., sprightly, youthful gait and high activity level) . . . (p. 208)

In other words, women's physical attractiveness is so highly valued because it serves as a biological marker of youth and health—in a word, *fertility*.

Buss (1995) admits that women also have faced the problem of identifying fertile mates. Although men's age is not linked to their fertility in the way women's is, men's fertility *is* associated with their overall health. Men's attractiveness could, therefore, serve as a guide for women in mate selection because of what it says about health (e.g., Gangestad & Simpson, 2000). Also, if we consider what resources might have been of value in the days of early humans (e.g., physical protection, hunting), we could argue that men's appearance could tell women something about their resources. Aspects of men's bodily appearance and skill (e.g., muscularity, strength, and athleticism) might have been reliable clues that they would be good protectors and providers (Wade, 2000). Still, the prevailing evolutionary perspective holds that women's attractiveness plays a more important role in mate selection than men's does, and this is proposed as a natural explanation for our greater emphasis on female beauty and bodies than on male beauty and bodies.

Biology and Beauty Trends

The evolutionary story told by Buss and Schmitt has certain logic to it, but it raises some questions as well. For example, if we focus on women's physical attractiveness purely because beauty indicates health and fertility, how is it that ideal standards of female beauty change with the decades and typically require modification of the natural female form? Surely, it isn't the case that in North America the full-figured, corseted shape was fertile in the late 19th century and the 1950s; the slender and boyish build, fertile in the 1920s and again in the 1960s; and the tall, thin physique with broad shoulders and breast implants, fertile today. In fact, some corsets damaged women's internal organs, thinness is associated with low fertility, and silicone breast implants have been suspected of causing various health problems, including immune system disorders and chronic fatigue.

The fickleness of fashion seems inconsistent with biologically based preferences, but most modifications that women make to their appearance do accentuate the characteristics that Buss and others say are fertility cues (e.g., makeup can make the skin look clearer, the eyes appear brighter, and the lips seem fuller). Even practices that may threaten women's reproductive health (e.g., wearing corsets, getting breast implants) may increase women's attractiveness in that they exaggerate secondary sex characteristics.

Still, across cultures and history we can find many beautifying practices that seem to have no apparent link to biology. For example, the long-neck women in the

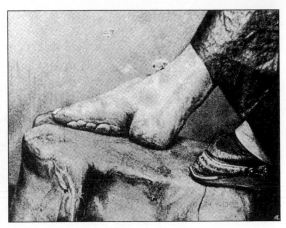

FIGURE 7.1
Beautifying practices with no apparent link to women's fertility.

Karen-Padaung tribes of Thailand wear spiral brass rings around their necks, beginning at about age 5 and increasing in length each year for several years thereafter. The result is that their collarbones are forced downward and they become dependent on the rings for support. Another practice that lasted for eight centuries in China, ending in the early 20th, was binding female feet beginning in childhood to create a 3-to-4-inch ideal "lotus foot" by adulthood (Wang, 2000).

Many physical modifications to women and men across cultures are made in pursuit of a beauty ideal, but they often are also intended to communicate something else about the person, such as group membership, role or status in a community, or gender.

Constructing Gender through Female Bodies

As discussed in Chapter 2, gender is socially constructed through our actions, our roles, our verbal and nonverbal language, and our cognitive processes. Gender is also socially constructed through physical appearance. That is, femininity and masculinity are expressed through clothing, hairstyle, and so forth; but the burden of gender construction is not equally borne by male and female bodies in our culture. By far, the majority of gender construction in contemporary industrialized cultures takes place through women's appearance. Women's appearance may be biologically significant because it hints at fertility status, but it is also culturally salient because of what it communicates about gender.

Consider a hypothetical scenario: Suppose a group of women and men were banished to the wilderness for several months with no mirrors, razors, grooming products, or labor-saving devices (and no reality-television crew lurking in the trees). Would the group come back to our civilization looking more feminine or more masculine? Well, let's see; they'd be hairier, dirtier, stronger smelling, more muscular. Doesn't sound much like our culture's idea of femininity. To us, more physically natural means more masculine; more groomed, scented, modified, and adorned means more feminine. In her book, *Beauty Bound*, clinical psychologist Rita Freedman (1986) put it this way:

> Not only is a woman socialized to act differently than a normal adult, but to look different as well—more like a female than a person. Her lips must be redder, lashes longer, waist smaller, skin smoother. . . . props and paint accentuate gender differences, creating some that have no basis in nature (blue eyelids) and exaggerating others that are minimal (hairless legs). Shape of brows, contour of feet, style of hair become potent substitutes for natural sex differences. (pp. 30, 53)

Clothing and accessories also communicate femininity. Overalls are gender-neutral, but if they have ruffles on them, they are feminine. Plain tie shoes are gender-neutral, but add a high heel and they are feminine. T-shirts are gender-neutral, but with a deeply scooped neck and cap sleeves, they are feminine. Jeans are gender-neutral, but if they are low-cut and leave the hips exposed, they are feminine. Skirts and dresses are feminine. Anything with bows or lace is feminine. Hair ornaments are strictly for the girls. In contrast, our culture no longer designates any clothing or accessories as clear signals of masculinity, except, perhaps, the jock strap.

Both femininity and masculinity are performances to some extent, but a feminine appearance is more of a put-on than a masculine appearance. Consider the case of male entertainers who impersonate women. Because femininity is a social construction, many female impersonators are successful at assuming an ideal feminine appearance (Tewksbury, 1994)—better than many real women I know. For example, the 1992 Miramax film *The Crying Game* created quite a buzz among moviegoers because of a shocking scene in which a very attractive and feminine woman character turns out to be a man. The Oscar-nominated role was artfully performed by female impersonator Jaye Davidson and fooled many viewers who found themselves slack-jawed when Davidson's sexual identity was revealed. Certainly, not all men could successfully feminize

FIGURE 7.2
As female impersonators demonstrate, a feminine appearance is largely constructed.

their appearance enough to pass as women, but female impersonators do have a more extensive bag of tricks than male impersonators.

Through alteration and adornment, women's bodies display femininity. In the process of assuming a feminine persona, a woman's body becomes more than her means of interaction with the material world; it becomes a visible marker serving to maintain socially constructed gender differences and gender roles. Because natural reproduction requires a functional male and a functional female, being able to distinguish between these two sexes is important, and secondary sex characteristics help us to do so. The gendered cues that we add to our naturally sex-differentiated appearances presumably facilitate this sorting out of the sexes, but a natural need to make distinctions does not necessitate that the bulk of differentiation must take place through female appearance. That *women's* bodies primarily serve as the canvas on which we paint gender may have to do with power.

Power and Objectification: The Male Gaze

British author Virginia Woolf (1929) wrote a humorous and telling account of an excursion she made to the British Museum library to research *women*,

> [I] opened a volume of the catalogue, and . . . . . the five dots here indicate five separate minutes of stupefaction, wonder and bewilderment. Have you any notion how many books are written about women in the course of one year? Have you any notion how many are written by men? Are you aware that you are, perhaps, the most discussed animal in the universe? . . . Why are women, judging from this catalogue, so much more interesting to men than men are to women? (p. 26–27, 29)

Woolf was amazed by the abundance of descriptions, analyses, opinions, and criticisms of women generated by male scholars and laypersons. She found no parallel collection of texts dissecting men from the point of view of women authors. Men were the observers; women the observed. The phenomenon of women being the ones observed, on display, or under scrutiny has been labeled the **male gaze**.

Cultural critic John Berger popularized the idea of the male gaze in his 1972 book and British television series, *Ways of Seeing*. In his comparison of nudes in European art to contemporary media images of women, he found many similarities. Nude women are usually pictured alone (with no male present), displaying a posture and facial expression that are intended to be sexually inviting, passive and nonthreatening to the viewer. Before the 20th century, artists felt compelled to represent nude women as mythological or allegorical figures because representations of *real* nude women were deemed morally unacceptable. Contemporary images of women are much more frankly sexual and, as Berger points out, the assumed spectator is always male. It is men's greater social power that positions them as the surveyors of women, according to Berger, and women's status as the surveyed requires them to be vigilantly preoccupied with how they appear to others. As Berger put it, "*[M]en act* and *women appear*. Men look at women. Women watch themselves being looked at" (p. 47). Recent psychological theory and research on women's self-objectification consistent with this idea is discussed later in this chapter.

The (heterosexual) male gaze is so pervasive in our popular culture that it may go unnoticed until it is challenged. The first time I became acutely aware of the male gaze—or rather the absence of a heterosexual female gaze—was when I saw the 1991 film *Thelma & Louise*. The film includes a scene between Brad Pitt and Geena Davis during which the camera pans Pitt's body so the viewer can take it all in. Wow! I was stunned. I realized that in decades of viewing hundreds of television programs and movies in which the camera zoomed in on, or seductively scanned over, body parts, *not once* had that body been male. How many times had the camera forced me to scrutinize a woman's curves, or watch her provocatively disrobe, or spy on her through a hole in the locker room wall? How many times had I watched scenes that featured gratuitous female nudity in the presence of a clothed or covered male? Why did the camera dictate that the only eyes I would see through would be those of a heterosexual male spectator?

Objectification in Popular Culture

Every day we gaze upon objectified images of women—women as objects of ideal beauty, women as sex objects, and women literally transformed into objects. To understand how pervasive objectified images of women are, it is worth considering examples of each of these forms of objectification in some detail. All the while, keep in mind the fact that Western popular culture is increasingly having a worldwide impact.

Beauty Images and Myths

Many authors have written books about the ubiquitous ideal of feminine beauty in Western popular culture. Some have theorized about the political underpinnings of our culture's commercialization of feminine beauty and how this "beauty system" (MacCannell & MacCannell, 1987) or "beauty myth" (Wolf, 1991) reinforces men's dominant status and sustains women's lesser status as objects on display.

In our culture, women and men have learned to equate female beauty with an artificial and rigorously maintained appearance. Consider the ever-present and pervasive beauty propaganda found in advertisements and other media (e.g., Kilbourne, 1999). Feminine beauty ideals from the early 19th century to the 20th include such disparate ideals as the boyish flapper and the buxom blonde a la Marilyn Monroe. The wide range of body sizes and shapes make clear how feminine beauty ideals have passed in and out of fashion (Banner, 1983). Consistent across the ideals, however, is the fact that none were attainable without alterations of women's natural appearance through special diets, clothing, makeup, or hairstyles. Whatever the current ideal, women learn from beauty merchandisers how they fall short of it and what products will remedy their inadequacy. For example, how many products have you seen to treat cellulite? Did you know that the vast majority of women have cellulite and that the term was first introduced in the United States by *Vogue* magazine in 1973 (Wolf, 1991)?

FIGURE 7.3

Source: For Better or For Worse Copyright © 1997 Lynn Johnston Productions. Distributed by Universal Press Syndicate. Reprinted with permission. All rights reserved.

Importantly, the beauty images that surround us every day not only require alteration of a natural appearance, but most are completely unrealistic. For years, the beauty and fashion industries have employed heavy makeup, deceptive clothing, artful lighting, careful posing of models, and photo retouching to create idealized images. The December 1990 cover of *Esquire* featured a headshot of actress Michelle Pfeiffer accompanied by the text, "What Michelle Pfeiffer needs . . ." When readers turned to the article, they found another photo and the rest of the caption, "is absolutely nothing." The irony of this headline was revealed in a memo from a photo lab that detailed the more than $5,000 worth of retouching that Pfeiffer's photo required, including softening facial lines, trimming her chin, and adding hair on the top of her head (Kilbourne, 2002).

More recently, actress Jamie Lee Curtis, publicly celebrated for her perfect body, exposed the techniques used in the creation of artificial beauty images when she posed at age 43 for *More* magazine with and without their application. In the natural shot, Curtis has flat hair, no makeup, and is wearing lycra shorts and a sports

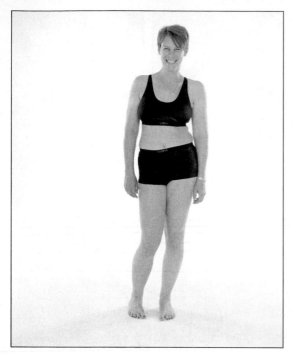

The natural Jamie.

The "glam" Jamie.

bra that reveal her bulging waist and less-than-sculpted legs; in other words, she looks quite ordinary. In the photo that was taken after a dozen experts worked on her for three hours, she looks like her familiar glamorous self. (When one of my Psychology of Women students shared this article with some male friends, they were incredulous. One of them exclaimed, "No way is that her! They put her head on another woman's body!" He was referring to the realistic photo.)

In the last 10 years, technology in photo retouching has advanced a tremendous amount. Now even amateur photographers can create completely false images. What this means for the beauty industry is that advertisers need not even use real women to sell products; instead they can create ideal beauty through seamless computer integration of features from several different imperfect models (Kilbourne, 2002), digital distortion of real images, or total electronic fabrication. In 2003, a group of Italian visionaries launched the first-ever virtual beauty contest, dubbed Miss Digital World, open only to virtual images of women created by graphic designers (Zampano, 2003). The creator of the contest claims that every age has its ideal of beauty and Miss Digital World is a search for the contemporary ideal. No real women look like the objects of beauty created through technology, not even the models whose parts inspire them.

Box 7.1 ∾

Hooters at the Mall of America

Before the Mall of America opened in Minnesota in 1992, planners announced that one of the merchants it would house was Hooters restaurant, a chain that originated in Florida in 1983. Of course, the name does not refer to vocalizations made by the owl in the company's logo; instead it makes reference to the slang term for breasts (and for those who miss the double entendre, the OO in the name looks suspiciously familiar). The restaurant is famous for its waitresses, the buxom "Hooters Girls," who dress in tight tank tops and skimpy orange shorts. On its Web site, the company explains,

> The element of female sex appeal is prevalent in the restaurants, and the company believes the Hooters Girl is as socially acceptable as a Dallas Cowboy cheerleader, Sports Illustrated swimsuit model, or Radio City Rockette.

Online and at the restaurant locations, customers can purchase merchandise, including Hooters Girls calendars, videos of Hooters Girls poolside, and T-shirts (including one for infants that reads "Life Begins at Hooters"). The company publishes its own magazine and has a television presence in the form of sports sponsorship and the Hooters swimsuit pageant.

When a local woman heard the news that the mall, a high-profile symbol of American consumer culture, would house Hooters, she was outraged and organized a citizen activist group that took on as its first project a boycott of the mall. Although the Give Hooters the Boot campaign was ultimately unsuccessful at keeping the restaurant out of the mall (or at making much of a dent in consumer enthusiasm for the place), it sent a strong message opposing sexual objectification of women's bodies in a context that was intended to be mainstream and have family appeal. Hooters is still thriving at the mall, just a short stroll away from the 14-screen movie theatre, and it is highly visible from many of the rides at Camp Snoopy, the indoor children's theme park.

Women's Bodies as Sexual Entertainment

"Sex sells," is the cliché attributed to advertisers who insist on using bodies to sell everything, even when the product has nothing to do with bodies (and sometimes in a strangely paradoxical way, such as Abercrombie and Fitch using nude bodies to sell clothing). As described in Chapter 3, most often women's bodies and sex appeal are used in advertising, and sometimes the women's bodies themselves are being sold. One need not venture into the world of adult entertainment to find women's bodies objectified for consumption.

Popular films and television shows emphasize women's bodies more than men's, and entire shows dedicated to women's bodies as sexually appealing entertainment are commonplace. Beauty pageants such as the relatively prim Miss America pageant and the more sexually charged Miss Universe competition have been televised regularly since Miss America hit the airwaves in 1954. Today, in addition to numerous derivative beauty pageants on broadcast and cable television, we have fitness competitions, swimsuit specials, and the Victoria's Secret Fashion Show (which debuted in 2001 on ABC, accompanied by a TV-14 warning to parents).

Magazine racks at grocery stores are filled with women's magazines with idealized beauty images of women gracing the covers. One recent content analysis found messages about women's bodily appearance on the covers of 78 percent of popular women's magazines they reviewed—only one-third of which were beauty or fashion magazines (Malkin, Wornian, & Chrisler, 1999). Alongside women's magazines, a relatively new genre of periodicals for men has emerged in the last few years, including titles such as *Maxim, Stuff, Razor,* and *FHM (For Him Magazine).* Filled with articles about celebrities, sports, health, and various lifestyle issues, these magazines invariably feature a scantily clad, sexually posed woman on the cover—and more inside. These magazines, and old standbys such as *Esquire* and the *Sports Illustrated* swimsuit issue, define women as one of many entertaining pastimes available to men.

The tradition of sexually objectifying individual women in popular entertainment has a long history; more recently, a new trend has made its way from the world of adult entertainment to Hollywood movies, television shows, and advertising: the sexual objectification of women in pairs. Portrayals of women engaged in same-sex liaisons has long been a popular theme in pornography for heterosexual men; for example, the December 2003 issue of *Playboy* featured twin sisters suggestively soaping each other in the shower. This theme, colloquially referred to as **faux lesbianism,** has made an appearance in recent ads for Gucci, Versace, Miu Miu, and other fashion manufacturers. The 2003 film *Anger Management* featured frequent sexual innuendo and behavior between two women characters who were supposed to be porn stars. Characters on the primetime television show *Friends* have made references to the appeal of girl-on-girl action. In a recent publicity portrait, former child stars and twin sisters Mary-Kate and Ashley Olsen posed with their legs intertwined, one of them mouthing the strand of pearls around the other's neck. Singers Madonna and Britney Spears made international news when they shared a theatrically staged open-mouthed kiss on the 2003 MTV Video Music Awards show. Women's sexual objectification is not about women expressing their own sexual desires; it is about women's bodies presented as sexually alluring commodities for heterosexual men. To date, there is no published psychological research on how these instances of paired objectification may prime sex stereotypes and/or affect perceptions of women's sexuality.

Distortion and Dehumanization

We are so accustomed to bodily objectification of women in popular culture that we may not notice when a representation of a woman's body has been altered in order to not even resemble a human being. We may also fail to notice cases in which women are objectified indirectly, without the involvement of a real human being. Advertisers routinely turn women's bodies or body parts into objects, but we rarely, if ever, see men's torsos as bottles of alcohol or men's legs as blades on a pair of

FIGURE 7.4a
Women's bodies dehumanized and distorted.

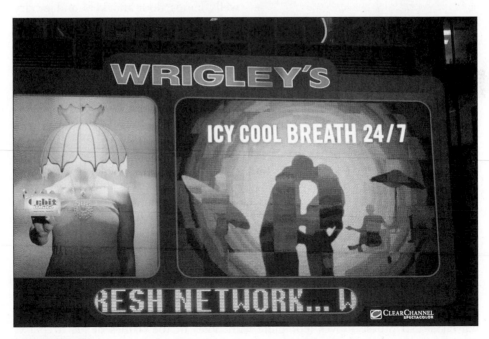

FIGURE 7.4b

FIGURE 7.4c

scissors (Kilbourne, 1999). Mirrored sexualized silhouettes of women figure prominently on the mud flaps of many a semi-truck. Cigarette lighters in the shape of women's bodies with breasts that light up when flicked are available at gas stations. Should they be so inclined, golfers can opt for Naked Lady tees. The original Barbie doll was inspired by a German novelty doll produced for adult men who put her on their dashboards or played with her at bars (Lord, 1994).

The transformation of women's bodies into objects is not a new phenomenon. The Art Nouveau period of design in the United States and Europe (circa 1890–1914) was characterized by extravagant representations of erotic decadence. This eroticism was communicated largely through the use of female nudes, which adorned, or served as, mundane objects such as candle holders, ashtrays, drawer pulls, inkwells, lamps, door knockers, and jewelry (Wood, 2000). Like today's female torso cigarette lighter, these objects required the user to hold or fondle the woman-object during routine use.

Turning women's bodies into objects is not a new activity; something that *is* relatively new is the objectification of *virtual* women. Since the early days of animation some seven decades ago, artists have given life to caricatures of women and female creatures (e.g., Minnie Mouse) and a few of these early characters were intended to be sex objects (e.g., Betty Boop). Over time, however, the sexualization of female cartoon characters has become commonplace. Compare Disney's *Snow White*, produced in 1937, with *The Little Mermaid*, produced in 1989, and the contrast is stark. Snow White's dress modestly covers her child like figure, while the hourglass-shaped mermaid is all but busting out of her shell-bra—and in one scene bursts out of the water, nude and in silhouette, bearing more than a slight resemblance to the aforementioned mud-flap women. In the G-rated Disney feature *The Hunchback of Notre Dame*, Judge Frollo agonizes over his sexual desire for the Gypsy woman Esmerelda while he imagines her performing a dance comprising classic striptease moves (complete with pole) in the flames of his fireplace. These animated ingénues are illustrated to be sexually appealing to real men. As the cartoon character Jessica Rabbit purred (in the husky voice of Kathleen Turner) to live actor Bob Hoskins in *Who Framed Roger Rabbit*, "I'm not bad. I'm just drawn that way."

Animated computer games such as *Tomb Raider* are marketed to adolescent boys and young men and commonly include hypersexualized representations of women. Actress Angelina Jolie, widely celebrated for her natural beauty, was required to wear foam breasts in the film adaptations of the "Tomb Raider" game because her human proportions could not measure up to the computerized standards. Recent ads for Steve Madden footwear feature photographs of models that have been digitally distorted to create extra-curvy minibodies with tiny waists and overly large heads, much like the currently popular Bratz dolls—and like the Bratz dolls, these Steve Madden models have grotesquely infantilized faces with wide foreheads, huge eyes, and small chins.

How does it impact women to be surrounded by idealized, sexualized, distorted, and dehumanized versions of themselves? How are women affected psychologically, behaviorally, and socially by constant messages about how important it is for them to be beautiful and how much they must modify their natural selves to be so? How are women's perceptions of their bodies shaped by their objectified status? How does the objectification of women's bodies affect their social interactions? Next, I explore the consequences of women's objectification.

Consequences of Objectification for Girls and Women

For several decades researchers have studied the impact of physical attractiveness in social interaction and its role in the self-concept. These two perspectives on physical attractiveness represent "the view from the outside" and the "view from the inside" (Cash, 1990). To understand women's experience as inhabitants of objectified bodies, it is important for us to consider both the inside and outside views, paying particular attention to gender-related differences that researchers have predicted and observed.

The Inside View: Body Image and Self-Esteem

The term ***body image*** refers to the mental picture we each have of our bodily appearance as well as the associated feelings we have about our perception of the size, shape, and attractiveness of our bodies (Dorian & Garfinkel, 2002). Many researchers have studied the link between body image and overall self-esteem and most have found that the link is stronger for women than it is for men.

Gender-Related Differences in Body Esteem

Women are more dissatisfied with their bodies than men are and, according to a recent meta-analysis, these differences are on the rise (Feingold & Mazzella, 1998). Women are more strongly invested in their physical appearance than men are, and there is evidence that women's heightened concern with their own appearance begins in childhood and extends across the lifespan (e.g., Murnen, Smolak, Mills, & Good, 2003).

Some researchers argue that men's dissatisfaction with their appearance has been underestimated. For example, in one study men reported as much dissatisfaction with their weight as women did; however, 55 percent of the men wanted to be heavier and 42 percent wanted to be lighter, whereas 93 percent of the women wanted to be lighter (Jacobi & Cash, 1994). As researchers take a closer look at men's body esteem, they are finding evidence that men do sometimes exhibit dissatisfaction with aspects of their bodies, such as muscularity and body size (e.g., Vartanian, Giant, & Passino, 2001), and these aspects are related to their self-esteem (Jacobi & Cash, 1994). Perhaps not surprisingly, the attributes about which men display insecurity are the same ones that could be linked to resources in the Pleistocene, as discussed earlier, and they also correspond to a recent increase in muscularity in idealized media images of men (Wade, 2000; Leit, Pope, & Gray, 2001). Still, body esteem is not as strongly related to overall self-esteem in men as it is in women, and men do not feel as negatively about their bodies as women do.

Effects of Media Images on Self-Esteem and Body Image

Beauty advertising aimed at women may lower self-esteem and body image. Most research on the impact of idealized beauty images on women's self-concepts has involved experiments of the same general form: Women are exposed to media images of attractive models and are then asked to report on their self-esteem, perceptions of their own attractiveness, and mood. In general, these studies find that exposure

FIGURE 7.5
Beauty ads contain more than pictures.

to ideal beauty images has negative effects on women's body satisfaction (e.g., Groesz, Levine, & Murnen, 2002), leads to distortion in self-perception of body size (e.g., Hamilton & Waller, 1993), and increases negative mood (e.g., Pinhas, Toner, Ali, Garfinkel, & Stuckless, 1999).

Most researchers have theorized that the negative effects of ideal images are the result of the *social comparison* process (Cattarin, Thompson, Thomas, and Williams, 2000). That is, idealized beauty images make women feel badly because their own appearance suffers by comparison. But there may be more going on than social comparison. Women usually encounter beauty images in advertisements for beauty products or articles in beauty magazines, but researchers have routinely presented the images without their original context. In doing so, they have overlooked the messages that typically accompany beauty images. These messages remind women that beauty is an important part of femininity, that beauty matters across all situations, that beauty is what matters most in women, and that women's beauty requires altering the natural body. Perhaps ideal images presented in the laboratory negatively impact women not merely because they set a high standard of comparison, but also because they serve as visual reminders of these messages and of women's objectified status.

A recent study offers support for the idea that women's bad feelings after viewing beauty images are not merely due to deciding, "She's got better legs than I do!" Adolescent women first viewed commercials related to female appearance and then completed measures of appearance schematicity, mood, body satisfaction, and self-confidence (Hargreaves & Tiggemann, 2002). *Appearance schematicity* refers to the belief that appearance is a very important part of the self and is a significant determinant of life outcomes (Cash & Labarge, 1996). In this study, appearance schematicity levels were higher in the women who had viewed the commercials than in the women who had not, whereas mood, body satisfaction, and self-confidence were all lower. The researchers suggested that beauty advertising temporarily heightens women's feelings about the importance of attractiveness and it is this heightened concern that is partially responsible for its negative effect on body satisfaction. Consistent with this explanation, individual differences in pre-existing appearance schematicity among the women participants moderated the impact of the images such that participants who were high in appearance schematicity at the outset were more susceptible to the negative effects.

In contrast to these results, some studies on women's responses to idealized images have found no effects or *positive* effects. Why do some women respond negatively to beauty images while others respond positively or with indifference? One factor that seems to matter is a woman's level of body dissatisfaction at the outset. Women who are more dissatisfied with their bodies respond more negatively to ideal images in experiments and in real life (e.g., Posavac, Posavac, & Posavac, 1998; Stice, Spangler, & Agras, 2001). So, the next question is why are some women more dissatisfied with their bodies in the first place?

One factor associated with body satisfaction is a woman's degree of gender typing. Women who are highly feminine report more body dissatisfaction than women who describe themselves as possessing more masculine characteristics, perhaps because appearance is central to the display of femininity (Forbes, Adams-Curtis, Rade, & Jaberg, 2001). Because attractiveness is based on a heterosexual norm, lesbian women might be expected to exhibit less body dissatisfaction than hetero-sexual women. Research comparing the body images of lesbian and heterosexual women is mixed. Some studies suggest that being involved in a lesbian social net-work in which beauty is defined differently than in mainstream culture may act as a buffer against the cultural influences that raise women's dissatisfaction with their bodies (Owens, Hughes, & Owens-Nicholson, 2003). Still, several studies have found that lesbian women, like heterosexual women, feel pressure to be thin (Cogan, 1999). Also like heterosexual women, lesbian and bisexual women who identify themselves as feminine, rather than masculine or androgynous, are the least satisfied with their bodies (Ludwig & Brownell, 1999).

Women's individual differences in body dissatisfaction also appear to be related to race, ethnicity, and culture. Researchers have made a variety of ethnic and cross-cultural comparisons of women's body esteem. African American women report higher levels of body esteem and lower levels of weight concern compared to Cau-casian American women, and their overall self-esteem is less impacted by their body esteem than it is in White women (e.g., Molloy & Herzberger, 1998; Henriques & Calhoun, 1999). The relatively higher level of body satisfaction displayed by African American women is typically attributed to the fact that fuller figures are val-ued as signs of beauty, status, and health in African communities (Ofosu, Lafreniere, & Senn, 1998). Franzoi & Chang (2002) found higher levels of body esteem in their Hmong women participants than in their Caucasian women participants, while Kowner (2002) found lower levels of body esteem among Japanese women com-pared to American women.

As Western media images of women spread across the globe, we may see more consistency in beauty ideals—and perhaps more consistency in women's body dis-satisfaction. Fashion magazines sold in Tibet these days have white European mod-els on the cover (Etcoff, 1999). In China, there is a massive marketing of cosmetics to help women create a Westernized appearance (Johansson, 2001). Interviews with Asian American women reveal that some of them have eyelid surgery because they believe that European-looking eyes appear more attractive and intelligent (Kaw, 1994).

Positive Effects of Beauty Images

A few studies have found that exposure to idealized beauty images leads to tempo-rary *increases* in body satisfaction among women. Both individual characteristics and situational context seem to be important in determining whether the exposure to beauty images is positive or negative.

In one study, ideal beauty images were shown to participants who were dieters or nondieters. After viewing the images, the dieters rated their current body sizes as smaller (more ideal in their minds) and were less inhibited about eating when given the opportunity. The body-image bolstering effect of the beauty images was en-hanced when researchers increased participants' beliefs that thinness is attainable. Apparently, the images temporarily enhanced dieters' perceptions that an ideal body was within their reach (Mills, Polivy, Herman, & Tiggemann, 2002).

Another study asked whether men's reaction to beauty images affects women. Women viewed idealized thin images with men present. The men either made brief positive comments about a few of the images or were silent. When men were present but silent, women's weight-related esteem was negatively impacted by the images; but, when men said "Nice," "Alright," and "Yeah," in response to the images, women showed *increases* in weight-related esteem. The researchers believe this happened because the women consciously put their defenses up when they overheard the men's comments, instead of letting the whole situation get them down (Henderson-King, Henderson-King, & Hoffman, 2001).

Are Media Beauty Images Really Ideal?

Analyses of *Playboy* centerfolds and fashion models document that since the 1960s the North American image of ideal female beauty has become increasingly thinner, so much so that many current models are thin enough to meet the weight criteria for anorexia (Garner, Garfinkel, Schwartz, & Thompson, 1980; Owen & Laurel-Seller, 2000). At the same time, body sizes of real women in the United States are on the increase (Spitzer, Henderson, & Zivian, 1999). As the gap between idealized media images and population norms increases, preferences regarding women's body size may change—but in what direction?

Researchers found an interesting pattern of results when they asked college-aged women and men to select their own and each other's ideals from a set of increasingly heavy silhouettes. Women indicated that their own ideal was thinner than their current body size. Men's ideal was the same as their self-perceived current body size. Both women and men misperceived what the other sex finds attractive: Men thought women prefer larger men than they do, and *women thought men prefer thinner women than they do* (Fallon & Rozin, 1985). Though this study was done two decades ago, more recent studies have replicated the finding (e.g., Demarest & Allen, 2000). It seems that the so-called ideal images of women—the extra-slender ones at least—may not reflect heterosexual men's actual preferences. Research by evolutionary psychologists on men's taste in women's figures is consistent with this idea. Men show a preference for a sexually mature shape with a waist-to-hip ratio of 0.7 or less; the higher the ratio, the more straight the shape (Singh & Young, 1995; Streeter & McBurney, 2003). In other words, men prefer curves. And, of course, women's curvy shapes come from body fat—or from surgical intervention. Studies on the thin media ideal have neglected to consider the idealized *proportions* of this ideal. Yes, the ideal is increasingly slim, yet it is still curvaceous. The ideal has thin arms, thin thighs, and a flat abdomen, but large breasts and a shapely rear. It is not an ideal promoting overall low body fat so much as it is an ideal about the most aesthetically strategic distribution of body fat on a slender frame. In a sample of college students, both women's and men's level of exposure to ideal images on television was correlated with their beliefs about the ideal bust, waist, and hip sizes for women. And both men and women who had more exposure to ideal images on television showed higher levels of approval for women's use of cosmetic surgeries such as breast augmentation and liposuction (Harrison, 2003).

The Outside-In View: Self-Objectification

According to psychologists Barbara Frederickson and Tomi-Ann Roberts (1997), girls and women are socialized to internalize an observer's perspective as a primary view of their physical selves. This perspective on self can lead to habitual body monitoring, which, in turn, can increase women's opportunities for shame and anxiety, reduce opportunities for peak motivational states, and diminish awareness of internal bodily states. (p. 1)

Frederickson and Roberts's *objectification theory* explains that in a sexually objectifying culture, girls and women learn to perceive themselves as objects and to adopt an observer's perspective on their own bodies. This idea is not original to Frederickson and Roberts—many writers and researchers before them have described a similar split in women's sense of self (e.g., Beauvoir, 1952; Berger, 1972; McKinley & Hyde, 1996), but objectification theory is important because it delineates the psychological and behavioral consequences of internalizing an objectified sense of self.

Self-objectification, they say, involves a habitual and chronic preoccupation with self-surveillance that disrupts a woman's connection to her subjective experiences and divides her attention. A woman's continual body monitoring not only creates a sort of splitting of self—between the subjective self and the self as object—but it also claims some proportion of her cognitive resources and interrupts her thoughts with feelings of concern about her appearance. Frederickson and Roberts do not think that women are naturally vain or self-absorbed. Instead they suggest that women *learn* to be vigilant about their appearance, a practical strategy in a culture in which women's appearance may significantly affect their life outcomes.

When women engage in habitual body monitoring, their subjective experience is disrupted in specific emotional and behavioral ways. For example, Fredrickson and Roberts suggest that research on gender-linked differences in the experience of *shame* can be understood in terms of self-objectification: The constant comparisons made between real women and ideal beauty images—both by women themselves and by others—may explain why women feel ashamed more often than men. Where is your attention focused when you feel ashamed? Do you feel like you want to hide or disappear? When we experience shame, our thoughts turn inward and our social skills suffer (Lewis, 1992). Frederickson and Roberts also suggest that experiences of objectification, or merely the concern that one's appearance will be scrutinized, lead to *anxiety*—not only anxiety about being attractive enough, but also anxiety about being too attractive and thereby inviting sexual harassment or assault.

These theorists suggest that girls' and women's behaviors are also affected by self-objectification because of how it interferes with motivation and redirects attention. Instead of living *in* their bodies, pursuing mental and physical activities in a purely subjective manner, girls and women find themselves self-consciously reminded of how they *appear* while they do these activities. Girls may become hesitant about doing sports, for example, because of concerns of appearing unattractive or unfeminine or in a compromising body position (Young, 1990). In one study of college women, approximately a third reported being preoccupied with concerns about their bodily appearance during sexual intimacy (Wiederman, 2000). Instead of attending to, and responding to, their internal desires and inclinations in an uninhibited manner, girls and women may learn to tune out internal sensations (such as sexual desire and hunger) and censor the corresponding behaviors, thus becoming alienated from their physical selves.

Not only does self-objectification direct attention away from internal states, but it divides attention between self-surveillance and other mental tasks. We know from cognitive psychology that our mental resources are limited. We can only think about so many things at once. Frederickson and Roberts suggest that as long as women are devoting some of their mental resources to the emotional and cognitive processing associated with self-objectification, fewer resources will be available for other applications. In one remarkable study, these same researchers and their colleagues measured women's and men's performance on math problems after trying on a sweater or a swimsuit. They found that men's math performance was unaffected by the experimental manipulation while women's math performance suffered in the swimsuit condition, which temporarily heightened their self-objectification (Frederickson, Roberts, Noll, Quinn, & Twenge, 1998). This finding has theoretical implications for women's mental productivity in educational or workplace settings in which they are reminded of their objectified status by such cues as sexually harassing comments, girlie calendars, and so forth.

Beauty Maintenance

Self-objectification taps women's cognitive energies, and it also leads to behaviors that consume women's physical energies, time, and money. Self-surveillance and its

"Watch yourself--he had lunch at Hooters."

FIGURE 7.6

Source: Reproduced by special permission of *Playboy* magazine. Copyright © 2003 by *Playboy*.

associated concerns and anxieties may inspire women to devote considerable effort to maintaining themselves as attractive objects. The beauty industry in the United States flourished after the turn of the 20th century with the popularization of cosmetics for everyday use by respectable women (Peiss, 1998). Today, women in the United States spend more than $15 billion annually on cosmetics, hair care, and skin care (Kline and Company, 2003) and several billion more on surgical and non-surgical cosmetic procedures, in an attempt to improve or remedy aspects of their bodies that they perceive as flawed.

Shame about appearance and a sense of self-objectification can explain the antagonistic relationship that many women have with their own bodies. Women's language about their bodies is frequently hostile and combative in tone. When women talk about their bodies, it is as if they are talking about a rebellious subordinate that must be kept in check or an enemy that must be defeated. Women talk about "watching" their weight and "fighting" their fat. They "tame" their hair and "control" their tummies. They "conceal" parts of their faces. We do not flinch when a woman says she "hates" her butt, thighs, tummy, breasts, wrinkles, and so forth. When was the last time you heard a man say he hated any part of his body?

Women's self-loathing paves the way for beauty-maintenance behaviors that are actually self-destructive. Though lung cancer is a serious risk, women smoke to curb their appetites. Heedless of the risk of melanoma, women in the United States visit tanning salons. Elsewhere in the world, dangerous skin-lightening products are becoming more popular among women of color who aspire to attractiveness ideals that equate higher social status with whiter skin (Browne, 2004). Some of the treatments to which women subject their own bodies seem almost like inhumane torture if one imagines them being inflicted by another person. For example, women limit their food intake, depriving themselves of nutrients required for development and functioning. They take dangerous drugs and supplements to alter their natural appetite and metabolism. They rip off or pluck out their body hairs. They use carcinogenic chemicals to color their hair (Zheng, 2004). They force their feet into high-heeled shoes that cause back and foot problems. They go under the scalpel to add, remove, or modify body parts. In a recent trend, some women are reportedly having toes surgically shortened to fit into extremely narrow-toed stiletto-heeled shoes (Harris, 2003).

The Outside View: Women's Bodies in Social Interaction

It may seem obvious that looks matter in social interaction, but psychologists did not get around to studying this until the 1960s. The topic was neglected partly because researchers did not want to find out that attractive people have an advantage in society (after all, we like to believe that "beauty is only skin deep" and we "can't judge a book by its cover"). Researchers were also hesitant to tackle it because they believed it was not possible to define *attractive* in a scientifically rigorous way; different people have different tastes and "beauty is in the eye of the beholder," right? Finally, this topic, like many others, may have been overlooked because the majority of researchers were men, and as men they likely did not feel the impact of their own physical attractiveness as intimately and powerfully as women do. Once a few pioneering social psychologists determined that physical attractiveness could and should be studied, a new research area was launched.

Since that time, many studies have explored the impact of physical attractiveness on social outcomes. More of these studies have focused on the impact of women's physical attractiveness than on the impact of men's attractiveness. In some cases, the researchers had a theoretical justification for emphasizing women's attractiveness and ignoring men's, but in most cases the researchers' assumption that only women's attractiveness matters was implied by their research designs. For example, Sigall and Aronson (1969) tested how an evaluator's attractiveness would affect receptivity to the evaluator's criticism by having an unattractive or attractive *woman* praise or criticize *male* participants; Dermer and Thiel (1975) looked only at the effects of *female* participants' attractiveness on their attributions about *women* of varying attractiveness; Cash, Kehr, Polyson, and Freeman (1977) studied the connection between physical attractiveness and attributions of psychological disturbance using only *female* targets—the examples could go on and on, and the bias continues to the present day.

Is there evidence, then, that women's attractiveness matters more in social interaction than men's does? Yes. For example, an early study found that when judging the quality of an essay ostensibly written by a woman, male perceivers rated the same essay higher when the attached author photo was attractive than when the author appeared unattractive (Kaplan, 1978). Female participants actually showed the opposite tendency; that is, they were more critical of the attractive woman's essay than they were of the unattractive woman's essay. When the author was a man, neither men's nor women's ratings were affected by the attractiveness of the author. The attractiveness of the male author did not play a discernible role in the judgment process; the attractiveness of the female author, however, cast a shadow (positive in the eyes of male perceivers; negative in the eyes of female perceivers) over her work. Social psychologists know that our culture promotes a stereotype that "what is beautiful is good" (Dion, Berscheid, & Walster, 1972), but in this study what is beautiful is good only if you are a woman perceived by a man; if you are woman perceived by another woman, what is beautiful is bad; if you are a man, beauty is neither good nor bad.

As this study suggests, in a culture where women are objectified, women's beauty matters—and it leads to both positive and negative outcomes. There are many other empirical investigations in which women's attractiveness has had stronger or more complex effects than men's attractiveness on others' perceptions. For example, this has been demonstrated in evaluations of job applicants (Pingitore, Dugoni, Tindale, & Spring, 1994), student evaluations of teachers (Buck & Tiene, 1989), therapists' evaluations of clients' self-concepts (Hobfall & Penner, 1978), and attributions of corporate success (Heilman & Stopeck, 1985). These studies have found that beauty is not always an advantage for women. Sometimes for women, beauty is a double bind.

Beauty as a Double-Bind

As described in Chapter 2 a double bind is a situation in which a person is "damned if she does and damned if she doesn't." It is easy to see how women are damned if they don't (have beauty or work on their appearance). It may not be so obvious how beauty can be a liability for women, but several studies from the early days of research on the "what is beautiful is good" stereotype suggest it can. These studies have found that attractive female targets were not perceived in a purely positive light.

In one study, attractive female targets were rated as more likely to be vain, snobbish, and poor marriage partners than less attractive female targets (Dermer & Thiel, 1975). In another, male and female targets were evaluated for managerial and nonmanagerial positions. Attractiveness was a consistent advantage for male candidates, but was only an advantage for women applying to a nonmanagerial position. The researchers hypothesized that more attractive women were perceived as more feminine and thus better suited for gender-stereotypical jobs (Heilman & Saruwatari, 1979). A different research team reported a similar pattern in perceptions of political candidates: Attractiveness was consistently advantageous for men, but more attractive women candidates were seen as more feminine and, thus, less qualified for the stereotypically masculine role of elected official (Sigelman, Thomas, Sigelman, & Ribich, 1986).

Another risk women run if they are attractive, or draw attention to their looks, is being the target of other women's animosity. Advertisements play upon women's beauty competition with slogans such as "Don't hate me because I'm beautiful"; "Maybe she's born with it—maybe it's Maybelline"; and "She's 40? Unbelievable!" When student researchers and I measured the impact of these ads on women, we found that women who had viewed beauty ads with competitive slogans reported significantly more hostility toward other women as compared to women who saw only the images with the slogans removed (Scott, Fenlon, Stevens, & Vaske, 2002). Women who are low in self-esteem and high in self-objectification are more hostile toward other women (Cowan, Neighbors, DeLaMoreaux, and Behnke, 2000; Cowan, *pers. comm.*). Teenage girls interviewed by Mimi Nichter (2000) admitted that when they saw a beautiful girl, they would label her a bitch and wanted to hurt, or even kill, her. They scrutinized potential rivals for any and all appearance flaws and were reluctant to form friendships with girls whom they perceived as perfect. It seems that the threat of beauty competition fuels women's hostile feelings toward other women (but you knew that already, didn't you?)

The F-Word: FAT

Obesity is stigmatized in our culture and negative attitudes toward overweight people are pervasive. Large people are ridiculed in movies and television shows, and this affects how we learn to view them from childhood (Cramer & Steinwert, 1998). Unlike other social prejudices that are now considered outdated, fat prejudice is rarely questioned or considered politically incorrect. Overweight women sometimes suffer socially and economically as a result of antifat attitudes. Being large is a liability for women in the workplace, where obesity may lead to bias in hiring (Pingatore, Dugoni, Tindale, & Spring, 1994) and is associated with self-reports of employment discrimination (Rothblum, Brand, Miller, & Oetjen, 1990), and lower pay (Maranto & Stenoien, 2000).

There are some differences between the fat attitudes of various populations in the United States. For example, obese African American women judge themselves and other women less harshly than Caucasian women do. In one study, White undergraduate women perceived large White women to be less intelligent, less attractive, and less potentially successful than their thinner counterparts, but Black undergraduate women did not exhibit this negative attitude toward large women, especially Black women (Hebl & Heatherton, 1998). This difference has been observed by other researchers as well and is typically attributed to cultural differences in standards of attractiveness and Black women's greater social distance from media beauty ideals that emphasize light skin and blonde hair.

Because of the pervasiveness of antifat attitudes, women who are at a healthy weight, or even underweight, report self-presentational concerns when eating in public—especially in front of men. In one set of studies, women participants had the opportunity to snack while interacting with a male confederate (Mori, Chaiken, & Pliner, 1987). In the first experiment, the researchers manipulated how desirable the male was as a potential romantic partner; women ate less in the presence of the desirable man, presumably to appear more attractive. In the second experiment, the researchers told the women participants that they had tested as either having highly feminine or highly masculine interests. Half of the women were then led to believe that a desirable male confederate had been informed of their interests. The women who believed that the man had been informed of their masculine interests ate less, presumably to appear more feminine. The teenage girls interviewed by Mimi Nichter (2000) reported eating less in front of boys because of their perception that girls should nibble, while guys could "inhale." They described how the boys would gossip about what they observed the girls eating, and would drop hints or make blatant remarks to the girls about how they should watch what they eat. Food ads often portray women's appetites and eating behaviors in moralistic terms. Women are given the message that it is bad or sinful to have an appetite—unless it is for diet foods, in which case it is possible to eat like a kid again (Kilbourne, 2002).

From Object to Subject: The Embodied Woman

This chapter has dealt with the countless ways that women's bodies are objectified and the consequences that objectification has for women. The next section discusses women's *embodied* experiences. The term *embodied* describes a sense of subjectivity instead of objectification, a feeling of being in one's body physically and psychologically, instead of monitoring one's body from the perspective of an observer. The next section explores how physical activities such as sports may promote women's sense of embodiment and discusses barriers that discourage girls' and women's participation in such activities.

The Contradiction between Femininity and Physical Activity

In *The Frailty Myth: Redefining the Physical Potential of Women and Girls,* Collette Dowling (2001) challenges the widely accepted notion that women are the weaker sex, instead blaming traditional feminine socialization for gender-related differences in strength and athleticism. Dowling describes how women's physical potential has been limited by laws and customs, dress codes and beauty standards, medical misinformation and misogyny. She suggests that a restrictive definition of *femininity*, rather than biology, makes women the weaker sex. Two centuries earlier, a similar opinion was expressed by British feminist foremother Mary Wollestonecraft in her 1792 treatise *A Vindication of the Rights of Woman*:

> [S]hould it be proved that woman is naturally weaker than man, whence does it follow that it is natural for her to labour to become still weaker than nature intended her to be? . . . To preserve personal beauty—woman's glory—the limbs and faculties are cramped . . . and the sedentary life which [women] are condemned to live, whilst boys frolic in the open air, weakens the muscles and relaxes the nerves. (pp. 127–128)

Are females the weaker sex? It is not easy to answer this question because the answer depends on what is being assessed. On average, men are taller than women, heavier than women, and have more muscle mass; so the average man can outperform the average woman in terms of absolute amount he can lift or distance he can jump; however, when ratios of body size to performance are calculated, some elite women outperform some elite men in sports such as sprinting and freestyle swimming (Dowling, 2000). Even when absolute performance is compared, without regard for differences in body size, women tend to outperform men in long-distance cold-water swims and endurance cycling (Dowling, 2000). Across cultures and time, women have been responsible for much, if not most, of the extremely physically challenging work of survival. We know women can be strong. Considering the disparity that still exists in training and skill development for girls compared to boys—and given the lessened physical demands of a modern lifestyle—we really cannot say at this point in history what women in our culture are capable of physically.

What we can say is that women's weakness relative to men has been highly prized among elite classes and in industrialized cultures for centuries. Only economically privileged women can afford to be weak. In the late 19th century United States, medical experts believed that intellectual activity and physical exertion would decrease women's fertility. Confinement to the home, and even to the bed, was commonly prescribed for middle- and upper-class women as a way to maximize their reproductive potential (and as a treatment to address psychological distress—more on this in Chapter 13). Women who wanted to challenge these restrictions did not have many options until the development of the safety bicycle in the 1880s—and even then, riding a bicycle wearing a corset and layers of skirts was no easy matter. Of course, weakness, passivity, and inactivity were not promoted for the women who served as domestic servants (nannies, maids, cooks) in the households of the idle middle- and upper-class ladies.

Since the modern Olympic Games were launched in 1896, amateur and professional athletics have increased in popularity worldwide. For the first 80 years of the growth of sports culture in the United States, the participation of girls and women was largely discouraged, significantly limited, or forbidden. It may be difficult for young women today to envision a world without women's sports and physical recreation, but it was only in 1972, with the passage of Title IX, that girls and women in the United States were assured equal opportunity to participate in sports in educational institutions.

Title IX is civil rights legislation that prohibits sex discrimination in access to educational programs at institutions that receive federal funds (which translates into most elementary and secondary schools and *all* colleges and universities). Title IX mandates equal athletic opportunities for the sexes. Schools must provide equal athletic scholarships, in terms of overall dollars, and participation slots that are in proportion to the gender makeup of the student body; however, schools need not provide identical athletic opportunities for females and males. Title IX has had a measurable positive impact on girls' sports participation, but, unfortunately, the majority of colleges and universities today are still noncompliant with it (Burton-Nelson, 2004).

Most girls and women living in the United States today have more personal freedom, more economic independence, more options in clothing and conduct, and many more opportunities to participate in organized sports and informal physical recreation than did the middle- and upper-class girls and women of the 18th and 19th centuries. Contemporary physiological research contradicts outdated beliefs about physical activity being detrimental to women's reproductive systems. Still, traditional feminine socialization continues to inhibit the development of physical skill and self-confidence in girls and women because its dominant message is that female bodies are valuable for their form, not their function.

When girls reach adolescence, their self-esteem may drop as they find their flesh figuratively and literally squeezed into the culture's rigid, narrow, and unrealistic beauty ideal (Pipher, 1994). The body that was once an ally in exploring and engaging the world now becomes an adversary that must be forced into submission to an artificial appearance standard. Girls learn that raw physicality is incompatible with the performance of femininity. It is unfeminine to have muscles, or to be strong, fast, tough, or better than boys. Engaging in sports that are dangerous, aggressive, and less aesthetically graceful than something like figure skating, is perceived to be particularly unfeminine (Koivula, 2001). See Box 7.2 for a description of the sport that best represents the contradiction between strength and a feminine appearance: women's competitive bodybuilding.

Girls' sports participation tends to dwindle as they grow older, and this is especially true for sports that are stereotypically masculine (Engel, 1994). Highly feminine gender-typed girls are more likely to drop out of masculine sports than less feminine girls are (Guillet, Sarrazin, & Fontayne, 2000). Girls who attend schools where physical education is taught in a co-ed context may be less likely to participate in sports than girls who take single-sex physical education classes (Engel, 1994). This may be due to heightened concerns about appearing feminine in the presence of boys, as well as concerns about being compared (unfavorably) with the boys.

We all are exposed to the message that girls as a group lack athletic skills whenever we hear the common insult leveled at boys (and girls) that they "throw [or run or play or hit] like a girl." Surrounded by discouraging messages like these, and lack of support for the development of their physical potential, many girls come to believe that they are the weaker sex. A meta-analysis of research on sex-related differences in physical self-confidence found an overall moderate effect size favoring males, particularly on masculine tasks (Lirgg, 1991). In part, this may have something to do with the way our culture defines *sports*.

Traditionally feminine physical activities, such as figure skating, are taken less seriously than traditionally masculine activities, such as football, though both are

BOX 7.2 ∾ Bev Francis and Rachel McLish in the 1980s

Bev Francis and Rachel McLish in the 1980s.

Women Pumping Iron: Barbells and Breast Implants

A decade after the film *Pumping Iron* (1976) introduced Arnold Schwarzenegger to the United States and legitimized competitive body building in the eyes of the American public, the filmmaker, George Butler, created a second documentary about the emerging sport of *women's* competitive body building. *Pumping Iron II: The Women* (1985) focuses on the quandary faced by judges of a competition in Las Vegas when they were faced with Bev Francis, an Australian power-lifter-turned-bodybuilder whose extreme success at the sport resulted in a physique that looked more prototypically male than female. Throughout the film, Francis is contrasted with the reigning woman bodybuilder of the time, Rachel McLish, whose petite build and pouty posturing fit very nicely into a conventional definition of femininity.

In one of the many scenes of judges arguing about how to evaluate women bodybuilders, Ben Weider, a founder of the International Federation of Body Builders (IFBB), opens a meeting with the following,

"We hope that this evening we can clear up the definite meaning, the analysis, of the word *femininity* and what you have to look for. This is an official IFBB analysis of the meaning of that word. What we're looking for is something that's right down the middle—a woman that has a certain amount of aesthetic femininity, yet has that muscle tone to show she's an athlete."

One of the judges retorts, "I object to being told that there is a certain point beyond which women

extremely physically demanding. Jumping rope is not considered a serious athletic pursuit unless the person jumping is a boxer working on his stamina and agility. Synchronized swimming and dance team are not taken as seriously, perhaps because the athletes wear makeup and glittery costumes and make their exertion look graceful and effortless. Women train for fitness competitions by engaging in heavy weightlifting and disciplined cardiovascular and flexibility routines, but these competitions appear more similar to beauty pageants or exotic dance revues than to prototypical sporting events.

Girls' feelings of athletic incompetence may also stem from the frustration they feel—consciously or unconsciously—when they must use equipment designed for males in settings that are male-dominated. When girls overcome the fear of getting too big and make their way to the weight room, they likely will find that the room

BOX 7.2   ~   Bev Francis and Rachel McLish in the 1980s (Concluded)

can't go in this sport. When you say they should look athletic but not too masculine, what does that mean exactly? I mean, it's as though the U.S. Ski Federation told women skiers that they could only ski so fast."

Weider responds, "We want what's best for our sport, and best for our girls. And we don't want to turn people off; we want to turn them on."

The judge replies, "We're in the 1980s, gentlemen. I mean, who are we to say what looks like a woman and what doesn't . . . The fact is that this is a watershed competition in the sense that in this competition—we all know this; there's no point in talking around it—there will be a female bodybuilding competitor who has gone beyond what any other woman bodybuilder has so far presented on stage."

Weider concludes, "We're here to protect the majority and protect our sport. If you have the majority of the girls that absolutely say, 'Hey, let's go for these big, grotesque muscles; let's go to the ultimate,' so be it. Okay? But we are following what the majority want. I just want to say that women are women and men are men and there's a difference, and thank God for that difference."

And, so goes the film. In the end, Bev Francis is awarded last place among the finalists—even though she is clearly the most successful bodybuilder of the bunch. After this experience, Francis got a nose job, dyed her mousy brown hair blonde, and wore pink bikinis in competition.

The world of women's competitive bodybuilding continues to struggle with the vivid visual contradiction between a highly developed muscular physique with extremely low body fat (which looks the same in women and men) and our culture's concept of femininity. Currently, the most popular way to resolve that contradiction is with large breast implants that are intended to signal that the bodies are indeed female.

The IFBB has dealt with the double bind by creating three categories for women competitors (whereas there is only one for men): bodybuilding, fitness, and figure. In its 2003 official rules, the IFBB includes a special appendix on assessing the female physique that flatly states women bodybuilders should not be penalized for being "too big" and that bodybuilding is not a conventional beauty contest. Figure competitors, in contrast, are required to wear high heels with their bikinis.

Source: Excerpt from *Pumping Iron II: The Women*, 1985. Reprinted by permission of George Butler, White Mountain Films.

is full of boys, the music blasting over the loudspeakers is woman bashing, the machines are designed for someone with longer legs or a longer reach, and the smallest increments between free weights is 5 pounds. The implicit message is "You don't belong here." There has been a trend in recent years to design sports equipment with female bodies in mind. For example, Minnesotan Pam Ryan has successfully marketed batting helmets for girls—with a hole to accommodate a ponytail. Players in the WNBA use a slightly smaller basketball than their male peers, one scaled in proportion to their smaller average hand size (but the court is the same length as the men's court and the baskets are just as high). Manufacturers of outdoor gear are finally making backpacks and sleeping bags tailored to the average shorter height of women adventurers, though like many other products and services, women's versions of the gear usually cost more than men's versions. Male bodies are the norm in sports.

Historically, femininity has been defined as inconsistent with physical strength and athleticism. Increasing numbers of girls and women are taking advantage of contemporary opportunities to participate in sports, and, in doing so, are behaving in ways that defy the traditional social construction of femininity; however, this defiant behavior has not led to a widespread redefinition of what it means to be feminine or womanly, or to greater acceptance of women athletes behaving in non-feminine or unattractive ways. Instead, spectators of women's sports are constantly reassured of the femininity and heterosexual appeal of women athletes through the language and images used to describe and represent them in popular media.

Constructing the Femininity and Heterosexuality of Women Athletes

Studies conducted over the last two and a half decades have consistently found that women's sports are underrepresented relative to rates of participation in both print and broadcast journalism. Women's sports are afforded significantly fewer photographs, fewer column inches, and less air time than men's sports (Kane, 1996; Koivula, 1999). Women who participate in sports considered sex appropriate (e.g., figure skating, gymnastics, tennis) are underrepresented, but they receive more coverage than women engaged in sex-inappropriate sports (Kane & Parks, 1990; Koivula, 1999). The quantity of coverage of women's athletics is different than men's, and so is the quality.

Describing Women Athletes

Media descriptions of women athletes differ from descriptions of men athletes in several ways. Women athletes and their sports are asymmetrically **gender marked** when reporters use terms such as *basketball* and *women's basketball* to refer to men's and women's sports, respectively; the underlying message here is that men's basketball is the norm while women's is the variation (Messner, Duncan, & Jensen, 1993). The relative social power of women and men is subtly communicated when commentators refer to female athletes as girls, but do not call male athletes boys, or when they use the women's first names (Anna, Serena, Svetlana) but the men's last names and title (Agassi or Mr. Agassi) (Koivula, 1999). Male athletes are praised more often than they are criticized, while female athletes are criticized more often than they are praised, thus subtly reinforcing men for their participation while punishing women for theirs (Billings, Halone, & Denham, 2002).

The behavior and accomplishments of women athletes are often described in gender stereotypical, infantilizing, or trivializing ways (Messner et al., 1993). When Sarah Hughes won first place in figure skating in the 2002 Winter Olympics, the *Boston Globe* described her gold medal as a "highly prized bauble," a term generally reserved for costume jewelry (*Boston Globe*, February 22). When high school basketball player Candace Parker became the first girl ever to win the McDonald's all-American slam dunk contest in 2004, one of the judges explained to a radio interviewer that Parker had raised the bar and now he expected a "bevy of lovely ladies" would soon follow in her footsteps (Block, 2004). While I watched televised coverage of women's cross-country skiing in the 2002 Olympics, I heard one male announcer point out that the woman leading the pack weighed only 95 pounds, wondering "How can anyone that small go so fast?" The other male announcer sighed, "95 pounds. Women everywhere are jealous."

Commentary about women athletes is not limited to their performance; women athletes are also subject to re-marks about their sexiness and physical appeal—or lack thereof (Kane, 1996). Anna Kournikova became a household name, not for her prowess at tennis, but for her blond hair and bikini body. In his coverage of skating at the 1992 Winter Olympics, commentator Verne Lundquist mentioned skater Christine Hough's nickname: "The world knows her as Toughie. It's hard to imagine someone that beautiful with that kind of nickname" (Daddario, 1994). In a cover story on volleyball superstar Gabrielle Reece, *Outside* magazine described her as a "powerhouse, all sweat and grinding teeth . . . [and] the cover girl, with her sultry, come-hither poses and mesmer-izing eyes . . ." (Karbo, 1995, p. 62).

Like other female public figures, fe-male athletes are more likely than male athletes to be identified as parents or spouses in media reports (Koivula, 1999). The implicit message is that these women may violate traditional gender roles with their athletic partici-pation, but they are still traditionally

FIGURE 7.7
Gabrielle Reece in *Outside* Magazine.

feminine—and heterosexual—so that makes their athleticism tolerable. Homo-phobia is rampant in the world of women's athletics. Most scholars have suggested that the primary reason for this is that lesbians in sport represent a serious challenge to a system based on heterosexual male privilege and power (Kane & Lenyski, 1998). By doing sports and partnering with other women, lesbian athletes are re-jecting traditional notions of femininity and refusing to be cast as sex objects for men. Lesbian athletes are not playing by the rules.

Picturing Women Athletes

Visual representations of women athletes also deemphasize their competence while highlighting their femininity and heterosexual appeal (Duncan, 1990; Fink & Kensicki, 2002). Women athletes are frequently pictured *not* engaged in their sports. Femininity cues such as jewelry, makeup, and revealing clothing are com-mon. Even strong, muscular women athletes appear petite when they are standing next to a larger man—often a boyfriend or husband. And when that man appears to be assisting them when they do pull-ups or lift weights, their relative weakness is implied.

BOX 7.3 ∽

When Olympians Pose for *Playboy*

Just after the conclusion of the 2004 summer Olympics, during which a dozen U.S. women competitors posed nude for *Playboy*, the satirical newspaper *The Onion* ran a story titled "Female Athletes Making Great Strides in Attractiveness." The following is an excerpt:

In the wake of the Summer Olympics, during which many American women achieved a level of media attention often reserved for men, sports fans are pleased to report that female athletes are continuing to make great strides in their personal appearances.

"As recently as 20 years ago, women's sports were for hardcore fans only, most of them women," Gary Hoenig, editor of *ESPN The Magazine*, said Monday. "But due in large part to the superior facial features of women like Maria Sharapova, the media have turned a spotlight on female athletics—and Americans of both genders are tuning in."

According to Hoenig, coverage of female athletes is no longer relegated to the back pages of sports magazines.

"Female players are finally being recognized by a larger audience—they're getting larger photos in the newspapers, appearing on talk shows, and taking the covers of magazines like *Maxim* and *Playboy*," Hoenig said. "As these ladies get prettier, that exposure will only grow." . . .

According to Frank Borne, author of *Great Strides*, "It's so refreshing to see more female athletes overcome hurdles . . . Thanks to their [appearance] many of these girls are achieving what would have been thought impossible a few decades ago. Perhaps someday, women athletes will be pretty enough to rank among the nation's top actresses and models."

Unfortunately, Borne said, professional sports organizations, by focusing on the women's athletic achievements, sometimes hamper the players' ability to draw a crowd.

Source: "Female Athletes Making Great Strides in Attractiveness," *The Onion*, Vol. 40, Issue 37, September 16, 2004. Reprinted with permission of *The Onion*. Copyright © 2004 by Onion, Inc. www.theonion.com

Women athletes are sexually objectified in pictorials that feature them wearing lingerie—or wearing nothing—in poses identical to those of the models in the *Sports Illustrated* swimsuit issue. The strength and athleticism of these women is not being celebrated in images that reduce them to objects for the consumption of heterosexual male viewers. Many women athletes willingly adopt sexy poses because they believe it is a way to draw positive attention to women's sports. But does this attention truly bolster support for women's athletics—or does it reduce women's athletics to just another form of women's bodies as sexual entertainment? When soccer star Brandi Chastain whipped off her jersey in a spontaneous moment of sheer triumphant exhilaration after kicking the winning goal at the 1999 FIFA Women's World Cup, the image of her in her black sports bra got as much attention as the victory itself. Her picture appeared on the covers of magazines and front pages of newspapers all over the United States. Did this widespread coverage of Chastain *un*covered help women's soccer? Apparently not. In 2003, the Women's United Soccer Association (WUSA) suspended operations for lack of revenue.

Effects of Media Coverage on Perceptions of Women Athletes

Although many studies have documented the discrepancies in coverage of women and men athletes described above, very few have addressed the perceptual and attitudinal impact of them. Are women athletes liked more when they are described as feminine and heterosexual? Is their competence underestimated when news reports minimize their accomplishments and focus on nonathletic aspects of their lives?

In one recent study, college student participants read a fictitious newspaper article that was either about a female or male athlete and either focused on physical attractiveness or athleticism (Knight & Giuliano, 2001). In the article focusing on physical attractiveness (which read like typical coverage of women athletes), the athlete was described as "becoming known as much for his [her] incredible body as for his [her] powerful strokes," as being among *People* magazine's 50 most beautiful people, and as having recently signed a modeling contract. The researchers found that when the woman athlete was described in terms of her attractiveness, both women and men readers perceived her as more attractive, while the perception of the male athlete's attractiveness was unaffected by the content of the description. Athletes described in terms of their attractiveness were seen as less heroic, and articles that focused on attractiveness were liked less than articles that focused on athleticism.

In another study, Knight and Giuliano (2003) investigated the impact of written information that either implied heterosexuality or was ambiguous about sexual orientation of the athlete. Interestingly, female athletes with an ambiguous sexual orientation were perceived as no less feminine and no more masculine than female athletes described as heterosexual; in contrast, male athletes with an ambiguous sexual orientation were perceived as more feminine and less masculine than male athletes described as heterosexual. Recall that it is women athletes whose heterosexuality is commonly implied or highlighted in media coverage because of the stereotype that all women athletes are lesbians. Overall, heterosexual athletes were viewed as more ideal, more physically attractive, and more respectable than those with an ambiguous orientation; but they were not perceived to be more athletically competent or likable.

One question that has not been answered by researchers yet is how media images that emphasize the appearance and sexuality of women athletes affect sedentary women's motivation to get active. Women's magazines like *Shape* and *Fitness* encourage women to exercise and engage in physical recreation, but the primary emphasis is still on how this activity will improve their appearance. Many models in these magazines appear thin and frail, not solid and strong. Those that do have an athletic frame frequently have had breast augmentation to add curves in the absence of body fat. These magazines promote embodied experience, but they do not challenge objectification. Magazines that have avoided the emphasis on appearance, such as *Sports Illustrated for Women* and *Women's Sports and Fitness* have been unable to stay in business. Is this because women readers are uninterested or because not enough advertisers will support content that helps women feel better about their bodies instead of inadequate? The promise of improved appearance may inspire women to begin an activity program, but research on exercise motivation suggests that more important in the long run is the intrinsic motivation that stems from subjective benefits such as psychological well-being, increased energy, and feelings of self-efficacy (Higgins & Oldenburg, 2003; Young et al., 2001).

Benefits of Embodied Experience for Girls and Women

The University of Minnesota is the host institution for a one-of-a-kind research institute, the Tucker Center for Research on Girls and Women in Sport. The Tucker Center directed the President's Council on Physical Fitness and Sport's (1997) comprehensive review of research on the benefits of sports participation for girls. Among the findings were that girls who participate in sports are at lowered risk for many chronic adult diseases, such as coronary heart disease, some cancers, and osteoporosis; they do better academically and are less likely to drop out of school; and, they have lower rates of stress and depression and higher self-esteem. Improved self-esteem among girls who participate in sports stems from feelings of physical competence, improved body image, and feeling less rigidly constrained by a feminine gender role (Richman & Shaffer, 2000). It is not only physically beneficial for girls and women to get active; it is psychologically beneficial to experience the body as instrumental instead of decorative.

Sports are not the only venue in which girls and women can challenge the limitations of femininity by actively inhabiting their bodies. Outdoor recreation is becoming increasingly popular for women (Henderson & Roberts, 1998) and may offer different benefits than sports. Like sports, outdoor recreation is consistent with traditional masculinity but not with traditional femininity. The idealized feminine form does not have mass or muscles. It is not dirty or sunburned or hairy or stinky. It does not assume unbecoming postures, such as those required in rock climbing. As described earlier in this chapter, put us all out to survive in the woods for a few months and we all would end up looking and acting a lot less feminine.

Trading media and mirrors for trees and trails can be a liberating experience for women whose relationship with their bodies is normally dictated by appearance concerns. Outdoor educator S. Copeland Arnold (1994) explains,

> My experiences in Outward Bound as a young woman deeply affected my sense of self-acceptance, self-esteem, and body image. I gained an appreciation for my strength and agility . . . Rather than an object to be adorned and perfected, my body became an ally. (pp. 43–44)

In contemporary industrialized cultures like the United States, we rarely have to rely on our bodies for survival. We have effort-saving appliances, automobiles, and infrastructure. Thinness, frailty, and passivity can be idealized only when women's strength and activity are not necessary for the work of living. Carrying her shelter, clothing, food supplies, and transportation on her back as she portages a canoe down a forest path can be an extremely challenging and empowering experience for a woman who has been taught to criticize her body instead of trust in it.

Making a Difference

Transforming Society: Challenging Objectification

At the societal level, women's objectification is a commercial enterprise. Advertisers routinely objectify women in their visual images; manufacturers create products that turn women's bodies or body parts into utilitarian objects; and service industries use Hooters Girls and "topless maids" to attract customers. Women's objectification is so common because it is profitable. We are unlikely to see significant change in the behaviors of profit-driven organizations until they receive the message that women's objectification is going to cost them.

As consumers, we have tremendous power to influence popular culture. I have heard people dismiss women's objectification with the convenient phrase, "Sex sells." This is not unlike dismissing sexual harassment or sexual violence against women with "Boys will be boys." Just because something happens doesn't mean it has to be accepted by society. And women's objectification is not sex; it is dehumanization of half the population, a process that strips women of their personhood and their sexual subjectivity. Ours is a society that is increasingly shaped by economic forces. If anything is going to change with regard to women's objectification in our commercially driven culture, well-informed consumers are going to have to use their voices—*and dollars*—to educate the people producing the images, the products, and the services that currently rely far too much on objectification of women to make a profit.

The Saga of Sally's. When a new restaurant named Sally's Saloon and Eatery opened near the University of Minnesota campus in 1993, perched on its logo was an extremely busty, barely dressed female rodent holding up a tray. A graduate student at the time, I wrote a letter to the owner explaining how I thought the logo was an example of the tired old tactic of women's sexual objectification being used to attract customers (and clearly not women customers). With the letter I enclosed a copy of his ad, now adorned with a sticker that read "This Insults Women." I explained that I would not be spending my dollars at the restaurant and that I would also inform others of the logo in an attempt to encourage them to buy their lunch at an establishment that didn't objectify women.

To his credit, the owner called me at home and explained that he had no clue the logo was sexist, that it had been drawn for him by a friend of his *who had formerly been an animator at Disney*, and that he had thought it was cute in that it reminded him of "that character in *Who Framed Roger Rabbit*." "Oh, you mean Jessica Rabbit?" I asked (while thinking, "My point exactly"). He explained that he had wanted the logo to be a girlfriend for Goldie Gopher, the University of Minnesota mascot. He said that some women customers had also complained, and he was committed to changing the logo as soon as he had enough money to do so.

Somehow the story made its way into the *Minneapolis Star Tribune* (February 19, 1993), the university's *Minnesota Daily* newspaper, and onto a local TV news broadcast. The logo was changed—her proportions were significantly toned down, her off-the-shoulder crop top was replaced with a long-sleeved sweater, and tennis shoes were added to make her look sportier and less provocative. See Figure 7.8 for the before and after versions.

This example may seem like less than a drop in the bucket considering how pervasive women's objectification is in our society, but we should never assume that our individual actions will have no impact. Every letter that an individual writes to a business or government official is generally considered to represent the opinions of several hundred people (who were too busy or discouraged to write their own letters). We also should not fall prey to the idea that there is something *wrong* with

Before   After

FIGURE 7.8

Sally's logo—before and after. In the final version, tennis shoes were added.

Source: Reprinted by permission of Sally's Saloon.

using our purchasing decisions to influence the culture. Students sometimes seem taken aback when I mention the concepts of a boycott—refusing to spend money at a business whose practices you dislike—and a girlcott—directing your money toward businesses whose practices you particularly admire. Yes, these could be construed as political acts, but they are not antipatriotic, anticapitalist, or anti-American. They are democracy in action.

Transforming Social Interactions: Seeing the Woman in the Body

Next time a woman says within your earshot, "I'm fat!" how will you respond to her? Will you quickly reassure her (validating her concern in the process) with, "No, you aren't!" Will you commiserate by criticizing yourself, "Me too!" Or, will you say, "So what?" or "I hadn't noticed" or "Funny, I thought you were smart, talented, and kind." How will you respond when she says, "I hate my hair (or butt, or . . .)"?

Next time you encounter a woman who has lost a noticeable amount of weight, has changed her hair color, or has decked herself out in eye-catching clothes, what will be the *first* thing you say to her? Will it be, "Have you lost weight? You look great" or "I love your hair!" What about, "Wow, it's good to see you. What's happening in your life? How did that project at work (or adventurous vacation, or situation with your family, or . . .) turn out?" When you meet a little girl, will you first ask her what she's learning in kindergarten or compliment her on her cute shoes?

One of the more subtle ways that women's objectification is reinforced is through our everyday interactions. As products of our socialization (and biology), we tend to perceive women in terms of their bodies and appearance. Admiration for a woman's altered appearance is considered a high compliment, although the unspoken corollary is that she looked bad or unacceptable before she modified herself. Talk about women's fat concern is scripted and takes on a ritualistic tone in our culture (Nichter, 2000). I once overheard a conversation in a psychology department restroom between a professor and two of her graduate students at a prestigious research university. They were talking about their bodies. The professor, who was accomplished and respected in her field, said something about her thighs. One of the grad students responded, "Not like you *have* any thighs!"

We can choose not to contribute to this form of objectification by making an effort to transcend women's appearance when we are interacting with them. We can look less and listen more. We can converse with women about topics other than body flaws and appearance strategies. We can value, prioritize, encourage, and reinforce women's nonappearance-related goals and accomplishments. Women are more than their bodies; our interactions with women can either contradict or support that fact.

Transforming Ourselves: Education and Embodiment

It is no easy task for a woman to live *in* her body in a society that has taught her from the time she was a girl to take a critical spectator's view on her physical self. Immersed every day in a cultural context that objectifies women, even a woman who is determined to resist social pressure may find that her relationship with her own body and her perceptions of other women's bodies are strongly influenced by this context. As a social psychologist, I think we can never underestimate the power of situations to influence our thoughts and behaviors. Thinking critically about situations is one way to diminish their effect on us, and seeking out alternative situations is another.

The first step toward being able to resist cultural messages is becoming aware of them. It is important to realize and recognize the ways in which women's bodies are sexually objectified, dehumanized, and distorted in order to understand the relationship many women have with their bodies. Textbooks like this one can help raise awareness, but ideally, critical thinking should start earlier, before girls have had to navigate their way through puberty and learn to inhabit a woman's (objectified) body. Parents can serve as cultural buffers, helping their daughters to process the unrealistic beauty standards and negative messages about their bodies that contribute to poor body image and disordered eating (Frank, 1999). Media literacy programs aimed at college women increase participants' skepticism about unrealistically thin beauty ideals, but they may be too late in the game to alleviate body image concerns (Irving & Berel, 2001).

Thinking critically about women's objectification is necessary, but perhaps not sufficient for women who want to truly transform their relationships with their bodies. A lifetime of internalized messages is unlikely to be thwarted by a few mental exercises alone. Women who aspire to heightened subjectivity must get up and move their muscles (and pull their sisters, daughters, and mothers along with them). They must defy critics who judge them negatively and label them as unwomanly because of their strength and self-esteem. Although it may be intimidating or unappealing at first, what might a woman learn about herself when she trades her makeup kit for a mountain bike? How might her perception of herself change when she turns off the television, closes the beauty magazines, and takes a walk through the woods? What if instead of carefully guarding her long, manicured nails she dug her hands into some clay and sculpted a full-figured goddess? Instead of spending a Saturday shopping for clothes, a group of women friends might spend the time kicking and punching their way through a martial arts class or learning swing dancing.

In the 1991 film *Fried Green Tomatoes*, the Southern-bred middle-aged character Evelyn Couch describes to her elderly friend, Mrs. Threadgood, how shedding feminine passivity in favor of active embodiment has affected her,

> I never get mad, Mrs. Threadgood. Never! The way I was raised it was bad manners. Well I got mad and it felt terrific! . . . Towanda, the Avenger! After I wipe out all the

punks of this world I'll take on the wife beaters . . . And I'll put tiny little bombs in Penthouse and Playboy, so they'll explode when you open 'em. And I'll ban all fashion models who weigh less than 130 pounds. I'll give half the military budget to people over 65 and declare wrinkles sexually desirable. Towanda, righter of wrongs, Queen beyond compare!

Evelyn Couch's personal transformation is incomplete at this point in the film. She's feeling heady (and especially aggressive) because for the first time ever in her life she is challenging the ways women's bodies are objectified, commercialized, targeted for violence, and devalued in later life. She is empowered by the realization that a woman can reject the cultural construction of femininity that robs her of her personhood and defines her merely in terms of her body.

Exploring Further

Brand, P. Z. (Ed.). (2000). *Beauty matters.* Bloomington, IN: Indiana University Press. Essays address why beauty matters and how gender, race, ethnicity, sexual orientation, and ability are related to our perceptions of beauty. Discussions of ideal appearance standards, cosmetic practices, and the beauty industry draw on feminist theory, philosophy, cultural history, and examples from the worlds of fashion and art.

Choi, P. Y. L. (2000). *Femininity and the physically active women.* New York: Routledge. Book addresses the contradiction between femininity and being the sporty type. Choi argues that the perception of athletes and athletic endeavors as masculine negatively affects girls' and women's participation in sports and recreational exercise.

Web Sites

The Tucker Center for Girls and Women in Sport (www.tuckercenter.org)

Melpomene Institute (www.melpomene.org)

MediaWatch (www.mediawatch.org)

PART 4

Gendered Life Paths

CHAPTER 8

Sex, Love, and Romance

∽

$\mathcal{S}$ex, love, and romance seem like natural events—instinctive, unlearned, and universal. For example, think about a kiss. Perfectly natural, right? In Western societies, kissing is seen as an instinctive way to express love and increase arousal. Yet in many cultures, kissing is unknown. When people from these cultures hear about our kissing customs, they agree that these practices are dangerous, unhealthy, or just plain disgusting. When members of one African community first saw Europeans kissing, they laughed and said, "Look at them—they eat each other's saliva and dirt" (Tiefer, 1995, pp. 77–78).

Strange as it may seem, sex, like kissing, is not a natural act. In other words, sexuality is not something that can be understood in purely biological terms. Instead, it is a social construct.

How Is Sexuality Shaped by Culture?

Individuals develop their own sense of sexual identity and desire in the context of their particular time in history, their social class, ethnic group, religion, and gender roles (Foucalt, 1978; Rubin, 1984). Every culture throughout the world controls human sexuality (Hyde & DeLamater, 1997). Because men have more social and political power, this control usually works to their benefit. For women, cultural constructions of sexuality lead to an ongoing tension between pleasure and danger (Joseph & Lewis, 1981; Vance, 1984).

What Are Sexual Scripts?

Each individual has a biological capacity for sexual arousal, but people learn rules that tell them how to have sex, with whom they may have it, what activities will be pleasurable, and when the individual is—and is not—allowed to take advantage of the biological potential for sexual enjoyment (Gagnon & Simon, 1973; Radlove, 1983). Together, the repertoire of sexual acts that is recognized by a particular social group, the rules or guidelines for expected behavior, and the expected punishments for violating the rules form the basis of *sexual scripts* (Laws & Schwartz, 1977).

Sexual scripts can be thought of as schemas for sexual concepts and events. For example, when college students were asked to list what people would typically do on a first date, they agreed on things such as worry about appearance, get dressed, go out, get to know each other by joking and talking, try to impress date, kiss goodnight, and go home. These first-date scripts featured men asking for the date and initiating physical contact (Rose & Frieze, 1989). Sexual scripts are used in guiding one's own behavior and in interpreting others' behavior.

Sexual scripts operate at societal, interactional, and individual levels. They are part of cultural institutions (e.g., sexual behaviors are regulated by law and religion), they provide norms for interpersonal behavior (e.g., the first-date script), and they are internalized by individuals (some behaviors come to be seen as exciting and others as disgusting). They are influenced by race and class as well as by gender

TABLE 8.1   Societal Scripts about Sexuality Differ in American Ethnic/Racial Groups, Even When Social Class Is Accounted For

Sexual Script	African American Male	African American Female	Mexican American Male	Mexican American Female	White Male	White Female
There's been a lot of discussion about the way morals and attitudes about sex are changing in this country. If a man and a woman have sex relations before marriage, do you think it is always wrong, almost always wrong, wrong only sometimes, or not wrong at all? (% Wrong)	25.5	38.3	27.7	41.8	21.6	30.3
What if they are in their teens, say 14 to 16 years old? In that case, do you think sex relations before marriage are always wrong, almost always wrong, wrong only sometimes, or not wrong at all? (% Wrong)	67.6	83.2	75.9	92.4	73.5	84.6
My religious beliefs have shaped and guided my sexual behavior. (% Agree)	49.5	69.2	51.8	60.9	44.4	56.6
I would not have sex with someone unless I was in love with them. (% Agree)	43.3	77.0	56.6	78.3	53.1	76.4

Source: From J. W. Mahay, E. O. Laumann & S. Michaels, 2000, "Race, Gender, and Class in Sexual Scripts," in E. O. Laumann & R. T. Michael (Eds.), *Sex, Love and Health: Private Choices and Public Policies*, pp. 197–238. Chicago: University of Chicago Press. Reprinted by permission.

(Mahay, Laumann, & Michaels, 2001). Table 8.1, based on a national U.S. sample, shows some normative scripts that differ among ethnic groups. Throughout this chapter, we consider women's sexuality and intimate relationships in terms of both biological potentials and the influences of society's sexual scripts.

How Do Sexual Scripts Differ across Cultures?

There is tremendous variability in cultural scripts about sex, love, and romance. For example, people in the United States believe that love is necessary for marriage. But in most of the world, marriages are arranged by family members, not by the bride and groom. Romantic love may be viewed as irrelevant or even destructive. In a study of college students in 11 cultures (India, Pakistan, Thailand, Mexico, Brazil, Japan, Hong Kong, the Philippines, Australia, England, and the United States), participants were asked whether they would marry someone they were not in love with, if the person had all the other qualities they desired. In India and Pakistan, about half said yes. In Thailand, the Philippines, and Mexico, about 10 to 20 percent agreed. However, in the other countries, including the United States, only a tiny minority of people said they would marry without love (Levine, Sato, Hashimoto, & Verma, 1995). Within each country, male and female respondents were quite similar in their beliefs.

Culturally influenced beliefs and expectations about sexuality lead to ethnic group differences in sexual behavior. For example, compared with American college students, Chinese students start dating at a later age, date less often, and are less likely to have sex with their dates (Tang & Zuo, 2000). A comparison of Asian and non-Asian students in a Canadian university showed that the Asian students were more conservative in their behavior (e.g., they were less likely to have had sexual intercourse or to masturbate, and they had fewer partners if sexually active) (Meston, Trapnell, & Gorzalka, 1996). In another study, ethnically diverse girls in grades 6 through 8 in the United States were asked what is the best age to have sex for the first time. Asian American girls gave the highest average age (21.7 years) and the African American girls the lowest (19.2 years). However, for all groups, the more a girl believed she could succeed in school and work, the less likely she was to predict early sexual activity for herself (East, 1998). Clearly, sexual scripts are part of larger life scripts, both of which are shaped by a person's social group and perceived opportunities.

Adolescent Sexuality

How Does Sexuality Emerge in the Teen Years?

With puberty comes a surge in sexual interest and behavior. During the last 40 years, there have been large changes in patterns of sexual activity in the teen years, both in the United States and around the world:

- More teens are having sexual intercourse outside of marriage.
- The increase has been greater for girls.
- First intercourse is occurring at an earlier age, on average.

However, there are ethnic group differences in the United States in age of first intercourse, and there are large variations from one country to another (Hyde & Delamater, 2003).

In the 1940s, only about 33 percent of females and 71 percent of males had intercourse outside marriage by the age of 25 (Kinsey, Pomeroy, & Martin, 1948; Kinsey, Pomeroy, Martin, & Gebhard, 1953). Today, about 79 percent of males and 74 percent of females are sexually experienced by age 19 (Hyde & DeLamater, 1997). The gender gap in sexual experience has almost disappeared; however, boys still have first sex at an earlier age than girls despite reaching puberty at a later age. African American teens have first-time sex at around 15.5 years of age, and whites at around 17 years; Latinos vary, with Cuban Americans and Puerto Ricans at 16.6 and Mexican Americans at 17. More than one in five teens experiences first intercourse between the ages of 11 and 14 (Becker, Rankin, & Rickel, 1998).

Comparisons of countries around the world show that the average age of first intercourse is similar (between 16 and 18 years in most countries). However, the percentage of unmarried women who have intercourse is lower in Latin American countries than in the United States or Africa, due to the influence of Catholicism. Increasingly, the influence of North American mass media around the world is contributing to changing sexual values and behavior so that intercourse outside marriage is becoming more widespread globally (Hyde & DeLamater, 2003).

What Factors Influence the Decision to Have Sex?

The initiation of sexual behavior depends very much on social factors. For both boys and girls, one of the strongest predictors of sexual activity is the *perceived* level of sexual activity of their best friends (DiBlasio & Benda, 1992; Furstenberg, Moore, & Peterson, 1986; Miller et al., 1997). In a study of more than 1,300 poor, urban middle schoolers, those who started having sex during sixth grade were more likely to believe that their peers were sexually active and that joining in would make them more popular (Kinsman, Romer, & Schwarz, 1998). But it is not just poor urban youth who are influenced by their beliefs about others' sex lives—most teens are. In other words, teens start having sex partly because they think their friends are doing it. In fact, perceptions about what peers are doing are more important predictors than the peers' actual behavior (Brooks-Gunn & Furstenberg, 1989). This raises troubling questions of free choice versus peer pressure, with differential effects on girls (Aarons & Jenkins, 2002). In a major national study, women of all racial and ethnic groups were significantly more likely than men to report that their first sex was unwanted (Laumann & Michael, 2000).

Parents have some influence on teens' sexual behavior (Miller et al., 1997). In a study of urban African American teens, girls' delaying of first intercourse was related to time spent with their mother and boys' was related to time with their father (Ramirez-Valles, Zimmerman, & Juarez, 2002). Both African American and white girls who feel close to their parents and talk to them about sex engage in less sexual behavior than girls who do not (Murry-McBride, 1996).

Although adults are quick to attribute teens' behavior to raging hormones, the relationship between hormones and sexual activity is complex. Hormonal levels have a strong effect on the level of a girl's sexual interests but only weak effects on her sexual behaviors (Udry, Talbert, & Morris, 1986). An earlier age of menarche has been associated with earlier sexual activity among both black and white adolescents (Smith, 1989; Zelnick, Kantner, & Ford, 1981), probably due to social pressures. As discussed in Chapter 6, early puberty means early gender intensification, which has many consequences for girls.

Are Teens Having Safer Sex?

Traditional sexual scripts focus on men's needs and condone male power and control in relationships. As a result, women often may be unable to assert a claim to safety during sexual activity (Chrisler, 2001; Gomez & Vanoss-Marin, 1996). The consequence is an increased risk of unwanted pregnancy and sexually transmitted diseases (STDs). These include bacterial infections such as chlamydia and gonorrhea, and viral infections such as herpes, genital warts, and HIV, which causes AIDS. All these STDs are transmitted by genital, anal, or oral sexual contact; and all can have serious health consequences beyond their immediate symptoms (Amaro, Raj, & Reed, 2001; Chrisler, 2001). Although STDs are a risk for sexually active people in any age group, teens are particularly vulnerable because they tend to have more partners and because they are inconsistent in using protection. One in four sexually active teens acquires an STD (Becker, Rankin, & Rickel, 1998).

The AIDS epidemic continues. The World Health Organization estimates that over 40 million people worldwide are infected, almost half of whom are women. In the United States, women now account for 25 percent of AIDS cases. Women of color are most at risk. Although black and Hispanic women together are less than 25 percent of U.S. women, they account for 78 percent of AIDS cases among women. The most common means of transmission for women is sexual intercourse with an infected man (38 percent) followed by injection drug use (25 percent). HIV/AIDS is now the third leading cause of death for African American women aged 25 to 44, and the fifth for all women in the same age group (Centers for Disease Control, 2002; Hyde & Delamater, 2003).

Condoms are the most effective means of preventing HIV infection during heterosexual contact. But many people do not use condoms consistently even when they know about their effectiveness in reducing STD risk. For example, interviews with 187 18- to 35-year-old Puerto Rican women in New York revealed that 64 percent engaged in unprotected sex with their primary partners (Dixon, Antoni, Peters, & Saul, 2001). In a study of African American women college students, 65 percent had never or rarely used condoms, although they knew about condom effectiveness (Mays & Cochran, 1988). In a study of white college students, 38 percent never used condoms (Boyd & Wandersman, 1991). Studies in many cultures show that large proportions of young heterosexuals still engage in unprotected sex. For example, a Nigerian study of a large sample of adolescents showed that only 21 percent of the girls and 36 percent of the boys used condoms, although they knew about condom effectiveness in STD prevention (Araoye & Adegoke, 1996).

Among teens in developed countries, the main reason for not using protection seems to be that safer sex is inconsistent with the romantic, spontaneous sex of scripted fantasies. In a study of 162 Australian students, 39 percent never used condoms even for casual sex with new partners, although they rated this activity as high risk. They were concerned that condom use would destroy the romance and afraid of negative implications ("What will he/she think of me if I start talking about condoms?") (Galligan & Terry, 1993).

College students underestimate their AIDS risk because they use inaccurate decision rules (Malloy, Fisher, Albright, Misovich, & Fisher, 1997). For example, many believe that it is OK to have unprotected sex with someone they know well and like (Williams et al., 1992). They may judge their risk of AIDS based on their partners' appearance ("He doesn't look sick" or "She is too good-looking to have AIDS"). And while they may use condoms for first-time sex with a new partner, they believe that when they are in a relationship, they do not have to worry about protection from STDs (Hammer, Fisher, Fitzgerald, & Fisher, 1996; Misovich,

Fisher, & Fisher, 1997). Of course, all these beliefs are dangerous. Young people tend to have a number of different partners during the college years; even if they are monogamous while in each relationship, their partners may have engaged in risky behavior in the past. In relationships, people are in effect having sex with every other person their partner has had sex with. Even if they do not have intercourse, other activities such as oral sex can transmit STDs. Because people value relationships, and want to trust their current partner, they may refuse to recognize the risks (Joffe, 1997; Misovich et al., 1997).

What can be done to reduce risky sexual behavior? Psychologists have developed strategies that work for a wide variety of groups, including urban minority teenagers and college students (Fisher & Fisher, 2000; Fisher, Fisher, Misovich, Kimble, & Malloy, 1996; Fisher, Williams, Fisher, & Malloy, 1999). Successful strategies depend on giving people *information* about how AIDS is transmitted, increasing their *motivation* to reduce their own risk, and teaching them *specific skills and behaviors*. These skills and behaviors might include practice in talking about condoms with a partner, avoiding drinking or drug use before sex, or learning how to buy and use condoms.

What works depends on the norms of the group. For example, messages that stress risk to the individual may work better in more individualistic cultures, whereas messages that stress harm to one's family may work better in more collectivist cultures (Murray-Johnson, Witte, Liu, Hubbell, Sampson, & Morrison, 2001). General appeals to "Just Say No" or to "Practice Safer Sex" simply do not change behavior. Most important, researchers need to develop feminist approaches that recognize the diverse realities of women's lives: Male control of sexual decision making, violence by male partners, dependence on men due to poverty, and drug addiction are all factors in risky behavior by women. Empowering women to control their own bodies is key to their sexual health (Amaro et al., 2001).

Experiencing Sexuality

First Intercourse: Less Than Bliss?

North American culture is more ambivalent and restrictive about women's sexuality than some European cultures, and this may affect how American young women experience their first sexual encounter. In a study of more than 400 American and Swedish college women, the Americans expressed significantly more negative reactions to their first experience of sexual intercourse (Schwartz, 1993). In a study of 1,600 American college students, women reported more guilt and less pleasure than men. When asked to rate the pleasure of their first sexual intercourse on a 1 to 7 scale, the women gave it an average score of 2.95 (Sprecher, Barbee, & Schwartz, 1995).

The gap between the ideal and the real is highlighted in the following two accounts. The first is from a Harlequin romance novel. The second is from a sexual autobiography written by a college sophomore, reproduced here exactly as she wrote it.

For a long timeless moment Roddy gazed down at the sleeping figure, watching the soft play of moonlight on her features . . . Gently he pulled back the blankets and lay down beside the motionless girl. She turned in her sleep, one hand flung out towards him. Tenderly he stroked a dark strand of hair from her face, then pulled her into his arms. . . . Still half drugged from brandy and sleep, she found herself stroking his hair. "Such a perfect dream," she murmured, her eyes already beginning to close again.

"No dream, my lady," and Roddy's mouth found hers, silencing her words. Tenderly he slipped the ribbon straps of her nightdress over her shoulders, and her body arched up towards him as his fingers traced a burning path across her breast. A groan vibrated deep in her throat as he threw her nightdress to the floor. Then his body was pressed along hers and she gasped at the feeling of skin on naked skin . . .

Driven now only by pure instinct, she moved against him, raining kisses down on his hair-roughened skin, tracing her fingers down the hard strength of his muscled chest. His breathing became ever more ragged, his hands slipping under her to pull her closer still, and she gave a tiny cry of surrender as he finally claimed her body, her fingers digging his shoulders as they moved together in frenzied rhythm. A vast well seemed to surge up within her, and as the room exploded into fragmented light she heard a voice crying "I love you" . . . (Elliot, 1989, pp. 116–118)

I don't think I will ever forget the night that I did lose my virginity. It was this past September (September 7th to be exact). My boyfriend and I had been going out for six months. I met him at a party late that night, but, by the time I had gotten there, he was extremely drunk. We came back to my room because my roommate was not going to be there. . . . Well, my boyfriend was very drunk and very amorous to say the least. Once we got into bed, I knew exactly what he had in mind, he was all hands and lips. I figured that we might as well have sex. . . . So, I made the decision to let him do whatever he wanted. For the actual act of sex itself, I hated it the first time. Not only was it painful but, it made a mess on my comforter. I hated my boyfriend at that time. I actually kicked him out of my room and sent him home. I was upset for a lot of reasons: My boyfriend was too drunk to remember the night so, I had made the wrong decision in letting him do whatever he wanted; there had been no feelings involved; I hadn't enjoyed it in the slightest; I had lost my virginity and betrayed my parents. I was upset for just a couple of days.

After that first night, the sex between my boyfriend and myself has been great. (Moffat, 1989, pp. 191–192)

How Do Women Experience Orgasm?

Women who do not have a great deal of sexual experience are sometimes unsure about whether they have had an orgasm because they do not know how it is supposed to feel. One way to get an idea of the subjective experience of orgasm is to ask women to describe their own behaviors and sensations. Shere Hite (1976) collected lengthy surveys from more than 3,000 women, but this represented responses from only about 3 percent of the questionnaires she distributed. There is no way to know how accurately the women who chose to respond represent all women. The major strength of Hite's work is that she used open-ended questions, and many of her respondents wrote lengthy, detailed answers. A few sample descriptions of orgasm are given in Box 8.1.

Is the experience of orgasm different for women and men? Research suggests that the experiences are similar. In a study in which college students were asked to

BOX 8.1   ∾   Women's Accounts of Orgasms

"There are a few faint sparks, coming up to orgasm, and then I suddenly realize that it is going to catch fire, and then I concentrate all my energies, both physical and mental, to quickly bring on the climax—which turns out to be a moment suspended in time, a hot rush—a sudden breathtaking dousing of all the nerves of my body in Pleasure—I try to make the moment last—disappointment when it doesn't."

"Before, I feel a tremendous surge of tension and a kind of delicious feeling I can't describe. Then orgasm is like the excitement and stimulation I have been feeling, increased, for an *instant*, a hundred-fold."

"It starts down deep, somewhere in the 'core,' gets bigger, stronger, better, and more beautiful, until I'm just four square inches of ecstatic crotch area!"

"The physical sensation is beautifully excruciating. It begins in the clitoris, and also surges into my whole vaginal area."

"It's a peak of almost, almost, ALMOST, ALMOSTTTT. The only way I can describe it is to say it is like riding a 'Tilt-a-Whirl.'"

"Just before orgasm, the area around my clitoris suddenly comes alive and, I can't think of any better description, seems to sparkle and send bright dancing sensations all around. Then it becomes focused like a point of intense light. Like a bright blip on a radar screen, and that's the orgasm."

"There is an almost frantic itch-pain-pleasure in my vagina and clitoral area that seems almost insatiable, it is also extremely hot and I lose control of everything, then there is an explosion of unbelievable warmth and relief to the itch-pain-pleasure! It is really indescribable and what I've just written doesn't explain it at all!!! WORDS!"

Source: From Shere Hite, 1976, *The Hite Report*. New York: Simon & Schuster. Copyright © 1976 by Shere Hite. Reprinted by permission of Fifi Oscard Agency, Inc.

write descriptions of their orgasms, judges (psychologists and physicians) could not reliably distinguish women's and men's descriptions (Vance & Wagner, 1976). In another study, students chose adjectives from a list to describe their experiences of orgasm (Wiest, 1977). Again, there were no significant differences in responses by women and men.

Evils of Masturbation or Joys of Self-Pleasure?

Stimulating one's own genitals is a very common sexual practice. Traditionally, this practice was given the clinical term *masturbation*, which made it seem like a disorder. Indeed, masturbation was thought to cause everything from dark circles under the eyes to insanity. However, the majority of people today believe that it is neither harmful nor wrong (Oliver & Hyde, 1993). More positive terms for masturbation include *self-pleasuring* and *self-gratification*.

Women usually masturbate by stimulating the clitoris, either by hand or with a vibrator. Other methods include pressing the clitoral area against a pillow or using a stream of water while in the bath or shower. Most women who masturbate engage in sexual fantasies while doing so. Hite's survey respondents described both their techniques and their fantasies (see Box 8.2).

Box 8.2   ∾   Women's Accounts of Masturbation

"To masturbate, I almost always need to be turned on by something like pornographic literature (and believe me it's hard to find anything halfway decent). I lie in bed, on my back, slide out of my panties or pajama bottoms because I like to be free to move. I rub my two middle fingers up and down and around the clitoral area. Sometimes I put two fingers of my other hand into my vagina. I rub for a few seconds and tense up my body. I can usually feel a definite fuzzy feeling when I know the orgasm is coming on and then I rub harder, mostly up and down. My legs are apart. The vaginal area is usually moistened as a result of my pornographic reading, otherwise I use spit or, very rarely, cold cream. I usually arch my back slightly when I am really turned on, at which point I take the fingers of my other hand out of my vagina and I push down on the uterine area just above the pubis."

"I lie down and begin to fantasize in my mind my favorite fantasy, which is a party where everyone is nude and engaging in group sex, lovely, lovely sex, all positions, kissing, caressing, cunnilingus, and intercourse. After about five minutes of this I am ready, very lubricated. I lift one knee slightly and move my leg to one side, put my middle finger on or around the clitoris and gently massage in a circular motion. Then I dream of being invited to this party and all those delicious things are happening to me. I try to hold out as long as possible, but in just a minute or two I have an orgasm. It is very simple, all in the mind. After the first orgasm I do not fantasize any longer, but concentrate entirely on the delicious feeling in my vagina and surrounding areas, continuing the same movement of my finger, but slightly faster and in about one minute I have another orgasm. I am very quiet, but do moan some during each orgasm. After several orgasms in this manner I start thinking of what's for dinner and the party is over."

"I don't masturbate like anybody else I ever heard of. I make a clump in the bedding about the size of a fist (I used to use the head of my poor teddy bear, but since I became too old to sleep with a teddy bear, a wad of the sheets has to suffice) and then lie on my stomach on top of it so that it exerts pressure on my clitoris. I then move my hips in a circular motion until I climax—very simple. It works with legs apart or together—either one, although when I am in a particularly frenzied state, together sometimes feels better. I usually end up sort of with my weight on my knees and elbows, so I can't do too much else with my hands."

There is a persistent gender difference in masturbation experience. Curiously, women do not report more negative attitudes toward masturbation, but they are definitely less likely to say they do it (Oliver & Hyde, 1993). Only about 42 percent of women in a national study reported that they had ever masturbated, compared to virtually all the men (Laumann, Gagnow, Michael, & Michaels, 1994). Little is known about the reasons for the gender difference in self-pleasuring, although some have suggested that it is due to women's body dissatisfaction. In a study of white and black women at a family planning clinic, the white women reported a higher overall frequency of self-pleasuring, and those who self-gratified more often had higher body satisfaction. However, there was no relationship between body satisfaction and self-gratification for black women (Shulman & Horne, 2003).

Experience in self-pleasuring has positive effects on women's sexual satisfaction. For example, in a study of married women aged 18 to 30, those who had experienced orgasm through self-gratification had more orgasms with their partners, greater sexual desire, more rapid arousal, higher self-esteem, and greater marital satisfaction than those who had not (Hurlbert & Whittaker, 1991). Self-pleasuring can be an important way for a woman to learn about her pattern of sexual arousal and satisfaction. Through practice, she can learn what fantasies are most arousing, what kinds and amounts of stimulation are most enjoyable, and what to expect from her body. For these reasons, sex therapists frequently use education in self-pleasuring for women who are unable to experience orgasm with a partner (LoPiccolo & Stock, 1986). Feminist writers have encouraged women to use self-gratification as a route to erotic skill and sexual independence (Dodson, 1987). The woman who can enjoy solo orgasms is not dependent on a partner for sexual pleasure and can enjoy sexual satisfaction without risk of pregnancy or STDs.

Lesbian and Bisexual Women

So far, the discussion in this chapter has been about heterosexuality, because it is the dominant, socially approved form of sexual expression and the one that has clear, pervasive scripts. Let's turn now to other sexual identities and experiences. First, I will discuss sexual orientation in historical and social context and then describe the process of developing a personal identity as a lesbian or bisexual woman.

A Social History of Lesbianism

Throughout the 19th century, many women in North American society had intense friendships, in which they spent weeks at each others' homes, slept in the same beds, and wrote passionate and tender letters to each other describing the joys of perfect loving harmony and the agonies of parting. These relationships sometimes were part of a lifelong commitment. No one labeled these women homosexuals or lesbians (Faderman, 1981; Smith-Rosenberg, 1975). Of course, we have no way of knowing how many of these relationships involved genital sex. They certainly involved romance, attachment, and intimacy. But homosexuality was not yet a concept in popular use.

By the early 20th century, lesbianism came to be seen as a serious form of pathology. The lesbian was "sick" with a grave "disease." The change in attitude may have come about because women were beginning to demand political and social equality with men. First-wave feminists were campaigning for women's education and the vote, and more women were entering the workforce. When women's friendships and attachments to other women had the possibility of leading to real alternatives to heterosexual marriage and dependence on men, they were stigmatized and controlled. Feminists, in particular, were likely to be diagnosed as suffering from the newly invented disease of lesbianism (Kitzinger, 1987).

The medical and psychiatric establishment continued to evaluate lesbianism as pathological until the second wave of feminism in the late 1960s. Responding to pressure from women's and gay liberation activists, the American Psychiatric Association conceded that there is no evidence that homosexuality in itself is a disorder and removed it from its official manual of psychiatric diagnoses in 1973. Overnight, millions of people who had had a psychiatric disorder became normal, a compelling example of the power of social institutions to construct—and reconstruct—reality.

Research has tended to echo society's model of lesbianism. When lesbianism was labeled a form of pathology, research by physicians, psychiatrists, sexologists, and psychologists focused on theories of causes (note that there is little research on the causes of heterosexuality), on juicy details of the deviant behaviors, and on various approaches to "curing" the disorder (Kitzinger, 1987). Bisexuals were usually lumped with gay men and lesbians or ignored altogether (Rust, 2000). The results of the first sex surveys were controversial and shocking: 28 percent of the women had engaged in some sort of lesbian sexual activity; 13 percent had had at least one sexual experience with another woman leading to orgasm (Kinsey et al., 1953). This is quite a lot of "pathological" women.

Later laboratory research showed that the pattern of physiological change in the sexual response cycle is the same regardless of whether one's partner is a woman or a man (Masters & Johnson, 1979). By the 1980s, lesbian sex came to be seen as more satisfying than heterosexual sex. Some sex researchers suggested that women are better at making love to women than men are, and that lesbians have more satisfying relationships. The effects on individuals of these rapid changes in the social construction of lesbianism can only be guessed at. Women born in the first decades of the 20th century have seen lesbianism transformed from an official psychiatric disorder to a "lifestyle choice" in their own lifetime.

Still, societal attitudes about gays, bisexuals, and lesbians remain negative. About 60 percent of Americans believe that sexual relations between two same-sex adults are always or almost always wrong (Hyde & DeLamater, 2003). Studies in several countries—including the United States, Norway, and Turkey—show that men's attitudes are more negative than women's (Anderssen, 2002; Herek, 2002; Sakalli, 2002). In more than 70 countries around the world, same-sex sexual acts are illegal and may be punished by imprisonment, beatings, or execution (Kitzinger, 2001). In the United States, antigay discrimination and harassment is common, which discourages lesbians and gay men from becoming socially visible.

Defining Sexual Orientations

Contemporary definitions of lesbianism reflect the political and social complexities of the category. Some definitions focus on lesbianism as a refusal to accept male dominance:

> Lesbian is a label invented by the Man to throw at any woman who dares to be his equal . . . who dares to assert the primacy of her own needs. (Radicalesbians, 1969, cited in Kitzinger, 1987, p. 43)

Others focus on intimacy and attachment:

> a woman who loves women, who chooses women to nurture and support and to create a living environment in which to work creatively and independently, whether or not her relations with these women are sexual. (Cook, quoted in Golden, 1987, p. 20)

Still others emphasize the individual's self-definition, as well as her behavior:

> a woman who has sexual and erotic-emotional ties primarily with women or who sees herself as centrally involved with a community of self-identified lesbians . . . and who is herself a self-identified lesbian. (Ferguson, quoted in Golden, 1987, p. 21)

Definitions of bisexuality are equally complex. A bisexual woman is capable of emotional and sexual attachment to both women and men. However, traditionally some researchers and clinicians have maintained that there is no such thing as a true bisexual, implying that they are just confused or indecisive and will eventually decide to be either gay or straight (Rust, 2000). Bisexuals may feel that they fit in with neither gay nor straight culture. They may be accused by the gay community of wanting to avoid the stigma of the homosexual label and of using cross-sex relationships to hide from their own homosexuality (Ault, 1996; Rust, 1993; 2000).

Some feminists argue that bisexuality is a revolutionary concept because it challenges the "little boxes" of sexual orientation and pushes society beyond dualistic thinking about sexuality (Firestein, 1998). Indeed, some people adopt bisexual identities to reflect their gender politics—they are attracted to *people*, not gender categories of males and females—or as a challenge to the belief that everyone can be neatly labeled (Rust, 2000). Nevertheless, individuals identifying as "bi" face difficult choices about how to present themselves in everyday life (Ault, 1996).

It is clear that women do not always mean the same things when they say "I am a lesbian" (or bisexual). A study done in England compared the explanations or stories about the experience of lesbianism given by 41 self-identified lesbians ranging in age from 17 to 58 (Kitzinger, 1987). Five viewpoints emerged from a close comparison of the accounts.

The first viewpoint was the idea of lesbianism as personal fulfillment. Women who viewed themselves primarily in this way were sure of being lesbians, were unashamed of their orientation, and thought of themselves as happy, healthy individuals:

> I have never stopped feeling relief and happiness about discovering myself and, you know, accepting about myself and finding all these other women, and it means that I'm happy almost every day of my life. . . . I've never regretted being a lesbian . . . (Kitzinger, 1987, p. 99)

A second viewpoint defined sexual preferences in terms of love: Lesbianism was seen as the result of falling in love with a particular person who just happened to be a woman. Though defining themselves as lesbian, these women felt that they could or would have a heterosexual relationship if they fell in love with a man. A third viewpoint had to do with the feeling of being "born that way," yet resisting sexual labeling:

> I'm me. I'm . . . a social worker; I'm a mother. I've been married. I like Tschaikowsky; I like Bach; I like Beethoven; I like ballet. I enjoy doing a thousand and one things, and oh yes, in amongst all that, I happen to be a lesbian; I love a woman very deeply. But that's just a *part* of me. (Kitzinger, 1987, p. 110)

The fourth view identified women who came to lesbianism through being radical feminists:

> It was only through feminism, through learning about the oppression of women by men and the part that the enforcement of heterosexuality, the conditioning of girls into heterosexuality plays in that oppression, it was through that I decided that whatever happens I will never go back to being fucked by men . . . that decision was made because I'm a feminist, not because I'm a lesbian. I take the label "lesbian" as part of the strategy of the feminist struggle. (Kitzinger, 1987, p. 113)

A final view identified women who saw their sexual orientation as a sin or weakness—a "cross to bear." These women were sometimes ashamed of being lesbians, said they would not have chosen it, and would be happier if they were heterosexual.

This study explored the multiple meanings women give to their sexuality and its relationship to the rest of their lives. Each of the ways these women subjectively experienced their sexuality had both costs and benefits for the individual.

Developing a Lesbian or Bisexual Identity

The process of **coming out**, or accepting lesbianism as a part of one's identity, may be slow and erratic. Gay, bisexual, and lesbian adolescents do not have an easy time. They are at higher risk for low self-esteem, emotional isolation, poor school performance, dropping out, and a variety of other problems. The suicide rate for lesbian and gay youths is two to three times higher than for other adolescents (Black & Underwood, 1998).

Coming out can take place at any time from middle childhood to late middle or old age. When it occurs later in life, it has been likened to a second adolescence. One woman, who came out as a 56-year-old grandmother, explained: "I simply did not know there was any other way to live than heterosexual. I knew I was pretty miserable, but I just accepted that as part of the way things had to be" (Lewis, 1979, p. 19). Being out is related to greater social support, improved relationships, and lower psychological distress in lesbians of all ages (Jordan & Deluty, 2000; Morris, Waldo, & Rothblum, 2001).

Women may first come into contact with lesbians or the idea of lesbianism in many ways. Before the gay rights movement, same-sex activity often occurred in a social vacuum. One woman recalled: "I was 16 when I first got sexually involved . . . I didn't think of it as being anything weird. I just thought of it as being neat, really something terrific. . . . I thought it was a unique thing we were doing" (Ponse, 1978, p. 187). Young women still struggle with the meaning of their desire for another woman and the dangers it represents (Ussher & Mooney-Somers, 2000). However, they now may read about the topic in the media or connect with a lesbian community and get involved in gay activism or politics.

Women's sexual identity seems to be potentially fluid and changeable (Bohan, 1996; Golden, 1987; Rust, 1993, 2000). Some women identify first as heterosexual, then as lesbian, later as bisexual. Others go through these changes in reverse. And labels and behaviors don't necessarily match. Some women say they are lesbians although their behavior is heterosexual or bisexual; still others say they are hetero-sexual although their behavior is lesbian or bisexual. Some women experience their sexual orientation as freely chosen, while others see it as beyond their control. Women's racial or ethnic identification is also intertwined with their development of a sexual identity.

In interviews with women college students, every possible grouping of feelings and activities existed within sexual identification categories (Golden, 1987). Among women who identified themselves to the researcher as lesbians, there were some who were sexually inexperienced, some whose sexual behavior was exclusively with other women, some with heterosexual experience, and some with bisexual experience. Like those who identify as lesbian, women who identify themselves as bisexual show a diversity of actual experience (Shuster, 1987). In a study of lesbians and bisexual women aged 14 to 21 years, self-identification had changed over time for many of the young women; more than half who identified as lesbian had identified as bisexual at some time in the past, and the majority had had sexual activity with both other women and with men (Rosario, Meyer-Bahlburg, Hunter, & Exner, 1996). In the first longitudinal study of lesbian and bisexual women, participants were first interviewed when they were 16 to 23 years old and followed up two years later. Half had changed their sexual orientation more than once, and one-third had changed between the two interviews—more evidence for the fluidity of women's sexual identities and behaviors (Diamond, 2000).

Almost all the research on lesbian and bisexual women has relied on all-white or predominantly white samples. Does identity development differ for women of different ethnic and racial backgrounds? Focusing on Latina lesbians, one re-searcher noted:

> Because as a Latino she is an ethnic minority person, she must be bicultural in Ameri-can society. Because she is a lesbian, she has to be polycultural among her own people. The dilemma for Latina lesbians is how to integrate who they are culturally, racially, and religiously with their identity as lesbians and women. (Espin, 1987a, p. 35)

Latina lesbians are perhaps more likely to remain in the closet, keeping their orien-tation secret from family and friends, than white lesbians because most members of their ethnic group strongly disapprove of lesbians. However, families who become aware of a daughter's lesbianism are unlikely to openly reject or disown her. They will remain silent, tacitly but not openly accepting the situation (Castaneda, 2000).

In a questionnaire study of 16 Latina (Cuban-born) lesbians, the respondents, like white participants in previous research, showed a wide range of subjective un-derstandings of their lesbianism. They also wrote eloquently about the difficulty of integrating their ethnic and sexual identities. This woman had earlier said that be-ing a Cuban and being a lesbian were equally important to her:

> I guess that if the choice were absolute, I would choose living among lesbians . . . but I want to point out that I would be extremely unhappy if all my Latin culture were taken out of my lesbian life. . . . I feel that I am both, and I don't want to have to choose. (Espin, 1987a, p. 47)

In interview studies, African American lesbians also have described issues of integrating multiple identities and group memberships: as lesbians, as members of the black community, and as part of the larger culture with its racism, sexism, and heterosexism:

> Diane (hesitated) to discuss her lesbian feelings while in college. The college she attended was predominantly White, and Diane relied a great deal on the Black community there for support. She considered that coming out to these individuals might jeopardize her acceptance in this group. Although Diane continued to explore her lesbian feelings internally, she also continued to date men. Several years later, as she did begin to come out to others, she feared that identification as a lesbian might pull her away from what she considered her primary reference group—Black Americans. (Loiacano, 1993, pp. 369–370)

African American families typically give strong support to their members in their struggles with racism, but may not have the same perspective about heterosexism. Also, African American religious groups have often been silent on issues of sexual orientation (Greene, 2000). Moreover, community values emphasize childbearing as a central role for women (Hatton, 1994). The small samples used in research to date make it difficult to generalize about African American lesbians and underscore the need for more research within the black community (Hatton, 1994). However, it is clear that, like other women of color, black lesbians "face the challenge of integrating more than one salient identity in an environment that devalues them on all levels" (Greene, 2000).

Asian American lesbians, too, face issues of multiple identities. Within Asian cultures, being a lesbian is viewed as a rejection of women's most important role, that of wife and mother. Moreover, the implication is that the lesbians' parents have failed and that the child is rejecting not only family values but Asian culture. In a study of 19 Asian American lesbians, the majority felt more comfortable in the lesbian community than the Asian American one, and reported that they had experienced more frequent discrimination as Asians than as lesbians. The researcher speculated that perhaps the stereotype of the passive but exotic Asian woman is so strong that the possibility that an Asian woman could be a lesbian is rarely considered; therefore, Asian lesbians experience more discrimination as women and Asians than as lesbians (Chan, 1993).

In a cross-cultural study of identity development, women aged 18 to 35 in Brazil, Peru, the Philippines, and the United States were asked "At what age did you realize that you would be heterosexual (or homosexual)?" In all four countries, lesbians reached this point of identity development at a later age than heterosexuals (Whitam, Daskalos, Sobolewski, & Padilla, 1998). Little is known about factors that contribute to developing a healthy lesbian identity. One study asked over 60 lesbian activists about factors that contributed to their successful coming-out process. These women mentioned being part of a gay community, using self-help and counseling, and acceptance by their families as important (Bringaze & White, 2001).

More research is needed on how women integrate sexual identity with other aspects of their sense of self. One model for integrating identities comes from Native

American cultures, where there is a tradition of accepting different sexes and sexualities, as Chapter 5 discussed. Some gay, lesbian, and bisexual Native Americans describe themselves as "two-spirit people." By taking this traditional name, they feel that they are returning to their Native American communities (Wilson, 1996).

Romantic Love and Sexual Pleasure

Romantic Love as a Cultural Script

Although there are few societal scripts for healthy homosexual relationships, heterosexuality is strongly scripted. One pervasive source of heterosexual scripting is the romance novels displayed in virtually every supermarket and shopping mall. Each of their covers features a woman (always young, white, beautiful) gazing rapturously up into the eyes of a tall, strong, handsome man. Their titles and their plots tell women that "Love Is Everything."

According to publishers' surveys, romance novels are read by almost 40 million American women. They account for 56 percent of mass-market paperback sales in the United States. More than 2,200 new titles are published every year. Romance novels aimed specifically at adolescents have been sold through school book clubs since about 1980, gaining in popularity every year. Although most romance novels are published in the United States, England, and Canada, their readership is global (Puri, 1997).

No one would claim that these novels are great literature. They follow a predictable script: "Woman meets (perfect) stranger, thinks he's a rogue but wants him anyway, runs into conflicts that keep them apart, and ends up happily in his arms forever" (Brown, 1989, p. 13). But their enduring popularity and appeal suggest that many women still believe (or want to believe) that love conquers all.

In romance novels, the heroine attracts the hero without planning or plotting on her part. In fact, she often fights her attraction, which she experiences as overwhelming, both physically and emotionally—her knees go weak, her head spins, her heart pounds, and her pulse quickens. The hero is often cold, insensitive, and rejecting, but by the end of the novel the reader learns that his coldness has merely been a cover for his love. The heroine is swept away and finally gives in to the power of love and desire.

What do young women learn from reading teen romances? A close analysis of a sample of 34 teen romances showed that the novels portrayed girls' sexuality as dangerous until it was channeled into heterosexual pairing. Girls' bodies were the site of a struggle for control among boyfriends, themselves, and their parents. In this struggle, the girl should appear passive: Girls responded to boys' cues but never took the lead themselves (Christian-Smith, 1994). In these novels, the lives of the heroines are made meaningful only by their heterosexual relationships.

Unfortunately, these relationships rarely include safe sex. Romance novels almost never depict the use of condoms in sexual encounters. And in a study of female college students, those who read the most romance novels had the most negative attitudes and intentions about condom use (Diekman, McDonald, & Gardner, 2000).

This study also showed that including safe-sex scripts in romance stories led to more positive attitudes towards condoms.

Romance novels are one of the many ways that women learn the cultural script that love defines a woman's existence. From earliest childhood, girls are encouraged to identify with heroines who are rescued by a handsome prince (Cinderella, Rapunzel), who are awakened from the coma of virginity by the love of a good man (Sleeping Beauty), or who transform an extremely unpromising prospect into a good catch through their unselfish devotion (Beauty and the Beast).

Why do so many women enjoy these fantasies? For adolescent girls, romance novels provide a way to make sense of their emerging sexuality (Christian-Smith, 1998). For hardworking wives and mothers, reading romances is an escape from humdrum reality into a reassuring fable of women's transforming men. Although the hero is initially cold, patronizing, sometimes even brutal, he actually loves the heroine; and it is the power of her love that transforms him into a sensitive and caring lover. In reading the romance, women may learn to interpret the insensitivity of their own boyfriends and lovers as evidence that underneath the gruff exterior is a manly heart of gold (Radway, 1984). Not surprisingly, this is an appealing fantasy.

What meanings do romantic scripts have for women who read romance novels in other cultural contexts? In India, dating is usually unacceptable, and women are expected to be virgins when they marry. Romantic love has little or nothing to do with choosing a life partner; most marriages are arranged by the couple's families. Yet India, where many middle-class women read English, may be the world's largest sales outlet for romance novels. A study of more than 100 young, single, middle-class Indian women suggested that reading romance novels is a form of cultural resistance. In them, women explored alternative, more liberated kinds of relationships with men. They also admired the spunky, feminine-but-strong heroines. And they gained information about sexuality. As one woman said, she had learned about the biology of sex at school, but it was from romance novels that she learned there is nothing wrong with sex—indeed, that it is pleasurable. For better and for worse, romance novels are part of the globalization of Western culture (Puri, 1997).

The Experience of Romantic Love

Given that the ideology of romance is directed largely at women, it might be expected that women are more romantic in their beliefs about relationships than men. The opposite seems to be true (see Figure 8.1). Studies (reviewed by Peplau and Gordon, 1985) show that, at least among the young predominantly white college students studied by most researchers, men are more likely to believe that true love comes only once, lasts forever, and overcomes obstacles such as religious differences. They are more likely to believe in love at first sight and to be game players, enjoying flirtation and pursuit. Consistent with their beliefs, men report falling in love earlier in a new relationship. They also feel more depressed, lonely, and unhappy after a breakup and are less likely to initiate the breakup than their female partners. Women are more likely to report feeling joy or relief after breaking up (Choo, Levine, & Hatfield, 1997).

FIGURE 8.1
Not what she bargained for.

Source: Copyright © 1987 by Nicole Hollander. Reprinted by permission.

Women, on the other hand, report more emotional symptoms of falling in love—feeling giddy and carefree, floating on a cloud, and being unable to concentrate. And once a relationship has moved beyond its first stages, they may become more emotionally involved in it than their male partners.

The reasons for these differences in the experience of romantic love are unclear (Peplau & Gordon, 1985). Men may fall in love more readily because they rely more on physical attractiveness to decide whom to love—a characteristic that is easy to see at the start of a relationship. They may also react more quickly because the cultural script says that men should initiate a dating relationship. Women traditionally may have been more pragmatic because, in choosing a mate, they were choosing a provider as well as a romantic partner. Yet they may appear more emotional because cultural norms allow them to admit to having feelings.

Gender-related differences in the experience of romantic love are not large, and there is a great deal of overlap in the beliefs and self-reported behaviors of women and men. But the differences are interesting because they do not always fit stereotypical expectations. Perhaps future researchers will examine them in more detail.

Do Romantic Scripts Affect Women's Sexual Experiences?

Young women, especially those of the dominant white culture, are exposed to many messages that tell them love is everything to a woman. At the same time, they learn that finding fulfillment and self in the love of a man is outside their control. In the romantic script, it is always the man who actively initiates and pursues; the woman passively offers token resistance but finally gives in to his desire.

These beliefs inform the sexual scripts of teens and young adults. Research on college students, other dating couples, and marital partners shows that men are more likely than women to initiate sex. People are especially vulnerable in sexual encounters; the woman who wants to initiate sex and the man who wants to say no may fear being rejected as future dates and labeled as deviants. It feels more comfortable and secure to follow familiar patterns, as expressed by this British 16-year-old being interviewed by a researcher:

INTEVIEWER: Do you think boys always take the lead?
RESPONDENT: Yeh.
I: Yeh? And do you want them to or—
R: Yeh! Definitely! It's tradition (laughs).
I: Yeh? Why? Does it feel better or does it—
R: I don't know? I just think they should.
I: Yeh.
R: 'Cause I wouldn't, so I would expect them to, really.
I: So why wouldn't you?
R: I don't know? 'Cause I am the girl? (both laugh). (Sieg, 2000, p. 501)

When the woman in a dating situation wants to respond positively to a man's sexual initiative, she may still feel that she ought to offer *token resistance*—in other words, to say no when she actually intends to have sex. Both women and men engage in token resistance for a variety of reasons: they want to test their partner's response, add interest to a boring relationship, or prevent being taken for granted (Muehlenhard & Rodgers, 1998). However, saying no when they really mean yes may have serious negative consequences for women. It discourages honest communication and perpetuates restrictive gender stereotypes. Most important, it may teach men to disregard women's refusals. If men learn from experience that no is often only a prelude to yes, they may become more aggressive with dates (Muehlenhard & Hollabough, 1988).

Romantic scripts also encourage people to think of lovemaking as something that "just happens." However, although sex may seem "perfectly natural," it is not naturally perfect (Tevlin & Leiblum, 1983). Women who take responsibility for their own pleasure and who take an active role in sex are much more likely to experience pleasure than those who are passive. Satisfying sex depends on communication, learning, and initiative on the part of both partners.

Women are encouraged to view sex in rosy, romantic terms, focusing on candlelight dinners, courtship, and soft caresses. Because many men do not require a romantic context for arousal, they may initiate intercourse with little romantic prologue. Romance novels portray men as the experts who make women come alive sexually. But men are likely to be expert only in the techniques and behaviors that bring *them* pleasure. Though men could benefit from learning about women's desires, sexual scripts can impede their development. Women who have not learned to acknowledge their own arousal and who do not feel entitled to initiate or direct sex are not in a good position to teach their male partners how to give them pleasure.

Do Romantic Scripts Lead to Sexual Dysfunction?

Because our society does not give women the same permission to be fully sexual that it gives men, women may experience less sexual joy. A meta-analysis showed that women express somewhat more anxiety, fear, and guilt about sex than men and are less accepting of casual and extramarital sex (Oliver & Hyde, 1993). However, the women and men did not report any overall difference in sexual satisfaction. Most of the participants in these studies were college-aged students. Other research suggests that adult women in heterosexual relationships experience less pleasure in sexual activity than their partners. In national samples, women were much more likely than men to report lack of interest or pleasure in sex (Laumann, Paik, & Rosen, 1999), and men reported more emotional and physical satisfaction in their relationships (Waite & Joyner, 2001).

Acceptance of traditional sexual scripts is implicated in women's sexual dysfunction and suppression of desire. Sexual pleasure and orgasm require an awareness of one's own needs plus a feeling that one is entitled to express those needs and have them met. Women's recognition of themselves as sexual beings is blocked in many ways by cultural influences. Women are more likely to feel guilty and ashamed about their bodies, as discussed in Chapter 7. They also may feel guilty about having needs and fear their partners' disapproval if they express their needs (Tevlin & Leiblum, 1983, p. 134).

Another script is that women are sexually passive; men, sexually aggressive. Adolescents and college students believe that males almost always want to have sex and females almost always want to avoid it. The effect of accepting this script is that sexual behaviors may proceed on his, not her, timetable, and the woman's pleasure is reduced. Because both sexes believe that it is natural for the man to initiate a sexual encounter and take the lead throughout, it is he who decides what activities the couple will (and will not) try, the duration of intercourse, and the sequence of events. With such little control, it is unlikely that the woman will have her needs met. If the man prefers only brief foreplay, the couple may proceed to penile penetration before the woman is aroused, making intercourse painful and unpleasant for her. (The term *foreplay* itself implies that penis-in-vagina is the main event, with hugging, kissing, talking, genital touching, and all other sexual activities merely a prologue.) Women typically need more stimulation to have an orgasm than men do. If intercourse seems to be over almost before it has begun, the woman who has accepted a passive role may be reluctant to ask for more stimulation. Repeatedly engaging in sex when one is not aroused and not satisfied may lead to clinical sexual problems (Tevlin & Leiblum, 1983).

One way to see that passivity is a learned script rather than a natural mode for women is to compare the behavior of the same women with both female and male partners. When bisexual women were with a male partner, they were much less active and initiating than when they were with a female partner (Masters & Johnson, 1979). Women who take an active, autonomous, and assertive part in sexual expression are more likely to be orgasmic (and multiorgasmic) (Radlove, 1983).

Another aspect of sexual scripts is the idea that women should focus entirely on their partner's pleasure. Some sex manuals instruct women to fake orgasm, act like prostitutes, or perform strip routines for their partners. To feminists, advice like this raises troubling questions of where consent ends and coercion starts. Faking arousal, pleasure, and orgasm may become so ingrained that the woman may not be able to distinguish between her own sexual desire and her desire to please, and her sex life may come to feel like a part she is acting or a service she must perform.

Sexuality in Social Context

Controlling Women's Sexuality

Radical feminist perspectives suggest that male dominance is fundamentally sexual. In other words, the power of men over women in society is expressed and acted out in male control of the very definition and meaning of sexuality (MacKinnon, 1994).

Genital Mutilation

An example of overt control of women's sexuality is the practice of ***female genital mutilation*** (also termed ***female circumcision,*** although it involves much more drastic procedures than male circumcision). Female genital mutilation is a common practice in at least 28 African countries as well as parts of Asia and the Middle East. It is usually done to young girls between the ages of 4 and 12. It may involve removal of part or all of the clitoris (***clitoridectomy***), cutting away the clitoris plus part or all of the inner lips of the vulva (***excision***), or in addition to excision, sewing the outer lips of the vulva together to cover the urinary and vaginal entrances, leaving only a small opening for the passage of urine and menstrual blood (***infibulation***). A woman who has undergone infibulation must be cut open for childbirth (Abusharaf, 1998).

The genital surgery is usually done by a midwife with no medical training under unsanitary conditions. Complications such as infection and hemorrhaging are common; the presence of open wounds makes women extremely vulnerable to HIV infection. Other long-term health consequences, especially for infibulated women, include chronic pelvic and urinary tract infections, childbirth complications, and depression. Because the clitoris is damaged or removed, circumcised women feel little or no sexual pleasure and do not have orgasms. "Circumcision is intended to dull women's sexual enjoyment, and to that end it is chillingly effective" (Abusharaf, 1998, p. 25).

According to Amnesty International, which has investigated genital mutilation as a human rights issue, 135 million women living today have been subjected to the process, and each year another 2 million girls are cut. Genital mutilation is spreading to countries where there are large numbers of refugees from Africa, Asia, and the Middle East. Great Britain outlawed the practice in 1985 when three girls bled to death after the procedure, but no one has ever been prosecuted under the law (Laurance, 2001).

Why does this custom persist? It is believed to purify women and control their sexuality, making them more docile and obedient. Women who remain uncut are disrespected, considered promiscuous, and may become social outcasts. The practice of genital surgery has been very resistant to change. However, studies show that the more educated women are, the less willing they are to allow their daughters to be cut. As women in developing countries make gains toward social equality, becoming less dependent on marriage for survival, their attitudes may change.

The custom of genital mutilation is the result of a cultural construction of sexuality that may seem barbaric to outsiders. However, it was actually a common practice in England and the United States only a century ago, when clitoridectomies were done by physicians to cure upper-class women of too much interest in sex, and one health expert advised parents of girls who masturbated to apply pure carbolic acid to the clitoris (Michael et al., 1994). And some current Western practices seem barbaric to outsiders, too. What counts as normal depends on one's cultural standpoint:

> Today, some girls and women in the West starve themselves obsessively. Others undergo painful and potentially dangerous medical procedures—face lifts, liposuction, breast implants, and the like—to conform to cultural standards of beauty and femininity . . . people in the industrialized world must recognize that they too are influenced, often destructively, by traditional gender roles and demands. (Abusharaf, 1998, p. 24)

Clearly, each culture exerts its own pressures.

Cultural Variations in the United States

Even within the United States, Western (European) ideas about sexuality and love are not shared by people from all ethnic backgrounds. Because almost all psychological research on romantic beliefs and behavior has relied on white heterosexual college students, there is much more to learn about the experiences of other groups of people.

Religion and social class separate cultural groups within the United States. Like their white peers, African American girls learn different lessons about sex and love, depending on their social class and religion. They may be brought up in strict homes, receiving explicit warnings from their mothers about men and sex, or in quite permissive ones where sexual activity is regarded as good and pleasurable (Joseph & Lewis, 1981). In several studies, African American teenage girls have reported strong conflicts between their sexuality and their plans for an education (Tolman & Brown, 2001). Behaviorally, African American women are more conservative in some ways than white women—less likely to masturbate or to engage in oral sex (Hyde & DeLamater, 2003). Attitudes may differ, too; some writers have suggested that black women may be less likely than their white counterparts to believe in romantic love as a woman's reason for living and more likely to maintain strong feelings of independence (Williams, 1997).

Like black women, Latinas in the United States are a diverse group with respect to social class. In addition, their families come from many different countries, including Cuba, Puerto Rico, Guatemala, and Mexico. Despite this diversity, there are some commonalities affecting romantic and sexual attitudes and behaviors. Because of historical influences and the Catholic religion, virginity is an important concept. In Hispanic cultures, the honor of a family depends on the sexual purity of its women. The Virgin Mary is presented as an important model for young women, and abstaining from sex before marriage is stressed (Castaneda, 2000; Espin, 1986).

The traditional Hispanic ideal for men is one of *machismo*—men are expected to show their manhood by being strong, demonstrating sexual prowess, and asserting their authority and control over women. Women's complementary role of *marianismo* (named after the Virgin Mary) is to be sexually pure and controlled, submissive, and subservient. Their main sources of power and influence are in their roles as mothers. These traditional roles vary widely with social class, urban versus rural locations, and generational differences (Castaneda, 2000). Nevertheless, the cultural imperatives of virginity, martyrdom, and subordination continue to exert influence over the experience of love for Hispanic women. This socialization pattern can create difficulties in sexual expression and increase vulnerability to partner violence and HIV infection (Espin, 1986; Raffaelli & Ontai, 2001; Salgado de Snyder, Acevedo, Diaz-Perez, & Saldivar-Garduno, 2000).

In Asian cultures the public expression of sexuality is suppressed, and sexual matters are rarely discussed. Yet sexuality is viewed as a healthy and normal part of life. The Confucian and Buddhist roots of Asian cultures stress women's roles as wives, mothers, and daughters and place strong importance on maintaining family harmony. Influenced by these traditions, Asian Americans tend to be more sexually conservative than people of other ethnic groups; for example, Asian American college students are less likely to be sexually active than their white peers (Chan, 2000). However, their views about abortion are liberal. Although their backgrounds differ, the majority are of Chinese origin and from non-Christian religions, and they view abortion as a socially responsible decision to avoid overpopulation and poverty (Hyde & DeLamater, 2003).

Cross-cultural and ethnic group differences in attitudes toward sexuality and sexual practices remind us that there is no right way to think about sexuality. Rather, sexuality, including beliefs, values, and behavior, is always expressed in cultural context. It is social, emergent, and dynamic (White, Bondurant, & Travis, 2000).

Attractiveness and Sexual Desirability

Physical attractiveness is an important factor in romantic relationships (Sprecher & Regan, 2000). Good looks are especially important to men who are choosing a prospective sexual partner or mate, as shown by research in many cultures. When college students in the United States (Nevid, 1984) and in India (Basu & Ray, 2001) were asked to rate physical, personal, and background characteristics they consider important in a sexual relationship, males tended to emphasize their partners' physical characteristics and females to emphasize personal qualities (see Figure 8.2). However, when rating characteristics they considered important in a long-term, meaningful relationship, both men and women emphasized personal qualities more than looks. And in both studies there was considerable overlap between the traits desired by women and men.

Because attractiveness is more important to men, variations from attractiveness norms are more stigmatizing for women. In one study, college students received a description of an obese or normal-weight person and then evaluated the person on aspects of sexuality. Students believed that an obese and a normal-weight man would have about the same sexual experiences and desirability; however, they viewed an obese woman as less sexually attractive and likable, and less likely to have pleasurable sexual experiences (Regan, 1996). Clearly, women's sexuality, more than men's, was being evaluated in terms of physical attractiveness. Of course, very few women can match the idealized images of femininity (Chapter 7), and no woman can do so as she grows older.

FIGURE 8.2

Source: For Better or For Worse Copyright © 1999 Lynn Johnston Productions. Distributed by Universal Press Syndicate. Reprinted with permission. All rights reserved.

Disability and Sexuality

Disabled girls and women, like nondisabled women, are judged by their attractiveness. Additionally, they are judged against an ideal of the physically perfect person who is free from weakness, pain, and physical limitations. In a study of attitudes about the sexuality of disabled and nondisabled women, Australian college students expressed much more negative attitudes about the disabled women's sexuality, and men were more negative than women (Chandani, McKenna, & Maas, 1989). Interviews with women who had cerebral palsy showed that one of the psychological tasks they faced was reconciling their bodies and experiences with society's norms for women (Tighe, 2001).

Women with disabilities confront stereotypes that sexual activity is inappropriate for them; that people with disabilities need caretakers, not lovers; that they cannot cope with sexual relationships; that they are all heterosexual and should feel grateful if they find any man who wants them; and that they are too fragile to have a sex life. When people around them express these stereotypical beliefs, it is difficult for women with disabilities to see themselves as potential sexual and romantic partners. These beliefs can interfere with disabled women's sexual expression and their chances for having relationships. In a national survey that compared women aged 18 to 83 with and without disabilities, the disabled women were less satisfied with the frequency of dating and perceived personal and societal barriers to dating relationships (Rintala et al., 1997). Indeed, disabled women are less likely to be married than disabled men, and more likely to be abandoned by their partners when a disability like multiple sclerosis is diagnosed (Chrisler, 2001; Fine & Asch, 1988).

Parental attitudes and expectations for daughters with disabilities can have important effects on daughters' sexual development. In a study of 43 women with physical and sensory disabilities (including cerebral palsy and spinal cord injury), many of the parents had low expectations of heterosexual involvement for their daughters because they saw them as unable to fulfill the typical role of wife and mother. Some of these daughters became sexually active partly out of rebellion and a desire to prove their parents wrong, while others remained sexually and socially isolated. In contrast, other parents saw their daughters as normal young women, with the disability only one of many unique characteristics. These young women became socially and sexually active as a matter of normal growing up. One interviewee reported:

> In childhood, I was led to believe that the same social performance was expected of me as of my cousins who had no disabilities. I was a social success in part because my mother expected me to succeed. In fact, she gave me no choice. (Rousso, 1988, p. 156)

Is Sex Talk Sexist?

A negative evaluation of female sexuality is deeply embedded in language, as Chapter 3 discussed. Linguists agree that languages develop an abundance of terms for concepts that are of particular interest or importance to a society. English has many terms describing women and their genitals in specifically sexual ways, and most of these are negative—*whore (ho)*, *bitch*, *cunt*, and *gash* are a few examples. One analysis found more than 200 terms for *prostitute* in English novels (Stanley, 1977). Absences in language are also revealing. For men, *virile* and *potent* connote positive masculine sexuality, as do other, more colloquial terms such as *stud, macho man*, and *hunk*. However, there is no English word for a sexually active woman that is not negative in connotation.

Slang words for sexual intercourse (*ramming, banging, nailing*) suggest that it is something violent and mechanical done to women rather than a mutual pleasure. The same verb can even be used to describe harm and sex—as in "she got screwed." One anthropologist who studied college students in their natural habitat (the dorm) reported that about one-third of the young men talked of women, among themselves, as "chicks, broads, and sluts." Their "locker-room style" was characterized by "its focus on the starkest physicalities of sex itself, stripped of any stereotypically feminine sensibilities such as romance, and by its objectifying, often predatory attitudes toward women" (Moffat, 1989, p. 183).

In a more recent study, New Zealand psychology students observed talk about sex in their daily life settings for a week and then analyzed the metaphors used. The four most common kinds of metaphor were food and eating (*munching rug; tasty; fresh muffin; meat market*); sport and games (*muff diving, getting to first base, chasing, scoring*); animals (*pussy, spanking the monkey, hung like a horse*); and war and violence (*whacking it in, sticking, pussy whipped, launching his missile*). Males were two and a half times more likely to be the active agent (*"He scored her sister"*) than females (*"She turns my crank"*) or both partners (*"They've been bonking away"*), reflecting the tendency to objectify women (Weatherall & Walton, 1999).

U.S. college students, too, have been asked to report the sexual language they used. Male students, especially those who were members of fraternities, were more likely than female students to report using degrading terms to refer to female genitals and aggressive terms to refer to sex acts. These same students next listened to a conversation in which one speaker told another about having sex with someone he or she had recently met. When the sex partner was talked about using the more degrading terms, he or she was viewed as less intelligent and moral (Murnen, 2000).

It is easy to see how women might become ambivalent about sexual pleasure when the very language of sex suggests that the female role is synonymous with being exploited or degraded. Negative language about women and sexual acts probably encourages both women and men to view women and their sexuality negatively. By making it hard to imagine alternatives, sexist language also inhibits social change. However, feminists have added new terms to the language, naming women's experiences (date rape, sexual harassment, girl power). Gay activists, too, have added to the language of sexuality (gay, straight, bi, coming out). Language change is an ongoing process (Crawford, 2001).

Studs and Sluts: Is There Still a Double Standard?

Traditionally, a *sexual double standard* was widely endorsed: Women were severely sanctioned for any sexual activity outside of heterosexual marriage, while for men such activity was expected and tolerated. Boys had to "sow their wild oats," while girls were warned that a future husband "won't buy the cow if he can get milk for free." Because sexual activity before marriage was viewed as wrong for women, fewer young women than young men were sexually active (Laumann & Michael, 2001).

For women, the double standard was often connected with a Madonna/whore dichotomy. Women were either "the pure, virginal, 'good' woman on her pedestal, unspoiled by sex or sin" or "her counterpart, the whore . . . consumed by desires of the flesh . . . dangerous and inherently bad" (Ussher, 1989, p. 14). A woman could not belong to both categories, and women who enjoyed sex were relegated to the "bad." Oliva Espin (1986) describes this dichotomy in Latin culture:

> To enjoy sexual pleasure, even in marriage, may indicate lack of virtue. To shun sexual pleasure and to regard sexual behavior exclusively as an unwelcome obligation toward her husband and a necessary evil in order to have children may be seen as a manifestation of virtue. In fact, some women even express pride at their own lack of sexual pleasure or desire. (p. 279)

By the 1970s, the double standard had decreased. Access to contraception, the sexual revolution, and women's liberation were said to have made women and men equally free to express themselves sexually outside of heterosexual marriage. Today, when people are asked to judge the sexual behavior of a hypothetical woman/man, the results may show little evidence of a double standard (Crawford & Popp, 2003).

However, although people may reject the double standard when asked about it hypothetically, they do not always behave that way in their daily lives. Researchers who have done their studies by interviewing their participants, meeting with them in small groups, or just hanging out with them find that the double standard is still used to control girls and women's sexual autonomy (Crawford & Popp, 2003). Behaviors that are acceptable for boys and men—having many partners, taking the sexual initiative, openly talking about sex—are less acceptable for girls and women (see Box 8.3). Sexual labels are still used to control and harass. For example, when middle-school students (ages 11 to 14) were observed in their daily interactions, the researchers reported that girls were often labeled whores, bitches, and sluts:

BOX 8.3 ❧ College Men Vote on the Double Standard

Between 1983 and 1987, more than 2,500 college men were asked a series of questions about the double standard by sex researcher Shere Hite. Here are the survey questions, along with their responses. Do you think that today's male college students would express similar or different attitudes?

1. Do you believe the double standard is fair? *No, according to 92 percent of men.*
2. If you met a woman you liked and wanted to date, but then found out she had had sex with ten to twenty men during the preceding year, would you still like her and take her seriously? *Most men were quite doubtful they could take her seriously; only 35 percent could.*
3. If one of your best male friends had sex with ten to twenty women in one year, would you stop taking him seriously and see it as a character flaw? *Definitely not—according to 95 percent of the men.*

4. Isn't this a double standard? And to equalize it, what should be done? Do you believe (a) men should stop being so "promiscuous" or (b) women should have as much sex as men do, with no negative feedback?

Most men found this a very difficult choice, but could see the logic of the question; the majority, approximately two-thirds, voted for (b), preferring giving women "equal rights" to changing their own view regarding sex. But many men also commented that of course the woman they would marry would probably not be one of those women who had chosen to have sex with that many men!

Source: From *Women and Love*, by Shere Hite. Copyright © 1987 by Shere Hite. Used by permission of Alfred A. Knopf, a division of Random House, Inc.

Joe and Hank walked over to a girl sitting at a table and repeatedly called her "slut-face" and "whore." They asked if her rates had gone down, or if they were still a quarter. They also told her they knew she'd "fuck any guy in the school". . . She finally said, "Fuck you," at which point Hank and Joe backed off and left her alone. (Eder, Evans, & Parker, 1995, p. 130)

Silencing Women's Desire

Because attitudes toward girls' sexuality are mixed, normal bodily desires may be denied and girls may learn to define their sexuality in others' terms.

What role do parents play in educating girls about their sexuality? Unfortunately, many parents are uncomfortable discussing sexuality with their adolescents. Parents may mislabel sexually important parts of the body or simply give them no names at all—especially for girls. Mothers are more reluctant to name the sexual parts of their daughters' anatomy than their sons' and do it at a later age. Few girls know they have a clitoris or that it is a separate organ from the vagina; many confuse the urinary opening with the vagina. Boys learn to personify their penises with names such as *johnson* or *dick*, to ascribe power and strength with names such as *cock* and *tool*, or to make everyday comparisons (testicles are *nuts* or *balls*). Girls learn to talk about their genitals, if at all, with terms such as *down there, privates, between your legs, nasty,* or *bottom.* It is not surprising that after years of objectification of their *bodies* and shamed silence about their sexual *embodiment,* many young women are far more prepared to look sexy than to be sexual.

Can schools fill the education gap? Sex education does not seem to help girls and women give voice to their own desire. Nearly three-quarters of the African American and white women participating in one community study reported that they had wanted more sex education when they were growing up (Wyatt & Riederle, 1994). In a British study, only 44 percent of a sample of more than 3,000 high school students considered their school sex education satisfactory. The majority thought it should start earlier, be taught in mixed-sex groups, and provide information on STDs and contraception. They did not want sex education left to parents (Mellanby, Phelps, Crichton, & Tripp, 1996).

In many U.S. schools, sex education has been shaped by pressures from some conservative parents and religious groups who believe that knowledge about sexuality encourages sexual activity. There is a "behind-the-scenes war" being waged between conservatives and liberals (Hyde & Jafee, 2000, p. 292), and adolescents are in the line of fire. Many schools have adopted federally funded programs such as *Sex Respect* that teach that abstinence is the only safe and moral approach to sexuality. Middle-school children are taught to chant slogans such as "Don't be a louse; wait for your spouse," and take chastity pledges in class (Hyde & Jafee, 2000).

These programs present heterosexual marriage as the sole place for sexual expression. They encode gender stereotypes of boys as sexually insatiable aggressors and girls as defenders of virginity (Hyde & Jafee, 2000). At best, girls are taught that they should avoid being victims—of teen pregnancy, STDs, or selfish males. They also learn that "good girls just say no" to sex. But nowhere do they hear the suggestion that girls and women might like, want, need, seek out, or enjoy sexual activity (outside of heterosexual marriage). Even in the more enlightened programs, girls see educational videos only about menstruation while boys are seeing films about wet dreams, erections, and penis size. And lesbian, gay, and bisexual students' need for information may be ignored altogether.

This kind of sex education does not allow young women to come to terms with their own feelings of sexuality. It "allows girls one primary decision—to say yes or no—to a question not necessarily their own" (Fine, 1988, p. 34). By emphasizing to girls the many ways that they can be victimized, it may also convey the idea that women are always weak and vulnerable, undermining their self-confidence (Marecek, 1986). Suddenly, a young girl's male companions, with whom she previously may have played freely, are transformed into slightly dangerous strangers. The neighborhood itself is no longer safe for her. bell hooks (1989) has poignantly described the consequences of this fear:

> I no longer felt the intimate sweet companionship with strange black men and even the old familiar faces. They were the enemies of one's virginity. They had the power to transform women's reality—to turn her from a good woman into a bad woman, to make her a whore, a slut. (p. 149)

This social construction of sexuality gives young women little opportunity to learn how to say no at whatever stage of sexual activity suits them, and no chance to learn when they would rather say yes—or be the one who asks. Because society constructs sexuality in terms of the presumably dangerous and uncontrollable urges of boys and men, girls and women are assigned the role of keeping everything under control by wanting only romance, never sex (Tolman & Brown, 2001). By assuming that girls and women are not active agents in their own sexuality, sex education contributes to muting women's desires:

> The naming of desire, pleasure, or sexual entitlement, particularly for females, barely exists in the formal agenda of public schooling on sexuality. When spoken, it is tagged with reminders of "consequences"—emotional, physical, moral, reproductive, and/or financial. . . . A genuine discourse of desire would invite adolescents to explore what feels good and bad, desirable and undesirable, grounded in experiences, needs, and limits. (Fine, 1988, p. 33)

There is resistance to this silencing. Some girls mock scripts about love and sexuality when they are around boys (Eder et al., 1995). Among some African American and Puerto Rican girls in one study, their comments often combined a sense of danger and desire. As one of them explained to the researcher: "Boys always be trying to get into my panties . . . I don't be needin' a man who won't give me no pleasure but takes my money and expect me to take care of him" (Fine, 1988, p. 35).

Women's sexual agency and desire also have been relatively invisible in sex education materials for adults. Up to the 1950s, sex manuals described women as slow to become aroused and capable of being sexually awakened only by the skill of their husbands in the security of marriage. Musical metaphors abounded, with women characterized as harps or violins that the male master musician could cause to give forth beautiful melodies. The sex manuals of the 1960s and 1970s urged women to be sexually free, but still on others' terms. After analyzing their contents, one feminist researcher asked, "Clearly, the new liberated woman is 'sensuous' and sexy—but is she sexual, on her own behalf?" (Altman, 1984, p. 123). Today, conservative marriage manuals such as *The Surrendered Wife* advise that no woman should refuse to have sex with her partner just because she doesn't feel like it.

Even in feminist theorizing, it is hard to find positive accounts of erotic experiences. A large proportion of feminist writing about sexuality has come from a radical perspective that views men and heterosexuality as oppressive. These writers explore sexual domination, but leave the question of how to represent women's experiences of heterosexual desire, power, and pleasure still open for debate.

Violence in Close Relationships

Dating and romantic relationships can provide a host of valuable experiences such as intimacy, companionship, sexual experimentation, and learning how to negotiate conflicts and differences (White, Donat, & Bondurant, 2001). However, courtship also has its dark side. Relationship problems can lead to anger, frustration, and confusion. Unfortunately, violence is an all-too-common means of exerting control in sexual encounters and romantic relationships. Here we look at verbal, physical, and sexual aggression in relationships.

Dating Violence

Violence between dating partners is so common that virtually everyone has witnessed a couple screaming, arguing, or yelling ugly names at each other, or one partner sulking resentfully or stomping off in a huff. In national surveys, over 80 percent of college students say they have been on the sending or receiving end of this kind of verbal aggression within the past year. Moreover, over one-third report having engaged in physical aggression during the same time period: grabbing, shoving, throwing something, or hitting. The rates are similar for women and men, across different ethnic groups, regions of the country, and types of colleges and universities. In sum, dating violence is a pervasive problem (White et al., 2001).

Although women and men report similar rates of aggression, their motives tend to be different. For men, staying in control is often an important relationship goal (Lloyd, 1991). Men are more likely to say that they aggress in order to intimidate and frighten the partner and control the relationship, while women say that they do so in self-defense or because they lost control of themselves (Campbell, 1992). Another motive for women's aggression is sensitization to the possibility of harm. Women who have experienced aggression in the past—for example, those who witnessed parental violence or were in a prior abusive relationship—may be primed to respond to aggression with more aggression, and even to initiate violence (White et al., 2001).

Is it possible to predict whether a partner is likely to be violent? Studies show a consistent pattern of characteristics in violence-prone men and women. For men, the characteristics are related to a need for dominance and control. Violent men are quick to anger and have used violence to get their way in the past. They believe that violence helps win arguments and that violence against a partner is justifiable. They hold untraditional rather than benevolent and protective beliefs about women. They are likelier than other men to use drugs, have divorced parents, and to be undergoing life stress. For women, the predictors are somewhat different: a history of child abuse, as well as anxiety, depression, and drug use, all increase the likelihood of being aggressive (White et al., 2001). However, there are some gender similarities: For both women and men, the single biggest predictor of aggressive behavior is having an aggressive partner. Truly, "violence begets more violence."

The consequences of courtship violence are more severe for women than for men. Women report more fear in violent situations, and they are three to four times as likely to sustain major emotional trauma and serious physical injuries due to dating violence than are men (Makepeace, 1986; Sugarman & Hotaling, 1989). The psychological effects can spread to virtually every area of life, affecting emotional states (hyperarousal, depression), cognitive functioning (lack of ability to concentrate, poor performance in school), and identity (low self-esteem). Dating violence also is associated with risk of further harm such as unwanted pregnancy, substance abuse, suicide, eating disorders, and high-risk sexual behaviors (Hanson, 2002; Silverman, Raj, Mucci, & Hathaway, 2001). In sum, being on the receiving end of dating violence can disrupt a young woman's healthy development in many serious ways.

Unfortunately, the ideology of romance encourages women to believe that they must stay in a relationship even if this means accepting violence and abuse (Carey & Mongeau, 1996). Studies of women who are in ongoing abusive relationships, compared to those who are not, show that they have more traditional attitudes toward women's roles and more romantic attitudes about love. They say they are committed to their partner and in love with him. They allow their partner to control them and often offer excuses for his abuse (Follingstad, Rutledge, McNeill-Hawkins & Polek, 1992). For these women, a romantic relationship has become a self-destructive trap (Carey & Mongeau, 1996). Belief in a fairy-tale ending can be harmful if it allows a woman to tolerate an abusive relationship (Jackson, 2001).

Sexual Coercion and Acquaintance Rape

Rape is defined as sexual penetration without the person's consent, obtained through force or threat of harm, or when the person is incapable of giving consent (Bachar & Koss, 2001). The more general terms *sexual assault* and *sexual coercion* include other kinds of unwanted sexual contact (such as groping and fondling) (White, Bondurant, & Donat, 2004). Here, we examine sexual coercion within relationships.

In national samples of adult women (Tjaden & Thoennes, 1998) and college students (Koss, Gidycz, & Wisniewski, 1987) in the United States, more than half of respondents report experiencing some form of sexual coercion. For example, in one survey, 54 percent of college women reported a history of sexual victimization. About 12 percent reported being verbally pressured into sexual intercourse, and an additional 14 percent reported unwanted contact such as forced sexual touching or kissing. Over 15 percent had experienced sexual penetration without their consent—in other words, they had experienced acts that meet the legal definition of rape—and another 12 percent had experienced attempted rape (Koss et al., 1987). However, 73 percent of the women who had experienced acts legally defined as rape did not label their experience as rape.

Most unacknowledged rapes are committed by someone known to the victim.

> Lenore stopped by her boyfriend's apartment to "hang out," but her boyfriend wasn't there. His roommate, a foreign exchange student, invited her in to wait for her boyfriend and then suggested that they watch a sex video. Lenore felt uncomfortable but thought that maybe he did not know how to act around American girls and did not want to embarrass him. She said no to the sex video by changing the subject. Then he proceeded to kiss and fondle her, although she said that her boyfriend might come back and that she wasn't interested in him in that way. He forced her to have sex on the couch and then held the door open for her to get up and leave. Lenore did not think she had been raped but she knew that she felt terrible because she had not wanted to have sex. (From an account told to me by an anonymous student, with her permission)

Sexual assault by a dating partner or someone known to the victim is termed *acquaintance rape.* Most of the public thinks of rape in terms of a stranger's jumping out of a dark alley, but acquaintance rape occurs far more often than stranger rape and has been called a hidden crime (Parrot & Bechhofer, 1991). Acquaintance rape is fostered by sexual scripts that encourage women to be passive and offer token resistance and encourage men to take the initiative physically and ignore a woman's refusals.

In a recent study of college students, about 20 percent of the sample reported experiences of sexual coercion. These included forced but nonpenetrative sex acts (i.e., a woman's date held her head down to force her to perform oral sex on him) and intercourse in situations where the woman was too impaired by alcohol or drugs to give consent:

> We were drunk. I didn't have control over myself & I didn't have the cognitive ability to say NO. I can't remember everything, but I know we had sex and if I were sober it would not have happened. I just could not control myself at all. (Kahn, Jackson, Kully, Badger, & Halvorsen, 2003, p. 241)

Women also commonly reported giving in to unwanted sex because a partner would not stop begging, whining, and pleading: "If he was really in the mood and I wasn't, he couldn't take no for an answer. We would just argue and argue about it until I gave in . . . (Kahn et al., 2003, p. 240). Even though some of the women's experiences qualified as rape, a woman was likely to use that term only if the man had used a high degree of force and intimidation or if she woke up to find him sexually penetrating her. If the assailant was a boyfriend, or the woman was too drunk to consent, she was less likely to call the incident rape. Some feminists argue that using the label "rape" is important; without it, the incident is not recognized as a crime and goes unreported and unpunished. Moreover, the woman is unlikely to get the help and support she needs. Others point out that a woman's choice of label may be part of how she copes with sexual assault, and she has the right to define her own experience (Kahn et al., 2003).

Whatever the label, such an experience has consequences for the survivor. Many studies have shown that victims of sexual coercion, like victims of other kinds of violence, suffer psychological consequences in such areas as emotional functioning (anxiety, phobias, depression), social relations (loss of trust, sexual dysfunction), and identity (lowered self-esteem). The physical aftereffects of rape include injuries sustained during the rape, unwanted pregnancy, and infection with an STD. The victim may also suffer from physical effects of trauma and anxiety, such as nightmares and inability to sleep. The psychological effects of rape are more severe when the assailant is an acquaintance or boyfriend than when he is a stranger, because acquaintance rape violates not only the woman's body but her trust, and because she is more likely to blame herself for what happened (Katz, 1991). The physical, emotional, and psychological aftereffects of rape interact with each other to impair the woman's ability to function, sometimes very severely (Koss & Kilpatrick, 2001).

Who is likely to inflict coercive sex? Unfortunately, there is no easy way to spot a potential rapist in advance, because most men involved in acquaintance rape look and act much like other men. However, certain factors in a man's background, personality, and social setting have been associated with sexual aggression toward women. Background factors include coming from a violent or abusive family, getting into trouble with the authorities as a teen, and being exceptionally sexually active at a young age. Personality factors include impulsivity, a need to dominate women, and low self-esteem. Factors in the social environment include involvement in a sports team or fraternity, alcohol use, exposure to pornography, and having friends who encourage sexual conquests and objectification of women (Frintner & Rubinson, 1993; Koss & Gaines, 1993; Seto, Maric, & Barbaree, 2001; White & Koss, 1993).

The possibility of sexual coercion means that, for women, relationships represent a conflict between pleasure and danger. Unfortunately, there are few positive cultural messages about women's right to know and enjoy their bodies and their sexuality.

Making a Difference

Sexual norms are changing rapidly in Western societies and these changes have global impact. The increasing acceptance of same-sex and extramarital sexual behavior has been liberating in some ways, but a sexual double standard remains; and women's sexuality is still suppressed, both overtly (genital mutilation) and covertly (the double standard). Relationship violence remains a major social problem. Here I will focus on efforts to end relationship violence as well as efforts to change cultural images of women's sexuality so that women are empowered to make sexual choices without coercion or shame.

Ending Relationship Violence

Dating violence is often rooted in earlier experiences of family violence and sexual abuse. Therefore, one important route to ending it is to reduce these earlier traumas. Educating adolescents about dating violence and acquaintance rape is important, too, but not all educational programs are equally effective.

Rape prevention programs on college campuses usually are aimed at women, offering advice on how to reduce the risk of assault (don't drink too much; don't be too trusting; say no clearly). However, there is little evidence that adopting these restrictions would actually protect woman from sexual assault; in reality, any woman is at risk for acquaintance rape. Also, advice on how not to be a victim might encourage a woman to blame herself if she is raped.

Programs for men aim for attitude change, too, with such advice as "No means no." But attitude change does not always lead to behavior change. Recent studies suggest that programs run *by* men *for* men are most effective in changing men's behavior. Some of these programs are organized through men's fraternities or athletic teams. For example, West Chester University of Pennsylvania has a peer education program for fraternity members (Mahlstedt, 1999), and Northeastern University sponsors a program for athletes, educating them to intervene when they witness relationship aggression of any kind (www.sportinsociety.org/mvp.html). Men can make an important contribution to feminism and to women's lives by working to end violence against women. This goal has spurred an international movement by men, the White Ribbon Campaign.

Sex as a Subject, Not an Object

Lily, a 17-year-old Latina interviewed in a study of girls' sexual desire, was asked what makes her feel sexy. Her reply referred to her boyfriend: "When he says that I look sexy, that's one of my sexy days." Though the interviewer repeatedly asked her how she herself felt, she continued to describe what her boyfriend thought (Tolman & Brown, 2001, p. 143).

In the midst of the pressures to experience sex on others' terms, it is well to remember that in spite of social pressures from all sides, some women, some of the time, do manage to love their bodies, define sexual pleasure in their own terms, and have good sex! Where can the missing discourse of women's sexual desire, action, and pleasure be found? Women's accounts of their sexual experiences, relationships, adventures, and fantasies offer possibilities (Hite, 1976, 1987). Celebrities such as Dr. Ruth and Susie Sexbright speak openly of the joys of sex; feminist therapists provide workshops on self-pleasuring and interventions to increase sexual pleasure (Dodson, 1987; Palace, 1999). Guides to women's health and sexuality such as *Our Bodies, Ourselves* have been written by women. Works of fiction and drama by women explore their naming and claiming of desire (see Box 8.4). Powerful and playful voices emerge from women's music, too, from the blues (Bessie Smith singing "You've Been a Good Ole Wagon") to Janis Joplin ("One Night Stand") and Ani DiFranco ("In or Out").

Such records of women's experiences remind us that the terms of sexual attraction and erotic arousal are not merely programmed into us. Often, they may even contradict the cultural stereotypes that surround us, as shown when some women develop healthy lesbian and bisexual identities. Future research on heterosexuality needs to explore how, "in spite of the patriarchal contours separating and opposing men and women, women do still desire and even celebrate sexual pleasure with men, and men still can renounce some of the . . . oppressive sexual practices which the sexual power divisions of our society produce and encourage in them" (Joseph & Lewis, 1981, pp. 238–239).

Exploring Further

∾

Boston Women's Health Book Collective. (1998). *Our bodies, ourselves for the new century.* New York: Simon & Schuster.
   This is the latest edition of the book that started a feminist revolution in women's health by establishing women as the experts on women's bodies. The diversity of women's sexual identities and expression is respected here.

Hyde, Janet S., & DeLamater, John. (2003). *Understanding human sexuality* (8th ed.) New York: McGraw-Hill.
   A matter-of-fact, nonsexist college text on human sexuality. This book, written with wisdom and humor, provides a great deal of factual information.

Kaschak, Ellyn, & Tiefer, Leonore (Eds.). (2001). *A new view of women's sexual problems.* Binghampton, NY: Hawthorne.

Box 8.4 ∞ V-Day

"I think that women have had it. They've had it with being abused, they've had it with being quiet, they've had it with bad sex, they've had it. I think they've reached a point where things have to change."[1] And Eve Ensler sought to make that change. It all began when she performed her award winning play, "The Vagina Monologues," in 1998 to a 20,000-seat audience in New York City. Ensler had gathered the material for her play through interviews with countless numbers of women across the country. Her monologues deal with topics ranging from rape to first sexual encounters to childbirth. Ensler then recognized that her play had both the powers to bring women's issues and sexuality to the public and be a catalyst for change through the founding of V-Day, a movement to end violence against women. V-Day activism entails raising funds to promote awareness and support existing antiviolence organizations. The V-Day College Initiative brings awareness to college campuses through student productions of "The Vagina Monologues" in which the proceeds go to benefit local antiviolence charities. V-Day also created The Afghan Women's Summit, The Stop Rape Contest, and Indian Country Project to further raise awareness about violence against girls and women that occurs internationally. V-Day is now celebrated each February 14 as a celebration of women's sexuality and a site of social change. What started out as one woman's play has become a movement. In 2001, V-Day was named one of 100 Best Charities by *Worth* Magazine and has raised over 14 million dollars in its first five years.

[1]Eve Ensler (2001) in "Virginia Braum in conversation with Eve Ensler: Public talk about 'private parts'" in M. Crawford & R. Unger (Eds.) *In our own words: Writings from Women's Lives* (pp. 288–293). Boston: McGraw Hill.

Sources: Virginia Braun in conversation with Eve Ensler (2001). Public talk about "private parts." In M. Crawford & R. Unger (Eds.), *In our own words: Writings from women's lives* (pp. 288–293). New York: McGraw-Hill. www.vday.org. Contributed by Meghan Deveau.

These innovative feminist thinkers demonstrate that standard views of sexuality are male centered, neglect the relational context of sexual expression, and ignore differences among women. They set out a new approach that balances psychological, social, and cultural factors with medical and biological factors. The book incorporates research and commentary from diverse points of view. A brilliant contribution to understanding women's sexual selves.

The Vagina Monologues (DVD). (2002). An HBO Production.
    Created and performed by Eve Ensler, this dramatic performance captures Ensler's unique performance of her controversial work. She performs interviews she conducted with other women about their vaginas, sex, orgasms, and menstruation.

CHAPTER 9

Commitments:

Women and Close Relationships

- **Marriage**
  Who Marries and When?
  Who Marries Whom?
  "Marrying Up" and "Marrying Down": The Marriage Gradient
  Varieties of Marriage
  Power in Marriage
  Happily Ever After? Marital Satisfaction and Psychological Adjustment
  What Makes a Marriage Last?

- **Lesbian Couples**
  Lesbian and Heterosexual Couples Compared
  What Are the Characteristics of Enduring Lesbian Relationships?
  Power in Lesbian Relationships
  Satisfaction in Lesbian Relationships

- **Cohabiting Couples**
  Who Cohabits and Why?
  Does Living Together Affect Later Marriage?

- **Ending the Commitment: Divorce and Separation**
  What Are the Causes and Consequences of Divorce?
  Breaking Up: When Relationships End without Divorce

- **Remarriage**

- **Domestic Violence: The Psychological and Physical Abuse of Women**
  Recognizing a Hidden Problem

- **Making a Difference**
  Ending Domestic Violence

- **Equality and Commitment**

- **Exploring Further**

She gave a gasp as he slid her underneath him. . . . By now Merril didn't want to talk any more. She simply wanted to fly, wherever Torrin chose to pilot her into the upper reaches of the seventh heaven.

But he lifted his head one last time. "Now will you tell me what it is I haven't asked you yet?"

"It's all right, I think you already have—" she breathed.

"And will you? Marry me, I mean?" he asked tenderly.

"Torrin, what are you doing?"

His voice was husky. "I'm giving you a lesson in love."

"Let it last forever, my dream lover," she whispered, moving sensually beneath his touch. "Like our marriage."

"And like my love for you," he murmured in velvet tones beside her head.

And as she moved against him, all notion of holding back now gone, she knew that, like love, their dream would last forever—because it was the real thing.

—The ending of *Fantasy Lover*, a Harlequin Romance (Heywood, 1989, p. 187)

for everyone?

Happy endings like the ones in romance novels appeal to women's hopes of finding the real thing and settling down to a lifetime of happiness. Romantic relationships lead—at least sometimes—to a desire to make a commitment to one partner. In our society that commitment often leads to marriage, and when people marry, they almost always hope it will last a lifetime. Not all enduring commitments to a partner take the form of marriage. Some lesbian couples choose long-term commitment, although they have not had the right to legal marriage. Some heterosexual couples choose to live together without formal marriage.

What do women want from these relationships? Research on close relationships shows that women want and need intimacy and equality. However, they may have difficulty meeting those needs within heterosexual relationships and may settle for less than they would prefer (Worell, 1988). Satisfaction in close relationships depends on *both* partners and also on social structural factors that couples cannot control. In this chapter we explore the kinds of commitments couples make to each other and the consequences of these commitments for women.

Marriage

As a very old joke puts it, "Marriage is an institution—but who wants to live in an institution?" This joke recognizes that marriage is a way that societies regulate private relationships between couples. Laws and statutes stipulate who may marry whom—for example, same-sex couples have been prohibited from marrying; in the past, interracial marriages were forbidden. Laws also regulate the minimum age for marriage, the division of property when marriages dissolve (indeed, whether they are permitted to dissolve), and the responsibilities of each partner within the marriage (what behaviors constitute grounds for divorce).

In cultures in which written law is less important, religious codes or social norms may serve the same regulatory function. For example, cross-cultural studies of preindustrial hunter-gatherer societies show that 79 percent of these societies allow men to have more than one wife. Few prohibit divorce and remarriage, but most punish married people for having sexual relations outside the marriage (Gough, 1984).

Although people in Western societies are aware that marriage is a legal contract subject to regulation by the state, they rarely think of it that way in relation to themselves. Rather, they are influenced by the ideology of romance, choosing their partners as individuals and expecting to live out their married lives according to their own needs and wishes. Nevertheless, the rights and responsibilities imposed by the state may have consequences for both partners, especially when the marriage ends.

As an institution, marriage has a strong patriarchal heritage (Grana, 2002). Historically, wealth and titles were passed on only through male heirs. In many countries, married women are still regarded as the property of their husbands. In the United States, most women still give up their own name and take their husband's name upon marriage. The institutional aspects of marriage shape behaviors and attitudes through cultural scripts:

> An institution is a way of life that is very resistant to change. People know about it; they can describe it; and they have spent a lifetime learning how to react to it. The idea of marriage is larger than any individual marriage. The role of husband or wife is greater than any individual who takes on that role. (Blumstein & Schwartz, 1983, p. 318)

Marriage, then, is both a personal relationship and a scripted social institution.

Who Marries and When?

More than 90 percent of people in Western societies marry at some time in their lives. However, marital patterns are diverging among ethnic groups. For example, African American women are the least likely of any group to be married (Dickson, 1993; Steil, 1997).

In general, women marry at younger ages than men do. Women in developing areas of the world marry very young. In many parts of Africa and Asia, the average age at first marriage is under 18 (United Nations, 1995). In contrast, the typical first-time bride in the United States now is about 25 years old; just one generation ago, she was 20 (Michael et al., 1994). A similar trend is occurring in other industrialized countries. Scandinavian countries lead the way in the trend to later marriage; for example, only 15 percent of 24-year-old Swedish women are married (Bianchi & Spain, 1986; Norton & Moorman, 1987).

Why are American women marrying later? The idea that women can have goals other than being a wife and mother is now widely accepted. Advances in contraception have made premarital sex and living-together arrangements less risky. For black women, there is a shortage of marriageable men, due to a number of socioeconomic forces (see Chapter 10 for more on African American family patterns). Economic factors may play a part, too; some young people find it difficult to become financially independent (Bianchi & Spain, 1986; Taylor, 1997).

Whatever the causes, the tendency to marry later has important implications for women, because the increased time between high school and marriage offers opportunities to broaden experience. A woman who enters her first marriage at an older age is less likely to exchange dependence on her parents for dependence on a husband. She is likely to have had some experience of independent living; has probably held jobs and supported herself; and has had time to get more education, which exposes her to a variety of viewpoints and experiences and also increases her employment opportunities. All in all, she is more likely than a younger woman to enter marriage with a well-developed sense of self and broad horizons for her life.

Who Marries Whom?

In a cross-cultural study, more than 9,000 people from 37 nations representing every part of the world were asked to assess the importance of 31 characteristics in a potential mate (Buss et al., 1990). The characteristics included good health, chastity, dependability, intelligence, social status, religious background, neatness, ambition, and sociability. The participants were young (their average age was 23) and typically urban, well educated, and prosperous—in other words, they are not representative samples from their countries. Nevertheless, their answers give an interesting picture of what women and men from diverse cultures look for in a potential marriage partner.

No two samples ordered the characteristics in exactly the same way. The biggest difference across cultures was in a cluster of characteristics reflecting traditional values such as chastity (the potential husband or wife should not have had previous sexual intercourse), being a good cook and housekeeper, and desire for a home and children. Samples from China, Indonesia, India, and Iran, for example, placed great importance on chastity, whereas those from Scandinavia considered it irrelevant.

Overall, cultural differences were much more important than gender differences. Men and women from the same culture were more similar in their mate preferences than were men from different cultures or women from different cultures. In fact, men's and women's rankings were virtually identical overall, with a correlation of +.95. This gender similarity suggests that each culture—whether Bulgarian, Irish, Japanese, Zambian, Venezuelan, or whatever—socializes men and women to know and accept its particular script for marriage. When all 37 cultures were considered, an overall picture of an ideal mate emerged. Women and men both rated mutual attraction and love, dependable character, emotional stability, and pleasing disposition as the four most important characteristics in a potential marriage partner.

There were some gender differences, however. Across cultures, women were somewhat more likely to emphasize a mate's earning capacity and ambition, and men to emphasize good looks and physical attractiveness. Do these differences reflect optimal mating strategies determined by evolution? Probably not. A later study found that women's preferences for men with material resources was greatest in countries where women had least ability to gain power on their own through access to education and jobs (Eagly & Wood, 1999). Clearly, there is more to choosing a mate than innate mating preferences (Miller, Putcha-Bhagavatula, & Pederson, 2002).

Many other studies have focused on spouse choices in the United States. In general, these studies, like the cross-cultural one just described, show that the desires of men and women are more similar than different. However, men remain somewhat more traditional in their thinking about marital scripts and roles. In a study of college students, the men were more conservative than the women on issues such as whether a mother should stay at home with an infant and willingness to move for a spouse's career (Novack & Novack, 1996). Overall, women appear to expect and desire more flexible marital patterns than men.

"Marrying Up" and "Marrying Down": The Marriage Gradient

Individual couples usually end up being closely matched on social class and ethnicity as well as on characteristics such as height, SAT scores, attractiveness, and age. Couples are similar in values, too: Religious people tend to marry other religious people, conservatives marry other conservatives, and feminists marry other feminists (Michael et al., 1994). When there are differences within a couple, it is usually the man who is older and better educated and has a more prestigious occupation; and this is true cross-culturally (United Nations, 1995).

The tendency for women to "marry up" and men to "marry down" by sorting themselves into couples in which the man has higher prestige and income potential is called the *marriage gradient* (Bernard, 1972). The marriage gradient probably came about because women had little access to education and high-status occupations and could achieve economic security only through marriage. In the United States, women's tendency to marry up has decreased as women have become more equal to men in earning power and educational opportunity. It also varies among groups of women. Black women, for example, are less likely than white women to marry up with respect to education (Schoen & Wooldredge, 1989).

Will the marriage gradient continue to exist, even though women have more equality today? Recent studies of U.S. college students suggest that both women and men value such attributes as intelligence, desire for children, and a pleasing personality most when choosing a mate—but that wealth and status are still important attributes for men (Regan, Levin, Sprecher, Christopher, & Cate, 2000; Stewart, Stinnett, & Rosenfeld, 2000). When playing a game in which they "designed" an ideal long-term mate by "purchasing" desirable characteristics, female students were willing to pay the most for status and resources when designing a man, and male students were willing to pay the most for physical attractiveness when designing a woman (Li, Bailey, Kenrick, & Linsenmeier, 2002). Even when young women are relatively empowered on their own, it seems that many still prefer a man with status and wealth—and men care less about their partner's money than her looks.

Varieties of Marriage

In the United States, many marriage patterns coexist (Blumstein & Schwartz, 1983). I will classify marriages into three types (traditional, modern, and egalitarian) based on three important characteristics: the division of authority, how spousal roles are defined, and the amount of companionship and shared activities they provide (Peplau & Gordon, 1985; Scanzoni & Scanzoni, 1976; Schwartz, 1994).

Traditional Marriage

In a *traditional marriage,* both husband and wife agree that the husband has (and should have) greater authority; he is the head of the family, or the boss. Even in areas in which the wife has some decision-making responsibility (such as household shopping), he retains veto power over her decisions. The wife is a full-time home-maker who does not work for pay. Clear distinctions are made between the husband's and wife's responsibilities. She is responsible for home and child care, and he is the breadwinner. Couples in these marriages may not expect to be best friends; rather, the wife finds companionship with other women—neighbors, sisters and other kin, or members of her church. The husband's friendship networks are with male kin and co-workers, and his leisure activities take place apart from his wife. Attitudes toward traditional marriage have changed a great deal in the past few decades (Steil, 2001). In national opinion polls in the 1970s and 1980s, about half of the population said that traditional marriage was the best lifestyle and that working mothers were bad for children. By 1996, 85 percent of married people thought that both partners should be earning income, and two-thirds endorsed sharing house-work equally (Steil, 2001).

These changes do not mean that marriages based on traditional beliefs and values are entirely a thing of the past. Even in the late 1990s, 30 percent of survey respondents agreed that "it is better for everyone if men are the achievers and women take care of the home" (Steil, 2001). Furthermore, certain religious groups strongly endorse the traditional marriage. For example, Orthodox Jews, Latter Day Saints (Mormons), some evangelical Christian sects, the Promise Keepers, and Nation of Islam insist that distinct gender roles and submission by the wife to her husband are necessary for marital and societal stability (Hewlett & West, 1998; Matthews, 1996). And women may find their marriages becoming more traditional than they expected if they temporarily leave paid employment to take care of young children. About 38 percent of women with children under the age of 6 and 28 percent of those with children under 18 are not employed (Gilbert & Rader, 2001; Steil, 2000).

Modern Marriage

In *modern marriage,* the spouses have a "senior partner–junior partner" or "near-peer" relationship. Modern wives work outside the home, but, by mutual agree-ment, the wife's job is less important than the husband's. He is the breadwinner, and she is working to help out or to provide extras. Moreover, it is expected that her paid employment will not interfere with her responsibilities for housework and child care. Within modern marriage, husbands and wives may spend an equal amount of time on paid work, but that work has different meanings because of the belief that the man is the real provider (Steil, 2001). Modern couples emphasize companionship and expect to share leisure activities. They value togetherness and may discuss husband/wife roles rather than taking them for granted as more tradi-tional couples do.

Modern marriage may seem to be a relationship of equality when compared with traditional marriage, but the equality is relative. Husbands still have more fi-nancial responsibility, and wives have more responsibility for the home and the chil-dren (see Figure 9.1). Modern wives do a *second shift* every day—they put in a day's

FIGURE 9.1

Let's make a deal . . .

Source: Sylvia by Nicole Hollander. Reprinted by permission of Source Books.

work for pay and another day's work when they get home (Hochschild, 1989). Men are considerably more satisfied than women with this arrangement (Baker, Kiger, & Riley, 1996). As one marital researcher put it, the men in these couples "support female equality but only up to the point it collides with their privilege" (Schwartz, 1994, p. 9). Women may be content with this arrangement because they want to be closely involved with their children, or they may put up with it because they do not know how to change it.

Egalitarian Marriage

Egalitarian marriage, once relatively rare, is becoming more common (Schwartz, 1994). In *egalitarian marriages*, the partners have equal power and authority. They also share responsibilities equally without respect to gender roles. For example, one partner's paid job is not allowed to take precedence over the other's. In practical terms, this means that either the husband or the wife might relocate to accommodate the other's promotion; either would be equally likely to miss work to care for a sick child. The ever-present tasks of running a household— cleaning, cooking, bill paying, errands—are allocated by interest and ability, not because certain jobs are supposed to be women's work and others men's work.

Although partners may be very involved in their careers, they may make career sacrifices to meet each other's and their children's needs because they believe in equity (Risman & Johnson-Sumerford, 1998). Such marriages are *post-gender relationships,* the partners have moved beyond using gender to define their marital roles.

More than any other type of marriage, an egalitarian relationship provides the couple with profound intimacy, intense companionship, and mutual respect. Egalitarian couples put their relationship first, ahead of work and other relationships (even family and children). Because they share a great deal, they understand each other, communicate well, and choose to spend a lot of time together. Often, each says that the other is his or her best friend, precious and irreplaceable, and that their relationship is unique (Risman & Johnson-Sumerford, 1998; Schwartz, 1994).

Power in Marriage

Different marriage types reflect different beliefs about what the duties of husband and wife should be and how they should view each other. Completely egalitarian marriages are still relatively rare. Although Americans like to think of marriage as an equal partnership, men end up having more power. Why is it that the result of a stroll down the aisle and the words "I do" is often a long-term state of inequality?

One definition of power is "the ability to get one's way, to influence important decisions" (Blumstein & Schwartz, 1983, p. 62). Accordingly, researchers have often compiled lists of types of decisions and asked one or both partners who usually makes the final decision about each type. In an important early study (Blood & Wolfe, 1960), more than 900 wives were asked who had the final say on whether the husband should change jobs (90 percent said husbands always did) and on how much to spend on food (41 percent reported that wives always did). Only 39 percent of the wives had decision-making power over whether or not they themselves should hold a paying job. Note that the decision with the most far-reaching consequences, the husband's job, is one on which husbands had virtually uncontested power. Another early study of Canadian households, 76 percent of wives said that the husband was the boss and only 13 percent said both had equal power (Turk & Bell, 1972).

More recent research confirms that norms have not changed very much. Even in dual-earner and dual-career marriages, there is still a consistent pattern of inequality; the roles and responsibilities are more balanced than in traditional marriages, but both partners seem to accept some level of male dominance. Even though women and men agree that women do far more housework and child care in most marriages, the majority of wives, both employed and stay-at-home, say that this imbalance is fair (Steil, 2001). Couples may construct a *myth of equality,* refusing to acknowledge how gender socialization and social forces have steered them toward traditional roles (Knudson-Martin & Mahoney, 1996).

How Do Couples Justify Marital Inequality?

These studies, and others like them, show that couples make meaning of their lives in the context of overall inequality. Power in marriage is both structural and ideological—it is related to societal structures that give men greater status and earning power and also to beliefs about who is better at nurturing or more suited to doing housework (Dallos & Dallos, 1997). How is marital power exerted and justified? How do couples create myths of equality and explain away inequalities in their own marriages?

When a sample of highly educated dual-career couples was asked about other couples' relationships, they defined equality in terms of task sharing. However, when asked about their own relationships, they talked less about who did the cooking and cleaning than about mutual respect and commitment (Rosenbluth, Steil, & Whitcomb, 1998). In fact, most of the couples had not achieved their ideal of equality: The women did more household work and their careers were secondary to their husbands' careers. But they did not focus on adding up who did what around the house, perhaps because it would make inequality painfully apparent. Redefining the situation is a common way to avoid perceiving injustice of all kinds (Steil, 2001).

In an in-depth study of 17 British couples, wives and husbands were interviewed together and then, 18 months later, separately (Dryden, 1999). The researcher was aware that married women are frequently in Catch-22 or double bind situations. Ideologically, they believe that marriage is supposed to be about love, sharing, and mutual respect. Practically, they might be unable to challenge inequalities in their own marriages because of being dependent on a husband's income or having very young children. Therefore, openly admitting their dissatisfactions might be emotionally almost "too hard to bear" (p. 58). For husbands, admitting inequality might lead to a loss of power and privilege. Therefore, the researcher analyzed the interview data for subtle ways that the women and men justified the status quo.

The women used distancing, talking about equality in vague, hypothetical terms rather than challenging their husbands openly ("*Some* men sit around watching the telly all day . . ."). They minimized conflict or blamed themselves when it happened ("It's only silly little things we fight about, and maybe I take them too seriously"). And they made positive comparisons between their husbands and other people's ("Some women have it really bad; their husbands don't do a thing to help, so I'm in a fairly equal situation"). These strategies helped the women create a vision of relative marital fairness for themselves as well as for the interviewer.

Although the women's challenges were indirect, minimal, and hedged with self-blame, the men often tried to deflect them, without actually mentioning inequality. Their strategies included describing their wives as inadequate ("If she were better organized, she could get all her work done with time left over") and themselves as "hard done by" (having to work long hours and needing more time out with the boys). The researcher noted that the husbands participated in reflecting back to their wives a negative identity that the wives had already created through self-blame—a "subtle undermining process that had the power to exacerbate in women a sense of lack of confidence, low self-esteem, and in some cases, depression" (p. 86). Clearly, these couples were doing gender in their marriages in ways that preserved and perpetuated marital inequality.

What Are the Sources of Men's Greater Power?

Many factors are associated with husband dominance in marriage (Steil, 1997). Social class and ethnicity make a difference: Black and working-class couples have less of a power differential than white middle- and upper-class couples. Wives who are employed have more power than those who work only at home. White middle-class women in traditional marriages may have less marital power than any other group of women.

One reason the power balance in marriage is weighted in favor of men is the influence of traditional beliefs and social norms. In a major study of American couples (Blumstein & Schwartz, 1983), couples were asked whether they agreed or disagreed that it is better if the man works to support the household and the woman stays home. In couples in which either spouse agreed, the husband was more powerful, regardless of how much money each partner actually earned. For example, Marlene and Art have been married for 30 years. She is an executive with the telephone company and he is a farm-equipment dealer; their incomes are about equal, although sometimes she earns more:

> MARLENE: Art makes the major economic decisions in our household. We are as
> consulting of one another as possible, but I realize that in the final push comes to
> shove that he is the one who shoulders the responsibility for this family . . .
>
> ART: I would say that I make the decision when it comes to money and I guess I would
> also say that if there is an argument and we cannot totally work it out so that we
> both agree, then I have more to say . . . someone has to finally make a decision
> and we have always done it this way. (Blumstein & Schwartz, 1983, pp. 57–58)

Another explanation for greater male power in marriage comes from *social exchange theory* (Thibault & Kelley, 1959). This theory proposes that the partner who brings greater outside resources to the relationship will have the greater influence in it. The partner who has less to offer, be it status, money, or knowledge, will inevitably take a back seat. Money establishes the balance of power in heterosexual relationships, even though this reality conflicts with American beliefs about equality:

> Most people like to think that the right to affect decisions is based on the demands of
> daily events, on which partner is wiser on a certain issue, or on special gifts of persua-
> sion. They do not like to think that income, something that comes into the relation-
> ship from the outside, imposes a hierarchy on the couple. But it does. (Blumstein &
> Schwartz, 1983, p. 53)

In American marriages, husbands usually bring more of three very important resources: money, education, and prestige. Husbands usually earn more than wives, even when both are employed full time, and are likely to have higher-status jobs. (This is true for a variety of reasons that I will discuss in Chapter 11.) As already noted, wives who have no income or employment of their own have the least power of any group of married women. Moreover, because of the marriage gradient, the husband in most marriages has a higher level of education than the wife. In American society, educational attainment brings status and prestige in itself and is also associated with higher income.

When the husband earns more, couples agree that he automatically has the right to make important financial decisions for the family. But the money he brings in also may give the husband the right to make other important decisions that have nothing to do with money. In a British study, one wife described how things changed only when she began to earn money on her own:

Before, I had five children and was very vulnerable, I avoided raising some issues because I was worried that he would stop giving me any money . . . he threatened it a couple of times and that was enough . . . now I'm earning things have changed, I'm not so quiet about things I don't like now. (Dallos & Dallos, 1997, p. 58)

Social exchange theory implies that if husband and wife have equal external resources, marital interaction will also be equal. But even in dual-career families, where the resources are fairly well matched, husbands still have more weight. For example, in a national sample of more than 1,500 dual-career, dual-earner, and traditional couples, wives in all three categories spent considerably more time in housework each week than their husbands. Dual-career husbands did not spend any more time each week doing housework than other men (Berardo, Shehen, & Leslie, 1987). Dual-career marriages also often fall short of being truly egalitarian in the relative importance attached to each partner's career. Which spouse, husband or wife, is more likely to move to a different location for career advancement or to relocate because the spouse had a job offer in a different place? When male and female psychologists (APA members) were surveyed, 42 percent of the men and only 19 percent of the women said they had moved for an increase in salary. However, 25 percent of the women and only 7 percent of the men had moved because of their partners' relocation (Gutek, 1989).

Social exchange theory is too limited; it has focused on economic exchange while ignoring the symbolic value of gender roles. For example, the provider role, still more important for men than women, means that men's capacity to earn money is more highly valued than their capacity to nurture children. For women, on the other hand, being there to provide emotional nurturance to husband and children is more valued than the ability to earn money. Even if a wife brings in as much money as her husband, she may not have equal power because her success is seen as undermining his provider role and interfering with her nurturing role. In other words, the same resource (in this case, earned income) may function differently for husband and wife (Howard & Hollander, 1997; Steil, 1994; Steil & Weltman, 1991).

Just how central is earning power to marital equality? And does its influence work the same way for husbands and wives? To answer these questions it is necessary to study couples in which the wives earn as much or more than their husbands. Couples like these used to be very rare, but today 20 percent of wives earn more than their husbands (Gilbert & Rader, 2001).

In one intriguing study, 30 couples in which the wife earned at least 33 percent more than the husband were compared with an equal number of couples in which the husbands earned at least 33 percent more than the wives (Steil & Weltman, 1991). Respondents were asked questions about the relative importance of careers ("Whose career is more important in the relationship?") and decision-making power ("Who has more say about household/financial issues?"). Consistent with social exchange theory, spouses who earned more saw their careers as more important and also had more say at home than spouses who earned less. Nevertheless, wives overall had less say in financial decisions, had more responsibility for children and housework, and felt that their husbands' careers were more important than their own. In another recent study, status-reversed couples, in which the wives earned more or were in higher-status occupations than their husbands, or both, showed a similar pattern (Tichenor, 1999).

In other words, equal access to money can be an equalizer of power in marriage—but even when wives earn more money than their husbands, beliefs about the appropriate roles of women and men still influence the balance of power in favor of men. This implies that in order to change power imbalances in marriage, both women's economic power and couples' gender ideology will have to change. Such shifts are occurring, and not only in the United States. A national study in Taiwan recently showed that Taiwanese wives' bargaining power in marriage has increased as their economic opportunities rise and traditional gender ideology falls (Xu & Lai, 2002).

Happily Ever After? Marital Satisfaction and Psychological Adjustment

"Happily ever after" is our society's romantic ideal of marriage. However, in *The Future of Marriage* (1972), Jessie Bernard maintained that marriage is not good for women. She suggested that every marriage is really two marriages, his and hers—and his is much more advantageous.

Which is closer to reality, the romantic ideal or the social scientists' seemingly cynical view? Does marriage bring happiness and fulfillment? We can examine the issue by looking at research on whether women (and men) are generally satisfied with the marriages they make, and whether marriage has any relationship to psychological adjustment.

Does Marital Happiness Change over Time?

The happiness and satisfaction of married women (and men) vary greatly across the life course of a marriage. Almost all studies of marital satisfaction over time show an initial honeymoon period followed by a substantial decline in happiness with the birth of the first child. Wives are more likely than husbands to become dissatisfied with the marriage over time. Satisfaction often hits its lowest point when the children are school-aged or adolescents. Some studies have shown that the happiness of the early years is regained or even surpassed in later life, when the children have grown and left home. In other studies, the happiness trend has been all downhill (Feeney, Peterson, & Noller, 1994; Schlesinger, 1982; Steinberg & Silverberg, 1987).

What accounts for the changes in marital happiness after the birth of children? When more than 700 women were studied during pregnancy and three months after the birth of their first child, they reported doing much more of the housework and child care than they had expected. Their negative feelings about their marriages were related to the violation of their expectancies of equal sharing. In other words, it was not the added domestic chores that made these new mothers less happy than they had been, but their feeling that the new division of labor was unfair. The more they had expected equality, the more dissatisfied they were (Ruble, Fleming, Hackel, & Stangor, 1988).

You might expect that happiness would decline less among women who feel respected and appreciated by their husbands, and this is just what was found in a study that followed couples for six years. Women whose marital satisfaction stayed the same or increased after giving birth were those who said that their husbands expressed love and were tuned in to their wives and their relationships. Those women whose marital satisfaction declined were those who perceived their husbands as negative or their lives as out of control and chaotic (Shapiro, Gottman, & Carrere, 2000).

Even when couples have been married 30 years or more, they look back at the child-rearing years as their least happy (Finkel & Hanson, 1992). When children leave home, couples have fewer demands on their money and time. Many couples experience this stage of their marriage as a time of greater freedom and flexibility, and therefore of increased marital happiness (Schlesinger, 1982).

Is Marriage Linked to Psychological Well-Being?

Studies in the 1970s showed that married women were more likely than married men to have psychological disorders and problems. Single women, on the other hand, had fewer disorders and problems than single men. In fact, for every type of unmarried person (ever-single, divorced, and widowed), most studies showed higher rates of psychological adjustment disorders for men than women. Only married women had more disorders than their male counterparts (Bernard, 1972; Gove, 1972; Steil & Turetsky, 1987b). Is marriage bad for women's mental health?

Recent research shows that marriage seems to be good for both women and men. People who are married or living together in a sexually exclusive relationship report greater emotional satisfaction and physical pleasure from sex than single people do (Waite & Joyner, 2001). Marriage is also associated with better psychological adjustment in both women and men. However, the benefits are unequally distributed: Men are more satisfied than women with their marriages and receive greater mental health benefits from being married (Fowers, 1991; Steil, 1997).

Why do husbands enjoy better psychological adjustment and well-being than wives? To answer this question we need to consider the different types of marriage. Several studies have shown that full-time homemakers have the poorest psychological adjustment, employed husbands have the best, and employed wives are intermediate (Steil, 1997; Steil & Turetsky, 1987b)—suggesting that something about being a homemaker in a traditional marriage is related to the occurrence of psychological disorders. (Of course, it is also possible that women with poorer adjustment are less likely to be in paid employment.)

We will look at women's work in homemaking and child care more closely in Chapters 10 and 11 and at psychological disorders in Chapter 13. For now, it is important to note that women may provide more social and emotional support for husbands than they receive in return. In one study of more than 4,000 married persons aged 55 and over, husbands said they were most likely to confide in their wives, while wives were less likely to confide in their husbands and more likely to turn to a friend, sister, or daughter. Both men and women who confided in their spouses had markedly higher marital satisfaction and overall psychological well-being than those who did not (Lee, 1988). The work of caring and emotional support that married women do may partly account for their husbands' better psychological adjustment.

Is Equality Linked to Well-Being in Marriage?

A great deal of research suggests that equality is beneficial for relationships (Steil, 1997). Couples who see their marriage as equal are more satisfied than more traditional couples, report better sexual adjustment and communication, and are less likely to use manipulative and indirect influence tactics with each other (Aida & Falbo, 1991; Steil, 1994, 1997). Perhaps it is not marriage per se that is bad for women's mental health but marriages in which women have little power and status (Dallos & Dallos, 1997).

A study of more than 800 dual-career professional couples tested the hypothesis that marital power is related to psychological well-being (Steil and Turetsky, 1987a). The researchers gathered information on each woman's earned income, her influence and responsibilities within the marriage, and her symptoms of psychological disorders. Because of earlier research connecting the presence of children to lowered marital happiness, they also compared childless women and mothers.

For childless women, the more equal a woman's marital relationship, the more satisfied she was with her marriage—and marital satisfaction was an important factor in overall psychological well-being. The mothers experienced their marriages as significantly less equal than the childless women did, and the perceived inequality was directly related to psychological symptoms. Although the dual-career professional couples in this sample are not representative of all married couples, this study suggests that relative power and equality play an important role in married women's well-being.

What Makes a Marriage Last?

What are the secrets of success of husbands and wives in enduring marriages? There is little research on long-lasting marriages, but as you might expect, these studies suggest that love, friendship, intimacy, and shared interests are important factors (Bachand & Caron, 2001; Goodman, 1999).

Lasting marriages also change over time. In one study of 581 adults who had been married an average of 18 years, participants were asked to remember how they had felt about their partner at the beginning of their love relationship and to describe how they felt now. They reported less erotic feelings and game-playing, an equal amount of friendship-based love, and (among the men) an increase in selfless, nurturing love (Grote & Frieze, 1998).

In a study of Canadian couples who had been married an average of 25 years and had at least one child, more than half the women said that they had started out their married lives with traditional role expectations, but only 20 percent still had such expectations at the time of the study. Over the course of their marriages their expectations had evolved to an ideal of shared responsibilities and more independence for themselves. Wives and husbands were asked to indicate the factors that had contributed to their staying together. Although they were interviewed separately, spouses agreed almost perfectly (Schlesinger, 1982). More recently, 147 U.S. couples who had been married at least 20 years were asked similar questions (Fenell, 1993). Table 9.1 shows the factors that both sets of couples thought were most important.

Of course, not all marriages that last a long time are happy marriages. In the Canadian study, about 10 percent of women and men indicated dissatisfactions with their relationships; for women, the dissatisfactions centered on sexual relations, finances, the husband's workload, and children (Schlesinger, 1982). Chronic marital dissatisfaction is related to problems of mental and physical health for older women (Levenson, Carstensen, & Gottman, 1993). Social norms may keep some unhappy marriages together. One study of couples found that those who were living together (but not legally married) were likely to break up when there was a pattern of inequality in the relationship; however, for married couples, inequality had no effect on whether the couple stayed together (Blumstein & Schwartz, 1983).

Psychological research on happiness in marriage points up some interesting discrepancies between the romantic ideal and the realities. Our society tells us that marriage and parenthood are more important routes to fulfillment for women than for men. Women are thought to be eager to catch a husband and men are thought to be caught reluctantly. Women may invest a great deal of energy in planning their weddings (have you ever seen a *Grooms* magazine on the newsstand?). Yet research suggests that Jessie Bernard was right when she proposed that there are two marriages in every marital union, his and hers, and that his is (at least sometimes, and somewhat) better than hers.

TABLE 9.1   Longtime Married Couples Cite Factors That Make Marriage Last

Canadian Couples	U.S. Couples
Respect for each other	Lifetime commitment to marriage
Trusting each other	Loyalty to spouse
Loyalty	Strong moral values
Loving each other	Respect spouse as best friend
Counting on each other	Commitment to sexual fidelity
Considering each other's needs	Desire to be a good parent
Providing each other with emotional support	Faith in God and spiritual commitment
Commitment to make marriage last	Desire to please and support spouse
Fidelity	Good companion to spouse
Give and take in marriage	Willingness to forgive and be forgiven

Source: Fenell, 1993; Schlesinger, 1982.

Lesbian Couples

In the past, lesbian and gay couples were a socially invisible minority; today, their relationships are increasingly open. This change is due to many factors, including the civil rights movement for lesbian, gay, and bisexual people and the destigmatization of homosexuality by the APA. In surveys of lesbians conducted over the last several decades, the great majority of respondents were currently in a steady relationship (Peplau & Spalding, 2000).

Lesbian and Heterosexual Couples Compared

When two women make a commitment to live together as lovers and friends, their relationship has some similarities to conventional marriage—but without the institutional aspects or the label. Lesbians (and gay men) have not had the right to marry legally, a situation that is just beginning to change. To date, there has been no research on legally married gay couples, because they are few and newly married. The great majority of lesbian and gay couples still do not have access to the features of marriage that make it seem desirable to become a couple and difficult to break up. For example, there is no standard way for them to have a public wedding ceremony or to establish reciprocal legal rights and responsibilities. There are no tax advantages or spousal insurance benefits. Lesbian partners may even be legally forbidden to see each other in the event of serious accident or hospitalization if their families of origin do not approve. Ending the relationship is not hampered by complicated divorce laws; nor does society urge same-sex couples to work at their relationships and remain loyal through the hard times.

This lack of institutional and societal support can give people the freedom to make their own rules, but it can also lead to instability. Some lesbian couples write their own wedding ceremonies, and some ask a minister or rabbi to perform a ceremony of union to bless their relationship. Occasionally, one partner legally adopts the other or the other's children. Many include each other in their wills and insurance policies, buy homes together, or draw up contracts delineating rights and responsibilities to each other. All these are ways of giving the relationship some legal and institutional status (Blumstein & Schwartz, 1983; Cabaj & Purcell, 1998). Gay rights activists are working for universal legal recognition of same-sex unions. The impact of these efforts has not yet been studied (Peplau & Spalding, 2000).

For many years, researchers and the public alike assumed that lesbian couples mimic traditional heterosexual roles, with one partner being the "husband" (butch) and the other the "wife" (femme). This belief applied a heterosexual script to lesbian relationships. Most research shows no clear preference for masculine/feminine roles among lesbians (Peplau & Spalding, 2000).

When lesbians do endorse butch/femme roles, it may be with different meanings than heterosexuals might assume. When a researcher asked a sample of 235 self-identified lesbians to define these concepts for themselves, the majority did identify as butch (26 percent) or femme (34 percent), with 40 percent of the sample being neutral. The higher a woman's education and income, the more likely she was to have an independent (not butch/femme) gender identity (Weber, 1996).

However, these women did not use butch/femme to represent husband/wife roles. To them, *butch* signified that they did not enjoy girly things such as makeup, dresses, and elaborate hairdos. *Femme* signified the freedom to enjoy makeup and other feminine aspects of personal style, while still being committed to loving women. They stressed that *butch* did not mean they were dominant, acted like men, or disliked being women, and *femme* had nothing to do with being submissive. In summary, the butch/femme dimension is important to some lesbians, and it is linked to social class, but it is not about relationship dominance.

What Are the Characteristics of Enduring Lesbian Relationships?

Lesbian relationships can be described on the same dimensions as heterosexual marriages: roles and the division of labor, companionship and communication, power and authority, and satisfaction. Most lesbians reject gender roles (Peplau & Spalding, 2000). When looking for a long-term partner, they prefer characteristics such as intelligence and interpersonal sensitivity (Regan, Medina, & Joshi, 2001).

Because same-sex couples cannot assign the breadwinner role on the basis of gender and because they tend to value independence, the importance of the work interests of each partner is much more likely to be fairly equal than in heterosexual marriages. In one study of more than 1,500 lesbian couples, 75 percent expressed the belief that both should work for pay (Blumstein & Schwartz, 1983). Less than 1 percent of these couples lived in a one-earner situation.

Just as they balance work roles, lesbians are highly likely to share household duties (Kurdek, 1993). They assign housekeeping chores on the basis of preference and ability, rather than roles. The basic principle is fairness. In the following interview, the speaker is an investment officer at a bank and her partner is a medical student:

> She feels very strongly about having an equitable situation and I think that comes from her having lived with men and feeling taken advantage of in the past, so she definitely feels it ought to be equitable. It's easy to slip into something where she does more because I am the only one working full time . . . but we see the dangers of that and we are keeping things in line so she doesn't get stuck with too much. (Blumstein & Schwartz, 1983, p. 150)

Same-sex couples tend to share more leisure activities than heterosexual couples. They are more likely to socialize with friends together, belong to the same clubs, and share hobbies and sports interests. Perhaps, due to socialization, two women are more likely to have interests in common than a woman and a man; or perhaps most people need same-sex best friends, and lesbians can find a same-sex friend and a spouse in the same person. The majority of lesbian couples say they want their relationship to be central to their lives, and they value companionship and communication (Blumstein & Schwartz, 1983).

Power in Lesbian Relationships

In general, most lesbians (like most heterosexuals) desire egalitarian relationships. In a study using matched samples of lesbians, gay men, and heterosexuals, all groups (and especially women, both lesbian and heterosexual) said that having an equal-power relationship was very important. However, only 59 percent of lesbians (and even fewer heterosexual women) reported that their current relationship was exactly equal (Peplau & Cochran, 1990).

Power differences in a lesbian relationship are usually due to the same factors that influence power in heterosexual relationships, such as one partner having greater resources of money, status, or education, or one partner being more committed than the other. However, the egalitarian ideal may be more important than status and money in determining power relations among lesbians. Unlike heterosexual couples, many of whom believe that the man should be the head of the family, the lesbian ideal is a relationship "where two strong women come together in total equality" (Blumstein & Schwartz, 1983, p. 310). Some studies suggest that lesbians may be more likely to establish egalitarian relationships than heterosexual women (Steil, 1994). Other studies show no differences. Further research is needed on factors affecting the balance of power in lesbian couples (Peplau & Spalding, 2000).

Satisfaction in Lesbian Relationships

Studies that compared the self-reported satisfaction and happiness of lesbian and heterosexual committed couples show few differences between the two types of couples (Peplau & Spalding, 2000). For example, when matched samples of lesbians and heterosexuals were compared, the lesbians, like the heterosexual women, reported that they both loved and liked their partners (Peplau & Cochran, 1980). Like heterosexual women, lesbians may be more likely than men to have a relational orientation toward sexuality, enjoying sex in committed relationships more than transient ones (Peplau & Garnets, 2000). Lesbian relationships tend to decline in satisfaction over time at about the same rate as those of married people (Peplau & Spalding, 2000). When partners have different levels of commitment to their careers, satisfaction is lower (Eldridge & Gilbert, 1990).

There are some subtle differences between lesbian and heterosexual couples, however. In a study of women in lesbian and heterosexual couples, the two groups were similar in their capacity for intimacy. However, a woman's capacity for intimacy made a difference only when her partner was a woman, when it led to a more intimate relationship and more direct communication strategies. In heterosexual couples, the woman's capacity for intimacy had no connection with the intimacy of the relationship, probably because men's greater power allows them to set the limits on intimacy (Rosenbluth & Steil, 1995).

External pressures affect relationships, too. Women who love women have to cope with prejudice and discrimination. Parents and other family members may reject or disown a lesbian daughter, remove her from a will, refuse to acknowledge the partner or the relationship, exclude the couple from family gatherings, or encourage them to break up.

One important factor in relationship satisfaction for lesbians is having a social support network. Receiving social support from friends and family is related to individual psychological adjustment as well as happiness in the relationship for both lesbian and gay male couples (Berger, 1990; Kurdek, 1988). This suggests that gay activists are right in encouraging lesbians to come out to friends and family despite the risk of rejection. However, the evidence is mixed. Although some studies show that women who are out to significant others in their lives (family, friends, employers) report more satisfaction with their partners, others find that relationship satisfaction is unrelated to disclosure about being a lesbian (Jordan & Deluty, 2000; Beals & Peplau, 2001).

Cohabiting Couples

Today many heterosexual couples choose to live together without being legally married. Sociologists give this arrangement the unromantic name *cohabitation.* Couples who do it usually call it *living together*—not a very precise term since roommates or parents and children can be said to live together, too. The absence of a suitable everyday term is one clue that the cohabitation relationship is not yet an institution in society.

Who Cohabits and Why?

Whatever the label, the practice of heterosexual couples living together without being officially married is more popular than ever in the United States. One of the most striking social changes of the past 40 years has been the rise in cohabitation. Among women born in the decade up to 1942, only about 6 percent lived with a man before getting married. (Michael et al., 1994). By the 1990s about half of all first marriages were preceded by living together (Forste & Tanfer, 1996). By the end of the 1990s about 25 percent of American women under the age of 39 were cohabiting (Popenoe & Whitehead, 1999). Black and Hispanic women are more likely than white women to cohabit, but there are differences among subgroups of Hispanic women. Mexican Americans, for example, are more disapproving of living together without planning to marry than are Puerto Ricans (Oropesa, 1996).

Although the increase in cohabitation is dramatic, the United States still has a lower proportion of cohabiting couples than many other industrialized countries. For example, virtually all Swedes cohabit before marriage, and a growing number never marry at all. Cohabitation is accepted both legally and morally even for couples who have children. As a result, half of all Swedish children are born to unmarried women (Trost, 1996). A common attitude is, "Why marry? It's our love that counts" (Popenoe, 1987).

In the United States, people choose to cohabit for a variety of reasons (Popenoe & Whitehead, 1999). For some, it is a prelude to marriage: "Let's see if we're compatible." Some cohabitants are divorced and not yet ready to remarry.

Some young people cohabit to show their independence from their parents. Some cohabit more as a matter of convenience than deep commitment; it's easier for two to pay the rent.

People who choose cohabitation tend to be liberal in attitudes about gender roles. They are more sexually experienced and sexually active than noncohabiters, and their relationships are less likely than married relationships to be monogamous. In a national sample of more than 1,200 women aged 20 to 37, cohabiters were five times more likely than married women to have sex with someone other than their partner—about one in five had sex with someone else while cohabiting. This was true for all ethnic groups studied (Forste & Tanfer, 1996).

Cohabiting couples usually have a division of labor similar to modern marriage. They almost always expect that both partners will work outside the home. However, as with most married couples, women do more housework than men (Blumstein & Schwartz, 1983). Liberal attitudes about gender roles do not always lead to liberated behavior.

Though many cohabiting women have egalitarian ideals (and choose to cohabit rather than marry partly because of those ideals), their goals of independence and autonomy within a relationship are usually only partly fulfilled. As with married couples, issues of money, power, and the division of labor inside and outside the home can be sources of conflict. Nevertheless, most cohabitants report high satisfaction with their arrangement, and a large majority plan to marry someday, though not necessarily their current partner (Murstein, 1986).

Does Living Together Affect Later Marriage?

One obvious potential outcome of living together is that the woman may become pregnant. Cohabitation is associated with premarital pregnancy among all ethnic groups, and the likelihood of pregnancy during cohabitation is greater for Puerto Rican than white or African American women. Does pregnancy push cohabiters toward marriage? This, too, depends on ethnic group. White women who get pregnant while cohabiting are very likely to marry; there is no effect for African American women; and for Puerto Rican women, pregnancy lowers the odds of marrying before the birth of the child. There is a long tradition of cohabiting in Puerto Rico, and having a child may solidify the union without leading to marriage. The data show that cohabiting has different meanings to different ethnic groups (Manning & Landale, 1996).

Is cohabitation related to later marital satisfaction? It would seem that if people use living together as a trial marriage, those who do go on to marry should be better adjusted and less likely to divorce. However, in the United States, Sweden, and Canada, studies show that former cohabitants are *more* likely to divorce, though their total time together is as long as the average married couple spends before divorcing (Teachman & Polenko, 1990). There may be ethnic and racial differences, too. In a study of about 200 black and 175 white couples in their first year of marriage, living together before marriage was unrelated to marital happiness for whites, but negatively related for blacks (Crohan & Veroff, 1989). Of course, a higher divorce rate for people who had previously cohabited is not necessarily an indication

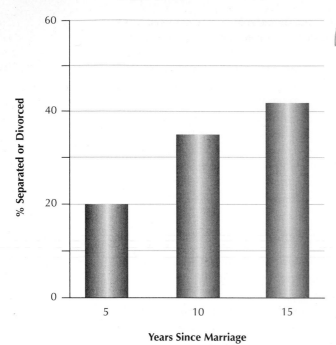

FIGURE 9.2

In the United States a large proportion of first marriages end within 15 years.

Source: First marriage dissolution, divorce, and remarriage: United States. (2001). National Center for Health Statistics.

that cohabitation is a mistake. Because women who cohabit (and their partners) are more unconventional, independent, and autonomous than those who do not, they may be more likely to leave a marriage that does not meet their expectations (Murstein, 1986).

Ending the Commitment: Divorce and Separation

The rise in divorces has probably gained more attention and caused more concern than any other social trend of our times. The United States has the highest divorce rate of any industrialized nation, a rate that more than doubled between 1960 and 1980 and has only recently leveled off or in some groups, declined slightly (Taylor, 1997). Between 40 percent and 50 percent of American marriages end within 15 years (see Figure 9.2), and the Department of the Census predicts that the U.S. divorce rate will continue to be among the world's highest. Black women are considerably more likely than white women to end a marriage through divorce or prolonged separation, and Hispanic women, less likely. Other countries have experienced similar increases in divorce rate, though none as extreme as the United States (Bianchi & Spain, 1986; McKelvey & McKenry, 2000; Norton & Moorman, 1987; Price & McKenry, 1988; Taylor, 1997).

What Are the Causes and Consequences of Divorce?

At the societal level, several factors have been correlated with rising divorce rates. Divorce rates rise along with women's participation in the paid workforce, both in the United States and in many other countries (Trent & South, 1989). Wives' paid employment is not usually a direct cause of divorce. Rather, it seems that when women have alternatives for economic survival other than dependence on a husband's income, they are less likely to stay in unsatisfactory marriages (Bianchi & Spain, 1986; Price & McKenry, 1988). Age at first marriage is also highly correlated with later divorce: The younger the man and woman are when they marry, the more likely they are to divorce (Bramlet & Mosher, 2001). Other

TABLE 9.2   Perceived Causes of Divorce: Women's and Men's Accounts

Cause	Women (%)	Men (%)
Infidelity	25	16
Incompatible	19	20
Drinking or drug use	14	5
Grew apart	10	9
Personality problems	8	10
Lack of communication	6	13
Physical or mental abuse	9	0
Loss of love	3	7
Not meeting family obligations	5	1
Employment problems	4	3
Don't know	0	9
Unhappy in marriage	3	3

Source: Adapted from Amato and Previti, 2003. Percentages have been rounded to nearest whole number.

factors related to the rising divorce rate are changes in laws and attitudes; divorce is no longer the social disgrace it once was, and no-fault laws make it easier.

At the personal level, women and men tend to give somewhat different reasons for the breakup of their marriages. In a recent study based on a national random sample of divorced people, women were more likely than men to mention their partner's infidelity, substance abuse, and mental or physical abuse as reasons for their divorce. Men were more likely to mention poor communication or say that they did not know the cause of the divorce. Other causes, such as incompatibility, were cited equally often by women and men (Amato & Previti, 2003). (See Table 9.2).

Events and feelings very early in a marriage may predict later divorce. In one recent study, those who were disillusioned within the first two years (as reflected in decreased love and affection and increased ambivalence) were more likely to end up divorced several years later (Huston, Caughlin, Houts, Smith, & George, 2001). Whatever the reasons for divorce, it has serious and long-lasting consequences for women. I will consider three types of consequences, each intertwined with the others in its effects: psychological adjustment, economic effects, and responsibility for children.

How Do People Psychologically Adjust to Divorce?

A considerable number of divorcing women (from 17 percent to 33 percent in different samples) describe their divorces as causing little or no psychological disturbance or pain. These women view their divorces as the end of a stressful or unbearable situation (e.g., abuse) and the beginning of increased freedom and competence. For most women, however, adjustment to divorce includes feelings of anger, helplessness, and ambivalence. Stress during divorce is related to a variety of physical health problems. (As with all correlational research, it is not possible to determine cause and effect in these studies.) Compared with married people, divorced people of both sexes have higher rates of illness, death, alcoholism, and serious accidents.

The divorce rate for older couples continues to rise (Taylor, 1997). Older women who have been in traditional marriages may be particularly vulnerable after divorce. When homemakers are divorced in middle or later life, they lose their source of financial support, have few marketable skills, and may view their divorce as a personal failure (Greenwood-Audant, 1984).

In general, however, the adjustment to divorce seems to be more difficult for men than for women. Although both divorced men and women are more likely to commit suicide than their married counterparts, divorced men are 50 percent more likely to do so than divorced women. They are also more likely to show serious psychological disturbances (Price & McKenry, 1988). Women appear to be better at building and maintaining networks of close friends and family during and following divorce (Gerstel, 1988), and men may miss their partner's caretaking more (see Figure 9.3). However, women and men are quite similar in their responses to divorce in many other ways (Gove & Shin, 1989). The question of whose divorce is worse, his or hers, is not easily resolved. Some researchers have suggested that men are more negatively affected in the short term, while women have more long-term problems to resolve (Price & McKenry, 1988).

Women's adjustment to divorce depends on the social support they receive, and this may differ for different groups of women. In a study using a national sample of divorced or separated women with at least one child, black women felt more positive about their personal ability to master their lives and their economic situation and were more likely than white women to receive support from a spiritual advisor such as a minister. White women were more likely to receive their support from friends and family and to start dating again sooner (McKelvey & McHenry, 2000).

Divorce is usually discussed as a personal and social tragedy. But divorce may be an important way that women counter marital inequality, a way out of an oppressive situation (Rice, 1994). In a study of successful egalitarian marriages, almost half were not first marriages, and most of the women said they had left their first marriage because of inequitable treatment (Schwartz, 1994). Divorce is a painful family transformation, but also a potential opportunity for growth and change (Stewart, Copeland, Chester, Malley, & Barenbaum, 1997).

What Are the Economic Effects of Divorce?

Divorce in the United States has been characterized as an economic disaster for women. The economic status of men improves upon divorce, while the economic status of women deteriorates (Price & McKenry, 1988). And no-fault divorce laws, designed to ensure equitable division of assets, have actually made the situation worse for women.

Why do women lose out financially with divorce? There are several reasons, but structural factors are probably more important than individual ones. The majority of state property laws assume that property belongs to the spouse who earned

"This is goodbye—there are one thousand, eight hundred, and twenty-five meals for you in the freezer."

FIGURE 9.3

Source: Copyright © The New Yorker Collection, 2004, Barbara Smaller, from cartoonbank.com. All rights reserved.

it. Since husbands usually have had greater earning power during the marriage, these laws result in men being awarded more of the couple's assets. The economic value of the wife's unpaid labor may not be considered. In other states, attempts to make divorce fairer for women have led to laws that order equal division of property. However, most divorcing couples (especially younger ones) have very little in the way of valuable property—perhaps a car (complete with loan payments), household furnishings, and a modest bank account, offset by credit card debt. Fewer than half have equity in a house. The biggest assets for the large majority of couples are the husband's education, pension benefits, and future earning power.

As we discussed earlier, the husband's career usually takes priority in both single-earner and dual-earner marriages. Couples invest their time, money, and energy in his advancement; frequently, the wife will postpone her education or career plans in order to put him through school, and she will do the unpaid work at home that allows him to concentrate on his paid job. Courts have been slow to recognize that the benefits husbands gain from traditional and modern marriage patterns translate into economic advantages upon divorce.

Only about 15 percent of all divorced women in the United States are awarded spousal support. Most awards are for a period of about two years; and in the past, less than half of the men ordered to provide such support have actually complied (Faludi, 1991; Price & McKenry, 1988).

Who Is Responsible for the Children?

The presence of children is an important factor in adjustment to divorce for women. Women of all social classes and marriage types are likely to be left with the financial responsibility and the day-to-day care of children when a marriage ends. The benefit of awarding custody to women is that most divorced women stay connected with their children and receive the emotional rewards of parenting more than most divorced men do. However, current custody arrangements also have costs for women.

Two-thirds of divorces involve children. More than half of all children in the United States will experience their parents' divorce before the age of 18, and they will then spend an average of about five years in a single-parent home, the great majority with their mothers (Arendell, 1997). Being a single parent is not easy. The single mother may feel overwhelmed with responsibility, guilty at having separated the children from their father, and compelled to be a supermom (L'Hommedieu, 1984).

The lack of a husband's income is a big handicap for divorced women and their children. About 60 percent of divorced mothers with custody of their children are awarded child support (Steil, 2001). However, the average amount paid as of the early 1990s was only about $3,600 a year (Arendell, 1997). Child support payments clearly do not cover the actual costs of bringing up a child.

Moreover, the majority of women entitled to child support do not receive it. Several national studies from the 1970s to the 1990s have shown that only 25 percent to 50 percent of men ordered to pay child support did so. No study has ever found that more than half of the fathers complied; many who comply do it irregularly and pay less than the designated amount; and one-fourth to one-third of fathers never make a single payment despite court orders. Black women are half as likely as white women to receive support, and the poorest, least-educated women are the least likely of all. Only 10 percent of welfare clients with children receive child support (Arendell, 1997; Costello & Stone, 1994; Price & McKenry, 1988).

Divorced women and their children must adjust to a lower standard of living. A woman's standard of living declines by about 30 percent to 40 percent on average (Duncan & Hoffman, 1991; Morgan, 1991). More than 25 percent of divorced women fall into poverty for some time within five years of divorce. Many more "balance on the brink of poverty" (Morgan, 1991, p. 96). For many women with children, the financial hardship that comes with divorce becomes the central focus of their lives, dictating where they can live, determining whether they and their children can afford health care, and affecting their psychological well-being (Arendell, 1997).

Breaking Up: When Relationships End without Divorce

In contrast to the large amount of research on divorce, few studies have examined the process or consequences when relationships end without a formal divorce. This can happen in several ways. Some spouses simply desert their families, leaving them without a division of assets or child support. Little is known about how these families fare. In others, partners agree to separate but do not get a divorce, a pattern that is more common in Black than in White communities (McKelvey & McHenry, 2000).

The ending of relationships between cohabiting men and women or between lesbian couples has not been studied much. The breakup rate for cohabiters is higher than the divorce rate for married couples, and this is true cross-culturally—for example, in the United States, Australia (Sarantakos, 1991), and Sweden. One study of Swedish couples attempted to sample only highly committed cohabiting couples by selecting only those who had had a child. Still, their breakup rate was three times the rate for comparable married couples (Popenoe, 1987).

For U.S. couples, the best comparisons of breakup rates come from a study in which couples were contacted a year and a half after participating in the original study and asked if they were still together (Blumstein & Schwartz, 1983). Figure 9.4 shows the percentage of married, cohabiting, and lesbian couples who had separated. Lesbians were the most likely to break up, a surprising finding given their emphasis on commitment and equality, but not so surprising when lack of social support for lesbian relationships is considered. When gay, lesbian, and heterosexual individuals who had broken up with a partner were asked why their relationship ended and how they felt about it, they gave similar reasons and reported similar levels of distress (Kurdek, 1997). People rarely talked about a breakup without sadness, anger, or regret.

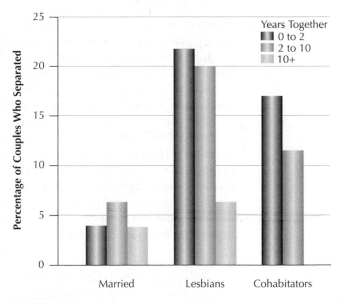

FIGURE 9.4

Separations over an 18-month period.

Source: Adapted from Philip B. Blumstein and Pepper S. Schwartz, *American Couples,* HarperCollins, 1983, fig. 53, p. 308 and fig. 54, p. 315. Copyright © 1983 by Philip B. Blumstein and Pepper S. Schwartz. Reprinted with permission from the publisher.

Remarriage

About two-thirds of women who get divorced remarry, about half of them within three years of the divorce. White women are more likely to remarry than black or Hispanic women. In the United States, about half of all marriages involve at least one partner who was previously divorced (Ganong & Coleman, 2000). A cynic might say that remarriages represent a triumph of belief over experience; women (and men, who are even more likely to remarry) do not question the institution of marriage after they have been divorced. Rather, they believe that they chose the wrong partner last time and now know how to choose the right one.

Women may remarry partly to escape divorce-induced poverty. Women with lower levels of education and income are more likely to remarry than those with more economic options. However, given the importance of power relations in marriage, the consequences of entering a new marriage from an impoverished "one-down" position are unlikely to be positive. Economic discrepancies may be related to the higher rate of spouse abuse in remarried families (Crosbie-Burnett & Giles-Sims, 1991).

Are second marriages more successful? In general, the level of satisfaction in second marriages is about the same as in first marriages; as in first marriages, husbands are more satisfied than their wives (Ihinger-Tallman & Pasley, 1987). Decision making may be more equal than in first marriages, but remarried women still do more housework than their partners (Ganong & Coleman, 2000). A Norwegian study of blended families showed that women did more child care regardless of whether they were the mother or the stepmother of the children in the family (Levin, 1997). Second marriages are even more likely to end in divorce than first marriages (Ganong & Coleman, 2000), with the result that well over half of women who remarry go on to experience a second divorce.

The complex family structures and dynamics of second marriages ("his," "hers," and "their" children, stepparents, ex-spouses, in-laws, and ex-in-laws) may be a source of stress. Financial problems may be increased by lack of support payments from former husbands, and many families have conflicts over how to allocate money to various household members (Ganong & Coleman, 2000; Ihinger-Tallman & Pasley, 1987). (Who should pay Tiffany's college tuition—mother, father, or stepparent?) Second marriages may also be less stable because, once having violated the societal and religious ideal of lifelong marriage, people are even less inclined to stay in unsatisfying relationships.

Some of the special problems of remarried couples—and the unshaken belief in the ideal—can be seen in the words of one couple, married less than two years at the time of the interview. She is a homemaker and he is a carpenter:

> WIFE: I feel anyone thinking about marrying a person who has been previously married should think very seriously about it. There are definitely special problems that accompany this type of marriage. . . . I feel my husband and I will always have his previous marriage overshadowing our marriage. My husband also feels guilty for not having his children with him. I in turn feel guilty and feel if it wasn't for me, maybe my husband would get back with his ex-wife and kids and live happily ever after.
>
> HUSBAND: I think everyone should find the right spouse the first time. I found mine the second time and the only thing that stops it from being perfect is my previous marriage. (Ihinger-Tallman & Pasley, 1987, p. 60)

Domestic Violence: The Psychological and Physical Abuse of Women

Millions of women around the world have been subjected to violence from their male partners. It is one of the most frequent causes of physical injury for women across cultures (United Nations Children's Fund, 2000). In the United States, researchers estimate that between 21 percent and 34 percent of women will be physically assaulted by a husband or boyfriend at least once in their lifetime, and that partners are responsible for the beatings of 2 to 4 million women every year (Smith, Smith, & Earp, 1999). Rates in Europe are similar to those in the United States (Neft & Levine, 1997), and rates in Africa, Asia, and Latin America are even higher (Pickup, 2001). Violence and aggression occur in gay/lesbian as well as in heterosexual relationships, and the rates are similar (Burke, Jordan, & Owen, 2002). However, the causes may be somewhat different (Miller, Greene, Causby, White, & Lockhart, 2001).

Statistics probably underestimate the actual incidence of wife abuse, which tends to be underreported due to shame, fear, and the belief that nothing will be done about it (Ellsberg, Heise, Pena, Augrto, & Winkvist, 2001). The violence inflicted on women in long-term relationships is now recognized as a major public health problem. For example, between one-third and one-half of all women seen in hospital emergency rooms have been injured by their husband or boyfriend (Warshaw, 2001).

Physical violence against a partner is almost always accompanied by psychological abuse—the woman may be threatened, publicly humiliated, criticized, and belittled. The abuser may be extremely jealous, using accusations of infidelity to keep her from seeing friends or going out. Psychological abuse may be equally as traumatic as physical abuse (Walker, 2000), and the combination of the two can be devastating, as a woman's life becomes governed by the threat of harm:

> But each day I lived in fear. I was afraid he was gonna come in while I was taking . . . I would wait to take a shower. I would hurry up and wash up. I mean, I know I wasn't getting clean enough, under my arms, between my legs but that was it, because I had to make it a minute and a half . . . because I was afraid he was gonna come in and just, you know, go off. (Smith et al., 1999, p. 184)

Recognizing a Hidden Problem

For many years, domestic violence was a hidden problem because it takes place within the privacy of the home. Moreover, traditional attitudes condone a man's right to dominate and control his wife or partner. Wife-beating was considered a normal, if regrettable, part of life. Even today, in countries where patriarchal ideology is strong, wife-beating may be viewed as a morally acceptable means of control (Haj-Yahia, 1998). In the United States, the scope and impact of partner violence has been made visible through two important kinds of research: random-sample surveys and studies of women in hospitals, courts, and battered women's shelters.

Surveys of the general population and studies of abuse survivors reveal different kinds and amounts of violence (Johnson, 1995).

In surveys, women and men both report inflicting violence on their partners about equally often (Straus, 1999). This kind of relatively gender-neutral violence has been called ***common couples violence*** (Johnson, 1995). It is relatively infrequent in a relationship, it rarely escalates over time, and it is sparked when the couple's coping skills are not sufficient for dealing with a particular conflict. In other words, common couple's violence results from a breakdown in the couple's ability to handle a conflict constructively, and it probably is as likely to occur in gay and lesbian as in heterosexual relationships. However, common couples' violence in heterosexual couples is not entirely gender-neutral. Women are much more likely to sustain physical injury than to inflict it, and their aggressive acts are often done in self-defense.

Studies of battered women show a pattern of severe, escalating male violence in which women rarely fight back and almost never initiate aggression. This kind of violence, termed ***patriarchal terrorism,*** has been the main focus of feminist research and activism (Johnson, 1995). It is much more frequent in a relationship than common couples' violence, pervading the whole context of the woman and man's interaction. Its motives are rooted in patriarchal tradition: the male perpetrator feels that he owns his woman and is entitled to control her by any means necessary. Both women who have been victims (Eisikovits & Buchbinder, 1999) and men who have been perpetrators (Anderson & Umberson, 2001; Reitz, 1999) report that without this control the batterer does not feel like a real man. To exercise and display his control, the abuser uses a variety of psychological techniques (see Figure 9.5). The ongoing psychological abuse is punctuated by episodes of physical violence, which escalate in intensity and frequency as time goes on. Thus, patriarchal terrorism is a continuous process for its victims, one that exposes them to prolonged and severe stress (see Figure 9.6). The following items, from a scale designed to measure women's experiences of battering (Smith et al., 1999, p. 189), were developed from battered women's own accounts:

> He makes me feel unsafe even in my own home.
> I feel ashamed of the things he does to me.
> I try not to rock the boat because I am afraid of what he might do.
> I feel like he keeps me prisoner.
> I hide the truth from others because I am afraid not to.
> He can scare me without laying a hand on me.
> He has a look that goes straight through me and terrifies me.

"Why Doesn't She Leave?"

Attitudes toward the abuse of women are changing. In U.S. studies, the majority of respondents believe that partner abuse is wrong (Drout, 1997; Locke & Richman, 1999). As a result of feminist activism, it is no longer a hidden problem; more people now acknowledge that abuse happens all too often and that any woman—rich, poor, middle-class, married, cohabiting, of any ethnic or racial group—is vulnerable. However, some myths about abuse remain. The most prevalent is the idea that

FIGURE 9.5

The power and control wheel.

Source: From R. J. Gelles & D. R. Loseke (Eds.), *Current Controversies on Family Violence*, pp. 47–62. Minnesota Program Development, Inc. Reprinted by permission.

there is a quick and easy solution for abuse: "Why doesn't she just leave?" Let's look at the evidence about ending an abusive relationship.

Women face many obstacles to leaving an abusive partner. Some of these are practical: She may have no money, no job, and no safe place to go. She may not have a car to leave in. If she takes the children out of school, she will upset them and draw the attention of authorities; if she leaves them behind, the abuser may harm them or she may lose custody.

One very important practical consideration is that attempting to leave may increase the violence. Research shows that a woman is more likely to be seriously injured or killed by her partner *after* she leaves him than when they are living together

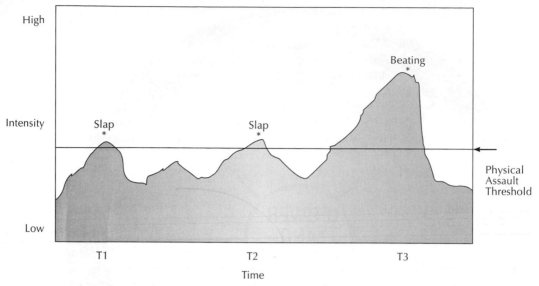

FIGURE 9.6   Battering as a Chronic and Continuous Process
Violence can include emotional and psychological abuse as well as physical assault. Research methods that measure only isolated physical assault incidents do not adequately account for all forms of violence, which underestimates how overwhelming and destructive is the phenomenon.

Source: From P. H. Smith, J. B. Smith & J. A. Earp, 1999, "Beyond the Measurement Trap: A Reconstructed Conceptualization and Measurement of Women Battering," *Psychology of Women Quarterly,* 23, pp. 177–193. Reprinted by permission of Blackwell Publishing Ltd.

(Jacobson & Gottman, 1998). It is chillingly common to open the Sunday paper, as I did recently, and see a headline such as "Man fatally shoots former wife, then self, police say" (Vosk, 2004). The article explained that the 47-year-old murdered woman had divorced her husband seven years earlier and moved to a different town, only to have him hunt her down. The article mentioned in passing that this incident was similar to another recent local murder in which a man used a shotgun to kill his wife who had separated from him. According to the U.S. Department of Justice (2000), 30 percent of all female murder victims—and only 3 percent of male murder victims—are killed by current or former partners. Violent men often make it clear that there is no escape:

> Everyday he'd put fear in me cause he'd always threaten me saying that if I decided to ever leave that he'd hunt me down like a dog and shoot me and the girls. And he knew I had nowhere to go, so I just had to stay there and put up with it. (Smith et al., 1999, p. 185)

In addition to the practical problems and risks, there are psychological issues involved in the decision to leave an abuser. Much (though not all) abuse is *cyclical:* The perpetrator goes through a period of increasing tension, a violent episode, and then a loving phase (Walker, 2000). A cyclical abuser is apologetic and repentant after an episode of violence, and the woman may believe his promises to change.

She may feel tied by love for him and their children, and she may accept the belief, based in romantic ideology, that it is a woman's job to stand by her man and transform him with her love.

After prolonged abuse, a woman may be so disempowered that she cannot conceive of making an escape. She feels trapped, worthless, and responsible for the violence. More than half of abused women become clinically depressed (Warshaw, 2001). As one battered woman said, "He programmed me over a long, long period of time" (Smith et al., 1999, p. 186). She may develop *battered women's syndrome,* a type of post-traumatic stress disorder, (Stein & Kennedy, 2001; Walker, 2000). She may become incapable of taking action on her own behalf.

Nevertheless, many women in abusive relationships do make active attempts to cope with the violence and get help. One coping strategy is "managing," in which a women tries to keep the peace by anticipating and avoiding anything that might make her partner angry. She takes on more and more responsibility and spends increasing energy on this task, becoming hyperalert to signs of impending violence. However, ultimately, the effort fails because the man retains control of defining what a good reason to be angry is. One battered woman concluded, "There was no way to tell what was going to happen because most of our arguments were not about anything serious . . . it was like, "you got the wrong kind of bread" or "I don't like that kinda candy bar." (Smith et al., 1999, pp. 184–185).

When coping strategies fail, women often seek help from clergy, family members, police, counselors, and helping agencies. When women turn to their families for help, they may be told that marriage is a sacred bond, that they should go home, apologize and try harder, or simply, "You made your bed, now lie in it." Often, they are disbelieved or blamed for the abuse, even by those trained to help (Dutton, 1996). Feminist therapy is a useful approach to helping women in abusive relationships because feminist therapists are likely to understand the patriarchal basis of wife abuse (see Chapter 13). However, not everyone can afford therapy or has access to a feminist therapist. And some groups of women, for example, immigrant and African American women, are distrustful of social services and do not want to take their troubles to a stranger (Joseph, 1997).

The limited research on long-term outcomes suggests that the great majority of women in abusive relationships do manage to end them (Schwartz, 1989). However, leaving is a long process, and some women go back to the abuser more than once before they are able to make a final break (Campbell, Rose, Kub, & Nedd, 1998). Perhaps this is partly due to the mixed messages they receive from the abusive spouse as well as from others.

Making a Difference

Ending Domestic Violence

Patriarchal ideology is a root cause of violence against women. To the extent that society accepts men's right to dominate women and women's second-class status, violence in heterosexual relationships is inevitable (Bograd, 1988). The ideology of patriarchy contributes to inequalities that make women vulnerable to violence. As discussed in this chapter, husbands usually earn more money, have higher-status jobs, and have more decision-making power than their wives. When women reach out for help, they may encounter patriarchal attitudes from social services, law enforcement, and the court system. In order to truly end relationship violence, it is necessary to change not just individuals, but social structures as well.

The **battered women's movement** is an international movement to educate the public about domestic violence, reform the legal system, and provide direct help to women whose partners are violent. In three decades of activism, this movement has made huge changes in society's view of partner abuse. For example, all 50 states have passed laws designed to protect battered women (Roberts, 1996). Police in many areas are now better trained to recognize domestic abuse and intervene to protect the woman. Physicians increasingly are being taught to screen for domestic abuse when interviewing women patients (Eisenstat & Bancroft, 1999). These changes make it easier for women to report abuse and get help, despite the powerlessness, shame, and fear they may feel.

Unfortunately, change is uneven. In most developing countries, abused women still have little legal protection (Levesque, 2001). In countries such as South Africa, the physical and sexual subordination of women, along with high rates of violence generally, are linked to high rates of HIV infection, injury, and death. In Asian countries, many people still defend a man's right to beat his wife (Pickup, 2001).

Battered women's shelters are refuges where a woman can find temporary safety, emotional support, information about their legal rights, and sometimes counseling. The first shelter for battered women opened in London in 1964, followed by the first U.S. shelter in 1974. Currently, there are about 2,000 shelters in the United States. Unfortunately, this is not nearly enough; thousands of women each year are turned away from shelters that have no space for them (Walker, 2001). Shelters are often underfunded, which means that they must rely on volunteers rather than trained staff, and staff spend much of their time fund-raising rather than offering services to women. Few shelters exist outside the United States, Canada, and Great Britain, although this is slowly changing. A recent study of battered women in South Africa showed that access to a shelter was crucial to their safety and their ability to change their situation (Angless, Maconachie, & Van Zyl, 1998). In 1993, I was fortunate to attend a feminist conference in Costa Rica, where participants celebrated the opening of the first battered women's shelter in that country.

In fostering the development of shelters, the battered women's movement created safe havens for women and saved many thousands of women (and children) from further harm. When asked what helped them the most in dealing with abuse, women most often say that it was access to a shelter (Gordon, 1996). However, the shelter initiative may be more useful in individualistic societies like the United States than in collectivist societies, where women are part of a much larger family structure. In Nepal or India, for example, a woman who left her family home would lose a web of vital social connections and her identity as a member of her society. In collectivist societies, and in working with more collectivist groups within our own society, such as African American and Native American women, other approaches need to be developed (Haaken & Yragui, 2003).

Shelters and counseling help the survivors of domestic abuse. Another feminist initiative is to focus on the perpetrators. This includes doing research to understand the attitudes, personality characteristics, and family histories of violent men. This research is difficult because most abusive men deny and minimize their violence and blame their wives or girlfriends for it. In one innovative study, men who were domestic violence offenders in court-ordered programs participated in interviews where they described their own perceptions of violent incidents they had perpetrated. One man had broken his wife's neck; another had held a knife in his wife's face and threatened her with death. These men framed relationships with other people as win/lose situations in which they either felt good, "up" and strong, or bad, "down" and weak (Reitz, 1999). From their perspective, the world was a threatening place where they could easily be rendered powerless:

> In a worldview where there is no equality, where identities are always polarized, always contested, and nonnegotiable, a person is constantly under threat of subjugation or annihilation unless he or she can first subjugate or annihilate the other. (Reitz, 1999, p. 163)

Such research has implications for counseling violent men. For example, cognitive therapy that helps men restructure their oppositional view of relationships may be useful, along with behavioral therapy that helps them manage anger.

To date, there have been few studies on the effectiveness of treatment programs for men. Few violent men volunteer to participate in programs aimed at changing them, and of those who do, many drop out. When court-ordered to attend, men who manage to complete a treatment program are less likely to be charged with abuse in the future, suggesting that such programs do help change patriarchal attitudes and behavior (Shepard, Falk & Elliott, 2002). It is also important that the criminal justice system take a firm stand against violence by arresting and prosecuting offenders. Research suggests that arrest and conviction effectively deters a man from perpetrating future abuse (Garner & Maxwell, 2000; Wooldredge & Thistlewaite, 2002). Clearly, the psychological and physical abuse of women in relationships is a complex problem demanding intervention on many fronts: changing patriarchal social structures, helping the victims, and stopping the perpetrators.

Equality and Commitment

A recurrent theme of this chapter has been that close relationships are important and can be beneficial to both women and men. Another theme has been that women in relationships with men almost always have less power than their partners—even when both partners believe in equality and want to work toward it.

This pattern seems to suggest that commitment and equality are incompatible, at least in heterosexual relationships. But studies of power in marriage have consistently found that a small number of couples do manage to have long-term egalitarian relationships. Although their numbers may be small, their existence tells us that the ideal is not beyond human power to achieve. Egalitarian marriage may be emerging as a new way to be married—a life pattern of the future (Risman & Johnson-Sumerford, 1998; Schwartz, 1994) (see Figure 9.7). The voices of women

FIGURE 9.7

Life in an egalitarian family.

Source: Sally Forth by Greg Howard. © Reprinted with special permission of King Features Syndicate.

and men in relatively egalitarian relationships tell us that these relationships can work. Here, the speaker is a man married for 16 years:

> I started out pretty traditional. But over the years it made sense to change. We both work, and so we had to help each other with the kids, and pretty soon they start asking for you—so only you will do, so you do some of that. And we worked together at church, and we both went whole hog into the peace program. So that got shared. I don't know; you can't design these things. You play fair, and you do what needs doing, and pretty soon you find the old ways don't work and the new ways do. (Schwartz, 1994, p. 31)

It is tempting to believe that equality in marriage or long-term cohabitation can be achieved simply by being willing to work at it. This belief is a variation of "Love conquers all." How many times have you heard people express the belief that "If two people love each other enough, and if they're both willing to compromise, they can have a good marriage"? A related belief is that if the husband does not *intend* to oppress or dominate the wife, oppression and domination will not occur. Happy marriage, then, should be mainly (or entirely) a matter of picking the right person. But one major conclusion that can be drawn from the research reviewed in this chapter is that power differentials between husbands and wives are *not* solely the result of individual differences. Rather, the institution of marriage has been organized around gender inequality, and attempts to change it have been only partially successful. Even couples who try very hard to change their own behavior have problems achieving gender balance in marriage. To understand how equality in marriage might become the rule rather than the exception, we need to look at both personal and structural factors.

To have an egalitarian marriage, both wife and husband must be willing to integrate their work and family responsibilities despite social pressures to conform to more traditional roles (Gilbert, 1993). Women who value their work outside the home and set limits on the sacrifices they make for husbands and children may be perceived as cold, unfeminine, and selfish; men who do housework and child care and set limits on their career involvement may be perceived as weak and unmasculine. (One of my children once *begged* my husband not to wear an apron in front of the child's friends!) Fortunately, attitudes toward the work and family roles of women and men have changed a great deal in the past 30 years and continue to become more flexible.

Women must lead the way to more egalitarian relationships because men are unlikely to fight a status quo that gives them many benefits. However, only when women perceive gender roles in relationships as unequal and unjust can they begin to change them. To recognize their position as unjust, women must be aware that other possibilities exist, must want such possibilities for themselves, must believe they are entitled to them, and must not feel personally to blame for not having them (Crosby, 1982; Steil, 1997).

Change involves negotiation. Roles are not engraved in stone, nor are they totally defined by society. Rather, they are expressed in day-to-day activities and can be negotiated between partners:

> Human beings are not just robots programmed by society. They are also willful actors, capable of choosing nonconformity and altering social structure if they so wish. . . . [There are] enormous possibilities for negotiation, compromise, and innovation [in marriage]. Individuals can construct their own realities to a surprising extent. (Thoits, 1987, p. 12)

What social factors give women more negotiating power in relationships with men? If society allows more flexible commitments to paid work by both women and men, there will be less likelihood that the man's job or career will take precedence. (The interaction of work and family life will be discussed further in Chapter 11.) Economic power is a key factor. The single biggest obstacle to egalitarian marriage and cohabiting relationships is men's greater earning power, which steers couples into investing in his career and leaving the work at home to her (Schwartz, 1994).

It is important for couples who are trying to create postgender relationships to build networks of like-minded people. Couples who spend time with other couples like them can learn from each other, provide havens from the criticism that more conservative people may aim their way, and provide role models of healthy alternatives to male dominance for themselves and their children. As the number of couples who are consciously trying to build egalitarian relationships increases, it should be easier for them to find each other and build supportive networks. Nontraditional arrangements are coming to be seen as legitimate, normal, and even routine (Thoits, 1987). Similar needs can be met for lesbian couples by being part of a lesbian community (Krieger, 1982).

The movement toward egalitarian relationships will bring benefits for both women and men. Men will be relieved of some of the economic burdens of traditional marriage and be freer to become involved with their children's growth and development. Women will experience better psychological adjustment. For both men and women, equality is linked to more satisfying relationships and greater intimacy. Equality and role flexibility in committed long-term relationships offer both women and men a chance to become more fully human.

Exploring Further

Feminism & Psychology: Special Issues on Marriage.

This noted journal asked feminist women and men to write about their views on gay and heterosexual marriage. The result is a superb collection of research articles, personal observations, and critical commentaries that spans three issues of the journal:

Volume 13, 4, November 2003.

Volume 14, 1, February 2004.

Volume 14, 2, May 2004.

Schewe, P. (2002). *Preventing violence in relationships: Interventions across the life span.* Washington, D.C.: APA.

This collection reviews research on violence in many kinds of relationships and focuses on what can be done to help victims and stop perpetrators.

CHAPTER 10

Mothering

∾

- **Images of Mothers and Motherhood**
- **The Decision to Have a Child**
  Why Do Women Choose to Have Children?
  The Motherhood Mandate
  Childless by Choice or Circumstance?
  How Does Society Restrict Women's Choices?
  Technology and Choice
- **The Transition to Motherhood**
  How Does Motherhood Change Work and Marital Roles?
  Do Mothers Face Impossible Ideals?
  Sexuality and Motherhood
  Psychological Effects of Bodily Changes during Pregnancy
  How Do Others React to Pregnant Women?
  Motherhood and Women's Identity
- **The Event of Childbirth**
  How Is the Meaning of Childbirth Socially Constructed?
  Is Childbirth a Medical Crisis?
  Family-Centered Childbirth
  Depression Following Childbirth: Why?
- **Experiences of Mothering**
  Teen Mothers
  Single Mothers
  Black Mothers and the Matriarchal Myth
  Lesbian Mothers
  Commonalities
- **Making a Difference**
  Transforming Social Policy: Redefining Family Values
  Transforming Social Meanings: Redefining Parenthood
- **Exploring Further**

> The day my husband and I took our newborn son home from the hospital I sat on my bed with him in my arms. All of a sudden, I realized I was in love. It is an indescribable love, comparable to nothing else in life. I never would have believed it before becoming a parent. . . . Now twelve, he knows exactly how to exasperate me, yet the love I feel for him today is as intense and passionate as when I held him in my arms on that beautiful fall day over a decade ago. (Deutsch, 1999, p. 228)

*M*otherhood is one of the most transforming events of a woman's life. It may seem the most natural thing in the world, a biological privilege accorded only to women. However, those aspects of society that seem most natural often are the ones most in need of critical examination. Like marriage, motherhood is an institution. Its meaning goes beyond the biological process of reproduction, encompassing many customs, beliefs, attitudes, rules, and laws. Like other institutions, it also has a powerful symbolic component. Yet women who become mothers are individuals. "Mother is a role; women are human beings" (Bernard, 1974, p. 7).

Motherhood raises troubling questions for feminist analysis. Liberal feminists have stressed that the institution of motherhood has been used to exclude women from public life, and they have shown how the myths and mystique of motherhood keep women in their place. Some radical and cultural feminists, on the other hand, have pointed out that motherhood is a woman-centered model of how people can be connected and caring (McMahon, 1995).

But the diversity of feminist opinion on motherhood need not be a problem. In this chapter, I will use a variety of feminist perspectives to address questions about mothering. What are the images and scripts that define mothers and motherhood? How do women go about choosing whether or not to have children, and to what extent are they allowed to choose? How does the transition to motherhood change women? What are women's experiences of birth and mothering? Finally, should motherhood be redefined?

Images of Mothers and Motherhood

Western society has strong beliefs about motherhood. The ideology of motherhood has been termed the *motherhood mystique.* It includes the following myths:

1. Motherhood is the ultimate fulfillment of a woman. It is a natural and necessary experience for all women. Those who do not want to mother are psychologically disturbed, and those who want to but cannot are fundamentally deprived.
2. Women are instinctively good at caregiving and should be responsible for infants, children, elderly parents, home, and husband. Good mothers enjoy this kind of work; a woman who doesn't is maladjusted or poorly organized.
3. A mother has infinite patience and the willingness to sacrifice herself to her children. If she does not put her own needs last, she is an inadequate mother.
4. A woman's intense, full-time devotion to mothering is best for her children. Women who work are inferior mothers (Hays, 1996; Hoffnung, 1989; Johnston-Robledo, 2000; Oakley, 1974).

FIGURE 10.1

The motherhood mystique internalized!

Source: Bringing Up Father © Reprinted with special permission of King Features Syndicate.

Although these beliefs may seem outdated, the motherhood mystique lives on (see Figure 10.1). It permeates advice to mothers, even from experts. An analysis of three best-selling child-rearing manuals showed that they held mothers primarily responsible for child care, prescribed intensive mothering, and glorified self-sacrifice (Hays, 1996).

The motherhood mystique may be a form of benevolent sexism in which women and men are seen as naturally having different roles and naturally being happy in them (Dallos & Dallos, 1997). It persists because it has important functions for *men* (Hays, 1996; Lorber, 1993b). Women are encouraged to sacrifice other parts of their lives for motherhood, which then creates economic dependence on men and is used to justify women's lower status and pay at work. "The social order that elevates men over women is legitimated by women's devotion to child care, since it takes them out of the running for top-level jobs and political positions and defuses their consciousness of oppression" (Lorber, 1993b, p. 170). The mystique may persist also because it is the one area in which Western society values connectedness and caring over individual achievement. But glorifying motherhood and defining it in ways that make many women feel guilty and burdened by it benefits groups that have the most power economically and politically.

The Decision to Have a Child

Having a child profoundly changes a woman's life, and in our society, children are not expected to produce much useful work or income for their parents or to support them financially in their old age. The cost of bringing up even one child is high. Yet the great majority of women have children.

Why Do Women Choose to Have Children?

There are practical reasons for having children, particularly in traditional societies. Children are necessary as workers (both at home and at jobs), as a path for passing on property and a customary way of life, and sometimes as a form of personal immortality. In postcolonial and underdeveloped societies, many children are lost to disease and malnutrition. Five or more children may have to be conceived for two to live to adulthood; these children may provide the only economic support available in their parents' old age.

As countries adopt industrialized ways of life, the birthrate drops. The best predictor of smaller families is not modernization itself, but attitudes toward modern science and medicine. As people begin to believe that science and medicine can deal with social problems, they may feel that it is not necessary to bear many children in order to have a few grow up. Nevertheless, because attitudes change more slowly than material conditions, there is a considerable lag between the development of better medical conditions and a drop in family size.

In industrialized societies, children have little economic value—in fact, they are a big economic liability—and psychological reasons for having children are given more weight. One traditional explanation for childbearing is the existence of a maternal instinct (Bernard, 1974). But if wanting children is instinctive, why are so many powerful socialization forces directed at instilling this "instinct" in girls? (For example, recall the girl-toys discussed in Chapter 6.) And why have abortion and infanticide been features of so many human societies throughout history? There are no inherent physiological benefits of motherhood for women, and there is no instinctive drive for pregnancy.

Rather than being instinctive, mothering is learned. Virtually all studies of single fathers show that when men cannot depend on women for child care (because of death, desertion, or divorce), they develop skills and behaviors very much like those of women. In addition, they come to see themselves as nurturing, compassionate, and sensitive to the needs of others, all stereotypically feminine traits (Risman, 1998). Biological theories assume that women are programmed to care for children; socialization theories assume that women are more nurturing because of early learning. But it is just as likely that a nurturing personality is created by being put into a nurturing role as an adult. The process of mothering is a kind of doing gender that produces womanly persons (McMahon, 1995).

The reasons for choosing to become a mother are different for women of different social classes. In an in-depth study of 59 white Canadian women, all employed full-time and mothers of a preschool child, the middle-class women talked about being ready to have a child only *after* they had met certain goals: maturity, the right relationship with a man, and career achievement. In contrast, the working-class women saw themselves as achieving adulthood *through* having a child. Their pregnancies, typically not planned, provided the opportunity to claim an identity as a mature, loving, and responsible person (McMahon, 1995).

Among the reasons our students mention when we discuss motherhood are the desire to experience pregnancy and birth, to participate in the growth of another human being, to please a husband or partner, to strengthen a relationship, to prove oneself an adult, to be needed and loved, and to pass on a family name or one's genes or one's values. Which of these reasons seems most compelling to you?

The Motherhood Mandate

There is considerable social pressure on women to have children, pressure that has been called the **motherhood mandate** (Russo, 1979) (see Figure 10.2). Americans surveyed in the 1950s through 1970s endorsed a strong norm against childlessness and one-child families (Baruch, Barnett, & Rivers, 1983; Unger, 1979a). Deliberately choosing not to have children was viewed as a sign of maladjustment in women. Stereotypes portrayed the only child as socially inadequate, self-centered, unhappy, and unlikable. (There is no evidence that only children actually are maladjusted.)

Has the motherhood mandate decreased because of feminism? Surveys in the late 1970s began to show more tolerance for people who chose not to have families. However, in the 1980s, the media rediscovered motherhood. In a backlash against the gains of the women's movement, women were warned that equality comes at a terrible cost—home and family (Faludi, 1991). Trend stories abounded—there is a new baby boom; women are all giving up

"So, have you two been doing anything reproductive?"

FIGURE 10.2

their careers for motherhood; day care is a pit of child abuse, and so on. The stories were based on biased anecdotes and sweeping generalizations, with little basis in reality. Each "trend" was a way of telling women that they must return to traditional roles or suffer dire consequences. "For women, the trend story was no news report; it was a moral reproach" (Faludi, 1991, p. 80). The decision to have a child still is made in the context of pressure to conform to the motherhood mandate.

Childless by Choice or Circumstance?

Throughout history, the childless woman has been regarded as a failed woman (Phoenix, Woollett, & Lloyd, 1991; Rich, 1976). Even in the 1990s, college students judged that women who remained childless by choice (even though they were happily employed) were less fulfilled, less acceptable role models, and more likely to be unhappy in later life (Mueller & Yoder, 1997).

Given the negative stereotype, why do some women choose not to have children? Reasons include financial considerations, a desire to pursue their education or career, the dangers of childbirth, the possibility of bearing a defective child, concerns about overpopulation, and a belief that they are not personally suited to nurturing and caring for children (Landa, 1990). Regardless of when the decision is made, it is common for women to have moments of doubt about it throughout their fertile years. Because the path of the childless woman has no clear map, "each woman seems to be traveling alone . . . unaware that others are on the same road ahead and behind her" (Morell, 2000, p. 321).

Of course, childlessness is not always a matter of choice. In a Canadian study of childless women and men over the age of 55, 72 percent attributed their childlessness to circumstance. Some people said they had not married because they had to take care of sick or elderly parents; others married late in life; others reported infertility or repeated miscarriages; and for others, it seemed to be simply fate: "It just didn't turn out that way" (Connidis & McMullin, 1996).

In the United States, about one woman in six experiences fertility problems, and only about half who seek medical treatment are able to conceive. Women who want to but cannot bear children may be stigmatized, leading to feelings of guilt and failure:

> His parents wouldn't leave me alone. They felt I wasn't trying. I was just feeling a failure—failure as a woman because you know this is what you are here for and I actually felt as though I had failed my husband because I wasn't giving him an heir to the throne. (Ulrich & Weatherall, 2001, p. 332)

Accepting childlessness is a gradual process. In a study of women who had given up trying to conceive a child after up to 15 years of treatment, participants reported coming to a point where they realized that further efforts were futile. After years of treatment, they felt exhausted and worn out. They felt profound grief and loss and a sense of emptiness. At the same time, however, they felt relief at being out of the "medical machinery" and recognized an opportunity to take back their lives, moving on to other goals (Daniluk, 1996).

Does not having children (by choice or by chance) lead to unhappiness? As discussed in Chapter 9, marital satisfaction drops with the birth of the first child and may not return to its original level until children leave home. In a major study of American women at midlife, whether a woman had children had no relationship to her psychological well-being (Baruch et al., 1983). The women in this study grew up in an era when the motherhood mandate was in full force, yet their well-being at midlife did not suffer because of childlessness. These results contradict the belief that children are central to a woman's happiness. Unless motherhood *and* refusal of motherhood are equally validated as normal and desirable, women are not yet liberated (Morell, 2000).

How Does Society Restrict Women's Choices?

Women's choices about child rearing do not take place in a social vacuum. Most societies regulate women's rights to have—and to choose not to have—children. Moreover, practical and economic factors restrict women's options, especially for poor and minority women. For example, a poor woman may have to choose a birth-control method based on its cost. Women who receive government benefits are more vulnerable to government monitoring and control of their reproductive choices. Because they have less access to lawyers and less of a public voice, they may be less able to challenge government restrictions of their rights. And they are more likely to be coerced into having (or not having) children (Roberts, 1998).

Feminists advocate ***reproductive freedom*** for all women, an ideal that has not yet been achieved. This concept includes a range of issues, such as the right to comprehensive and unbiased sex education, access to safe and reliable contraception, an end to forced sterilization and forced birth control for poor and minority women, and access to safe and legal abortion (Baber & Allen, 1992; Bishop, 1989).

At the heart of the concept of reproductive freedom is the idea that all choices about reproduction should be made by the woman herself: It is her body and her right to choose. For this reason, feminist perspectives on reproductive freedom are often termed ***pro-choice***. Because reproductive freedom affects every aspect of a woman's life, it has been a key component of every feminist movement throughout history. "Without the ability to determine their reproductive destinies, women will never achieve an equal role in social, economic, and political life and will continue to be politically subordinate to and economically dependent on men" (Roberts, 1998).

Contraception

Accidental pregnancies can be the result of a number of factors: contraceptive failure, lack of contraceptive knowledge or skill, lack of access to contraceptives, failure to use contraception, and unplanned or coerced sexual activity. Moreover, although women are expected to take most of the responsibility for safer sex, psychological factors, lack of power within heterosexual relationships, and sexual scripts make it difficult for many women, particularly young ones, to take control in this area.

Every form of contraception has drawbacks. Some methods are messy, inconvenient, and interfere with spontaneity (foam, condoms, and diaphragms). Some may cause nausea and weight gain, require daily remembering, or have the potential for long-term side effects (the pill). Some offer no protection against STDs (see Chapter 8). Some are expensive and not covered by insurance (see Box 10.1). Hormonal contraceptives such as Norplant and Norplant 2 can be implanted under the skin to ensure infertility for up to five years, but the up-front cost is high (over $500).

Problems with using contraceptives effectively are compounded for poor women and women in developing countries. For example, some methods cannot be used by women who are breastfeeding; but in countries without hygienic water supplies, breastfeeding is the only safe way to nourish an infant. Other contraceptive methods require supervision by medical professionals, which is prohibitive for the majority of the world's women (Owen & Caudill, 1996).

Information about contraception is widely available to middle-class U.S. women, everywhere from *Glamour* magazine to the *New York Times*. However, some groups of women are much less likely to get the information they need and want. Young women just beginning to be sexually active are disadvantaged: Only 13 states

BOX 10.1   ∾   Viagra Bias

Viagra bias? The initial rush of some insurers to pay for Viagra, the so-called erection pill, is leaving women (and their doctors) crying foul. Nearly 40 years after the advent of the birth control pill, only 56 percent of Pill prescriptions are covered by insurers. Why the disparity? The American College of Obstetricians and Gynecologists (ACOG) says the fact that the financial burden of birth control is borne by women, not insurers, is a clear case of gender discrimination. In fact, the cost of covering contraception would more than pay for itself in savings on abortion, prenatal care and delivery. "Contraception isn't optional," says Anita Nelson, an associate professor of obstetrics and gynecology at UCLA School of Medicine. "Women need it to protect their health and quality of life, and the prohibitive cost is partly to blame for the high number of unintended pregnancies in this country."

The Equal Employment Opportunity Commission has ruled that excluding contraceptives from health insurance coverage is sex discrimination. Twenty states now require equal coverage for contraceptives. But federal legislation is needed, because not all states are complying with the ruling. The Equity in Prescription Insurance and Contraceptive Coverage Act (EPICC), introduced in Congress in 1997, would require insurers who pay for prescription drugs to cover all FDA-approved contraceptives, as well as related doctor visits. It still has not been made law.

Source: Courtesy of *Glamour*, Conde Nast Publications, Inc., *Glamour*, September 1998; and The Center for Reproductive Rights, www.crlp.org/pub_fac_epicc.html

mandate sex education in the schools, and not all of these programs discuss contraception. Virtually no information is available in diverse languages, even in areas with large numbers of recent immigrants and ethnically diverse populations (Watson, Trasciatti, & King, 1996).

Family Health International's field studies have found that controlling one's fertility is often a mixed blessing in developing countries (Waszak, Severy, Kafafi, & Badawi, 2001). For example, in Egypt, family planning services are easily accessible, and public acceptance is high. However, if a wife does not conceive a child soon after marriage, her husband's family may start looking for a replacement wife and pressuring her husband to divorce her. Family planning empowers women, but it may also increase their anxiety and psychological distress when they live in contexts of gender inequality. For contraception services to be effective, women's psychological needs and cultural contexts must be taken into account.

Abortion

Of the world's estimated 210 million pregnancies annually, about 40 percent are unplanned. In the United States, about 1.3 million abortions take place each year, representing about 30 percent of pregnancies. Eighty-eight percent of these abortions take place within the first 12 weeks of pregnancy.

Women choosing abortion tend to be young, poor, and unmarried. The percentage of pregnancies that are aborted varies greatly by race/ethnicity: 16 percent for White women, 22 percent for Hispanic women, and 38 percent for Black women. These differences suggest that women of color are experiencing more unwanted pregnancies than white women—perhaps because they have less access to contraception or less sexual and contraceptive decision-making power (Alan Guttmacher Institute, 2002; Hyde & Delamater, 2003; Travis & Compton, 2001).

Abortion has been legal in the United States since 1973, when the Supreme Court, ruling in *Roe v. Wade*, affirmed that women have a right to decide whether to terminate their pregnancies on the basis of the constitutional right to privacy. Abortion, the Court ruled, is a matter to be decided between a woman and her physician. Although the principle of choice was affirmed by this ruling, in practice there are many limitations and legal restrictions on women's choices.

How is abortion restricted? The *Hyde Amendment,* in effect since 1976, prohibits the use of federal Medicaid money for abortions except when the mother's life is (medically) endangered. Because Medicaid provides health care for low-income families, many poor women were forced to choose between paying for an abortion out of their own inadequate incomes and carrying an unwanted fetus to term. The Medicaid restriction has resulted in some poor women delaying abortion until they can afford to pay for it or resorting to illegal abortion, thus increasing the risk of complications (Bishop, 1989; Miller, 1996). Today, 99 percent of the money spent on abortions for poor women must come from state (rather than federal) funds. But states may do little to provide for poor women, even those who are victims of incest or rape (Daley & Gold, 1993). Many states have enacted restrictive laws directed at all women seeking abortions. These laws may require the consent of a husband or partner, mandatory waiting periods, and supposedly "educational" requirements designed to discourage women from seeking abortions (Lublin, 1998). Parental notification and consent for minors is now mandatory in 32 states (Alan Guttmacher Institute, 2002). Abortion is safest when it is performed early in the pregnancy; laws that delay it affect women's health (Miller, 1996).

A new and effective nonsurgical abortion procedure, developed in Europe in the 1980s, is *mifepristone* (Mifeprex), formerly known as RU-486. This drug safely induces abortion early in pregnancy by causing the uterine lining to slough off. Antiabortion groups prevented legalization of RU-486 in the United States for over a decade because they believed that it would make abortions more private (the patient simply goes to her doctor's office for the pill, not to an abortion clinic) and therefore less vulnerable to political pressure (Hyde & Delamater, 2003). After a long campaign by women's health advocates, Mifeprex was finally, in 2000, made available to American women. However, the Bush administration and conservative legislators immediately sought to restrict its availability, especially to poor women (Wallace, 2001). A Federal agency recently refused approval for Plan B, a type of morning-after pill, for use without a prescription on the grounds that it might encourage young women to have unprotected sex (Harris, 2004). (See Figure 10.3.)

A different kind of restriction comes from harassment and violence at abortion clinics. The number of doctors who perform abortions has dropped 18 percent since 1982, partly because of stalking, death threats, Internet hit lists, and murders of physicians and clinic staff (Cozzarelli & Major, 1998; Vobejda, 1994). Picketing, bomb threats, and demonstrations affect clients, too. Studies of women who

FIGURE 10.3

Source: Copyright © 2003 Signe Wilkinson, The Washington Post Writers Group. Reprinted with permission.

encountered antiabortion protesters as they went to a clinic show that the encounters made women feel angry, intruded on, and guilty. However, they had no effect on the women's decision to have an abortion (Cozzarelli & Major, 1998).

Each year, about 46 million abortions occur worldwide, about 20 million of them illegally. In many developing countries in Africa and Asia, safe abortion is unavailable because medical facilities are scarce. When a developing country has restrictive laws, wealthy women can obtain abortions under medical supervision, but poor women may attempt self-induced abortion by taking caustic drugs or inserting objects into the vagina. In these countries, abortion mortality rates are hundreds of times higher than in the United States (Alan Guttmacher Institute, 2002).

Women in some European countries face restrictions on their abortion options. Poland had readily available abortions until 1994, when the legislature passed one of the most restrictive policies in Europe, largely as a result of pressure from Polish Catholic Church leaders. Other European countries have high fees, waiting periods, and requirements for women to have two doctors' opinions before obtaining an abortion (Darnton, 1993). Ireland has a complete ban on abortions as well as contraceptives.

The politics of abortion in the United States affect women around the world. U.S. law forbids using U.S. tax dollars to fund abortions abroad. On his first day in office in 2001, President George W. Bush extended that restriction by signing an order banning U.S. aid to global organizations that use their own funds to provide abortions or abortion counseling to poor women in developing countries. In 2002, he eliminated U.S. contributions to UN family planning programs. These programs provide not only abortion counseling but also contraceptive education, HIV and AIDS prevention, and general health education to women and children in over 140 poor and developing countries (Helmore, 2002).

Science, Censorship, and the Information Wars

One argument used in efforts to restrict abortion is that it has harmful physical and/or psychological consequences. In their zeal to abolish abortion, opponents have put political pressure on government agencies to misrepresent the scientific evidence showing that abortion is safe for women. Many scientists and elected officials are concerned about the governmental manipulation of science to achieve political ends (Sluzki, 2003; www.house.gov/reform/min/politicsandscience).

One example is the claim that abortion causes breast cancer, a claim that has no scientific basis. The Web site of the National Cancer Institute formerly provided accurate information on this topic, citing a study of 1.5 million women that showed *no* association between abortion and breast cancer; that information has been magically replaced by a statement that "the evidence is inconclusive" (Sluzki, 2003).

Another example of misinformation is the claim that women who have an abortion typically suffer guilt, shame, and lasting psychological damage—a ***post-abortion syndrome*** (Miller, 1996; Russo, 2000). This so-called fact has been widely disseminated on the Web by abortion opponents. Although psychology cannot resolve moral differences of opinion about abortion, empirical research can answer questions of the relationship between abortion and psychological well-being. Let's look at the evidence for and against "post abortion syndrome."

To determine the effects of abortion on women's mental health, the American Psychological Association commissioned a study of all the scientific research published in the United States since abortion was legalized in 1973. This research review established that the legal termination of an unwanted pregnancy does not have major negative effects on most women. Measurements of psychological distress usually drop immediately following the abortion and remain low in follow-ups after several weeks (Public Interest Directorate, 1987). When a woman freely chooses a legal abortion, the typical emotion that follows is relief. In fact, abortion may be a milestone for a woman in taking control over her own life (Travis & Compton, 2001).

This does not mean that women are always perfectly well-adjusted after an abortion. In different studies, between 0.5 percent and 15 percent of abortion clients have experienced psychological problems that lasted from one week to 10 years following the abortion. But the most important factor in a woman's adjustment after abortion is her adjustment prior to the abortion (Russo, 2000). A woman is more likely to have psychological problems following an abortion if she has a history of prior emotional problems, has received little support from her family or friends, felt pressured into the abortion decision, has strong antiabortion religious beliefs, or believed in advance that she would have problems in coping (Public Interest Directorate, 1987). Women obtaining abortions have a much higher rate of past physical, sexual, and emotional abuse than other women, a factor that strongly affects their pre-abortion well-being and makes them more vulnerable to the effects of any life stress (Russo, 2000). Encounters with antiabortion demonstrators at the time of the abortion also have negative effects. The more intense the protest outside the clinic when a woman tried to enter, the more depressed she was after the abortion (Cozzarelli & Major, 1998).

Most women contemplating an abortion have mixed feelings about it. Women who experience severe distress following abortion may want to obtain psychological counseling. However, women should not have to deny their conflicts for fear of being labeled emotionally disturbed:

> Abortion, like other moral dilemmas, does cause suffering in the individuals whose lives are impacted. That suffering does not make the choice wrong or harmful to the individual who must make the choice, nor should the individual be pathologized for having feelings of distress. In fact, the shouldering of such suffering and of responsibility for moral choices contributes to psychological growth. (Elkind, 1991, p. 3)

The Society for the Psychology of Women, Division 35 of APA, has countered the misleading information about "post-abortion syndrome" by launching an informative section on the Pro-Choice Forum Web site (www.prochoiceforum.org).

Technology and Choice

Controversies about contraception and abortion show that the development of new reproductive technology does not always increase choices for women. The reality is that reproductive technology has introduced many troublesome questions of ethics, morality, power, and choice. Indeed, the body may be the major battleground of women's rights for decades to come.

Selective Abortion

Blood tests, amniocentesis, and other new technologies allow selective abortion of "defective" fetuses. The great majority of women who find that they are carrying a Down syndrome fetus, for example, choose to abort; and a majority of Americans endorse that choice (Wertz, 1992). Is abortion justified for disorders that cause mental retardation? What about those that may cause social (but not cognitive) problems, such as the sex chromosomal variations discussed in Chapter 5?

Some people believe that pregnant women do not have the right to end a potential life simply because the child will be less than perfect (Lee, 2000). On the other hand, women are the ones who bear the burden of child rearing. Disability activists argue that if social supports were available, parenting a disabled child would not involve the sacrifices it now does. And what counts as a disability? In a study in the U.K., many students expressed fears about widening the definition of disability. (Recall the selective abortion of female fetuses discussed in Chapter 6.) As one student said, "The danger is that choice can end up being unlimited. . . . It would mean that people could act out their prejudices about what makes a good person such as white children or straight children" (Lee, 2000, p. 398).

Fetal "Rights"

Under the U.S. constitution, legal rights for individuals begin at birth. However, there is increasing political pressure from conservatives to define fetuses as persons and endow them with rights. In 2002, the Bush administration proposed to change health insurance regulations in order to define *children* to include fetuses from conception onward. The administration claimed that this would allow health coverage for low-income pregnant women, but pro-choice advocates claimed it was a ploy to undermine women's right to choose. Abortion rights advocates fear that a federal court might rule that the rights of a fetus take precedence over the rights of a pregnant woman (Kemper, 2002).

Because of political pressures, the monitoring of women's behavior during pregnancy is increasing (Baber & Allen, 1992; Kline, 1996; Pollit, 1998). In at least 17 states, women have been charged with child abuse for using drugs or alcohol during pregnancy, although fetuses are not children under the law. Meanwhile, media reports typically ignore the fact that there are almost no treatment programs available for pregnant women who are addicted to drugs. This form of social control falls more heavily on poor women; those who can afford private health care are not monitored or tested against their will. (One physician pointed out that if these were middle-class women, they would be referred to the Betty Ford Clinic, not sent to jail.)

Feminist health-care activists are concerned about the slippery slope: Will women soon be jailed for smoking, failing to take their medication, or not getting enough exercise during pregnancy? And they point out that the concept of fetal rights places responsibility solely on women instead of on both parents and their community. The best way to foster infant health is to help pregnant women by providing low-cost prenatal care, drug treatment programs, and social support services—not by punishing women for being less than perfect incubators.

In Vitro Fertilization

Some couples who are unable to conceive a child use technologies such as ***in vitro fertilization,*** or ***IVF,*** commonly known as the test-tube baby procedure. A woman's ovaries are stimulated with strong fertility drugs so that they produce multiple eggs, which are then surgically removed. Her partner's sperm (obtained by masturbation) is combined with the eggs in a glass dish. If fertilization occurs, the embryos are inserted into the woman's uterus to develop (Williams, 1992).

IVF carries many risks. The fertility drugs and surgeries can lead to unpleasant and dangerous side effects and complications. The emotional costs are high, as women put their lives and careers on hold to concentrate on getting pregnant, and the success rate is low.

Women who choose to undergo IVF describe themselves as desperate to have children at any cost. Their strong desire to become biological mothers is usually seen as natural. The media frequently feature heart-rending stories of a woman's quest for a child, but rarely do these stories analyze how the need to have children is socially constructed. In an analysis of 133 news articles on IVF, 64 explicitly endorsed the belief that bearing children is the single most important accomplishment of adult life, and only two articles countered that belief (Condit, 1996). "To what extent does our society *create* a market for IVF by placing so many important meanings on fertility that to be infertile indeed becomes an unbearable problem?" (Williams, 1992, p. 262).

Studies exploring women's motivations for seeking IVF suggest that these women have been strongly influenced by the motherhood mandate: The majority believe that parenthood is an essential part of a woman's life. Moreover, they report having experienced strong external pressures to bear children (Williams, 1992). Indeed, some women may undergo IVF partly because only after IVF fails can they be accepted by others as childless due to fate, not choice (Koch, 1990). On the other hand, those who succeed in having a child through IVF or other medically assisted methods generally report more positive relationships between mother, father, and child than comparison mothers who conceived naturally, and IVF children are as well-adjusted as others (Hahn, 2001).

Other Methods of Conception

IVF is only one of the reproductive technologies being used to allow couples to have children. Some methods are decidedly low-tech, with the kitchen turkey-baster the favored means of insemination and the couples themselves in control of the technology. In one case, a lesbian couple had a child with sperm donated by one partner's father to the other partner. Both genetic and social ties of grandparent to grandchild were thus created.

Some couples use reproductive technologies in order to pay others to breed children for them. Many feminists believe that this practice exploits women (Baber & Allen, 1992; Raymond, 1993); others argue that contract pregnancy can have substantial benefits to all parties if it is stringently regulated (Purdy, 1992). As currently practiced, contract pregnancy raises seemingly insoluble ethical dilemmas. The following are descriptions of actual cases:

> Robert M. contracts for a baby with Elvira J. without telling her that he is considering divorcing his wife Cynthia M. On learning of the pending divorce, Elvira refuses to give up the baby for adoption, although she allows the Ms to take the baby home with them on the condition that they seek marriage counseling. Six months later, Robert M. files for divorce, triggering a three-way custody battle between biological father, biological mother, and caretaker mother. Who is being exploited here? Does the fact that Elvira is a Latina with only a seventh-grade education make a difference? (Nelson, 1992)

> Mark C. and Cristina C. hire Anna J. to gestate an embryo grown from their sperm and egg. Finding herself attached to the child, Anna seeks visitation rights. A judge rules that Anna is not the child's mother (although it is she who has given birth), but merely a temporary foster mother, and denies her request. Anna is a black single mother; the Cs' are white and Asian-American, respectively. (Purdy, 1992)

These cases illustrate the ethical and social dilemmas created by reproductive technologies. Many feminists argue that women are at risk for exploitation by technologies that separate the genetic and physiological aspects of pregnancy. Women's bodies are manipulated and experimented on. More than ever, women may be viewed solely as egg providers and incubators, and motherhood defined only in biological terms (Baber & Allen, 1992; Raymond, 1993; Ulrich & Weatherall, 2000).

The Transition to Motherhood

Becoming a mother changes a woman's life perhaps more than any other single life transition. Pregnancy, birth, and the transition to motherhood include both biological and social events. These events interact to produce changes in life circumstances, lifestyle, and involvement in paid work, as well as changes in relationships with partners, parents, and others. Once a woman becomes a mother, the role is hers for life; and she will be defined largely through that role, much more than men are defined through their roles as fathers. It is not surprising that motherhood profoundly affects a woman's sense of self (Ussher, 1989). Let's look more closely at some of the changes that occur with pregnancy and motherhood and their effects on women's identities.

How Does Motherhood Change Work and Marital Roles?

More than 20 longitudinal studies have shown that the birth of a child can negatively affect family relationships, reducing psychological well-being and marital satisfaction (Walzer, 1998). Husbands and wives become more different from each other; studies using large national samples show that parenthood results in bigger changes in women's lives than in men's, as women take on more child care and housework (Sanchez & Thomson, 1997).

Many women experience the change from paid worker to unpaid at-home mother as stressful. The changes from a nine-to-five schedule to being on call 24 hours a day, from adult company to isolation with an infant, from feeling competent to feeling overwhelmed with new tasks, all require adjustments. The difficulties may be offset by the rewards of getting to know one's growing baby, the belief that caring for one's children is worthwhile and important, and the sense of mastery that comes from learning how to do it well. Women who return to paid work have their own stresses, juggling many demands. For both groups, conflicts occur.

A major source of conflict is the discrepancy between women's expectations of their partners' involvement and men's actual behavior once the child is born. Studies suggest that although many men are positive about the idea of becoming a father, they do not follow through with a fair share of the work (Nicolson, 1990). In one study, new mothers kept time-use diaries and were also interviewed twice. Their workdays ranged from 11 to 17½ hours a day, and they spent an average of six hours a day alone with their babies. Although they cited the babies' fathers as their main source of support, fathers actually contributed only zero to two hours a day of primary care (Croghan, 1991). In another study women described the kinds of help they received: "If I'm at the end of the rope, he'll step in and take over." "At dinner time he pitches in . . . entertains the baby" (Rhoades, 1989, pp. 131–141).

These studies suggest that new mothers are stressed by inequality in marital roles. Women may enter motherhood with expectations of equality in parenting, but these expectations collide with reality (Ruble, Fleming, Hackel, & Stangor, 1988). It is difficult for women and men to change parenting relationships because cultural images and social structures constantly reinforce the idea that mothers, not fathers, should have day-to-day responsibility for children (Walzer, 1998). (See Figure 10.4.) Myths of motherhood still imply that women should be fulfilled through self-sacrifice and grateful for any small contribution their husbands might make (Croghan, 1991).

Do Mothers Face Impossible Ideals?

Mothers are encouraged to evaluate themselves against images of ideal mothers such as the radiant, serene Madonna and the superwoman who juggles the demands of house, children, husband, and job while providing her children with unfailing love and plenty of quality time (Ussher, 1989). Women often are not prepared for negative and ambivalent feelings and may feel like failures when they occur. It is likely that a majority of women experience decreased emotional well-being at some

"Of course I want to have kids, Claire—just not all the time."

FIGURE 10.4

Source: Copyright © The New Yorker Collection, 2003, David Sipress, from cartoonbank.com. All rights reserved.

point during pregnancy and early motherhood (Condon, 1987; Ruble et al., 1988; Ussher, 1989; Wells, Hobfall, & Lavin, 1997). Some women have described the conflicts that come from experiencing negative feelings they knew did not live up to the ideals:

> Motherhood wasn't what I expected—unadulterated wonder. The shock of the isolation and much of the sheer slog and boredom were exacerbated by the fact that I felt I wasn't supposed to feel dissatisfied. (Wandor, 1980, cited in Ussher, 1989, p. 84)
>
> Being brought up in the traditional way, I always feared something terrible would happen if I went away, like the house would burn down. I felt I would be punished for leaving the children, even to go to work. Especially to go to work. (A single mother; Hall, 1984, pp. 17–18)
>
> I couldn't seem to do anything right; I felt so tired, the baby kept crying, and I kept thinking that this was supposed to be the most fulfilling experience of my whole life. It felt like the most lonely, miserable experience. (A mother three weeks after the birth of her first child, cited in Ussher, 1989, p. 82)

The best strategies for coping with role changes during pregnancy seem to be active assertion and seeking communal relationships with other women. In a study of white employed pregnant women, these were associated with reduced depression and anger (Wells et al., 1997). In another study, women who received social support during pregnancy showed many beneficial physical and psychological outcomes that persisted through the first year of motherhood (Oakley, 1992).

Sexuality and Motherhood

When women become pregnant, they are confronted with many of the contradictions about sexuality that characterize Western society. The Madonna ideal—pure and serene—exists at the cost of desire: The Madonna must be a virgin (Young, 1998). (See Figure 10.5.) The idea of a mother who has sexual desires and acts on them conflicts with the ideal of maternal selflessness. Becoming pregnant and giving birth highlight a woman's sexuality. At the same time society, may downplay the sexuality of the

FIGURE 10.5

This photo of model Jerry Hall by noted photographer Annie Leibovitz is disturbing to many viewers because Hall's sexuality and the maternal behavior of breastfeeding a baby are both on display. With it, Leibovitz asks the viewer to think about our sentimental images of mothers.

pregnant woman or the mother, fostering a split between the woman's body and sense of self (Ussher, 1989, p. 92).

One example of this split is the disconnection between desire and behavior during pregnancy. Many women experience increased sexual desire while pregnant, especially in the middle three months (Kitzinger, 1983). This may reflect physical changes such as an increased blood supply to the pelvic area, as well as psychological factors. (For one thing, the woman and her partner needn't worry about contraception!) Yet women may engage in sexual activities less often, out of fear of harming the fetus, feeling unattractive, or physical awkwardness.

In a normal pregnancy, intercourse and orgasm are safe until four weeks before the due date; these activities do not harm the fetus or cause miscarriage (Masters & Johnson, 1966). When women were surveyed about their physicians' advice, however, 60 percent had received no information at all, and another 10 percent were told they should not have intercourse after their seventh month (Gauna-Trujillo & Higgins, 1989). Perhaps the medical profession perpetuates the myth of the asexual mother because doctors, themselves influenced by the myth, are reluctant and embarrassed to discuss sex with pregnant women (Ussher, 1989).

Psychological Effects of Bodily Changes during Pregnancy

The hormonal changes of pregnancy are much greater than those of the menstrual cycle. The levels of progesterone and estrogen in pregnant women are many times higher than in nonpregnant women, and many of the physical experiences of early pregnancy may be related to rapid increases in these hormones. These include breast tenderness, fatigue, and "morning sickness" (which can actually occur at any time of the day): nausea, revulsion at the sight or odor of food, and sometimes vomiting.

In addition, other physiological changes may alter the functioning of the central nervous system. The level of the neurotransmitter norepinephrine drops during pregnancy while the levels of stress-associated hormones rise (Treadway, Kane, Jarrahi-Zadeh, & Lipton, 1969). Norepinephrine and progesterone have both been related to depression. In a study of mood changes during pregnancy, women were interviewed both before and during their pregnancies and compared with a control group of women who did not become pregnant. For the pregnant group, changes in mood increased compared with both their prepregnancy baseline and the control group, mainly during the first third of the pregnancy (Striegel-Moore, Goldman, Garvin, & Rodin, 1996).

Pregnancy is also a time of dramatic weight gain and changes in body shape. Many women feel extremely ambivalent about these changes (Ussher, 1989). Reactions include feeling temporarily free from cultural demands to be slim, feeling awe and wonder, feeling afraid and disgusted by their size, and feeling alienated and out of control (see Box 10.2). In a study of more than 200 women, changes in body image were among the most frequently reported stressors of pregnancy and early motherhood, second only to physical symptoms (Affonso & Mayberry, 1989). Recent research suggests that body image concerns are increasing; some women are

BOX 10.2 ❧ "A Brand New Body": One Woman's Account of Pregnancy

Suzanne Arms (1973) kept a journal during her first pregnancy. Her reactions to her changing body are captured in these journal entries, ranging from early to late in her pregnancy.

I have the feeling that I brought a brand new body home from the doctor's office. I'm a new me. Nobody else would look at me and call me pregnant, but it's wonderful to know that I really am, and I look for every tiny sign to prove it's true. My developing breasts are encouraging, and my nipples have become much larger. My nipples stand erect at times, and they're at least three shades darker. (p. 13)

I have never felt beautiful but I've always liked my face and filled-out body. . . . But looking at pictures of me crying last week really hurt. They're so un-me. Just a pudgy woman. Today I don't feel like that at all. I've tied my hair back, vowed not to wear those baggy farmer jeans till after the baby comes, and put on a dress; I really do feel beautiful. In fact, I feel like I'm a pretty good place for a baby to stay and grow in. Nice, round, firm, with just enough fat all over to make it really soft and safe for the baby. (p. 29)

I've been getting more and more pleasure from my sensual feelings. There's some old tightness in me that seems to be losing its hold at last, and I feel all of me expanding. (p. 35)

I rub cocoa butter on my tummy and breasts every morning after showering. The skin has become pink and smooth and I can't help feeling it all the time. The other day we were in the bookstore, and I was absent-mindedly rubbing myself and staring into space. A young woman with a child called to me from across the store, "That's a lovely belly you have there!" (p. 40)

I've begun to feel huge. I remember hearing other pregnant women hassle themselves about getting fat. I never could figure it out. To me they looked beautiful, round and blooming. I assured myself that I would never feel that way, and I would love my tummy and all the extra pounds. Well, that's great in theory—but suddenly the day comes when I look in the mirror and my face is round and I really do look like an orange! even holding my stomach in. So yesterday I spent the whole day feeling fat, ugly, and unlovable. Despite every nice thing John has said, I knew he would soon see how unappealing I am. (p. 44)

A very full feeling today, I'm thick and stuffed like a bulging cabbage. (p. 59) I never thought it would come to this. I can't reach over my stomach to get to my feet. John has to lace up my hiking boots! (p. 63)

Sometimes it seems as though I've been pregnant all my life. I can't remember being unpregnant. (p. 64)

Suzanne Arms' pregnancy was planned and wanted, and she was in a stable relationship with a supportive male partner. How might the reactions of women to their changing bodies differ in differing social circumstances?

Source: From Suzanne Arms, 1993, *A Season to Be Born.* Copyright © 1993 by Suzanne Arms. Reprinted by permission of Suzanne Arms.

choosing not to become pregnant because of fears about how it would change their bodies (Garner, 1997).

Indeed, the pregnant woman does lose some control over her body. Changes will occur no matter what she does. She is helpless (short of terminating the pregnancy) to govern her own body. And yet, as discussed throughout this book, society defines her largely in terms of her body. Thus, it should not be surprising if pregnant women feel unfeminine, moody, or insecure, even apart from hormonal causes.

How Do Others React to Pregnant Women?

Pregnant women are powerful stimuli for the behavior of others. "A woman begins to assume the identity of mother in the eyes of society almost as soon as she is visibly pregnant, ceasing to be a single unit long before the birth of her child" (Ussher, 1989, p. 81). Her body symbolizes the eternal power of women:

> The atmosphere of approval in which I was bathed—even by strangers on the street, it seemed—was like an aura I carried with me, in which doubts, fears, misgivings, met with absolute denial. This is what women have always done. (Rich, 1976, p. 26)

Pregnant women may be genuinely cherished. One woman, who married into a Puerto Rican family, was delighted by her special status when she became pregnant:

> I'm treated like a precious, fragile person by my in-laws. I . . . get the best seat on the couch and am served dinner first. When my mother-in-law found out I was pregnant with my first child, she created a special ritual for me that involved a warm, scented candle-lit bath. She placed my husband's baby picture on the mirror and told me all about her experiences with pregnancy and birth. (Johnston-Robledo, 2000, pp. 132–133)

On the other hand, pregnancy may elicit benevolent sexism because pregnant women are seen as fragile and dependent, and therefore less threatening. Pregnancy may even be a kind of stigma: People react very differently to pregnant and nonpregnant women, and their reactions may lead to change in the women's behavior in return. This was illustrated in an intriguing experiment in which two female experimenters alternated between appearing pregnant (with the help of a little padding) or carrying a box the same size as the "pregnancy" (Taylor & Langer, 1977). The women stood in elevators and measured the distance that other passengers stood from them. Both men and women stood closer to the nonpregnant woman. Men, especially, avoided the pregnant woman. She was also stared at more; both men and women spent considerable time furtively looking at her stomach, so much so that both experimenters felt very uncomfortable when playing the pregnant role.

The public presence of pregnant women has since become more acceptable. Actress Demi Moore even appeared nude and very pregnant on the cover of *Vanity Fair* in 1991. Are pregnant women still stigmatized? With the help of a little padding, perhaps some intrepid female researchers will conduct another study.

Motherhood and Women's Identity

Pregnancy and mothering affect women's sense of self. In a Canadian study, for example, the women experienced themselves as profoundly changed. Middle-class women described the changes in terms of personal growth and self-actualization; working-class women described them in terms of "settling down." For both groups, motherhood involved a moral transformation in which they became deeply connected to their babies. However, the flip side of such connectedness—feeling responsible for the child—was described as one of the hardest things about motherhood (McMahon, 1995).

In another study that followed newly married couples over a three-year period, the birth of a child changed both parents' identities: Men became more masculine and women more feminine on dimensions that defined masculinity and femininity for themselves. In other words, the changes in marital roles and activities following the birth of a child deepened their sense of themselves as feminine women and masculine men (Burke & Cast, 1997).

An intensive case study of one woman's pregnancy illustrates the experience of change (Smith, 1991). Clare's identity change during early pregnancy involved imagining the child-to-be:

> In one respect, it's—it's a person, a whole person that just happens to be in there, and in another way, it's something different. (p. 231)

In the middle phase, Clare experienced a growing sense of psychological relatedness with others—partner, mother, sister. Near the end of the pregnancy, Clare sees herself as very changed:

> I'm one of two and I'm one of three. . . . An irrevocable decision, the steps have been made that mean that my other identities, if you like as a mother and a partner, make up that essential me now. (p. 236)

The transition to motherhood involves losses as well as gains. The woman ceases to be seen as an autonomous individual and is instead viewed as an expectant mother and then mother. It is not surprising that feelings of loss are experienced. It is hard to change from being "Joy Williams, secretary/jogger/painter/daughter/ spouse and more" to being "Timmy's mom." I remember my own feelings of sadness and loss shortly after the birth of my first child when the nurses in the hospital referred to all the women in the maternity unit as Mother ("Mother, are you ready for your lunch tray?") rather than by our names. It seemed as if everything that had gone before was now to be put aside for the all-encompassing identity and job of Mother.

Because feelings of loss conflict with the motherhood mystique, women may be ashamed of them, label themselves as ill or abnormal, or believe that "baby blues" are inevitable and biologically determined. One of the ways cultural constructions of motherhood may oppress women is that they are not allowed to mourn or grieve the old, lost self (Nicolson, 1993).

So far, we have been talking about the transition to motherhood mainly as it has been constructed for white middle-class women exposed to the motherhood mystique. What does the identity of mother mean for poor women? An eloquent expression of class and color differences in ideals of womanhood and motherhood comes from a famous speech attributed to Sojourner Truth, a crusader for abolition and suffrage and an ex-slave, to the Akron Convention for Women's Rights in 1852:

> That man over there says that women need to be helped into carriages, and lifted over ditches and have the best place everywhere. Nobody ever helps me into carriages, or over mud puddles or gives me any best place, and ain't I a woman? Look at me! Look at my arm! I have ploughed, and planted, and gathered into barns, and no man could head me! And ain't I a woman? I could work as much and eat as much as a man—when I could get it—and bear the lash as well! And ain't I a woman? I have borne thirteen children, and seen them most all sold off to slavery, and when I cried out with my mother's grief, none but Jesus heard me. And ain't I a woman? (Adapted from Ruth, 1990, pp. 463–464)

Attitudes toward pregnant women still vary by social class. Middle-class women in heterosexual marriages may be treated as delicate and special, but poor single women are labeled welfare moms, undeserving of respect. Middle-class mothers are urged to stay home with their children, but poor mothers are forced to look for paid employment (see Figure 10.6). Heterosexual women's connectedness with their children is seen as positive, but lesbians' connectedness with theirs is pathologized. Identity is affected not only from within, but also by the social context of mothering.

FIGURE 10.6

Source: Copyright © 2003 David Horsey. Tribune Media Services, Inc. All rights reserved.

The Event of Childbirth

If a woman were training to run a marathon, climb a cliff, or go on an Outward Bound trek, she would probably think of the upcoming event as a challenge. She would acknowledge that her body would be worked hard and stressed, her courage tested, and her life put at some risk. Yet she could feel in control and prepare for the challenge. She might undertake the experience as a way of knowing her own self or of developing her strengths and resources. Childbirth is a normal physical process with some of the same potential for empowerment, yet women are rarely encouraged to think of it in this way (Rich, 1976). Instead, they are taught to think of it as an event in which they will be dependent, passive, subject to authority, and in need of expert medical intervention.

How Is the Meaning of Childbirth Socially Constructed?

In virtually all cultures, birth is associated with fear, pain, awe, and wonder; it is viewed as both the worst pain anyone could suffer and as a peak experience. Yet there are surprisingly few accounts of childbirth *by women*, and women's experiences of childbirth are invisible in Western art. Images of war and death are innumerable, but images of birth are nonexistent (Chicago, 1990). Artist Judy Chicago's Birth Project is a collective effort by women artists and crafters to represent images of birth (see Figure 10.7).

FIGURE 10.7
Judy Chicago's image "Crowning" represents the moment the baby's head first becomes visible at the vaginal opening.

Popular culture gives us its own version: Many prime-time situation comedies have shown their stars giving birth. A study of books, magazines, newspaper articles, TV shows, and movies in the 1980s and early 1990s showed that these media usually portrayed a woman giving birth as a passive patient, not an active agent, and showed a very strong preference for hospital births over birthing centers or home births (Sterk, 1996). It seems that women are in charge of childbirth only when they write science-fiction novels (see Box 10.3).

Is Childbirth a Medical Crisis?

In some countries, birth is considered a natural phenomenon that needs no medical intervention in the majority of cases. For example, in the Netherlands the laboring woman is believed to need only "close observation, moral support, and protection against human meddling." A healthy woman can best accomplish her task of birthing her baby if she is self-confident, in familiar surroundings—preferably her own home—and attended by a birth specialist such as a midwife. Women at risk of complications are hospitalized, but most babies are born at home (MacFarlane, 1977, p. 29).

In contrast, virtually all U.S. births take place in hospitals. As recently as 1935, the majority of babies were born at home, but by the end of the 1970s, 99 percent of births took place in hospitals (Nelson, 1996). Today, nurse-midwives attend about 7 percent of U.S. births, with the rest attended by physicians (NCHS, 1999). Even the language of childbirth reflects the centrality of the physician: People routinely speak of babies being *delivered* by doctors instead of birthed by women.

Is the medical model of birth best for women? On the one hand, basic health care and education for pregnant women can save lives and improve maternal and infant health. On the other hand, the medical monopoly may lead to women being regarded as incompetent and passive patients, depriving them of control during one of life's most awesome experiences. Many of the customary procedures surrounding birth in the United States are virtually unknown in other societies and are not necessarily in the best interest of mother or baby. For example, in hospital births the woman lies on her back during delivery, whereas in most cultures women give birth in a squatting or semiseated position. The supine position puts pressure on the spine, may slow labor, works against gravity, increases the risk of vaginal tearing, and makes it more difficult for the woman to push actively during the process. Why, then, do hospitals insist on this position? It is easier for the physician, who can view the birth more conveniently.

American women have experienced childbirth with feet in the air, drugged, shaved, purged with an enema, denied food and water, hooked up to machines and sensors, and psychologically isolated to a degree that is virtually unknown in other parts of the world (Nelson, 1996). Research shows that giving birth in an unfamiliar environment, being surrounded by strangers, and being moved from one room to another late in labor affect the birth process adversely even in nonhuman animals, yet these practices are routine in medicalized childbirth (MacFarlane, 1977; Newton, 1970).

In the United States, women have also been routinely taught that they will need pain relief during normal birth. The use of tranquilizers, barbiturates, and

BOX 10.3   ∾   Takver Gives Birth

In this passage from her novel *The Dispossessed*, acclaimed science-fiction writer Ursula LeGuin movingly describes the work and the triumph of giving birth.

Takver got very big in the belly and walked like a person carrying a large, heavy basket of laundry. She stayed at work at the fish labs till she had found and trained an adequate replacement for herself, then she came home and began labor. Shevek arrived home in midafternoon. "You might go fetch the midwife," Takver said. "Tell her the contractions are four or five minutes apart, but they're not speeding up much, so don't hurry very much."

He ran to the block clinic, arriving so out of breath and unsteady on his legs that they thought he was having a heart attack. He explained. They sent a message off to another midwife and told him to go home, the partner would be wanting company. He went home, and at every stride the panic in him grew, the terror, the certainty of loss. . . . Takver had no time for emotional scenes; she was busy. She had cleared the bed platform except for a clean sheet, and she was at work bearing a child. She did not howl or scream, as she was not in pain, but when each contraction came she managed it by muscle and breath control, and then let out a great houff of breath, like one who makes a terrific effort to lift a heavy weight. Shevek had never seen any work that so used all the strength of the body.

He could not look on such work without trying to help in it. He could serve as handhold and brace when she needed leverage. They found this arrangement very quickly by trial and error, and kept to it after the midwife had come in. Takver gave birth afoot, squatting, her face against Shevek's thigh, her hands gripping his braced arms. "There you are," the midwife said quietly under the hard, engine-like pounding of Takver's breathing, and she took the slimy but recognizably human creature that had appeared. A gush of blood followed, and an amorphous mass of something not human, not alive. The terror he had forgotten came back into Shevek redoubled. It was death he saw.

Takver had let go of his arms and was huddled down quite limp at his feet. He bent over her, stiff with horror and grief.

"That's it," said the midwife, "help her move aside so I can clean this up."

"I want to wash," Takver said feebly.

"Here, help her wash up. Those are sterile cloths—there."

"Waw, waw, waw," said another voice.

The room seemed to be full of people. . . .

Somehow in this extreme rush of events the midwife had found time to clean the infant and even put a gown on it, so that it was not so fishlike and slippery as when he had seen it first. The afternoon had got dark, with the same peculiar rapidity and lack of time lapse. The lamp was on. Shevek picked up the baby to take it to Takver. Its face was incredibly small, with large, fragile-looking, closed eyelids. "Give it here," Takver was saying. "Oh, do hurry up, please give it to me."

He brought it across the room and very cautiously lowered it onto Takver's stomach. "Ah!" she said softly, a call of pure triumph.

"What is it?" she asked after a while, sleepily.

Shevek was sitting beside her on the edge of the bed platform. He carefully investigated, somewhat taken aback by the length of gown as contrasted with the extreme shortness of limb. "Girl."

The midwife came back, went around putting things to rights. "You did a first-rate job," she remarked, to both of them. They assented mildly. "I'll look in in the morning," she said leaving. The baby and Takver were already asleep. Shevek put his head down near Takver's. He was accustomed to the pleasant musky smell of her skin. This had changed; it had become a perfume, heavy and faint, heavy with sleep. Very gently he put one arm over her as she lay on her side with the baby against her breast. In the room heavy with life he slept.

anesthetics during childbirth has become routine; but it is also controversial. On the one hand, drugs can spare women unnecessary pain. On the other hand, there are "a number of well-documented dangerous effects on both mother and infant" (Hyde & DeLamater, 2003, p. 165). For example, anesthetics in the mother's bloodstream are passed to the infant and may slow development for up to four weeks. Anesthetics may prolong labor by inhibiting contractions and making the mother unable to help push the baby through the birth canal. Psychologically, they reduce the woman's awareness and her ability to control one of the most meaningful events of her life.

The medical model of birth encourages physicians and pregnant women to focus on possible complications and emergencies and may cause them to react to even remote possibilities with drastic medical interventions. In the past 25 years, there has been a dramatic increase in the number of cesarean (surgical) births in the United States, from about 4 percent to over 24 percent of all births (Martin, Park, & Sutton, 2002). This rate is much higher than in other developed countries such as Great Britain (where it is about 10 percent) and is *not* associated with lower infant mortality). Other medical procedures such as fetal monitoring, ultrasound, and artificial induction of labor are also rising dramatically in the United States (NCHS, 1999).

The reasons for the epidemic of medical intervention are unclear. Some critics have rather cynically suggested that scheduled surgical births are more convenient and profitable for physicians. Others have attributed the increase to physicians' fear of malpractice suits. When birth is defined as a medical event, helping and supporting the laboring woman seems inadequate, and heroic medical measures seem desirable. It has also been suggested that the high rate of surgical deliveries is an attempt by the medical profession to keep its dominant role in childbirth, despite women's increasing insistence on viewing birth as a normal process.

Family-Centered Childbirth

The medicalization of birth reached its height in the United States in the 1950s and 1960s. After undergoing male-managed childbirth, many women began to write about their experiences and work toward more woman- and family-centered birthing practices. Women organizers founded the International Childbirth Education Association in 1960. Widely read books such as *Our Bodies, Ourselves; Immaculate Deception; Of Woman Born;* and *The Great American Birth Rite* helped change public attitudes in the 1970s.

At about the same time, methods of ***prepared*** or ***natural childbirth*** were introduced to the American public. The most popular type of prepared childbirth is the ***Lamaze method,*** named after a French obstetrician. Women who use this approach learn techniques of relaxation and controlled breathing. Relaxation helps to reduce tension and the perception of pain and conserves energy during labor. Controlled breathing helps the woman work with, not against, the strength of each uterine contraction. The Lamaze method does not rule out the use of pain-relieving drugs, but it emphasizes that with proper preparation they may not be needed, and it leaves the choice to the laboring woman.

Another part of the Lamaze technique is the help of a "coach," or trusted partner—usually the baby's father—during labor and birth. The coach helps the mother with relaxation and controlled breathing and provides emotional support and encouragement. Men had been banished from the delivery room at the heyday of the medical model, regarded as unhygienic, superfluous, and likely to get in the way (MacFarlane, 1977). Today, many men feel that participating in the birth of their child is an important part of being a father.

Studies comparing women who used Lamaze and other methods of childbirth education and training with women who had no special preparation have shown benefits associated with prepared childbirth. These include shorter labor, fewer complications, less use of anesthetics, less reported pain, and increased feelings of self-esteem and control (Hyde & DeLamater, 2003). These studies must be interpreted carefully. Perhaps women who sign up for Lamaze training are largely those who are motivated to experience childbirth positively under any circumstances. In other words, the studies do not rule out the sampling bias of self-selection.

One study of support during childbirth does rule out self-selection effects (Kennell, Klaus, McGrath, Robertson, & Hinkley, 1991). More than 600 pregnant women, mostly Hispanic, poor, and unmarried, were randomly assigned to one of three groups. One group received emotional support during labor from a specially trained woman helper. The helpers, who were recruited from the local community, stayed with the laboring women to provide encouragement, explain the birth process, and offer soothing touch and handholding. A second group had a non-interactive female observer present, and the third group had standard hospital care.

Women in the emotional support group had a cesarean rate of 8 percent, compared with 13 percent in the observed group and 18 percent in the standard procedure group. They experienced less pain in labor: The standard group was almost seven times as likely to need anesthesia as the emotional support group. Moreover, their labor time was shorter, and they and their babies spent less time in the hospital. Clearly, emotional support made a large difference. The study's director estimated that investing small amounts of money in providing this kind of support would save $2 billion a year in hospital costs.

Women's efforts to regain control of the event of birth have resulted in many changes from the extreme medical model of 30 years ago. Today, fathers are more likely to be with the birthing woman. More births are taking place in homelike birth centers, attended by nurse-midwives. Women and their partners are far more likely to be educated about the normal processes and events of pregnancy and birth. Such knowledge reduces fear and helplessness and thus reduces discomfort. Learning techniques to use during labor can replace passive suffering with active involvement and coping. However, new technology is continually being introduced, and each new intervention can readily be overused.

Women's struggle for choice and control in childbirth parallels the struggle for self-determination in general and is part of a social revolution that is not yet complete. The medical model of birth illustrates the way social institutions can decrease the power of women. When real control is lacking, women perceive themselves as helpless and passive, and this perception in turn contributes to powerlessness. Treating birth as a normal, woman- and family-centered event, rather than a medical one, could prove very beneficial to women, their partners, and their children.

Depression Following Childbirth: Why?

The first weeks following childbirth (the ***postnatal period***) are often characterized as a time of mood swings and depression. For the first few days after giving birth, most women feel elated: The labor is over and the baby has arrived. Soon, however, they experience depression and crying spells. Between 50 percent and 80 percent of women experience mood swings for only a day or two. Longer-lasting depression (six to eight weeks) occurs in about 13 percent of women; it includes feelings of inadequacy and inability to cope, fatigue, tearfulness, and insomnia. The most severe form, a clinical psychosis, affects one-tenth of 1 percent of new mothers (Hyde & DeLamater, 2003; Mauthner, 1998).

Are postnatal mood disorders due to hormonal changes? Birth is followed by dramatic decreases in the high levels of estrogen and progesterone that characterize pregnancy. However, hormone changes have not been shown to *cause* depression; in fact, there is no direct link between postnatal hormone levels and mood (Johnston-Robledo, 2000; Treadway et al., 1969). The hormonal changes of pregnancy and the postnatal period are real. They give rise to bodily changes and sensations that must be interpreted by the woman who is experiencing them. But the social context of interpretation is crucial; postnatal depression may be more of a social construction than a medical condition. It is virtually unknown in many countries, including India, China, Mexico, and Kenya, suggesting that the causes are at least partly cultural (Mauthner, 1998).

Many social and interpersonal factors may contribute to depression and mood swings among new mothers: dissatisfaction with body size and shape, feeling incompetent to care for a newborn, a sense that one's real self is lost in the role of mother, disappointment with a partner's lack of support, and so on. In an intensive study of a small sample of English women experiencing postnatal depression, a key factor was conflicts between their expectations of motherhood and their actual experiences. Different mothers resolved these conflicts in different ways, but in all cases a woman's recovery was a process of accepting herself and rejecting the impossible ideals of motherhood. Often, this came about through talking with other women (Mauthner, 1998). Women who find it difficult to relate to others because of their personality styles or their past experiences may experience more depressive symptoms (Lutz & Hock, 1998).

As a mother, I believe that sleep deprivation has been overlooked as a factor in postnatal mood disorders. During the last weeks of pregnancy, a woman may not sleep well due to the discomfort caused by the heavy, restless fetus. Next, the hard physical work and stress of birthing a child are followed by many consecutive nights of disturbed sleep. Babies rarely sleep for an unbroken six- to seven-hour period before they are 6 weeks old, and some take much longer to settle down. I know of no studies of postnatal depression that have examined sleep deprivation as a factor or compared moodiness in new mothers with moodiness in a sleep-deprived comparison group. Going without sleep for a few days can make anyone cranky and depressed. The lack of attention to this possibility is a striking example of how sociocultural influences are often overlooked in studying women's lives.

Countries in which postnatal depression is rare offer a period of rest and special care for the new mother, practical and emotional support from other women, and positive attention to the mother, not just the baby (Johnston-Robledo, 2000; Mauthner, 1998). For example, in Guatemala, a new mother gets an herbal bath and a massage. In Nigeria, she and her baby are secluded in a "fattening room" where her meals are prepared by others. Customs like these may help the new mother interpret her bodily changes and sensations more positively and ease her adjustment to motherhood. One U.S. psychologist who studied new mothers suggests, "Next time a friend or relative has a baby, in addition to a gift for the baby, bring her a meal and offer to help around the house" (Johnston-Robledo, 2000, p. 139). And maybe somebody else could get up with the baby so she can get a good night's sleep.

Experiences of Mothering

The realities of mothering are as different as the social circumstances of women who mother. In this section, let's look at what motherhood involves for diverse groups of women.

Teen Mothers

Each year in the United States more than a million young women under the age of 20 become pregnant. Most of these teens are unmarried. Over half of teen pregnancies result in the birth of a child; about 30 percent are terminated by abortion, and the rest end in miscarriage (Hyde & DeLamater, 2003). The rate of births to teen mothers is much higher for Hispanic and Black groups than for whites (Martin et al., 2002).

The rate of teen pregnancy dropped dramatically throughout the 1990s for all ethnic groups (Martin et al., 2002). However, the teen pregnancy rate in the United States is still much higher than in comparable countries (see Figure 10.8). U.S. teens are not more sexually active than their European counterparts, but they are much less likely to use contraception reliably and effectively (Alan Guttmacher Institute, 2002).

What factors put girls at risk for early pregnancy? First and foremost, teen pregnancy and childbearing are related to social class disadvantages. Living in a poor or dangerous neighborhood, growing up in a poor family with a single parent, and being sexually abused are all linked to teen pregnancy. Parents who supervise and regulate their teens' activities and teach them to avoid unprotected sex may lower the risk to some extent (Miller, Benson, & Galbraith, 2001).

Adolescent motherhood has serious consequences for the young women involved, their children, and society as a whole. These include interrupted education and lowered job opportunities for the mothers, health problems for the babies, and the costs of public assistance

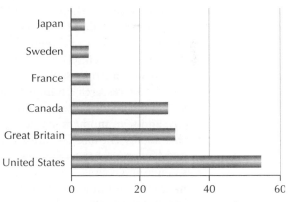

Birth Rate per 1,000 Women Aged 15–19

FIGURE 10.8   U.S. Teenagers Have Higher Birthrates Than Adolescents in Other Developed Countries

Source: Reproduced with the permission of The Alan Guttmacher Institute from: The Alan Guttmacher Institute (AGI), *Facts in Brief: Teenagers' Sexual and Reproductive Health,* New York: AGI, 2002.

and interventions (Elise, 1995). In one major study, 281 teen mothers in Indiana were followed through pregnancy and when their children were aged 3, 5, and 8. The average age of the mothers at the time of childbirth was 17; almost two-thirds were African American, one-third white, and 4 percent Hispanic. Although most of the children were of normal weight and health at birth, they suffered increasing physical, emotional and behavioral problems. By the age of 8, more than 70 percent were having problems in school. The mothers were suffering disadvantages, too. They did not know very much about taking care of children and did not have the cognitive maturity to be skilled parents. Five years after their child's birth, most remained undereducated, underemployed, and weighed down by depression, anxiety, and stress.

However, there was a great deal of variability in the group. About 18 percent of the mother-child pairs were thriving: The mothers were working, had continued their education, and showed high self-esteem and little depression or anxiety. Their children were developmentally normal. Another 20 percent of the women were also doing well, although their children were struggling with developmental or behavioral problems. The women who had managed to overcome the disadvantages of early motherhood were those who started off with more advantages in the first place (e.g., they had more education before they got pregnant), those who received emotional support from a partner, and those whose coping skills and cognitive readiness for parenthood were high (Whitman, Borkowski, Keogh, & Weed, 2001).

Another study focused on a group of very disadvantaged inner-city teens from New York. These women ranged in age from 14 to 19; most were African American or Puerto Rican; two-thirds came from families on welfare. The young mothers who were doing best at a five-year follow-up had active lives that typically involved working, going to school, spending time with their partner and families, and taking care of their children. What contributed to their strengths? In-depth interviews revealed themes of having been raised in a strict home environment, receiving support from their family with the expectation that they would make something of themselves, having role models and support for education, and having confidence, a strong will, and a passion to succeed (Leadbeater & Way, 2001).

These research findings show that statistics alone do not convey the meaning of teen pregnancy. Teen pregnancy is often used as a symbol of moral and social decay, and teen mothers are accused of undermining family values. Research shows that adolescent mothers are a diverse group who are often struggling to overcome disadvantages that go far beyond just having a baby. Many teen mothers show resilience and courage in overcoming the obstacles they face. Surprisingly, adolescent motherhood does not always result in permanent disadvantage. The majority of teen mothers eventually finish high school, get stable jobs, move into their own apartments or houses, and raise children who do not go on to become teen parents themselves (Leadbeater & Way, 2001).

I am not arguing that early childbearing is desirable. But its meaning and consequences depend on its cultural context. Though teen pregnancy is seen as a huge social problem today, rates were actually higher in the 1950s than now (Nettles & Scott-Jones, 1987). It was less of an issue then, because most teen mothers were married, or hastily got married on becoming pregnant.

Today, there are ethnic and cultural differences in the acceptance of teen pregnancy. Most African American teen mothers live with and receive support from their own mothers. Among Hispanic families, teen pregnancy may not be seen as problematic as long as it results in marriage. Some young women see any child as a gift from God, no matter how unfortunate the circumstances of its birth (Leadbetter & Way, 2001; Whitman, et al., 2001). And some teen mothers become inspired to better their lives for the sake of their child (Leadbetter & Way, 2001).

Young mothers need access to programs to help them learn parenting skills, complete their education, and take control of their contraceptive use. Moreover, they need support from their families, their communities, and the educational system. There is also a great need for more research on teen fathers—it takes two to make a baby. A particular need is programs that help fathers take responsibility for birth control, family planning, and their children's economic and social support. With help, the negative effects of early childbearing can be overcome (Elise, 1995; Henly, 1997; Leadbetter & Way, 2001; Whitman et al., 2001).

Single Mothers

The number of families headed by single women has increased dramatically over the past 25 years. Minority children are more likely to grow up in single-parent families; 23 percent of white, 31 percent of Hispanic, and 55 percent of African American children are in single-parent households, the great majority headed by women (only 4 percent of children in single-parent families live with their fathers). The reasons for this increase are diverse, too. For whites, the primary reason for single parenthood is the high separation and divorce rate (see Chapter 9). For Hispanic and black women, the primary reason is a rise in births to single women (Steil, 2001).

Single mothers, whether they are unmarried, separated, or divorced, are more likely to be holding down jobs than women with husbands present in the home. Yet families headed by women are far more likely to be poor than other families are. Over half of all black and Hispanic woman-headed families and over one-third of white woman-headed families are living in poverty. Poverty among women and children is one of the most serious social problems in the United States today (See Chapter 6).

Why are women-headed households so likely to be poor? Some of the reasons for women's poverty are the same as men's: They may lack education or job skills, or live in an area in which there are few jobs. But women are poor for gender-related reasons as well: because they receive little economic support from absentee fathers after divorce (Chapter 9) and because they are underpaid and underemployed (Chapter 11). Perhaps most important, public policy does not reflect the needs of women and children.

Even women who have full-time employment may not be able to earn enough to keep themselves and their families out of poverty. The story of one single working mother illustrates the dilemmas of being both nurturer and provider. Lori P. worked full time as a secretary at a university, earning about $800 a month. When her partner left her and their 4-year-old son, she was unable to pay her monthly bills, which included $500 for child care. Although Lori started out with advantages—health-care coverage, good child care, safe housing, occasional child-support contributions from the absent partner, and middle-class respectability—she barely manages to survive:

> I don't know what I'm going to do. My dad helped last month, but rent's due next Wednesday and I don't have any money. I mean I don't. I just paid all my bills. It's the end of the month now and I don't get paid for two more weeks. I have $2.50 in my account; two dollars and fifty cents! Rent's $545—I get paid in two weeks again, but that will only be $400 . . . I need help—I feel like I'm sinking. (Polakow, 1993, pp. 82–83)

Ashamed to be on welfare, Lori wants to get her college degree so that she can get a better job, but she cannot afford to pay for child care while she attends night classes. For now, she is relying on another poor single mother, who babysits for $2 an hour.

As Lori's story shows, men's failure to provide financial support is a major source of single mothers' economic burdens. In addition, the lack of publicly subsidized child care makes it impossible for a single working mother to get ahead. Even if she works full time at minimum wage, child care for one child will consume between 37 percent and 78 percent of her income (Polakow, 1993). Of all the Western industrialized nations, only the United States fails to provide family-support benefits as a matter of public policy (Lorber, 1993b).

Most single mothers want to work, and most do have jobs (Youngblut, Singer, Madigan, Swegart, & Rodgers, 1997; Steil, 2001). But finding good child care is a worry. Many low-income mothers are raising their children in high-risk environments where the need for quality care is crucial. In a study of low-income African American single mothers who were former welfare recipients, concerns about child care were linked with mothers' depression and negative feelings about their children (Jackson, 1997).

The primary response to the feminization of poverty in the United States seems to be to blame the victims. Women who accept welfare benefits are accused of causing the very problems they are trying to cope with. Since the 1980s, public aid programs to help people help themselves out of poverty have been repeatedly cut (Polakow, 1993; Sapiro, 1994). In 1996, welfare reform legislation mandated that mothers of young children who receive benefits find paid employment, and the current political climate is even harsher. Consider that many middle-class mothers, with safe homes, good child care, decent jobs, and husbands at home find it difficult or impossible to manage full-time employment when they have babies or toddlers—then think about doing it alone, poor, at a minimum-wage job, and in a dangerous neighborhood.

Many conservative policymakers assume that marriage is the answer to poverty among women and children. However, the majority of women who have children outside of marriage are poor before they become pregnant. Even if these women married the fathers of their babies, they would still be poor, because the fathers are likely to be unemployed and living in economically depressed areas (Dickerson, 1995). And many of the fathers are simply not available, or have so many problems of their own that they cannot help support a family. For example, in a major study of inner-city young mothers, by the time their first child was 6, 10 percent of the fathers were dead, 25 percent were in jail, and 24 percent were selling or using drugs. Others were irresponsible, abusive, or involved in a new relationship. Only a few couples managed to stay together (Leadbetter & Way, 2001). Even among middle-class divorced women, remarriage is not always an option for mothers of small children, and second marriages are more likely than first marriages to end in divorce (Chapter 9).

But there is more to single-mother families than poverty and despair. Studies show that single mothers are proud that they are handling a difficult job well. They are just as satisfied with motherhood as married mothers are (Smith, 1997). Among white families, single-parent homes seem to be less gender typed than two-parent homes. They encourage more gender-neutral play in children and create more flexible attitudes about gender roles (Smith, 1997). This result makes sense when we consider that fathers are more prone than mothers to treating children in gender-stereotypical ways (Chapter 6), and that children of single mothers see their moms as both the provider and nurturer. Among African American single-parent families, strengths include role flexibility (many adults may "mother" a child), spirituality (relying on inner strength rather than material possessions for happiness), and a sense of community ("It takes a village to raise a child") (Randolph, 1995).

Little research has been done on single parents in other countries. In a recent study of single parents in China, one-third were men; the majority had arrived at single parenthood through divorce, and the others through the death or desertion of a spouse. (Pregnancy outside of marriage is extremely rare in China.) Virtually all were employed and they had an average of one child. In this sample, the psychological adjustment of both single mothers and fathers was positively related to the amount of emotional and practical support they received. This study shows that the social context of single parenthood differs across cultures and suggests that the same factors influence psychological well-being in single moms and dads when they are in comparable situations (Cheung & Liu, 1997).

Black Mothers and the Matriarchal Myth

African women were brought to the United States to work as slaves and to produce more slaves, sometimes through rape and forced childbearing. If they were given a few days off from slave labor after childbirth, it was more to protect the owner's investment than to allow them to rest and recover. They were able to care for their own children only after all their other work was done and, as Sojourner Truth eloquently testified, were likely to see their children sold away from them (Almquist, 1989).

African Americans, under slavery, experienced the systematic, widespread destruction of their families. In addition to this legacy of slavery, there has since been a scarcity of black men to be providers and husbands. The causes for this scarcity include migration from the South, high death rates from poor health care, and the effects of poverty and discrimination, leading to drug use, imprisonment, and violent death. Thus, black women have been (and still are) more likely than white women to be raising families without a resident father/husband. For African

American women, motherhood is not equated with being dependent on a man (Collins, 1991; Dickerson, 1995).

Black women have coped with oppression in many ways. They often form extended households, with two or three generations living together and sharing resources. Grandmothers, sisters, cousins, and aunts care for the children of young mothers. Black families are less likely than white ones to give children up for adoption by strangers, and more likely to take in the children of friends and relatives. In the black community, these informal adoptions are seen as better than stranger adoption, because children can stay in contact with their mothers and live with people they know and trust (Almquist, 1989). This collective, cooperative child rearing may reflect a West African heritage (Collins, 1991; George & Dickerson, 1995; Greene, 1990).

Unfortunately, black women have been judged against a white middle-class norm of female submission and traditional marriage arrangements (Collins, 1991). Sociologists and psychiatrists have accused them of castrating their husbands and sons by being unfeminine and domineering (Giddings, 1984). The infamous Moynihan Report (Moynihan, 1965) attributed the problems of the urban black community to the "matriarchal" social organization of black families.

Blaming black women for social problems avoids confronting the real problems of racism, classism, and sexism. Moreover, it obscures the unique contributions of African American family patterns. Black women's involvement in social activism often stems from their definition of motherhood: A good mother does not just take care of her own offspring; she works to meet the needs of her entire community (Collins, 1991; Naples, 1992).

Lesbian Mothers

About one lesbian in six is a mother (Strommen, 1993). Some women who marry or cohabit with men and have children within these relationships later identify as lesbian and bring up their children in lesbian households. Other lesbians have a child through adoption or artificial insemination. What are the special issues and stresses that confront lesbian mothers?

One of the biggest potential problems is negotiating the marginalized identity of lesbian with the mainstream identity of mother (Hequembourg & Farrell, 1999). Although there is increasing acceptance of lesbians, many people consider a lesbian family unnatural:

> Vicky's parents had a party to introduce their grandchild to the family, but they refused to acknowledge me as the other parent; rather, they chose to identify me as a very good friend who is helping Vicky raise the baby. I wept for hours and knew that I would never again hide the nature of our relationship. (Mercer, 1990, p. 233)

Economic strains also exist. Like single mothers, lesbian mothers have to manage without a man's greater earning power. Their income is often so low that lack of money is a source of daily stress. If the mother has to deal with a welfare department, there is the added strain of a state agency making judgments about her lesbian lifestyle (Crawford, 1987).

Lesbian families may experience isolation. Lesbian mothers may feel little in common with the heterosexual families of their children's friends. Turning to the lesbian community for support, they may find that the lives of their child-free lesbian friends are very different from their own. As more lesbians decide to have children, support groups and networks of lesbian families are growing.

Finally, lesbian mothers may confront problems of internalized homophobia:

> Lesbians should not be surprised or ashamed to find themselves grappling with questions such as: Is this natural? Is it okay for lesbians to have kids? Am I hurting my children . . . is it unfair to bring them into a homophobic world? Am I a woman who is able to mother like other women? These . . . are questions that have been answered in positive ways by many lesbian mothers over the years. (Crawford, 1987, p. 197)

Do lesbians raise children differently than heterosexual mothers, and do their children turn out differently? Research suggests that the children of lesbian families are remarkably similar to those of heterosexual families.

One study of African American women compared the attitudes of 26 heterosexual and 26 lesbian mothers. The two groups were similar in the value they placed on independence and self-sufficiency for their children. The lesbian mothers, however, were more tolerant about rules, less restrictive of sex play, less concerned with modesty, and more open in providing sex education. They also viewed boys and girls as more similar to each other than the heterosexual mothers did and expected more traditionally masculine activities from their daughters (Hill, 1987). Given the costs of feminine socialization for girls, these may be healthy attitudes.

In the United Kingdom, children in a representative sample of lesbian families were compared with those in two-parent and single-mother heterosexual families. Parents, teachers, and a child psychiatrist assessed the children's adjustment. There were few differences in lesbian and heterosexual mothers' parenting styles except that the lesbian mothers hit their children less often and engaged in more imaginative play with them. Overall, the children of lesbian mothers were well adjusted and had positive relationships with their parents and peers (Golombok et al., 2003). Another British study tracked 78 children, half raised by lesbian mothers and half by heterosexual single mothers, from middle childhood to young adulthood (Tasker & Golombok, 1997). As young adults, these participants were asked to look back on their family life. Children of lesbians were more positive about their family life than children of heterosexuals, especially if their mother was open about her sexual orientation and active in lesbian politics. Children of lesbians were no more likely to identify as gay or lesbian, but those who did were more likely to be involved in a relationship than were gay children of heterosexuals. Children raised by lesbians reported that their mothers had been more open and comfortable communicating with them about sexual development and sexuality as they were growing up. There was no difference in psychological adjustment in the two groups. On the whole, it seems that lesbian family life produces children who are very much like children from heterosexual families. Research reviews (Falk, 1993; Tasker, 1999) have found no detrimental effects of lesbian parenting on children's psychological adjustment or gender-role development.

Despite the research evidence, courts have often assumed that lesbians are unfit mothers. In 1993, the American Psychological Association argued for a lesbian mother in a Virginia case in which the court had awarded custody of a 2-year-old boy to his grandmother. There was no evidence that Sharon Bottoms was a poor mother or that her son Tyler was suffering any problems; her relationship with another woman was the only custody issue. Typically, lesbians stand a 50–50 chance of losing their children in custody disputes (Falk, 1993). In this case, an appeals court, influenced by the APA brief and psychologists' expert testimony, overturned the earlier verdict and returned Tyler to his mother and her partner (Sleek, 1994).

Commonalities

The experiences of women who mother are shaped by social class, sexual orientation, economic status, and many other factors. Are there any overall similarities? Many mothers have written of their feelings and thoughts about motherhood. Several themes emerge in these accounts. Here are examples of five such themes in the words of mothers who told their stories in *Balancing Acts*, a book edited by Katherine Gieve (1989).

1. Becoming a mother results in large, significant, and permanent changes in identity and life circumstances.

   Daniel is seven, Matthew, five, and when I think about the past seven years I feel like a person watching the dust begin to settle after an earthquake. (p. 41)
   I did not imagine the force or the excitement—nor how I would willingly be taken over by my children. . . . I look at the world with different eyes and inward with a new vision. I feel riven, torn apart, and made again. (p. 51)
   I am not where I was before—not in a single detail. I have learned to pride myself on new abilities, some I had never considered of value. I was blown wide open by motherhood and by the emotions that came with it. . . . I had no idea that I could love that well. . . . Conversely, other abilities by which I had set great store, producing words on time, selling an idea, keeping myself fired up . . . seem useful but little more than that. (pp. 127–128)

2. Motherhood can involve feelings of intense love, competence, and achievement (see Figure 10.9).

   The rewards of motherhood were immediate and lasting. I have established a relaxed physical intimacy with both my children which tolerates anger and laughter, built up over a decade of washing them, reading to them, and tumbling about with them. (p. 114)
   Pregnancy had suited me, I enjoyed giving birth, but nothing prepared me for the reality of the new baby. I was almost paralyzed by the joy that shot through me as I looked through the plastic (hospital crib) that morning . . . it's just impossible to put into words . . . I was transported. (p. 124)
   She's brought into a room. . . . Not much hair, toothless, a fat bald child in a scratchy pink dress. It is love at first sight. . . . I feel as if I've been waiting all my life for this moment, for this child. . . . The "I" who adopts this four-month-old baby is forced to recognize that, physically and symbolically, she is another being, formed by other bodies, in relationships I know nothing of. But in my imagination, she is the missing part of myself, at last returned. I am complete. (pp. 138–139)

3. Motherhood is a constantly changing relationship, as both child and
mother grow and develop. Mothers
and children move from a relationship of profound inequality to one
of (ideally) equality. Throughout
the process, the mother moves from
meeting physical needs to meeting intellectual ones; emotional demands remain a constant.

It was not the hard work of child care
that I found so difficult (probably because I shared it with others) but the
constantly changing relationship which
continued in terms not chosen by me at
an unpredictable and changeable pace.
It required constant reassessment and
with it pain, anger, and remorse, as well
as excitement and pleasure. Daniel elicited from me both my greatest love and
generosity and my darkest anger and
frustration. (p. 45)

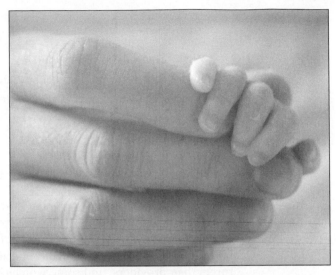

FIGURE 10.9
The intense love of mother and child can be a uniquely
rewarding human experience.

As our children grow and change, and new pleasures, new battles, take the place of
the early ones, I feel I live in a constant state of surprise and suspense. It is like reading
the best of novels, combined with being in love; I want things to stand still yet can't wait
to see what will happen next. And, above all, I don't want the story to end. (p. 159)

4. Both child and mother must confront the limitations of love and care.

With all my love, I cannot be everything she wants and needs any more than I can shield
her from pain . . . indeed I must add to her pain. . . . My fantasy, that if I love her enough
nothing else matters, has to give way. (p. 140)

"You are not my real mother," says my daughter to me. I did not feel either that my
mother was my real mother, perhaps every daughter, every child, has this doubt. . . . The
gap between the ideal Mother, and the mother we actually have, is perhaps always there.
If the Mother is the fixed perfect image of the ideal, a mother (small m) is always what
falls short of that image. (pp. 143–144)

5. Mothers and children must adapt to a society that is structured as though children did not exist and does not provide necessary support for those who care
for the young.

The world suddenly became a much more dangerous place once I had a baby dependent
on me for his very life. For the first time I was thrown into a world that did not recognize my physical, emotional, social, and political needs. This applied to design, ar-
chitecture, roads, public transport, dangerous machinery; not to mention lack of
community child care facilities. . . . it isn't the child that makes your life hard, it is the
adult world and the powers that be. Usually, it is the very people who sentimentalize and
idealize motherhood who stop listening. (pp. 53–54)

> Motherhood . . . has made me aware of time in many different ways. In particular how women's time is taken for granted so that there is little concordance between the way time is structured in the so-called public world and the rhythm of time associated with caring for a young child. (p. 77)

These five commonalities emerged from the writings of diverse women about their experiences of motherhood. Perhaps you can think of others.

Making a Difference

Bringing up children is an awesome responsibility. Traditionally, in Western societies it has been divided into a nurturing role, assigned to women, and a provider role, assigned to men. This arrangement has many limitations. It does not allow for individual differences in personality and ability—some men might make better nurturers than providers, and some women better providers than nurturers. It keeps women and children economically dependent on men; when men default, families live in poverty. It overlooks the diversity of families. Single-parent families, gay and lesbian families, and families from different cultural traditions do not conform to the patriarchal ideal. Social change over the past several decades has been uneven. Although the majority of women now participate in the provider role, men have not correspondingly increased their participation in nurturing. How might our society support mothers and children and help fathers develop their parenting potential?

Transforming Social Policy: Redefining Family Values

Public policy on families in the United States lags behind policies in every other industrialized country in the world (Crittenden, 2001). The United States needs better-paid parental leave, subsidized child care, and flexible working hours. One initiative in this direction is the organization MOTHERS (Mothers Ought to Have Equal Rights). Founded in 2002, MOTHERS seeks to recognize the vital contribution mothers and other caregivers make to society by working to provide them with economic and social recognition. Its agenda includes gaining social security credit for primary caregivers of children and establishing a national policy of six months' paid family leave when parents give birth or adopt a child (Heitner, 2003). To learn more about activism on behalf of those who care for children, see http://www.mothersoughttohaveequalrights.org. At present, however, respect and security for caregivers barely register on the national political agenda, despite rhetoric about family values. The political activism to bring about these changes is unlikely to be effective until the changes are as relevant to powerful men as to women (Silverstein, 1996).

Transforming Social Meanings: Redefining Parenthood

Our society has assigned mothers responsibility for their children's psychological well-being to an extent that few other cultures around the world or throughout history have done. It has asked them to fulfill their responsibilities in relative isolation, often without the support they need. Moreover, it has created myths that disguise the realities of parenting. Despite their enormous responsibilities and lack of resources, mothers get blamed for everything that goes wrong with children.

"Mother-blaming is like air pollution"—so pervasive that it often goes unnoticed (Caplan, 1989, p. 39). Psychology and psychiatry have a long tradition of viewing Mom as the source of all problems. A review of 125 articles published in major mental health journals between 1970 and 1982 found that mothers were blamed for 72 different kinds of problems in their offspring. The list included aggressiveness, agoraphobia, anorexia, anxiety, arson, bad dreams, bedwetting, chronic vomiting, delinquency, delusions, depression, frigidity, hyperactivity, incest, loneliness, marijuana use, minimal brain damage, moodiness, schizophrenia, sexual dysfunction, sibling jealousy, sleepwalking, tantrums, truancy, an inability to deal with color blindness, and self-induced television epilepsy (Caplan & Hall-McCorquodale, 1985)!

Where are the fathers when blame is handed out? They seem to be invisible. Psychology has contributed more than its share to the father-invisibility problem. A review of 544 empirical research studies of children's psychological disorders published between 1984 and 1991 found that only 1 percent focused exclusively on fathers, while 48 percent focused exclusively on mothers. Another 25 percent included both parents but did not analyze for sex differences or interactions (Phares & Compas, 1993). When the studies including fathers were examined separately, clear effects were found: Fathers do play a role in children's psychopathology. Children whose fathers sexually molest them, abuse alcohol, or are depressed are particularly at risk for psychological disorders.

Fathering is being recognized as a feminist issue. As long as a good father is defined simply as a good provider, men will have more privilege both at home and in public life and will continue to be deprived of intimacy and emotional connection with their families. Many feminists have called for redefining fatherhood and helping men become good fathers. There is more to being a father than providing a paycheck; good fathers are responsive and emotionally available to their children (Silverstein, 2002). (See Figure 10.10.) At present, much of the poverty and dysfunction among women and children in the United States can be linked to men who father children and then fail to take care of them. Rather than condemn these men as "deadbeat dads," our society could consider them "dads in training" and provide social programs to help them be better fathers (Leadbetter & Way, 2001).

What are the payoffs for redefining parenthood? Research reviews have shown that a father's love is good for children, whose cognitive and emotional development is better when their fathers are involved in their lives (Rohner & Veneziano, 2001; Silverstein, 1996). Father involvement is good for couples, who report greater marital satisfaction, and for mothers, who report decreased stress. And it is good

FIGURE 10.10
A father who is emotionally involved with caring for his child fosters the child's healthy development.

for fathers themselves, who report higher self-esteem and satisfaction with their role as parents (Deutsch, 1999). Redefining fatherhood could go a long way toward reducing mother-blaming, too, by shattering the myth that anyone can be a perfect parent.

Redefining motherhood *and* fatherhood is a revolution that is past due. What is needed is a postgender definition that allows for flexibility and diversity of family patterns (Silverstein & Auerbach, 1999).

Exploring Further

Cusk, Rachel. (2002). *Life's work: On becoming a mother.* New York: Picador.
    An intense introspection on the transition to motherhood by a gifted writer. It's not always a pretty story, but it has the raw edge of truth.

Crittenden, Ann. (2001). *The price of motherhood: Why the most important job in the world is still the least valued.* New York: Henry Holt.

An eye-opening analysis of how society exploits those who care for children. A strength of this book is its many specific ideas for changing U.S. society so we can "bring children up without putting women down."

Atwood, Margaret. (1986). *The handmaid's tale*. New York: Anchor Books.

Atwood's futuristic novel imagines a world where women are enslaved so that their reproductive services can be controlled and their offspring offered to men in power. It is frightening and eerily relevant as fundamentalist governments in many countries severely curtail women's roles.

Casa de los Babys. (2003).

Director John Sayles portrays six North American women who go to Mexico to adopt babies, and the Mexican families whose choices are constrained by poverty. This film asks hard questions about who is qualified to be a mother.

CHAPTER 11

Work and Achievement

❧

$\mathcal{W}$ork is a part of almost every woman's life, but the world of work is a gendered world. Often, women and men do different kinds of work, face different obstacles to satisfaction and achievement, and receive unequal rewards. This chapter examines the unpaid and paid work of women, women's values about work and achievement, explanations for the differing work patterns of women and men, and factors affecting women's achievement. We listen to the voices of women as they talk about their work: its problems, its satisfactions, and its place in their lives.

If She Isn't Paid, Is It Still Work?

Much of the work women do is unpaid and not formally defined as work. When women's work caring for their homes, children, and husbands is taken into account, virtually everywhere in the world women work longer hours than men and have less leisure time (United Nations, 2000). Because women's work in the home is invisible to the larger society, there are many misconceptions about it (Vanek, 1984). Let's look first at this invisible work: women's contributions in housework, meeting others' emotional needs, and enhancing the status of their male partners.

Housework: The Double Day

Scrubbing floors and toilets, shopping for food and cooking meals, changing beds, washing, ironing, and mending clothes, doing household planning and record keeping—all the chores required to keep a household functioning—are classified as housework. Though fewer women today than in the past make housework a full-time job, it is still a part of life for most women around the world.

Women's work in the home demands more hours each day than many paid jobs. In developing countries, housework may include gathering firewood, carrying water over long distances, and grinding grain for cooking. In industrialized countries, technology (household electricity, running water, appliances) has made the work less dirty and arduous than it used to be, and the smaller size of modern families means less work, but new tasks have taken the place of old ones. Traveling for errands, shopping, and transporting children takes up hours each week. Having bigger houses and more possessions means that there is more "stuff" to take care of. And standards have risen, as icons of domesticity such as Martha Stewart encourage women to cook gourmet meals, grow their own vegetables, and obsess over decorating details.

Is Housework Shared?

Chapters 9 and 10 documented that equality in the domestic realm is rare. Housework and child care remain largely the responsibility of women (Phillips & Imhoff, 1997) (see Figure 11.1). Chores tend to be assigned by gender: Men do outside work, women do inside work, and women tend to do the chores that come up most often. A survey of more than 1,200 U.S. households showed that 93 percent of the women usually did the meal planning, 88 percent usually did the food shopping,

FIGURE 11.1

Source: Copyright © Baby Blues Partnership. Reprinted with special permission of King Features Syndicate.

and 90 percent usually did the cooking—percentages that had not changed much since the 1970s (Harnack, Story, Martinson, Neumark-Sztainer, & Stang, 1998). Women's chores are more stressful because often they have to be done on a tighter schedule—you can put off washing the car until it's convenient, but it's not so easy to put off making dinner (Barnett & Shen, 1997). In a random sample of married or cohabiting couples in which both partners worked for pay, women still did about twice as much housework (14.89 hours each week) as men (6.81) (Stevens, Kiger, & Riley, 2001). A survey of more than 2,700 U.S. couples showed that only when both husbands and wives share egalitarian beliefs do husbands do more than the minimum (Greenstein, 1996).

In short, for most women, work outside the home is followed each day by another round of work at home—the second shift.

The prevailing pattern—overworked women and resistant to moderately involved men—is quite consistent across cultures and ethnic groups, including African American (Hossain & Roopmarine, 1993) and Mexican American families (Hartzler & Franco, 1985; Williams, 1990). In an Australian study of 128 wives' attempts to get their husbands more involved in housework, only four wives experienced any lasting success (Dempsey, 1997). UN studies of daily time use in developing countries consistently show that, compared with men, women are doing less paid work, more unpaid work, and working longer hours overall (United Nations, 2000).

Is Housework Trivial?

Within individual families, the unpaid domestic work of women is often accorded very little value:

> The garbage could overflow and no one would dump it, or the dog may need to be fed . . . and everybody relies on mother to do it . . . some days I feel that they're taking me for granted. They know I'm not going out into the work force, and every once in a while I hear one of my sons say, "Well, you don't do anything all day long." . . . If they didn't have clean clothes or their beds weren't changed or something like that they might realize that their mother does do something. But most of the time they don't. I don't think men feel that a woman does a day's work. (Whitbourne, 1986, p. 165)

The devaluation of housework is also apparent at the societal level. The phrases *working woman* and *working mother* suggest that a woman is not really a worker unless she is in the paid workforce. Unpaid housework is not listed in the U.S. Department of Labor's Dictionary of Occupational Titles. Its monetary value is not computed into the gross national product—an "official denial that this work is socially necessary" (Ciancanelli & Berch, 1987).

Obviously, families could not thrive without the unpaid work of women. But exactly how much is her work worth? Its monetary value is difficult to compute. One way is to estimate the cost of replacing her services with paid workers—cook, chauffeur, babysitter, dishwasher, janitor, and so forth. But many women feel that their services could not be replaced with paid workers because the work demands loving care and an intimate knowledge of the family. Who could calculate the appropriate pay for planning a small child's birthday party or the "overtime" involved when a woman takes charge of children, pets, house, bills, and yard work while her husband travels on business? Women's homemaking responsibilities involve not only skills but also personal involvement.

Another method is to calculate the wages the homemaker loses by working at home instead of at a paid job. If she could earn $250 a week as a bank clerk, for example, that is the value of 40 hours of housework. By this method, however, housework done by a woman who could earn $140 an hour as an attorney is worth 20 times as much as the identical chores done by a woman who could only earn $7 an hour as a food server (Vanek, 1984).

Neither method of calculating the value of housework really captures the unique characteristics of homemaking, because it does not fit androcentric definitions of work. Imagine how a "help wanted" ad for a homemaker might look:

> WANTED: Full-time employee for small family firm. DUTIES: Including but not limited to general cleaning, cooking, gardening, laundry, ironing and mending, purchasing, bookkeeping, and money management. Child care may also be required. HOURS: Avg. 55/wk but standby duty required 24 hours/day, 7 days/wk. Extra workload on holidays. SALARY AND BENEFITS: No salary, but food, clothing, and shelter provided at employer's discretion; job security and benefits depend on continued goodwill of employer. No vacation. No retirement plan. No opportunities for advancement. REQUIREMENTS: No previous experience necessary, can learn on the job. Only women need apply.

The homemaker's job looks unattractive indeed in this description. Women do find it unsatisfying in many ways. They dislike the boring, repetitive, and unchallenging nature of much of the work. On the other hand, they enjoy the rewards that come from taking care of their children and husbands (Baruch et al., 1983). In the rare cases in which men take primary responsibility for housework and child care, their feelings about the job are similar to women's—they like the emotional involvement with their families and dislike the housework (Rosenwasser & Patterson, 1984–1985).

Relational Work: Keeping Everybody Happy

Women are largely responsible for caring for others' emotional needs. Keeping harmony in the family has long been defined as women's work (Parsons & Bales, 1955). In a study of marital interaction in which more than 100 couples kept diaries about their communication patterns, wives did more relational work than husbands. They focused on their husbands, friends, and family; spent time talking and listening with them; talked about relationships more; and worked to keep harmony in the family (Ragsdale, 1996). In another study of dual-earner couples, both partners were asked about how much time they and their spouse spent confiding thoughts and feelings, trying to help the partner get out of a bad mood, trying to talk things over when there was a problem, and so on. Women reported doing more of this "emotion work" than men did and were less satisfied with the division of emotion work between the partners (Stevens, Kiger, & Riley, 2001). The time and energy necessary for this work may be considerable, as everyone relies on Mom to smooth emotional crises.

Part of the reason mothers do more child care than fathers may be because they are believed to be the relationship specialists (see Figure 11.2). And this does not change when mothers work for pay. When full-time homemakers and full-time paid workers were surveyed, the employed women were doing just as many child-care activities as the homemakers, except for watching TV with their children. Working mothers were equally likely to read to their child, play games, offer praise, and stop their own activity to play with the child (DeMeis & Perkins, 1996).

Relational work goes beyond a woman's immediate family to a wider network of relatives (Baruch et al., 1983; Di Leonardo, 1987). Women are in charge of visits, letters, and phone calls to distant family members. They buy the presents and remember to send the card for Aunt Anna's birthday. They organize weddings, family reunions, and holiday celebrations, negotiating conflicts and allocating tasks. Although the specifics of the family rituals vary according to social class and ethnic group, families' dependence on women's labor is similar, whether they are upper-class Mexican, working-class African American, middle-class Italian American, migrant Chicano farm workers, or immigrants to America from rural Japan (research reviewed in Di Leonardo, 1987).

Like housework, the relational work of women is largely ignored in traditional definitions of work. But it requires time, energy, and skill, and it has economic and social value. Exchanging outgrown children's clothes with a sister-in-law or sending

FIGURE 11.2

Source: Jump Start reprinted by permission of United Feature Syndicate, Inc.

potential customers to a cousin's business firm are ways of strengthening relationships that also help families maximize financial resources (Di Leonardo, 1987).

Perhaps most important, relational work fosters marital satisfaction and happiness. But women do not want to do it all. Couples who balance emotional work, with each partner doing about the same amount, are more satisfied with their marriages than couples in which one person is responsible for doing it all (Holm, Werner-Wilson, Cook, & Berger, 2001; Stevens, Kiger, & Riley, 2001).

Status Work: The Two-Person Career

Women's unpaid work benefits the careers of their husbands. The terms *status-enhancing work* and *two-person career* describe situations in which wives serve as unofficial (and often unacknowledged) contributors to their husbands' work (Papanek, 1973; Stevens et al., 2001). The most studied example is the corporate wife (e.g., Kanter, 1977); the wives of clergymen and college presidents are other very visible examples. The male graduate student whose wife supports him by working for pay, typing his papers, and keeping household problems out of his way so he can study is also receiving the benefits of a two-person career. So is the politician, whose wife must be able to "give the speech when he can't make it but to shut her mouth and listen adoringly when he is there" (Kanter, 1977, p. 122).

The role of helper to a prominent man may be rewarding, but it restricts a woman's freedom of action and ties her fate to her spouse's. Consider that Hillary Rodham Clinton, who did not take her husband's name when she married, was later pressured into doing so for political reasons (Marshall, 1997). When she took on the important task of health-care reform, the press seemed more interested in her hairstyle than her health-care plan. And as First Lady, she was subjected to hostile jokes and public humiliation over her husband's sexual activities. Only when her husband left public office was Rodham Clinton able to build her own political career.

What kinds of work do women do in the service of their husbands' careers? The specific tasks vary, depending on the husband's job and career stage (Kanter, 1977). She may entertain clients in her home and make friends with people who can be useful in advancing her husband's career. She is expected to be available at any time for complete care of their children so that he can travel or work evenings and weekends. She often participates in volunteer or community service related to his position. She may also contribute direct services in place of a paid employee—typing, taking sales calls, keeping books or tax records for his small business, or scheduling his travel. Finally, she provides emotional support. She is expected to listen to his complaints, help him work through problems at work, cheerfully accept his absences and work pressures, avoid burdening him with domestic trivia, and motivate him to achieve to his fullest potential. She is, indeed, "the woman behind the man."

What Are the Costs and Benefits of Invisible Work?

Obviously, housework, relational work, and the ladies' auxiliary do not provide a paycheck. Traditionally, women were supposed to be rewarded by a sense of *vicarious achievement* (Lipman-Blumen & Leavitt, 1976). In other words, a woman is supposed to identify with her husband and feel gratified by his successes. Many women do report this kind of gratification; others feel exploited. One corporate wife complained to an interviewer, "I am paid neither in job satisfaction nor in cash for my work. I did not choose the job of executive wife, and I am heartily sick of it" (Kanter, 1977, p. 111).

Women who achieve through their husbands are vulnerable. If the marriage ends through the husband's death or divorce or if he does not achieve fame and glory, she may have little to put on a resume and few skills that prospective employers would regard as valuable. Increasingly, women are insisting that divorce courts recognize that their unpaid work is vital to their husband's success (see Box 11.1).

The availability of some women as unofficial employees for their husbands' companies also has implications for women who are employed and competing with men. There is no corporate husband position to match that of the corporate wife. Indeed, the world of work assumes that workers are men and that these men have wives to take care of them (Wajcman, 1998). The female employee may appear less talented and motivated than her male colleague because she lacks his invisible support staff. If she is married, her husband is unlikely to invest his future in vicarious achievement. A study of more than 1,600 U.S. corporate employees showed that men at the highest executive levels were significantly more likely to have spouses who were full-time homemakers than men at lower levels and women at all levels (Burke, 1997). Similar results were found in a U.K. study of high-level managers: 88 percent of the married women and only 27 percent of the married men had partners who were employed full-time. In other words, the career success of men is given an invisible boost by their at-home support staff. Corporations know this very well; men are seen as bringing two people to their jobs, and women, because of their family duties, as bringing less than one (Wajcman, 1998).

Gay men and lesbians also are disadvantaged in the workplace by the expectation that everyone has a wife at home. A gay friend of mine in graduate school shared the feelings of many career-oriented women, lesbian and heterosexual, single and married, when he observed, "I need a wife!"

Working Hard for a Living: Women in the Paid Workforce

More women are working outside the home than ever before, a worldwide social change (United Nations, 2000). A majority of American women, including most mothers of young children, now work for a living. According to U.S. census data, about 62 percent of white women, 59 percent of black women, and 53 percent of Hispanic women are working for pay (Gutek, 2001b). Women's and men's employment rates are converging. By 2005, the percentage of all American women who engage in paid work is expected to rise to nearly 62 percent, compared with a projected decline from 75 percent to 73 percent for men (Gutek, 2001b; National Association of Working Women, 2000).

BOX 11.1   ∾   It's Her Job, Too

Lorna Wendt: If marriage isn't a partnership between equals, why get married?

Once upon a time, a good corporate wife was to be seen and not heard. She was to make sure nothing, but nothing, came between her man and his work. She was to shield him from the tedious and distracting details of domestic life. She was to raise beautiful, well-mannered children and maintain a beautiful, well-appointed home, making it look effortless. She was to work the charity circuit—to be the belle of the charity ball and also its unpaid CEO. She was to smile through scores of business dinners. And she was never, ever, to make a stink. Even in the worst of times, even when things unraveled, she was expected to know her place and,

if need be, to slip quietly offstage. Lorna Wendt did all of these things except the last. When her 32-year marriage to GE Capital CEO Gary Wendt came apart two years ago, she raised a big ruckus. She wanted half of the $100 million she estimated he was worth. She wanted to tap what she considered her rightful share of the treasure-trove of stock options and pension benefits accumulated during the marriage but not due until later in his career. She wanted respect. She wanted acknowledgment, just once and writ large, that society valued all those things she'd done on the home front. As with executive pay, the amount one needs to live on wasn't the issue. The money was merely a way of keeping score.

And Lorna Wendt did score. . . . She came away with $20 million—far less than the $50 million she'd sought, but far more than the $8 million plus alimony that Wendt had originally offered. She got half the hard assets—breaking the glass ceiling that often exists in uppercrust divorces, where wives are more likely to get what the judge thinks they need according to a practice known in the divorce bar as "enough is enough."

The Wendt case has launched a thousand cocktail-party conversations and struck fear in the hearts of primary breadwinners everywhere. A lot of men are still incredulous of her demands. In a big-bucks case like hers, "the question becomes, Is the person who is making the money—is that person's contribution greater than the person who stays at home and runs the house?" says Robert Stephan Cohen, a New York divorce lawyer. "I'll tell you, having represented a number of

(Continued on next page)

BOX 11.1 ⌒ It's Her Job, Too (Concluded)

high-net-worth individuals—they think the contribution of the at-home spouse is important, but not equal." Yet Lorna Wendt has elicited cheers from lots of career women and stay-at-home women alike. No matter the unlikelihood of this very proper, soft-spoken, 54-year-old woman straight out of another era becoming a feminist symbol. Her case has struck a chord.

Lorna Wendt is rich, privileged, hardly Everywoman. But as the woman behind the success story, she has come to stand for the many things that wives still mostly end up doing and that society seems mostly to take for granted: child rearing, tending a family's emotional and spiritual needs, and the unglamorous stuff like car pools, doctor's appointments, sympathy notes. Lorna Wendt has become a lightning rod for the tensions that swirl around what has traditionally been called women's work. "I complemented him by keeping the home fires burning and by raising a family and by being the CEO of the Wendt corporation and by running the household and grounds and social and emotional ties so he could go out and work very hard at what he was good at," she says. "If marriage isn't a partnership between equals, then why get married? If you knew that some husband or judge down the road was going to say, 'You're a 30% part of this marriage, and he's a 70% part,' would you get married?"

Source: From "It's Her Job Too," by Betsy Morris, *Fortune*, February 2, 1998, pp. 65–67. Copyright © 1998 Time, Inc. All rights reserved.

Sex Segregation

In 1900, the three main occupations available to women were schoolteacher, factory worker, and household servant (Perun & Bielby, 1981). Though women's job options have expanded a great deal, the workplace is still characterized by *sex segregation.* The workforce separation of women and men "extends to all regions and countries irrespective of the level of economic development, the political system, or the religious, social or cultural environment" (United Nations, 2000, p. 128). We will look at two varieties: *horizontal sex segregation,* the tendency for women and men to hold different jobs, and *vertical sex segregation,* the tendency for women to be clustered at the bottom of the hierarchy within occupations.

Horizontal Segregation

There are few occupations in which the proportion of women and men is about equal. Instead, there are women's jobs and men's jobs (Lorber, 1993b). Ninety-eight percent of all secretaries, 93 percent of nurses, and 84 percent of elementary schoolteachers are women. Ninety-nine percent of auto mechanics, more than 90 percent of engineers, and 70 percent of computer scientists are men (Gilbert & Rader, 2001). Nearly 60 percent of all employed women work in service, clerical, administrative support, technician, and sales fields. Less than one-third of employed women are in the higher-paying managerial and professional occupations. Some occupations have an overall equal ratio of women and men but remain segregated at the level of the individual workplace or task (Lorber, 1993b; Gutek, 2001b).

For example, in retail sales, men more often sell appliances, computers, and cars (the big-ticket items), while women more often sell clothing. Women are more likely to work in fast-food chains and diners; men are more likely to be waiters and chefs in expensive restaurants.

The fact that workplaces tend to be "his" or "hers" is a product of the gender system. The jobs where women are clustered tend to be relatively low in pay and status, with little job security and few opportunities for career advancement. Most are service oriented and associated with stereotypical feminine characteristics such as caring (United Nations, 2000). In 1990, "for every one woman lawyer, there were 101 women doing clerical work, 33 women operating factory machines, 30 sales clerks, 9 nurses aides, and 8 waitresses" (Yoder, 2002).

The good news is that horizontal sex segregation has declined considerably since the 1970s. Most of the decline has been in professional and management areas. Sex segregation has been more persistent in jobs held by high school graduates. Overall, horizontal sex segregation is still substantial, and women made fewer gains in the 1990s relative to the 1970s and 1980s (Gutek, 2001b).

Vertical Segregation

Vertical sex segregation is present when men tend to hold positions that have higher status and better pay than the jobs women hold within an organization or occupation (Gutek, 2001b; Lorber, 1993b). For example, in the health-care industry, the nurses' aides, abortion clinic workers, social workers, laboratory technicians, and nurses are likely to be women; physicians and hospital administrators are more likely to be men. The closer to the top of the hierarchy, the fewer women there are. In a recent study of more than 500 companies in the United Kingdom, only 8 percent of top executives were female; in the United States, only about 5 percent of senior executives are women, and this hardly changed during the 1990s (Gilbert & Rader, 2000; Valian, 1998; Wajcman, 1998). Women hold between 1 and 5 percent of top executive positions in Canada, Brazil, and Germany (United Nations, 2000). In fact, there is not a single field open to both women and men in which there are more women than men at the top, in any country in the world.

The pervasive phenomenon of women being blocked from advancement has been called the ***glass ceiling:*** The woman can see her goal, but she bumps into a barrier that is both invisible and impenetrable (Lorber, 1993b). Women are not totally excluded, but they find it difficult to move past midlevel positions in business and the professions. Women on their way up perceive the glass ceiling as very real, but men in power do not agree. In one survey of women corporate vice presidents, 71 percent said there was a glass ceiling for women in their organization. However, 73 percent of the male chief executive officers in the same organizations said there was not (Federal Glass Ceiling Commission, 1998).

Women's Work as Extension of Family Roles: "It's Only Natural"

Many women's paid jobs are characterized by service to others in ways that are similar to the unpaid work wives and mothers do. Women provide food and cleaning services in hotels, restaurants, and hospitals. Nurses are expected to provide tender, loving care to patients, manage the unit like good housekeepers, and serve as hand-maidens to physicians (Cassell, 1997; Corley & Mauksch, 1988). Teachers provide emotional nurturance to young children, and social workers care for the poor and needy.

Even when women and men are in equivalent jobs, such as corporate management, women are expected to be more caring and supportive than men, creating extra demands on their time and energy (Wajcman, 1998). Though it is expected, their caring is simultaneously devalued. For example, one psychologist who received excellent teaching evaluations was described by her department chair as being "mama-ish" and "charming" in the classroom—hardly the qualities valued by the tenure and promotion committee (Benokraitis, 1997).

Because caring fits into a feminine stereotype, it is often seen as a natural by-product of being female rather than an aspect of job competence. This contributes to the devaluation of women's work: If women perform certain functions naturally, the reasoning goes, virtually any woman can do them; and the woman who does so deserves no special recognition. Recently, the *New York Times* described new customer-service software that can detect an irate caller, suggesting that the software could be used to route "an angry man on the line" to "a soothing female operator" ("Press 1 If You're Steamed," July 7, 2002). Reading this, I wondered if the female operators will get bonuses or raises for their "soothing" skills. Somehow, I doubt it. After all, women just naturally know how to calm down angry men.

The devaluation of caring costs women money. The female-dominated fields of nursing, social work, and teaching may be very rewarding; but they are chronically underpaid. Despite the fact that they require advanced degrees, they do not typically lead to high income; instead, they are characterized by "learning without earning" (Betz & Fitzgerald, 1987). People who take care of zoo animals earn, on average, $2,500 a year more than those who take care of children in child-care centers. Ninety-five percent of child-care workers are women, and 33 percent are women of color (Murray, 1997; Noble, 1993).

The Wage Gap

Women earn less money than men. Indeed, as Figure 11.3 shows, no group of women has a median income that comes close to the median income of white men. Journalist Barbara Ehrenreich has documented just how hard it is to get by on the jobs available to ordinary working women (see Box 11.2). And the difference between men's and women's wages holds for every level of education. Although young people are urged to get a college education to increase lifetime earnings, the financial payoff of education is much greater for men. (See Figure 11.4.) Overall, women college graduates earn about $7,800 less annually than college-educated men (U.S. Department of Labor, 2002).

The gender gap in wages has decreased slightly over the past 40 years. As shown in Figure 11.5, this is partly because women are earning more and partly because men are earning less. Women now earn about 76 cents for every dollar of men's earnings, and the earnings of African American women are catching up to

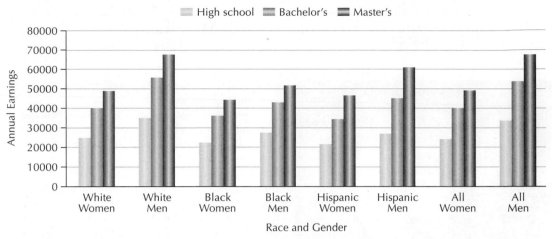

FIGURE 11.3

Median annual full-time earnings by race, gender, and education: 2001.

Source: National Committee on Pay Equity, 2002.

FIGURE 11.4

Source: Copyright © Steve Kelley. Reprinted by permission.

BOX 11.2 ∾ Undercover at Wal-Mart: Life as a Low-Wage Worker

Can America's low-wage workers survive on their weekly paychecks? This is the question journalist Barbara Ehrenreich set out to answer when she went undercover as a minimally skilled laborer. Shedding the privileges of her education and social class, Ehrenreich took on the identity of a homemaker of modest education and job skills attempting to reenter the job market. Ehrenreich traveled to several states, spending approximately one month in each location and working at jobs such as housecleaner, waitress, and sales clerk. Using only the money she earned from her jobs, Ehrenreich attempted to pay for housing, food, transportation, and other living expenses.

Ehrenreich soon learned that minimum wage does not equate to living wage. Although she was physically fit, a native English speaker, and had no dependents, she had difficulty financially sustaining her simple needs on her earnings. Even working two jobs, seven days a week did little to help. Additionally, being short of money created many unforeseen problems for Ehrenreich, who found it difficult to obtain safe, inexpensive housing and reliable transportation and maintain a healthy diet. For example, because she could not afford security deposits for an apartment, Ehrenreich had to live in a motel, which cost more and was less safe. Living in a motel room created additional hardships. Lacking a refrigerator or stove, Ehrenreich had to make do with fast food, an expense she had not anticipated.

Ehrenreich's experience makes it clear that those who fill the low-wage rung on Americas economic ladder are greatly disadvantaged. This includes especially the millions of women forced into the workforce because of welfare reform. The American dream of attaining wealth through hard work does not take into account the reality of the working poor, whose hard labor is not even enough to pay the bills.

Sources: Barbara Ehrenreich, *Nickel and dimed: On (not) getting by in America.* Contributed by Roxanne Donovan, University of Connecticut.

those of white women. But the gap between all women's earnings and those of white men is still very large (National Committee on Pay Equity, 2004). And 24 cents out of every dollar has huge lifetime costs to women. If the current wage gap continues, a woman who is now 25 and works full-time for the next 40 years will earn a lifetime total of $523,000 less than the average 25-year-old man. (You can check out your own loss on the Internet: Go to www.aflcio.org/issuespolitics/women/equalpay/calculate.cfm, key in your age, education, and current income, and the consequences of your personal wage gap will be calculated for you.) Around the world, the wage gap is even greater, with women earning about 66 cents for every dollar earned by men (United Nations, 2000).

FIGURE 11.5

Median annual full-time earnings by race, gender, and education: 2001.

Source: National Committee on Pay Equity, 2004.

Why this large and persistent inequity in earnings? One traditional explanation is that women invest less in their work roles than men—they are less committed to their work, less likely to obtain extra training and education, more likely to be absent or to quit a job. However, little evidence exists to support these claims. On the contrary, the gender gap in earnings remains substantial when variables such as education, absences, number of hours worked, and years on the job are controlled (Gutek, 2001b; Tsui, 1998; Valian, 1998; Wajcman, 1998). The individual investment hypothesis also does not explain why women's jobs that require high levels of education and skill (like preschool teacher) pay less than men's jobs with lower requirements (like drywall installer).

Another explanation focuses on the jobs rather than the gender of the worker—secretaries and clerks are paid less than electricians and truck drivers, and since more women choose to be secretaries and clerks, they earn less on average. It is certainly true that women are clustered in a few low-paying job sectors, but is this entirely a matter of choice? Moreover, there are substantial wage differences when women and men do exactly the same jobs. Female truck drivers earn 76 percent, and female computer programmers and engineers 89 percent, of what their male counterparts earn (U.S. Department of Labor, 2002).

It is hard to escape the conclusion that men are paid more for whatever they do simply because they are men (Betz and Fitzgerald, 1987). The income discrepancy between women and men is part of a larger pattern of overvaluing whatever is male and undervaluing whatever is female (see Figure 11.6). A UN study (cited in Landrine & Klonoff, 1997) of 140 people who had sex-change operations found

FIGURE 11.6
Sex discrimination—the power of a good allegory.

Source: Sally Forth © Reprinted with special permission of King Features Syndicate.

that all the women who changed to men had higher salaries after the change, whereas all but two of the men who changed to women received much lower salaries.

Doing Gender in the Workplace

Women's position in the workplace is not just a static aspect of social structure. Rather, it is continually re-created as people make workplace decisions influenced by gender. Chapter 2 discussed how men and women do gender within groups, describing some of the cognitive and social processes that sustain inequality. Let's take a closer look at how sexism operates in the world of work. In particular, how does gender influence evaluations of work? How does it influence hiring and advancement?

Attributions for Success and Failure

When faced with an example of a woman or a man who has succeeded at some achievement, people very often come up with different reasons to explain her or his success. Men's success is more likely to be seen as the result of high ability ("he succeeded because he's talented or smart"). Women's success is more likely to be attributed to luck (Deaux & Emswiller, 1974). When the task cannot be attributed entirely to luck (such as becoming a physician), people are still reluctant to judge women equal to men in ability. Instead, they attribute the woman's success more to hard work (Feldman-Summers & Kiesler, 1974).

How do people explain situations in which a male or female attempts achievement but fails? Several studies show that they are likely to blame a woman's failure on lack of ability and a man's failure on bad luck or the quirks of the situation, such as an unusually difficult task (Cash, Gillen, & Burns, 1977; Etaugh & Brown, 1975).

It is easy to see how the typical pattern of attributing males' successes to ability and females' to luck disadvantages women in the workplace. A manager is probably far more likely to hire or promote someone who is perceived as very able than as someone who just got lucky. Similarly, an employer might view an isolated failure as confirmation of a woman's lack of ability but as only a temporary setback for a man. The assumption behind the typical pattern of attribution seems to be that men are basically competent; whether they succeed or fail, that belief remains intact. Women, on the other hand, are basically incompetent, and that belief, too, can be maintained whether they succeed or fail.

Devaluing Women's Performance

"Are women prejudiced against women?" is a question asked in a study that set off a wave of research on how people judge the performance of women versus men (Goldberg, 1968). Female college students were asked to rate the quality and importance of several professional articles. Some of the articles were from stereotypically female professions, such as dietetics; others from stereotypically male professions, such as city planning; and others from relatively gender-neutral areas. Each article was prepared in two versions, as though written either by "John MacKay" or "Joan MacKay." Except for the authors' names, the two versions of each article were identical. The students rated the articles more highly when they thought they had been written by a man, including the articles from stereotypically feminine fields. Other researchers found that male raters showed similar prejudice (Paludi & Bauer, 1983; Paludi & Strayer, 1985).

Sometimes highly competent performance by a woman is actually evaluated more positively than comparable performance by a man—as though female competence has more value because it is unexpected (Abramson, Goldberg, Greenberg, & Abramson, 1977). In general, though, many laboratory studies from the 1960s to the recent past made a convincing case that work attributed to a woman is often devalued. For example, a classic study used psychologists as the participants. Fictitious sets of credentials for psychologists were sent to psychology department chairpersons; the credentials were identical except for the gender of the applicant. The chairpersons were asked how likely they would be to hire the individual described and what level of job they might offer. When the chairpersons thought they were evaluating a female psychologist, "she" was rated less favorably and considered qualified for a lower-level position than when "he" was evaluated (Fidell, 1970).

Are these experimental studies relevant to real job settings today? A meta-analysis of supervisors' ratings of employees showed little overall bias. In other words, controlling for employees' education, experience, and other relevant variables, supervisors did not typically devalue female employees. However, pro-male biases did show up when the raters were all male and when the rating dimensions were masculine (e.g., leadership ability). Pro-female bias showed up when the rating dimensions were feminine (e.g., concern for others) (Bowen, Swim, & Jacobs, 2000). These results suggest that traditional gender attitudes held by many men may affect their evaluations of women's work, and that gender stereotypes associated with the measures used to rate employees may produce bias.

Women's own stories about their experiences at work suggest that evaluation bias affects how they are treated on a daily basis. "Women report that their comments and suggestions are ignored or ridiculed; that men making the identical comments receive praise whereas they do not, and that they are excluded from meetings, networks, lunches and other activities that are part of the 'old boy' network and of the road to career advancement" (Landrine & Klonoff, 1997, p. 11). For women of color, sexism may be compounded by racism. In a study of a matched sample of 200 African American and European American women in professional and managerial positions, the majority of both groups reported differential treatment at work due to their gender, and a majority of the African American women also perceived differential treatment due to their race (Weber & Higginbotham, 1997).

Discrimination in Hiring and Promotion

Sex discrimination in employment has been illegal since 1964, when the Civil Rights Act was passed. Before that time, many employers discriminated as a matter of policy. For example, AT&T allowed women to work only up to certain levels and in a limited range of tasks (Gutek & Larwood, 1987). Many states had laws that "protected" women by excluding them from certain jobs. For example, women were banned from jobs that required working at night, working around chemicals, serving drinks, or lifting more than 30 pounds (McCormick, 2002). (And just how much does the average 3-year-old weigh?)

Although employers today cannot directly refuse to hire or promote applicants because of race or gender, a great deal of discrimination still occurs. One source of evidence comes from studies of evaluation bias that used simulated job resumes or applications. A recent meta-analysis of 49 such studies showed a strong preference for men when the job was seen as masculine, and a somewhat weaker preference for women when the job was seen as feminine (Davison & Burke, 2000). Unfortunately, leadership roles are still usually perceived as masculine (Eagly & Karau, 2002).

More direct evidence of discrimination comes from sex-discrimination lawsuits. Companies that have been sued (and the costs of the settlements) include State Farm ($200 million), Home Depot ($104 million), Lucky Stores ($95 million), AT&T ($66 million) and Mitsubishi Motors ($34 million). As I write this chapter, a sex-discrimination suit against Wal-Mart, the largest employer in the United States, is making headlines. According to the lawsuit, filed on behalf of 1.6 million women workers (past and present), Wal-Mart has kept women in the lowest-paying jobs and favored male managers in hiring and promotion. Although 65 percent of Wal-Mart's low-level employees are female, only 33 percent of its managers are (Abelson, 2004; Greenhouse & Hays, 2004). Time will tell if the case, the largest of its type in U.S. history, stands up in court, but the pattern is one familiar to many women. In a U.S. sample of more than 1,200 women, over 40 percent said that at some time in their lives they had been denied a raise, a promotion, or some other deserved reward at work because they were women. One in five (and more women of color than white women) had experienced such discrimination within the past year (Landrine & Klonoff, 1997).

Many other studies indicate that equally qualified women are less likely than men to be hired or are offered lower-paying, less-desirable jobs (Betz & Fitzgerald, 1987; Eagly & Karau, 2002; Fassinger, 2002). Sexism today is unfortunately alive and well; however, unlike sexism of the past, it is more likely to be subtle than blatant. Often, it is not even intentional (Benokraitis, 1997).

In addition to gender discrimination, lesbians may also face discrimination on the basis of sexual orientation. They may be fired, not hired, or not promoted due to stereotypes about lesbians being maladjusted, mentally ill, or child molesters. In a survey of 203 lesbians in a metropolitan area (mainly white collar, middle class, and highly educated), 25 percent reported specific instances of formal or informal discrimination, including being fired or forced to resign when their personal life became known. Others were denied raises or promotions. Informal discrimination included taunts, gossip, ridicule, social rejection, and even physical violence (Levine & Leonard, 1984). In several large-sample surveys, between 13 percent and 62 percent of lesbian and gay adults reported that they had experienced employment discrimination (Badgett, 1996).

Lesbians and gay men are faced with a classic double bind in deciding whether to be open about their sexual orientation at work. Being out is linked to greater job satisfaction and better interpersonal relationships at work (Driscoll, Kelley, & Fassinger, 1996; Ellis, 1996); on the other hand, it may lead to even more discrimination (Croteau, 1996; Fassinger, 1996).

Unfortunately, patterns of discrimination are often very hard to see. For example, if you are a woman with a bachelor's degree who has been with a company for five years and you are not promoted, you might compare yourself with a male co-worker who was promoted. Suppose this man has been with the company for only three years but he has a master's degree: It's hard to decide whether or not you have been discriminated against. But suppose you look further in the company and find a man who was promoted with only a high school diploma and 10 years of service and a woman who was not promoted with two years of college and eight years of service. A pattern begins to form. But that pattern is apparent only when many cases are averaged, and discrimination is usually examined one case at a time (Crosby, Clayton, Alksnis, & Hemker, 1986). One important function of affirmative action programs is to keep records so that patterns of discrimination become evident over time. You can't fix a problem if nobody knows the problem exists (Crosby, 2003).

Social Reactions to Token Women

From the local fire department or welding shop to the U.S. Senate, the corporate boardroom, and everywhere in between, women in nontraditional careers are likely to work mostly with men. They are a minority in workplaces where the environment is highly masculine. Just by being numerically rare, a woman in a male-dominated field is sure to stick out (see Figure 11.7). This is true for other

AFFIRMATIVE DISTRACTION

FIGURE 11.7

Affirmative distraction.

disadvantaged groups, too. The "odd person," whether black, Hispanic, disabled, or female, becomes a **token**. Generally, researchers define a token as a member of a group that is less than about 15 percent of the larger group. Female firefighters and male nurses, for example, are usually tokens in their workplaces.

Tokens are highly visible and may feel as though they are on display. Marian Pour-El, a mathematician, described her reception as a graduate student in the math department at Harvard in the 1970s:

> My first colloquium at Harvard University was a memorable event. The tea, which preceded the actual lecture, was held in the library and was a rather formal affair. As I entered, all eyes sank lower into the teacups in a great effort not to seem to notice me. Needless to say, no one talked to me at all. At the end of the tea the chairman . . . turned to me and said with a twinkle in his eye, "Your presence is noted here." (Pour-El, 1974, p. 36)

Because of this visibility, tokens feel a great deal of performance pressure. As one woman commented, "If it seems good to be noticed, wait until you make your first major mistake" (Kanter, 1977, p. 213). When a white male employee makes a mistake, it is interpreted as an individual error and no more; if the token woman or minority makes a similar mistake, it may be taken as evidence that "those people" should not have been hired and are bound to fail. Paradoxically, the token must also worry about being too successful. Since all eyes are on her, if she performs well enough to show up members of the dominant group, she may be criticized for being a workaholic or "too aggressive."

Tokens are also socially isolated. Often, members of the dominant group avoid them. The very presence of a token may remind dominant group members of what they have in common. For example, when a lone female engineer joins the working group, men may actually spend more time talking about topics that exclude her, such as their military experiences, than they did when there were no women around (Gutek, 2001c). This isolation adds to the stress of the token position (see Box 11.3).

BOX 11.3 ∾ The Effects of Tokenism: A Case Study

Social psychologist Janice Yoder has written a moving description of her experiences as a visiting faculty member at a U.S. military academy. Yoder's token status was extreme on several dimensions: She was one of sixteen women among 545 faculty members, 97 percent of whom were military officers. Her visibility, isolation, and relegation to negative roles were correspondingly extreme:

> My differences as a civilian, a researcher, and a woman created uncertainty among my colleagues and threatened to disrupt the team. . . . I frequently was isolated from group discussions. . . . One subgroup (of the department) dubbed itself the "Wolf Gang," used "We eat sheep!" as their motto, and howled when called upon to make group presentations. The depart-

mental theme song chosen was "Macho Man," hardly appropriate for an academic department that included two female officers and myself. The gossip about my sexuality ranged from lesbian to heterosexually promiscuous. . . .

> I was assigned to one of two female roles: "wife" or "feminist/libber." In the former role, I was invited to a luncheon for wives. . . . While this was mildly amusing, the effects of my second label as "feminist/libber" were not. . . . I watched as my colleagues began to get restless when I raised my hand, rolled their eyes as I spoke, and concluded by ignoring. . . . I became totally ineffectual, yet unwilling to keep quiet and thus implicitly condone these actions. My role as a deviate became predictable, unwelcome, and ignored. (pp. 64–65)

Yoder described the psychological effects of token treatment in a journal entry made after only three months of such treatment:

> What does happen to the deviate? The deviate can convert, but short of a sex-change operation . . . and a personality overhaul, conversion seems out of the question for me. . . . What can I do? Yet, the failure is placed squarely on my shoulders. "What's wrong with you?" "Why can't you get along?" These questions haunt me, undermining my self-image to a point where I am reduced to crying at home alone at night. . . . I feel impotent, I can't sleep, but I am never clear-headed and fully awake. I have an eye infection. Daily problems have become insurmountable difficulties. . . . I can't work. I can't go out and have fun. . . . I have become bad in my eyes; the attributions of blame have been internalized. (p. 66)

Janice Yoder resigned from her visiting professorship after one semester.

Source: From Janice Yoder, 1985, "An Academic Woman as a Token: A Case Study," *Journal of Social Issues,* 41, pp. 61–72. Reprinted by permission of Blackwell Science.

Finally, tokens are often stereotyped. They get pigeonholed into familiar roles such as mother, wife, or sex object. One female commercial pilot reported that her copilot questioned whether she was following the directions from air traffic control, saying "Oh well my wife gets lost when she goes to the supermarket" (Davey & Davidson, 2000, p. 213).

When the token does not play along with stereotyped roles, she may be cast as the archetypal unfeminine "iron maiden" or "bitch." (Gutek, 2001c). (There is even a corporate training program, Bully Broads, aimed at women executives who are perceived as too aggressive. Its goal is to help them relearn indirect, manipulative techniques such as crying, wearing more provocative clothing, and pretending to be incompetent. Personally, I don't think this is progress for women!) Tokens are usually eager to fit in and may choose not to challenge the values and practices of the men in power—indeed, they may outdo the men in enforcing the status quo (Lorber, 1993b). Or they may want to support other women and make the workplace more welcoming but are so stressed by their own token status that they cannot (Yoder, 2002).

Women and minorities are much more likely than white men to experience token status. However, when white men are the tokens, they suffer no disadvantages. In a field study of workers in a zoo park, new employees were randomly assigned to work groups in which they were tokens (e.g., a man assigned to a gift shop staffed by women) or to gender-balanced groups. Only female tokens were negatively evaluated. In fact, male tokens advanced more quickly than men in gender-balanced groups (Yoder & Sinnett, 1985).

Moreover, men earn more than women whether they are in male-dominated, female-dominated, or gender-balanced occupations (Budig, 2002). Men in female-dominated occupations (nurse, librarian, elementary teacher, and social worker) fare better than women in the same occupations in several ways—they are more satisfied with their jobs, get better evaluations, and advance faster. This has been dubbed the *glass escalator* to contrast with the glass ceiling experienced by women (Williams, 1992).

Comparisons of male and female tokens show that the negative effects of being a token are not due just to numbers. Rather, they reflect differences in status and power. When women or ethnic minorities enter a group that was formerly all White and male, it is perceived as a kind of infiltration by less-desirable people (see Figure 11.8). The negative effects of tokenism for women and ethnic minorities decrease once the formerly tokenized group is about 35 percent of the larger group (Yoder, 2002). But numbers alone are not the answer, because tokens are still lower in status.

How can women tokens become more respected and effective? A recent study reaffirms that just getting the job and having the expertise to do it are not enough. When women were appointed leaders of all-male task groups and supplied with task-relevant expertise to help them lead the groups, they still were not very successful or appreciated as leaders. Only when a male experimenter specifically told group members that the woman leader had special training and useful information for their task was the woman able to be effective (Yoder, Schleicher, & McDonald, 1998). While it is worrisome that women's leadership still needs to be

© UFS, Inc.

FIGURE 11.8

Source: Dilbert Copyright © by Scott Adams. Reprinted by permission of United Feature Syndicate, Inc.

given legitimacy by high-status men, this study suggests one way that fair-minded men can use their organizational power on behalf of competent women.

Role Models and Mentors

Role models are members of one's own reference group who are visibly successful (Yoder, Adams, Grove, & Priest, 1985). Just knowing that other women have managed to overcome the obstacles to success may help the newcomer (Basow & Howe, 1980; O'Connell & Russo, 1980). For example, female graduate students who had female professors as role models described themselves as more career oriented, confident, instrumental, and satisfied than those who had male role models (Gilbert, Galessich, & Evans, 1983). In a recent study of over 400 undergraduate psychology students, having a good relationship with a supportive role model was an important factor in helping the students decide their future career goals (Perrone, Zanardelli, Worthington, & Chartrand, 2002).

Unlike white men, women and minority men have had few role models. Lack of role models probably contributes to loneliness and feelings of deviance. Adding a few token women to the workplace does not solve the role model problem. In fact, pressure to be a role model adds to the pressures on the token.

Role models may be admired from afar; **mentors** are people who take a personal interest in the newcomer (Yoder et al., 1985). Knowing the formal rules in a workplace is rarely enough. Whether you are working in a corporation, factory, hospital, or office, there is inside knowledge that is never written down in the employee manual. Instead, workers rely on informal social networks to work the system to their advantage (Lorber, 1993b). Successful older men frequently serve as mentors to young men on their way up, providing them with introductions to important people, special training, and hints about office politics. They may also stand up for the young man if he makes a controversial decision and raise his status simply by associating with him.

Having a mentor increases job satisfaction and career advancement for both women and men. The beneficial effects of mentoring have been shown for many groups, including adults from diverse ethnic backgrounds in professional careers (Gutek, 2001c). A study of 231 female attorneys showed that those who had had mentors earned more money, were more successful, and were more satisfied in their careers than those who had not (Wallace, 2001). A study of women psychologists showed that those who had a research mentor were more likely to do research and also to become research mentors for others (Dohm & Cummings, 2002).

Having a white man as mentor may be especially beneficial to future income. In one study, graduates of business administration (MBA) programs who had established a mentoring relationship with a white man earned $16,840 more annually than those who did not. Having a woman or a minority man for a mentor had no effect on salary. African American and Hispanic graduates of both sexes, and white women, were less likely to have white male mentors (Dreher & Cox, 1996). For attorneys, too, those with male mentors end up earning more than those with female mentors (Wallace, 2001).

Why do women have more difficulty finding a mentor than men do? One reason is that women lack access to the **old-boy network,** with its "bands of brothers" who look out for each other's interests (Lorber, 1993b). As one female corporate executive put it: "It's always been men at the top of this company and the top of the company I was in before. They all know each other. They've all come up the same route together, all boys together" (Wajcman, 1998, p. 97).

Often, high-status men are reluctant to mentor women. Quite simply, they feel more comfortable with people they perceive as more similar to themselves. Also, young women may not always realize the importance of finding mentors (Kanter, 1977; Nieva & Gutek, 1981). Or they may be reluctant to ask senior men for mentoring because they fear the relationship would be misinterpreted as sexual (Gutek, 2001c).

What about women mentoring other women? In the past, only a few women were in positions that would enable them to mentor other women, and the pressures of their token status may have prevented them from reaching out (Yoder, 2002). The scarcity of mentors is probably easing, as old-girl networks have grown. For example, APA's psychology of women division matches beginning researchers with accomplished ones for mentoring. And MentorNet, a national e-mail network, offers opportunities for women in engineering, math, and science to connect with supportive experts in their fields (www.mentornet.net). Women may be better mentors for women in creating a professional self-image, empowerment, and supportive personal counseling (Burke & McKeen, 1997; Gaskill, 1991; Gilbert & Rossman, 1992). Among a sample of female attorneys, those mentored by men earned more; but those mentored by women reported less conflict between work and family and greater career satisfaction, and they were more likely to intend to continue practicing law (Wallace, 2001).

Leadership: Do Women Do It Differently?

Clearly, there are barriers that prevent many women from achieving positions of leadership. But despite the obstacles, more women are moving into positions of leadership. Once they are in leadership positions, do women lead differently from men?

Contrary to stereotype, there are no dramatic gender differences in leadership style. In a meta-analysis of 370 previous comparisons, women were somewhat more democratic and participative leaders than men. However, the difference depended on the situation—for example, it was larger in laboratory studies than real-life settings (Eagly & Johnson, 1990). In laboratory studies, people are usually strangers to each other and the manager role is simulated; gender roles may be salient. In actual workplaces, people have clear job titles and roles and long-term relationships; the demands of the manager role may be more important than gender roles (Eagly & Johannesen-Schmidt, 2001).

Are women more effective as leaders? Effectiveness is usually defined as how well the leader helps the group reach its stated goals. A meta-analysis of 76 studies of leadership effectiveness showed that there were no gender differences except in the military, where men were more effective (Eagly, Karau, & Makhijani, 1995). Again, the effect of situation is apparent—military leadership takes place in an extremely masculine realm where women are a small minority of each work group. In another measure of effectiveness, studies of woman-owned businesses (reviewed by Hooijberg & DiTomaso, 1996) show that they are equally likely to survive and thrive as businesses owned by men.

In contrast to these findings of overall similarity, a recent study of managers from the United States and eight other countries found some significant gender differences. Women were rated higher on several positive attributes such as motivating others, showing optimism about goals, mentoring others, being considerate, and rewarding others for good performance. Men were more likely to be critical about others' mistakes, to be absent or uninvolved during a crisis, and to wait until problems were severe before trying to solve them. Overall, in this study the women were perceived as more effective managers (Eagly & Johannesen-Schmidt, 2001).

In summary, the evidence suggests that once women are seen as legitimate leaders, they behave similarly to men in the same kinds of positions and they are equally likely to succeed. However, where there are differences in leadership style, the styles that women are more likely to use may enhance the effectiveness of their organizations. But any advantage that women may have in leadership style may be offset by the resistance of men in power to accept women's leadership. As more women enter formerly masculine domains, however, the salience of gender will diminish in leadership contexts.

Sexual Harassment from Nine to Five

Sexual harassment has been around for a long time, but it has been formally defined and studied only in the past 25 years (Gutek & Done, 2001). Second-wave feminist activists and researchers first named it as a form of sex discrimination, drawing public attention and stimulating research on the topic. What used to be considered just part of life for a working woman is now recognized as harmful and classified as illegal.

Defining Sexual Harassment

The legal definition of sexual harassment distinguishes two kinds (EEOC, 1980). *Quid pro quo* harassment is unwanted sexual advances or behavior that is a condition of employment. In other words, the harasser makes it clear that the employee will be fired, given unpleasant tasks, receive a negative evaluation, or otherwise suffer bad consequences unless she complies with sexual demands. For example, one woman reported, "This man went after every girl in the office and he went after me. Every female who worked in the office was subjected to this guy. We got fired if we did not go out with him" (Gutek, 1985, p. 82).

The second kind of harassment is the creation of a *hostile work environment*. This could include obscene remarks, demeaning jokes about women, or suggestive comments about the worker's sexuality or personal life, as well as threatening or aggressive sexually toned materials in the workplace. In one case, a shipyard worker was subjected to pornographic pictures and graffiti at work, and her male co-workers put up a dartboard drawn like a woman's breast with the nipple as the bulls-eye (Fitzgerald, 1993).

There is room for confusion and disagreement even in legal definitions. What seems like an unwanted advance or a hostile environment to one person may seem like a friendly invitation or innocent fun to another. The Supreme Court has changed and enlarged its definitions several times over the past two decades to encompass changing social definitions of harassment and will most likely continue to do so (Gutek & Done, 2001). Some researchers have created psychological definitions that differ from the legal ones, classifying a behavior as sexual harassment if the recipient perceives it as offensive and detrimental to her well-being (Fitzgerald, Swan, & Magley, 1997). In the courts, both the victim's perspective and the outsider's perspective are taken into account. The victim must show that the behavior is severe or pervasive and detrimental to her well-being, and the behavior must be such that a reasonable person would call it harassment (Gutek & Done, 2001).

These legal and psychological definitions are important in distinguishing sexual attention from sexual harassment; the latter must be severe, pervasive, and unwanted. For example, if a supervisor asks an employee to go out on a date, it is not sexual harassment (although it may be unwise, divisive in the office, or contrary to company policy). However, if the employer repeatedly asks for a date despite the worker's evident dismay or disinterest, or suggests directly or indirectly that she might get that raise or that vacation time if they got together, the employer is violating the law and committing sexual harassment. In the case of hostile environment harassment, an occasional sexist joke or lewd remark does not qualify as a hostile climate, but a pattern of sexist behavior that interferes with work does.

The Prevalence of Harassment

Anyone can be subjected to sexual harassment. It is evident in every culture where researchers have inquired about it, although it may take different forms in different cultures (Barak, 1997). Cross-cultural comparisons show that it is more prevalent in the United States than in comparable countries in Europe (Gruber, 1997).

A recent meta-analysis showed that when women are asked directly if they have been sexually harassed, the reported rate is much lower than when they are presented with a list of sexually harassing behaviors and asked to check any that have happened to them (Ilies, Hauserman, Schwochau, & Stibal, 2003). Like other forms of violence against women, harassment is likely to go unrecognized and under-reported, and cases that go to court usually involve only the most severe forms. In general, random-sample surveys indicate that "35 percent to 50 percent of women have experienced sexual harassment at some point in their working lives" (Gutek & Done, 2001, p. 373). Some of the most consistent data come from periodic random sample surveys of federal employees (USMSPB, 1981, 1987, 1995). In these surveys, 42 to 44 percent of women workers reported that they had experienced harassment within the past 24 months, a proportion that remained steady over the 14 years covered by these studies. Men can be sexually harassed, too, although this happens much less often than male-to-female harassment. In these cases, the harasser is likely to be another man, and there are fewer negative consequences (Gutek & Done, 2001; Waldo, Berdahl, & Fitzgerald, 1998).

Although anyone may be vulnerable to harassment, some factors may elevate a person's risk. For example, women in male-dominated occupations are particularly likely to experience harassment (Gutek & Done, 2001). Younger women and those who are unattached to men (unmarried and divorced women and lesbians) are more likely to be harassed than older, married women. Women of color may be more likely to be harassed than white women, although too few studies have been done to reach a definite conclusion. Ethnic minority women may be particularly vulnerable because stereotypes portray them as sexually available (African Americans and Latinas) or docile and submissive (Asian Americans). Women of color as a group also hold less power and status in the workplace than white women, which may increase their risk (Murrell, 1996). Sexual harassment often, but not always, goes downward in the power hierarchy. In about half the cases, the harasser is a supervisor, but may also be a co-worker or a customer (Gutek & Done, 2001).

What Are the Causes of Harassment?

There are several theories about the causes of sexual harassment. The *sex-role spillover theory* suggests that harassment occurs when a woman's gender is more salient than her role as a worker so that men see her first and foremost as a sex object. Gender is most salient when the woman is in a token position; thus, this theory predicts that the more male-dominated the occupation, the more harassment will occur. Gender can also be salient when the job has objectification built in to it—as when waitresses are required to wear short skirts or tight T-shirts.

Another theory stresses that sexual harassment is an abuse of power. Men have more formal power in organizations and often have more informal influence as well. They can misuse their power to treat women and sex objects or to belittle and insult them, then claim that the incidents never occurred or that the woman invited harassment or was trying to "sleep her way to the top." This theory is consistent with evidence that sexual harassment is more prevalent in more hierarchical organizations such as the military than in organizations with smaller power differentials such as universities (Ilies et al., 2003).

A third theory points to the broader sociocultural context of male dominance. Men are still being socialized toward being dominant, taking the sexual initiative, being sexually persistent, and feeling entitled to have what they want. Women are still being socialized toward compliance, nurturance, taking the role of sexual gatekeeper, and putting others' needs first. Thus, according to the sociocultural theory, sexual harassment at work is just part of a larger pattern of societal dominance by men. Each of these theories has been supported by some research, suggesting that sexual harassment may stem from all these causes and differ from one setting to another.

The Consequences of Harassment

The economic consequences of workplace sexual harassment are enormous. A U.S. government agency estimated that sexual harassment of federal employees cost $327 million in two years due to workers' being less productive, taking sick leave to cope with the effects of harassment, or changing jobs (USMPSB, 1995). In surveys, more than one woman in five reports that she has quit a job, gotten transferred, been fired, or stopped trying to get a job because of harassment (Gutek, 1985).

The psychological consequences of harassment can be even more devastating. Harassment interferes with women's commitment to their jobs and the satisfaction they get from doing them, as shown by studies done in many different occupations. In a large utility company, harassment was linked to women's being absent more often and wanting to leave the company (Fitzgerald, Drasgow, Hulin, Gefland, & Magley, 1997); in a sample of office workers, sexual harassment was linked to lower job satisfaction (Piortrkowski, 1998); in Navy personnel, it was linked to dissatisfaction with the Navy and plans to leave military service (Rosenfeld, Newell, & Le, 1998).

The negative consequences of harassment extend to many psychological domains. The woman's initial reactions may include self-doubt, confusion, and guilt, as she asks herself if she did anything to cause or encourage the harassment. She may worry about losing her job or fear that the harassment will escalate into rape, and her anxiety may become chronic. Her self-confidence and self-esteem drop. Several studies have shown that the experience of sexual harassment can lead to depression, irritability, physical symptoms (extreme fatigue, headaches), and psychological distress (Gutek & Done, 2001). A national study of over 3,000 women found that prior harassment was linked with major depression and posttraumatic stress disorder (PTSD). The effects were large: only 9 percent of nonharassed women, and nearly 30 percent of those who had been harassed, suffered from PTSD (Dansky & Kilpatrick, 1997). The more severe the harassment, the more likely it is to cause psychological damage, and this occurs whether or not the woman labels her experience as harassment (Gutek & Done, 2001).

Sexual harassment is not inevitable. Organizations can reduce it by educating people about the problem, and many have developed policies and programs designed to do so. However, these programs may be designed primarily to protect the company from potential lawsuits. This kind of education is not enough in itself and may even be counterproductive. In one recent study, faculty and staff at a university were given a 30-minute program that included a video about the university's policies, an oral presentation, and discussion. When participants were then compared to a control group of nonparticipants, they had more knowledge about harassment—a positive result. However, men who had participated in the training were *less* likely than control-group men to recognize sexual harassment or say they would report it, and *more* likely to blame the victim (Bingham & Scherer, 2001). In this case, the educational effort seems to have backfired, making men more resistant to recognizing the problem.

Educating people about the definition of harassment is not enough. Organizations must also having a strong policy in place, send clear messages to employees that harassment will not be tolerated, and punish those who violate standards (Gutek, 1985). Moreover, they should provide support systems for women who have been harassed and protect them from retaliation when they report it. Preventing sexual harassment is more than just a matter of preventing lawsuits; it is a matter of creating an organizational climate that is healthy for all workers.

Women's Career Development: Are There Obstacles from Within?

So far, our discussion of obstacles to women's job and career satisfaction has focused on forces in the social environment. We now turn to psychological factors—individual differences in beliefs, values, motives, and choices.

Do Women Have Different Values and Interests?

Do women workers want and need different rewards than men? Do they end up in feminized occupations because these occupations fit with their personal values? A great deal of research has attempted to answer these questions: A recent meta-analysis found 242 different samples totaling well over half a million people (Konrad, Ritchie, Lieb, & Corrigall, 2000). Aggregating these many studies has provided a clearer picture of what women and men value in their jobs.

In general, sex differences were small. Women tended to value intrinsic rewards more highly—those rewards that come from actually doing the job, such as intellectual stimulation, a chance for creativity, a sense of accomplishment, and feeling that the work is meaningful. Men tended to value different intrinsic rewards, such as freedom, challenge, and power. They also valued extrinsic rewards more highly—those that come after the job is done or as a by-product of the job, such as pay and promotion, fringe benefits, and job security. Women placed higher value on a pleasant working environment—friendly co-workers, comfortable surroundings, commuting ease, and convenient hours. Perhaps women value comfort and friendliness on the job more than men because many women leave paid work at the end of the day for a second full-time job of homemaking and child care.

Women's and men's values seem to be converging, especially when they occupy similar positions. In the meta-analysis just described, attributes like wanting responsibility became more important to women in the 1980s and 1990s, and many sex differences found in the 1970s disappeared, suggesting that women's aspirations have risen with their opportunities (Konrad et al., 2000). In a recent study of senior managers of multinational corporations, women and men agreed that a sense of achievement and enjoying the job were their most important motives. In fact, they agreed on every motive they were asked about—respect from colleagues, developing other people, meeting goals, and so on. The only gender differences were that women were slightly more likely than men to care about having power and slightly less likely to care about money (Wajcman, 1998). Thus, it is highly unlikely that the wage gap or the glass ceiling can be attributed to differences in values (Gutek, 2001b).

Although values may help determine one's occupational setting, the occupational setting may also affect one's values. When a person is given opportunities to advance, he or she is likely to develop a strong work commitment and aspirations for promotions and raises. A person placed in a job with little upward mobility tends to become indifferent, to complain, and to look for extrinsic satisfactions. Thus, the social structure of the workplace is a powerful force in shaping values and behavior. But its effects are often overlooked. When women in dead-end jobs develop poor attitudes, these attitudes are sometimes seen as characteristic of women as a group instead of a human response to blocked opportunities. As one organizational researcher put it, "What the clerical worker with low motivation to be promoted might need is a promotion; what the chronic complainer might need is a growthful challenge. But who would be likely to give it to them?" (Kanter, 1977, p. 158).

Are Women Less Motivated to Achieve?

For more than 50 years, psychologists have explored the question of why some people strive for success. *Achievement motivation* is the desire to accomplish something valuable and important and to meet high standards of excellence. Starting in the 1950s, researchers devised tests for measuring achievement motivation and predicting achievement-oriented behavior (McClelland, Atkinson, Clark, & Lowell, 1953). Achievement behaviors of any sort—from running a marathon to winning a beauty contest—could theoretically be predicted by one's score on an achievement-motivation measure. For research purposes, however, scores were used to predict performance in academic settings and competitive games in the laboratory.

Early research showed that achievement-motivation scores predicted the achievement behavior of men but not women. Reflecting the strong gender bias of research at that time, the intriguing question of why women behaved less predictably than men was not explored. Instead, researchers just excluded women from their future studies, concluding that they must lack achievement motivation (Unger, 1979a; Veroff, Wilcox, & Atkinson, 1953).

Today, it is recognized that women and men have similar motivation to achieve, but that motivation may be channeled in different directions. As they are growing up, girls and boys continually make choices, both consciously and unconsciously, about how they will spend their time and efforts. This decision making is complex and multidimensional (Hyde & Kling, 2001). The most important current theory for understanding these choices and their relationship to achievement motivation is the *expectancy X value model* (Eccles, 1994).

The expectancy part of the theory involves the individual's *expectations of success*. Research shows that junior high and high school students consistently have gender-linked expectations for success: Boys are more confident in math, and girls in English. But even if a girl believes she can succeed at a task, she is unlikely to attempt it unless it is important to her—this is where the value part of the theory comes in. The *subjective value* of various options (Do I enjoy English more than math? Will I really need math for my chosen career?) strongly affects decision making; for example, girls typically view math as less useful and important to them than boys do.

Expectancies and values are shaped by parental attributions (my daughter got an A in math because she works hard; my son, because he's bright), gender-role beliefs (scientists are nerdy guys), and self-perceptions (I can't do physics). Because gender socialization affects values, definitions of success, and the kinds of activities seen as crucial to one's identity, it affects virtually every aspect of achievement-related decision making.

One example of differently socialized values is the importance placed on being a parent. Gender differences in the subjective value of having children, and its effects on career planning, were demonstrated in an interesting study of college students (Stone & McKee, 2000). When they responded to surveys, both women and men were strongly career oriented. However, interviews with the same students gave a different picture. Men consistently planned to put their career first, whereas most of the women planned to cut back or stop their careers once they had children. As one said, "Once I'm a parent, my career is on hold." Perhaps because of these differences in the value attached to parenthood, women had much less knowledge than men did about the fields they planned to enter (the graduate training needed, how much they could earn) and were gaining much less relevant work experience while in college. Although they expected to work and to be successful, the women's values were affecting the attention they gave to their career future. Do you think that results would be similar or different on your campus?

Exceptional Work Lives

Achievement in the Professions

Until recently, women professionals worked mostly in education, social work, and nursing. Today many women continue to enter these professions. Meanwhile, others are entering formerly male-dominated professions—law, medicine, psychology, science and engineering, the military, and business management. For example, women went from 3 percent of all attorneys in the 1970s to about 25 percent in the 1990s (Valian, 1998). It is still the case that relatively few women achieve professional success. Yet despite the many obstacles, some women do. How are these women different? What factors in their personalities and backgrounds make the difference?

What Factors Affect Women's Career Development?

Although high-achieving women in the professions are few in number, they provide potential role models for other women. Their backgrounds suggest ways to bring up girls without limiting their aspirations and development, and their achievements represent the possibility of breaking down sex segregation in the workplace. If a few women can make it, a world of equal power and status for all women and men becomes easier to imagine.

   In general, high-achieving women come from backgrounds that provide them with a relatively unconstricted sense of self and an enriched view of women's capabilities (Lemkau, 1979, 1983). Their families and their upbringing are unusual in positive ways (see Table 11.1). As social learning theory would predict, girls who are exposed to less gender-stereotyped expectations are more likely to become high achievers. Attending all-girls' schools and women's colleges can provide role models and opportunities for leadership. Not surprisingly, parents play an important

TABLE 11.1   Characteristics Associated with Achievement in Women

Individual Variables	Background Variables
High ability	Working mother
Liberated sex role values	Supportive father
Instrumentality	Highly educated parents
Androgynous personality	Female role models
High self-esteem	Work experience as adolescent
Strong academic self-concept	Androgynous upbringing
Educational Variables	**Adult Lifestyles Variables**
Higher education	Late marriage or single
Continuation in mathematics	No or few children
Girls' schools and women's colleges	

Source: From Betz & Fitzgerald,, 1987, *The Career Psychology of Women*, p. 143. Academic Press. Copyright © 1987 by Elsevier. Reprinted with permission.

role. Employed mothers—especially when they enjoy their work and are successful at it—provide an important model for achievement. Because fathers usually encourage gender typing in their children more than mothers do and usually have more family power, a father who supports and encourages his daughter's achievements may be especially influential (Weitzman, 1979). One African American woman who became a distinguished physician provided an eloquent description of her parents' belief in her:

> As a woman, I was told, I would be able to do whatever I wanted. I was taught that my skin had a beautiful color. This constant, implicit reinforcement of positive self-image was my parents' most valuable gift to me. I grew up loving my color and enjoying the fact that I was a woman. . . . In school, I performed well because my mother and father expected it of me. When I entered high school, I elected the college preparatory program as a matter of course. (Hunter, 1974, pp. 58–59)

Setting high goals and persisting despite setbacks are important factors in women's career development. In a survey of more than 200 African American women attorneys, 80 percent said that their families and teachers had encouraged them to work hard and set high goals. They also said they had benefited from having access to black women role models and to equal opportunity programs (Simpson, 1996). In a longitudinal study, an ethnically diverse group of high school girls who expressed interest in math/science careers in 1980 were followed up to 13 years later. Those who had achieved their goals had taken more elective math and science in high school, set high standards for themselves, and stressed how important it is to "hang in there" when difficulties arise. Those who had experienced their parents' divorce were especially motivated to be financially independent because they had seen what happens to women who have to support their children on their own. Among the group that had not achieved their goals, some were stopped by family socialization (they were taught that the most important goal for a woman is marriage) or critical life events such as an unplanned pregnancy (Farmer et al., 1997).

Variations among Successful Women

The research summarized in Table 11.1 has been very useful in helping psychologists understand the dynamics of achievement in women, but it does have limitations. Obviously, all these characteristics are not true of all high-achieving women. Some women who do not have any of them manage to succeed anyway, and some even report having been spurred on by a disapproving parent or an attempt to hold them back (Weitzman, 1979). In one study, black and white women who came from poor families in which neither parent had finished high school were extensively interviewed. Despite their disadvantaged backgrounds, these women had achieved extraordinary success in business, academia, or government service. The odds-defying achievers had an unusually strong belief in their ability to control their lives. They believed that "you can do anything if you put your mind to it" (Boardman, Harrington, & Horowitz, 1987).

Research on high-achieving women has been done mostly on white women. More research is needed on diverse groups of women achievers to give a complete profile of successful women. Family background and socialization probably affect

Hispanic, Asian American, and African American women differently. For example, black women generally grow up expecting to support themselves; traditional Asian American culture discourages women from independence and rewards subservience.

It is likely that racism and sexism interact to impede the career development of women of color. Black women, for example, have higher aspirations than black men or white women during high school, but, like white women, their career goals decline during college. Black women are more likely than black men, but less likely than white women, to achieve success in a profession. Compared with white women, they are more likely to be in a traditional woman's profession, especially teaching (Betz & Fitzgerald, 1987).

Models of career development based on heterosexuals may have limited applicability to lesbian and bisexual women. Recent research suggests that the process of coming out and accepting a lesbian identity (see Chapter 8) is personally demanding and, in some cases, may delay career development. However, coming out is a normal phase for lesbian and bisexual women, one that should be taken into account in career counseling (Boatwright, Gilbert, Forrest, & Ketzenberger, 1996).

Cause—or Effect?

Studying the factors leading to success by looking at successful women is an example of retrospective research in which participants look back at factors influencing them at an earlier time. It can show us what characteristics successful women tend to share. However, it can also lead us to assume that we know the *causes* of success when we may be observing its *results.*

In other words, women who—for whatever reason—have the opportunity to test themselves in a demanding career may develop high self-esteem, assertiveness, independence, and achievement motivation as a consequence of their success. From this perspective, opportunity creates a "successful" personality, rather than vice versa (Kanter, 1977). Retrospective memory is not always accurate, either. Successful women may remember more achievement emphasis in their backgrounds than less-successful women simply because this dimension is relevant to them as adults (Nieva & Gutek, 1981).

Blue-Collar Women

During the 1970s and 1980s, federal affirmative-action guidelines, discrimination suits from workers, and unions all pressured employers to open opportunities for women in blue-collar fields (Harlan & O'Farrell, 1982). Women began to enroll in apprentice programs in the skilled trades and to take jobs as coal miners, police officers, truck drivers, welders, carpenters, and steelworkers (Braden, 1986; Deaux & Ullman, 1983; Hammond & Mahoney, 1983; Martin, 1988). (See Figure 11.9.)

Most women who became skilled blue-collar workers in male-dominated areas did not plan to do so (Deaux & Ullman, 1983; Martin, 1988). Rather, they often started out in other occupations and changed to meet perceived opportunities. Those who pioneered in entering the trades before affirmative-action mandates have been described by themselves and their co-workers as fighters: brave, rugged, tough, aggressive, confident, and willing to take risks (Harlan & O'Farrell, 1982). Even today, women entering blue-collar work are more assertive, less gender typed, and more likely to use active, direct problem-solving strategies than women in other kinds of work (Nash & Chrisler, 2001). They have a strong sense of self and a desire to be independent (Greene & Stitt-Gohdes, 1997).

In one study, 470 African American, white, and Hispanic women who entered programs in which more than 80 percent of the students were male were compared with women who entered programs with a preponderance of female students. The biggest difference between the two groups was that women in the nontraditional group (regardless of ethnic background) had received more support and encouragement from female and male friends, family, teachers, and counselors. They were also more instrumentally oriented (Houser & Garvey, 1985). Another study showed that economic need was the biggest factor in women's decision to move to blue-collar jobs, and this was especially true for black women (Padavic, 1991). Thus, individual background, personality factors, and current contexts may interact to influence women's employment choices.

FIGURE 11.9
Blue-collar women are an important group because they challenge stereotypes of passivity and represent one way that women break out of the pattern of low earnings.

Blue-collar women generally report a high level of satisfaction with their jobs. They like the variety and challenge of the work. They are proud of their competence and autonomy, have high levels of self-esteem, and often aspire to promotion and advancement (Deaux & Ullman, 1983; Ferree, 1987; Hammond & Mahoney, 1983; O'Farrell & Harlan, 1982). Being well paid is an important part of job satisfaction for blue-collar women. In one study, two-thirds of a sample of black, white, and Hispanic women steelworkers had children at home, and 61 percent of these were the sole wage earners for their families (Deaux & Ullman, 1983). One coal miner remembered her experience as a waitress: "I thought there must be a better way—here I am making $1.45 an hour and $1.00 an hour in tips. Jesus, there's gotta be another way." She described her decision to become a coal miner in vivid terms: "I can wash off coal black but I can't wash off those damn bill collectors" (Hammond & Mahoney, 1983, p. 19).

Of course, we do not know whether the woman shapes the job or the job shapes the woman—a problem with retrospective research discussed earlier. It does seem that proving oneself in a job that requires physical strength and endurance is empowering. One woman mechanic/ship fitter described her early fears but also reported how she learned to deal with "static" from male co-workers, one of whom told her, "This is no place for a woman; you ought to be outside taking care of your kids."

> I got angry one day, and I told one of the guys that I had to feed my damn kids just like he did, that's why I was there, and I never had too much trouble after that. (Braden, 1986, p. 75)

Blue-collar women do face some disadvantages. They are workplace tokens, few in number and low in status. Male co-workers and supervisors may feel threatened by their presence. Physical strength, endurance, and courage are central components of manhood. If mere women can handle their jobs, how are these men to distinguish themselves as men? Women may be taunted and ridiculed, subjected to hazing, threatened with physical injury, deliberately given unsafe equipment, and exposed to hostile, violent pornography on the job (Fitzgerald, 1993). A survey of blue-collar women (compared with school secretaries) showed that they experienced more sexual harassment and gender discrimination, more adverse working conditions, higher stress, and lower satisfaction. The black women in the sample also reported more racial discrimination than their counterparts who were secretaries (Mansfield et al., 1991). On-the-job stress creates psychological symptoms for blue-collar women (Goldenhar, Swanson, Hurrell, Ruder, & Deddens, 1998). Clearly, the satisfaction of doing a tough job and getting paid well for it can be offset by the burden of working in a hostile environment.

Putting It All Together: Work and Family

Women's increasing involvement in paid work has been one of the strongest social trends of the past 30 years. According to U.S. census data, in 1970 only 30 percent of married women with children under the age of 6 worked outside the home; by the mid-1990s, 63 percent of these women were working, along with 71 percent of married women with school-age children (Gilbert & Rader, 2001). Moreover, as discussed in Chapters 9 and 10, many mothers are single and must provide all or most of the financial support of their children.

It is interesting that women's work became a research issue only in the 1970s, when middle-class white women began entering the workforce in greater numbers. The fact that working-class, black, and some Hispanic women had always held paid jobs had not been considered worthy of psychological research. Unlike most research on work, which focuses on men, research on the problems of combining work and family has focused almost exclusively on women, especially on white, upper-middle-class women who are pursuing careers in business and the professions.

When psychologists first began studying working women, they emphasized the social and personal costs of multiple roles, rather than their rewards (Crawford,

1982; Gilbert & Rader, 2001). For example, researchers investigated whether women's work was detrimental to their mental health or their marriages. They were much less likely to ask whether family involvement or a happy marriage may make one a better and more productive worker. Researchers are now examining work and family from a broader perspective, looking at how women's and men's activities at work and at home converge.

Although people sometimes say that "you shouldn't bring your work home from the office" or "you shouldn't let personal problems affect your work," they do affect each other. Men's and women's work and family roles function as a system, with each component affecting every other (Gilbert & Rader, 2001; Lorber, 1993b). A woman's involvement in her paid work may depend not only on whether she has young children but also on whether she has a partner. If so, can her partner stay home from work with a sick child? How do both partners define housework responsibilities? Each partner's involvement in paid work depends on the other. If one earns a high salary, the other may feel less tied to a particular job; if one job is only part-time, the other may put in overtime. Combining the multiple obligations of spouse, parent, and worker has often been described as a balancing act. Let's look at some costs and benefits of the balancing act for working women and their families.

What Are the Costs of the Balancing Act?

There is no doubt that combining work and family is hard for both women and men, and that the "double day" of paid and unpaid work done by many women is particularly demanding. *Role conflict* refers to the psychological effects of being faced with sets of incompatible expectations or demands; *role overload* describes the difficulties of meeting these expectations. The secretary who is asked to work overtime on short notice and must scramble to find child care may experience both conflict (feeling guilty and torn between her two obligations) and overload (as she calls babysitters while typing the overdue report). Because her mother and worker roles are incompatible, there is no really satisfactory resolution of the conflict, and it may lead to guilt, anxiety, and depression. Chronic overload may lead to fatigue, short temper, and lowered resistance to physical illness.

Research has consistently shown that women workers experience role conflict (Crosby, 1991; Gilbert, 1993; Wajcman, 1998). In some studies, men also report role conflict. However, women are much more likely than men to adjust their jobs around their family responsibilities (Mennino & Brayfield, 2002). For example, women are more likely to arrange flextime schedules, work part-time, turn down opportunities for promotion or overtime, and use their own sick days to care for others. Women also adjust their family lives around their paid work by limiting the number of children they have, cutting back on housework, hiring live-in child-care workers, and so on. Of course, these trade-offs affect their partners, too. Some couples work out mutual strategies such as sharing child care and housework or hiring someone else to do chores.

Though both women and men make trade-offs to keep up with the balancing act, their choices may be shaped more by sociocultural aspects of gender than by their own attitudes and beliefs. When more than 900 men and women in a national survey were asked about the trade-offs they made and their gender-role attitudes, individual attitudes had little effect. In other words, more traditionally oriented people did not make different choices than more egalitarian people. However, both women and men in male-dominated occupations made more trade-offs that put family needs second to work needs. For example, they were more likely to take on extra work and to miss a family event. These results suggest that "male-typed occupations, regardless of whether they are held by women or men, are less accommodating to job-family balance" (Mennino & Brayfield, 2002, p. 251).

There is very little research on the costs of the balancing act among people who are not heterosexual, economically privileged, or white. In a study of lesbians, most of whom currently had a partner, 41 percent reported conflicts between their relationship and work roles—usually problems in allocating time and energy. Moreover, 33 percent reported conflicts at work in feeling socially unacceptable. They felt unable to be themselves or to discuss their partner or home life, and they reported pressure to dress and act in stereotyped heterosexual ways (Shachar & Gilbert, 1983).

What Are the Benefits of the Balancing Act?

Effects on Women and Men

Side by side with research showing widespread problems with role conflict and overload is a great deal of research showing *benefits* associated with multiple roles. Indeed, study after study shows that involvement as a spouse, parent, and worker is beneficial for both women and men. The value of the balancing act is reflected in better mental health, physical health, and relationship quality (Barnett & Hyde, 2001).

Why does involvement in many roles benefit well-being? One reason may be that paid work in itself is generally a source of increased self-esteem, more social involvement, and an independent identity (Steil, 1997). When women make paid work part of their lives, they gain more than just an income.

Another reason is that success in one domain may help people keep a sense of perspective about the other domains (Crosby, 1982, 1991). In a study of more than 200 managers, both women and men believed that their roles as parents and active members of their community had more positive than negative effects on their performance at work (Kirchmeyer, 1993). Being passed over for promotion might seem less of a disaster if one is happily involved in leading a Girl Scout troop; dealing with a difficult teenager at home may be made easier by being respected at the office. Women who juggle home and work develop good coping strategies, such as choosing the most rewarding aspects of each job and delegating the others. Having a paid job can provide a handy excuse for a woman not to do things she didn't want to do in the first place (Baruch et al., 1983).

Employment also increases women's power in the family (see Chapter 9). And it provides families with higher incomes, which benefits everyone and reduces the pressure on husbands (Barnett & Hyde, 2001). Men who get involved with the care of their children are often surprised to find how deeply rewarding this role can be and say that they would never give it up (Deutsch, 1999).

However, multiple roles may be beneficial only up to a point, after which overload and psychological distress may prevail. Role quality is important, too. A woman's job is unlikely to bring her satisfaction if she is subject to sexual harassment or discrimination (Barnett & Hyde, 2001).

There are some limitations to the research in this area. Research samples are self-selected—people have sorted themselves into employed and nonemployed groups before being studied. It is possible that multiple roles and happiness go together simply because better-adjusted people are more likely to attempt multiple roles in the first place. Furthermore, most of the research on the benefits of multiple roles has been done on people who have the advantages of high income and professional status. Role conflict and overload may contribute to burnout in jobs such as nursing and teaching (Greenglass & Burke, 1988; Statham, Miller, & Mauksch, 1988).

Effects on Children

What about the children? Do they suffer when both parents work outside the home? It's easy to find conservative commentators and experts who claim that working mothers (but never working fathers) contribute to juvenile delinquency, behavior problems, and poor adjustment in children. Day-care scare articles tell parents that their children will be abused and neglected if they are not home with mom. And employed mothers are sometimes viewed as second-class mothers, with the stay-at-home mom still the ideal. These views echo the long tradition of mother-blaming discussed in Chapter 10.

However, research does not confirm the popular wisdom. A recent meta-analysis of 59 studies confirmed that children cared for by their mothers did not differ developmentally in any important way from those cared for by other adult caretakers (Erel, Oberman, & Yirmiya, 2000). In general, children in day care do not suffer from disruption of their bond with their mothers; they may experience increased intellectual growth and development, especially if they come from low-income homes that cannot provide an enriched environment; and they are at least as socially skilled as other children (Scarr, 1998; Scarr, Phillips, & McCartney, 1990). And as for juvenile delinquency, a study of over 700 adolescents showed that mothers' work status (both when the teens were preschoolers and currently) was unrelated to the teens' delinquency (Vander-Ven, Cullen, Carrozza, & Wright, 2001). For many families today, the issue is not whether Mom and Dad should both work, but how to find affordable good-quality child care (see Figure 11.10).

Researchers may have overlooked potential benefits associated with working mothers—an example of bias in the framing of research questions. Child care can provide enrichment and foster intellectual and social development. In some cases, good child care may help offset poor parenting (Scarr, 1998; Silverstein, 1991). Furthermore, in many families, mothers' incomes are a matter of necessity. Two-thirds of mothers are working to keep their families out of poverty, and this proportion is increasing (Scarr, 1998).

Employed mothers also provide alternative role models for their children. Several studies have shown that daughters of employed women are more independent and self-confident. Both daughters and sons of employed women hold more egalitarian attitudes about women and view women (including their own mothers) as more competent (Steil, 1997). The benefits of a mother who models many areas of competence may be especially great for girls. As adults, daughters of employed

FIGURE 11.10
Day-care fantasies and realities.

women are more likely to become high achievers (Betz & Fitzgerald, 1987). As yet, there is no research on how fathers who care for their children and do a fair share of housework affect their children's attitudes or behavior.

Making a Difference:
Women, Work, and Social Policy

Clearly, the world of work presents women with many problems. As feminist leader Bella Abzug once said, "It is shocking that as women, we have to beg . . . for family support systems, decent wages, and the dignity to do what men have always done." (Herman, 1988, p. x)

The problems may seem large and unsolvable, but equity for women workers is not an impossible dream. How to go about achieving that dream is, however, an open question. Different ideas about the causes of inequity lead to different proposed solutions. Some researchers and policymakers focus on the individual level, others on the interpersonal or intergroup level, and still others on the structural level.

At the individual level, there is an emphasis on problems within women themselves: Women may lack the skills or motivation to succeed. According to this model, the best way to change women's work situation is to provide self-improvement and training programs to help women overcome their deficiencies. Examples are assertiveness training and time-management courses for women (Crawford, 1995). Individual change may be helpful for some women, but, as we have seen, there is little evidence that women as a group lack ability or motivation. The individual-deficit model runs the risk of blaming the victim by ignoring social factors that are beyond the control of the individual (Fassinger, 2002). It leaves the work of change to women, without questioning the masculine values that underlie both corporate culture and the double day at home.

A structural-level approach focuses on the impact of organizations on the people in them. It proposes that the situation a person is placed in shapes behavior. From this perspective, low expectations and lack of ambition may be adaptive adjustments to reality and will change if real opportunities for advancement become available. The system, not the individual, must change for equity to be achieved. Rather than viewing women as unique, it sees their problems as similar to problems faced by other disadvantaged groups such as racial and ethnic minorities. Legislation for equal opportunity and affirmative action is one route to change (Crosby, 2003). According to the structural approach, equal opportunity leads to equal performance. Family leave policies and affordable, high-quality child care are important structural changes, too.

A final approach is based on intergroup power, which has been stressed throughout this book and is the focus of Chapter 2. From this perspective, when men have more social power, women are treated as an outgroup. This model explains why women's work is devalued, why male career patterns and definitions of work and achievement are taken as the norm, and why occupations so frequently end up segregated by sex. Stereotypes about differences between women and men reinforce the ingroup-outgroup distinction.

The intergroup perspective views change in the workplace as dependent on societal change. Educating people about stereotyping might help in the short run, but fundamental change depends on altering the power structure. Power-oriented strategies include passing and enforcing equal-opportunity legislation, increasing women's political power, and forming women's organizations and networks to exert pressure for social change. Many women and men today are engaged in these strategies.

By showing how discrimination works, psychological research can help point the way to change. How can gender bias in hiring and promotion be eliminated? Both individuals and organizations must change (Valian, 1998):

- Ensure that women's performance is accurately evaluated by teaching people about attribution biases.
- Develop clear, specific criteria for performance evaluation and make people responsible for meeting the criteria.

- Allow enough time and attention for performance evaluations. The quicker and more automatic the decision making, the more people rely on cognitive biases that disadvantage women.
- Increase the number of women in the pool, which reduces the salience of gender.
- Appoint leaders who are committed to gender equity.
- Develop clear institutional policies about gender equity and sexual harassment and make sure they are communicated and implemented consistently.

Parallel changes are also needed to eliminate bias due to race, ethnic group, sexual orientation, age, disability, and other dimensions of disadvantage.

The information and analysis in Chapters 9 to 11 show that women's and men's experiences in relationships, families, and workplaces are interdependent. Women who cannot achieve economic parity at work are disadvantaged by having less power in their marriages. Much of the work women do is unpaid and undervalued. Sex discrimination at work affects productivity and quality of life. If women are to have the same career opportunities as men, they must be able to decide if and when they will bear children. Families suffer when social policy is based on myths of motherhood instead of the realities of contemporary life. These are just a few examples of the complex relationships among family roles and workplace issues. Models of change that focus on gendered social structures and power inequities are more useful than those that stress changing women's attitudes and values.

Exploring Further

Crosby, Faye. (2003). *Affirmative action is dead: Long live affirmative action*. New Haven: Yale University Press.
   Affirmative action is probably the most misunderstood social policy of our times. Crosby's clear thinking and lively writing clear up misconceptions and show why affirmative action is still needed.

Hays, Sharon. (2003). *Flat broke with children*. New York: Oxford University Press.
   The impact of welfare reform seen through the eyes of welfare recipients, most of whom are poor women forced into the labor market in low-wage jobs with few benefits. Hays's study is based on interactions with welfare recipients and caseworkers.

Prime Suspect I. (1991).
   Now available on DVD, this British thriller stars an ace female detective (Helen Mirren) who captures a serial killer while coping with everyday sexism. A realistic, gripping portrayal of gender and status in the predominantly male world of police work.

CHAPTER 12

The Second Half:
Midlife and Aging

- Cynthia, who is White, was born in 1930. As a teenager, she felt attraction to other women but had no words for it and no idea anyone else might feel the same way. She was 41 when the gay rights movement began, 45 when homo-sexuality was removed from the DSM, and 70 when the TV character Ellen "came out" on TV. After many years of secrecy and stress, Cynthia feels that she has a positive lesbian identity in her old age (Kimmel & Martin, 2001).
- Rebecca W. is white, upper-middle-class, 58 years old and has been married for 40 years. Her husband, aged 67, is a retired executive. When their five children were still at home, she took care of Mr. W's father, who lived with them for several years until his death. Now Mrs. W. takes care of her 84-year-old mother, who is forgetful and resentful and has many physical limitations. She always hoped that she would travel and take up new interests when her children left home, but that is not possible. Mrs. Wood suffers from stress and depression (Brody, 2004, pp. 190–191).
- Dorothy, who is African American, was born in 1925 in a small southern town and grew up under racial segregation. She earned a high school diploma and wanted to be a secretary, but at that time, only white women could get clerical jobs. She worked all her life cleaning the houses of white families. Now that she is widowed, she is surviving on $6,000 a year and has to ask her family to help out with basic needs such as food and medicine (Ralston, 1997).
- Mercedes is a Mexican American woman now in her late 60s. When she was growing up, her father did not see the point of sending a daughter to school. She married very young and remembers wanting to play jump rope with her friends but having to cook beans for her husband instead. She had six children, all of whom now live nearby. People call her *la abuela*, the grandmother, a sign of respect. Mercedes is sought out by many in her community as a *curandera*, one who can heal mind and body (Facio, 1997).
- Annette, born in 1947 to a middle-class white family, is a baby boomer, one of the large group of Americans born between 1946 and 1964. Hers was the first generation to have the Pill and she was in no hurry to get married. She has worked outside the home ever since her only child started school. After some early struggles against sex discrimination at work, she had a satisfying career as a social worker. Divorced, living alone, and with little money saved, she is looking forward to retirement with mixed feelings (Scott, 1997).

It is often said that age is the great leveler—it happens to everyone. However, as these real-life examples show, individuals experience aging differently depending on social class and ethnic background. Another important factor is an individual's **age cohort**—the group of people born in about the same decade. Different age cohorts have different experiences as a group. My mother's cohort, for example, grew up during the Great Depression and lived through World War II as young adults; these experiences shaped their values in many ways.

In this chapter, we explore the lives of women at midlife and beyond. Midlife is usually defined as the period that begins at 45 years of age and ends at 65 years of age and old age as the period beyond age 65. However, some researchers divide the old into the "young old" (65–75), the "old old" (75–85), and the "oldest old" (beyond 85).

Psychology traditionally has paid less attention to the second half of life than the first, particularly where women are concerned. This is unfortunate because women and men experience aging somewhat differently, and the accumulated inequities of a lifetime can leave older women vulnerable to many problems. However, the second half of a woman's life can be as full of surprises, challenges, and rewards as the first. Let's start by looking at how age is socially defined and evaluated.

Not Just a Number: The Social Meanings of Age

To a teenager, a 40-year-old may seem ancient; but my 82-year-old aunt says that *old* is anyone five years older than she is. How would you define *old?* Are you old once you reach a certain age? Does it happen when you become a grandparent? When you retire? Or are you "only as old as you feel"? Each of these definitions is possible. Age is subjective. Its meaning is defined by social consensus, and the criteria differ from one time and place to another (Sokolovsky, 1997). In our own society, we tend to use chronological age as a marker. However, age in years is only loosely correlated with abilities or roles; at best, it is convenient shorthand that lumps together quite different people. One 80-year-old woman might be in a nursing home, whereas another is volunteering as a helper to the elderly.

Is There a Double Standard of Aging?

Many people hold a **double standard of aging.** They think women are old at an earlier age than men, and they see being old as more negative for women. Historically, women's value and status have often depended on their reproductive ability. Men's status, in contrast, has been derived from their achievements, money, and power. Therefore, a woman was old when she could no longer reproduce, whereas a man was not old until he became mentally or physically incapacitated.

The double standard of aging can often be seen in the portrayal of older women and men in the mass media. I'll discuss media images in more detail shortly, but for now here is one example. In an in-depth analysis of a British magazine aimed at older people, the female models in the ads were all well under the age of 50, except for one gray-haired older woman shown using a vacuum cleaner. In contrast, a gray-haired older man was featured in an ad for a senior railpass, which showed him in a wetsuit, carrying a large surfboard into the waves. The ad claimed, "60 isn't what it used to be. There are sights to see, friends to visit, waves to catch" (Blytheway, 2003, p. 46).

Do people apply the double standard to themselves? An interesting study of a random national sample of people aged 20 to 85 years in Sweden examined perceptions of age (Öberg, 2003). Figure 12.1 shows the proportion of people over 30 who said they were disturbed by age-related changes in their appearance. You can see that there is a significant gender gap; women expressed more body dissatisfaction than men did. However, the gap does not increase with age. In other words,

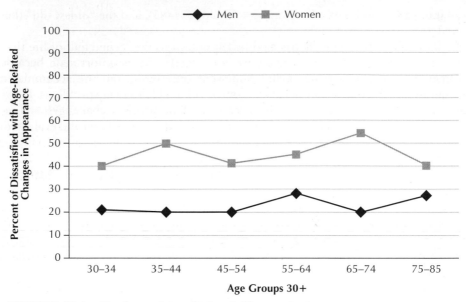

FIGURE 12.1   Gender and Age-Related Changes in Appearance

In a study of Swedish adults, women in every age group were more likely than men of the same age to be dissatisfied with the effects of age on their appearance. Do you think the results would be similar or different in the United States?

Source: Adapted from P. Öberg, 2003, *Aging Bodies: Images and Everyday Experiences*, p. 118, Fig. 4.4. New York: Alta Mira Press. Reprinted by permission.

younger and older women were similar in being less satisfied with their aging bodies than men were. In an interview study done in England, the double standard was evident in a slightly different form. Older women were more distressed about changes in *appearance*, and older men by changes in their bodies' *function* (loss of stamina, running speed, etc.). Men spoke of their aging bodies as a holistic entity, whereas women spoke of parts (legs, thighs, neck) (Halliwell & Dittmar, 2003). Both these studies' results reflect the pervasive objectification of the female body discussed in Chapter 7.

Although the double standard of aging is important, we should be careful not to oversimplify it (Öberg, 2004). The double standard may differ considerably across cultures and ethnic groups. Moreover, as women gain occupational status more similar to men's, and are judged on similar dimensions, the double standard of aging may be lessening (Calasanti & Slevin, 2001).

Ageism

Prejudice and discrimination based on age is termed ***ageism***. Like other forms of bias, ageism characterizes individuals on the basis of their membership in a group and can affect beliefs, attitudes, and behavior toward group members.

As a form of oppression, ageism has the potential to touch everyone, even those who are most privileged. Aging happens to everyone who lives long enough, be they female or male, rich or poor, ethnic minority or white. In a recent survey of people over the age of 60, nearly 80 percent of respondents reported experiencing ageism. The most common form of ageism was being told jokes that made fun of older people. However, ageism was sometimes more personal. Respondents reported that others assumed they had memory problems, ignored them, or did not take them seriously because of their age (Palmore, 2001).

Most people, especially younger people, barely notice that age is being made into a form of stigma. But the message that being old is repulsive, embarrassing, or unthinkable is visible everywhere in our society. Writing this chapter, I became more sensitized to small examples of ageism. In the space of a few days, I heard a tiny apartment described as a granny flat, came across several cartoons depicting old women with drooping breasts, skinny legs, and wrinkled faces; and heard a memory lapse described as a "senior moment." (When a 20-year-old forgets the car keys, we don't call it a "young adult moment"!). Next, my copy of the *New Yorker* arrived in the mail. The artist had titled this cover "Spring Break." The cover art—intended to be funny—showed a grumpy-looking elderly woman about to slip on a banana peel.

Cross-Cultural Differences

White American culture is extremely individualistic and materialistic. These values work best for the young and strong. Those at midlife usually can cope fairly well, but "the old are bound to fail" when judged on "rugged individualism" (Cruikshank, 2003, p. 10). The older one gets, the less possible it is to maintain total autonomy and independence. Aging brings the need for help from others, and in U.S. culture this need is often seen as shameful. In cultures that value interdependence and connection, the willingness to rely on others may not be so different for older people than for younger ones. Thus, the meaning of old age depends on culture.

Furthermore, in rapidly changing modern societies, the knowledge held by the old may seem unimportant. In contrast, some cultures, past and present, have respected and venerated the old as keepers of knowledge. For example, Buddhist tradition honors old teachers, and Native American tribes relied on the old to pass on crucial knowledge such as where to find medicinal plants. The "wise elder," most often personified as male, is an ancient archetype still with us (think Obi-Wan Kenobi and Gandalf).

When old people have meaningful tasks and roles in a society, there is less emphasis on their bodies and more on their contributions. The old may have special status as peacekeepers, mediators, or keepers of tradition. In some Asian societies, spiritual power is thought to increase as the body becomes frailer. Old women are honored with the right to name children in some African and Native American groups.

In North American society, meaningful roles for the old are most evident in minority communities. For example, Native American women often become important leaders and artists in old age, and older African American women are an important source of influence in churches and civic groups. In contrast, mainstream American society views age largely as a physical condition, which fosters the marginalization of old people (Cruikshank, 2003).

Nevertheless, the idea that old people are always venerated elsewhere compared to our own society is oversimplified. In preindustrial societies, just as in our own, how an old person is treated depends on his or her gender, status, and power, aside from age. In poor and developing countries, old people may have to do hard physical labor as long as they can, and retirement is an unknown concept. Old women may be valued only as caregivers for others, a role that is increasingly difficult to fill as one gets older. Religious beliefs may stress respect for the old, but this does not always happen in practice. Physical infirmities, illness, and disabilities seem to lower one's status almost everywhere. Still, most cross-cultural research suggests that the status of the old in the United States is lower than in many other cultures, past and present (Cruikshank, 2003).

Self-Identity and Social Identity

Like other forms of bias, ageism can be internalized, affecting the individual's identity and self-esteem. "This is the heart of ageism: We deny that we are aging, and when we are forced to confront it, we treat it as ugly and tragic" (Calasanti & Slevin, 2001, p. 186).

People engage in a great deal of denial about their own aging. For example, a 65-year-old may refuse to go to a senior citizen center or retirement community because she does not want to be around "all those old people." A common research finding is that older people have a pessimistic view of the health of others in their age group, but consider themselves the lucky exceptions (Cruikshank, 2003).

In one study, older adults in Finland were asked to look in a mirror and describe their reflection. One 79-year-old woman said, "It isn't a reflection of me. I know myself pretty well. . . . Spiritually I don't feel old, like 'oh dear how old I am.' But I can see it in the appearance" (cited in Öberg, 2004, p. 107). This woman is making a distinction between her *self identity* (her own subjective feeling of age) and her *social identity* (the way she looks to others).

The discrepancy between self and social identities was explored in a Swedish study (Öberg, 2004), in which participants aged 20 to 85 answered these questions:

> In my inner self I feel as if I am ____ years old.
> I would most like to be ____ years old.
> I think that other people see me as ____ years old.

Figure 12.2 shows that every age group except the 20-year-olds reported a difference between their chronological age and their subjective age. The great majority of people said they felt younger, wanted to be younger, and thought that others saw them as younger than they actually were. The gaps between self, ideal, and social identities increased with age. Respondents in their 80s wanted to be 50, felt like 60, and thought that they looked like 70 to others.

Distancing yourself from your age may be a form of resistance against the social stigma of being old. "If I emphasize that I differ from the 'typical' old who are deteriorating, I try to dodge the scorn often heaped on them. . . . And the more I claim difference, the better I feel about myself" (Cruikshank, 2003, p. 11). However, when each old person thinks of himself or herself as the exception, it is

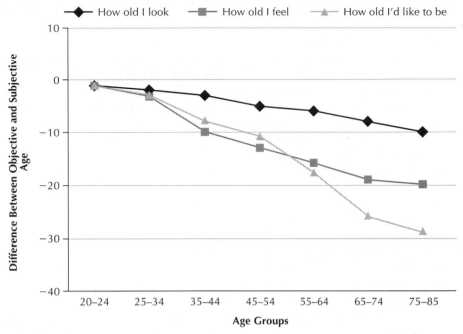

FIGURE 12.2

The discrepancy for respondents in different age groups between how old they think they look, how old they feel, and how old they would like to be.

Source: Öberg and Tomstam, 2001, as summarized in Öberg, 2003.

unlikely that older people will bond with each other or act collectively to change the sociocultural forces that construct *old* age so negatively. Instead, the politics of aging encourage each of us to believe that getting old is something that only happens to other people.

Images of Older Women

Think about the last few TV dramas or sitcoms you watched. Were there any women over 40 in leading roles? If so, how were they portrayed? Older women in the mass media are few and far between, and those who do appear are often stereotyped as unattractive, useless, and boring (Markson & Taylor 2000).

Invisibility

As women grow older, they become less visible in all forms of mass media, as though they are so repulsive that no one would want to look at them. Older men, too, are underrepresented, but to a much lesser degree. The double standard of aging can be seen in television, in films, and in advertising. For example, one study of television ads showed that only 12 percent of the characters were people over 50, and 75 percent of those were men (Quadagno, 1999). In films, older men are given lead roles more often than older women. Men in their 50s, 60s, and even older are portrayed as sexually desirable and active; but when older women are present at all, they are most often shown as asexual and unattractive (Markson & Taylor, 2000).

The most invisible aspect of older women is their sexuality. Although young women's bodies are sexually objectified and exploited by the mass media, old women are almost never portrayed as sexual, unless their sexual desire is the butt of jokes and ridicule. The bodies of young women are used to sell everything from fishing tackle to vodka, but the bodies of old women are evaded. This invisibility "deprives women of all ages from knowing what old bodies look like . . . the ways beauty can be expressed through old female forms is yet to be known" (Cruikshank, 2003, p. 149).

Two recent exceptions prove the rule: Nude scenes for young actresses are so commonplace that they are unremarkable, but when Diane Keaton (age 58) briefly appeared nude in the 2003 movie *Something's Gotta Give*, she was lauded as a brave, risk-taking pioneer by the press. A 2004 episode of *NYPD Blue* featured a 60ish woman who was happily sexual, but her character was played for laughs as inept Officer Medavoy managed to bed her. And, unlike the steamy nude sex scenes of the young characters in this series, their sex scene showed only a jiggling bed and two pairs of legs—from the knees down.

Older lesbian, gay, bisexual, and transgendered (LGBT) people are invisible not only in mainstream media but even in media aimed at the gay community. In an analysis of LGBT magazines such as *Out* and *The Advocate*, there were only two articles on older people in 542 pages of text. Images of men were more numerous than those of women, and there were no images of anyone of either sex who looked to be 60 or older (Apuzzo, 2001).

Grannies and Witches: Stereotypes of Older Women

Like other stereotypes, age stereotypes vary on the dimensions of competence and warmth. Much like disabled and retarded people, elderly people are seen as "doddering but dear" (Cuddy & Fiske, 2002). Is there a double standard in stereotypes of old people? Are images of old women more negative than those of old men?

Some research shows that age stereotypes are similar for women and men. For example, when college students rated a middle-aged or old man, woman, or person (sex unspecified) on a list of traits, they rated the old—both women and men—less positively than the middle-aged. Women were seen as warmer and more emotional, and men as more powerful, but they were seen as more similar than different overall (Sherman, 1997). In other studies, older women have been viewed as less competent, intelligent, wise, and independent than older men, but also as more nurturing, warm, and sensitive (Canetto, 2001). These studies suggest that gendered stereotypes of the old are an extension of gender stereotypes applied to young people rather than a sharply different double standard.

Age stereotyping is usually triggered by appearance. Many experimental studies show that the physical characteristics of age (wrinkles, gray hair) are rated more negatively for women than for men—clear evidence of a double standard (Canetto,

2001). In interview studies, older women repeatedly say that their aging bodies are the first cues that others use to classify them. When they are with friends and family, they are treated as individuals; but when they interact with strangers in public settings, "all anyone seems to see is an old woman."

One of the most pervasive images of old women is the kindly grandmother, an image that is consistent with trait stereotypes of warmth and nurturance (Canetto, 2001). Granny images are reinforced by the clothes and props assigned to older women in media representations. The Granny figure wears a housedress, a shawl, or an apron. She sits in a rocking chair, knitting, or stirs a pot over the stove. Her gray hair, worn in a tight bun, and her outdated, unfashionable clothes signify that she has not kept up with the times. This grandmother figure abounds in films made over the past six decades. A comic variation is the outrageous granny (think Beverly Hillbillies) (Markson, 2003).

Other prototypes of older women in the media are the mother-in-law from hell (*Sex and the City*'s Bunny), the manipulative, selfish elderly mother (Livia in *The Sopranos*), and the comical but powerless "little old lady" (Cruickshank, 2003) (See Figure 12.3.). A recent analysis of Disney movies concluded that old women were depicted as ugly, evil, greedy, power-hungry, and crazy (Perry, 1999).

"It sounds like Osama bin Laden, but it could be your mother."

FIGURE 12.3

Source: Copyright © The New Yorker Collection, 2003, Frank Cotham, from cartoonbank.com. All rights reserved.

Everyday language reflects stereotypes of old people, and old women in particular. The very word *old* is so unpleasant that it is avoided whenever possible with terms like *senior citizen* and *golden ager.* Some terms trivialize, derogate, or patronize the old—such as *geezer, little old lady,* and *dirty old man.* In Sweden, dances for older people are popularly called *raisins disco* (Öberg, 2004); in England, domestic violence against the elderly is called *granny bashing.* Terms for old women are particularly harsh. There are few terms for older men that rival *old hag, old biddy,* and *old bag* in negativity.

The Effects of Age Stereotypes

One effect of age stereotypes is apparent in social interaction: When people talk to the elderly, they sometimes switch to ***elderspeak*** (Ruscher, 2001). Elderspeak is like baby talk (the speech addressed by adults to young children) or the speech people use when they talk to their pets: It is grammatically simplified, repetitious, slowed down, and exaggerated in pitch. Only listeners who suffer from hearing loss or dementia are likely to find elderspeak helpful.

Elderspeak can be very patronizing, conveying the expectation that the listener is not competent to understand normal speech. When people speak to elders as though they are incompetent, they may create a self-fulfilling prophecy. Because elderspeak is simplified, it conveys less information, thereby leading the old person to respond in a more simplistic way and reinforcing the belief in his or her incompetence (Ruscher, 2001).

Exposure to ageist stereotypes can have insidious effects on judgments about older people. In one recent study, college students listened to a taped lecture read by a gender-neutral and age-neutral voice and rated the "professor" on teaching skills. Some were told that the professor was a male or female under age 35, and others that he/she was over age 55. Although the lecture was identical for all participants, students rated the professor as more enthusiastic, vocally expressive, and showing more interest when they thought he was young and male than in any other condition (Arbuckle & Williams, 2003). This study shows the interaction of age and gender stereotypes: Students' evaluations were filtered through their stereotypes about older professors as well as female professors.

What would happen if positive stereotypes of the elderly were substituted for negative ones? In one interesting study, participants ranging in age from 63 to 82 played a video game that exposed them to either positive or negative stereotypes about the old. Before and after the game, their speed and style of walking were measured. Those who had been exposed to positive stereotypes walked faster and more energetically—suggesting that the slower gait of older people may be partly due to internalized stereotypes and not entirely to the physical changes of aging (Hausdorff, Levy, & Wei, 1999).

In an Aging Woman's Body

I was conversing with a middle-aged friend . . . the talk turned to personal matters, and she told me about using herbs to manage her hot flashes, while I shared some concerns about my arthritis and needing a cane to get around. We laughed when we realized that though we are past worrying about having periods and getting pregnant, we never really are free of concerns about our bodies. (A woman in her 70s, quoted in Doress-Worters & Ditzion, 1998)

As bodies grow older, they change. Acknowledging and accepting this is an important part of aging. There are physical differences between women and men as they age, but the meaning of an aging body is not just a matter of its physical state; it depends on the social context. Track and field athletes are relegated to Masters status at age 35 (women) and 40 (men). In contrast, symphony conductors often lead major orchestras into their 80s, and some U.S. senators have served into their 90s (Calasanti & Slevin, 2001). Because women, more than men, are evaluated throughout their lifetimes by their bodies, living in an aging body is a particular challenge for women.

Physical Health in Middle and Later Life

Measures of women's health in later life are somewhat contradictory. On the one hand, women as a group have a long life expectancy, outliving men on average. On the other hand, women are more likely than men to have chronic illnesses and disabilities as they age (Canetto, 2001). Here we look at some of the most common health problems of older women.

Heart Disease

What is your best guess about the three leading causes of death for U.S. women? Many people's list would include breast cancer. Although one woman in nine will be diagnosed with breast cancer during her lifetime, the three leading causes of death for women in industrialized countries are the same as for men: heart disease, all types of cancer, and stroke (Canetto, 2001). Over the past 35 years, death from heart disease has actually decreased for men while increasing for women, and the death rate is higher for African American and Latina women than for other women. Currently, 6.4 million American women have a diagnosed heart disease condition (Marcuccio, Loving, Bennett, & Hayes, 2003).

Because most research on heart disease was conducted with men, there has been a shortage of information about women's symptoms (which may differ from men's) and a gender gap in treatment. Far more men than women have diagnostic tests and surgery, and women are less likely to be referred to a cardiac rehabilitation program even when their symptoms are identical to men's (Chrisler, 2001).

The effects of gender bias in the diagnosis and treatment of heart disease were evident in a survey of over 200 female patients, most between the ages of 40 and 79 (Marcuccio et al., 2003). Almost half of the sample had been unaware that they were at risk for heart disease before their diagnosis. Over half the women were dissatisfied with their treatment, citing physicians who were rude, condescending, abrupt, or inattentive. Over 1 in 10 who were dissatisfied said that their condition was initially misdiagnosed as panic disorder, menopausal symptoms, or hypochondria; and they resented being told in effect, "It's all in your head." Only 60 percent of the sample were referred to a cardiac care program. Despite knowing that their disease put their lives at risk, fewer than 15 percent made significant changes toward a healthier lifestyle, probably because they were not given enough support and information about how to do so. The researchers noted that other studies also have shown that women receive very little counseling about exercise, diet, and weight control, and much less than men do, after heart disease is diagnosed.

Chronic Illnesses

Midlife and older women are likely to live with chronic illnesses such as arthritis and diabetes. Conditions that limit activity (spinal degeneration, varicose veins, and joint problems) are two to three times more prevalent in women over 75 than in men of the same age group. Because the probability of all these conditions increases with age, it is not uncommon for a woman in the oldest-old group to have three or more chronic health concerns simultaneously, such as arthritis, heart disease, high blood pressure, back pain, and diabetes (Canetto, 2001).

Chronic illness has psychological effects on identity. After a short-term illness like the flu, a person stops focusing on the disruptive body and goes back to normal, once again taking a working body for granted. Chronic illness forces a continued focus on the body, as it fluctuates between good days when daily life goes on with relative ease, and bad days when the damaged body defines the person (Gubrium & Holstein, 2004). The patient must face the fact that her disorder cannot be cured. Instead, she must cope with whatever physical pain and limitations it brings, along with changes in activities and roles. For example, a woman with diabetes may no longer be able to enjoy cooking favorite foods, taking her children and grandchildren out to dinner, or feasting at family gatherings. It is not surprising that many people with chronic illnesses also experience depression (Chrisler, 2001).

Chronic illness also increases dependency and the need for help with daily living. When an older woman can no longer take care of herself, she may not have anyone to turn to. Women with diseases such as multiple sclerosis and cancer are more likely to be abandoned by their partners than men with the same problems (Chrisler, 2001). Although only 5 percent of people over 65 are in nursing homes at any given time, women are 75 percent of those who are.

Shortcomings of the U.S. health care system aggravate the problems of the chronically ill. Critics point out that "there is a sharply increasing population of older women who are economically and socially deprived" (Carp, 1997, p. 261), and yet providing home help and services seems to be a very low priority for government spending. Critics also charge that many older people with chronic illnesses are overmedicated (Cruikshank, 2003). The U.S. medical system is better at spectacular one-time interventions (like heart transplants) than at managing long-term conditions and helping people maintain wellness as they age.

Ethnicity and Health

Women of Hispanic and African American heritage report poorer health than European American women, and they are more likely to die from diseases that could be treated and managed if they had access to good health care. For example, 34 percent of black women, and only 19 percent of white women, have high blood pressure, which can lead to strokes (Cruikshank, 2003). Diabetes is the fourth-ranked cause of death among African American, Native American, and Hispanic women, but ranks seventh among European Americans (Canetto, 2001).

Socioeconomic status is the single most important determinant of health in old age, and probably is the root cause of many ethnic differences in health status. Poverty is linked to ill health in adults for the same reasons it is in children (Chapter 6): It is connected to many stressors such as unemployment, crowding, poor diet, unsanitary living conditions, pollution, and violence (Chrisler, 2001). Moreover, the lack of universal health care insurance in the United States means that poor people are unlikely to get consistent high-quality care for the chronic illnesses associated with poverty. The effects of low socioeconomic status accumulate over a lifetime and lead to a shortened life.

Menopause and Hormone Replacement Therapy

The U.S. medical system does seem eager to cure one huge problem affecting millions of women. Unfortunately, the "problem" is not a disease or disorder but a natural aspect of aging, and the "cure" may be unnecessary and even harmful.

Menopause refers to the end of the menstrual cycle and monthly periods. It is caused by a decrease in the production of estrogen and progesterone by the ovaries. It can occur any time between the mid-40s and the late 50s, but the average age is 51.

Physical Signs of Menopause

The menopausal transition takes place over several years, as periods become less regular. A woman can be sure that she has reached menopause when she has not had a period for a full year.

Other bodily changes may accompany menopause. In Western societies, about 50 to 85 percent of all women experience *hot flashes,* brief episodes of suddenly increasing heart rate, warmth, and sweating. Hot flashes may occur as infrequently as once a month or as often as several times an hour. They are caused by the decline in estrogen that triggers menopause. Over time, the body accommodates to lower estrogen levels and hot flashes disappear. However, there are cross-cultural differences that call into question whether hot flashes have a single biological cause. For example, women in Japan and Mayan women in Mexico very rarely experience hot flashes with menopause (Beyene, 1989; BWHBC, 1998). Is this because of dietary differences or because menopause is less stressful in cultures that value old women more than our own does? This question is still unanswered.

Many women also experience vaginal changes with menopause: The skin and membranes in this area become thinner and drier, which may make sexual penetration by a partner uncomfortable. However, this can be remedied with lubricating gels. In a community-based study, 20 percent of postmenopausal women reported this condition, and of those, only 15 percent reported it as bothersome (BWHBC, 1998).

Psychological Experiences of Menopause

There is a long history of attributing women's psychological distress to their reproductive systems. Starting in the 1860s, psychiatry developed diagnostic categories for the supposed craziness of postmenopausal women, including "old maid's insanity" and "involutional melancholia," a form of midlife depression (Markson, 2003).

The belief that women become depressed, moody, irritable, and hypersensitive at menopause is still prevalent among health-care providers and women themselves (Avis, 2003).

Contrary to these beliefs, research shows no evidence that the onset of menopause leads to depression or that women suffer more depression after menopause than before (Avis, 2003). Instead, the evidence suggests that depression during the menopausal transition is predicted by a prior history of depression, health problems, and social factors (see Figure 12.4). Depression is not a normal part of menopause.

Menopause may be linked with short-term moodiness and irritability in some women. This may be partly due to physical changes; when sleep is disturbed by hot flashes, irritability can result. It may also be due to expectations created by

"I was on hormone replacement for two years before I realized that what I really needed was Steve replacement."

FIGURE 12.4

Source: Copyright © The New Yorker Collection, 2001, Jack Ziegler, from cartoonbank.com. All rights reserved.

stereotypes. If everyone expects a menopausal woman to be moody, mood changes caused by stressful life events may be misattributed to her hormones.

An old expression for menopause is "change of life." Indeed, like menarche, it marks a major life change that is unique to females. In one study of 2,500 women, the majority experienced this change with neutral or positive feelings (Avis & McKinlay, 1991). In studies comparing African and European American women, the black women had more positive attitudes than the white women, viewing menopause as a normal and unremarkable part of life (Sampselle, Harris, Harlow, & Sowers, 2002; Sommer et al., 1999). A woman may be relieved that she no longer can become pregnant and can stop using birth control; she may be happy to say goodbye to pads, tampons, and cramps. Very few 50-year-olds want to have a baby.

Most women cope with the signs of menopause with little fuss. In one study, about half of the participants reported hot flashes, but not everyone was bothered by them (McKinlay, Brambilla, & Posner, 1992). One woman described lying in bed on a cold winter night, dreading a necessary trip to the bathroom:

> Then I had a hot flash and, all of a sudden, it was very easy to leave my warm bed! For the rest of the winter I used my nighttime hot flashes this way. My friends laughed when I told them that hot flashes are not all bad! (BWHBC, 1998, p. 557)

The Medicalization of Menopause

Despite the fact that it is a normal part of aging for women, there is a long history of pathologizing menopause. Psychiatric diagnoses such as involutional melancholia were part of the myth that women are mentally unstable because of their reproductive hormones: Raging "PMS" hormones made us unfit in our reproductive years, and waning hormones did so at midlife and after (BWHBC, 1998). Even today, physicians sometimes misdiagnose serious conditions such as hypertension and heart disease as menopausal symptoms, and some still overprescribe tranquilizers and antidepressants to midlife women rather than listen to their concerns about their changing bodies (BWHBC, 1998).

Because menopause happens to over 50 percent of the adult population, there is a great deal of money to be made in treating it as a disease. Increasingly, U.S. society defines age as a sickness that can be treated and cured (Calasanti & Slevin, 2001). This trend was apparent in the use of reproductive hormones to relieve signs of menopause and prevent signs of aging, termed ***estrogen replacement therapy (ERT)*** or ***hormone replacement therapy (HRT)***, depending on whether estrogen alone or a combination of hormones is used. Proponents argued that ERT/HRT could prevent osteoporosis (bone density loss), heart disease, and some types of cancer. Some claimed that it also could prevent age-related changes in cognition (memory loss and dementia) and appearance (wrinkles and weight gain). Pharmaceutical companies, some scientists, and many physicians urged women to stay forever young by taking hormones to offset menopause.

However, these claims were made before there was sufficient research. Recently, a very large national study of women aged 50 to 79 (N = 25,000) set out to examine the effect of diet, exercise, and ERT/HRT on heart disease, cancer, and osteoporosis. The HRT part of the study was ended early when results showed that

HRT was associated with a slightly *increased* risk of breast cancer, heart attack, and stroke (Cruikshank, 2003). Soon after, the ERT results were analyzed and also showed that the risks outweighed the benefits. ERT was linked to an increased risk of stroke and had no effect on preventing heart disease (Women's Health Initiative Steering Committee, 2004). Moreover, both HRT and ERT were linked to increased cognitive impairment such as memory loss and dementia (Espeland et al., 2004; Shumaker et al., 2004). Women's health activists are outraged that this "therapy" was prescribed to so many women in the absence of scientific evidence for its benefits. In the process, many women have probably been harmed.

These results should give pause to those who think that aging can be stopped or reversed by medical interventions. The signs of menopause, such as hot flashes, usually can be controlled with simple measures such as wearing layers, exercising, and meditation (BWHBC, 1998). If hot flashes or vaginal dryness are very severe, short-term, low-dose ERT or an estrogen cream applied to the vaginal area may offer relief.

Women can have more control over their own lives by resisting the medicalization of menopause and aging. When menopause and midlife are defined as illnesses, every woman over a certain age becomes a perennial patient in a system that is not designed to respect and value women.

Constructing the Object of Desire

Increasingly, both women and men are expected to spare no effort to disguise or eliminate the bodily changes that come with age. For men, Viagra is aggressively marketed as a way to restore the sexual vigor of youth. For women, much more than a pill is required.

As a woman ages, the ideal female face and body become more and more impossible to achieve. To look young is good; to look old is ugly, bad, and contemptible. In response, many women view their bodies as the site of an ever-more laborious project in which the goal is to masquerade as a younger woman (Calasanti & Slevin, 2001).

Of course, attempts to avoid old age are ultimately futile. Nevertheless, attempts to avoid the *appearance* of old age are rapidly increasing in Western societies, aided by aggressive marketing of antiaging products. Older women use more age-concealment techniques than older men and also report that they are likely to do so in the future (Harris, 1994). They have plenty to choose from. There are 1,700 skin creams alone, advertised with slogans such as "Don't deny it, defy it" and "Lie about your age. Hide the evidence." The woman is exhorted to go to war with her own body, to "fight," "resist," and "outwit" aging.

These messages are directed most strongly to white middle-class and affluent women. Research suggests that the most privileged women are most concerned about their appearance and most invested in treating their body as an improvement project, while working-class women regard their body more in terms of how well it functions (Calasanti & Slevin, 2001).

The number of cosmetic surgery procedures performed in the United States has increased greatly since the 1990s. Medical techniques such as Botox (injections of a neurotoxin that paralyzes facial muscles) are marketed at parties, and women are encouraged to have them every few months to avoid the dreaded appearance of facial lines. TV programs such as *The Swan* and *Extreme Makeover* are raising the bar, justifying even the most radical, gruesome, and painful surgical procedures in the quest for perfect (youthful) features. Cosmetic surgery is expensive and usually not covered by health insurance; it carries risks of disfigurement and death; and it must be repeated periodically to maintain the effect. The increasing demand for cosmetic surgery suggests that feminism has had little impact on attitudes about aging. As Botox-stiffened and surgically tightened faces become the norm, the less we will know of the real range and variety of aging faces (Cruikshank, 2003).

Some women respond to the pressure to maintain a youthful appearance by opting out at midlife. If society is saying that they must do what they manifestly cannot do (be slim, smooth-skinned, and young), they choose not to participate in the game of objectification. Instead, they wear relaxed clothes and comfortable shoes, defining a feminine appearance in terms of ease and freedom of movement (see Figure 12.5). Author Carolyn Heilbrun quipped that she was glad when she reached 50 because she could stop wearing drag.

Exercise, Sport, and Fitness

One of the most important factors in maintaining good health in the second half of life is regular exercise. The many benefits of exercise are both psychological (mood stability, energy levels) and physical (lowering the risk of life-threatening conditions such as diabetes, high blood pressure, obesity, and heart disease). Exercise relieves hot flashes and arthritis pain, maintains strength and posture, strengthens the immune system, benefits thinking and memory, and improves skin tone. In the elderly, exercise helps prevent the loss of muscle tone that causes falls, broken bones, and permanent disability. "Scientific evidence definitely proves the benefits of exercise for older people," including not only those who are already fit but those who have been sedentary for years and even those in their 90s (Cruikshank, 2003, p. 70; BWHBC, 1998).

In every age group, women exercise less than men. This gender difference may be related to socialization and to the fact that women have less leisure time. Women's lower incomes also contribute to the difference because they are less likely to have money for gym memberships, sports equipment, and active vacations. Lack of exercise contributes to the high rate of debilitating conditions among older women; it is estimated that regular exercise could cut the age-related decline in physical functioning by half (Canetto, 2001).

Fortunately, it is never too late to start exercising. Physicians in the past often responded to older people's reports of weakness, lack of energy, and poor stamina by saying, "What do you expect, at your age? Get used to it." However, strength training can not only delay but actually reverse the process of muscle loss. Pioneering studies at Tufts University showed that men in their 60s and 70s gained 100 to 175 percent in muscle strength after 12 weeks of a high-intensity strength-training program. The research program was then extended to women and men who were nursing-home residents ranging in age from 86 to 96. In eight weeks, these frail

FIGURE 12.5

Source: Copyright © The New Yorker Collection, 2004, Roz Chast, from cartoonbank.com. All rights reserved.

elders increased their strength on average by 175 percent. Their walking speed and balance greatly improved. Later studies recruited healthy postmenopausal women, also with dramatic results: After a one-year program, the exercise group, compared to a no-treatment control group, gained bone density; improved their balance; lost inches; and became more active, energetic, and physically flexible (Nelson, 2000).

Given the strong and consistent evidence that exercise is key to health and well-being in the second half of life, one might expect that the health-care system would be sponsoring many programs and providing many opportunities for older people to become more active. This is not the case. Instead, exercise programs, where they exist at all, are often small, short-lived, and underfunded, lasting only until a grant runs out (Cruikshank, 2003).

Women are taking matters into their own hands to foster fitness. The National Black Women's Health Project, prompted by the lower life expectancy and higher rates of heart disease, diabetes, and breast cancer among African American women, sponsors Walking for Wellness (www.blackwomenshealth.org). This program has been going on since 1990 and has inspired over 12,000 women to incorporate walking into their lives.

Sexuality in Middle and Later Life

Visualize an old woman wearing a miniskirt. What is your first reaction to this image? What reaction do you think your friends would have?

A miniskirted old woman is deviant because she dares to appear sexual past her reproductive years (Calasanti & Slevin, 2001). Sexuality and sexual activity in older people are widely considered disgusting or ridiculous, and this is conveyed in jokes and stories (see Figure 12.6). However, even these are gender biased—there are plenty of approving jokes about "dirty old men" and Viagra, but an immense cultural silence about the sexuality of older women.

Older adults have been almost entirely neglected in the sex research described elsewhere in this book. In the Hite Report on women, only 19 out of over 1,800 participants were over 60. Most recently, the NHSLS report, an otherwise excellent national survey, excluded men and women over 60. However, medical and behavioral studies show that many old people desire and are capable of enjoying sexual intimacy. The biggest factors influencing sexual activity and interest in older people are age, health, past sexual activity and enjoyment, and the availability of a partner (Calasanti & Slevin, 2001).

Gender Ratios and Gendered Norms

Because women live longer than men, the gender ratio at age 65 is 149 women for every 100 men. By the age of 85, there are 259 women for every 100 men (Hatch, 1995). Moreover, women tend to marry men older than themselves. For both these reasons, heterosexual women are likely to spend the last decades of their lives without a marital or sexual partner (Fields & Casper, 2001). African American women are twice as likely as White women to be divorced, separated, or widowed in later life and have even lower chances of remarrying because of early mortality among African American men (Ralston, 1997).

Opportunities to remarry are limited not just because of a numerical shortage of men, but because available men usually choose younger partners. It is socially acceptable for older men to enter relationships with women many years younger than they are. In a recent TV example, 60ish Detective Andy Sipowicz (*NYPD Blue*) married a woman in her 30s and soon fathered a child; in movies, Jack Nicholson (60) has been romantically paired with Helen Hunt (34), and Michael Douglas (53)

"See that man sitting right over there? He gives me fever."

FIGURE 12.6

with Gwyneth Paltrow (25). In contrast, older woman/younger man relationships are much less common, both in the media and in real life.

Older Lesbians

> Now in my 50s, I am 18 years into what I hope will be a lifelong relationship with a woman. Sex for us is a steady friend. During our busy work week, we cuddle and that's good. On weekends and on vacations, we make time for lovemaking and cherish how it reconnects and refreshes us. (BWHBC, 1998, pp. 563–564)

There has been very little research on sexuality among older lesbians and bisexual women. Among older cohorts, women who have had lifelong emotional attachments to other women often do not use the word *lesbian* to describe themselves and may not be included in research. In one survey that included 119 self-identified lesbians and bisexual women with an average age of 68, about half the women were currently living with a partner. Compared with those who lived alone, those living with a partner reported better mental health, higher self-esteem, and less loneliness (Grossman, D'Augelli, & O'Connell, 2001). Although this study did not assess sexual activity directly, it demonstrates the importance of long-term intimate relationships in these older women's lives.

BOX 12.1 ❧ Sex and the Senior Citizen

"Before I turn 67—next March—I would like to have a lot of sex with a man I like. If you want to talk first, Trollope works for me." Jane Juska, a retired English teacher, placed this personal ad in the *New York Review of Books* in the fall of 1999. She writes in her book which chronicles this experience, *A Round-Heeled Woman: My Late Life Adventures in Sex and Romance*, "At age sixty, I had put myself out to pasture after thirty-three years of thriving on a live audience: 150 kids during the day and one feisty son at night. So I was okay. Except there was no one for me to touch and no one to touch me." Breaking from the stereotype that older women are void of desire or are not sexual beings, Juska took matters into her own hands and sought what she wanted: Sex. One may argue that Juska is falling into the trap of "needing a man" to find happiness. However, she writes that her life is very rich with her family, friends, hobbies, and work, but that she also wanted passion. Yet finding sex at an older age is difficult because of the lack of men in her age group and the idea that an elder woman does not need or want sex. In our culture, a double standard exists in which men can be older and still distinguished and sexy (i.e., Sean Connery) whereas, after menopause, women are seen as sexually "over the hill." It could be said that Juska reclaimed what was rightfully hers—her sexuality—and has paved the way for other older women to become sexual agents. Juska serves as a reminder that one can have gray hair, bifocals *and* sexual desires.

Source: Witchell, A. (2003, April 27). Sex and the single senior. *The New York Times*, p. 9.1. Contributed by Meghan Deveau.

Sexual Activity and Satisfaction

Due to both skewed gender ratios and social norms, fewer older women than older men are sexually active (Grambs, 1989; Öberg, 2003). The gender differences in sexual attitudes and behavior may be partly due to age cohort; men who are now in the 65-and-up age group were allowed much more sexual freedom in their younger years than women were at the time. As more recent cohorts age, these women may have very different attitudes. Still, some things are slow to change, as this woman points out:

> I'm no longer worried about pregnancy; the children are gone; my energy is released. I have a new surge of interest in sex. But at the same time the culture is saying, "You are not attractive as a woman; act your age. . . ." It's a terrible bind for a middle-aged woman. (BWHBC, 1998, p. 563)

Although there are still many taboos, women are beginning to speak about and reclaim their sexuality at midlife and beyond. (See Box 12.1.)

Relationships: Continuity and Change

There is much more to the second half of life than changes in the physical self. Midlife is often a time of major changes in relationships with partners, friends, and family. Children grow up and leave home. Grandchildren are born. A husband may become dependent on his wife for daily help and care. Here we look at some important relationships for women in middle and later life.

Friends and Family

Older women tend to be involved with rich networks of friends and family. Compared to men in the same age group, they have more friends and feel closer to their friends (Canetto, 2001). Women friends, in particular and friends who have been close for a long time provide companionship and support for older women (Adams, 1997). Close friends may be particularly important for older lesbians; in one recent study of lesbian and bisexual women in their 60s, friends were named as the number one source of support (Grossman et al., 2001).

Consistent with their extended family patterns, African American women are more involved with family than are European American women. Older Black women are closer to their adult children and have more frequent contact with them than do older white women. They are also more involved with their grandchildren and may develop a particularly close guiding relationship with a granddaughter (Ralston, 1997).

For older women of all ethnic groups, relationship with sisters can be a vital source of social support. Sibling relationships are unique because of their long duration, similar family history, shared memories, and same age cohort. This was brought home to me when my mother-in-law Mary's younger sister died at the age of 83. Mary said sadly, "I knew her for 83 years; we went through life together." In studies of sibling relationships, sister-sister dyads are the most consistently rated as the most positive and intimate, whereas brother-brother dyads are more often hostile or distant (Scott, 1997). (The relative lack of closeness among older male siblings may be a late-life legacy of raising boys to be independent and competitive.) The positive quality of relationship between sisters in later life has been documented not only in the United States but also in Canada, Eastern and Western Europe, and Israel. Relationships with sisters may intensify in old age, after a woman is widowed. Having a sister nearby is related to life satisfaction and mental health in old age (Scott, 1997).

Involvement with friends and family has costs as well as rewards. Like the younger women discussed in Chapters 9 and 10, older women provide more care and more different kinds of care for other people than older men do, regardless of whether they also work outside the home (Canetto, 2001). We will return shortly to a discussion of the costs and benefits of care work.

Becoming a Grandmother

The grandmother is one of the few positive images of older women. She is easy to visualize: White haired, kindly, and warm, she dishes out homemade cookies, babysits for free, and indulges her grandchildren. Even Barbara Bush took advantage of the image by calling herself "everyone's grandmother."

Adapting to a New Role

Grandparenting gives midlife and older women a meaningful and important place in their families. Grandmothers are often relied on for advice, babysitting, help in a crisis, emotional support, financial assistance, and maintaining family customs and rituals. All these provide an important cushion for young families. For the grandparents, it can be very satisfying to see the family line continue and to once again experience the love of a small child (Scott, 1997). (See Figure 12.7.) However, becoming a grandmother is an involuntary role change. Its meaning and its effects on women's lives are more complex than its image suggests.

FIGURE 12.7
The benefits of being a grandmother.

A woman may become a grandmother at any time from her 30s to her 70s. The timing of grandparenthood is an important factor in how women adapt to this new role. Younger grandmothers may not be ready:

> When my daughter called me from Florida to tell me I was now a grandmother, I was not in the least elated. I had recently remarried and was seeing myself as a young, passionate lover. I didn't want to think of myself as a grandmother. (Doress-Worters & Siegal, 1994, pp. 139–140)

A grandmother who is still working full-time may have little spare time to be involved with babies and young children. Cohort effects are important, too. Baby-boom grandmothers may lead active lives that leave little time to be a traditional grandma (Scott, 1997).

Because the role expectations for grandmothers are so strong, some grandmothers feel the need to set limits. For example, in a study of middle-age Chicanas, one woman said about being a grandmother, "I love it, but I'm not the kind of grandma where I'm going to sit down and only knit little things." Another said that she would help out when needed, but not "stay home and take care of children so (the daughter) could have a good time . . . grandparents have the right to be free and enjoy themselves when they're old" (Facio, 1997, p. 343). These women recognized that a grandmother's caregiving may be taken for granted, and they insisted on the right to define grandparenthood for themselves.

Ethnicity, Social Class, and Grandmothers' Roles

A woman's ethnicity is a key determinant of how she will experience her grandmotherly role. Among Native American families, the grandmother is the center of the family and the one who holds it all together. Native American women often become grandmothers at a young age, and this transition is seen more even more important than becoming a mother because of the symbolic responsibilities it carries. Relationships between grandmother and grandchildren are characterized as very warm and loving, and the grandmother is not just a caregiver but a storyteller and teacher who passes on tribal knowledge to the next generation. In Native American communities, it is not unusual for a child to ask to live with his or her grandparents, and the request is usually granted (John, Blanchard, & Hennessy, 1997).

In African American communities, too, extended multigenerational families offer scope for grandparental involvement in grandchildren's daily lives. The greater contact and involvement of black grandparents holds even when socioeconomic status is controlled, implying that it is a cultural difference rather than an economic one (Ralston, 1997).

Due to divorce, as well as HIV/AIDS and drug epidemics in poor and minority communities, increasing number of grandparents are taking primary responsibility for grandchildren. Some grandmothers provide full-time day care for working single moms; others take in their grandchildren and raise them, with or without legal custody. Women in ethnic minority groups are much more likely than European American women to have primary responsibility for one or more grandchildren. The number of grandparent-headed households increased 53 percent in the 1990s, and about 6 percent of all children now live in such households. More than 75 percent of all grandparents raising children are women; almost half do not have a spouse; and over half are above the age of 55 (Calasanti & Slevin, 2001). Many grandmothers who became full-time caregivers report that it was a nondecision; faced with grandchildren whose parents were incapacitated by drug addiction, physical illness, or mental disability, the grandmother's attitude was "you do what you have to do" (Scott, 1997).

Over 57 percent of grandmother-alone households are poor (Calasanti & Slevin, 2001). Women in this situation have multiple stressors that detract from physical health, emotional well-being, and financial security (Scott, 1997). They report more depression and poorer physical health than other grandparents (Calasanti & Slevin, 2001). Grandmothers bringing up children often mourn their dreams of financial security and freedom in later life. These women are unsung heroes who give to the next generation, often at their own expense:

> I was in my late 30s and my other children were all in high school when one of my daughters developed a drug problem, and I had to take her two little ones to raise. I was afraid I couldn't do it. I thought I was done raising kids, and they were babies! But I felt it was my responsibility because they were my blood. I didn't want them to go to foster care . . . I raised them both . . . and they still call me Ma . . . I am proud that both of my grandkids are doing well now, and that I was able to raise them. (BWHBC, 1998, p. 553)

Caregiving: Its Costs and Rewards

As discussed in Chapters 9 through 11, women provide a great deal of work in caring for others. Much of this work is invisible and undervalued. Women's care work does not stop when their children are grown. As I have just noted, many women step in and become primary parents to their grandchildren. I turn now to other aspects of women's care work in middle and later life.

Caring for Elderly Parents

The great majority of caregivers to the old—about 75 percent—are women. This is true across all ethnic groups except Asian Americans, where men are almost as likely to be care providers for elderly parents as women are (Calasanti & Slevin, 2001).

Women who take responsibility for elderly parents, in-laws, and other relatives are often called "women in the middle" because they are most often in their middle years; they are the middle generation in their families; and they are caught in the middle between the requirements of being a wife, parent, worker, and care giver (Brody, 2004). They are also in the middle of conflicting values, because society currently tells them that women should work outside the home, yet traditional values still prescribe care work as their responsibility.

Women in the middle are a very diverse group in ethnicity and social class as well as in other ways. Some have young children of their own; others are in their 70s. Their numbers and their problems have been virtually ignored by society until quite recently.

There is more and more need for care work for the elderly because their numbers are increasing. According to national surveys, about 17 percent of people over 65 have some form of disability that requires long-term help from others (Brody, 2004). What kind of help do older people need? Those with disabilities may need assistance with basic personal care, such as getting in and out of bed, bathing, dressing, eating, and toileting, as well as help with life tasks such as cooking, housework, shopping, transportation, and money management.

Most women who care for elderly relatives do the job willingly and derive many benefits from it: satisfaction from fulfilling a big responsibility, following religious teachings, expressing their love, and returning care received from the parent in the past, as these two daughters express:

> I never regret caring for her. She's the only mother I have. (Brody, 2004, p. 118)

> He (her father) gave me so much and so caringly, and so completely. There's no way there's too much I could be doing. It's not an exchange. He just deserves it. (Brody, 2004, p. 137)

However, care work takes a toll on a woman's psychological well-being, physical health, family relationships, lifestyle, and career. Of all these negative effects, symptoms of emotional strain are the most prevalent. In study after study, caregivers report depression, anger, anxiety, guilt, feelings of helplessness, and emotional exhaustion (Brody, 2004).

Women often try to enlist others in helping with care work, but with limited success. One husband rigged up buzzers so that his wife could respond immediately whenever his 95-year-old mother called from her upstairs room—but did not offer to respond himself. Another women, desperately needing a respite, sent her mother to her sister's house for a visit, but reported that "after a couple of weeks, my brother-in-law put her in a taxi back to us" (Brody, 2004, p. 105). Although some family members do share care, it is most often left to a daughter who is perceived as suitable by others—or who is the only one who offers.

Caring for a Spouse

Because women marry men older than themselves and men have shorter life expectancies, it is highly likely that the husband in a heterosexual couple, rather than the wife, will receive spousal care during his old age and final illness (Calasanti & Slevin, 2001). Our society assumes that old women will be responsible for their even older husbands. The older a married woman is, the more likely she will take on the physical and emotional work of elder care despite health problems of her own.

Lucy's story is typical of a white, working-class caregiver:

"Her husband is bedridden and his entire care is left up to her. She feels tremendous pressure from this responsibility, and she attributes her heart problems to it. Inadequate finances, approximately $500 a month for the two of them, also contribute to her unhappiness. . . ." At 74, Lucy wishes she were still working not just because she needs the money but also because she needs to get out of the house. She told an interviewer that her only trips outside the home were to the doctor, the pharmacy, and the grocery store. "Honey, I haven't been in a store downtown for years." (Calasanti & Slevin, 2001, p. 136)

Caring for an elderly spouse can be heartbreaking when it involves prolonged deterioration of physical or mental abilities. One woman, Sara, spoke of her concerns in a support group for Alzheimer's caregivers:

Can I ever finally close him out of my life and say, "Well, it's done. It's over. He's gone"? How do I really know that the poor man isn't hidden somewhere, behind all that confusion, trying to reach out and say, "I love you Sara"? (Faircloth, 2004, pp. 217–218)

Lesbian couples have similar experiences of care work as heterosexual couples do, but they may also have to cope with heterosexist treatment that adds to their stress. Getting help for a partner may mean coming out about the relationship, and the partner's relatives may withhold help because they do not approve of the relationship (Hash, 2001).

Why Do Women Do More Care Work?

Care work penalizes employed women who are forced to cut back their work hours, turn down promotions, or retire early. Not only do they lose wages directly, but they suffer long-term economic losses because their retirement pensions and Social Security benefits are affected. In one survey, researchers estimated that the lifetime cost of care work for a woman was well over half a million dollars in lost wages and retirement benefits (Brody, 2004). This huge sacrifice on the part of women is taken for granted by society.

Given its psychological and economic costs, why do women continue to do care work, even into their old age? Some psychologists and sociologists have argued that women do more care work because nurturing is more central to their identity. Others have said that women have less attachment to their paid work and therefore are freer to do unpaid work. However, research shows that personality makes little difference in who gets assigned care work, and over half of female caregivers keep on working despite their caregiving responsibilities (Martire & Stephens, 2003).

Care work is not just a free choice. Rather, responsibility for caring for the ill, especially the elderly, is structured by the gender-based division of labor in families, the devaluing of unpaid work, and the reluctance of society to provide social services for those in need. Paid care is too expensive for most families, and federal funding has been cut back over several decades. As one researcher said, women's lifelong devotion to taking care of others "may seem 'natural' and a 'choice,' but what are the alternatives?" In the words of female caregivers themselves, "Who else is going to do it?" (Calasanti & Slevin, 2001, p. 149).

Work and Achievement

For women who are socioeconomically privileged, midlife can be a very positive and fulfilling time. Moreover, women in recent age cohorts are likely to be invested in multiple roles as partner, mother, and paid worker, and having multiple roles is associated with better psychological adjustment. Is midlife the prime of life for (some) women?

Women in Their Prime

Several studies have shown that for college-educated women midlife typically is a time of self-confidence, achievement, and happiness. A sample of Canadian women between the ages of 45 and 65 described themselves as satisfied with themselves and their accomplishments and optimistic about growing older (Quirouette & Pushkar, 1999). Samples of U.S. women show similar results. For example, in a longitudinal study, women's positive identity and self-confidence in their personal power increased from their 20s to their 60s. A woman's belief that she was contributing to the world and caring for the next generation increased up to midlife and then leveled off (Zucker, Ostrove, & Stewart, 2002).

In another study of college graduates between the ages of 26 and 80, women in their early 50s had the highest life satisfaction. Compared with other age groups, both older and younger, these midlife women had fewer child-care responsibilities, better health, and higher income. They were self-confident and involved in the world (Mitchell & Helson, 1990). The researchers suggested that women's prime time of life is their 50s.

For some women, midlife is a chance to explore new career directions or return to school. Psychological theories of personality development have overlooked this sort of developmental pathway because they have largely been based on a (white middle-class) male norm of completing education and investing heavily in a career during young adulthood. For women, the stimulus for making a change varies. For some, the death or serious illness of a friend or family member who is near their own age prompts the realization that time is limited and that it is important to make the most of it. For other women, divorce is the catalyst for forging a new path. Still

FIGURE 12.8
For some women, midlife is a time to achieve long-postponed goals.

others, relieved of child-care responsibilities for the first time, decide to follow a long-postponed dream:

> All my life I had wanted to be a nurse but instead was a secretary. Finally, at age 57, when the youngest of our children graduated from college, I took a year from the workaday world to attend school and become a licensed practical nurse. I made the highest grade in our class on the state board exam. (BWHBC, 1998, p. 552)

Midlife patterns of change vary by socioeconomic class. Women from poor or working-class backgrounds often experience health problems sooner than more advantaged women do because they do more physically demanding and hazardous work and have poorer health care. For these women, slowing down, not speeding up, may be a major midlife goal (BWHBC, 1998). However, for others, education becomes an important means of redefining the self. Some of the most hard-working and dedicated college students are older working-class women who are making up for the education they could not afford at 18 (Cruickshank, 2003). Education can be a lifelong process (see Figure 12.8).

Retirement

Psychological theories of retirement among men conceptualize it as a major life change. The retiree's social status, power, and income drop. His daily activities and interpersonal interactions change drastically as he gains large amounts of free time but loses daily contact with co-workers.

This model of retirement is a poor fit for women (Calasanti & Slevin, 2001; Canetto, 2001) for several reasons. Until quite recently, very few women had the kinds of jobs that provide high status, power, and income. Retirement for women more often meant leaving low-status work and subordinate positions. Furthermore, women, more often than men, make the decision to retire because of events unrelated to work itself: A husband retires and pressures his wife to do so, or someone in the family needs care. And many low-income workers must keep working as long as possible to make ends meet. Often, low-income women work "off the books" into their old age, without accumulating pensions or benefits (Cruikshank, 2003).

When women, especially working-class women, retire from paid work, their total workload may not change a great deal because of all the unpaid work they do. For a woman who is caring for her elderly parent, cooking and cleaning for her husband, and babysitting for active grandchildren, retiring from her job may make little difference. In fact, her unpaid work may expand. As one woman said in an interview, she liked being retired because "Now I got time to do my work" (Calasanti & Slevin, 2001, p. 130).

When a man retires, he rarely does more work around the house unless his wife becomes severely disabled. When men speak of the freedom of retirement, they mean not having to go to the office or report to a supervisor. Women, in contrast, describe the freedom to do the laundry at any time of day. However, this may be most true for white couples; African American families appear to be more flexible than white families in midlife gender roles (Calasanti & Slevin, 2001).

Divorced or never-married women tend to work longer than married women, probably because they cannot afford to retire as early. There has been very little research on retirement among gay and lesbian individuals or couples. In one recent study, lesbian couples had a lower average income before retirement than gay male, heterosexual married, or heterosexual cohabiting couples. However, they reported doing the least financial planning for retirement of any of the groups (Mock, 2001). Lesbians are more likely to have been continuously employed through their adult years than heterosexual women, but their long years of work may not lead to a financially secure retirement (Kitzinger, 2001).

In the media's images, retirees are eager consumers of travel and leisure products—healthy, smiling seniors cycling country roads, going on cruises, and sipping wine in outdoor cafes. The reality may differ. Retirement is part of wider sociocultural patterns of economic advantage and disadvantage. "Retirement is not simply leisure, the early bird special, and senior discounts on Tuesday; it is a mechanism for income reduction" (Cruikshank, 2003, p. 130). And it is a mechanism that is biased by age, gender, and social class—one that may maintain and even magnify the gender hierarchies of young adulthood.

Vulnerabilities of Middle and Later Life

Loss of a Life Partner

In the United States today, there are 8.5 million widowed women over 65, and about 2 million widowed men (Brody, 2004). The widowhood rate is higher for African American women than for other ethnic groups (Bradsher, 1997). The average widow lives for more than 15 years after her partner's death (Canetto, 2001).

Losing a spouse to death is one of life's most difficult experiences. However, women seem to cope with this loss better than men do. Although they report high levels of emotional pain and distress, they have less severe depression and fewer serious physical health problems than men in similar circumstances. They are less likely to abuse alcohol, suffer a heart attack, or commit suicide following the death of a spouse (Canetto, 2001; Stroebe, Stroebe, & Schut, 2001).

The gender difference in coping with spousal loss may be due to several factors. First, women have better-developed support networks than men; widows typically rely on close friends, children, and grandchildren throughout the grieving process. Second, men who lose a wife lose a caregiver, whereas women who lose a husband usually have been providing work on his behalf. Finally, women may cope better because widowhood occurs at a younger age than for men and "women expect to spend part of their lives as widows" (Canetto, 2001, p. 187). It is sad but true that almost every woman over 60 knows others her age that have been widowed and to some degree may mentally prepare for becoming a widow.

When older women are widowed, they are much less likely to remarry than widowed men in their age group. One result is that older women are increasingly likely to live alone. Loneliness and isolation are potential problems for widows; however, for many, living alone is a positive choice, bringing independence and freedom from care work (Canetto, 2001).

As with all aspects of growing older, ethnicity and social class shape different experiences of widowhood. Among Latina women, for example, a widow is expected to respect the memory of her marriage by refraining from sexual activity for the rest of her life and devoting herself to taking care of others. *La abuela* is asexual; to be otherwise is shameful (Facio, 1997). However, some Latinas resist this form of social control. Maria G. has been widowed for 10 years and has a "friend" despite her daughter's disapproval:

> Your kids think that once you're old, you're dead or something. They get very jealous. And the first thing they say is, "What about my father?" Well, what about their father, he's dead, may he rest in peace, but I'm not! (Facio, 1997, p. 346)

Little is known about partner loss in lesbian couples. Although lesbians have an advantage in that their partner is likely to live longer, coping with the loss of a lesbian life partner is made more difficult by heterosexism (Cruikshank, 2003). If the couple has not been "out" to friends and family, the grief may have to be borne alone. Others do not recognize that the friend who died was more than just a friend. This deprives the surviving partner of the support network that helps heterosexual women cope with bereavement.

Poverty

Poverty in old age may reflect the accumulation of a lifetime of gender-linked inequities. Women now in old age have earned less than men for their work and are far less likely to have held the kinds of jobs that provide pensions. They have probably taken time out from paid work for child raising or worked part-time. For every year a woman works taking care of her children, her spouse, or her elderly family members, a zero is entered into her Social Security account, unless she has done over 35 years of paid work. "Defining an older woman's caregiving years as 'zero years' is blatant gender discrimination. Women are penalized for doing the work society expects of them" (Cruikshank, 2003, p. 128).

About two-thirds of all poor older adults in the United States are women, and the majority of these are ethnic minority women (Canetto, 2001). Poverty among old women is a problem in less-developed nations due to sex discrimination in education, employment, and access to wealth such as land and inherited property. However, the United States is alone among industrialized nations in having large numbers of old women living in poverty. In Sweden, France, and the Netherlands, the poverty rate of old women living alone is less than 2 percent; in the United States, it is 18 percent (Cruikshank, 2003).

Older married women are better off than single or widowed women of the same age because of their partner's economic resources. However, a middle-class woman who is relying on her husband's pension may slip into poverty as she ages. Often, savings are depleted during his final illness. His pension may end with his death, and her Social Security benefits drop. Older women living alone have a poverty rate five times higher than older men living alone (Canetto, 2001).

Social class makes a huge difference in the odds that a woman will be poor in her old age. Cruikshank (2003) illustrates the cascade of class-linked inequities:

> A middle-class professional woman in her twenties can afford to buy an IRA (retirement saving fund) each year, but the woman who cleans her office cannot. Forty-five years later, the former may have accumulated several hundred thousand dollars, the latter nothing. To acquire this wealth, all the first woman has to do is keep breathing. . . . Her husband has a secure job that will provide a pension. . . . The working-class woman's parents will probably need her caregiving help sooner. . . . In late life, home ownership is often the key to financial security, but when working-class people of color own a home, it may have declining value in an inner-city neighborhood. (pp. 116–117)

The plight of old women who are poor is not what anyone would look forward to in the last years of life:

> I try to buy the cheapest things. I always make my own milk from powder . . . If I need clothes I go across the street to the thrift shop. I watch for yard sales . . . If I have 80 cents I can go to the Council on Aging for a hot lunch. But the last two weeks of the month are always hard . . . I'm down to my last $10, and I've got more than two weeks to go. (A woman in her 70s, in Doress-Worters & Siegal, 1994, p. 192)

(See Box 12.2.)

Will future cohorts of women escape poverty in old age? Economists calculate that even today's working women face a steep climb to save enough money to cover basic living expenses in retirement. According to their computations, women now at the lowest income levels could not save enough no matter how soon they started or how hard they tried. More than a third of baby-boomer women will be single when they retire over the next few decades. In 2001, the median net worth of households headed by single women was $27, 850, compared to with $140,000 for households of married couples. Only 35 percent of single women had retirement accounts. The gender gap in retirement resources reflects the fact that women's lifetime earnings are still very much lower than men's (Duenwald & Stamler, 2004).

Elder Abuse

Violence against the elderly, termed **elder abuse,** may involve physical injury, emotional stress, sexual violence, neglect, and misappropriating the victim's possessions or money (Carp, 1997). Most of the harm caused by elder abuse is borne by women, and most elder abuse occurs when the older person lives with family members. Old

---

BOX 12.2 ∽ Victims of Poverty and Isolation

The number of older people living alone is on the rise, which is cause for concern because, for the elderly, living alone may mean living—and dying—in isolation. Because our society is so mobile (20 percent of the population moves every year), older people are commonly separated from their children and grandchildren.

The isolation of older people puts them in danger, particularly during natural crises, such as heat waves. During the heat wave in France in 2003, more than 11,000 people were left dead within the first two weeks of August, most of them elderly. In Chicago in 1995, more than 700 people died from the heat.

Most victims of heat waves are also poor, leaving them unable to afford air conditioners or, in some cases, the electricity to run them. Like officials in Chicago in 1995, the French government was slow to react to the heat crisis of 2003. But unlike Chicago and the rest of the United States, the French see this devastating number of deaths as a social issue. The country is even considering canceling one of its national holidays and using the increased tax revenue from wages to provide more money to care for the elderly.

In the United States, these types of deaths are usually attributed to natural disasters, acts of God,

or, in some cases, the failure of individuals to take care of themselves. In 1995, Chicago's commissioner of human services at the time, Daniel Alvarez, actually blamed the victims, calling them people "who die because they neglect themselves." A comment like that by a French official would probably cause uproar in the government, but in the States it was hardly noticed.

Some view the death of the elderly from causes such as a heat wave as an indication that it is time for these people to go—that this is a graceful way to pass. But what is graceful about dying a slow, agonizing death, only to be discovered by neighbors days later when an odor is noticed?

American society fails to address the poverty and isolation issues of older citizens, the majority of whom are women. Those with money are able to live in assisted-living centers, which are usually comfortable and may even be luxurious. But it is only those with money who have the privilege to entertain such an option, giving them a chance to live out their full lifespan.

Source: Adapted from Brock, F. (2003, September 14). Victims of heat. Victims of isolation. *The New York Times*, section 3, p. 8. Contributed by Michelle R. Kaufman, University of Connecticut.

---

people are reluctant to complain about abuse when complaining could mean losing their home, and family members are reluctant to report each other (Carp, 1997).

Elder abuse has much in common with other forms of intimate violence. It reflects patriarchal power imbalances; it takes place in private settings; and it is fostered by secrecy and the isolation of its victims (White et al., 2001). Like other forms of domestic violence, elder abuse can be chronic yet still remain a family secret.

Too few studies have been done to fully assess the prevalence of elder abuse, but one random-sample study in a northeastern city found that 2 percent of people over 65 had been physically abused by a caregiver (Pillemer & Finkelhor 1988). In other studies, estimates of abuse range from .5 percent to 32 percent. The higher estimates come from surveys of physicians, nurses, and social workers who report seeing cases of elder abuse among their patients (Carp, 1997).

Sexual abuse of old people is still largely a taboo topic, although it is beginning to receive attention. One study in the U.K. reported that the victims were female by a 6:1 ratio, and the perpetrators were usually family members, more often sons than husbands. Elderly women in nursing homes may be raped and sexually abused. Memory impairment and physical frailty in nursing-home residents make their victimization easy and prosecution unlikely (White et al., 2001). Although the overall risk of violence against women generally declines with age, those women who live into very old age, have significant physical or mental disabilities, or are dependent on others for survival are particularly vulnerable to all forms of elder abuse.

Making a Difference

Age is a dimension of life that is both biological and cultural. Physical, psychological, and social factors all interact to define a person's age and its meaning. Although aging and death are inevitable, poor quality of life in later years is not.

Transforming Society: Elder Activism

Social policy in the United States discriminates against older people, particularly older women, and political activism is an important route to change.

Because older people are an increasingly large proportion of the population, their political clout is growing. The proportion of the U.S. population over age 65 is increasing dramatically. At the beginning of the 20th century, older people made up about 4 percent of the population; by the year 2030, they will be 20 percent—some 70 million people. One researcher joked, "It will be Florida all over the country" (Dobrof, 2001). The oldest old are the most rapidly growing population of all. There will be 19 million people over 85 in the population by the year 2050 (Brody, 2004).

Activism on behalf of older people is definitely a women's issue, but it is particularly important for women of color. Table 12. 1 shows how many more years a person can expect to live once he or she reaches 65. You can see from the table that, in every ethnic group, women tend to live longer than men, but some groups are disadvantaged relative to others. African-American women have the lowest life expectancy of any group of women, probably due to the combined effects of racism and low socioeconomic status.

There are many organizations dedicated to political activism on behalf of people over 60. However, these organizations have sometimes treated the old as a gender-neutral group, ignoring issues of particular concern to women. Women's organizations have often focused on issues crucial to younger women, such as reproductive rights. Moreover, organizations dedicated to women's issues and those dedicated to older people's issues have sometimes failed to connect. Thus, the problems of aging women in our society are only beginning to be recognized and addressed.

TABLE 12.1   If You Are 65, How Much Longer Is Your Life Expectancy?

Race/Ethnicity	Men	Women
European American	16.1	19.2
African American	14.4	17.5
Hispanic	18.5	21.8
Asian/Pacific Islanders	18.8	22.9
American Indian	14.9	18.3

Data for each group reflects different years—American Indians 1993; Asian/Pacific Islander and Hispanics, 1997; European Americans and African Americans 1998.

Sources: Hendley and Bilimoria, 1999; John, 1999; U.S. Bureau of the Census, 2000. Adapted from Calasanti and Slevin, 2001, p. 31.

Maggie Kuhn is one example of a woman who has made a difference for older people. When she was forced to retire at the age of 70, Kuhn founded the multigenerational activist group now known as the Gray Panthers and became one of its most visible spokespersons. Kuhn was proud to be what she called "an elder of the tribe." When then-President Gerald Ford introduced her as a young lady, she stood up and said, "Mr. President, I am not a young lady. I've lived a long time. I'm an old lady" (Doress-Waters & Siegal, 1994, pp. 428, 439). Maggie Kuhn called upon young and old people to join together in working for a better world. When she died in 1995 at the age of 89, she left a thriving organization and a legacy of successful activism on issues such as forced retirement, pension rights, and nursing-home reform (Kuhn, 1991).

Activism on behalf of older women and men is likely to increase dramatically as baby boomers reach midlife and aging becomes personally relevant. This cohort grew up with the civil rights movement, the women's movement, and the peace and environmental movements. They are better educated than previous cohorts, they expect a higher standard of living, and they know that "the squeaky wheel gets the grease" when it comes to changing social policy. Moreover, thanks to pioneers like Maggie Kuhn, they have a well-established network of organizations already in place to educate and advocate for older people (see Box 12.3).

Transforming Social Interaction: Taking Charge of the Second Half

Among the current cohort of midlife women are some who are envisioning new paths for their later years. Women are more likely to be single, widowed, or divorced at midlife now than in previous cohorts, and such women are realizing that they cannot look forward to a spouse's companionship—or retirement benefits—in old age. Some women are choosing to live collectively with other women for companionship, mutual support, and economic benefits. This option builds on one of women's strengths, their lifelong bonds with women friends (Adams, 1997).

> ### BOX 12.3 ⁓ Resources for Activism
>
> There are many ways for you to become an activist on behalf of older women. Below are some national organizations committed to the social advancement of women, particularly issues of women's health and well-being later in life.
>
> www.blackwomenshealth.org
> *Black Women's Health Imperative:* An African American health education, research, advocacy, and leadership development institution. This organization is the leading force for health for African American women, promoting optimum health for black women across the lifespan—physically, mentally, and spiritually.
>
> www.graypanthers.org
> *Gray Panthers:* A national organization of intergenerational activists dedicated to changing social policy on issues such as peace, employment, housing, antidiscrimination (ageism, sexism, racism), and family security. Over the years, the Gray Panthers have stopped forced retirement at age 65, exposed nursing-home abuse, and worked towards universal health care.
>
> www.latinahealth.org
> *National Latina Health Organization:* Works toward the goal of bilingual access to quality health care and self-empowerment of Latinas through culturally respectful educational programs, health advocacy, outreach, research, and public policy.
>
> www.nsclc.org
> *National Senior Citizens Law Center:* Provides legal services support for poor senior citizens. Advocates to promote the independence and well-being of low-income elderly and those with disabilities.
>
> www.4woman.gov
> *National Women's Health Information Center:* A service of the Office on Women's Health in the Department of Health and Human Services, this Web site provides an array of women's health information and resources, including minority women's health.
>
> www.nwhn.org
> *National Women's Health Network:* Develops and promotes a critical analysis of health issues in order to affect policy and support consumer decision making.
>
> www.sageusa.org
> *Senior Action in a Gay Environment (SAGE):* World's oldest and largest organization devoted to meeting the needs of aging gay, lesbian, bisexual, and transgender elders.
>
> Contributed by Michelle R. Kaufman, University of Connecticut.

A recent *New York Times* article (Gross, 2004) profiled some women who are teaming up for old age. Christine P., a contractor in her 60s, built a house for herself and three friends to share, complete with exercise room and hot tub. Two other women in their mid-60s bought adjoining apartments in a city high-rise, planning to help each other enjoy life as long as they are able. I know one collective-living group that consists of one heterosexual married couple, one lesbian couple, and two single women. This group pooled their resources to buy a house in a warm climate; they designated private living space for each individual or couple, as well as shared space. Most of the group is not yet retired, but as incomes drop with retirement, they plan to pool the cost of helpers for the house and garden. Like other pioneers of the new collective living, this group consulted attorneys and drew up an agreement that protects individual financial assets. They also purchased long-term-care insurance individually so that they would not become burdens to each other.

There are no official statistics on how many older women are creating family-of-choice living arrangements, but interest in this option is growing rapidly. Baby boomer women often have previous experience of communal living and are used to controlling their own lives. Laura Young, executive director of the Older Women's League, commented, "We lived together in dorms and sororities. We shared apartments after graduation. We traveled together. We helped each other through divorce and the death of our parents. Why not take it to the next level?" (Gross, 2004, p. A1).

At present, the new collective living seems to be largely a middle-class trend. However, activists for the elderly have long pointed out that publicly subsidized housing usually is designed on the assumption that tenant will be either a married couple or a woman living alone. Why not have units for two women, designed with both private and shared space? (Cruikshank, 2003). Because friendship is so important to women, the quality of older women's lives may depend very much on being free to choose how and with whom they would like to live. The stakes are high, as women (and some men) seek to avoid isolation and poverty in old age.

Transforming Ourselves: Resisting Ageism

As members of an ageist society, none of us can claim to be completely free of ageism. However, we can try to analyze and resist it. How often do we stereotype old women? When we compliment someone by saying "you don't look your age" the implicit message is that if she did look her age it would be a misfortune. When we praise an older woman for being active or busy all the time, we are forgetting that young people do not have to stay frantically busy in order to be seen as worthwhile people. When you meet a person who says she is retired, do you think she has nothing much to talk about? Do you stay silent when someone uses the word *old* as a putdown?

Even stereotypes that seem positive can be harmful because they treat all members of the category as if they are alike and set standards for behavior. The media tend to pay attention only to seniors who run marathons or go bungee jumping, implying that older people who are not superbly healthy or incredibly active are somehow not aging successfully or productively. Another positive but perhaps insidious image is the wise elder stereotype. Not everyone who is old is wise! A better way to honor the old is to value them as individuals (Cruikshank, 2003).

The authors of an excellent resource book on women and aging (Doress-Worters & Siegal, 1994) spoke as older women in an ageist society:

> We proudly claim our age and experience as demonstrating our right to define who we are and what we need to live lives of dignity, activity, and involvement in our communities; decent health care and housing; an income sufficient to enjoy, rather than simply to endure, our later years; and the recognition that we are important members of society with much to contribute. (p. 439)

As a society, we owe no less to our elders.

Exploring Further

∽

Cruikshank, Margaret. (2003). *Learning to be old: Gender, culture, and aging*. Westport, CT: Greenwood Press.
As its title says, this book puts gender first in its analysis of aging. Its feminist perspective leads to many new insights about women's aging and many concrete suggestions for social change.

Delaney, Sarah Louise, Delaney, A. Elizabeth, et al. (1993). *Having our say: The Delaney sisters' first 100 years*. New York: Kodansha International.
At the ages of 101 and 103, two African American sisters talk about their lives as pioneering black professionals (a teacher and a dentist respectively). They are wise and funny, and their story recounts their triumphs over racial and gender inequities.

Friedan, Betty. (1993). *The fountain of age*. New York: Simon & Schuster.
Friedan, an influential second-wave feminist activist, was in her 70s when she wrote this insightful analysis of women's aging. Her passion for social change has not diminished with age.

PART 5

Gender and Well Being

CHAPTER 13

Psychological Disorders, Therapy, and Women's Well-Being

Chapter contributed by Britain Scott, Ph.D.

$\mathcal{R}$ead the title of this chapter. What do you think it means? Does it imply that women's disorders are cured by therapy, thereby enhancing their well-being? Not exactly. Does it suggest a simple list of topics that will be addressed in turn: first, women's psychological problems, then how to treat them, and then something about women's psychological health? Not quite. Replace *and* with *versus* and you'll get a better sense of the gist of much of this chapter. Before I discuss how feminist therapy contributes to women's well-being and how you can make differences in society and in yourself that do the same, I will first address the ways that traditional psychiatry and psychological practice have sometimes done the opposite. Topics include sexist bias in the diagnosis of disorders, the ways in which gender roles and stereotypes interact with our understanding of disordered behaviors, and some history of how psychiatrists have responded to women's nonconformist behavior by incarcerating or sedating them. After illustrating how traditional approaches to mental health have largely been less than woman-friendly, I will turn to a discussion of feminist alternatives.

Sexist Bias in Defining Disorders

In her autobiographical memoir *Girl, Interrupted*, Susanna Kaysen (1993) contemplates the etiology or causes of mental illness. She invites the reader to select from a list of explanations for atypical behavior, including that the person in question is "possessed," "a witch," "bad," "ill," "a victim of society's low tolerance for deviant behavior," and "sane in an insane world." Most of us living in the United States today would be unlikely to invoke demon possession or witchcraft as explanations for unusual behavior. We are much more comfortable with the idea of mental illness, which we now attribute to biological and social causes, rather than spiritual ones. We consider mental distress and disorders treatable and individuals suffering from them deserving of treatment. But how do we decide who is mentally ill and who is normal? As the last two explanations on Kaysen's list suggest, sometimes the decision depends not on the behavior itself, but on society's perception of that behavior.

The Social Construction of Abnormality

Normal is a relative term. We can define something as normal based on statistical probability. We could say, for example, that if it falls within a certain range of the population mean, then it is normal. This may seem like an objective way to define normality, but in everyday life we rarely know the statistical probability of a characteristic or behavior before we label it. And even when we do have a sense of the numbers, we are not necessarily guided by them. To use a nonbehavioral example, the average height of women in the United States is 5 feet 3.7 inches (National Center for Health Statistics, 2004); yet petite sizes begin at 5 ft 4 inches. Why are sizes for average women labeled with a special designation? Social factors (in this case, fashion industry standards) affect whether something that is statistically probable is considered normal.

Social factors also influence whether a behavior is statistically probable in the first place. Behaviors vary with culture and historical period. For example, tattoos and body piercing are much more common in urban industrialized settings today than they were just a couple of decades ago, or than they have been in traditional cultures around the world for thousands of years. Just 20 years ago, a waitress with a nose ring would have been considered abnormal by conventional standards, whereas today she may be seen as a bit alternative, or hip, but not so far outside the norm.

The norm itself is also determined by social factors such as the status and relative power of the persons making the judgment and the persons being judged. Those of dominant status in the population are in a position to designate what is normal and will likely define the norm in relation to themselves. In patriarchal societies such as the United States, there is a pervasive tendency to consider males the norm and females a special category (Tavris, 1992). This can have negative consequences for women. For example, our legal system employs a "reasonable man" standard to evaluate behavior in both civil and criminal cases. Battered women who have protected themselves and their children by attacking their batterers when the batterers were relatively defenseless (e.g., while asleep), have been unable to justify their actions as self-defense, because the reasonable man standard holds that self-defense only occurs spontaneously; the androcentric standard ignores the fact that many women are physically weaker than their batterers—and so will choose to act when they have a better chance of success—and are acting in response to long-term abuse (Raitt & Zeedyk, 2000; Zeedyk & Raitt, 1997).

Women's Behavior as Abnormal

In general, women have been labeled as the unreasonable and crazy ones in androcentric cultures. Feminine "madness" has been contrasted with masculine "rationality" in science, religion, literature, art, and humor (Showalter, 1986; Ehrenreich & English, 1973). Women have been called mad for challenging the limitations of a traditional feminine gender role, and they have experienced genuine psychological distress as a result of how this devalued role has limited their access to education, economic independence, sexual self-expression, and political power.

In psychology, the male-as-norm perspective has influenced researchers' and clinicians' views of women's behavior. In one of the first studies of gender stereotypes, practicing clinical psychologists were asked to choose the traits that characterized a healthy adult male and a healthy adult female (Broverman, et al., 1970). Their profiles of a healthy adult and healthy adult male matched each other and were discrepant from the healthy adult female. Until feminist scholarship gained a solid foothold in the discipline of psychology in the late 1970s, psychiatrists and psychologists routinely labeled women's behavior as disordered or deficient when compared to a male standard, and attributed the disorder to reproductive pathology and natural feminine frailty (e.g., Chesler, 1997; Ussher, 1992; Showalter, 1986).

A male-as-norm bias has permeated not only academic psychology, but pop psychology as well. Most advice columns and self-help books are aimed at

FIGURE 13.1
Photo that has circulated around the Internet accompanied by the tag line "Don't say we didn't warn ya!"

women. Women are told they have low self-esteem and are too emotional and too dependent—compared to whom? If *women* were the standard of comparison, would there be more self-help books for men, guiding them to temper their inflated self-esteem, develop sensitivity skills, and become less overly independent? Instead of women reading books about *Men Who Can't Love* and *Women Who Love Too Much*, might men read books about how to love as much as women do? Perhaps men would be the target audience for self-help books in general, instead of women constantly getting the message that they are the ones who need to change.

The Diagnostic and Statistical Manual (DSM)

The *Diagnostic and Statistical Manual of Mental Disorders (DSM)* is produced by the American Psychiatric Association for use by clinicians. It catalogs recognized disorders, listing them with background information and diagnostic criteria. Including the first *DSM*, published in 1952, there have been six versions (I, II, III, III-Revised, IV, and IV-Text Revision). Revisions have been necessary in some cases because of new research findings that have clarified known disorders or suggested new ones. Revisions have also occurred because of the subjective factors that influence judgments of normality, as described above. For example, until 1973, homosexuality was included in the *DSM* as a mental illness. Whether due to advances in research on sexual orientation, political pressure, or both, the American Psychiatric Association opted to exclude it from *DSM-III*. Activists for gay and lesbian rights interpreted this to mean that homosexuality had officially been declared normal (Caplan, 1995).

A "mental disorder," according to the *DSM-IV-TR*, is

> a clinically significant behavioral or psychological syndrome or pattern that occurs in an individual and that is associated with present distress (e.g., a painful symptom) or disability (i.e., impairment in one or more important areas of functioning) or with a significantly increased risk of suffering death, pain, disability, or an important loss of freedom. In addition, this syndrome or pattern must not be merely an expectable and culturally sanctioned response to a particular event, for example, the death of a loved one. Whatever its original cause, it must currently be considered a manifestation of a behavioral, psychological, or biological dysfunction in the individual. Neither deviant behavior (e.g., political, religious, or sexual) nor conflicts that are primarily between the individual and society are mental disorders unless the deviance or conflict is a symptom of a dysfunction in the individual, as described above. (p. xxxi)

Several of the terms in this definition are open to subjective interpretation. Who decides whether something is "clinically significant," a "syndrome," "an expectable and culturally sanctioned response," or a "symptom of dysfunction in the individual"?

Some feminist critics of the *DSM* have suggested that gender, race/ethnicity, and class all affect whether a behavior is tolerated from particular individuals within a given cultural context. They object to the sharp lines delineating normal from abnormal and distinguishing one disorder from another, claiming that such pigeonholing obscures the complex variability of behavior and its causes in a given social environment (e.g., Caplan, 1995). For example, at what point should a clinician conclude that a woman's unhealthy pattern of desperate dieting and depriving herself of adequate nutrition is an eating disorder? If a college student lives in a dorm where binging and purging are accepted and even encouraged as a reasonable way to respond to social pressure to be thin, is she suffering from bulimia nervosa if she joins in?

Another concern raised by critics of the *DSM* approach is that the manual has the potential to legitimize labels that have far-reaching implications, even when sound scientific support for the labels is lacking. For example, one of the appendices in the *DSM* lists provisional categories needing further study. Even though diagnostic labels in this appendix are pending, they may be applied by clinicians. Caplan (1995) tells an interesting story about a category that appeared in this appendix in *DSM-III-R*, but was excluded from *DSM-IV*. The category was called "self-defeating personality disorder (SDPD)." Caplan and others found the label extremely troubling for a few reasons: It would undoubtedly be applied nearly exclusively to women, the diagnostic criteria were characteristics commonly observed in women who have been victims of abuse, the category could be tied to Freudian tradition that labeled women masochistic by nature, and there was a marked dearth of empirical support for the category. Essentially, Caplan and

BOX 13.1 ∽ **Paula Caplan's Story of Self-Defeating Personality Disorder (SDPD)**

Diagnostic Criteria from the DSM-III-R:

1. You choose people and situations that lead to disappointment, failure, or mistreatment.
2. You reject offers of help.
3. You respond to good news or success with depression, guilt, or actions that produce pain.
4. You provoke others to reject or be angry with you, and then feel hurt, defeated, or humiliated.
5. You turn down opportunities for pleasure.
6. You are able to do well but you keep sabotaging your own objectives.
7. You reject people who treat you well; e.g., you are turned off by considerate sexual partners.
8. You like to play the martyr, sacrificing your own interests for others who do not solicit or need your help.

When the American Psychiatric Association began its work on DSM-IV, Paula Caplan and her graduate student Maureen Gans were working on a review of published and unpublished data relevant to SDPD. They volunteered their information to the work group that would be reviewing SDPD for the DSM-IV. Caplan and Gans had concluded that the category was unsubstantiated by research and should be excluded from the DSM-IV. Although the committee agreed that empirical support was lacking and decided not to move SDPD to the main body of DSM-IV, it appeared that they planned to tweak the criteria and retain the category in the appendix (Caplan, 1995). Then, in 1992, a series of events occurred that Caplan believes altered the course of SDPD.

Margaret Jensvold was a psychiatrist who claimed she had experienced sexual harassment and sex discrimination while working at the National Institutes of Mental Health (NIMH). She filed a lawsuit and also asked her boss to recommend a therapist for her to see. Ultimately, she learned that her boss was also the therapist's boss—though neither had mentioned that to her—and had recorded in his notes that Jensvold suffered from SDPD. This was potentially a perfect defense for those at NIMH accused of sexually harassing and discriminating against Jensvold: as Caplan puts it, "Her mental disorder made us do it!"

Jensvold went public with her case, bringing bad publicity to the NIMH and to SDPD. Shortly thereafter, the work group voted to exclude SDPD from the DSM-IV. Nothing had changed in terms of the empirical support—or lack thereof—for this category. The outcome in this case, removal of a questionable category, is one that feminists might applaud, but the case also suggests that the process of labeling is sometimes more political than scientific. In her 1995 book, *They Say You're Crazy: How the World's Most Powerful Psychiatrists Decide Who's Normal*, Caplan offers other examples that lead the reader to wonder what "disorder" will be created next for women.

others feared that this diagnosis could be used in clinical and legal contexts to blame women for their own victimization. See Box 13.1 for Caplan's story about SDPD.

Blaming Women for Distress and Disorders

When Sigmund Freud came to the United States in 1909 and delivered a series of lectures on his psychoanalysis, many progressive individuals were excited about his candid acknowledgment of human sexuality. Feminists thought his early ideas about female sexuality held promise and encouraged him to write more about women; however, when he did, many women were dismayed at his formulation of femininity. Freud defined female sexuality and the feminine personality in terms of their difference from a male norm. According to Freud, in the process of resigning themselves to their inferior genitalia, females develop specific feminine personality characteristics, including masochism (Freud, 1933). Masochism is defined as deriving pleasure from one's own pain.

The idea that women are masochistic caught on, perhaps because it provided a rationalization for women's subordinate status and the pain they experienced at the hands of abusive men; if women like to suffer, then there is no need to critically examine the circumstances that promote their suffering. Like-minded psychoanalysts embraced Freud's proposition, and so did many other psychiatrists and psychotherapists. The assumption that women are naturally masochistic leads logically to the conclusion that they bring their problems onto themselves by seeking out unhealthy relationships and damaging situations. Caplan (1985) relates a vivid example in her book *The Myth of Women's Masochism*,

> [A graduate student] had been doing an internship at a local hospital, seeing patients for psychotherapy. One of her patients was Sylvia, a woman whose first husband, after they married, had refused to have any sexual relationship with her at all and had also begun to beat her. They were soon divorced and, some time later, Sylvia married another man. While married to her second husband, she became bulimic, going on massive eating binges and then forcing herself to vomit until her throat began to bleed. [The supervising psychiatrist explained] that Sylvia was a masochist. "You see how beautifully her masochism works," he said. "When her first husband isn't there to beat her anymore, she *becomes* her first husband and forces herself to vomit until she bleeds. He's not there to hurt her, so she hurts herself." (p. 192)

Take a moment to engage in some critical thinking. What other explanations might there be for Sylvia's bulimia besides "she is a masochist"?

Women have been blamed for their own distress and disorders, and they have also been blamed for the distress and disorders of others around them. In particular, mothers have been blamed for the psychological problems of their children. The mother-blaming described in Chapter 10 has a long history. An early example appears in the book *The Borderland of Insanity*, published in 1875 in London. The author claimed that insanity is inherited from the mother twice as often as it is inherited from the father; however, he had no scientific evidence to support this assertion (Russell, 1995). In the United States, mother-blaming became fashionable within psychiatry and psychology and among the general public during and after World War II.

Mothers were considered responsible not only for the well-being of their own children, but for the health of society in general. One of the more popular authors to point the finger at mothers for society's problematic behavior was Phillip Wylie, who, in his 1942 book, *A Generation of Vipers*, put it this way,

Mom got herself out of the nursery and the kitchen . . . she also got herself the vote and, although politics never interested her (unless she was exceptionally naïve, a hairy foghorn, or a size forty scorpion), the damage she forthwith did to society was so enormous and so rapid that even the best men lost track of things. Mom's gracious presence at the ballot box was roughly concomitant with the start toward a new all-time low in political scurviness, hoodlumism, gangsterism, labor strife, thuggery, moral degeneration, civic corruption, smuggling, bribery, theft, murder, . . . financial depression, chaos, and war. (pp. 188–189)

Of course, it wasn't the mothers themselves that were engaging in antisocial behavior, but Wylie (and others) held them responsible. Wylie's hostile tirade continues with a description of the typical middle-aged, middle-class mother as a useless, repulsive, smothering, and manipulative drain on society whose demand for devotion from her son saps him of his masculine autonomy. The American man was a coddled, simpering, emasculated mother-worshiper, according to Wylie and his contemporaries.

This epidemic flight from manhood that mothers were supposedly causing was deemed especially severe among African Americans because of the Black Matriarchy (Buhle, 1998). African American men were criticized for being childlike, impulsive, manipulative, and irrational—and these characteristics were attributed to the fact that most African American families were headed by relatively economically independent working mothers. The role of systemic racism in shaping the behaviors of African American men—and in distorting perceptions of them—was overlooked by the mother-blamers.

During the post–World War II baby boom, mothering was elevated to the status of patriotic public service. Women had been called to the paid workforce while men were away fighting during both World Wars, and had often been the primary breadwinners while men were unemployed during the Great Depression between the wars. After World War II, women were encouraged (even pressured) to resume their place in the domestic sphere. The country as a whole was counting on population growth and scientific technology to restore the prosperity and progress that had been disrupted by the wars and the depression. In the home, science was applied not only through innovations in gadgetry, but also through expertise-based approaches to child rearing. Mothering was in the limelight, and mothers faced unprecedented scrutiny of their efforts. Women's magazines regularly featured authoritative warnings about the dangers of improper parenting, from sources such as the now legendary Dr. Benjamin Spock (Walker, 1998). More than ever before, physicians and psychologists emphasized the primary influence of mothers to raise psychologically healthy—or unhealthy—children.

Within the discipline of psychiatry, Wylie's smothering mother became the schizophrenogenic mother. Though not all theorists took an environmental stance on the etiology of schizophrenia, among those who did were several who pointed specifically to overprotective and domineering mothering (Hartwell, 1996). Mothers have been blamed for many other disorders as well by psychiatrists, psychologists, and social workers (Caplan & Hall-McCorquodale, 1985; Caplan, 2000). Dr. Edward Strecker, author of the mother-blaming book *Their Mothers' Sons: The Psychiatrist Examines an American Problem*, gave a lecture to 700 medical students at Bellevue Hospital in 1946 in which he identified various types of (unfit) mothers who were responsible for the nearly 2 million men found psychologically unfit to serve in World War II and for the 600,000 psychiatric discharges (Hartwell, 1996). Apparently, the depression and the horrors of a Second World War were not as compelling an explanation for these men's psychopathology.

Gender-Linked Psychological Disorders

Among the diagnostic labels used today, several are applied at different rates to women and men. The primary categories in which women are overrepresented relative to men are eating disorders, mood and anxiety disorders, and some personality disorders. On the other hand, women are underrepresented relative to men in diagnostic frequency for substance abuse disorders, some antisocial conduct disorders, and all of the sexual paraphilias. First we will consider some general reasons why these sex-related differences in diagnostic rates may exist, and then we will take a closer look at explanations for why specific disorders appear more often in women.

Why Are There Sex-Related Differences in the Rates of Some Disorders?

Before answering the question about why sex-related differences in rates exist, we must first consider the possibility that the reported sex ratios are inaccurate. Clinical samples are not random and may not represent the sex ratios in the general population (Hartung & Widiger, 1998). The samples employed in research studies on disorders also are typically nonrandom and nonrepresentative. When this is the case, the bias in sampling can lead to bias in the understanding of the disorder, which can then lead to bias in diagnostic criteria, which may lead to differences in application of the criteria—it is a vicious cycle. For example, what is now diagnosed as *somatization disorder,* characterized by the presence of physical symptoms with no known physical cause, was originally diagnosed as *hysteria,* which, literally translated, means "wandering womb" (Hartung & Widiger, 1998). The name of the disorder was changed, but the diagnostic criteria continued to include reproduction-related symptoms that applied only to women (e.g., irregular menstruation). In an effort to prevent diagnostic sex bias, the authors of the *DSM-IV* added what they considered a parallel set of symptoms for men (e.g., erectile dysfunction), *but this was not based on any research with men.* The current diagnostic criteria are based entirely on research with samples of all women and, therefore, may lead to more frequent diagnosis in women, whether or not the disorder actually occurs more often in women.

Assuming that at least some of the reported sex ratios in disorders are fairly accurate, it may be tempting to name biology as the source of the differences. It would be convenient to conclude, for example, that women get depressed because of their hormones and men develop sexual paraphilias because of theirs. Certainly, biological factors predispose some individuals to particular psychological disorders, but for the most part these factors are found in both women and men; for example, both women and men can have a genetic predisposition for depression. There is some evidence that the genetic and hormonal differences between the sexes may contribute to a few specific sex-related differences in disorders, such as the tendency for women with bipolar disorder to cycle more rapidly between bouts of depression and mania than men do (Leibenluft, 1996). Still, most sex-related differences in psychological disorders have thus far not been adequately accounted for by biological factors.

Some disorders may be diagnosed more frequently in women because women may be more likely to report their distress and seek help; help-seeking is more consistent with a feminine gender role than with a masculine one in our culture (e.g., Good, Dell, & Mintz, 1989; Addis & Mahalik, 2003). Some studies comparing women's and men's relative likelihood to seek psychological help have found that women report greater willingness (e.g., Johnson, 1988; Kessler, Brown, & Broman, 1981); however, the fact that some disorders are diagnosed more frequently in *men* suggests that even if women are typically more willing than men to seek psychological or psychiatric care, this is an inadequate explanation for all the observed sex-related differences in diagnosis frequency.

A careful examination of which disorders are diagnosed at significantly different rates in the sexes reveals a pattern consistent with traditional gender roles and gender stereotypes. For example, Rosenfield (2000) suggests that women's higher rates of *internalizing disorders,* where negative affect is turned inward, and men's higher rates of *externalizing disorders,* where negative behavior is expressed outwardly, are tied to gender socialization. Moodiness and fear are more characteristic of stereotypical femininity, whereas heavy drinking, aggression, and sexual expression are seen as more masculine behaviors.

Gender stereotypes may influence not only the contrasting behaviors that women and men exhibit, but the way the same behaviors are perceived and labeled differently when exhibited by a woman versus by a man. Therapists' own preconceptions about gender may color their interpretations of female and male clients differently, causing them to overdiagnose certain conditions in women and underdiagnose others. For example, given the same set of symptoms, clinicians may be more inclined to diagnose depression in women than in men (Potts, Burnam, & Well, 1991), or to diagnose a woman with "borderline personality disorder" and a man with "antisocial personality disorder" (Becker & Lamb, 1994). Stereotypes about women may lead to paradoxical diagnostic biases in that they will sometimes contribute to clinicians' misperception of psychopathology in women—because women are the crazy ones, and sometimes lead clinicians to overlook women's actual problems—because, after all, emotional distress is common in women, right? (Lopez, 1989; Robinson & Worell, 2002).

Finally, some disorders may be diagnosed more frequently in women because they actually occur more frequently in women—not because of biology, but because of gender roles and gender prejudice. For example, women may be more likely to develop eating disorders because of the strong link between femininity and appearance pressure (Martz, Handley, & Eisler, 1995). They may be more prone to other disorders, including depression and anxiety, because of gender-specific stressors such as sex discrimination and sexual violence. Support for this idea was found by

Klonoff, Landrine, and Campbell (2000) when they compared women and men on psychiatric symptoms, after collecting self-report data from the women regarding how frequently they had experienced sexist events, such as being called a sexist name (e.g., bitch, chick) or hearing sexist jokes. When *all* the women were compared to the men, the typical sex-related differences were in evidence: Women reported significantly more symptoms of anxiety, depression, and somatization; however, when level of exposure to sexist stressors was taken into account, only the women who had frequently experienced sexist stressors reported more symptoms than the men.

Which Disorders Are Diagnosed More Frequently in Women?

The disorders discussed next all are diagnosed at higher rates in women than in men. Although they are discussed separately, keep in mind that they are not unrelated to one another. These disorders commonly occur together; women who suffer from depression often exhibit anxiety disorders, eating disorders, and borderline and dependent personality disorders (Sprock & Yoder, 1997; Widiger & Anderson, 2003).

Depression

Women are twice as likely as men to suffer from **major depressive disorder** and two to three times as likely to experience the more long-lasting variant, **dysthymic disorder** (DSM-IV-TR). Both of these disorders are characterized by chronically low mood and disabling symptoms such as marked loss of interest in activities, appetite changes, sleep disruption, fatigue, inability to concentrate, and excessive negative thinking. The higher incidence of depression in women is first evident in adolescence and has been found cross-culturally (Weissman, et al., 1996). Explanations for higher rates of depression in girls and women have focused on many different factors, including genetics and hormones, cognitive styles, and external social factors such as discrimination, poverty, and violence.

Depression and other mood-related disorders have a genetic component. For example, individuals who inherit the tendency to have low levels of the neurotransmitter serotonin are more likely to suffer from depression than individuals with average levels of serotonin. Depression runs in families, but there is little support for the idea that the genetic predisposition for depression is passed down to women more than to men (Sprock & Yoder, 1997). Some recent research suggests that sex hormones may affect the availability and activity of relevant neurotransmitters and so may have an indirect effect on depression, but, in general, hormonal explanations are insufficient to fully account for the sex-related difference in depression (Kessler, 2003).

Many studies suggest that girls and women subjectively experience more negative life events than boys and men do (Hankin & Abramson, 2001). Cognitive explanations for the sex-related difference in depression suggest that girls and women, more so than boys and men, may then respond to these negative life events with thinking patterns that contribute to low mood. For example, women engage more than men in ***rumination,*** passively dwelling on distress, its causes and consequences, instead of actively distracting themselves or seeking social support (see Nolen-Hoeksema, 1995, for review). Rumination predicts depression. Nolen-Hoeksema and her colleagues suggest that women's tendency to ruminate more than men is tied to their subordinate social status. Women feel less control than men do over their life circumstances and emotions and yet more responsible for maintaining positive relationships with others; therefore, they worry rather than act (Nolen-Hoeksema, Larson, & Grayson, 1999; Nolen-Hoeksema & Jackson, 2001). The attributions people make to explain negative life events may also make them vulnerable to depression. Women, more so than men, tend to exhibit a hopeless style, attributing negative events to stable, global, internal causes instead of thinking, "Well, it's a one-time event, it's just one aspect of my life, and it wasn't my fault!" (Abramson, Metalsky, & Alloy, 1989; Hankin & Abrahmson, 2001).

FIGURE 13.2

Women's lower social status relative to men may predispose them to rumination, which is predictive of depression.

Although the *DSM-IV-TR* reports that the prevalence of depression appears to be unrelated to ethnicity, income, marital status, or education, many have suggested that these factors do, in fact, contribute to women's higher rates of depression, especially when they interact with sexism. Ethnic prejudice is a problem for both minority women and men, but when coupled with sexism, women find themselves in double jeopardy. Poverty is becoming a women's issue because an increasing proportion of people living below the poverty line are women and children. Poverty is correlated with depression, especially among mothers with small children (Belle & Doucet, 2003).

Another external factor that is predictive of women's depression is interpersonal violence (e.g., Campbell, Kub, Belknap, & Templin, 1997; Golding, 1999; Koss, Bailey, Yuan, Herrera, & Lichter, 2003). Child sexual abuse, rape, and battering are all associated with elevated levels of depression in women (Koss et al., 2003). Recent studies suggest that this is true for women from varied cultural backgrounds, including African American women (Banyard, Williams, Siegel, & West, 2002), Native American women (Bohn, 2003), and Chinese American women (Hicks & Li, 2003). Post-traumatic stress disorder and dissociative disorders, both associated with abuse, are also diagnosed more often in women, though this is not acknowledged in the *DSM-IV* (Hartung & Widiger, 1998).

Anxiety Disorders

Generalized anxiety disorder is somewhat more common in females than in males, but a more pronounced sex-related difference is found for panic disorder. *Panic disorder* is diagnosed when an individual has experienced repeated, unexpected periods of sudden intense fear or discomfort (accompanied by physical symptoms such as heart palpitations, dizziness, trembling, and a feeling of choking) followed by at least a month of worry about having another panic attack. Because these attacks can occur in public, it is not surprising that panic disorder is associated with *agoraphobia,* which is intense fear of being in places from which it might be difficult or embarrassing to escape (e.g., outside the home alone, in a crowd, traveling on an airplane) (*DSM-IV-TR*). Panic disorder without agoraphobia is diagnosed twice as often in women as in men, and panic disorder with agoraphobia is diagnosed three times as often in women (*DSM-IV-TR*).

Some explanations for the sex-related difference in diagnosis of agoraphobia focus on gender, suggesting, for example, that feminine socialization may contribute to women's greater fear of being in public spaces. Traditionally, girls and women have been encouraged to reside in the domestic, private sphere and discouraged from asserting themselves in the public sphere. Also, public places can be aversive for women due to the sex discrimination, sexual objectification, sexual harassment, and sexual violence that they may encounter. Other explanations for the sex-related diagnostic difference also focus on gender, but suggest that the difference may be an artifact: Perhaps men also fear public spaces, but, because of masculine gender role expectations that they boldly enter the arena of the public sphere, men may be unwilling to admit their fear and instead choose to mask it with coping behaviors such as drinking alcohol (see Bekker, 1996, for review).

In addition to agoraphobia, most other phobias are about twice as common in women as in men, but the sex ratios vary across phobia type. For example, 75 to 90 percent of individuals with natural environment and animal phobias are women (*DSM-IV-TR*). This is particularly interesting, given the long tradition in many cultures and religions of associating women more closely than men with nature as nurturers and creators of life (Merchant, 1995). Earth-based spiritual traditions honor earth goddesses and Mother Nature, yet women in the United States today are much more likely than men to exhibit an intense fear of nature. Perhaps the roots of women's natural environment and animal phobias lie in gender socialization that discourages girls from exploring wild places and accepting their natural physical selves.

Eating Disorders

More than 90 percent of individuals diagnosed with *anorexia nervosa* are female and at least 90 percent of those diagnosed with *bulimia nervosa* are female (*DSM-IV*). The word *anorexia* refers to a loss of appetite, but individuals with anorexia nervosa do not usually lose their appetites; instead, they exert rigorous control over their food intake and physical activity level to achieve a lower than minimally normal body weight. Distorted perception of body shape and size is typical. Although widespread concern about the prevalence of anorexia nervosa among girls and women is relatively recent among medical professionals and the general public, self-starvation behaviors among women have been documented as far back as the Middle Ages (Bemporad, 1996; Brumberg, 2000; Liles & Woods, 1999). Like anorexia, bulimia is related to extreme concern about weight gain, but individuals exhibiting bulimia are very often of normal weight or above normal weight. They do not tend to restrict their food intake, instead engaging in food binges followed by purging through vomiting or use of laxatives. Many girls and women engage in unhealthy eating habits and suffer from distressing body preoccupation but do not meet the specific diagnostic criteria for these disorders. (See Box 13.2.)

Both depression and anxiety in women often co-occur with body dissatisfaction and eating disorders (e.g., Bulik, Sullivan, Carter, & Joyce, 1996; Fava et al., 1997), though the precise nature of the relationship is unclear. Given the appearance pressures on women described in Chapter 7, it seems reasonable to suppose that body dissatisfaction may lead to both eating disorders and depression in some women. Some studies of nonclinical samples of undergraduate women suggest that the culture's emphasis on thinness and beauty for women does increase women's negative feelings about their bodies and, in turn, their eating disorder symptoms (e.g., Noll & Fredrickson, 1998; Stice & Shaw, 1994). It is also possible that depression predisposes women to body dissatisfaction (Keel, Mitchell, Davis, & Crow, 2001) instead of the other way around. All of the research on the associations between these

---

Box 13.2   ∼

DSM-IV **Diagnostic Criteria for Anorexia**

A. Refusal to maintain body weight at or above a minimally normal weight for age and height.

B. Intense fear of gaining weight or becoming fat, even though underweight.

C. Disturbance in the way in which one's body weight or shape is experienced, undue influence of body weight or shape on self-evaluation, or denial of the seriousness of the current low body weight.

D. In postmenarcheal females, amenorrhea (i.e., the absence of at least three consecutive menstrual cycles).

DSM-IV **Diagnostic Criteria for Bulimia**

A. Recurrent episodes of binge eating. An episode of binge eating is characterized by both of the following:

(1) Eating, in a discrete period of time (e.g., within any two-hour period), an amount of food that is definitely larger than most people would eat during a similar period of time and under similar circumstances.

(2) A sense of lack of control over eating during the episode (e.g., a feeling that one cannot stop eating or control what or how much one is eating).

B. Recurrent inappropriate compensatory behavior in order to prevent weight gain, such as self-induced vomiting; misuse of laxatives, diuretics, enemas, or other medications; fasting; or excessive exercise.

C. The binge eating and inappropriate compensatory behaviors both occur, on average, at least twice a week for three months.

D. Self-evaluation is unduly influenced by body shape and weight.

E. The disturbance does not occur exclusively during periods of anorexia nervosa.

Source: Reprinted with permission from the *Diagnostic and Statistical Manual of Mental Disorders*, 4th Edition, Text revision. Copyright © 2000 American Psychiatric Association.

factors is correlational, and so it is difficult for researchers to determine whether there are simple causal links between them or more complex relationships.

What we do know is that the associations between depression, anxiety, body dissatisfaction, and eating disorders vary in different populations of women. For example, a study of Mexican American women found that endorsement of U.S. societal values (which include the emphasis on thinness for women) was significantly correlated with bulimic symptoms, while a study of African American women conducted by the same researchers found no association between these factors, nor between depressive symptoms and bulimic symptoms (Lester & Petrie, 1995; 1998). One study with post-partum women found that weight gained during pregnancy is associated with depression for White women, but not for African American women (Cameron et al., 1996), perhaps because African American women are less likely than Caucasian women to perceive body changes related to pregnancy negatively (Walker, Timmerman, Kim, & Sterling, 2002).

Cross-cultural variation is evident in the prevalence of eating disorders in general. They are more common in industrialized societies, perhaps because of beauty standards that emphasize thinness and also because of the greater wealth of food that allows women the luxury of refusing and abusing food. Within the United States, rates of eating disorders show cultural variation, occurring most often among white women, but recent studies suggest that eating disorders may be increasing among populations of minority women.

Some populations of women may be less prone to eating disorders because of their greater social distance from the mainstream beauty ideal. The ideal is young, white, heterosexual, and middle-class; it may be easier for women who do not fit into these categories to reject the dominant standard. Recently, researchers have paid particular attention to how *acculturation* affects rates of eating disorders in girls and women of color in the United States. Becoming more adapted to the dominant culture (e.g., speaking English as a primary language even though one is not a native English speaker) is related to increased risk of eating disorders among girls and women of color (e.g., Gowen et al., 1999; Cachelin, Veisel, Barsegarnazari, & Striegel-Moore, 2000). As girls and women become more acculturated, their social distance from the mainstream ideal decreases.

Not all of the theories about eating disorders focus exclusively on social context. Some emphasize individual differences in personality traits that may lead to disordered eating. Different individuals may respond differently to the social context. For example, in a study of more than 1,000 female twins, perfectionism (in the form of high concern about making mistakes) was related to symptoms of both anorexia and bulimia (Bulik et al., 2003). Perhaps girls and women with perfectionist tendencies are more vulnerable to cultural ideals for appearance and behavior.

Borderline and Dependent Personality Disorders

Several personality disorders show sex-related discrepancies in prevalence rates, including antisocial and narcissistic disorders (diagnosed more in men) and dependent and borderline disorders (diagnosed more in women). There is a large body of literature debating whether these differences are artifacts of imprecise sampling, the result of bias in diagnostic constructs or criteria, or due to assessment bias by clinicians or self-report instruments. Some evidence supports all of these explanations, depending on the disorder in question (Widiger, 1998).

Borderline personality disorder (BPD), the diagnosis applied to the author of *Girl, Interrupted*, is characterized by a pattern of instability in relationships, self-concept, and emotions accompanied by impulsivity and a severe fear of abandonment (*DSM-IV-TR*). Seventy-five percent of the individuals diagnosed with BPD in clinical settings are female; however, some studies of BPD prevalence in the general population find no gender difference, so there may be a sampling bias (Skodol & Bender, 2003). Taking the clinical rates as representative, several researchers have explored the possibility that the diagnostic criteria for BPD are sexist. In one study, undergraduate students sorted the diagnostic criteria for the personality disorders on the basis of how characteristic they were of women versus of men (Sprock, Blashfield, & Smith, 1990). All of the BPD criteria were rated as more characteristic of women, with the exception of the criterion describing intense, inappropriate anger.

Dependent personality disorder (DPD) is characterized by an excessive need to be cared for that leads to submissive and clingy behavior. (*DSM-IV-TR*). Individuals with dependent personality traits experience intense longings to be loved, nurtured, and protected. They have extreme trouble making independent decisions, even minor daily ones, and they require a lot of reassurance and advice. They have difficulty expressing disagreement with others because they fear it will lead to a loss of support or approval. They have trouble initiating projects because of low self-confidence in their abilities. Importantly, these dependent behaviors are to be considered signs of the personality disorder only when they exceed age-appropriate or culturally appropriate norms. What about gender-appropriate norms? How about differences in gender socialization and gender roles? And what about factors confounded with gender, such as economic dependence and being the victim of domestic abuse? The *DSM-IV-TR* doesn't offer any guidance to clinicians on these points except to say that "societies may differentially foster and discourage dependent behaviors in males and females" (p. 723).

Some Other Disorders Diagnosed More Frequently in Women

A few other disorders are diagnosed more frequently in women than in men according to the *DSM-IV-TR*. One of these is *factitious disorder*, which involves intentionally producing or feigning psychological or physical symptoms in order to meet a psychological need to assume the sick role; only the most serious variant is diagnosed more frequently in men. (Keep *factitious disorder* in mind when you read in the next section about the cult of invalidism among privileged American and Western European women in the late 19th century.) Another disorder worth mentioning here is *depersonalization disorder*, feeling an extreme sense of detachment or estrangement from oneself as if one is an observer of one's own mental processes or body; this disorder is diagnosed at least twice as often in women as in men in clinical samples (*DSM-IV-TR*). Chapter 7 discussed how self-objectification is common among women. Might depersonalization represent a more extreme form of women's common out-of-body state? Some bulimic women report feelings of dissociation following eating binges (*DSM-IV-TR*).

The *DSM-IV* includes an appendix of ***culture-bound syndromes*** that are not officially recognized by the American Psychiatric Association, but are well known in other cultures. Listed among these are two that are reportedly observed more often in women than in men. *Latah* is a Malaysian term to describe hypersensitivity to sudden fright that leads to dissociative or trancelike behavior. The syndrome goes by different names in the many regions of the world where it is recognized, including in Thailand, Japan, and the Philippines. In Malaysia, Latah is most common in middle-aged women. *Mal de ojo*, literally "evil eye" in Spanish, is widely found in Mediterranean cultures. Sufferers exhibit fitful sleep, crying for no apparent reason, and intestinal distress. Though it is most frequently reported in children, *mal de ojo* tends to strike women more often than men when it occurs in adults.

Sexist Bias in the Treatment of Psychological Disorders

Broadly speaking, treatment for psychological disorders can be defined in terms of two general approaches: a psychiatric model that utilizes medical therapies, including drugs and hospitalization, and a nonmedical psychotherapeutic approach. Psychoanalysis, the therapy originally developed by Sigmund Freud, falls into both categories in that it is a nonmedical talk therapy but is primarily practiced by a (relatively small) subset of psychiatrists. Both the psychiatric and psychotherapeutic approaches have suffered from gender bias. This section will first address the sexism that has pervaded psychiatric institutionalization and drug therapies. Then I will describe criticisms of traditional psychotherapy.

Institutionalizing Women

Residential facilities for severely mentally ill or developmentally disabled people serve important caretaking and rehabilitative functions in our society today. Sometimes, however, people are wrongfully incarcerated in these institutions (e.g., Szasz, 1973; 2002). A look at the history of women's institutionalization in the United States and Europe reveals a pattern of unwarranted involuntary commitment as punishment for socially deviant behavior and unwillingness to conform to the limits of a socially prescribed feminine gender role (Showalter, 1986; Ripa, 1990; Chesler, 1997; Ussher, 1992).

Charcot, Freud, and the Salpêtrière

From the 17th to the 19th centuries, the Salpêtrière in Paris was an infamous institution housing primarily women. Initially built as a gunpowder factory, it was remodeled and expanded under the reign of Louis XIV into an almshouse to shelter some of the 40,000 homeless Parisians, 10 percent of the city's population (Vallois, 1998). Many of the women forcibly housed in the Salpêtrière were prostitutes who were later shipped to Louisiana and Canada to help populate France's new territories. Women considered (in the parlance of the time) feeble-minded or deranged were routinely chained to the walls. Things changed, however, under the direction of Phillipe Pinel, who, perhaps inspired by the humanitarian themes of the French Revolution, unchained the insane at the Salpêtrière in the last years of the 18th century.

Women who were homeless, suspected or known prostitutes, or merely deviant in their behavior (e.g., were loud or aggressive) were likely candidates for involuntary commitment in the Salpêtrière during the 19th century. Jean-Martin Charcot, the founder of modern neurology, opened a clinic in the Salpêtrière to study individuals who displayed *hysterical symptoms,* physical problems with no apparent organic cause. Charcot disagreed with predecessors who thought hysteria was caused by a wandering womb (he saw hysteria in men as well), but he did attribute hysteria to sexual dysfunction.

The majority of Charcot's patients were women. The most famous and favored of these was Blanche Wittmann, nicknamed the "Queen of Hysterics," whose dramatic displays of hysteria on demand served Charcot well in his theatrical lectures to colleagues, as depicted in André Brouillet's painting *Une leçon clinique à la Salpêtrière* (see Figure 13.3). Charcot documented hysterical fits in his patients with the use of photography, a cutting-edge technology at that time. Some photographs were spontaneous, while others documented hysterical episodes induced by hypnosis (Didi-Huberman, 2003). The original photographs are archived at the Charcot library; for those not headed to Paris anytime soon, digital images of them

FIGURE 13.3

(*Iconographie photographique de la Salpêtrière*) can be viewed online at http://charcot. bum.jussieu.fr.

Charcot's work on hysteria was highly influential to a certain young physician who came to work with him for a few months in 1885. That physician's name was Sigmund Freud. Freud was impressed with Charcot's ability to use hypnosis to produce and relieve hysterical symptoms. Here was the first hint that the unconscious mind might be connected to some forms of physical distress. Freud was also impacted when he overheard Charcot assert quietly to a colleague that the cause of hysteria "*c'est toujours la chose genitale . . . toujours . . . toujours . . . toujours*" (translation: "It is always something genital . . . always . . . always . . . always) (Freud, 1914, p. 14).

It was while in residence at the Salpêtrière that Freud first developed his own ideas about hysteria and its origins in childhood sexual trauma. Later, Freud retracted his claim that the hysteria he observed in his women patients at his clinic in Vienna was due to actual childhood sexual trauma and developed the alternative explanation that the symptoms stemmed from unconscious conflict regarding wishful sexual fantasies. This about-face in Freud's thinking may have been due to the negative reaction his theory elicited from his peers in the medical community; after all, he was essentially claiming that childhood sexual abuse was commonplace in their high-status households (Masson, 1984). Undoubtedly, this shift had a significant impact on the treatment received by women who actually had been abused.

True Women and Madwomen in the Victorian Era

In the mid-to-late-19th century United States, involuntary commitment of mad-women by their husbands or other family members who found their attitudes or behaviors inconvenient, unacceptable, or uncontrollable was not unheard of among the middle and upper classes. At the time, economically privileged women were expected to aspire to "True Womanhood," to be passive, pious, domestic, and morally pure (Welter, 1966). According to medical wisdom of the time, intellectual activity—such as that required when pursuing higher education or engaging in social reform activism—was contraindicated for women. The only recommended activity was childbearing; however, this was somewhat of a double bind due to the fact that pregnancy and lactation were also seen as causes of women's mental illness (Geller & Harris, 1994).

A cult of invalidism flourished among affluent women in the United States and Europe during the latter 19th century and into the beginning of the 20th (Ehrenreich & English, 1973). With their physical and intellectual exercise severely limited by corsets and conventions, fashionable women manifested chronic sickness in the form of vague nervous ailments. Frailty, weakness, and acute sensitivity came to be romanticized as a variation on the True Woman ideal (Geller & Harris, 1994). Like the True Woman, the so-called neurasthenic woman was no threat to a patriarchal household or society.

Because women's reproductive organs were believed to be the primary source of their mental distress, physicians used woman-specific therapies, including the surgical removal of ovaries, electrical shocks to the uterus, hot water injections into the vagina, and clitoral cauterization (Geller & Harris, 1994; Russell, 1995). An influential doctor named S. Weir Mitchell popularized the rest cure, months of confinement in bed with no activity. Mitchell's idea was that women enjoyed being ill and that making the conditions of illness extremely aversive would hasten their recovery. His approach treated women as unruly children in need of paternal discipline. In her short story *The Yellow Wallpaper*, suffragist and feminist foremother Charlotte Perkins Gilman (1892) relates a first-person account of a woman's descent into madness *caused* by her physician husband's implementation of the rest cure:

FIGURE 13.4
Charlotte Perkins Gilman

> If a physician of high standing, and one's own husband, assures friends and relatives that there is really nothing the matter with one but temporary nervous depression—a slight hysterical tendency—what is one to do? . . . I am absolutely forbidden to "work" until I am well again . . . Personally, I believe that congenial work, with excitement and change, would do me good. (p. 1)

The woman in the story proceeds to develop delusions about a female prisoner lurking behind the garish designs on the peeling wallpaper in the nursery where she has been residing. Perkins Gillman herself was institutionalized and put on the rest cure by Weir Mitchell for a month in 1887. She suffered from nervous prostration following the birth of her daughter (today she would probably be diagnosed with postpartum depression). When she was sent home, she was instructed to live as domestic a life as possible, to limit her intellectual activity to two hours per day, and never to write another word. After complying with this protocol for several months, Gilman, "came perilously near to losing [her] mind." She recovered after her divorce. See Box 13.3 for stories from other women confined to asylums during the latter 19th century.

Institutionalization of girls and women who defied socially imposed limits on their behavior is not a horror of only the distant past. The recent Miramax film *The Magdalene Sisters* (2003) is a fictionalized account of real abuses suffered by many of the 30,000 girls in Ireland who were sent (against their will) to live and work as laundresses in the Magdalene asylums between the 1880s and the 1990s (Gordon, 2003). These institutions were built by the Sisters of Mercy as spiritual refuges for

BOX 13.3 ～ Women's Voices from the 19th-Century Asylum

My youngest brother I loved with all the tender love of a sister, and I wanted him to have an education, and I worked in the factory to get money to help educate him; and is it possible that a brother, or a human being, could be so hardened or cruel, on account of difference of religion, to put a sister in prison and hire men to try experiments, and to commit rape on a sister, and to delight in her sufferings! . . . Is this the state of our country, that the rights of a female are trampled upon . . .

—*Elizabeth T. Stone (1840–1842)*

It is now twenty-one years since people found out that I was crazy, and all because I could not fall in with every vulgar belief that was fashionable . . . I find that active nervous temperaments that are full of thought and intellect want full scope to dispose of their energy, for if not they will become extremely excitable. Such a mind cannot bear a tight place, and that is one great reason why women are much more excitable than men, for their minds are more active; but they must be kept in a nut-shell because they are women.

—*Phebe B. Davis (1850–1853)*

It was in a Bible-class . . . that I defended some religious opinions . . . which brought upon me the charge of insanity. . . . Early on the morning of the 18th of June, 1860, as I arose from my bed, preparing to take my morning bath, I saw my husband approaching my door with two physicians, both members of his church and of our Bible class . . . Fearing exposure I hastily locked my door . . . [but] my husband forced an entrance into my room through the window with an axe! . . . And I, for shelter and protection against exposure in a state of almost entire nudity, sprang into bed . . . The trio approached my bed, and each doctor felt my pulse, and without asking a single question both pronounced me insane.

—*Elizabeth Parsons Ware Packard (1860–1863)*

Here, women of intelligence, of spirit, of refinement, with homes, with families, and possessing the power to comfort, cherish, and adorn these, are left to stagnate . . . they are prisoners. It is very generally believed . . . that an asylum confines only the violent, dangerous, or utterly imbecile . . . This is a remarkably wide-spread error.

—*Adeline T. P. Lunt (Date unknown)*

Source: All excerpts from Geller, J. L., and Harris, M. (1994). *Women of the asylum. Voices from behind the walls, 1840–1945.* New York: Anchor Books.

morally shamed girls (e.g., girls who were seen as too promiscuous, girls who were considered too attractive, girls whose reputations had suffered as a result of rape, girls who had become pregnant before marriage); instead, as portrayed in the film, girls were subject to severe psychological and physical cruelty inflicted by the nuns and priests staffing the institutions. Although these asylums may not seem to have much to do with mental illness from a contemporary perspective, it is important to keep in mind that during the 19th century, when the Magdalene asylums first opened, hypersexuality in females was considered by European and American doctors to be a form of psychopathology (Lunbeck, 1994).

Women and Deinstitutionalization

In the 1960s and 1970s, a number of writers in the United States and Europe penned antipsychiatry critiques that focused on the social construction of madness and the authoritarian abuses perpetrated by psychiatric institutions (e.g., Goffman, 1961; Laing, 1970; Szasz, 1970). The claim that the mentally ill were yet another marginalized group, labeled and punished for their nonconformist behavior, had a particular appeal against the backdrop of the civil rights movement and counter-culture activism. There followed a trend promoting the deinstitutionalization of mental patients and reliance on community-based care facilities. Unfortunately, these facilities were underfunded and limited in number. The result was that many psychologically distressed individuals ended up homeless (Isaac & Armat, 1990).

Deinstitutionalization has had particular implications for women. When family and community care take the place of institutional care, who are the primary caregivers? Most of the time, they are women (Ascher-Svanum & Sobel, 1989; Bachrach, 1984; Thurer, 1983). Deinstitutionalization is related to women's role as the primary caregivers in their families in another way as well: Women with serious mental disorders are more likely to be at home raising their children than they were when community-based outpatient services were unavailable (Oyserman, Mowbray, Meares, & Firminger, 2000). And deinstitutionalized women may be more likely to become mothers than women living within a facility that provides family planning services (Bachrach, 1984).

Medicating Women

Like institutional care, when properly applied, psychotropic drugs can serve as an effective component in treatment programs for many forms of psychological distress such as depression and generalized anxiety. As in the case of institutionalization, however, a historical look at the use of psychiatric medications suggests that women have been disproportionately targeted as candidates for this form of therapy, especially when they experienced distress related to their traditional feminine roles as mothers and homemakers.

Sedatives for Stepford Wives

Since tranquilizers and sedatives were first introduced for widespread use in the 1950s, they have been prescribed more often for women than for men (e.g., Balter, Levine, & Manheimer, 1974; Women's Task Force of the Michigan Department of Mental Health,1984; Graham & Vidal-Zaballos, 1998). This difference may be due, in part, to women's higher rates of disorders appropriately treated with these types of drugs, but it can also be attributed to a sexist bias toward calming women perceived as disruptive to the social order. Concurrent with the mid-century mother-blaming described earlier in this chapter, tranquilizers hit the U.S. market in the 1950s and were promoted in magazines such as the *Ladies' Home Journal* and *Cosmopolitan* as the cure for women's frigidity, infidelity, single status, career-mindedness, and rejection of motherhood (Metzl, 2003).

Miltown, a muscle relaxant, was introduced to the American public in 1955. Demand for it soon exceeded that for any previous prescription drug. By the end of 1956, 1 in 20 Americans, the majority women, were taking tranquilizers (Metzl, 2003). In 1969, Valium became the most widely prescribed medication in the United States with 1 in 10 Americans taking it, three-quarters of whom were women (Chambers, 1972). Tranquilizers were so commonly prescribed to married, middle-class women in North America and Europe that they earned the nickname

FIGURE 13.5 *"Mother's Little Helpers" by Judy Olausen*

"mother's little helper," popularized in the 1966 Rolling Stones song by the same name:

> Mother needs something today to calm her down
> And though she's not really ill
> There's a little yellow pill
> She goes running for the shelter of a mother's little helper
> And it helps her on her way, gets her through her busy day . . .
>
> *(Lyrics excerpted from "Mothers Little Helper")*

In the 1950s, 1960s, and 1970s, tranquilizers were recommended for women not only to relieve their own distress, but also to relieve the distress men experienced living with troublesome women. Single women, married women whose husbands considered them sexually frigid, and career-minded women were all targets for sedation (Metzl, 2003).

Advertising Drugs to Psychiatrists

Long before it was legal to advertise prescription drugs directly to consumers, pharmaceutical companies targeted physicians through ads in medical journals. Still today more than 80 percent of promotional funds are spent on advertising to physicians (U.S. General Accounting Office, 2002). Researchers have found gendered patterns in the content of these ads that contradict reality.

A study of more than 200 ads for a variety of prescription drugs from American medical journals found that when both women and men were pictured, women were twice as likely to be portrayed as consumers, though national health statistics at the time suggested that women made fewer office visits and spent fewer days in hospitals than men did (Hawkins & Aber, 1993). Consistent with the face-ism in advertising described in Chapter 3, just parts of women's bodies were pictured significantly more often than just parts of men's, and women appeared naked four times as often as men. An analysis of portrayals of women in U.S. and Canadian medical journals found that drug advertisements reinforced negative stereotypes of women (Ford, 1986). For example, one ad pictured a male bus driver on one page, with the copy, "He is suffering from estrogen deficiency"; on the next page was a picture of an older woman passenger who appeared to be talking loudly, and the rest of the copy, "She is the reason why." Other ads portrayed women as childlike, complaining, and unable to cope.

In a study of psychotropic drug advertisements in primary psychiatry journals from North America and Great Britain, women were overrepresented compared to psychiatric epidemiological data, especially in U.S. journals (Munce, Robertson, Sansom, & Stewart, 2004). An analysis of all the psychotropic drug advertisements appearing in a family physician journal for a period of four years revealed that 77 percent of them depicted women patients (Hansen & Osborne, 1995). In this family practice journal and a psychiatry journal the researchers also analyzed, nearly all of the ads for antidepressant medications portrayed women consumers—100 percent and 80 percent, respectively. These percentages are distinctly inconsistent with the typical 2:1 sex ratio of depression diagnosis.

Ads for antidepressants distort reality in that they tend to portray stereotypically idealized life circumstances, subtly discouraging physicians from exploring the social causes of women's depression such as sexism, poverty, and domestic violence (Nikelly, 1995). Ads for psychiatric medications also neglect racism as a source of psychological distress. An ad that appeared in the *Archives of General Psychiatry* in 1974 pictured an African American woman, dressed in professional clothing, looking menacing and raising a fist, with the heading, "Assaultive and belligerent? Cooperation often begins with HALDOL" (Metzl, 2003). This ad, which ran during the heyday of the civil rights movement and the feminist second wave, implied that the remedy for African American women's outrage was medication rather than social change. Although such blatantly racist images are rare today, a recent study found that 88 percent of the people pictured in a sample of ads from psychiatric journals were White—and so would not bring racism to mind (Munce et al., 2004).

Selling Drugs Directly to Women

In 1985, the U.S. Food and Drug Administration (FDA) lifted its moratorium on direct-to-consumer advertising for prescription drugs. According to the current FDA guidelines, drug manufacturers may solicit consumers with three types of advertisements: *product claim ads*, which describe the drug and what it does and must include information about risks and side effects; *reminder ads*, which mention the drug by name but do not make any claims about what it does, and so do not have to include risk information; and *help-seeking ads*, which describe a disorder or condition without mention of a specific drug and are not regulated by the FDA (U.S. General Accounting Office, 2002).

In a recent content analysis of 10 leading U.S. magazines, researchers found that prescription drug advertisements appeared more often in the publications aimed at women than in those geared toward men or general readership (Woloshin, Schwartz, Tremmel, & Welch, 2001). What are women readers to conclude when they routinely encounter Prozac antidepressant ads in magazines such as *Self* and *Marie Claire* alongside articles about how to be more attractive and how to find love (Metzl, 2003)? Paxil, another antidepressant, was the fourth most frequently advertised drug in 2000—at about the same rate as Viagra, for impotence (GAO, 2002). Print ads for Paxil, which have appeared since 1993, have overwhelmingly featured women—who happen to be young, white, conventionally attractive, thin, well dressed, and heterosexual (Hanganu-Bresch, 2004). In one of these ads, a woman is standing separated from her helpless looking husband and son, and the text reads, "What's standing between you and your life?" In the "after" picture, she is crouched next to her son, hugging him and gazing happily upward (at her husband?). Her normal life as a mother and wife has been restored.

Not long ago, while I was waiting in a women's health clinic, a brochure caught my eye. On the cover was a smiling woman, her hair and clothes blowing in the wind. Above her were the words "mood swing," with "mood" crossed out. Underneath, in smaller text, it said, "Think it's PMS? Think again. It could be PMDD." Inside the brochure were more pictures of smiley women and the words "Irritability," with "Irrit" crossed out, and "low energy," with "low" crossed out. There were also three pages of text asking the reader whether she has mood swings, bloating, breast tenderness, and other symptoms in conjunction with her menstrual cycle—and then encouraging her to ask her doctor whether medication for premenstrual dysphoric disorder (PMDD) might be right for her. Nowhere in this help-seeking brochure did the pharmaceutical company who produced it identify PMDD as a psychiatric diagnosis—but it is.

PMDD currently appears in a *DSM-IV* appendix of potential categories needing further study. It does not appear as an official category because of insufficient support; however, it can still be used by psychiatrists and other doctors as a diagnosis. Controversy continues to rage regarding the inclusion of PMDD in the *DSM*. Supporters claim it is an identifiable clinical syndrome and its inclusion in the *DSM* is important to legitimize some women's cyclical suffering (e.g., Endicott, 2000). Some critics agree that the validation of women's experience is important, but assert that women should not require a mental illness diagnosis to receive medication for physical and emotional symptoms commonly associated with menstruation. Also, the existence of this diagnostic category may reinforce the stereotype of premenstrual women as emotionally unstable (Nash & Chrisler, 1997).

Because of the gender biases that exist in the use of psychotropic drugs, some psychiatrists and psychologists are advocating feminist psychopharmacology (e.g., Hamilton & Jensvold, 1995; Marsh, 1995). They argue that a feminist perspective will help counter sexism in psychiatric diagnosis and prescription patterns. In addition, they suggest that a feminist perspective would add social and cultural context to biologically focused research on sex-related differences in responses to psychotropic drugs and their effectiveness. Especially lacking from outcome research is a consideration of ethnic and racial factors; psychopharmacological treatment for women of color has been studied very little, although psychiatrists seem particularly inclined to favor drugs over other forms of therapy for people of color (Jacobsen, 1994). A contemporary feminist approach would consider ethnic and racial factors along with gender.

Traditional Psychotherapy

Critics of traditional psychotherapy are referring not only to psychological treatment before the rise of feminist practice in the 1970s, but also to the work of contemporary clinicians who fail to adopt a nonsexist or feminist approach. The primary criticisms that have been leveled at traditional psychotherapy include the following:

1. The theoretical orientation and/or personal perspective that informs the therapist's appraisal of the client's distress and guides the treatment may be based on gender stereotypes and sexist attitudes.
2. Traditional psychotherapeutic orientations focus on the individual as the source of the psychological distress with little or no consideration of social contextual factors that may contribute to the client's problems, such as sexism and racism.
3. The relationship between the therapist and client is an unequal one in which the therapist is the more powerful expert and the client is in a subordinate and vulnerable position.

The second two criticisms listed apply to prefeminist psychotherapy in general, whereas the first one applies to individual therapists or primarily to psychoanalysis and its offshoots.

Sexism in Therapy

The influence of Freudian thinking on American and European psychiatry and psychology should not be underestimated. Although most therapists today are not psychoanalytically oriented per se, Freud's notions about things such as women's masochism may still exert an influence on their thinking (Caplan, 1985). Women who undergo Freudian psychoanalytic therapy will likely come to understand that they are maladjusted if they are ambitious (this is a sign of penis envy, according to Freud), immature if they have not transferred the focus of their sexuality from the clitoris to the vagina, and have unresolved unconscious conflicts if they report memories of childhood sexual abuse (which are most likely fantasies, according to Freud). For these reasons and more, most feminists in the United States have rejected psychoanalysis as a beneficial therapeutic approach for women; however, French feminism and postfeminism draw heavily on psychoanalysis (relying more on the work of French psychoanalyst Jacques Lacan than on Freud). And, as will be discussed in the section on feminist therapy, there are feminist psychoanalytic clinics in the United States and England.

Most therapists today are eclectic in their orientations, borrowing from classic behavioral therapy, cognitive therapy, Freudian and post-Freudian psychodynamic thought, and so on. The most popular single approach is cognitive-behavioral therapy, in which the therapist and client work on changing not only maladaptive behavioral patterns, but also destructive thought patterns. This approach is not in itself sexist; however, it may be biased if the therapist thinks in sex-stereotypical ways. For example, a traditional cognitive-behavioral therapist might respond to a woman client's continual fears about her mothering with the suggestion that she take a parenting class to bolster her skills, instead of critically examining the unrealistic and idealized version of mothering that pervades our popular culture. The cognitive-behavioral approach may be less than optimal for women unless the therapist infuses it with a distinctly feminist orientation (e.g., Hurst & Genest, 1995; Srebnik & Saltzberg, 1994).

Whether a therapist is eclectic, cognitive-behavioral, psychoanalytic, or otherwise, if that therapist is traditionally schooled and does not employ a feminist approach, he or she will tend to ignore how the client's gender, sexual orientation, race, ethnicity, disability, or other social categories may affect her experience. By focusing only on intrapsychic factors, such as personality and counterproductive thought patterns, a traditional therapist will overlook factors outside the individual that may be contributing to her distress. Instead of challenging those factors, perhaps working with the client to change the ones that are under her control and to find new ways to deal with those that are not, a traditional therapist would more likely focus on the client's maladaptive response to her situation. The goal of traditional therapy is to adapt the client to the social context, not critically examine the social context itself.

Sexual Misconduct by Therapists

When people seek psychotherapy, they are in a needy position, which automatically makes them less powerful relative to the therapist from whom they desire treatment. They are psychologically distressed and eager to feel better, so they are probably more open and trusting than they might normally be in a new relationship with a stranger. Add to this the therapist's impressive title and academic credentials, and the relationship ends up very unbalanced, indeed. This power differential need not necessarily be a problem—after all, there are many circumstances under which people need to make themselves vulnerable to others; however, some therapists have abused their higher status. The most egregious form of abuse is sexual misconduct between the therapist and client, which in the vast majority of cases involves male therapists and female clients.

In national studies, about 7 percent of male therapists report having had sexual relationships with their clients, compared to 1.5 percent of women therapists (Pope, 2001). The therapist-client relationship is an intimate one, and sexual attraction between therapists and clients is not uncommon; however, professional ethical guidelines for both psychologists and psychiatrists in the United States prohibit sexual interaction with clients. Every state in the United States prohibits therapist-client sexual relationships through licensing regulations; offenders may be sued for malpractice in civil court and in some states may be charged with criminal conduct (Pope, 2001). Sexual interaction between therapists and their clients is considered unethical precisely because of the power imbalance between them.

Sexual relationships between therapists and clients are potentially psychologically damaging to the clients, and may, of course, have repercussions for the therapist and his family as well. Women who have had sexual relationships with their therapists later report feeling emotionally unstable, ashamed, guilty, angry, and less able to trust (Somer & Saadon, 1999; Pope, 2001). In a survey of 958 patients who had been sexually involved with their therapists, 90 percent reported having been harmed by the experience, 14 percent attributed suicide attempts to their experience, and 11 percent required hospitalization during their recovery from it (Pope & Vetter, 1991). Chesler (1997) interviewed women who had been in sexual relationships with their therapists. Common themes running through their accounts included feelings of responsibility for the sexual interaction and feelings of abandonment when the therapist ended the sexual relationship (which he did in the majority of the cases). One woman's account highlights the abuse of power very well:

> I know I needed him very, very badly. It was like he was God. . . . He was mistreating me, and I didn't want to admit that, because I needed him badly. I loved him . . . then he offered me a job as his typist but he wouldn't sleep with me anymore. I was so depressed and upset and I wanted some help and called up, hysterical, "Please talk to me on the phone," and he said, "I can't talk to you now, I'll call you back." And he never called back. I felt deserted and all alone . . . (Chesler, 1997, p. 174)

Feminist Therapy

The characteristics that define feminist therapy read like a list of remedies to the problems of traditional therapy described above. The general principles of feminist therapy have been outlined by several authors (e.g., Hill & Ballou, 1998; Worell & Johnson, 2001; Worell & Remer, 2003). From a feminist therapy perspective,

1. Women's subjective experiences are valid and important to consider given the androcentrism that has pervaded psychological theory.
2. Not all problems originate in the individual and "personal" problems are not merely personal but are sometimes social and political.
3. Therapy should be collaboration between therapist and client rather than a hierarchical relationship.
4. The goals of therapy are to help women feel positively about themselves and empowered to make social change, not to educate them about what is wrong with them.
5. It is imperative for the therapist to be cognizant of the fact that women are diverse and their experiences are affected by social factors such as their age, race, ethnicity, sexual orientation, class, disability, and so on.

Feminist therapy is not a theoretical orientation in the same way as cognitive behaviorism or psychoanalysis; rather, it is a set of values that may be applied in a variety of therapeutic contexts.

Conducting Feminist Therapy

In a survey study of feminist therapists, Hill & Ballou (1998) asked whether the therapists had "adapted a specific therapeutic strategy so that it is feminist." Their respondents explained how they had taken traditional tools, such as cognitive techniques and dream analysis, and revised them to incorporate feminist principles. For example, one therapist challenges women to question whether their negative thinking may be a learned response to gender expectations; another teaches self-hypnosis as a skill under the control of the client, instead of using standard hypnosis that can lead to feelings that the therapist is controlling the client. See Box 13.4 for an example of psychoanalytic practice informed by feminist principles.

BOX 13.4 ∾ Feminist Psychoanalytic Therapy

Luise Eichenbaum

Women's Therapy Centre (WTC) in London. The orientation of the Centre's therapists is psychoanalytic, but fundamental to their approach is an understanding of how social issues affect women's lives at the individual and institutional level. These social issues include not only gender, but race, class disability, and sexuality. The WTC makes a concerted effort to provide services to women who do not usually have access to therapy; thus, they reserve half of their slots for women from black and minority ethnic communities, young women, disabled women, and low-income women. The staff is culturally diverse and they offer therapy in several languages other than English.

When students and I visited the WTC as part of our study-abroad Psychoanalysis and Feminism course, we met in small groups with the analysts. A burning question we had was how they resolved the inconsistencies between Freudianism and feminism. We wondered what it meant to them to practice psychoanalytic therapy within a woman-centered context. One analyst responded by highlighting their diverse training; not all of them were grounded in Freudian psychoanalysis but

In 1976, inspired by the second wave of feminism in the United States and England, psychotherapists Luise Eichenbaum and Susie Orbach founded the

Studies comparing the practices of therapists who identify as feminist and those who do not suggest that, even when traditional tools are used, feminist therapy is distinctly different from nonfeminist therapy. Feminist and nonfeminist therapists respond differently to items such as "I consider my clients' problems through a gender-role perspective" (Worell & Johnson, 2001). In one study, clients who had worked with feminist therapists reported that they felt more respected, validated, and empowered than did those who worked with nonfeminist therapists (Piran, 1999).

BOX 13.4 ~ Feminist Psychoanalytic Therapy *(Concluded)*

used the work of other analysts, such as object-relations theorist Melanie Klein, to guide their work. Another offered an example of how a psychodynamic understanding was often helpful in highlighting unproductive patterns in group therapy: She found that when working with groups of women, men often came to represent the "bad object" and, as a result, the group spent all their time blaming men for their distress instead of focusing on constructive change—both personal and political. In general, these analysts found no contradiction between thinking psychoanalytically about women's internal worlds and thinking as feminists (though they may not label themselves as such) about women's external circumstances.

Five years after founding the WTC, Eichenbaum and Orbach, with Carol Bloom, cofounded the Women's Therapy Centre Institute (WTCI) in New York City. The WTCI offers some group therapy for eating and body-image problems, but focuses primarily on training therapists in the integration of contemporary psychoanalysis and feminism.

For more information about the work of the psychodynamic therapists at the WTC, see Marilyn Lawrence and Marie Maguire's (1999) edited volume, *Psychotherapy with women: Feminist perspectives*. (Florence, KY: Taylor & Francis/Routledge).

Susie Orbach

Though feminist therapists use mostly traditional techniques that they have adapted to be consistent with the principles of feminist therapy, some are employing novel techniques that may not be well established in traditional psychotherapy but seem particularly suited to the goals of feminist therapy. One such example is exercise therapy. Only since the 1980s has there been much research on the use of exercise in treating mental illness (Rejeski & Thompson, 1993). Some of this research has shown exercise to be effective in treating anxiety and depression (for review, see Salmon, 2001), both of which are more common in women than in men.

But it is not merely the antidepressant and anxiety-reducing effects of exercise that make it appealing to some feminist therapists. Exercise can contribute to the goals of feminist therapy because of its empowering effects, and because women's engagement in exercise can be considered a form of resistance to the oppressive idea that strength and activity are unfeminine (Chrisler & Lamont, 2002). As discussed in Chapter 7, physical activity may serve as an antidote to the negative psychological effects of self-objectification; therefore, exercise therapy may hold particular promise for treating women's body-related problems such as eating disorders (Chrisler & Lamont, 2002).

Although exercise therapy has the potential to benefit women especially, therapists who utilize it should be aware of cultural factors that may affect individual women's attitudes toward exercise. For example, exercise may be viewed differently by African American women than by Caucasian American women (e.g., Hall, 1998), or by veiled Muslim women than by women who are accustomed to presenting themselves less modestly. Many other things may also affect a woman's receptivity to exercise therapy and what form it might take for her; such factors might include her socioeconomic status (does she have leisure time and access to recreational facilities?), her family situation (e.g., if she is a stay-at-home mother of small children, does she have child care while she exercises?), and her physical condition. Fortunately, because exercise can take so many different forms (e.g., walking, swimming, dancing, yoga, weight-lifting), it can potentially be adapted as a positive form of feminist therapy for almost any woman.

Feminist Therapy for a Diversity of Women

One of the unifying principles of feminist therapy is sensitivity on the part of the therapist to characteristics of the individual such as age, race, ethnicity, sexual orientation, class, and disability. Certainly this is not an exhaustive list of the social contextual factors that influence women's experience, but they are the primary ones addressed in the feminist therapy literature. This section will briefly address just a few of the issues that arise in feminist therapy with three particular populations of women: older women, women of color, and lesbian and bisexual women.

Aging Women

It may seem peculiar to refer to age as a diversity characteristic. Most women (if they are so fortunate) will eventually fall into the category of "older" or "elderly." Yet older women are relatively invisible within the clinical context just as they are in our broader social context. For example, when researchers study body-image concerns, they often focus on young women at risk for eating disorders, even though the physical appearance changes that come with aging are a source of concern for many women (Chrisler & Ghiz, 1993; Hurd, 2000; Crose, 2002). As women in our youth-oriented society reach their 50 and 60s, they may experience what Pearlman (1993) refers to as "late midlife astonishment," a sudden awareness that in the eyes of the culture they have become stigmatized as unimportant and undesirable, especially because of their perceived loss of physical attractiveness and sexual appeal.

FIGURE 13.6
Feminist therapists must be sensitive to diversity among women.

Changes in physical appearance are by no means the only, or most important, potential sources of psychological distress for women as they grow older. As women mature into the middle and latter stages of their lives, they may have to deal with issues that were not as immediate, or perhaps not even relevant, when they were younger. Thinking back to the previous chapter, can you recall some of these issues? They include retirement and economic stress, loss of a life partner (and diminishing prospects for new partners), loss of peers, physical limitations, caretaking of elderly parents (and perhaps children at the same time), health concerns, living alone, ageism—the list could go on.

Just as developmental researchers must be cognizant of cohort effects when they make comparisons between participant samples of different ages, so too must therapists be mindful of cohort factors when working with older women. For example, women who are in their 70s today were in their 40s during the women's movement of the 1970s; they are likely to have lived a more gender-traditional life than a young therapist and may be somewhat resistant to some feminist ideas. This may present a particular challenge for feminist therapists who encourage women to question traditional gender roles. On the other hand, it would be a mistake to assume that older women will have less-than-positive attitudes toward feminism—just as it is a mistake to assume anything else about them.

Feminist therapists are already well aware of the ways in which gender stereotypes can color perceptions and behaviors; when treating older women, they must be equally attuned to effects of age stereotypes. Therapists seeking to understand the sources of an older woman's psychological distress may not think to explore certain possibilities if they rely on age stereotypes. For example, just because a woman is older and is in a relationship with an older partner does not mean that she is not battered (Vinton, 2001). Just because she is someone's grandmother does not mean she isn't struggling with an addiction to alcohol or other drugs (Katz, 2002). She may be well past menopause and living in a nursing home, but that does not mean that her sexual functioning is unimportant to her (Aizenberg, Weizman, & Barak, 2002). The narrow thinking and patronizing attitude sometimes displayed by traditional health-care providers working with older women (Feldman, 1999) are potentially minimized when the provider adopts an age-aware, feminist perspective.

Women of Color

Feminist therapists working with women of color must first understand one basic fact: Women "of color" often have common experiences, such as being the target of racial or ethnic prejudice, but the experiences of women identified by this label also vary tremendously (Comas-Díaz & Greene, 1994). Issues of central importance to Native American women will likely be different than the concerns of recent Somali refugee immigrant women. African American women come from a very different cultural background than Asian American women. Catholic Latina women living in Texas are worlds apart from Muslim Arab women living in Minnesota. And yet all of these women—and many more—are typically considered women of color in the United States.

Some women of color are more reluctant than white women to seek mental health care. This is sometimes due to cultural norms against seeking help. For example, Asian American women who enter therapy may feel that they are admitting personal failure and bringing shame to their families (Bradshaw, 1994). Women of color may also be hesitant to seek therapy because it is very probable that their only option will be to work with a White therapist of European descent. This therapist probably will have little personal experience with racism, will not likely be fluent in any language other than English, will be highly educated and financially comfortable, and will have only limited knowledge of ethnic or religious cultures other than her own. The therapist is likely to have learned stereotypes about the client's nationality, race, culture, religion, and so on.

Of particular relevance in feminist therapy is the potential gap between feminist ideals—originally formulated by mostly White middle-class women within a Western European tradition—and the ideas about gender that women of color may bring with them from their cultures of origin. Women from India may subscribe to very rigid gender roles in which girls are considered property from birth and are prepared throughout childhood for an eventual arranged marriage (Jayakar, 1994), whereas Native American women may be accustomed to a variety of flexible gender roles such as the bold and assertive manly hearted role for postmenopausal women among the Canadian Blackfeet and the *berdache* or *two-spirit* role for gender-bending men in many North American Indian cultures that was described in Chapter 5 (LaFramboise, Berman, & Sohi, 1994). Also relevant are the preconceived notions that the therapist may have regarding gender roles in the client's culture of origin. For example, what is your stereotype of gender relations within Latina/Latino cultures? Do you think of dominant *macho* men and submissive, second-class women? Many scholars have characterized Latina/Latino cultures in this way, yet some studies have suggested that this stereotype is an exaggeration and overgeneralization (Vasquez, 1994). Feminist therapists must be careful not to assume that they know how a woman of color feels about gender. At the same time, a feminist therapist will be more prepared than a nonfeminist therapist to deal with the intersections between gender, race, and ethnicity for women of color.

Lesbian and Bisexual Women

Throughout traditional psychological theory and practice, healthy sexuality has been very narrowly defined. Assumptions regarding heterosexuality and homosexuality permeate the literature (Worell & Remer, 2003; Garnets & Peplau, 2001; Peplau & Garnets, 2000). Heterosexuality has been viewed as normal, while homosexuality and bisexuality have been pathologized. Sexual orientation has been presumed stable across the lifetime, casting a suspicious light on deviations later in life. Gender and sexual orientation have been confounded (much as they are in common stereotypes) such that lesbian women have been assumed more masculine than feminine women. Sexual orientation has been conceptualized as an attribute of the individual, rather than a variable pattern of erotic and romantic attractions that are influenced by the social and cultural context of women's lives (Garnets & Peplau, 2001).

Garnets and Peplau (2001) recommend that therapists abandon these outdated models of women's sexual orientation in favor of a model in which women's sexual orientation cannot be categorized nor attributed to a single cause. They suggest that much of the theorizing about sexual orientation has been based on a male norm, and that women's sexual orientation may be more variable across the lifespan than men's; therefore, therapists should not be surprised if a woman client who felt her sexual identity was well established ends up confused and distressed when she experiences changes in her sexual attractions. And when a woman does experience such changes, according to Garnets and Peplau, the therapist should not assume that the client's new sexual orientation is her true identity.

A Word about Feminist Therapy for Men

Can men benefit from feminist therapy? Several feminist therapists think so, some of whom are men themselves (Remer & Rostosky, 2001a; 2001b). For example, Carlton Parks and his colleagues have described the use of feminist therapy with gay and bisexual adult male sexual assault survivors (Parks, Woodson, Cutts, & Flarity-White, 2000–2001). As an approach that is sensitive to sexual orientation, feminist therapy may have more to offer gay and bisexual men than a traditional approach would. Other feminist therapists have suggested that heterosexual men may benefit from a relationship with a female feminist therapist because it can help illuminate some aspects of their relationships with women that a gender-blind or gender-stereotypical therapist might miss (Remer & Rostosky, 2001b). Finally, feminist therapists may be able to help increase male clients' awareness of the costs of rigidly conforming to a traditional masculine gender role (Remer & Rostosky, 2001a).

Evaluating Feminist Therapy

In principle, feminist therapists strive to remedy the shortcomings of traditional therapy, but are they successful? At this point we have very little formal data on the effectiveness of the feminist therapeutic approach (Worell & Johnson, 2001). Anecdotally, feminist clinicians have been very successful at identifying and treating psychological distress specific to women, such as trauma experienced by survivors of sexual assault, incest, and battering—all things that were unnamed and untreated by prefeminist therapists (Chesler, 1997; Marecek, 1999). If the international growth of feminist therapy since the 1970s is any indication, there is a substantial demand for woman-friendly, gender-aware, and diversity-sensitive therapy (Chesler, 1997). It is important, however, to generate support for feminist therapy effectiveness that goes beyond mere anecdote. Psychotherapies are typically evaluated by *outcome studies* that measure reductions in personal distress. Judith Worell (2001) suggests that assessment of feminist therapy should also measure empowerment; that is, she considers feminist therapy successful if it not only makes a woman feel better, but also inspires her to work for social change in her community.

Feminist therapy is not without its critics. Even supporters of the approach have highlighted its limitations. Ussher (1992) points out that as highly educated, professionally credentialed individuals, feminist therapists, like traditional therapists, still represent a privileged group. She warns that feminist theory generated by elite academics and activists may not be applicable or accessible to all women. The academics and clinicians who write about and practice feminist therapy constitute a less-diverse group than women in general.

Speaking of women *in general*, some have warned against the tendency of some feminist therapists to think of all women as sharing characteristics unique to their sex (e.g., Cosgrove, 2003). For example, when researchers interviewed a sample of feminist therapists about their practice, many of them implied a belief in a fundamental feminine or womanly nature, referring to "the essence of being a woman" and "the feminine character" (Marecek & Kravetz, 1998, p. 18). Assuming that all women share a uniquely feminine perspective ignores diversity among women and can contribute to biased attitudes favoring women as a group with special qualities—effectively reversing the sexism characteristic of traditional therapy.

Making a Difference

By now you have a better sense of why I introduced this chapter with the idea that traditional clinical practice may be at odds with women's well-being. Feminist therapy is a step in the right direction toward improving the mental health context for women. Equally important is social change that will challenge the perception of women's madness relative to a male norm, and will lead to a reduction in the external factors that contribute to women's real psychological distress.

Transforming Ourselves: Finding a Feminist Therapist

Not all feminist therapists are alike. In fact, not all therapists who call themselves feminist are necessarily feminist. Why would a therapist adopt the feminist label if his or her work is not truly informed by feminist therapy principles? Hypothetically, an unscrupulous clinician might do so in order to attract business (Caplan, 1992), but a self-named feminist therapist might *seem* not feminist because of different ideas about what feminism means.

There are many flavors of feminism and potentially as many different varieties of feminist therapy. So, how does one find the *right* feminist therapist? Besides referrals from family, friends, or other clinicians, an individual in search of a feminist therapist could consult some of the several therapist search engine sights on the Internet, most of which list "Feminist Therapy" as a specialty option. Some larger metropolitan areas have woman-centered social services that can direct people to feminist clinicians, such as the Feminist Therapy Referral Project (FTRP) in Berkley, Calif.

Transforming Social Relations: Challenging the "Crazy Woman" Stereotype

How many times have you heard someone make a wisecrack about women being "nuts" when they are "on the rag"? Have you ever had a guy (or his new girlfriend) tell you with a shudder that all of his ex-girlfriends were "psycho"? Do you and your friends agree that your mothers are all "crazy"? The idea that women as a group are mentally ill permeates our culture. From now on, pay attention to the examples you encounter in everyday conversation, movies and television, crime reports, advice columns, stand-up comedy routines, and so on. Take note when women's behavior is pathologized relative to a male standard of rationality and wellness. And then challenge it! Challenge yourself and your acquaintances to steer clear of the loony women comments and jokes. Treat women's perspectives and experiences with the respect that they deserve (including your own, if you are a woman). Question the experts that would have us believe that women are irrational, illogical, too dependent, and emotionally overwrought.

Transforming Society: Promoting Women's Psychological Well-Being

Clearly, women's well-being is intimately tied to their social circumstances. Sexism, racism, poverty, violence—all of these are significant contributors to women's psychological distress. Women have long been told that the remedy for their distress is individual change (or medication or hospitalization), but no amount of therapy for an individual woman is going to alleviate her symptoms if the source of the problem is economic inequality, sexual harassment, or domestic abuse. Feminist therapists encourage their clients to seek relief through social change. By engaging in activism to address the social problems that women face, you, too, can work to promote women's mental health.

Exploring Further
∾

Chesler, P. (1997). *Women and Madness* (25th anniversary edition). New York: Four Walls Eight Windows.
   First published in 1972, this groundbreaking book challenges traditional definitions of madness and critiques the use of psychiatry as a form of social control over women.

Showalter, E. (1986). *The Female Malady: Women, Madness, and English Culture, 1830–1980.* New York: Pantheon Books.
   Book explores sexism embedded in psychiatric practices from the 19th and 20th centuries, including institutionalization, medication, and psychosurgery.

Films
∾

Girl, Interrupted
The Magdalene Sisters

CHAPTER 14

Making a Difference:
Toward a Better Future for Women

- **Contemporary Feminism**
- **The Backlash against Feminism**
  Negative Images of Feminists
  Feminism as a "Woman's Problem"
  Women's Attitudes toward Feminism
- **Feminist Psychology and Social Change**
  The Changing Face of Psychology
  Imagine a World . . .
  What Can One Student Do?

$\mathcal{T}$hroughout history, women have struggled to have their voices heard, their injustices recognized, and their contributions to society accepted. For over 150 years, the women's movement has provided a powerful force for change.

The first wave of feminist activists included the suffragists who achieved the vote for women in the early 1900s. The second wave, whose activism began in the 1960s, worked on issues such as reproductive rights, workplace equality, sexism in the media, nonsexist child raising, the integration of women into science and politics, and an end to violence against women. Today, third-wave feminists continue the tradition, working on some of the same inequities that second-wave feminism tackled, and adding new ones: the continued objectification of women, reproductive rights in a high-tech era, global trafficking in girls and women, and many more.

Contemporary Feminism

Feminists are a diverse group on dimensions such as nationality, ethnicity, social class, and religion. This diversity is a strength because it encourages people to work for social change in many areas and to use a variety of strategies. Throughout this book, we have seen that the problems faced by working-class women are quite different from those faced by professional women. Older women experience different forms of sexism than younger women. Women who mother run into a different kind of stereotyping and inequality than those who do not. Anyone whose sexual orientation is different from the heterosexual norm may encounter prejudice and discrimination on that basis. People whose bodies are marked by difference are beginning to claim a right to their own dimensions of diversity, as shown by activism for the rights of intersex and transgender people.

Increasingly, feminism is a global social movement. International conferences bring women together to learn from each other about the particular forms that patriarchy takes in each society and to share effective strategies for change (see Figure 14.1). In this book, we have looked at issues such as the global influence of Western beauty ideals, sex trafficking, the invisible and unpaid work of women around the world, and the social meaning of aging in different cultures.

Making the women's movement, and feminist psychology, more inclusive is not an easy task. Much of feminist theory has assumed that gender is the primary source of oppression for all women. If this were true, being inclusive would consist simply of studying how sexism affects women of color, disabled women, and any other defined group of women. However, many women do not consider gender the primary source of oppression in their lives. They urge other women to become more aware of how sexism varies or interacts with other kinds of oppression and privilege (Greene & Sanchez-Hucles, 1997).

Women of color argue that feminist theory and research should go beyond analyzing the position of white women in relation to white men. It should also analyze the position of white women in relation to women of color, white women to men of color, and people of color to white men. These analyses would help white feminists confront and change their own unacknowledged racism and ethnocentrism. As a

FIGURE 14.1
Feminism is a global movement for empowering women.

start, each white feminist might ask herself, "What privileges does my white skin give me?" (Fine, Weis, Powell, & Wong, 1997; McIntosh, 1988). Similarly, each heterosexual feminist might ask, "How has my heterosexuality affected my feminist politics?" (Wilkinson & Kitzinger, 1993).

One Asian American third-wave feminist, Jee Yeun Lee, eloquently stated the importance of women-of-color perspectives:

> Women of color do not struggle in feminist movements simply to add cultural diversity, to add the viewpoints of different kinds of women. Women of color feminist theories challenge the fundamental premises of feminism, such as the very definition of "women," and call for recognition of the constructed racial nature of all experiences of gender. . . . These days, whenever someone says the word "women" to me, my mind goes blank. What "women"? What is this "women" thing you're talking about? Does that mean me? Does that mean my mother, my roommates, the white woman next door, the checkout clerk at the supermarket, my aunts in Korea, half the world's population? . . . Sisterhood may be global, but who is in that sisterhood? None of us can afford to assume anything about anybody else. This thing called "feminism" takes a great deal of hard work, and I think this is one of the primary hallmarks of young feminists' activism today: We realize that coming together and working together are by no means natural and easy. (Lee, 1995)

Women of color who believed that white women had omitted recognition of their issues articulated the womanist perspective in feminism. In response, white women have tried harder to overcome the racism that is part of our society and to work together with women of color. Similarly, lesbians and bisexual women criticized feminist organizations for focusing on straight women's issues, and older women wrote about ageism within the women's movement. As a result of these criticisms, the women's movement has made respect for differences a cornerstone of feminist philosophy and activism.

Along with their respect for diversity, feminists also have other shared values and goals. At the most basic level, a feminist is one who believes in the worth and value of women. As a 1970s bumper sticker proclaimed, "Feminism is the radical notion that women are people." Moreover, feminists recognize that social change is necessary and that no one can create social justice by herself. And they believe that people should work together to change society so that women can lead more secure, satisfying, and fulfilling lives. This belief in *collective action,* or group solidarity toward social change, is part of what differentiates feminism from just individual women achieving success.

The Backlash against Feminism

Like other progressive movements for social justice, feminism has met with resistance from those who benefit from inequality. Each time that feminist perspectives have gained power, there has been a *backlash*—attempts to put women, and particularly feminists, back in their place (Faludi, 1991). The backlash has taken different forms at different times in history, but some characteristic patterns emerge repeatedly. One form of backlash is to label feminists and their ideas as crazy. As noted in Chapter 13, 19th century Western women were labeled mad if they wanted to think independently or enlarge their world beyond that of wife and mother. Another form of backlash is to claim that feminism is a mere quarrel among women, of no importance to men. Let's look more closely at each of these forms of resistance to feminism.

Negative Images of Feminists

When first-wave feminists began organizing to win the right to vote, political cartoonists depicted them in ways that seem very familiar today. Figure 14.2 shows suffragists as ugly, cigar-smoking, angry women who foist their babies off on men. Their exposed legs represent their dangerously out-of-control sexuality. The text tells us that they are brassy, sharp-tongued man-tamers.

In the 1970s, these images resurfaced. The media image of second-wave feminists was quite negative:

> News reports and opinion columnists created a new stereotype, of fanatics, "braless bubbleheads," Amazons, "the angries," and "a band of wild lesbians." The result is that we all know what feminists are. They are shrill, overly aggressive, man-hating, ball-busting, selfish, hairy, extremist, deliberately unattractive women with absolutely no sense of

PUBLISHED BY CURRIER & IVES.   Entered according to Act of Congress A.D.1869, by Currier & Ives, in the Clerks Office of the District Court of the United States, for the Southern District of New York.   152 NASSAU ST. NEW YORK.

THE AGE OF BRASS.

FIGURE 14.2
Backlash against first-wave feminists.

humor who see sexism at every turn. They make men's testicles shrivel up to the size of peas, they detest the family and think all children should be deported or drowned. Feminists are relentless, unforgiving, and unwilling to bend or compromise; they are single-handedly responsible for the high divorce rate, the shortage of decent men and the unfortunate proliferation of Birkenstocks in America. (Douglas, 1994, p. 7)

By the 1980s, at least some women had made some gains toward equality. The media then turned to declaring feminism outdated, claiming that equal rights had been fully achieved, society was now in a so-called postfeminist era, and women were abandoning feminism because it had terrible costs. In the 1980s version of backlash, everything from infertility to the breakdown of society was blamed on feminism, and its time was declared long past (Faludi, 1991).

Today, the public image of feminists has both positive and negative aspects. For example, a study of British male high school students and adult men revealed that they had "Jekyll and Hyde" views: Feminists are reasonable women who just want equality *and* ugly, man-hating lesbians who go around "banging and shouting" and just want men to "jump in the river." Surprisingly, many men held *both* these contradictory views (Edley & Wetherell, 2001). U.S. studies also show that feminists are viewed positively as women working together to achieve goals and negatively as

FIGURE 14.3

Responding to the backlash.

Source: Copyright © 1992 by Nicole Hollander. Reprinted by permission.

man-hating, masculine-appearing extremists (Alexander & Ryan, 1997). Conservative men in power play to the negative view. Recently, the newly appointed Roman Catholic Archbishop of Boston preached that feminism is an evil ideology. In an Easter Week sermon, he denounced it along with the "drug culture," the "sexual revolution," "consumerism," the "breakdown of authority," and other "threats" to the Church and society (McNamara, 2004).

In the mass media, conservative commentators try to scare men and turn women away from working together for equality by referring to "feminazis" and characterizing any criticism of the status quo as "male-bashing" (see Figure 14.3). A favorite right-wing term is *militant feminist*, though what it means is unclear. Personally, I have never met a feminist with an assault weapon or heard of any feminist armies about to march on Congress, the Rotary club, or the football stadium. Feminism, of course, is not about "bashing" or making war on men; it is about disliking—and working to end—male *privilege* and its costs to girls and women.

Feminism as a "Woman's Problem"

One of the ways that feminists and their ideas are trivialized is to treat equality as an issue that only women need to care about. I remember when sexual harassment on college campuses was first defined and specified as a violation of academic integrity. Across the country, universities began to develop sexual harassment policies and procedures and disseminate them to faculty. Each time my university mailed an informational brochure to faculty, I would find a dozen or more copies of the brochure stuffed in my mailbox. What happened was that my male colleagues would glance at it in the mailroom, think "women" and immediately pass it on to me! After all, I was the "woman person" and the token feminist on the faculty.

If it weren't so annoying, this might have been funny. I certainly wasn't harassing anyone and was already quite familiar with the guidelines—I'd helped to draft them. The professors who really needed the information—those who might have to counsel a student who had been harassed or whose own behavior might step over the line at some point—were able to dismiss the need to inform themselves by mentally classifying the problem as a "woman's issue."

If feminism is only for women, the next step in dismissing it is to portray women as fighting with each other over it (Douglas, 1994). Any woman who attacks the ideals and practices of feminism is almost guaranteed a hearing in the news media. It is even better if she claims to be a feminist, and it seems to matter little if her expertise on the issues is minimal. This prevents male social theorists and political analysts from having to study and consider feminist ideas themselves and allows them to claim that sensible women see through feminism and reject it.

In the 1970s, the media ignored the many groups of women working collectively for women's rights. Instead, they focused on Gloria Steinem, a feminist journalist and activist, versus Phyllis Schlafly, a conservative activist who called feminists a "bunch of bitter women seeking a constitutional cure for their personal problems." The effect was to make feminism seem like a disagreement between two female ideologues rather than a widespread social movement. Respected national media such as *Time* and *Newsweek* referred to the debate over the Equal Rights Amendment to the U.S. Constitution as "women versus women" and "the war between the women." In the 1992 presidential campaign, Barbara Bush and Hillary Rodham Clinton were portrayed as polar opposites—the good wife and mother versus the selfish career woman. Today, conservative media celebrities such as Dr. Laura pit stay-at-home and working mothers against each other. In short, "the catfight remains an extremely popular way for the news media to represent women's struggles for equality and power" (Douglas, 1994, p. 243).

Women's Attitudes toward Feminism

The societal images of feminism and feminists clearly influence women. On the one hand, studies during the 1980s and 1990s show that college women describe feminists as strong, caring, capable, open minded, knowledgeable, and intelligent (Berryman-Fink & Verderber, 1985; Buhl, 1989). On the other hand, being labeled feminist brings a certain stigma (see Figure 14.4). In one study, women made less positive statements about the feminist movement than about the women's movement, demonstrating that simply adding the "f-word" (feminist) caused them to think more negatively about women's activism (Buschman & Lenart, 1996). When college women were asked to report their own beliefs and those of a typical feminist, even those who identified themselves as feminists felt that the typical feminist was more extreme in beliefs than they themselves were (Liss, Hoffner, & Crawford, 2000). And many women are reluctant to label themselves feminists. In one recent study, 78 percent of college women said they were not feminists, although the majority agreed with some or most of the goals of the women's movement (Liss et al., 2001). And even the feminists reported that they didn't always admit to being feminists in public!

Negative depictions of feminism have done their work: Women who support gender justice seem to be quite aware that a feminist may be seen as an angry woman who hates men, and feminism as a radical, destructive ideology. What factors predict whether a woman will choose to identify as a feminist? Exposure to feminist ideas, having a generally positive view of feminists, and recognizing that discrimination exists are important. In addition, those who call themselves feminists

FIGURE 14.4

Source: Stone Soup Copyright © 1999 Jan Eliot. Distributed by Universal Press Syndicate. Reprinted with permission. All rights reserved.

support the goals of the women's movement, believe in collective action, and tend not to hold conservative beliefs (Liss et al., 2001; Myasovsky & Wittig, 1997).

I invite you to think critically about the ways that feminists and feminism are portrayed in our society. Personally, I am proud to call myself a feminist, and I find it disturbing that the media focus on the ideas of feminism only through the distortions and attacks of antifeminists. Consider this question: Whose interests does it serve if a movement to end sexism is made to seem irrational, wrong, and futile?

Despite the attacks, feminism is a vital arena of theory and research. Women's rights are human rights. They are so important that, far from holding to an inflexible party line, feminists have always encouraged debate and a plurality of viewpoints. In writing this book, I have tried to present a variety of feminist perspectives with the goal of encouraging you to think critically about them.

Feminist Psychology and Social Change

The second wave of the women's movement has had important effects on psychology. One of the most basic changes has been the number of women in psychology and their status within the field. Even more important than numbers is the influence of feminist theory and research.

The Changing Face of Psychology

Only a few short years ago, psychologists who happened to be women could not get hired by high-status universities and were rarely taken seriously as scientists or theorists (Unger, 1998b). Today, women earn the majority of higher degrees in psychology, lead well-established professional organizations, produce many books and journals, and participate in every aspect of psychological research, education, and practice.

I saw a small example of the changing gender norms within psychology recently. At my university, there are regular lunchtime research talks for faculty and graduate students. At one, the speakers were a married couple (with different last names) from a nearby college who do their research jointly. With them were their two children, a 4-year-old son and a 1-month-old infant. The man in the couple started their research presentation, while Mom took the children to play outside. Sexist? Not exactly. Halfway through the talk, she returned, Dad took the kids outside, and she concluded the presentation and discussion of their research. A lunchtime psychology program became an example of collaborative research, shared parenting, and the balancing act of multiple roles for both women and men.

Progress is uneven, however. It will probably be a while before such a scene occurs regularly enough that it is taken for granted.

Imagine a World . . .

Imagine a world that is free of domestic violence. Imagine a world where husbands do half the housework, every child is protected from sexual abuse, and no old woman is forced to end her life in poverty. Imagine a world where half of the CEOs, judges, generals, and members of parliament or congress are women—in every country. What would the world be like if all pregnancies were chosen and all children wanted? If the human capacity for emotion and empathy were considered manly as well as womanly? If all body shapes and sizes were accepted, and no woman felt she had to do gender by starving herself?

It's true that none of these visions is close to becoming reality. But nobody expected it would be easy to remedy the patriarchal power imbalances that shape women's lives. The psychology of women and gender that has developed over the past 30 or so years has made a huge contribution toward a more just society. Its contribution began with naming androcentrism and sexism in psychological theories and research. It continued with the development of many new research topics and theories—think back for a moment to the hundreds of research articles described in this book. These are just a sample of the important scientific research that forms the basis of feminist psychology. Feminist psychologists also founded organizations (such as Division 35 and AWP), started new research journals, and developed feminist approaches to counseling and therapy.

All these efforts have made a positive difference for girls and women. However, there are signs that women and feminist perspectives have not yet been fully integrated into psychology. Publishing one's research in a psychology of women journal still may have less impact than if it were published in a "mainstream" journal. Despite the wealth of feminist books and journals now available, college textbooks and course syllabi too often still exclude gender, women, ethnicity, and diversity (Bronstein & Quina, 2003). The continued lack of integration of feminist scholarship is a serious problem because, throughout history, women's contributions have often been curtailed by their exclusion from powerful positions and erased by their omission from the history books.

What Can One Student Do?

> Never doubt that a small group of thoughtful, committed people could change the world. Indeed, it's the only thing that ever has.
>
> —*Margaret Mead*

Over the years, I have encountered some students who seem disconnected from their courses in psychology. Although they are psychology majors, they don't seem to feel a part of their major or department, and they don't see themselves as active shapers of their own educational experience. I believe that this is partly a legacy of psychology's past as a science defined and controlled by a dominant social group. Today, the entire field of psychology is becoming more diverse, and you can participate in creating a psychology of all people.

You can make a difference as a student by contributing to research and by using your knowledge of the psychology of women and gender to work for change. When you have a choice of topic, you can write term papers on women or gender in your psychology, history, and literature courses. You can do an independent study or thesis on women and gender. You can ask questions in class when women are excluded or trivialized in readings and lectures. These strategies do not add much to the time and effort you put into your education, but they can help raise consciousness for yourself and others.

You can join an organization for women's equality or volunteer at the women's center on your campus. If your campus has no women's center or women's studies program, start asking why. By taking courses that focus on women and gender and recommending them to others, you can show the administration that there is a demand for this knowledge.

Your knowledge of the psychology of women and gender can help in your career planning. If you are planning to apply to graduate schools in psychology (or any other area), look carefully at the number of women faculty in the programs you consider and find out how many have tenure. Look for courses on women and gender in the catalog, and find out whether there are women's studies and ethnic studies programs and a women's center. When visiting, ask about the level of support for feminist scholarship on campus. Psychology students (both male and female) can find information and support on a variety of gender issues by joining the Association for Women in Psychology (www.awpsych.org) or Division 35 of APA (www.apa.org/about/division/div35.html) as student affiliates. These organizations allow students to become part of networks of people with similar concerns. Through organizations like these, you can develop friendships with others who share your values and work together for social change.

If you are seeking employment after graduation, look carefully at the gender-related policies and family sensitivity of the companies you consider. Do they have flextime, on-site day care, parental leave, and benefits for same-sex partners? Does the health-care plan cover women's reproductive needs? What proportion of management are women? How often do women get promoted from inside the company? Is there ethnic and racial diversity? What is the company's record on sexual harassment complaints? Ask questions based on your knowledge of the psychology of women and gender.

One of the most important things you can do is to continue to educate yourself on the issues facing girls and women. Even though you have completed this book and your current course, continue to challenge the androcentrism in your education and the world around you. This will help you think critically about what you read and hear in other textbooks, classes, and from the popular media. It also will help you become an equal partner in relationships, an effective employee, and a responsible citizen after graduation.

Psychological research and theory have provided a wealth of evidence and reason on why women want and deserve full human rights. I offer the research and theory in this book as a resource and a gift. This gift can be made meaningful only by the one who receives it. How will you use your knowledge of psychology to make a difference?

References

Aarons, S. J., & Jenkins, R. R. (2002). Sex, pregnancy, and contraception-related motivators and barriers among Latino and African-American youth in Washington D.C. *Sex Education, 2,* 5–30.

ABC/Nepal. (1996). *Red light traffic: The trade in Nepali girls.* NGO report (3rd ed.). Kathmandu, Nepal: ABC/Nepal.

ABC News. (2003). *American porn: Corporate America is profiting from porn—quietly.* January 28 on Abcnews.com.

Abelson, R. (2004, June 23). Bias suit a hope to move up at Wal-Mart. *The New York Times,* pp. C1, C8.

Abramson, L. Y., Metalsky, G. I., & Alloy, L. B. (1989). Hopelessness depression: A theory-based subtype of depression. *Psychological Review, 96,* 358–372.

Abramson, P. E., Goldberg, P. A., Greenberg, J. H., & Abramson, L. M. (1977). The talking platypus phenomenon: Competency ratings as a function of sex and professional status. *Psychology of Women Quarterly, 2,* 114–124.

Abusharaf, R. M. (1998, March/April). Unmasking tradition. *The Sciences,* 22–27.

Adams, R. C. (1997). Friendship patterns among older women. In J. M. Coyle (Ed.), *Handbook on women and aging* (pp. 400–417). Westport, CT: Greenwood Press.

Ader, D. N., & Johnson, S. B. (1994). Sample description, reporting and analysis of sex in psychological research: A look at APA and APA division journals in 1990. *American Psychologist, 49,* 216–218.

Addis, M. E., & Mahalik, J. R. (2003). Men, masculinity, and the contexts of help seeking. *American Psychologist, 58,* 5–14.

Adult Video News. (2002). *The 25 events that shaped the first 25 years of video porn.* Available at AdultVideoNews.com.

Affonso, D. D., & Mayberry, L. J. (1989). Common stressors reported by a group of childbearing American women. In P. N. Stern (Ed.), *Pregnancy and parenting* (pp. 41–55). New York: Hemisphere.

Aguilera, R. J. (2000). Disability and delight: Staring back at the devotee community. *Sexuality and Disability, 18,* 255–261.

Aida, Y., & Falbo, T. (1991). Relationships between marital satisfaction, resources, and power strategies. *Sex Roles, 24,* 43–56.

Aizenberg, D., Weizman, A., & Barak, Y. (2002). Attitudes toward sexuality among nursing home residents. *Sexuality and Disability, 20,* 185–189.

Alan Guttmacher Institute (2002). *Facts in brief: Teenagers' sexual and reproductive health.* New York: Author.

Alexander, S., & Ryan, M. (1997). Social constructs of feminism: A study of undergraduates at a women's college. *College Student Journal, 31,* 555–567.

Algoe, S. B., Buswell, B. N., & DeLamater, J. D. (2000). Gender and job status as contextual cues for the interpretation of facial expression of emotion. *Sex Roles, 42,* 183–208.

Alindogan-Medina, N. (2001). Women's studies: A struggle for a better life. In M. Crawford, & R. Unger (Eds.), *In our own words: Writings from women's lives* (pp. 45–57). Boston: McGraw-Hill.

Almquist, E. M. (1989). The experiences of minority women in the United States: Intersections of race, gender, and class. In J. Freeman (Ed.), *Women: A feminist perspective* (4th ed., pp. 414–445). Mountain View, CA: Mayfield Publishing.

Altman, M. (1984). Everything they always wanted you to know. In C. S. Vance (Ed.) *Pleasure and danger: Exploring female sexuality* (pp. 115–130). Boston: Routledge & Kegan Paul.

Amaro, H., Raj, A., & Reed, E. (2001). Women's sexual health: The need for feminist analyses in public health in the decade of behavior. *Psychology of Women Quarterly, 25,* 324–334.

Amato, P. R., & Previti, D. (2003). People's reasons for divorcing: Gender, social class, the life course, and adjustment. *Journal of Family Issues, 24,* 602–626.

American Association of University Women Educational Foundation. (2001). *Hostile hallways: Bullying, teasing and sexual harassment in school.* Washington, DC: Author.

American Psychiatric Association (APA) (1994). *Diagnostic and statistical manual of mental disorders* (4th ed.). Washington, DC: American Psychiatric Association.

American Psychiatric Association (2000). *Diagnostic and statistical manual of mental disorders: DSM-IV-TR* (4th ed.). Washington, DC: Author.

American Psychiatric Association. (2000). *Diagnostic and statistical manual of psychological disorders* (4th ed.). Washington, DC: Author.

Anderson, C. A., Berkowitz, L., Donnerstein, E., Huesmann, L. R., Johnson, J. D., Linz, D., et al. (2003). The influence of media violence on youth. *Psychological Science in the Public Interest, 4,* 81–110.

Anderson, K. J., & Leaper, C. (1998). Meta-analysis of gender effects on conversational interruptions: Who, what, when, where, and how. *Sex Roles, 39,* 225–252.

Anderson, K. L., & Umberson, D. (2001). Gendering violence: Masculinity and power in men's accounts of domestic violence. *Gender & Society, 15,* 358–380.

Anderssen, N. (2002). Does contact with lesbians and gays lead to friendlier attitudes? A two year longitudinal study. *Journal of Community and Applied Social Psychology, 12,* 124–136.

Angless, T., Maconachie, M., & Van Zyl, M. (1998). Battered women seeking solutions: A South African study. *Violence Against Women, 4,* 637–658.

Apuzzo, V. M. (2001). A call to action. In D. C. Kimmel, & D. L. Martin (Eds.), *Midlife and aging in gay America: Proceedings of the SAGE conference 2000* (pp. 1–11). New York: Harrington Park Press.

Araoye, M. O., & Adegoke, A. (1996). AIDS-related knowledge, attitude and behaviour among selected adolescents in Nigeria. *Journal of Adolescence, 19,* 179–181.

Arbuckle, J., & Williams, B. D. (2003). Students' perceptions of expressiveness: Age and gender effects on teacher evaluations. *Sex Roles, 49,* 507–516.

Archer, D., Iritani, B., Kimes, D. D., & Barrios, M. (1983). Faceism: Five studies of sex differences in facial prominence. *Journal of Personality and Social Psychology, 45,* 725–735.

Arendell, T. (1997). A social constructionist approach to parenting. In R. Arendell (Ed.), *Contemporary parenting: Challenges and issues* (pp. 1–44). Thousand Oaks, CA: Sage.

Arima, A. N. (2003). Gender stereotypes in Japanese television advertisements. *Sex Roles, 49,* 81–90.

Arnold, D. H., & Doctoroff, G. L. (2003). The early education of socioeconomically disadvantaged children. In S. T. Fiske, D. L. Schacter, & C. Zahn-Waxler (Eds.), *Annual Review of Psychology* (Vol. 54, pp. 517–545). Palo Alto, CA: Annual Reviews.

Arnold, S. C. (1994). Transforming body image through women's wilderness experiences. *Wilderness Therapy for Women: The Power of Adventure* (pp. 43–54) (originally published as volume of *Women & Therapy*). In Cole, E.

Erdman, & E. Rothblum (Eds.). New York: Hayworth Press, Inc., 1994.

Aronson, J., Lustina, M. J., Good, C., Keough, K., Steele, C. M., & Brown, J. (1999). When White men can't do math: Necessary and sufficient factors in stereotype threat. *Journal of Experimental Social Psychology, 35,* 29–46.

Ascher-Svanum, H. & Sobel, T. S. (1989). Caregivers of mentally ill adults: A woman's agenda. *Hospital and Community Psychiatry, 40,* 843–845.

Ault, A. (1996). Ambiguous identity in an unambiguous sex/gender structure: The case of bisexual women. *The Sociological Quarterly, 37,* 449–463.

Avis, N. E., & McKinlay, S. M. (1991). A longitudinal analysis of women's attitudes toward the menopause: Results from the Massachusetts women's health study. *Maturitas, 13,* 65–79.

Baber, K. M., & Allen, K. R. (1992). *Women and families: Feminist reconstructions.* New York: Guilford.

Bachand, L. L., & Caron, S. L. (2001). Ties that bind: A qualitative study of happy long-term marriages. *Contemporary Family Therapy: An International Journal, 23,* 105–121.

Bachar, K., & Koss, M. (2001). Rape. In J. Worell (Ed.), *Encyclopedia of women and gender* (pp. 893–903). San Diego, CA: Academic Press.

Bachrach, L. L. (1984). Deinstitutionalization and women: Assessing the consequences of public policy. *American Psychologist, 39,* 1171–1177.

Baculinao, E. (2004, September 14). China grapples with legacy of its "missing girls": Disturbing demographic imbalance spurs drive to change age-old practices. Retrieved September 21, 2004, from http://www.msnbc.com/id/5953508/print/1/displaymode/1098/

Badgett, M. V. L. (1996). Employment and sexual orientation: Disclosure and discrimination in the workplace. In A. L. Ellis and E. D. B. Riggle (Eds.), *Sexual identity on the job: Issues and services* (pp. 29–52). New York: Harrington Park Press.

Bailey, D. S. (2004). Number of psychology PhDs declining. *Monitor on Psychology, 35,* 18–19.

Baker, R., Kiger, G., & Riley, P. J. (1996). Time, dirt, and money: The effects of gender, gender ideology, and type of earner marriage on time, household-task, and economic satisfaction among couples with children. *Journal of Social Behavior and Personality, 11,* 161–177.

Balter, M. B., Levine, J., & Manheimer, D. I. (1974). Cross-national study of the extent of anti-anxiety/sedative drug use. *New England Journal of Medicine, 290,* 769–774.

Bandura, A. (1965). Influence of model's reinforcement contingencies on the acquisition of imitative responses. *Journal of Personality and Social Psychology, 1,* 589–595.

Bandura, A., & Walters, R. H. (1963). *Social learning and personality development.* New York: Holt, Rinehart & Winston.

Banner, L. W. (1983). *American beauty*. Chicago: University of Chicago Press.

Bannon, L. (2000, March). More kids' marketers pitch number of single-sex products. *The Wall Street Journal*, pp. B1, 4.

Banyard, V. L., Williams, L. M., Siegel, J. A., & West, C. M. (2002). Childhood sexual abuse in the lives of Black women: Risk and resilience in a longitudinal study. *Women & Therapy, 25*, 45–58.

Barak, A. (1997). Cross-cultural perspectives on sexual harassment. In W. O'Donohue (Ed.), *Sexual harassment: Theory, research, and treatment* (pp. 263–300). Boston: Allyn & Bacon.

Barak, A., Feldman, S., & Noy, A. (1991). Traditionality of children's interests as related to their parents' gender stereotypes and traditionality of occupations. *Sex Roles, 24*, 511–524.

Bargad, A., & Hyde, J. S. (1991). Women's studies: A study of feminist identity development in women. *Psychology of Women Quarterly, 15*, 181–201.

Barnett, R. C., & Hyde, J. S. (2001). Women, men, work, and family: An expansionist theory. *American Psychologist, 56*, 78–96.

Barnett, R. C., & Shen, Y.-C. (1997). Gender, high- and low-schedule-control housework tasks, and psychological distress: A study of dual-earner couples. *Journal of Family Issues, 18*, 403–428.

Barreca, G. (1991). *They used to call me Snow White . . . but I drifted: Women's strategic use of humor.* New York: Viking.

Barrett, L. F., Lane, R. D., Sechrest, L., & Schwartz, G. E. (2000). Sex differences in emotional awareness. *Personality and Social Psychology Bulletin, 26*, 1027–1035.

Bart, P. B. (1971). Sexism and social science: From the gilded cage to the iron cage, or, the perils of Pauline. *Journal of Marriage and the Family, 33*, 734–735.

Bartsch, R. A., Burnett, T., Diller, T. R., & Rankin-Williams, E. (2000). Gender representation in television commercials: Updating an update. *Sex Roles, 43*, 735–743.

Baruch, G. K., Barnett, R. C., & Rivers, C. (1983). *Lifeprints: New patterns of love and work for today's women.* New York: New American Library.

Basow, S. A., & Howe, K. G. (1980). Role model influence: Effects of sex and sex-role attitude in college students. *Psychology of Women Quarterly, 4*, 558–572.

Basu, J., & Ray, B. (2001). Friends and lovers: A study of human mate selection in India. *Psychologia: An International Journal of Psychology in the Orient, 44*, 281–291.

Baumgardner, J., & Richards, A. (2000). *Manifesta: Young women, feminism, and the future.* New York: Farrar, Straus and Giroux.

Bazzini, D. G., McIntosh, W. D., Smith, S. M., Cook, S., & Harris, C. (1997). The aging woman in popular film: Underrepresented, unattractive, unfriendly, and unintelligent. *Sex Roles, 36*, 531–543.

Beals, K. P., & Peplau, L. A. (2001). Social involvement, disclosure of sexual orientation, and the quality of lesbian relationships. *Psychology of Women Quarterly, 25*, 10–19.

Beauvoir, S. (1953). *The second sex.* (H. M. Parshley, trans.). New York: Knopf.

Becker, D., & Lamb, S. (1994). Sex bias in the diagnosis of borderline personality disorder and post traumatic stress disorder. *Professional Psychology: Research and Practice, 25*, 55–61.

Becker, E., Rankin, E., & Rickel, A. U. (1998). *High-risk sexual behavior: Interventions with vulnerable populations.* New York: Plenum.

Beggs, J. M., & Doolittle, D. C. (1993). Perceptions now and then of occupational sex typing: A replication of Shinar's 1975 study. *Journal of Applied Social Psychology, 23*, 1435–1453.

Bekker, M. (1996). Agoraphobia and gender: A review. *Clinical Psychology Review, 16*, 129–146.

Belle, D. (2004). Poor women in a wealthy nation. In J. C. Chrisler, C. Golden, & P. D. Rozee (Eds.), *Lectures on the psychology of women* (3rd ed., pp. 28–42). New York: McGraw-Hill.

Belle, D., & Doucet, J. (2003). Poverty, inequality, and discrimination as sources of depression among U.S. women. *Psychology of Women Quarterly, 27*, 101–103.

Bem, S. L. (1981). Gender schema theory: A cognitive account of sex typing. *Psychological Review, 88*, 354–364.

Bem, S. L. (1983). Gender schema theory and its implications for child development: Raising gender-aschematic children in a gender-schematic society. *Signs, 8*, 598–616.

Bem, S. L. (1993). The lenses of gender. New Haven, CT: Yale University Press.

Bem, S. L. (1998). *An Unconventional Family.* New Haven, CT: Yale University Press.

Bemporad, J. R. (1996). Self-starvation through the ages: Reflections on the pre-history of anorexia nervosa. *International Journal of Eating Disorders, 19*, 217–237.

Benbow, C. P. (1988). Sex differences in mathematical reasoning ability in intellectually talented preadolescents: Their nature, effects, and possible causes. *Behavioral and Brain Sciences, 11*, 169–132.

Benbow, C. P., & Stanley, J. C. (1980). Sex differences in mathematical ability: Fact or artifact? *Science, 210*, 1262–1264.

Benokraitis, N. V. (Ed.). (1997). *Subtle sexism: Current practice and prospects for change.* Thousand Oaks, CA: Sage.

Berardo, D. H., Shehen, C. L., & Leslie, G. R. (1987). A residue of tradition: Jobs, careers, and spouses' time in housework. *Journal of Marriage and the Family, 49*, 381–390.

Berenbaum, S. A., & Hines, M. (1992). Early androgens are related to childhood sex-typed toy preferences. *Psychological Science, 3*, 203–206.

Berger, J. (1972). *Ways of seeing.* London: Penguin Books.

Berger, P. L., & Luckmann, T. (1966). *The social construction of reality: A treatise in the sociology of knowledge.* Garden City, NY: Doubleday.

Berger, R. M. (1990). Passing: Impact of the quality of same-sex couple relationships. *Social Work, 35,* 328–332.

Bernard, J. (1972). *The future of marriage.* New York: World.

Bernard, J. (1974). *The future of motherhood.* New York: Penguin.

Berns, N. (1999). My problem and how I solved it: Domestic violence in women's marriages. *Sociological Quarterly, 40,* 85–108.

Berryman-Fink, C., & Verderber, K. S. (1985). Attributions of the term feminist: A factor analytic development of a measuring instrument. *Psychology of Women Quarterly, 9,* 51–64.

Best, D. L. (2001). Cross-cultural gender roles. In J. Worell (Ed.), *Encyclopedia of Women and Gender* (pp. 279–290). San Diego, CA: Academic Press.

Betz, N. E., & Fitzgerald, L. E. (1987). *The career psychology of women.* New York: Academic Press.

Beyene, Y. (1989). *From menarche to menopause: Reproductive lives of peasant women in two cultures.* Albany: State University of New York Press.

Bianchi, S. M., & Spain, D. (1986). *American women in transition.* New York: Russell Sage Foundation.

Biernat, M., & Kobrynowicz, D. (1999). A shifting standards perspective on the complexity of gender stereotypes and gender stereotyping. In W. B. Swann, Jr., J. H. Langlois, & L. A. Gilbert (Eds.), *Sexism and stereotypes: The gender science of Janet Taylor Spence* (pp. 75–106). Washington, DC: American Psychological Association.

Bigler, R. S. (1999). Psychological interventions designed to counter sexism in children: Empirical limitations and theoretical foundations. In W. B. Swann Jr., J. H. Langlois, & L. A. Gilbert (Eds.), *Sexism and stereotypes in modern society: The gender science of Janet Taylor Spence* (pp. 129–151). Washington, DC: American Psychological Association.

Billings, A. C., Halone, K. K., & Denham, B. E. (2002). "Man, that was a pretty shot": An analysis of gendered broadcast commentary surrounding the 2000 Men's and Women's NCAA Final Four Basketball Championships. *Mass Communication and Society, 5*(3), 295–315.

Bing, V. M., & Reid, P. T. (1996). Unknown women and unknowing research: Consequences of color and class in feminist psychology. In N. R. Goldberger & J. M. Tarule (Eds.), *Knowledge, difference, and power: Essays inspired by "Women's Ways of Knowing"* (pp. 175–202). New York: Basic Books.

Bingham, S. G., & Scherer, L. L. (2001). The unexpected effects of a sexual harassment educational program. *The Journal of Applied Behavioral Science, 37,* 125–153.

Bishop, N. (1989). Abortion: The controversial choice. In J. Freeman (Ed.), *Women: A feminist perspective* (4th ed., pp. 45–56). Mountain View, CA: Mayfield.

Black, J., & Underwood, J. (1998). Young, female, and gay: Lesbian students and the school environment. *Professional School Counseling, 1,* 15–20.

Bleier, R. (Ed.). (1986). *Feminist approaches to science.* Elmsford, NY: Pergamon Press.

Block, M. (2004). Interview: Sonny Hill discusses this week's win of a high school slam dunk contest by Candace Parker, the first female to do so. *All Things Considered.* National Public Radio, March 31.

Blood, R. O., & Wolfe, D. M. (1960). *Husbands and wives.* New York: Free Press.

Blumstein, P., & Schwartz, P. (1983). *American couples.* New York: William Morrow.

Blytheway, B. (2003). Visual representations of late life. In C. A. Faircloth, (Ed.), *Aging bodies: Images and everyday experiences* (pp. 11–49). New York: AltaMira Press.

Blytheway, B. (1993). Aging and biography: The letters of Bernard and Mary Berenson. *Sociology, 27,* 153–165.

Boardman, S. K., Harrington, C. C., & Horowitz, S. V. (1987). Successful women: A psychological investigation of family class and education origins. In B. A. Gutek & L. Larwood (Eds.), *Women's career development* (pp. 66–85). Newbury Park, CA: Sage.

Boatwright, K. J., Gilbert, M. S., Forrest, L., & Ketzenberger, K. (1996). Impact of identity development upon career trajectory: Listening to the voices of lesbian women. *Journal of Vocational Behavior, 48,* 210–228.

Bograd, M. (1988). Feminist perspectives on wife abuse: An introduction. In K. Yllo & M. Bograd (Eds.), *Feminist perspectives on wife abuse* (pp. 11–26). Berkeley, CA: Sage.

Bohan, J. S. (1996). *Psychology and sexual orientation: Coming to terms.* New York: Routledge.

Bohn, D. K. (2003). Lifetime physical and sexual abuse, substance abuse, depression, and suicide attempts among Native American women. *Issues in Mental Health Nursing, 24,* 333–352.

Bolin, A. (1996). Transcending and transgendering: Male-to-female transsexuals, dichotomy, and diversity. In G. Herdt (Ed.), *Third sex, third gender: Beyond sexual dimorphism in culture and history* (pp. 447–485). New York: Zone Books.

Bornstein, K. (1994). *Gender outlaw: On men, women, and the rest of us.* New York: Routledge.

Boston Women's Health Book Collective (1998). *Our bodies, our selves for the new century.* New York: Simon & Schuster.

Boswell, S. L. (1979). *Nice girls don't study mathematics: The perspective from elementary school paper.* Presented at the meeting of the American Educational Research Association, San Francisco, CA.

Boswell, S. L. (1985). The influence of sex-role stereotyping on women's attitudes and achievement in mathematics. In S. F. Chipman, L. R. Brush, & D. M. Wilson (Eds.), *Women and mathematics: Balancing the equation* (pp. 175–198). Hillsdale, NJ: Erlbaum.

Bowen, C. C. Swim, J. K., & Jacobs, R. R. (2000). Evaluating gender biases on actual job performance of real people: A meta-analysis. *Journal of Applied Social Psychology, 30,* 2194–2215.

Boxer, A. M., Cook, J. A., & Herdt, G. (1999). Experiences of coming out among gay and lesbian youth: Adolescents alone. In *The adolescent alone: Decision making in health care in the United States* (pp. 121–136). Cambridge, England: Cambridge University Press.

Boyd, B., & Wandersman, A. (1991). Predicting undergraduate condom use with the Fishbein and Ajzen and the Triandis attitude-behavior models: Implications for public health interventions. *Journal of Applied Social Psychology, 21,* 1810–1830.

Brabant, S., & Mooney, L. (1986). Sex role stereotyping in the Sunday comics: Ten years later. *Sex Roles, 14,* 141–148.

Brabant, S., & Mooney, L. A. (1997). Sex role stereotyping in the Sunday comics: A twenty year update. *Sex Roles, 37,* 269–281.

Braden, A. (1986). Shoulder to shoulder. In J. B. Cole (Ed.), *All American women: Lines that divide, ties that bind* (pp. 74–80). New York: Macmillan.

Bradshaw, C. K. (1994). Asian and Asian American women: Historical and political considerations in psychotherapy. In L. Comas-Díaz & B. Greene (Eds.), *Women of color: Integrating ethnic and gender identities in psychotherapy* (pp. 72–113). New York: Guilford Press.

Bradsher, J. E. (1997). Older women and widowhood. In J. M. Coyle (Ed.), *Handbook on women and aging* (pp. 418–429). Westport, CT: Greenwood Press.

Bramlet, M. D., & Mosher, W. D. (2001). *First marriage dissolution, divorce, and remarriage: United States.* Hyattsville, MD: National Center for Health Statistics.

Bringaze, T. B., & White, L. J. (2001). Living out proud: Factors contributing to healthy identity development in lesbian leaders. *Journal of Mental Health Counseling, 23,* 162–173.

Brodsky, A. (1973). The consciousness-raising group as a model for therapy with women. *Psychotherapy: Theory, Research, and Practice, 10,* 24–29.

Brody, E. M. (2004). *Women in the middle: Their parent care years* (2nd ed.). New York: Springer.

Brody, L. R., & Hall, J. A. (2000). Gender, emotion, and expression. In M. Lewis & J. Haviland-Jones (Eds.), *Handbook of emotions* (pp. 338–349). New York: Guilford.

Bronstein, P. (in press) The family environment: Where gender role socialization begins. In J. Worrell & C. Goodheart (Eds.), *Handbook of girls' and women's psychological health.* New York: Oxford University Press.

Bronstein, P., & Quina, K. (Eds.). (2003). *Teaching gender and multicultural awareness: Resources for the psychology classroom.* Washington, DC: American Psychological Association.

Brooks-Gunn, J. (1988). Antecedents and consequences of variations in girls' maturational timing. *Journal of Adolescent Health Care, 9,* 365–373.

Brooks-Gunn, J., & Furstenberg, F. F., Jr. (1989). Adolescent sexual behavior. *American Psychologist, 44,* 249–257.

Broverman, I. K., Broverman, D. M., Clarkson, F. E., Rosenkrantz, P. S., & Vogel, S. R. (1970). Sex-role stereotypes and clinical judgments of mental health. *Journal of Consulting and Clinical Psychology, 34,* 1–7.

Broverman, I. K., Vogel, S. R., Broverman, D. M., Clarkson, F. E., & Rosenkrantz, P. S. (1972). Sex-role stereotypes: A current appraisal. *Journal of Social Issues, 28,* 59–78.

Brown, E. A. (1989, June 9). Happily ever after. *Christian Science Monitor,* 13.

Brown, L. M. (1998). *Raising their voices: The politics of girls' anger.* Cambridge, MA: Harvard University Press.

Brown, L. M., & Gilligan, C. (1992). *Meeting at the crossroads: Women's psychology and girls' development.* Cambridge, MA: Harvard University Press.

Browne, K. (2004). An unhealthy idea of beauty: Big business tells women whiter is better. *Ms., 13,* 60–62.

Brumberg, J. J. (2000). *Fasting girls: The history of anorexia nervosa.* New York: Vintage Books.

Buck, S., & Tiene, D. (1989). The impact of physical attractiveness, gender, and teaching philosophy on teacher evaluations. *Journal of Educational Research, 82,* 172–177.

Budig, M. J. (2002). Male advantage and the gender composition of jobs: Who rides the glass elevator? *Social Problems, 49,* 258–277.

Buhl, M. (1989, September/October). The feminist mystique. *View,* 16.

Buhle, M. J. (1998). *Feminism and its discontents: A century of struggle with psychoanalysis.* Cambridge, MA: Harvard University Press.

Bulik, C. M., Sullivan, P. F., Carter, F. A., & Joyce, P. R. (1996). Lifetime anxiety disorders in women with bulimia nervosa. *Comprehensive Psychiatry, 37,* 368–374.

Bulik, C. M., Tozzi, F., Anderson, C., Mazzeo, S. E., Aggen, S., & Sullivan, P. F. (2003). The relation between eating disorders and components of perfectionism. *American Journal of Psychiatry, 160,* 366–368.

Bullock, H. E., Wyche, K. F., & Williams, W. R. (2001). Media images of the poor. *Journal of Social Issues, 57,* 229–246.

Burke, P. J., & Cast, A. D. (1997). Stability and change in the gender identities of newly married couples. *Social Psychology Quarterly, 60,* 277–290.

Burke, R. J. (1997). Alternate family structures: A career advantage? *Psychological Reports, 81,* 812–814.

Burke, R. J., & McKeen, C. A. (1997). Gender effects in mentoring relationships. In R. Crandall (Ed.), *Handbook of gender research* (pp. 91–104). Corte Madera, CA: Select Press.

Burke, T. W., Jordan, M. L., & Owen, S. S. (2002). A cross-national comparison of gay and lesbian domestic violence. *Journal of Contemporary Criminal Justice, 18,* 231–257.

Burton-Nelson, M. (2004, March). *The courage to compete: How title IX and the women's sports revolution are transforming women, men, and society.* Lecture delivered at the University of St. Thomas, St. Paul, MN.

Buschman, J. K., & Lenart, S. (1996). "I am not a feminist but . . .": College women, feminism, and negative experiences. *Political Psychology, 17,* 59–75.

Buss, D. M. (1995). Psychological sex differences: Origins through sexual selection. *American Psychologist, 50,* 164–168.

Buss, D. M., et al. (1990). International preferences in selecting mates: A study of 37 cultures. *Journal of Cross-Cultural Psychology, 21,* 5–47.

Buss, D. M., & Schmitt, D. P. (1993). Sexual strategies theory: An evolutionary perspective on human mating. *Psychological Review, 100,* 204–232.

Bussey, K., & Bandura, A. (2004). Social cognitive theory of gender development and functioning. In A. H. Eagly, A. E. Beall, & R. J. Sternberg (Eds.), *The psychology of gender* (pp. 92–119). New York: Guilford Press.

Byers, M. (2003). Buffy the Vampire Slayer: The next generation of television. In R. Dicker & A. Piepmeier (Eds.), *Catching a wave: Reclaiming feminism for the 21st century* (pp. 171–188). Boston: Northeastern University Press.

Cabaj, R. P., & Purcell, D. W. (Eds.). (1998). *On the road to same-sex marriage: A supportive guide to psychological, political, and legal issues.* San Francisco: Jossey-Bass.

Cachelin, F. M., Veisel, C., Barzegarnazari, E., & Striegel-Moore, R. H. (2000). Disordered eating, acculturation, and treatment-seeking in a community sample of Hispanic, Asian, Black, and White women. *Psychology of Women Quarterly, 24,* 244–253.

Calasanti, T. M., & Slevin, K. F. (2001). *Gender, social inequalities, and aging.* New York: AltaMira Press.

Cameron, D. (1995). *Verbal Hygiene.* London: Routledge.

Cameron, D. (1996). The language-gender interface: Challenging co-optation. In V. L. Bergvall, J. M. Bing, & A. F. Freed (Eds.), *Rethinking language and gender research: Theory and Practice* (pp. 31–53). New York: Addison-Wesley.

Cameron, D. (1997). Performing gender identity: Young men's talk and the construction of heterosexual masculinity. In S. Johnson & U. H. Meinof (Eds.), *Language and masculinity* (pp. 47–64). Cambridge, MA: Blackwell.

Cameron, R. P., Grabill, C. M., Hobfoll, S. E., & Crowther, J. H. (1996). Weight, self-esteem, ethnicity, and depressive symptomatology during pregnancy among inner-city women. *Health Psychology, 15,* 293–297.

Campbell, A. (1992). *Men, women, and aggression.* New York: Basic Books.

Campbell, J. C., Kub, J., Belknap, R. A., & Templin, T. N. (1997). Predictors of depression in battered women. *Violence Against Women, 3,* 271–293.

Campbell, J. C., Rose, L., Kub, J., & Nedd, D. (1998). Voices of strength and resistance. A contextual and longitudinal analysis. *Journal of Interpersonal Violence, 13,* 743–762.

Canetto, S. S. (2001). Older adult women: Issues, resources, and challenges. In R. K. Unger (Ed.), *Handbook of the psychology of women and gender* (pp. 183–197). New York: Wiley.

Caplan, P. (1985). *The myth of women's masochism.* New York: E. P. Dutton.

Caplan, P. (1995). *They say you're crazy: How the world's most powerful psychiatrists decide who's normal.* Reading, MA: Perseus Books.

Caplan, P. (2000). *The new don't blame mother: Mending the mother-daughter relationship.* New York: Routledge.

Caplan, P. J. (1989). Don't blame mother. New York: Harper & Row.

Caplan, P. J. (1992). Driving us crazy: How oppression damages women's mental health and what we can do about it. *Women & Therapy, 12,* 5–28.

Caplan, P. J., & Hall-McCorquodale, I. (1985). Mother-blaming in major clinical journals. *American Journal of Orthopsychiatry, 55,* 345–353.

Carey, C. M., & Mongeau, P. A. (1996). Communication and violence in courtship relationships. In D. D. Cahn & S. A. Lloyd (Eds.), *Family violence from a communication perspective* (pp. 127–150). Thousand Oaks, CA: Sage.

Carli, L. L. (1990). Gender, language, and influence. *Journal of Personality and Social Psychology, 59,* 941–951.

Carli, L. L. (2001). Gender and social influence. *Journal of Social Issues, 57,* 735–741.

Carp, F. M. (1997). Retirement and women. In J. M. Coyle (Ed.), *Handbook on women and aging* (pp. 112–128). Westport, CT: Greenwood Press.

Cash, T. F. (1990). The psychology of physical appearance: Aesthetics, attributes, and images. In T. F. Cash & T. Pruzinsky (Eds.), *Body images: development, deviance, and change* (pp. 51–79). New York: Guilford.

Cash, T. F., Gillen, B., & Burns, D. S. (1977). Sexism and "beautyism" in personnel consultant decision making. *Journal of Applied Psychology, 62,* 301–310.

Cash, T. F. Kehr, J. A., Polyson, J. & Freeman, V. (1977). Role of physical attractiveness in peer attribution of psychological disturbance. *Journal of Consulting and Clinical Psychology, 45,* 987–993.

Cash, T. F., & Labarge, A. S. (1996). Development of the Appearance Schemas Inventory: A new cognitive body-image assessment. *Cognitive Therapy and Research, 20,* 37–50.

Cassell, J. (1997). Doing gender, doing surgery: Women surgeons in a man's profession. *Human Organization, 56,* 47–52.

Castaneda, D. (2000). Gender issues among Latinas. In J. C. Chrisler, C. Golden, & P. D. Rozee (Eds.), *Lectures on the psychology of women* (pp. 193–208). Boston: McGraw-Hill.

Cattarin, J. A., Thompson, J. K., Thomas, C., & Williams, R. (2002). Body image, mood, and televised images of attractiveness: The role of social comparison. *Journal of Social and Clinical Psychology, 19*, 220–239.

CBS News 60 Minutes (2003 November 23). *Porn in the USA: Adult entertainment industry becoming mainstream.*

Centers for Disease Control. (2002). *HIV/AIDS among US women.* Washington, DC: Center for Disease Control and Prevention, National Center for HIV STD, and TB Prevention, Division of HIV/AIDS Prevention.

Chambers, C. (1972). An assessment of drug use in the general population. In J. Sussman (Ed.), *Drug Use and Social Policy.* New York: AMS.

Chan, C. S. (1993). Issues of identity development among Asian-American lesbians and gay men. In L. D. Garnets & D. C. Kimmel (Eds.), *Psychological perspectives on lesbian and gay male experiences* (pp. 376–388). New York: Columbia University Press.

Chan, C. S. (2000). Asian American women and adolescent girls: Sexuality and sexual expression. In J. C. Chrisler, C. Golden, & P. D. Rozee (Eds.), *Lectures on the psychology of women* (pp. 149–162). Boston: McGraw-Hill.

Chandani, A. T., McKenna, K. T., & Maas, F. (1989). Attitudes of university students towards the sexuality of physically disabled people. *British Journal of Occupational Therapy, 52*, 233–236.

Charlesworth, W. R., & LaFreniere, P. (1983). Dominance, friendship utilization and resource utilization in preschool children's groups. *Ethology and Sociobiology, 4*, 175–186.

Chesler, P. (1972). *Women and madness.* New York: Doubleday.

Chesler, P. (1997). *Women and madness* (25th anniversary ed.). New York: Four Walls Eight Windows.

Cheung, C., & Liu, E. S. (1997). Impacts of social pressure and social support on distress among single parents in China. *Journal of Divorce & Remarriage: International Studies, 26*, 65–82.

Chicago, J. (1990, March). *The birth project.* Women's History Month Lecture, Trenton State College, Trenton, NJ.

Chipman, S. F., & Thomas, V. G. (1985). Women's participation in mathematics: Outlining the problem. In S. F. Chipman, L. R. Brush, & D. M. Wilson (Eds.), *Women and mathematics: Balancing the equation* (pp. 1–24). Hillsdale, NJ: Erlbaum.

Chodorow, N. (1978). *The reproduction of mothering.* Berkeley, CA: University of California Press.

Chodorow, N. (1979). Feminism and difference: Gender relation and difference in psychoanalytic perspective. *Socialist Review, 46*, 42–64.

Chodorow, N. J. (1995). Gender as a personal and cultural construction. *Signs: Journal of Women in Culture and Society, 20*, 516–544.

Choo, P., Levine, T., & Hatfield, E. (1997). Gender, love schemas, and reactions to romantic break-ups. In R. Crandall (Ed.), *Handbook of gender research* (pp. 143–160). Corte Madera, CA: Select Press.

Chow, E. N-L. (1996). The development of feminist consciousness among Asian American women. In E. N-L. Chow, D. Wilkinson, & M.B. Zinn (Eds.), *Race, class, & gender: Common bonds, different voices* (pp. 251–264). Thousand Oaks, CA: Sage.

Chrisler, J. C. (2001). Gendered bodies and physical health. In R. K. Unger (Editor), *Handbook of the psychology of women and gender* (pp. 289–302). New York: Wiley.

Chrisler, J. C., & Ghiz, L. (1993). Body image issues of older women. *Women & Therapy, 14*, 67–75.

Chrisler, J. C., & Lamont, J. M. (2002). Can exercise contribute to the goals of feminist therapy? *Women and Therapy, 25*, 9–22.

Christian-Smith, L. K. (1994). Young women and their dream lovers: Sexuality in adolescent fiction. In J. M. Irvine (Ed.), *Sexual cultures and the construction of adolescent identities* (pp. 206–227). Philadelphia: Temple University Press.

Ciancanelli, P., & Berch, B. (1987). Gender and the GNP. In B. B. Hess and M. M. Ferree (Eds.), *Analyzing gender: A handbook of social science research* (pp. 244–266). Newbury Park, CA: Sage.

Cogan, J. C. (1999). Lesbians walk the tightrope of beauty: Thin is in, but femme is out. *Journal of Lesbian Studies, 3*, 77–89.

Cohen, B. P., Berger, J., & Zelditch, M. (1972). Status conceptions and interactions: A case study of developing cumulative knowledge. In C. McClintock (Ed.), *Experimental social psychology* (pp. 408–411). New York: Holt, Rinehart, & Winston.

Cole, E. R., Zucker, A. N., & Duncan, L. E. (2001). Changing society, changing women (and men). In R. K. Unger (Ed.), *Handbook of the psychology of women and gender* (pp. 410–423). New York: Wiley.

Cole, S. G. (1987). *Pornography and harm.* Toronto: Metro Action Committee on Public Violence Against Women and Children.

Coley, R. J. (2001). *Differences in the gender gap: Comparisons across racial/ethnic groups in education and work.* Princeton: Educational Testing Service.

Collaer, M. L., & Hines, M. (1995). Human behavioral sex differences: A role for gonadal hormones during early development? *Psychological Bulletin, 118*, 55–107.

Collins, P. H. (1991). The meaning of motherhood in Black culture and Black mother-daughter relationships. In P. Bell-Scott, B. Guy-Sheftall, J. J. Royster, J. Sims-Wood, M. DiCosta-Willis, & L. P. Fultz (Eds.), *Double stitch: Black women write about mothers and daughters* (pp. 42–60). New York: HarperCollins.

Collins, P. H. (1997). Pornography and black women's bodies. In L. L. O'Toole & J. R. Schiffman (Eds.), *Gender violence: Interdisciplinary perspectives* (pp. 395–399). New York: New York University Press.

Coltrane, S., & Adams, M. (1997). Work-family imagery and gender stereotypes: Television and the reproduction of difference. *Journal of Vocational Behavior, 50,* 323–347.

Coltrane, S., & Messineo, M. (2000). The perpetuation of subtle prejudice: Race and gender imagery in 1990s television advertising. *Sex Roles, 42,* 363–389.

Comas-Dìaz, L., & Greene, B. (1994). *Women of color: Integrating ethnic and gender identities in psychotherapy.* New York: Guilford.

Condit, C. M. (1996). Media bias for reproductive technologies. In R. L. Parrott & C. M. Condit (Eds.), *Evaluating women's health messages* (pp. 341–355). Thousand Oaks, CA: Sage.

Condon, J. (1987). Psychological and physical symptoms during pregnancy: A comparison of male and female expectant parents. *Journal of Infant and Reproductive Psychology, 5,* 207–220.

Connidis, I. A., & McMullin, J. A. (1996). Reasons for and perceptions of childlessness among older persons: Exploring the impact of marital status and gender. *Journal of Aging Studies, 10,* 205–222.

Corley, M. C., & Mauksch, H. O. (1988). Registered nurses, gender, and commitment. In A. Statham, E. M. Miller, & H. O. Mauksch (Eds.), *The worth of women's work: A qualitative synthesis* (pp. 135–150). Albany, NY: State University of New York Press.

Cosgrove, L. (2003). Resisting essentialism in feminist therapy theory: Some epistemological considerations. *Women & Therapy, 25,* 89–112.

Costello, C., & Stone, A. J. (Eds.). (1994). *The American woman 1994–1995: Where we stand—Women and health.* New York: Norton.

Costos, D., Ackerman, R., & Paradis, L. (2002). Recollections of menarche: Communication between mothers and daughters regarding menstruation. *Sex Roles, 46,* 49–59.

Cowan, G. (1992). Feminist attitudes toward pornography control. *Psychology of Women Quarterly, 16,* 165–177.

Cowan, G., and Campbell, R. R. (1994). Racism and sexism in interracial pornography: A content analysis. *Psychology of Women Quarterly, 18,* 323–338.

Cowan, G., Neighbors, C., DeLaMoreaux, J., & Behnke, C. (1998). Women's hostility toward women. *Psychology of Women Quarterly, 22,* 267–284.

Coyle, J. M. (Ed.). (1997). *Handbook on women and aging.* Westport, CT: Greenwood Press.

Cozzarelli, C., & Major, B. (1998). The impact of antiabortion activities on women seeking abortions. In L. J. Beckman & S. M. Harvey (Eds.), *The new civil war: The psychology, culture, and politics of abortion* (pp. 81–104). Washington, DC: American Psychological Association.

Craig, R. S. (1992). The effect of television day part on gender portrayals in television commercials: A content analysis. *Sex Roles, 26,* 197–211.

Cramer, E., & MacFarlane, J. (1994). Pornography and abuse of women. *Public Health Nursing, 11,* 268–272.

Cramer, P. & Steinwert, T. (1998). Thin is good, fat is bad: How early does it begin? *Journal of Applied Developmental Psychology, 19,* 429–451.

Crawford, M. (1981, August). Emmy Noether: She did Einstein's math. *Ms.,* 86–89.

Crawford, M. (1982). In pursuit of the well-rounded life: Women scholars and the family. In M. Kehoe (Ed.), *Handbook for women scholars* (pp. 89–96). San Francisco: Americas Behavioral Research.

Crawford, M. (1988). Gender, age, and the social evaluation of assertion. *Behavior Modification, 12,* 549–564.

Crawford, M. (1989). Agreeing to differ: Feminist epistemologies and women's ways of knowing. In M. Crawford & M. Gentry (Eds.), *Gender and thought* (pp. 128–145). New York: Springer Verlag.

Crawford, M. (1995). *Talking difference: On gender and language.* London: Sage.

Crawford, M. (2000). Editor's introduction: How to make sex and do gender. *Feminism & Psychology, 10,* 7–10.

Crawford, M. (2001). Gender and language. In R. K. Unger (Ed.), *Handbook of the psychology of women and gender* (pp. 228–244). New York: Wiley.

Crawford, M., & Chaffin, R. (1986). The reader's construction of meaning: Cognitive research on gender and comprehension. In E. Flynn & P. Schweikart (Eds.), *Gender and reading: Essays on reader, text, and context* (pp. 3–30). Baltimore: Johns Hopkins University Press.

Crawford, M., & English, L. (1984). Generic versus specific inclusion of women in language: Effects on recall. *Journal of Psycholinguistic Research, 13,* 373–381.

Crawford, M., & Kimmel, E. (1999). Promoting methodological diversity in feminist research (pp. 1–6). In M. Crawford & E. Kimmel (Eds.), Innovations in feminist research (special issue). *Psychology of Women Quarterly, 23,* 1.

Crawford, M., & Marecek, J. (1989). Psychology reconstructs the female. *Psychology of Women Quarterly, 13,* 147–166.

Crawford, M., McCullough, M., & Arato, H. (1983, June). *Do women's studies classes change attitudes in women but not men?* Paper presented at the annual meeting of the National Women's Studies Association, Bloomington, Indiana.

Crawford, M., & Popp, D. (2003). Sexual double standards: A review and methodological critique of two decades of research. *The Journal of Sex Research, 40,* 13–26.

Crawford, M., Stark, A., & Renner, C. (1998). The meaning of *Ms.*: Social assimilation of a gender concept. *Psychology of Women Quarterly, 22,* 197–208.

Crawford, S. (1987). Lesbian families: Psychosocial stress and the family-building process. In *Boston Lesbian Psychologies Collective, Lesbian psychologies* (pp. 195–214). Urbana, IL: University of Illinois Press.

Crick, N. R., & Rose, A. J. (2000). Toward a gender-balanced approach to the study of social-emotional development: A look at relational aggression. In P. H. Miller & E. K.

Scholnick (Eds.), *Toward a feminist developmental psychology* (pp. 153–168). New York: Routledge.

Crist, G. (2003, May 9). Upperclassmen's power theme in AFA sex probe. *Rocky Mountain News (Denver, CO)*, p. 30A.

Crittenden, A. (2001). *The price of motherhood.* New York: Metropolitan Books.

Croghan, R. (1991). First-time mothers' accounts of inequality in the division of labour. *Feminism & Psychology, 1,* 221–246.

Crohan, S. E., & Veroff, J. (1989). Dimensions of marital well-being among white and black newlyweds. *Journal of Marriage and the Family, 51,* 373–383.

Crosbie-Burnett, M., & Giles-Sims, J. (1991). Marital power in stepfather families: A test of normative-resource theory. *Journal of Family Psychology, 4,* 484–496.

Crosby, F. J. (1982). *Relative deprivation and working women.* New York: Oxford University Press.

Crosby, F. J. (1991). *Juggling: The unexpected advantages of balancing career and home for women and their families.* New York: Free Press.

Crosby, F. J. (2003). *Affirmative action is dead: Long live affirmative action.* New Haven, CT: Yale University Press.

Crosby, F. J., Clayton, S., Alksnis, O., & Hemker, K. (1986). Cognitive biases in the perception of discrimination: The importance of format. *Sex Roles, 14,* 637–646.

Crosby, F. J., Iyer, A., Clayton, S., & Downing, R. A. (2003). Affirmative action: Psychological data and the policy debates. *American Psychologist, 58,* 93–115.

Crose, R. G. (2002). A woman's aging body: Friend or foe? In F. K. Trotman & C. M. Brody (Eds.), *Psychotherapy and Counseling with Older Women* (pp. 17–40). New York: Springer Publishing Company.

Croteau, J. M. (1996). Research on the work experiences of lesbian, gay, and bisexual people: An integrative review of methodology and findings. *Journal of Vocational Behavior, 48,* 195–209.

Cruikshank, M. (2003). *Learning to be old: Gender, culture, and aging.* Lanham, MD: Rowman & Littlefield.

Cuddy, A. J. C., & Fiske, S. T. (2002). Doddering but dear: Process, content, and function in stereotyping of older persons. In T. D. Nelson (Ed.), *Ageism: Stereotyping and prejudice against older persons* (pp. 3–26). Cambridge, MA: MIT Press.

Daddario, G. (1994). Chilly scenes of the 1992 Winter Games: The mass media and the marginalization of female athletes. *Sociology of Sport Journal, 11,* 275–288.

Daley, D., & Gold, R. B. (1993). Public funding for contraceptive, sterilization, and abortion services, fiscal year 1992. *Family Planning Perspectives, 25,* 244–251.

Dallos, S., & Dallos, R. (1997). *Couples, sex, and power: The politics of desire.* Philadelphia: Open University Press.

Daniluk, J. C. (1996). When treatment fails: The transition to biological childlessness for infertile women. *Women & Therapy, 19,* 81–98.

Dansky, B. S., & Kilpatrick, D. G. (1997). Effects of sexual harassment. In W. O'Donohue (Ed.), *Sexual harassment: Theory, research and treatment* (pp. 152–174). Boston: Allyn & Bacon.

Darling-Wolf, F. (1997). Framing the breast implant controversy: A feminist critique. *Journal of Communication Inquiry, 21,* 77–97.

Darnton, J. (1993, March 11). Tough abortion law provokes dismay in Poland. *The New York Times,* p. A13.

Darwin, C. (1872/1998). *The expression of emotions in man and animals.* New York: Oxford University Press.

Davey, C. L., & Davidson, M. J. (2000). The right of passage? The experiences of female pilots in aviation. *Feminism and Psychology, 10,* 195–225.

Davies, P. G., Spencer, S. J., Quinn, D. M., & Gerhardstein, R. (2002). Consuming images: How television commercials that elicit stereotype threat can restrain women academically and professionally. *Personality and Social Psychology Bulletin, 28,* 1615–1628.

Davis, D. M. (1990). Portrayal of women in prime-time network television: Some demographic characteristics. *Sex Roles, 23,* 325–332.

Davis, T. L. (1995). Gender differences in masking negative emotions: Ability or motivation? *Developmental Psychology, 31,* 650–667.

Davis, S., Crawford, M., & Sebrechts, J. (Eds.). (1999). *Coming into her own: Encouraging educational success in girls and women.* San Francisco: Jossey-Bass.

Davison, H. K., & Burke, M. J. (2000). Sex discrimination in simulated employment contexts: A meta-analytic investigation. *Journal of Vocational Behavior, 56,* 225–248.

Deaux, K., (1984). From individual differences to social categories: Analysis of a decade's research on gender. *American Psychologist, 39,* 105–116.

Deaux, K., & Emswiller, T. (1974). Explanations of successful performance on sex-linked tasks: What's skill for the male is luck for the female. *Journal of Personality and Social Psychology, 29,* 80–85.

Deaux, K., & Lewis, L. L. (1984). The structure of gender stereotypes: Interrelationships among components and gender labels. *Journal of Personality and Social Psychology, 46,* 991–1004.

Deaux, K., & Major, B. (1987). Putting gender into context: An interactive model of gender-related behavior. *Psychological Review, 94,* 369–389.

Deaux, K., & Ullman, J. C. (1983). *Women of steel.* New York: Praeger.

Deaux, K., Winton, W., Crowley, M., & Lewis, L. L. (1985). Level of categorization and content of gender stereotypes. *Social Cognition, 3,* 145–167.

Demarest, J. & Allen, R. (2000). Body image: gender, ethnic, and age differences. *Journal of Social Psychology, 140,* 465–472.

DeMeis, D. K., & Perkins, H. W. (1996). "Supermoms" of the nineties: Homemaker and employed mothers' performance and perceptions of the motherhood role. *Journal of Family Issues, 17,* 776–792.

Dempsey, K. (1997). Trying to get husbands to do more work at home. *Australian and New Zealand Journal of Sociology, 33,* 216–225.

Denmark, F. L., Russo, N. F., Frieze, I. H., & Sechzer, J. A. (1988). Guidelines for avoiding sexism in psychological research: A report of the ad hoc committee on nonsexist research. *American Psychologist, 43,* 582–585.

Dermer, M. & Theil, D. L. (1975). When beauty may fail. *Journal of Personality and Social Psychology, 31,* 1168–1176.

Desmarais, S., & Curtis, J. (1997). Gender differences in pay histories and view on payment entitlement among university students. *Sex Roles, 37,* 623–642.

Deutsch, F. (1999). Halving it all: How equally shared parenting works. Cambridge, MA: Harvard University Press.

Devine, P. G. & Monteith, M. J. (1999). Automaticity and control in stereotyping. In S. Chaiken & Y. Trope (Eds.), Dual-process theories in social psychology (pp. 339–360). New York: Guilford.

Devor, H. (1997). MTF: Female-to-male transsexuals in society. Bloomington, IN: University of Indiana Press.

Diamond, L. M. (2000). Sexual identity, attractions, and behavior among young sexual-minority women over a 2-year period. *Developmental Psychology, 36,* 241–250.

DiBlasio, F. A., & Benda, B. B. (1992). Gender differences in theories of adolescent sexual activity. *Sex Roles, 27,* 221–239.

Dickson, L. (1993). The future of marriage and family in Black America. *Journal of Black Studies, 23,* 472–491.

Dickerson, B. J. (Ed.). (1995). African-American single mothers. Thousand Oaks, CA: Sage.

Didi-Huberman, G. (2003). *The invention of hysteria: Charcot and the photographic iconography at the Salpêtrière* (Alisa Hartz Trans.). Cambridge, MA: MIT Press.

Diekman, A. B., McDonald, M., & Gardner, W. L. (2000). Love means never having to be careful: The relationship between reading romance novels and safe sex behavior. *Psychology of Women Quarterly, 24,* 179–188.

Dietz, T. L. (1998). An examination of violence and gender role portrayals in video games: Implications for gender socialization of aggressive behavior. *Sex Roles, 38,* 425–442.

Di Leonardo, M. (1987). The female world of cards and holidays: Women, families, and the work of kinship. *Signs, 12,* 440–453.

Dion, K. E., Berscheid, E. & Walster, E. (1972). What is beautiful is good. *Journal of Personality and Social Psychology, 24,* 285–290.

Dion, K. L. (1987). What's in a title? The Ms stereotype and images of women's titles of address. *Psychology of Women Quarterly, 11,* 21–36.

DiPalma, L. M. (1994). Patterns of coping and characteristics of high-functioning incest survivors. *Archives of Psychiatric Nursing, 8,* 82–90.

Disch, E. (1999). Encouraging participation in the classroom. In S. N. Davis, M. Crawford, & J. Sebrechts (Eds.), *Coming into her own: Educational success in girls and women* (pp. 139–154). San Francisco: Jossey-Bass.

Dittmann, R. W., Kappes, M. E., & Kappes, M. H. (1992). Sexual behavior in adolescent and adult-females with congenital adrenal hyperplasia. *Psychoneuroendocrinology, 17,* 153–170.

Devine, P. G. & Monteith, M. J. (1999). Automaticity and control in stereotyping. In S. Chaiken & Y. Trope (Eds.), Dual-process theories in social psychology (pp. 339–360). New York: Guilford.

Dixon, D. A., Antoni, M., Peters, M., & Saul, J. (2001). Employment, social support, and HIV sexual-risk behavior in Puerto Rican women. *AIDS and Behavior, 5,* 331–342.

Dobrof, R. (2001). Aging in the United States today. In D. C. Kimmel & D. L. Martin (Eds.), *Midlife and aging in gay America: Proceedings of the SAGE conference 2000* (pp. 15–17). New York: Harrington Park Press.

Dodson, B. (1987). *Sex for one: The joy of self-loving.* New York: Crown.

Dohm, F. A., & Cummings, W. (2002). Research mentoring and women in clinical psychology. *Psychology of Women Quarterly, 26,* 163–167.

Doress-Worters, P., & Ditzion, P. (1998). Women growing older. In *Our bodies, ourselves for the new century: The Boston women's health book collective* (pp. 547–589). New York: Simon & Schuster.

Doress-Worters, P. B., & Siegal, D. L. (1994). *The new ourselves growing older.* New York: Simon & Schuster.

Dorian, L., & Garfinkel, P. E. (2002). Culture and body image in Western society. *Eating and Weight Disorders, 7,* 1–19.

Douglas, S. J. (1994). *Where the girls are: Growing up female with the mass media.* New York: Times Books/Random House.

Dovidio, J. F., Ellyson, S. L., Keating, C. F., Heltman, K., & Brown, C. E. (1988). The relationship of social power to visual displays of dominance between men and women. *Journal of Personality and Social Psychology, 54,* 233–242.

Dowling, C. (2001). *The frailty myth: Redefining the physical potential of women and girls.* New York: Random House.

Dreher, G. F., & Cox, T. H., Jr. (1996). Race, gender, and opportunity: A study of compensation attainment and the establishment of mentoring relationships. *Journal of Applied Psychology, 81,* 297–308.

Driscoll, J. M., Kelley, F. A., & Fassinger, R. E. (1996). Lesbian identity and disclosure in the workplace: Relation to occupational stress and satisfaction. *Journal of Vocational Behavior, 48,* 229–242.

Drout, C. E. (1997). Professionals' and students' perceptions of abuse among married and unmarried cohabiting couples. *Journal of Social Behavior and Personality, 12*, 965–978.

Dryden, C. (1999). *Being married, doing gender.* New York: Routledge.

Duenwald, M., & Stamler, B. (2004, April 13). On their own, in the same boat. *The New York Times*, p. B13.

Dugger, C. W. (2001, April 22). Abortions in India spurred by sex test skew the ratio against girls. *The New York Times*, p. 12.

Duncan, G. J., & Hoffman, S. D. (1991). A reconsideration of the economic consequences of marital dissolution. *Demography, 22*, 485.

Duncan, L. E. (1999). Motivation for collective action: Group consciousness as mediators of personality, life experiences, and women's rights activism. *Political Psychology, 20*, 611–635.

Duncan, M. C. (1990). Sports photographs and sexual difference: Images of women and men in the 1984 and 1988 Olympic games. *Sociology of Sport Journal, 7*, 22–43.

Durik, A., Hyde, J. S., Marks, A., Roy, A., Anaya, D., & Schultz, G. (2002). *Ethnicity and gender stereotypes of emotion.* Manuscript submitted for publication.

Dutton, D. G. (1996). Patriarchy and wife assault: The ecological fallacy. In L. K. Hamberger, & C. Renzetti (Eds.), *Domestic partner abuse* (pp. 125–151). New York: Springer.

Duval, L. L., & Ruscher, J. B. (1994, July). *Men use more detail to explain a gender-neutral task to women.* Poster presented at the annual meeting of the American Psychological Society, Washington, DC.

Eagly, A. H. (1987). *Sex differences in social behavior: A social role interpretation.* Hillsdale, NJ: Erlbaum.

Eagly, A.H., & Johannesen-Schmidt, M.C. (2001). The leadership styles of women and men. *Journal of Social Issues, 57*, 781–797.

Eagly, A. H., & Johnson, B. T. (1990). Gender and leadership style: A meta-analysis. *Psychological Bulletin, 108*, 233–256.

Eagly, A. H., & Karau, S. J. (2002). Role congruity theory of prejudice toward female leaders. *Psychological Review, 109*, 573–598.

Eagly, A. H., Karau, S. J., & Makhijani, M. (1995). Gender and the effectiveness of leaders: A meta-analysis. *Psychological Bulletin, 117*, 125–145.

Eagly, A. H., & Mladinic, A. (1993). Are people prejudiced against women? Some answers from research on attitudes, gender stereotypes, and judgments of competence. In W. Strobe & M. Hewstone (Eds.), *European review of social psychology* (pp. 1–35). New York: Wiley.

Eagly, A. H., & Wood, W. (1999). The origins of sex differences in human behavior: Evolved dispositions versus social roles. *American Psychologist, 54*, 408–423.

East, P. L. (1998). Racial and ethnic differences in girls' sexual, marital, and birth expectations. *Journal of Marriage and the Family, 60*, 150–162.

Eccles, J. S. (1989). Bringing young women to math and science. In M. Crawford and M. Gentry (Eds.), *Gender and thought: Psychological perspectives* (pp. 36–58). New York: Springer-Verlag.

Eccles, J. S. (1994). Understanding women's educational and occupational choices: Applying the Eccles et al. model of achievement-related choices. *Psychology of Women Quarterly, 18*, 585–610.

Eccles, J. S., Adler, T. F., Futterman, R., Goff, S. B., Kaczala, C. M., Meece, J. L., et al. (1985). Self-perceptions, task perceptions, socializing influences, and the decision to enroll in mathematics. In S. F. Chipman, L. R. Brush, & D. M. Wilson (Eds.), *Women and mathematics: Balancing the equation* (pp. 95–122). Hillsdale, NJ: Erlbaum.

Eccles, J. S., Barber, B., Jozefowicz, D., Malenchuk, D., & Vida, M. (2000). Self-evaluations of competence, task values, and self-esteem. In N. G. Johnson, M. C. Roberts, & J. Worell (Eds.), *Beyond appearances: A new look at adolescent girls* (pp. 53–83). Washington DC: American Psychological Association.

Eccles, J. S., & Jacobs, J. E. (1986). Social forces shape math attitudes and performance. *Signs, 11*, 367–389.

Eckes, T. (1994). Features of men, features of women: Assessing stereotypic beliefs about gender subtypes. *British Journal of Social Psychology, 33*, 107–123.

Eder, D., Evans, C., & Parker, S. (1995). *School talk: Gender and adolescent culture.* New Brunswick, NJ: Rutgers University Press.

Edley, N., & Wetherell, M. (2001). Men's construction of feminism and feminists. *Feminism & Psychology, 11*, 439–458.

Edmonson, G. (2003, August 30). Poll: 1 in 5 female cadets assaulted; Most Air Force Academy cases not reported. *The Atlanta Journal-Constitution*, p. 3C.

Edwards, C. P., Knoche, L., & Kumru, A. (2001). Play patterns and gender. In J. Worell (Ed.), *Encyclopedia of women and gender* (pp. 809–815). San Diego, CA: Academic Press.

Ehrenreich, B., & English, D. (1973). *Complaints and disorders: The sexual politics of sickness.* New York: The Feminist Press.

Eichler, M. (1988). *Nonsexist research methods.* Boston: Allen & Unwin.

Eisenstat, S. A., & Bancroft, L. (1999). Domestic violence. *New England Journal of Medicine, 341*, 886–892.

Eisikovits, Z., & Buchbinder, E. (1999). Talking control: Metaphors used by battered women. *Violence Against Women, 5*, 845–868.

Eldridge, N. S., & Gilbert, L. A. (1990). Correlates of relationship satisfaction in lesbian couples. *Psychology of Women Quarterly, 14*, 43–62.

Elfenbein, H. A., & Ambady, N. (2003). Universals and cultural differences in recognizing emotions. *Current Directions in Psychological Science, 12*, 159–164.

Eliason, M., Donelan, C., & Randall, C. (1992). Lesbian stereotypes. *Health Care for Women International, 13*, 131–144.

Elise, S. (1995). Teenaged mothers: A sense of self. In B. J. Dickerson (Ed.), *African American single mothers* (pp. 53–79). Thousand Oaks, CA: Sage.

Elkind, S. N. (1991, Winter). Letter to the editor. *Psychology of Women, 18,* 3.

Elliot, R. (1989). *Song of love.* New York: Harlequin.

Elliott, S. (2003, February 24). Stars of pornographic films are modeling in a campaign for Pony, the shoe company. *New York Times,* secton C, p.9.

Ellis, A. L. (1996). Sexual identity issues in the workplace: Past and present. In A. L. Ellis & E. D. B. Riggle (Eds.), Sexual identity on the job: Issues and services (pp. 1–16). New York: Harrington Park Press.

Ellsberg, M., Heise, L., Pena, R., Agurto, S., & Winkvist, A. (2001). Researching domestic violence against women: Methodological and ethical considerations. *Studies in Family Planning, 32,* 1–16.

Elman, R. A. (2001). Mainstreaming immobility: Disability pornography and its challenge to two movements. In C. M Renzetti, J. L. Edleson, and R. K. Bergen (Eds.), *Sourcebook on violence against women* (pp. 193–207). Thousand Oaks, CA: Sage.

Endicott, J. (2000). History, evolution, and diagnosis of premenstrual dysphoric disorder. *Journal of Clinical Psychiatry, 61,* 5–8.

Engel, A. (1994). Sex roles and gender stereotyping in young women's participation in sport. *Feminism & Psychology, 4,* 439–448.

Erel, O., Oberman, Y., & Yirmiya, N. (2000). Maternal versus nonmaternal care and seven domains of children's development. *Psychological Bulletin, 126,* 727–747.

Erkut, S., Fields, J. P., Sing, R., & Marks, F. (1997). Diversity in girls' experiences: Feeling good about who you are. In B. J. R. Leadbeater & N. Way (Eds.), *Urban girls: Resisting stereotypes, creating identities* (pp. 53–64). New York: New York University Press.

Espeland, M. A., Rapp, S. R., Shumaker, S. A., Brunner, R., Manson, J. E., & Sherwin, B. (2004). Conjugated equine estrogens and global cognitive function in postmenopausal women: Women's health initiative memory study. *Journal of the American Medical Association, 291,* 2959–2968.

Espin, O. M. (1986). Cultural and historical influences on sexuality in Hispanic/Latin women. In J. Cole (Ed.), *All American women: Lines that divide, ties that bind* (pp. 272–284). New York: Free Press.

Espin, O. M. (1987). Issues of identity in the psychology of Latina lesbians. In Boston Lesbian Psychologies Collective (Ed.), *Lesbian psychologies: Explorations and challenges* (pp. 35–55). Urbana: University of Illinois Press.

Etaugh, C., & Brown, B. (1975). Perceiving the causes of success and failure of male and female performers. *Developmental Psychology, 11,* 103.

Etaugh, C., & Liss, M. B. (1992). Home, school, and playroom: Training grounds for adult gender roles. *Sex Roles, 26,* 129–147.

Etcoff, N. (1999). *Survival of the prettiest: The science of beauty.* New York: Anchor Books/Doubleday.

Evans, G. W. (2004). The environment of childhood poverty. *American Psychologist, 59,* 77–92.

Evans, L., & Davies, K. (2000). No sissy boys here: A content analysis of the representation of masculinity in elementary school reading textbooks. *Sex Roles, 42,* 255–270.

Evans, P. C. (2003). "If only I were thin like her, maybe I could be happy like her": The self implications of associating a thin female ideal with life success. *Psychology of Women Quarterly, 27,* 209–214.

Facio, E. (1997). Chicanas and aging: Toward definitions of womanhood. In J. M. Coyle (Ed.), *Handbook on women and aging* (pp. 335–350). Westport, CT: Greenwood Press.

Faderman, L. (1981). *Surpassing the love of men: Romantic friendship and love between women from the Renaissance to the present.* New York: William Morrow.

Fagot, B. I., & Leinbach, M. D. (1995). Gender knowledge in egalitarian and traditional families. *Sex Roles, 32,* 513–526.

Faircloth, C.A. (Ed.). (2003). *Aging bodies: Images and everyday experiences.* New York: AltaMira Press.

Falk, P. J. (1993). Lesbian mothers: Psychosocial assumptions in family law. In L. D. Garnets & D. C. Kimmel (Eds.), *Psychological perspectives on lesbian and gay male experiences* (pp. 420–436). New York: Columbia University Press.

Fallon, A. E., & Rozin, P. (1985). Sex differences in perceptions of desirable body shape. *Journal of Abnormal Psychology, 94,* 102–105.

Faludi, S. (1991). *Backlash: The undeclared war against American women.* New York: Doubleday.

Farrell, B. (2003). American TV raises the stars and strips: The major US networks are doing the unthinkable—putting porn in their schedules. *The Observer,* August 17, p. 8.

Farmer, H. S., et al. (Eds.). (1997). *Diversity & women's career development: From adolescence to adulthood.* Thousand Oaks, CA: Sage.

Fassinger, R. E. (1996). Notes from the margins: Integrating lesbian experience into the vocational psychology of women. *Journal of Vocational Behavior, 48,* 160–175.

Fassinger, R. E. (2002). Hitting the ceiling: Gendered barriers to occupational entry, advancements, and achievement. In L. Diamant & J. A. Lee (Eds.), *The psychology of sex, gender, and jobs: Issues and resolutions* (pp. 21–46). Westport, CT: Praeger.

Fausto-Sterling, A. (2000). *Sexing the body: Gender politics and the construction of sexuality.* New York: Basic Books.

Fava, M., Abraham, M., Clancy-Colecchi, K., & Pava, J. A. (1997). Eating disorder symptomatology in major depression. *Journal of Nervous and Mental Disease, 185,* 140–144.

Favreau, O. E. (1997). Sex and gender comparisons: Does null hypothesis testing create a false dichotomy? *Feminism and Psychology, 7,* 63–81.

Federal Glass Ceiling Commission. (1998). Working women face barriers to advancement. In M. E. Williams (Ed.), *Working women: Opposing viewpoints* (pp. 64–72). San Diego, CA: Greenhaven Press.

Feeney, J., Peterson, C., & Noller, P. (1994). Equality and marital satisfaction in the family life cycle. *Personal Relationships, 1,* 83–99.

Feinberg, L. (1996). *Transgender warriors: Making history from Joan of Arc to Dennis Rodman.* Boston: Beacon.

Feingold, A., & Mazzella, R. (1998). Gender differences in body image are increasing. *Psychological Science, 9,* 190–195.

Feldman, S. (1999). Please don't call me "dear": Older women's narratives of health care. *Nursing Inquiry, 6,* 269–276.

Feldman-Summers, S., & Kiesler, S. J. (1974). Those who are number two try harder: The effects of sex on attributions of causality. *Journal of Personality and Social Psychology, 30,* 846–855.

Fenell, D. L. (1993). Characteristics of long-term first marriages. *Journal of Mental Health Counseling, 15,* 446–460.

Ferree, M. M. (1987). She works hard for a living: Gender and class on the job. In B. B. Hess & M. M. Ferree (Eds.), *Analyzing gender: A handbook of social science research* (pp. 322–347). Newbury Park, CA: Sage.

Ferris, D. (1996). *Duke Nukem 3d.* Review available at http://www.gamerevolution.com/games/pc/action/dnuke.htm

Fidell, L. S. (1970). Empirical verification of sex discrimination in hiring practices in psychology. *American Psychologist, 25,* 1094–1098.

Fields, J., & Casper, L. (2001, June). America's families and living arrangements 2000: Population characteristics. *U.S. Department of Commerce: Economics and Statistics Administration.* Retrieved July 8, 2004, from http://www.census.gov/prod/2001pubs/p20-537.pdf

Filardo, E. K. (1996). Gender patterns in African American and White adolescents' social interactions in same-race, mixed-gender groups. *Journal of Personality and Social Psychology, 71,* 71–82.

Fine, M. (1985). Reflections on a feminist psychology of women: Paradoxes and prospects. *Psychology of Women Quarterly, 9,* 167–183.

Fine, M. (1988). Sexuality, schooling, and adolescent females: The missing discourse of desire. *Harvard Educational Review, 58,* 29–53.

Fine, M., & Asch, A. (1988). *Women with disabilities: Essays in psychology, culture, and politics.* Philadelphia: Temple University Press.

Fine, M., Weis, L., Powell, L. C., & Wong, L. M. (Eds.). (1997). *Off white: Readings on race, power, and society.* New York: Routledge.

Fink, J. S., & Kensicki, L. J. (2002). An imperceptible difference: Visual and textual constructions of femininity in *Sports Illustrated* and *Sports Illustrated for Women. Mass Communication and Society, 5,* 317–339.

Finkel, J. S., & Hanson, F. J. (1992). Correlates of retrospective marital satisfaction in long-lived marriages: A social constructivist approach. *Family Therapy, 19,* 1–16.

Firestein, B. A. (1998, March 7). Bisexuality: A feminist vision of choice and change. Paper presented at the annual meeting of the Association for Women in Psychology, Baltimore, MD.

Fischer, A. H., & Manstead, A. S. R. (2000). The relation between gender and emotion in different cultures. In A. H. Fischer (Ed.), *Gender and emotion: Social psychological perspectives* (pp. 71–94). Cambridge, England: Cambridge University Press.

Fisher, J. D., & Fisher, W. A. (2000). Theoretical approaches to individual-level change in HIV risk behavior. In J. L. Peterson, R. J. DiClemente (Eds.), *Handbook of HIV prevention, AIDS prevention and mental health* (pp. 3–55). New York: Kluwer Academic/Plenum.

Fisher, J. D., Fisher, W. A., Misovich, S. J., Kimble, D. L., & Malloy, T. E. (1996).Changing AIDS risk behavior: Effects of an intervention emphasizing AIDS risk reduction information, motivation, and behavioral skills in a college student population. *Health Psychology, 15,* 114–123.

Fisher, W. A., Williams, S. S., Fisher, J. D., & Malloy, T. E. (1999). Understanding AIDS risk behavior among sexually active urban adolescents: An empirical test of the information-motivation-behavioral skills model. *AIDS and Behavior, 3,* 13–23.

Fiske, A. P., Haslam, N., & Fiske, S. T. (1991). Confusing one person with another: What errors reveal about the elementary forms of social relations. *Journal of Personality and Social Psychology, 60,* 656–674.

Fiske, S. T. (1993). Controlling other people: The impact of power on stereotyping. *American Psychologist, 48,* 621–628.

Fiske, S. T., Bersoff, D. N., Borgida, E., Deaux, K., & Heilman, M. E. (1991). Social science research on trial: Use of sex stereotyping research in *Price Waterhouse v. Hopkins. American Psychologist, 46,* 1049–1060.

Fiske, S. T., Xu, J., Cuddy, A. C., & Glick, P. (1999). (Dis)respecting versus (dis)liking: Status and interdependence predict ambivalent stereotypes of competence and warmth. *Journal of Social Issues, 55,* 473–489.

Fitch, R. H., & Denenberg, V. H. (1998). A role for ovarian hormones in sexual differentiation of the brain. *Behavior and Brain Science, 21,* 311–352.

Fitzgerald, L. F. (1993). Sexual harassment: Violence against women in the workplace. *American Psychologist, 48,* 1070–1076.

Fitzgerald, L. F., Drasgow, F., Hulin, C. L., Gelfland, M. J., & Magley, V. J. (1997). Antecedents and consequences of sexual harassment in organizations: A test of an integrated model. *Journal of Applied Psychology, 82,* 578–589.

Fitzgerald, L. F., Swan, S., & Magley, V. J. (1997). But was it really sexual harassment? Legal, behavioral, and psychological definitions of the workplace victimization of women. In W. O'Donohue (Ed.), *Sexual harassment: Theory, research, and treatment* (pp. 5–28). Boston: Allyn & Bacon.

Fivush, R. (1989). Exploring sex differences in the emotional content of mother-child conversations about the past. *Sex Roles, 20,* 675–692.

Fivush, R., Brotman, M. A., Buckner, J. P., & Goodman, S. H. (2000). Gender differences in parent-child emotion narratives. *Sex Roles, 42,* 233–253.

Fivush, R., & Buckner, J. P. (2000). Gender, sadness, and depression: The development of emotional focus through gendered discourse. In A. H. Fischer (Ed.), *Gender and emotion: Social psychological perspectives* (pp. 232–254). Cambridge, England: Cambridge University Press.

Flanders, L. (1997). *Real majority, media minority: The costs of sidelining women in reporting.* Monroe, ME: Common Courage Press.

Focus on the Family. (1989). *Fatal addiction: Ted Bundy's final interview with James Dobson* (Videotape). Pomona CA: Author

Follingstad, D. R., Rutledge, L. L., McNeill-Hawkins, K., & Polek, D. S. (1992). Factors related to physical violence in dating relationships. In E. C. Viano (Ed.), *Intimate violence: Interdisciplinary perspectives* (pp. 121–135). New York: Hemisphere.

Forbes, G. B., Adams-Curtis, L. E., Rade, B., & Jaberg, P. (2001). Body dissatisfaction in women and men: The role of gender-typing and self-esteem. *Sex Roles, 44,* 461–484.

Ford, A. R. (1986). When women outlive their ovaries. *New Internationalist, 165.*

Foreit, K. G., Agor, A. T., Byers, J., Larue, J., Lokey, H., Palazzini, M., et al. (1980). Sex bias in the newspaper treatment of male-centered and female-centered news stories. *Sex Roles, 6,* 475–480.

Forste, R., & Tanfer, K. (1996). Sexual exclusivity among dating, cohabiting, and married women. *Journal of Marriage and Family, 58,* 33–47.

Foucault, M. (1972). *The archaeology of knowledge.* New York: Pantheon.

Foucault, M. (1978). *The history of sexuality.* New York: Pantheon.

Fouts, G., & Burggraf, K. (2000). Television situation comedies, female weight, male negative comments, and audience reactions. *Sex Roles, 42,* 925–932.

Fowers, B. J. (1991). His and her marriages: A multivariate study of gender and marital satisfaction. *Sex Roles, 24,* 209–221.

Fox, D., & Prilleltensky, I. (1997). *Critical psychology: An introduction.* London: Sage Publications.

Frank, M. L. (1999). Raising daughters to resist negative cultural messages about body image. *Women and Therapy, 22,* 69–88.

Franzoi, S. L., & Chang, Z. (2002). The body esteem of Hmong and Caucasian young adults. *Psychology of Women Quarterly, 26,* 89–91.

Fraser, L. (2002, December 1). The islands where boys grow up to be girls: In the South Pacific, the fa'fafine men who spend their lives as women—turn gender roles upside down. *Marie Claire, 9* (12), 72–78.

Frederickson, B. L., & Roberts, T. (1997). Objectification theory: Toward understanding women's lived experiences and mental health risks. *Psychology of Women Quarterly, 21,* 173–206.

Frederickson, B. L., Roberts, T., Noll, S. M., Quinn, D. M., & Twenge, J. M. (1998). That swimsuit becomes you: Sex differences in self-objectification, restrained eating, and math performance. *Journal of Personality and Social Psychology, 75,* 269–284.

Freedman, R. (1986). *Beauty bound.* Lexington, MA: Lexington Books.

French, H. W. (2003, June 29). Victims say Japan ignores sex crimes committed by teachers. The *New York Times,* p. A4.

Freud, S. (1914). *On the history of the psycho-analytic movement.* New York: W. W. Norton, Inc., 1966.

Freud, S. (1933). Femininity. In J. Strachey (Ed.), *New introductory lectures on psycho-analysis* (pp. 112–135). New York: W. W. Norton, 1965.

Frintner, M. P., & Rubinson, L. (1993). Acquaintance rape: The influence of alcohol, fraternity membership, and sports team membership. *Journal of Sex Education and Therapy, 19,* 272–284.

Frisch, R. E. (1983a). Fatness, menarche, and fertility. In S. Golub (Ed.), *Menarche: The transition from girl to woman* (pp. 5–20). Lexington, MA: Lexington Books.

Furnham, A., & Mak, T. (1999). Sex-role stereotyping in television commercials: A review and compendium of fourteen studies done on five continents over twenty-five years. *Sex Roles, 41,* 413–437.

Furstenberg, F. F., Jr., Moore, K. A., & Peterson, J. L. (1986). Sex education and sexual experience among adolescents. *American Journal of Public Health, 75,* 1221–1222.

Gagnon, J. H., & Simon, W. (1973). *Sexual conduct: The social sources of human sexuality.* Chicago: Aldine.

Galliano, G. (2003). *Gender: Crossing boundaries.* Belmont, CA: Wadsworth/Thomson Learning.

Galligan, R. F., & Terry, D. J. (1993). Romantic ideals, fear of negative implications, and the practice of safe sex. *Journal of Applied Social Psychology, 23,* 1685–1711.

Ganahl, D. J., Prinsen, T. J., & Netzley, S. B. (2003). A content analysis of prime time commercials: A contextual framework of gender representation. *Sex Roles, 49,* 545–551.

Gangestad, S. W., & Simpson, J. A. (2000). The evolution of human mating: Trade-offs and strategic pluralism. *Behavioral and Brain Sciences, 23,* 573–644.

Gannon, L. R., Luchetta, T., Rhodes, K., Pardie, L., & Segrist, D. (1992). Sex bias in psychological research:

Progress or complacency? *American Psychologist, 47,* 389–396.

Ganong, L. H., & Coleman, M. (2000). Remarried families. In C. Hendrick & S. S. Hendrick (Eds.), *Close relationships: A sourcebook* (pp. 155–170). Thousand Oaks, CA: Sage.

Garland, A. W. (1988). *Women activists: Challenging the abuse of power.* New York: Feminist Press.

Garner, D. M. (1997, February). The 1997 body image survey results. *Psychology Today,* 30–44.

Garner, D. M., Garfinkel, P. E., Schwartz, D., & Thompson, M. (1980). Cultural expectations of thinness in women. *Psychological Reports, 47,* 483–491.

Garner, J. H., & Maxwell, C. D. (2000).What are the lessons of the police arrest studies? *Journal of Aggression, Maltreatment & Trauma, 4,* 83–114.

Garnets, L. D. (2004). Life as a lesbian: What does gender have to do with it? In J. C. Chrisler, C. Golden, & P. D. Rozee (Eds.), *Lectures on the Psychology of Women Third Edition* (pp. 170–188). Boston: McGraw-Hill.

Garnets, L. D., & Peplau, L. A. (2001). A new paradigm for women's sexual orientation: Implications for therapy. *Women & Therapy, 24,* 111–121.

Gaskill, L. R. (1991). Same-sex and cross-sex mentoring of female proteges: A comparative analysis. *Career Development Quarterly, 40,* 48–63.

Gauna-Trujillo, B., & Higgins, P. G. (1989). Sexual intercourse and pregnancy. In P. N. Stern (Ed.), *Pregnancy and parenting* (pp. 31–40). New York: Hemisphere.

Gazmarian, J., Petersen, P., Spitz, A., Goodwin, M., Saltzman, L., & Marks, J. (2000). Violence and reproductive health: Current knowledge and future research directions. *Maternal and Child Health Journal, 4,* 79–84.

Ge, X., Conger, R. D., & Elder, G. H., Jr. (2001). Pubertal transition, stressful life events, and the emergence of gender differences in adolescent depressive symptoms. *Developmental Psychology, 37,* 404–417.

Geary, D. C. (1996). Biology, culture, and cross-national differences in mathematical ability. In T. Ben-Zeev & R. J. Sternberg (Eds.), *The nature of mathematical thinking* (pp. 145–171). Hillsdale, NJ: Erlbaum.

Geller, J. L., & Harris, M. (1994). *Women of the asylum: Voices from behind the walls, 1840–1945.* New York: Anchor Books.

Gender verification suspended on trial basis at Sydney Olympics. Retrieved April 10, 2000, from http://www.isna.org

Gentry, M. (1989). Introduction: Feminist perspectives on gender and thought: Paradox and potential. In M. Crawford & M. Gentry (Eds.), *Gender and thought* (pp. 1–16). New York: Springer-Verlag.

George, S. M., & Dickerson, B. J. (1995). The role of the grandmother in poor single-mother families and households. In B. J. Dickerson (Ed.), *African American single mothers* (pp. 146–163). Thousand Oaks, CA: Sage.

Gerbner, G. (1997). Gender and age in prime-time television. In S. Kirschner & D. A. Kirschner (Eds.), *Perspectives on psychology and the media* (pp. 69–94). Washington, DC: American Psychological Association.

Gerbner, G., Gross, L., Morgan, M., & Signorielli, N. (1993). Growing up with television: The cultivation perspective. In J. Bryant & D. Zillman (Eds.), *Media effects: Advances in theory and research.* Hillsdale, NJ: Erlbaum.

Gerstel, N. (1988). Divorce, gender, and social integration. *Gender & Society, 2,* 343–367.

Giddings, P. (1984). *When and where I enter: The impact of black women on race and sex in America.* New York: Morrow.

Gieve, K. (1989). *Balancing acts: On being a mother.* London: Virago.

Gilbert, L. A. (1993). *Two careers/One family: The promise of gender equality.* London: Sage.

Gilbert, L. A., Galessich, J. M., & Evans, S. L. (1983). Sex of faculty role model and students' self-perceptions of competency. *Sex Roles, 9,* 597–607.

Gilbert, L. A., & Rader, J. (2001). Current perspectives on women's adult roles: Work, family, and life. In R. Unger (Ed.), *Handbook of the psychology of women and gender* (pp. 156–170). New York: Wiley.

Gilbert, L. A., & Rossman, K. M. (1992). Gender and the mentoring process for women: Implications for professional development. *Professional Psychology: Research and Practice, 23,* 233–238.

Gilman, C. P. (1892). The yellow wallpaper. Reprinted in *The Yellow Wallpaper and Other Stories.* Mineola, New York: Dover Publications, 1997.

Gladstone, V. (2003, September 28). Barbie dances, with help from City Ballet. *The New York Times,* p. AR9.

Glick, P., Diebold, J., Bailey-Werner, B., & Zhu, L. (1997). The two faces of Adam: Ambivalent sexism and polarized attitudes toward women. *Personality and Social Psychology Bulletin, 23,* 1323–1334.

Glick, P., & Fiske, S. T. (1996). The Ambivalent Sexism Inventory: Differentiating hostile and benevolent sexism. *Journal of Personality and Social Psychology, 70,* 491–512.

Glick, P., & Fiske, S. T. (2001). An ambivalent alliance: Hostile and benevolent sexism as complementary justifications for gender inequality. *American Psychologist, 56,* 109–118.

Goffman, E. (1961). *Asylums: Essays on the social insituation of mental patients and other inmates.* New York: Doubleday.

Goldberg, P. A. (1968). Are women prejudiced against women? *Transaction, 5,* 28–30.

Golden, C. (1987). Diversity and variability in women's sexual identities. In Boston Lesbian Psychologies Collective (Eds.), *Lesbian psychologies* (pp. 18–34). Urbana: University of Illinois Press.

Golden, C. (2000). Still seeing differently, after all these years. *Feminism & Psychology, 10,* 30–35.

Goldenhar, L. M., Swanson, N. G., Hurrell, J. J., Ruder, A., & Deddens, J. (1998). Stressors and adverse outcomes for female construction workers. *Journal of Occupational Health Psychology, 3,* 19–32.

Golding, J. M. (1999). Intimate partner violence as a risk factor for mental disorders: A meta-analysis. *Journal of Family Violence, 14,* 99–132.

Golombok, S., Perry, B., Burston, A., Murray, C., Mooney-Somers, J., Stevens, M., & Golding, J. (2003). Children with lesbian parents: A community study. *Developmental Psychology, 39,* 20–33.

Gomez, C. A., & Vanoss-Marin, B. (1996). Gender, culture, and power: Barriers to HIV-prevention strategies for women. *Journal of Sex Research, 33,* 355–362.

Gonzales, P. M., Blanton, H., & Williams, K. J. (2002). The effects of stereotype threat and double-minority status on the test performance of Latino women. *Personality & Social Psychology Bulletin, 28,* 659–670.

Good, G. E., Dell, D. M., & Mintz, L. B. (1989). Male role and gender role conflict: Relations to help seeking in men. *Journal of Counseling Psychology, 36,* 295–300.

Gooden, A. M., & Gooden, M. A. (2001). Gender representations in notable children's picture books: 1995–1999. *Sex Roles, 45,* 89–101.

Goodman, C. (1999). Intimacy and autonomy in long term marriage. *Journal of Gerontological Social Work, 32,* 83–97.

Gordon, J. S. (1996). Community services of abused women: A review of perceived usefulness and efficacy. *Journal of Family Violence, 11,* 315–329.

Gordon, M. (2003, August 3). How Ireland hid its own dirty laundry. *The New York Times,* section 2, p. 1.

Gough, K. (1984). The origin of the family. In J. Freeman (Ed.), *Women: A feminist perspective* (3rd ed., pp. 83–99). Palo Alto, CA: Mayfield.

Gould, S. J. (1980). *The panda's thumb.* New York: Norton.

Gould, S. J. (1981). *The mismeasure of man.* New York: Norton.

Gove, W. R. (1972). The relationship between sex roles, marital status, and mental illness. *Social Forces, 51,* 34–44.

Gove, W. R., & Shin, H. C. (1989). The psychological well-being of divorced and widowed men and women: An empirical analysis. *Journal of Family Issues, 10,* 122–144.

Gowen, L. K., Hayward, C., Killen, J. D., Robinson, T. N., & Taylor, C. B. (1999). Acculturation and eating disorder symptoms in adolescent girls. *Journal of Research on Adolescence, 9,* 67–83.

Grady, K. E. (1977, April). *The belief in sex differences.* Paper presented at the meeting of the Eastern Psychological Association, Boston.

Grady, K. E. (1981). Sex bias in research design. *Psychology of Women Quarterly, 5,* 628–636.

Graham, K., & Vidal-Zaballos, D. (1998). Analysis of use of tranquilizers and sleeping pills across five surveys of the same population (1985–1991): The relationship with gender, age and use of other substances. *Social Science and Medicine, 46,* 381–395.

Grambs, J. D. (1989). *Women over forty: Visions and realities.* New York: Springer.

Grana, S. J. (2002). *Women and (In)justice: The criminal and civil effects of the common law on women's lives.* Boston: Allyn & Bacon.

Gray, H. M., & Phillips, S. (1998). *Real girl real world: Tools for finding your true self.* Seattle, WA: Seal Press.

Greene, B. (2000). African American lesbian and bisexual women. *Journal of Social Issues, 56,* 239–250.

Greene, B., & Sanchez-Hucles, J. (1997). Diversity: Advancing an inclusive feminist psychology. In J. Worell & N. G. Johnson (Eds.), *Shaping the future of feminist psychology: Education, research, and practice* (pp. 173–202). Washington, DC: American Psychological Association.

Greene, B. A. (1990). Sturdy bridges: The role of African-American mothers in the socialization of African-American children. In J. P. Knowles & E. Cole (Eds.), *Motherhood: A feminist perspective* (pp. 205–225). New York: Haworth.

Greene, C. K., & Stitt-Gohdes, W. L. (1997). Factors that influence women's choices to work in the trades. *Journal of Career Development, 23,* 265–278.

Greenglass, E. R., & Burke, R. J. (1988). Work and family precursors of burnout in teachers: Sex differences. *Sex Roles, 18,* 215–229.

Greenhouse, S., & Hays, C. L. (2004, June 23). Wal-Mart sex-bias suit given class-action status. *The New York Times,* pp. A1, C8.

Greenstein, T. N. (1996). Husbands' participation in domestic labor: Interactive effects of wives' and husbands' gender ideologies. *Journal of Marriage and the Family, 58,* 585–595.

Greenwood-Audant, L. M. (1984). The internalization of powerlessness: A case study of the displaced homemaker. In J. Freeman (Ed.), *Women: A feminist perspective* (3rd ed., pp. 264–281). New York: Mayfield.

Gremaux, R. (1996). Woman becoming man in the Balkans. In G. Herdt (Ed.), *Third sex, third gender: Beyond sexual dimorphism in culture and history* (pp. 241–281). New York: Zone Books.

Groesz, L. M., Levine, M. P., & Murnen, S. K. (2002). The effect of experimental presentation of thin media on body satisfaction: A meta-analytic review. *International Journal of Eating Disorders, 31,* 1–16.

Gross, J. (2004, February 27). Older women team up to face future together. *The New York Times,* p. A1.

Grossman, A. H., D'Augelli, A. R., & O'Connell, T. S. (2001). Being lesbian, gay, bisexual, and 60 or older in North America. In D. C. Kimmel & D. L. Martin (Eds.), *Midlife and aging in gay America: Proceedings of the SAGE Conference, New York City, 2000* (pp. 23–40). New York: Harrington Park Press.

Grossman, A. L., & Tucker, J. S. (1997). Gender differences and sexism in the knowledge and use of slang. *Sex Roles, 37*, 101–110.

Grossman, F. K., Gilbert, L. A., Genero, N. P., Hawes, S. E., Hyde, J. S., & Marecek, J. (1997). Feminist research: Practice and problems. In J. Worell & N. G. Johnson (Eds.), *Shaping the future of feminist psychology: Education, research, and practice* (pp. 73–91). Washington, DC: American Psychological Association.

Grossman, J. B., & Tierney, J. P. (1998). Does mentoring work? An impact study of the Big Brothers Big Sisters program. *Evaluation Review, 22*, 403–426.

Grossman, M., & Wood, W. (1993). Sex differences in intensity of emotional experience: A social role interpretation. *Journal of Personality and Social Psychology, 65*, 1010–1022.

Grote, N. K., & Frieze, I. H. (1998). "Remembrance of things past": Perceptions of marital love from its beginnings to the present. *Journal of Social and Personal Relationships, 15*, 91–109.

Gruber, J. E. (1997). An epidemology of sexual harassment: Evidence from North America and Europe. In W. O'Donohue (Ed.), *Sexual harassment: Theory, research and treatment* (pp. 84–98). Boston: Allyn and Bacon.

Gubrium, J. F., & Holstein, J. A. (2003). The everyday visibility of the aging body. In C.A. Faircloth (Ed.), *Aging bodies: Images and everyday experiences* (pp. 205–227). New York: AltaMira Press.

Guillet, E., Sarrazin, P., & Fontayne, P. (2000) "If it contradicts my gender role, I'll stop": Introducing survival analysis to study the effects of gender typing on the time of withdrawal from sport practice: A 3-year study. *European Review of Applied Psychology, 50*, 417–421.

Gutek, B. A. (1985). *Sex and the workplace.* San Francisco: Jossey-Bass.

Gutek, B. A. (1989). Relocation, family, and the bottom line: Results from the Division 35 survey. *Psychology of Women Quarterly, 16*, 5–7.

Gutek, B. A. (2001). Women and paid work. *Psychology of Women Quarterly, 25*, 379–393.

Gutek, B. A., & Done, R. S. (2001). Sexual harassment. In R. K. Unger (Ed.), *Handbook of the psychology of women and gender* (pp. 367–387). New York: Wiley.

Gutek, B. A., & Larwood, L. (Eds.). (1987). *Women's career development.* Newbury Park, CA: Sage.

Guthrie, R. V. (1976). *Even the rat was white: A historical view of psychology.* New York: Harper & Row.

Haaken, J., & Yragui, N. (2003). Going underground: Conflicting perspectives on domestic violence shelter practices. *Feminism & Psychology, 13*, 49–71.

Hahn, C. S. (2001). Review: Psychosocial well-being of parents and their children born after assisted reproduction. *Journal of Pediatric Psychology, 26*, 525–538.

Hair-raising experience (2003, September). *Boston Magazine*, 30.

Haj-Yahia, M. M. (1998). Beliefs about wife beating among Palestinian women: The influence of their patriarchal ideology. *Violence Against Women, 4*, 533–558.

Hall, J. A. (1996). Touch, status, and gender at professional meetings. *Journal of Nonverbal Behavior, 20*, 23–44.

Hall, J. A., Carter, J. D., & Horgan, T. G. (2000). Gender differences in nonverbal communication of emotion. In A. H. Fischer (Ed.), *Gender and emotion: Social psychological perspectives* (pp. 97–117). New York: Cambridge University Press.

Hall, K. (1995). Lip service on the fantasy lines. In K. Hall & M. Bucholtz (Eds.), *Gender articulated* (pp. 183–216). New York: Routledge.

Hall, N. L. (1984). *The true story of a single mother.* Boston: South End Press.

Hall, R. L. (1998). Softly strong: African American women's use of exercise in therapy. In K. F. Hays (Ed.), *Integrating exercise, sports, movement and mind: Therapeutic unity* (pp. 81–100). Binghamton, NY: Haworth.

Hall, R. L. (2004). Sweating it out: The good news and the bad news about women and sport. In J. C. Chrisler, C. Golden, & P. D. Rozee (Eds.), *Lectures on the Psychology of Women Third Edition* (pp. 56–76). Boston: McGraw-Hill.

Halliwell, E., & Dittmar, H. (2003). A qualitative investigation of women's and men's body image concerns and their attitudes toward aging. *Sex Roles, 49*, 675–684.

Halpern, D. F. (1992). *Sex differences in cognitive abilities* (2nd ed.). Hillsdale, NJ: Erlbaum.

Hamilton, J. A., & Jensvold, M. F. (1995). Sex and gender as critical variables in feminist psychopharmacology research and pharmacotherapy. *Women & Therapy, 16*, 9–30.

Hamilton, K. & Waller, G. (1993). Media influences on body size estimation in anorexia and bulimia: An experimental study. *British Journal of Psychiatry, 162*, 837–840.

Hamilton, M. C. (1991). Masculine bias in the attribution of personhood: People = male, male = people. *Psychology of Women Quarterly, 15*, 393–402.

Hammer, J. C., Fisher, J. D., Fitzgerald, P., & Fisher, W. A. (1996). When two heads aren't better than one: AIDS risk behavior in college-age couples. *Journal of Applied Social Psychology, 26*, 375–397.

Hammond, J. A., & Mahoney, C. W. (1983). Reward-cost balancing among women coalminers. *Sex Roles, 9*, 17–29.

Hanganu-Bresch, C. (2004). *Advertising depression: The case of Paxil.* Paper presented at the Conference on College Composition and Communication, San Antonio, TX.

Hankin, B. L. & Abramson, L. Y. (2001). Development of gender differences in depression: An elaborated cognitive vulnerability-transactional stress theory. *Psychological Bulletin, 127*, 773–796.

Hansen, F. J., & Osborne, D. (1995). Portrayal of women and elderly patients in psychotropic drug advertisements. *Women & Therapy, 16*, 129–141.

Hanson, R. (2002). Adolescent dating violence: Prevalence and psychological outcomes. *Child Abuse and Neglect, 26,* 449–453.

Harad, A. (2003). Reviving Lolita; or, because junior high is still hell. In R. Dicker & A. Piepmeier (Eds.), *Catching a wave: Reclaiming feminism for the 21st century* (pp. 81–101). Boston: Northeastern University Press.

Harasty, A. S. (1997). The interpersonal nature of social stereotypes: Differential discussion patterns about in-groups and out-groups. *Personality and Social Psychology Bulletin, 23,* 270–284.

Harding, S. (1986). *The science question in feminism.* Ithaca, NY: Cornell University Press.

Hare-Mustin, R. T., & Marecek, J. (Eds.). (1990). *Making a difference: Psychology and the construction of gender.* New Haven, CT: Yale University Press.

Hargreaves, D. & Tiggemann, M. (2002). The effect of television commercials on mood and body dissatisfaction: The role of appearance-schema activation. *Journal of Social and Clinical Psychology, 21,* 287–308.

Harlan, S. L., & O'Farrell, B. (1982). After the pioneers: Prospects for women in nontraditional blue-collar jobs. *Work and Occupations, 9,* 363–386.

Harlow, H. (1971). *Learning to love.* New York: Albion.

Harnack, L., Story, M., Martinson, B., Neumark-Sztainer, D., & Stang, J. (1998). Guess who's cooking? The role of men in meal planning, shopping, and preparation in U.S. families. *Journal of the American Dietetic Association, 98,* 995–1000.

Harris, B. J. (1984). The power of the past: History and the psychology of women. In M. Lewin (Ed.), *In the shadow of the past* (pp. 1–5). New York: Columbia University Press.

Harris, G. (2003, December 7). If the shoe won't fit, fix the foot? Popular surgery raises concerns. *The New York Times,* late Sunday edition, section 1, p. 1.

Harris, G. (2004, May 8). Morning-after-pill ruling defies norm. *The New York Times,* p. A13.

Harris, S. (1994). Racial differences in predictors of college women's body image attitudes. *Women and Health, 21,* 89–104.

Harrison, K. (2003). Television viewers' ideal body proportions: The case of the curvaceously thin woman. *Sex Roles, 48,* 255–265.

Hartung, C. M., & Widiger, T. A. (1998). Gender differences in the diagnosis of mental disorders: Conclusions and controversies of the DSM-IV. *Psychological Bulletin, 123,* 260–278.

Hartwell, C. E. (1996). The schizophrenogenic mother concept in American psychiatry. *Psychiatry: Interpersonal and Biological Processes, 59,* 274–297.

Hartzler, K., & Franco, J. N. (1985). Ethnicity, division of household tasks and equity in marital roles: A comparison of Anglo and Mexican American couples. *Hispanic Journal of Behavioral Sciences, 7,* 333–344.

Harville, M. L., & Rienzi, B. M. (2000). Equal worth and gracious submission: Judeo-Christian attitudes toward employed women. *Psychology of Women Quarterly, 24,* 145–147.

Hash, K. (2001). Preliminary study of caregiving and post-caregiving experiences of older gay men and lesbians. In D. C. Kimmel & D. L. Martin (Eds.), *Midlife and aging in gay America: Proceedings of the SAGE Conference, New York City, 2000* (pp. 87–94). New York: Harrington Park Press.

Haskell, M. (1997). *Holding my own in no man's land: Women and men and film and feminists.* New York: Oxford University Press.

Haslett, B. B., & Lipman, S. (1997). Micro inequities: Up close and personal. In N. V. Benokraitis (Ed.), *Subtle sexism: Current practice and prospects for change* (pp. 34–53). Thousand Oaks, CA: Sage.

Hatch, L. R. (1995). Gray clouds and silver linings: Women's resources in later life. In J. Freeman (Ed.), *Women: A feminist perspective* (5th ed., pp. 182–196). Mountain View, CA: Mayfield.

Hatton, B. J. (1994, March). *The experiences of African American lesbians: Family, community, and intimate relationships.* Poster presented at the Southeastern Psychological Association Convention. New Orleans, LA.

Hausdorff, J., Levy, B. R., & Wei, J. Y. (1999). The power of ageism on physical function in older persons: Reversibility of age-related gait changes. *Journal of the American Geriatric Society, 47,* 1346–1349.

Hawkins, J. W., & Aber, C. S. (1993). Women in advertisements in medical journals. *Sex Roles, 28,* 233–242.

Hays, S. (1996). *The cultural contradictions of motherhood.* New Haven, CT: Yale University Press.

Hebl, M. R. & Heatherton, T. F. (1998). The stigma of obesity in women: The difference is black and white. *Personality and Social Psychology Bulletin, 24,* 417–426.

Hecht, M. A., & LaFrance, M. (1998). License or obligation to smile: The effect of power and sex on amount and type of smiling. *Personality and Social Psychology Bulletin, 24,* 1332–1342.

Hedges, L. V., & Becker, B. J. (1986). Statistical methods in the meta-analysis of research on gender differences. In J. G. Hyde & M. C. Linn (Eds.), *The psychology of gender: Advances through meta-analysis* (pp. 14–50). Baltimore: Johns Hopkins University Press.

Heenan, C. (2002). Special issue: The reproduction of mothering: A reappraisal. *Feminism and Psychology, 12,* 5–53.

Heilman, M. E., & Saruwatari, L. R. (1979). When beauty is beastly: The effects of appearance and sex on evaluations of job applicants for managerial and non-managerial jobs. *Organizational Behavior and Human Performance, 23,* 363–372.

Heilman, M. E., & Stopeck, M. H. (1985). Attractiveness and corporate success: Different causal attributions for males and females. *Journal of Applied Psychology, 70,* 379–388.

Heise, L., Ellsberg, M., & Gottemoeller, M. (1999). *Ending violence against women* (Population Reports, Series L. 11). Baltimore: Johns Hopkins University School of Public Health.

Heitner, K. (2003). MOVIExperience: A tool to empower girls. *The Feminist Psychologist, 30,* 18.

Heitner, K. (2003). Feminist psychologists and motherhood: Reaching out to find support. *The Feminist Psychologist, 30,* 21–23.

Helmore, E. (2002, June 30). U.S. aid cut hits world birth control. *The Observer,* p. 1.

Helwig, A. A. (1998). Gender-role stereotyping: Testing theory with a longitudinal sample. *Sex Roles, 38,* 403–424.

Henderson, K. & Roberts, N. (1998). An integrative review of the literature on women in the outdoors. In K. M. Fox, L. H. McAvoy, & M. D. Bialeschki (Eds.) *Coalition for Education in the Outdoors Fourth Research Symposium Proceedings* (pp. 9–21). Bradford Woods, IN: Coalition for Education in the Outdoors.

Henderson-King, D., Henderson-King, E., & Hoffman, L. (2001). Media images and women's self evaluations: Social context and importance of attractiveness as moderators. *Personality and Social Psychology Bulletin, 27,* 1407–1416.

Henley, N. M. (1973). Status and sex: Some touching observations. *Bulletin of the Psychonomic Society, 2,* 91–93.

Henley, N. M. (1977). *Body politics: Power, sex, and nonverbal communication.* Englewood Cliffs, NJ: Prentice-Hall.

Henley, N. M. (1989). Molehill or mountain? What we do know and don't know about sex bias in language. In M. Crawford & M. Gentry (Eds.), *Gender and thought* (pp. 59–78). New York: Springer-Verlag.

Henley, N. M., Meng, K., O'Brien, D., McCarthy, W. J., & Sockloskie, R. (1998). Developing a scale to measure the diversity of feminist attitudes. *Psychology of Women Quarterly, 22,* 317–348.

Henley, N. M., Miller, M., Beazley, J. (1995). Syntax, semantics, and sexual violence: Agency and the passive voice. *Journal of Language and Social Psychology, 14,* 60–84.

Henriques, G. R., & Calhoun, L. G. (1999). Gender and ethnic differences in the relationship between body esteem and self-esteem. *Journal of Psychology, 133,* 357–368.

Henry, C. (1998, May 10). Community voices—women in the '90s: Names. *The Philadelphia Inquirer,* p. E6.

Hequembourg, A. L., & Farrell, M. P. (1999). Lesbian motherhood: Negotiating marginal-mainstream identities. *Gender and Society, 13,* 540–557.

Herdt, G. (1997). *Same sex, different cultures.* Boulder, CO: Westview.

Herek, G. M. (2002). Gender gaps in public opinion about lesbians and gay men. *Public Opinion Quarterly, 66,* 40–66.

Herman, A. (1988). Foreword. In A. Statham, E. M. Miller, & H. O. Mauksch (Eds.), *The worth of a women's work: A qualitative synthesis* (pp. ix–xi). Albany, NY: State University of New York Press.

Hernandez, D. G. (1994, May 21). Good and the bad about women's news in newspapers. *Editor and Publisher,* pp. 17, 41.

Herrett-Skjellum, J., & Allen, M. (1996). Television programming and sex stereotyping: A meta-analysis. In B. Burleson (Ed.), *Communication yearbook 19* (pp. 157–185). Thousand Oaks, CA: Sage.

Hewlett, S. A., & West, C. (1998). *The war against parents: What we can do for America's beleaguered moms and dads.* Boston: Houghton Mifflin.

Heywood, S. (1989). *Fantasy lover.* Ontario, Canada: Harlequin.

Hicks, M. H. R., & Li, Z. (2003). Partner violence and major depression in women: A community study of Chinese Americans. *Journal of Nervous and Mental Disease, 191,* 722–729.

Higgins, L. C., & Oldenburg, B. (2003). Predictors of progression and regression in exercise adoption in young women. *Journal of Applied Social Psychology, 33,* 716–729.

Hill, M. (1987). Child-rearing attitudes of black lesbian mothers. In Boston Lesbian Psychologies Collective (Eds.), *Lesbian psychologies* (pp. 215–225). Urbana: University of Illinois Press.

Hill, M., & Ballou, M. (1998). Making therapy feminist: A practice survey. *Women & Therapy, 21,* 1–16.

Hill, S. A. (2002). Teaching and doing gender in African American families. *Sex Roles, 47,* 493–506.

Hines, M. (2004). *Brain gender.* Oxford, England: Oxford University Press.

Hite, S. (1976). *The Hite report.* New York: Macmillan.

Hite, S. (1987). *The Hite report: Women and love: a cultural revolution in progress.* New York: Knopf.

Hobfall, S. E. & Penner, L. A. (1978). Effects of physical attractiveness on therapists' initial judgments of a person's self concept. *Journal of Consulting and Clinical Psychology, 46,* 200–201.

Hoburg, R., Konik, J., Williams, M., & Crawford, M. (2004). Bisexuality among self-identified heterosexual college students. *Journal of Bisexuality, 4,* 25–36.

Hochschild, A. R. (1989). *The second shift: Working parents and the revolution at home.* New York: Viking.

Hoffnung, M. (1989). Motherhood: Contemporary conflict for women. In J. Freeman (Ed.), *Women: A feminist perspective* (4th ed., pp. 157–175). Mountain View, CA: Mayfield.

Hogue, M., & Yoder, J. D. (2003). The role of status in producing depressed entitlement in women's and men's pay allocations. *Psychology of Women Quarterly, 27,* 330–337.

Holm, K. E., Werner-Wilson, R. J., Cook, A. S., & Berger, P. S. (2001). The association between emotion work balance and relationship satisfaction of couples seeking therapy. *American Journal of Family Therapy, 29,* 193–205.

Hooijberg, R., & DiTomaso, N. (1996). Leadership in and of demographically diverse organizations. *Leadership Quarterly, 7,* 1–19.

hooks, b. (1984). *Feminist theory: From margin to center.* Boston: South End Press.

hooks, b. (1989). *Talking back: Thinking feminist, thinking black.* Boston: South End Press.

hooks, b. (2000). *Feminism is for everybody: Passionate politics.* Cambridge, MA: South End Press.

Hossain, Z., & Roopmarine, J. L. (1993). Division of household labor and child care in dual-earner African-American families with infants. *Sex Roles, 29,* 571–584.

Houser, B., & Garvey, C. (1985). Factors that affect nontraditional vocational enrollment among women. *Psychology of Women Quarterly, 9,* 105–118.

Howard, J. A., & Hollander, J. A. (Eds.). (1997). *Gendered situations, gendered selves: A gender lens on social psychology.* Thousand Oaks, CA: Sage.

Hrdy, S. B. (1988, April). Daughters or sons. *Natural History,* 64–82.

Huang, J. (1993). An investigation of gender differences in cognitive abilities among Chinese high school students. *Personality and Individual Differences, 15,* 717–719.

Hunter, G. T. (1974). Pediatrician. In R. B. Kundsin (Ed.), *Women and success: The anatomy of achievement* (pp. 58–61). New York: Morrow.

Hunter, J., & Mallon, G. P. (2000). Lesbian, gay, and bisexual adolescent development: Dancing with your feet tied together. In B. Greene & G. L. Croom (Eds.), *Education, research, and practice in lesbian, gay, bisexual, and transgendered psychology* (pp. 226–243). Thousand Oaks, CA: Sage.

Hurd, L. C. (2000). Older women's body image and embodied experience: An exploration. *Journal of Women and Aging, 12,* 77–97.

Hurlbert, D. F., & Whittaker, K. E. (1991). The role of masturbation in marital and sexual satisfaction: A comparative study of female masturbators and nonmasturbators. *Journal of Sex Education and Therapy, 17,* 272–282.

Hurst, S. A., & Genest, M. (1995). Cognitive-behavioural therapy with a feminist orientation: A perspective for therapy with depressed women. *Canadian Psychology, 36,* 236–257.

Huston, T. L., Caughlin, J. P., Houts, R. M., Smith, S. E., & George, L. J. (2001). The connubial crucible: Newlywed years as predictors of marital delight, distress, and divorce. *Journal of Personality and Social Psychology, 80,* 237–252.

Hyde, J. S., & DeLamater, J. (1997). *Understanding human sexuality* (6th ed.). New York: McGraw-Hill.

Hyde, J. S., & DeLamater, J. D. (2003). *Understanding human sexuality* (8th ed.). New York: McGraw Hill.

Hyde, J. S., Fennema, E., Ryan, M., Frost, L., & Hopp, C. (1990). Gender comparisons of mathematics attitudes and affects: A meta-analysis. *Psychology of Women Quarterly, 14,* 299–324.

Hyde, J. S., & Jaffe, S. R. (2000). Becoming a heterosexual adult: The experiences of young women. *Journal of Social Issues, 56,* 283–296.

Hyde, J. S., & Kling, K. C. (2001). Women, motivation, and achievement. *Psychology of Women Quarterly, 25,* 364–378.

Hyde, J. S., & Linn, M. C. (Eds.). (1986). *The psychology of gender: Advances through meta-analysis.* Baltimore: Johns Hopkins University Press.

Hyde, J. S., & McKinley, N. M. (1997). Gender differences in cognition: Results from meta-analyses. In P. J. Caplan, M. Crawford, J. S. Hyde, & J. T. E. Richardson (Eds.), *Gender differences in human cognition* (pp. 30–51). New York: Oxford University Press.

Hyde, J. S., Rosenberg, B. G., & Behrman, J. (1977). "Tomboyism." *Psychology of Women Quarterly, 2,* 73–75.

Ihinger-Tallman, M., & Pasley, K. (1987). *Remarriage.* Beverly Hills, CA: Sage.

Ilies, R., Hauserman, N., Schwochau, S., & Stibal, J. (2003). Reported incidence rates of work-related sexual harassment in the United States: Using meta-analysis to explain reported rate disparities. *Personnel Psychology, 56,* 607–631.

India's religious leaders condemn sex selection practices. Retrieved July 14, 2001, from http://womenshealth. medscape.com

Inzlicht, M., & Ben-Zeev, T. (2000). A threatening intellectual environment: Why females are susceptible to experiencing problem-solving deficits in the presence of males. *Psychological Science, 11,* 365–371.

Irving, L. M., & Berel, S. R. (2001). Comparison of media-literacy programs to strengthen college women's resistance to media images. *Psychology of Women Quarterly, 25,* 103–111.

Isaac, R. J., & Armat, V. C. (1990). *Madness in the streets: How psychiatry and the law abandoned the mentally ill.* New York: Simon & Schuster.

Jacklin, C. N. (1981). Methodological issues in the study of sex-related differences. *Developmental Review, 1,* 266–273.

Jackson, A. P. (1997). Effects of concerns about child care among single, employed black mothers with preschool children. *American Journal of Community Psychology, 25,* 657–673.

Jackson, S. (2001). Happily never after: Young women's stories of abuse in heterosexual love relationships. *Feminism and Psychology, 11,* 305–321.

Jacobi, L., & Cash, T. F. (1994). In pursuit of the perfect appearance: Discrepancies among self-ideal percepts of multiple physical attributes. *Journal of Applied Social Psychology, 24,* 379–396.

Jacobs, A. (1998, September 13). His debut as a woman. *The New York Times Magazine,* 48–51.

Jacobsen, F. M. (1994). Psychopharmacology. In L. Comas-Diaz & B. Green (Eds.), *Women of color: Integrating ethnic and gender identities in psychotherapy*. New York: Guilford.

Jacobson, N. S., & Gottman, J. M. (1998). *When men batter women*. New York: Simon & Schuster.

James, D., & Drakich, J. (1993). Understanding gender differences in amount of talk: A critical review of research. In D. Tannen (Ed.), *Gender and conversational interaction* (pp. 281–312). New York: Oxford University Press.

James, J. (1999). The contribution of women's studies programs. In S. Davis, M. Crawford, & J. Sebrechts (Eds.), *Coming into her own: Encouraging educational success in girls and women* (pp. 23–36). San Francisco: Jossey-Bass.

Jamieson, K. H. (1995). *Beyond the double bind: Women and leadership*. New York: Oxford University Press.

Jayakar, K. (1994). Women of the Indian subcontinent. In L. Comas-Díaz & B. Greene (Eds), *Women of color: Integrating ethnic and gender identities in psychotherapy* (pp. 161–181). New York: Guilford Press.

Jhally, S. (1995). Writer, editor, and narrator. *Dreamworlds II: Gender/Sex/Power in music video* (videotape). Northampton, MA: Media Education Foundation.

Joffe, H. (1997). Intimacy and love in late modern conditions: Implications for unsafe sexual practices. In J. M. Ussher (Ed.), *Body talk: The material and discursive regulation of sexuality, madness and reproduction* (pp. 159–175). New York: Routledge.

Johansson, P. (2001). Selling the "modern woman": Consumer culture and Chinese gender politics. In S. Munshi (Ed.), *Images of the modern woman in Asia: Global media, local meanings* (pp. 94–122). Richmond, Surrey, UK: Curzon Press.

John, B. A., & Sussman, L. E. (1989). Initiative taking as a determinant of role-reciprocal organization. In R. K. Unger (Ed.), *Representations: Social constructions of gender* (pp. 259–272). Amityville, NY: Baywood.

John, R., Blanchard, P. H., & Hennessy, C. H. (1997). Hidden lives: Aging and contemporary American Indian women. In J. M. Coyle (Ed.), *Handbook on women and aging* (pp. 290–315). Westport, CT: Greenwood Press.

Johnson, M. E. (1988). Influences of gender and sex role orientation on help-seeking attitudes. *Journal of Psychology, 122*, 237–241.

Johnson, M. P. (1995). Patriarchal terrorism and common couple violence: Two forms of violence against women. *Journal of Marriage and the Family, 57*, 283–294.

Johnston-Robledo, I. (2000). From postpartum depression to the empty nest syndrome: The motherhood mystique revisited. In J. C. Chrisler, C. Golden, & P. D. Rozee (Eds.), *Lectures on the psychology of women* (pp. 129–148). Boston: McGraw-Hill.

Jordan, J. V., Kaplan, A. G., Miller, J. B., Stiver, I. P., & Surrey, J. L. (1991). *Women's growth in connection*. New York: Guilford.

Jordan, K. M., & Deluty, R. H. (2000). Social support, coming out, and relationship satisfaction in lesbian couples. *Journal of Lesbian Studies, 4*, 145–164.

Joseph, G. I., & Lewis, J. (1981). *Common differences: Conflicts in black and white feminist perspectives*. Boston: South End Press.

Joseph, J. (1997). Woman battering: A comparative analysis of black and white women. In G. Kaufman Kantor & J. L. Jasinski (Eds.), *Out of darkness: Contemporary perspectives on family violence* (pp. 161–169). Thousand Oaks, CA: Sage.

Jost, J. T. (1997). An experimental replication of the depressed entitlement effect among women. *Psychology of Women Quarterly, 21*, 387–393.

Kahn, A. S., Jackson, J., Kully, C., Badger, K., & Halvorsen, J. (2003). Calling it rape: Differences in experiences of women who do or do not label their sexual assault as rape. *Psychology of Women Quarterly, 27*, 233–242.

Kahn, A. S., & Jean, P. J. (1983). Integration and elimination or separation and redefinition: The future of the psychology of women. *Signs, 8*, 659–670.

Kahn, A. S., & Yoder, J. D. (1989). The psychology of women and conservatism: Rediscovering social change. *Psychology of Women Quarterly, 13*, 417–432.

Kaiser Family Foundation. (2001). Victoria Rideout, *Generation Rx.com: How young people use the Internet for health information*. (Publication No. 3202), New York, N.Y.

Kane, M. J. (1996). Media coverage of the post Title IX female athlete: A feminist analysis of sport, gender, and power. *Duke Journal of Gender Law & Policy, 3*, 95–127.

Kane, M. J., & Lenskyi, H. J. (1998). Media treatment of female athletes: Issues of gender and sexualities. In L. A. Wenner (Ed.), *MediaSport* (pp. 186–201). New York: Routledge.

Kane, M. J., & Parks, J. B. (1990). Mass media images as a reflector of historical social change: The portrayal of female athletes before, during and after Title IX. In L. Vander Velden & J. H. Humphrey (Eds), *Psychology and Sociology of Sport: Current Selected Research, 133*, 146–147.

Kanter, R. M. (1977). *Men and women of the corporation*. New York: Basic Books.

Kaplan, R. M. (1978). Is beauty talent? Sex interaction in the attractiveness halo effect. *Sex Roles, 4*, 195–204.

Karbo, K. (1995). The Übergirl cometh. *Outside, 20*, 60–68, 145.

Karraker, K. H., Vogel, D. A., & Lake, M. A. (1995). Parents' gender stereotyped perceptions of newborns: The eye of the beholder revisited. *Sex Roles, 33*, 687–701.

Katz, B. L. (1991). The psychological impact of stranger versus nonstranger rape on victims' recovery. In A. Parrot & L. Bechhofer, (Eds.), *Acquaintance rape: The hidden crime* (pp. 251–269). New York: Wiley.

Katz, P. A. (1996). Raising feminists. *Psychology of Women Quarterly, 20*, 323–340.

Katz, R. S. (2002). Older women and addictions. In S. L. A. Straussner & S. Brown (Eds.), *The handbook of addiction treatment for women* (pp. 272–297). San Francisco, CA: Jossey-Bass.

Kaw, E. (1994). "Opening" faces: The politics of cosmetic surgery and Asian American women. In N. Sault (Ed.). *Many mirrors: Body image and social relations* (pp. 241–265). New Brunswick, NJ: Rutgers University Press.

Kaysen, S. (1993). *Girl, interrupted.* New York: Turtle Bay Books, a Division of Random House.

Keel, P. K., Mitchell, J. E., Davis, T. L., & Crow, S. J. (2001). Relationship between depression and body dissatisfaction in women diagnosed with bulimia nervosa. *International Journal of Eating Disorders, 30,* 48–56.

Kelle, H. (2000). Gender and territoriality in games played by nine-to-twelve-year-old schoolchildren. *Journal of Contemporary Ethnology, 29,* 164–197.

Keller, J. (2003, September). The H-Bomb. *Boston Magazine,* pp. 70–78.

Keltner, D., Capps, L., Kring, A. M., Young, R. C., & Heerey, E. A. (2001). Just teasing: A conceptual analysis and empirical review. *Psychological Bulletin, 127,* 229–248.

Keltner, D., Gruenfeld, D., & Anderson, C. (2003). Power, approach, and inhibition. *Psychological Review, 110,* 265–284.

Kemper, V. (2002, February 1). Proposal calls fetus a 'child' for health care funding: Bush says rule change would let states offer prenatal services to poor. Abortion rights groups criticize move. *Los Angeles Times,* p. A30.

Kendall-Tackett, K. A. (2001). Victimization of female children. In C. M. Renzetti, J. L. Edelson, & R. K. Bergen (Eds.), *Sourcebook on violence against women* (pp. 101–116). Thousand Oaks, CA: Sage.

Kennell, J., Klaus, M., McGrath, S., Robertson, S., & Hinkley, C. (1991). Continuous emotional support during labor in a US hospital. *Journal of the American Medical Association, 265,* 2197–2201.

Kennelly, I. (1999). "That single-mother element": How white employers typify black women. *Gender and Society, 13,* 168–192.

Kessler, R. C. (2003). Epidemiology of women and depression. *Journal of Affective Disorders, 74,* 5–13.

Kessler, R. C., & Brown, R. L., & Broman, C. L. (1981). Sex differences in psychiatric help-seeking: Evidence from four large-scale surveys. *Journal of Health and Social Behavior, 22,* 49–64.

Kessler, S. J. (1990). The medical construction of gender: Case management of intersexed infants. *Signs, 16,* 3–26.

Kessler, S. J. (1998). *Lessons from the intersexed.* New Brunswick, NJ: Rutgers University Press.

Kessler, S. J. (2002, October). *Intersexuality in the 21st century: Medical emergency or medical invention?* Colloquium presented to the Social Psychology Division, University of Connecticut, Storrs.

Kessler, S. J., & McKenna, W. (1978). *Gender: An ethnomethodological approach.* New York: John Wiley.

Kilbourne, J. (1999). *Deadly persuasion: Why women and girls must fight the addictive power of advertising.* New York: The Free Press.

Kilbourne, J. (2002). *Killing us softly 3: Advertising's image of women* (Videotape). Northampton, MA: Media Education Foundation.

Kimball, M. M. (1995). *Feminist visions of gender similarities and differences.* New York: Harrington Park Press.

Kimball, M. M. (2001). Gender similarities and differences as feminist contradictions. In R .K. Unger (Ed.), *Handbook of the psychology of women and gender* (pp. 66–83). New York: Wiley.

Kimmel, D. C., & Martin, D. L. (Eds.). (2001). *Midlife and aging in gay America: Proceedings of the SAGE Conference, New York City, 2000.* New York: Harrington Park Press.

Kimmel, E. (1999). Feminist teaching: An emergent practice. In S. Davis, M. Crawford & J. Sebrechts (Eds.), *Coming into her own: Encouraging educational success in girls and women* (pp. 57–76). San Francisco: Jossey-Bass.

Kimmel, E. B. (1989). The experience of feminism. *Psychology of Women Quarterly, 13,* 133–146.

Kinsey, A. C., Pomeroy, W. B., & Martin, C. E. (1948). *Sexual behavior in the human male.* Philadelphia: Saunders.

Kinsey, A. C., Pomeroy, W. B., Martin, C. E., & Gebhard, P. H. (1953). *Sexual behavior in the human female.* Philadelphia: Saunders.

Kinsman, S. B., Romer, D., & Schwarz, D. F. (1998). Early sexual initiation: The role of peer norms. *Pediatrics, 102,* 1185–1192.

Kirchmeyer, C. (1993). Nonwork-to-work spillover: A more balanced view of the experiences and coping of professional women and men. *Sex Roles, 28,* 531–552.

Kitayama, S., Markus, H. R., & Kurokawa, M. (2000). Culture, emotion, and well-being: Good feelings in Japan and the United States. *Cognition and Emotion, 14,* 93–124.

Kitzinger, C. (1987). *The social construction of lesbianism.* London: Sage.

Kitzinger, C. (2001). Sexualities. In R. K. Unger (Ed.), *Handbook of the psychology of women and gender* (pp. 272–285). New York: Wiley.

Kitzinger, S. (1983). *Women's experience of sex.* London: Dorling Kindersley.

Kling, K. C., Hyde, J. S., Showers, C., & Buswell, B. (1999). Gender differences in self-esteem: A meta-analysis. *Psychological Bulletin, 125,* 470–500.

Kline, K. N. (1996). The drama of in utero drug exposure. In R. L. Parrott & C. M. Condit (Eds.), *Evaluating women's health messages* (pp. 61–79). Thousand Oaks, CA: Sage.

Kline and Company. (2003). *Cosmetics and toiletries U.S.A.: Continuing industry analysis.* Retrieved February 2004, from Kline Group Web site: http://www.klinegroup.com

Klomsten, A. T., Skaalvik, E. M., Espnes, G. A. (2004). Physical self-concept and sports: Do gender differences still exist? *Sex Roles, 50,* 119–127.

Klonoff, E. A., & Landrine, H. (1995). The schedule of sexist events: A measure of lifetime and recent sexist discrimination in women's lives. *Psychology of Women Quarterly, 19,* 439–472.

Klonoff, E. A., Landrine, H., & Campbell, R. (2000). Sexist discrimination may account for well-known differences in psychiatric symptoms. *Psychology of Women Quarterly, 24,* 93–99.

Knight, J. L., & Guiliano, T. A. (2001). He's a Laker; she's a "Looker": The consequences of gender-stereotypical portrayals of male and female athletes by the print media. *Sex Roles, 45,* 217–229.

Knight, J. L. & Guiliano, T. A. (2003). Blood, sweat, and jeers: The impact of the media's heterosexist portrayals on perceptions of male and female athletes. *Journal of Sport Behavior, 26,* 272–284.

Knudson-Martin, C., & Mahoney, A. R. (1996). Gender dilemmas and myth in the construction of marital bargains: Issues for marital therapy. *Family Process, 35,* 137–153.

Koch, L. (1990). The fairy tale as a model for women's experience of in vitro fertilization. In H. B. Holmes (Ed.), *Issues in reproductive technology I* (pp. 303–320). New York: Garland.

Kohlberg, L. (1966). A cognitive-developmental analysis of children's sex role concepts and attitudes. In E. E. Maccoby (Ed.), *The development of sex differences* (pp. 82–173). Stanford, CA: Stanford University Press.

Koivula, N. (1999). Gender stereotyping in television media news coverage. *Sex Roles, 41,* 589–604.

Koivula, N. (2001). Perceived characteristics of sports categorized as gender-neutral, feminine and masculine. *Journal of Sport Behavior, 24,* 377–393.

Kong, M. E. (1997). The portrayal of women's images in magazine advertisements: Goffman's gender analysis revisited. *Sex Roles, 37,* 979–996.

Konrad, A. M., Ritchie, J. E., Lieb, P., & Corrigall, E. (2000). Sex differences and similarities in job attribute preferences: A meta-analysis. *Psychological Bulletin, 26,* 593–641.

Koss, M. P., Bailey, J. A., Yuan, N. P., Herrera, V. M., & Lichter, E. L. (2003). Depression and PTSD in survivors of male violence: Research and training initiatives to facilitate recovery. *Psychology of Women Quarterly, 27,* 130–142.

Koss, M. P., & Gaines, J. A. (1993). The prediction of sexual aggression by alcohol use, athletic participation, and fraternity affiliation. *Journal of Interpersonal Violence, 8,* 94–108.

Koss, M. P., Gidycz, C. A., & Wisniewski, N. (1987). The scope of rape: Incidence and prevalence of sexual aggression and victimization in a national sample of higher education students. *Journal of Consulting and Clinical Psychology, 55,* 162–170.

Koss, M. P., & Kilpatrick, D. G. (2001). Rape and sexual assault. In E. Gerrity, T. M. Keane, & T. Garis (Eds.), *The mental health consequences of torture* (pp. 177–193). New York: Plenum.

Kowner, R. (2002). Japanese body image: Structure and esteem scores in a cross-cultural perspective. *International Journal of Psychology, 37, 149–159.*

Koyama, E. (2002, January 7). Intersex activists respond to the Vagina Monologues. E-mail posted to Women's Studies Listserv.

Kramarae, C., & Treichler, P. A. (1985). A feminist dictionary. Boston: Pandora.

Kravetz, D. (1980). Consciousness-raising and self-help. In A. M. Brodsky & R. Hare-Mustin (Eds.), *Women and psychotherapy* (pp. 267–283). New York: Guilford.

Krieger, S. (1982). Lesbian identity and community: Recent social science literature. *Signs, 8,* 91–108.

Kuhn, M. (1991). *No stone unturned: The life and times of Maggie Kuhn.* New York: Ballantine.

Kurdek, L. A. (1988). Perceived social support in gays and lesbians in cohabitating couples. *Journal of Personality and Social Psychology, 54,* 504–509.

Kurdek, L. A. (1993). The allocation of household labor in gay, lesbian, and heterosexual married couples. *Journal of Social Issues, 49,* 127–139.

Kurdek, L. A. (1997). Adjustment to relationship dissolution in gay, lesbian, and heterosexual partners. *Personal Relationships, 4,* 145–161.

LaFramboise, T. D., Berman, J. S., & Sohi, B. K. (1994). American Indian women. In L. Comas-Díaz & B. Greene (Eds.), *Women of color: Integrating ethnic and gender identities in psychotherapy* (pp. 30–71). New York: Guilford.

LaFrance, M. (1992). Gender and interruptions: Individual infraction or violation of the social order? *Psychology of Women Quarterly, 16,* 497–512.

LaFrance, M. (2001). Gender and social interaction. In R. K. Unger (Ed.), *Handbook of the Psychology of Women and Gender* (pp. 245–255). New York: Wiley.

LaFrance, M., & Hecht, M. A. (2000). Gender and smiling: A meta-analysis. In A. H. Fischer (Ed.), *Gender and emotion* (pp. 118–142). Cambridge, England: Cambridge University Press.

Laing, R. D. (1970). *The divided self.* New York: Random House.

Lamb, S., & Keon, S. (1995). Blaming the perpetrator: Language that distorts reality in newspaper articles on men battering women. *Psychology of Women Quarterly, 19,* 209–220.

Lambdin, J. R., Greer, K. M., Jibotian, K. S., Wood, K. R., & Hamilton, M. C. (2003). The animal = male hypothesis: Children's and adult's beliefs about the sex of non-sex specific stuffed animals. *Sex Roles, 48, 471–483.*

Landa, A. (1990). No accident: The voices of voluntarily childless women–An essay on the social construction of fertility choices. In J. P. Knowles & E. Cole (Eds.), *Motherhood: A feminist perspective* (pp. 139–158). New York: Haworth.

Landrine, H. (1985). Race x class stereotypes of women. *Sex Roles, 13*, 65–75.

Landrine, H., & Klonoff, E. A. (1997). *Discrimination against women: Prevalence, consequences, remedies.* Thousand Oaks, CA: Sage.

Landrine, H., Klonoff, E. A., Gibbs, J., Manning, V., & Lund, M. (1995). Physical and psychiatric correlates of gender discrimination: An application of the schedule of sexist events. *Psychology of Women Quarterly, 19*, 473–492.

LaRossa, R., Jaret, C., Gadgil, M., & Wynn, G. R. (2001). Gender disparities in Mother's Day and Father's Day comic strips: A fifty-four year history. *Sex Roles, 44*, 693–718.

Larson, M. S. (2003). Gender, race, and aggression in television commercials that feature children. *Sex Roles, 48*, 67–76.

Laumann, E. O., Gagnon, J. H., Michael, R. T., & Michaels, S. (1994). *The social organization of sexuality: Sexual practices in the United States.* Chicago: University of Chicago Press.

Laumann, E. O., & Michael, R. T. (Eds.). (2000). *Sex, love, and health in America: Private choices and public policies.* Chicago: University of Chicago Press.

Laumann, E. O., Paik, A., & Rosen, R. C. (1999). Sexual dysfunction in the United States: Prevalence and predictors. *JAMA, 281*, 537–544.

Laurance, J. (2001, August 22). Doctors must refuse to collude in this abusive practice: "Genital mutilation is one of many harmful practices affecting women in traditional societies." *The Independent*, p. 5.

Laws, J. L., & Schwartz, P. (1977). *Sexual scripts.* Hinsdale, IL: Dryden.

Leadbeater, B. J. R., & Way, N. (2001). *Growing up fast: Transitions to early adulthood of inner-city adolescent mothers.* Mahwah, NJ: Erlbaum.

Leaper, C. (2000). The social construction and socialization of gender during development. In P. H. Miller & E. K. Scholnick (Eds.), *Toward a feminist developmental psychology* (pp. 127–152). New York: Routledge.

Leaper, C., Anderson, K., & Sanders, P. (1998). Moderators of gender effects on parents' talk to their children: A meta-analysis. *Developmental Psychology, 34*, 3–27.

Lee, E. (2000). Young people's attitudes toward abortion for abnormality. *Feminism & Psychology, 10*, 396–399.

Lee, G. R. (1988). Marital intimacy among older persons: The spouse as confidant. *Journal of Family Issues, 9*, 273–284.

Lee, J. (1995). Beyond bean counting. In B. Findlen (Ed.), *Listen up! Voices from the next feminist generation* (pp. 205–211). Seattle, WA: Seal Press.

Lee, J. (2003). Menarche and the (hetero)sexualization of the female body. In R. Weitz (Ed.) *The politics of women's bodies* (2nd ed.) (pp. 82–99). Oxford, England: Oxford University Press.

Leibenluft, E. (1996). Women with bipolar illness: Clinical and research issues. *American Journal of Psychiatry, 153*, 163–173.

Leit, R. A., Pope, H. G., & Gray, J. J. (2001). Cultural expectations of muscularity in men: The evolution of *Playgirl* centerfolds. *International Journal of Eating Disorders, 29*, 90–93.

Lemkau, J. P. (1983). Women in male-dominated professions: Distinguishing personality and background characteristics. *Psychology of Women Quarterly, 8*, 144–165.

Leonhardt, D. (2003, November 16). Sugar and spice, and sour dads. *The New York Times*, p. BU 4.

Lester, R., & Petrie, T. A. (1995). Personality and physical correlates of bulimic symptomatology among Mexican American female college students. *Journal of Counseling Psychology, 42*, 199–203.

Lester, R., & Petrie, T. A. (1998). Physical, psychological, and societal correlates of bulimic symptomatology among African American college women. *Journal of Counseling Psychology, 45*, 315–321.

Levenson, R. W., Carstensen, L. L., & Gottman, J. M. (1993). Long-term marriage: Age, gender, and satisfaction. *Psychology and Aging, 8*, 301–313.

Levesque, R. J. R. (2001). *Culture and family violence.* Washington, DC: American Psychological Association.

Levin, I. (1997). The stepparent role from a gender perspective. *Marriage & Family Review, 26*, 177–190.

Levine, M. P., & Leonard, R. (1984). Discrimination against lesbians in the work force. *Signs, 4*, 700–710.

Levine, R., Sato, S., Hashimoto, T., & Verma, J. (1995). Love and marriage in eleven cultures. *Journal of Cross-Cultural Psychology, 26*, 554–571.

Lewis, J. (2002). *Playing the human part: Lupe Ontiveros on how not to be a diva.* Retrieved August 25, 2002, from http://www.laweekly.com/ink/02/16/cover-lewis2.php

Lewis, M. (1992). *Shame: The exposed self.* New York: Free Press.

Lewis, S. (1979). *Sunday's women: Lesbian life today.* Boston: Beacon.

L'Hommedieu, T. (1984). *The divorce experiences of working and middle class women.* Ann Arbor: UMI Research Press.

Li, N. P., Bailey, J. M., Kenrick, D. T., & Linsenmeier, J. A. W. (2002). The necessities and luxuries of mate preferences: Testing the tradeoffs. *Journal of Personality and Social Psychology, 82*, 947–955.

Liles, E. G., & Woods, S. C. (1999). Anorexia nervosa as viable behaviour: Extreme self-deprivation in historical context. *History of Psychiatry, 10*, 205–225.

Lindsey, E. W., & Mize, J. (2001). Contextual differences in parent-child play: Implications for children's gender role development. *Sex Roles, 44*, 155–176.

Lindsey, E. W., Mize, J., & Pettit, G. (1997). Differential play patterns of mothers and fathers of sons and daughters: Implications for children's gender role development. *Sex Roles, 37*, 643–662.

Linz, D., Donnerstein, E., & Penrod, S. (1987). Sexual violence in the mass media: Social psychological implications. In P. Shaver & C. Hendrick (Eds.), *Review of Personality and Social Psychology: Vol. 7. Sex and gender* (pp. 95–123). Newbury Park, CA: Sage.

Lipman-Blumen, J., & Leavitt, H. J. (1976). Vicarious and direct achievement patterns in adulthood. The Counseling Psychologist, 6, 26–31.

Lirgg, C. D. (1991). Gender differences in self-confidence in physical activity: A meta-analysis of recent studies. *Journal of Sport and Exercise Psychology, 13*, 294–310.

Liss, M., Hoffner, C., & Crawford, M. (2000). What do feminists believe? *Psychology of Women Quarterly, 24*, 279–284.

Lloyd, S. A. (1991). The dark side of courtship. *Family Relations, 40*, 14–20.

Locher, P., Unger, R. K., Sociedade, P., & Wahl, J. (1993). At first glance: Accessibility of the physical attractiveness stereotype. *Sex Roles, 28*, 729–743.

Locke, L. M., & Richman, C. L. (1999). Attitudes toward domestic violence: Race and gender issues. *Sex Roles, 40*, 227–247.

Loiacano, D. K. (1993). Gay identity issues among Black Americans: Racism, homophobia, and the need for validation. In L. D. Garnets & D. C. Kimmel (Eds.), *Psychological perspectives on lesbian and gay male experiences* (pp. 364–375). New York: Columbia University Press.

Lopez, S. R. (1989). Patient variable biases in clinical judgment: Conceptual overview and methodological considerations. *Psychological Bulletin, 106*, 184–203.

LoPiccolo, J., & Stock, W. E. (1986). Treatment of sexual dysfunction. *Journal of Consulting and Clinical Psychology, 54*, 158–167.

Lorber, J. (1993b). *Paradoxes of gender.* New Haven, CT: Yale University Press.

Lord, M. G. (1994). *Forever Barbie: The unauthorized biography of a real doll.* New York: William Morrow and Company.

Lott, B. (1987). Sexist discrimination as distancing behavior: I. A laboratory demonstration. *Psychology of Women Quarterly, 11*, 47–58.

Lott, B. (1989). Sexist discrimination as distancing behavior: II. Primetime television. *Psychology of Women Quarterly, 13*, 341–355.

Lott, B., & Rocchio, L. M. (1997). Individual and collective action: Social approaches and remedies for sexist discrimination. In H. Landrine & E. A. Klonoff (Eds.), *Discrimination against women: Prevalence, consequences, remedies* (pp. 148–171). Thousand Oaks, CA: Sage.

Lottes, I., Weinberg, M., & Weller, I. (1993). Reactions to pornography on a college campus: For or against? *Sex Roles, 29*, 69–89.

Lovelace, L., & McGrady, M. (1981). *Ordeal.* New York: Berkley Books.

Lubinski, D., Benbow, C. P., Shea, D. L., Eftekhari Sanjani, H., & Halvorson, B. J. (2001). Men and women at promise for scientific excellence: Similarity not dissimilarity. *Psychological Science, 12*, 309–317.

Lublin, N. (1998). *Pandora's box.* New York: Rowman & Littlefield.

Ludwig, M. R., & Brownell, K. D. (1999). Lesbians, bisexual women, and body image: An investigation of gender roles and social group affiliation. *International Journal of Eating Disorders, 25*, 89–97.

Lueptow, L. B., Garovich, L., & Lueptow, M. B. (1995). The persistence of gender stereotypes in the face of changing sex roles: Evidence contrary to the sociocultural model. *Ethology & Sociobiology, 16*, 509–530.

Lunbeck, E. (1994). *The psychiatric persuasion: Knowledge, gender, and power in modern America.* Princeton, NJ: Princeton University Press.

Lunney, K. (2003, April 17). Air force: Sex assault scandal confined to the academy. *Government Executive Magazine.* Retrieved from http://www.govexec.com/dailyfed/0403/041703m1.htm.

Lutz, W. J., & Hock, E. (1998). Factors that influence depressive symptoms in mothers of infants. *Psychology of Women Quarterly, 22*, 499–503.

Lytton, H., & Romney, D. M. (1991). Parents' differential socialization of boys and girls: A meta-analysis. *Psychological Bulletin, 109*, 267–296.

MacCannell, D., & MacCannell, J. F. (1987). The beauty system. In N. Armstrong & L. Tennenhouse (Eds.), *The ideology of conduct: essays on literature and the history of sexuality.* (pp. 206–238). New York: Methuen.

Maccoby, E. E. (1980). *Social development: Psychological growth and the parent-child relationship.* New York: Harcourt Brace Jovanovich.

Maccoby, E. E. (1998). *The two sexes: Growing up apart, coming together.* Cambridge, MA: Belknap Press of Harvard University Press.

Maccoby, E. E., & Jacklin, C. (1974). *The psychology of sex differences.* Stanford, CA: Stanford University Press.

MacFarlane, A. (1977). *The psychology of childbirth.* Cambridge, MA: Harvard University Press.

MacKinnon, C. A. (1994). Sexuality. In A. C. Herrmann & A. J. Stewart (Eds.), *Theorizing feminism: Parallel trends in the humanities and social sciences* (pp. 257–287). Boulder, CO: Westview Press.

MacKinnon, C., & Dworkin, A. (Eds.). (1997). *In harm's way: The pornography civil rights hearings.* Cambridge, MA: Harvard University Press.

Mahalingam, R. (2003). Essentialism, culture, and beliefs about gender among the Aravanis of Tamil Nadu, India. *Sex Roles, 49*, 489–496.

Mahay, J. W., Laumann, E. O., & Michaels, S. (2001). Race, gender, and class in sexual scripts. In E. O. Laumann & R. T. Michael (Eds.), *Sex, love, and health: Private choices and public policies* (pp. 197–238). Chicago: University of Chicago Press.

Mahlstedt, D. (1999). *Men's work: Fraternity brothers stopping violence against women.* New York: Insight Media.

Major, B. (1994). From social inequality to personal entitlement: The role of social comparisons, legitimacy appraisals, and group membership. In M. P. Zanna (Ed.), *Advances in experimental social psychology, Vol. 26* (pp. 293–355). New York: Academic Press.

Major, B., Barr, L., Zubek, J., & Babey, S. H. (1999). Gender and self-esteem: A meta-analysis. In W. B. Swann Jr., J. H. Langlois, & L. A. Gilbert (Eds.), *Sexism and stereotypes in modern society: The gender science of Janet Taylor Spence* (pp. 223–253). Washington, DC: American Psychological Association.

Major, B., Gramzow, R. H., McCoy, S. K., Levin, S., Schmader, T., & Sidanius, J. (2002). Perceiving personal discrimination: The role of group status and legitimizing ideology. *Journal of Personality & Social Psychology, 82*, 269–282.

Major, B., Schmidlin, A. M., & Williams, L. (1990). Gender patterns in social touch: The impact of setting and age. *Journal of Personality and Social Psychology, 58*, 634–643.

Makepeace, J. M. (1986). Gender differences in courtship violence victimization. *Family Relations: Journal of Applied Family and Child Studies, 35*, 383–388.

Malkin, A. R., Wornian, K., & Chrisler, J. C. (1999). Women and weight: Gendered messages on magazine covers. *Sex Roles, 40*, 647–655.

Malloy, T. E., Fisher, W. A., Albright, L., Misovich, S. J., & Fisher, J. D. (1997). Interpersonal perception of the AIDS risk potential of persons of the opposite sex. *Health Psychology, 16*, 480–486.

Mama, A. (2002). Gender, power, and identity in African contexts. *The Wellesley Centers for Women Research and Action Report, 23*, 6–15.

Manning, W. D., & Landale, N. S. (1996). Racial and ethnic differences in the role of cohabitation in premarital childbearing. *Journal of Marriage and the Family, 58*, 63–77.

Mansfield, P. K., Koch, P. B., Henderson, J., Vicary, J. R., Kohn, M., & Young, E. W. (1991). The job climate for women in traditionally male blue-collar occupations. *Sex Roles, 25*, 63–79.

Maranto, C. L., & Stenoien, A. F. (2000). Weight discrimination: A multidisciplinary analysis. *Employee Responsibilities and Rights Journal, 12*, 9–24.

Marcuccio, E., Loving, N., Bennett, S. K., & Hayes, S. N. (2003). A survey of attitudes and experiences of women with heart disease. *Women's Health Issues, 13*, 23–31.

Marecek, J. (1986, March). *Sexual development and girls' self-esteem.* Paper presented at the Seminar on Girls: Promoting Self-Esteem, sponsored by the Girls' Coalition of Southeastern Pennsylvania, Swarthmore, PA.

Marecek, J. (1989). Introduction to special issue: Theory and method in feminist psychology. *Psychology of Women Quarterly, 13*, 367–378.

Marecek, J. (1999). Trauma talk in feminist clinical practice. In S. Lamb (Ed.), *New versions of victims: Feminists struggle with the concept.* New York: New York University Press.

Marecek, J., Crawford, M., & Popp, D. (2004). On the construction of gender, sex, and sexualities. In A. H. Eagly, A. E. Beall, & R. J. Sternberg (Eds.), *The psychology of gender* (2nd ed.) (pp. 192–216). New York: Guilford.

Marecek, J. & Kravetz, D. (1998). Power and agency in feminist therapy. In I. B. Seu & M. C. Heenan (Eds.), *Feminism and psychotherapy: Reflections on contemporary theories and practices* (pp. 13–29). Thousand Oaks, CA: Sage.

Markson, E. W. (2003). The female aging body through film. In C. A. Faircloth (Ed.), *Aging bodies: Images and everyday experiences* (pp. 77–102). New York: AltaMira Press.

Markson, E. W., & Taylor, C. A. (1993). Real versus reel world: Older women and the Academy Awards. In N. D. Davis, E. Cole, & E. D. Rothblum (Eds.), *Faces of women and aging* (pp. 157–172). Binghamton, NY: Harrington Park Press.

Markson, E. W., & Taylor, C. A. (2000). The mirror has two faces. *Aging and Society, 20*, 137–160.

Markus, H. R., & Kitayama, S. (1991). Culture and the self: Implications for cognition, emotion, and motivation. *Psychological Review, 98*, 224–253.

Marsh, M. (1995). Feminist psychopharmacology: An aspect of feminist psychiatry. *Women & Therapy, 16*, 73–84.

Marshall, A. (1997). Who's laughing? Hillary Rodham Clinton in political humor. In N. V. Benokraitis (Ed.), *Subtle sexism: Current practice and prospects for change* (pp. 72–90). Thousand Oaks, CA: Sage.

Martin, C. L., & Fabes, R. A. (2001). The stability and consequences of young children's same-sex peer interactions. *Developmental Psychology, 37*, 431–446.

Martin, C. L., Fabes, R. A., Evans, S. M., & Wyman, H. (1999). Social cognition on the playground: Children's beliefs about playing with girls versus boys and their relations to sex segregated play. *Journal of Social & Personal Relationships, 16*, 751–771.

Martin, C. L., & Halverson, C. F. (1983). The effects of sex-typing schemas on young children's memory. *Child Development, 54*, 563–574.

Martin, C. L., & Ruble, D. (2004). Children's search for gender cues. *Current Directions in Psychological Science, 13*, 67–70.

Martin, J. A., Park, M. M., & Sutton, P. D. (2002). Births: Preliminary data for 2001. *National vital statistics reports, 5.* Hyattsville, MD: Nation Center for Health Statistics.

Martin, S. E. (1988). Think like a man, work like a dog, and act like a lady: Occupational dilemmas of policewomen. In A. Statham, E. M. Miller, & H. O. Mauksch (Eds.), *The worth of women's work: A qualitative synthesis* (pp. 205–224). Albany, NY: State University of New York Press.

Martire, L. M., & Stephens, M. A. P. (2003). Juggling parent care and employment responsibilities: The dilemmas of adult daughter caregivers in the workforce. *Sex Roles, 48,* 167–173.

Martz, D. M., Handley, K. B., & Eisler, R. M. (1995). The relationship between feminine gender role stress, body image, and eating disorders. *Psychology of Women Quarterly, 19,* 493–508.

Masson, J. M. (1984). *The assault on truth: Freud's suppression of the seduction theory.* New York: Harper Perennial.

Masters, W. H., & Johnson, V. (1966). *Human sexual response.* Boston: Little, Brown.

Masters, W. H., & Johnson, V. (1979). *Homosexuality in perspective.* Boston: Little, Brown.

Matthews, A. P. (1996). How evangelical women cope with prescription and description. In C. C. Kroeger, J. R. Beck, et al. (Eds.), *Women, abuse, and the Bible: How scripture can be used to hurt or to heal* (pp. 86–105). Grand Rapids, MI: Baker Books.

Matthews, S. H. (1979). *The social world of old women.* Beverly Hills: Sage.

Mauthner, N. S. (1998). "It's a woman's cry for help": A relational perspective on postnatal depression. *Feminism & Psychology, 8,* 325–355.

Mayall, A., & Russell, D. (1993). Racism in pornography. *Feminism and Psychology, 3,* 275–281.

Mays, V. M., & Cochran, S. D. (1988). Issues in the perception of AIDS risk and risk reduction activities by black and Hispanic/Latina women. *American Psychologist, 43,* 949–957.

McClelland, D. C., Atkinson, J. W., Clark, R. A., & Lowell, E. L. (1953). *The achievement motive.* Englewood Cliffs, NJ: Prentice Hall.

McCormick, M. J. (2002). The search for the ideal heterosexual role play. In L. Diamant & J. A. Lee (Eds.), *The psychology of sex, gender, and jobs: Issues and resolutions* (pp. 155–170). Westport, CT: Praeger.

McCreary, D. R., & Rhodes, N. D. (2001). On the gender-typed nature of dominant and submissive acts. *Sex Roles, 44,* 339–350.

McGuffey, C. S., & Rich, B. L. (1999). Playing in the gender transgression zone: Race, class, and hegemonic masculinity in middle childhood. *Gender & Society, 13,* 608–627.

McHugh, M. D., Koeske, R. D., & Frieze, I. H. (1986). Issues to consider in conducting nonsexist psychological research: A guide for researchers. *American Psychologist, 41,* 879–890.

McIntosh, P. (1988). *Understanding correspondence between white privilege and male privilege through women's studies work.* (Working paper No. 189). Wellesley, MA: Center for Research on Women, Wellesley College.

McKelvey, M. W., & McKenry, P. C. (2000). The psychosocial well-being of Black and White mothers following marital dissolution. *Psychology of Women Quarterly, 24,* 4–14.

McKinlay, S. M., Brambilla, D. J., & Posner, J. G. (1992). The normal menopause transition. *American Journal of Human Biology, 4,* 37–46.

McKinley, N. M., & Hyde, J. S. (1996). The objectified body consciousness scale: Development and validation. *Psychology of Women Quarterly, 20,* 181–215.

McMahon, M. (1995). *Engendering motherhood.* New York: Guilford.

McNamara, E. (2004, April 11). Linking evil to feminism. *The Boston Globe,* p. B1.

Meier, E. (2000). Legislative efforts to combat sexual trafficking and slavery of women and children. *Pediatric Nursing, 26,* 216–211.

Mellanby, A. R., Phelps, F. A., Crichton, N. J., & Tripp, J. H. (1996). School sex education, a process for evaluation: Methodology and results. *Health Education Research, 11,* 205–214.

Mennino, S. F., & Brayfield, A. (2002). Job-family trade-offs: The multidimensional effects of gender. *Work and Occupations, 29,* 226–256.

Mercer, R. T. (1990). *Parents at risk.* New York: Springer.

Merchant, C. (1995). *Earthcare: Women and the Environment.* New York: Routledge.

Merritt, R. D., & Kok, C. J. (1995). Attribution of gender to a gender-unspecified individual: An evaluation of the people = male hypothesis. *Sex Roles, 33,* 145–157.

Merskin, D. (1999). Adolescence, advertising, and the ideology of menstruation. *Sex Roles, 40,* 941–957.

Messner, M. A., Duncan, M. C., & Jensen, K. (1993). Separating the men from the girls: The gendered language of televised sports. *Gender & Society, 7,* 121–137.

Meston, C. M., Trapnell, P. D., & Gorzalka, B. B. (1996). Ethnic and gender differences in sexuality: Variations in sexual behavior between Asian and non-Asian university students. *Archives of Sexual Behavior, 25,* 33–72.

Metzl, J. (2003). *Prozac on the couch: Prescribing gender in the era of wonder drugs.* Durham: Duke University Press.

Michael, R. T., Gagnon, J. H., Laumann, E. O., & Kolata, G. (1994). *Sex in America: A definitive survey.* Boston: Little Brown.

Miller, B. C., Benson, B., & Galbraith, K. A. (2001). Family relationships and adolescent pregnancy risk: A research synthesis. *Developmental Review, 21,* 1–38.

Miller, B. C., Norton, M. C., Curtis, T., Hill, E. J., Schvaneveldt, P., & Young, M. H. (1997). The timing of sexual intercourse among adolescents. *Youth & Society, 29,* 54–83.

Miller, B. D. (2001). Female-selective abortion in Asia: Patterns, policies, and debates. *American Anthropologist, 103,* 1083–1095.

Miller, D. H. (1996). Medical and psychological consequences of legal abortion in the United States. In R. L. Parrott & C. M. Condit (Eds.), *Evaluating women's health messages* (pp. 17–32). Thousand Oaks, CA: Sage.

Miller, D. H, Greene, K., Causby, V., White, B. W., & Lockhart, L. L. (2001). Domestic violence in lesbian relationships. *Women & Therapy, 23,* 107–127.

Miller, J. B. (1986). *Toward a new psychology of women* (2nd ed.). Boston: Beacon.

Miller, L. C., Putcha Bhagavatula, A., & Pedersen, W. C. (2002). Men's and women's mating preferences: Distinct evolutionary mechanisms? *Current Directions in Psychological Science, 11,* 88–93.

Mills, J. S., Polivy, J., Herman, C. P., & Tiggeman, M. (2002). Effects of exposure to thin media images: Evidence of self-enhancement among restrained eaters. *Personality and Social Psychology Bulletin, 28,* 1687–1699.

Mintz, S. B. (2003). In a word, *Baywatch.* In R. Dicker & A. Piepmeier (Eds.), *Catching a wave:Reclaiming feminism for the 21st century* (pp. 57–81). Boston: Northeastern University Press.

Mischel, W. (1966). A social learning view of sex differences in behavior. In E. Maccoby (Ed.), *The development of sex differences* (pp. 56–81). Stanford, CA: Stanford University Press.

Mischel, W. (1970). Sex-typing and socialization. In P. H. Mussen (Ed.), *Carmichael's manual of child psychology* (pp. 3–72). New York: Wiley.

Misovich, S. J., Fisher, J. D., & Fisher, W. A. (1997). Close relationships and elevated HIV risk behavior: Evidence and possible underlying psychological processes. *Review of General Psychology, 1,* 72–107.

Mitchell, V., & Helson, R. (1990). Women's prime in life: Is it the 50's? *Psychology of Women Quarterly, 14,* 451–470.

Mitten, D. (1996). A philosophical basis for a women's outdoor adventure program. In K. Warren (Ed.), *Women's Voices in Experiential Education* (pp. 78–84). Dubuque, IA: Kendall Hunt.

Moayedi, R. (1999). Mentoring a diverse population. In S. Davis, M. Crawford, & J. Sebrechts (Eds.) *Coming Into Her Own: Educational Success in Girls and Women* (pp. 229–243). San Francisco: Jossey-Bass.

Mock, S. E. (2001). Retirement intentions of same-sex couples. *Journal of Gay & Lesbian Social Services, 13,* 81–86.

Moffat, M. (1989). *Coming of age in New Jersey.* New Brunswick, NJ: Rutgers University Press.

Moller, L. C., & Serbin, L. A. (1996). Antecedents of toddler gender segregation: Cognitive consonance, gender-typed toy preferences, and behavioral compatability. *Sex Roles, 35,* 445–460.

Mollica, R., Donelan, K., Tor, S., Lavelle, J., Elias, C., Frankel, M., et al. (1993). The effect of trauma and confinement on functional health and mental health status of Cambodians living in Thailand-Cambodia border camps. *JAMA, 270,* 581–586.

Molloy, B. L., & Herzberger, S. D. (1998). Body image and self-esteem: A comparison of African-American and Caucasian women. *Sex Roles, 38,* 631–643.

Money, J., & Ehrhardt, A. (1972). *Man and woman, boy and girl.* Baltimore: Johns Hopkins University Press.

Monteith, M. J., & Czopp, A. M. (2003, October). *Confronting prejudice: Making social and personal norms against prejudice salient by meeting prejudice head-on.* Symposium conducted at the conference of the Society of Experimental Social Psychology, Boston, Massachusetts.

Montgomery, H. (2001). *Modern Babylon: Prostituting children in Thailand.* New York: Berghahn.

Morell, C. (2000). Saying no: Women's experiences with reproductive refusal. *Feminism and Psychology, 10,* 313–322.

Morgan, B. L. (1998). A three generational study of tomboy behavior. *Sex Roles, 39,* 787–800.

Morgan, K. P. (1996). Describing the emperor's new clothes: Three myths of educational (in) equity. In A. Diller, B. Houston, K. P. Morgan, & M. Ayim (Eds.), *The gender questions in education: Theory, pedagogy, and politics* (pp. 105–122). Boulder, CO: Westview.

Morgan, L. A. (1991). *After marriage ends: Economic consequences for midlife women.* London: Sage.

Mori, D., Chaiken, S., & Pliner, P. (1987). "Eating lightly" and the self-presentation of femininity. *Journal of Personality and Social Psychology, 53,* 693–702.

Morier, D., & Seroy, C. (1994). The effect of interpersonal expectancies on men's self-presentation of gender role attitudes to women. *Sex Roles, 31,* 493–504.

Morris, J. (1974). *Conundrum.* New York: Harcourt Brace Jovanovich.

Morris, J. F., Waldo, C. R., & Rothblum, E. D. (2001). A model of predictors and outcomes of outness among lesbian and bisexual women. *American Journal of Orthopsychiatry, 71,* 61–71.

Moynihan, D. P. (1965). *The Negro family: The case for national action.* Washington, DC: U.S. Department of Labor.

Muehlenhard, C. L., & Hollabough, L. C. (1988). Do women sometimes say no when they mean yes? The prevalence and correlates of women's token resistance to sex. *Journal of Personality and Social Psychology, 54,* 872–879.

Muehlenhard, C. L., & Rodgers, C. S. (1998). Token resistance to sex: New perspectives on an old stereotype. *Psychology of Women Quarterly, 22,* 443–463.

Mueller, K. A., & Yoder, J. D. (1997). Gendered norms for family size, employment, and occupation: Are there personal costs for violating them? *Sex Roles, 36,* 207–220.

Munce, S. E., Robertson, E. K., Sansom, S. N., & Stewart, D. E. (2004). Who is portrayed in psychotropic drug advertisements? *Journal of Nervous & Mental Disease, 192,* 284–288.

Murnen, S. K. (2000). Gender and the use of sexually degrading language. *Psychology of Women Quarterly, 24,* 319–327.

Murnen, S. K., Smolak, L., Mills, J. A., & Good, L. (2003). Thin, sexy women and strong, muscular men: Grade-school children's responses to objectified images of women and men. *Sex Roles, 49,* 427–437.

Murphy, E. M. (2003). Being born female is dangerous for your health. *American Psychologist, 58,* 205–210.

Murray, S. B. (1997). It's safer this way: The subtle and not-so-subtle exclusion of men in child care. In N. Benokraitis (Ed.), *Subtle sexism* (pp. 135–153). Thousand Oaks, CA: Sage.

Murray-Johnson, L., Witte, K., Liu, W. Y., Hubbell, A. P., Sampson, J., & Morrison, K. (2001). Addressing cultural orientation in fear appeals: Promoting AIDS-protective behaviors among Mexican immigrant and African American adolescents and American and Taiwanese college students. *Journal of Health Communication, 6,* 335–358.

Murry-McBride, V. (1996). An ecological analysis of coital timing among middle-class African American adolescent females. *Journal of Adolescent Research, 11,* 261–279.

Murstein, B. I. (1986). *Paths to marriage.* Beverly Hills, CA: Sage.

Mwangi, M. W. (1996). Gender roles portrayed in Kenyan television commercials. *Sex Roles, 34,* 205–214.

Myaskovsky, L., & Wittig, M. A. (1997). Predictors of feminist social identity among college women. *Sex Roles, 37,* 861–883.

Nanda, S. (1990). *Neither man nor woman: The* hijras *of India.* Belmont, CA: Wadsworth.

Naples, N. A. (1992). Activist mothering: Cross-generational continuity in the community work of women from low-income urban neighborhoods. Special issue: Race, class, and gender. *Gender & Society, 6,* 441–463.

Nash, H. C., & Chrisler, J. (1997). Is a little (psychiatric) knowledge a dangerous thing? The impact of premenstrual dysphoric disorder on perceptions of premenstrual women. *Psychology of Women Quarterly, 21,* 315–322.

National Association of Working Women. (2000). Retrieved August 17, 2002, from http://www.9to5.org/profile.html

National Center for Health Statistics. (1999). *Trends in the attendant, place, and timing of births, and in the use of obstetric interventions, United States, 1989–97.* Hyattsville, MD: Author.

National Center for Health Statistics. (2004). Unpublished data from the National Health and Nutrition Examination Survey. Retrieved May 2004 from Center for Disease Control Web site: http://www.cdc.gov/nchs/fastats/bodymeas.htm.

National Committee on Pay Equity. (2004). *Wage gap widens.* Retrieved October 1, 2004, from http://www.pay-equity.org

Neft, N., & Levine, A. D. (1997). *Where women stand: An international report on the status of women in 140 countries.* New York: Random House.

Nelson, A. (2000). The pink dragon is female: Halloween costumes and gender markers. *Psychology of Women Quarterly, 24,* 137–144.

Nelson, E. J. (1996). The American experience of childbirth. In R. L. Parrott & C. M. Condit (Eds.), *Evaluating women's health messages* (pp. 109–123). Thousand Oaks, CA: Sage.

Nelson, H. L. (1992). Scrutinizing surrogacy. In H. B. Holmes (Ed.), *Issues in reproduc-tive technology* (pp. 297–302). New York: Garland.

Neto, F., & Pinto, I. (1998). Gender stereotypes in Portuguese television advertisements. *Sex Roles, 39,* 153–164.

Nettles, S. M., & Scott-Jones, D. (1987). The role of sexuality and sex equity in the education of minority adolescents. *Peabody Journal of Education, 64,* 183–197.

Nevid, J. S. (1984). Sex differences in factors of romantic attraction. *Sex Roles, 11,* 401–411.

Newton, N. (1970). The effect of psychological environment on childbirth: Combined crosscultural and experimental approach. *Journal of Cross-Cultural Psychology, 1,* 85–90.

Nichter, M. (2000). *Fat talk: What girls and their parents say about dieting.* Cambridge, MA: Harvard University Press.

Nicolson, P. (1990). A brief report of women's expectations of men's behavior in the transition to parenthood: Contradictions and conflicts for counselling psychology practice. *Counselling Psychology Quarterly, 3,* 353–361.

Nicolson, P. (1993). Motherhood and women's lives. In D. Richardson & V. Robinson (Eds.), *Thinking feminist: Key concepts in women's studies* (pp. 201–224). New York: Guilford.

Niemann, Y. F., Jennings, L., Leilani, R., Richard, M., Baxter, J. C., & Sullivan, E. (1994). Use of free responses and cluster analysis to determine stereotypes of eight groups. *Personality and Social Psychology Bulletin, 20,* 379–390.

Nieva, V. F., & Gutek, B. A. (1981). *Women and work: A psychological perspective.* New York: Praeger.

Nigro, G. N., Hill, D. E., Gelbein, M. E., & Clark, C. L. (1988). Changes in the facial prominence of women and men over the last decade. *Psychology of Women Quarterly, 12,* 225–235.

Nikelly, A. G. (1995). Drug advertisements and the medicalization of unipolar depression in women. *Health Care for Women International, 16,* 229–242.

Noble, B. P. (1993, April 18). Worthy child-care pay scales. *The New York Times,* p. 25.

Nolen-Hoeksema, S., Larson, J., & Grayson, C. (1999). Explaining the gender difference in depressive symptoms. *Journal of Personality and Social Psychology, 77,* 1061–1072.

Nolen-Hoeksema, S. (1995). Epidemiology and theories of gender differences in unipolar depression. In M. V. Seeman (Ed.), *Gender and psychopathology* (pp. 63–87). Washington, DC: American Psychological Association.

Nolen-Hoeksema, S., & Jackson, B. (2001). Mediators of the gender difference in rumination. *Psychology of Women Quarterly, 25*, 37–47.

Noll, S. M., & Fredrickson, B. L. (1998). A mediational model linking self-objectification, body shame, and disordered eating. *Psychology of Women Quarterly, 22*, 623–636.

Norton, A. J., & Moorman, J. E. (1987). Current trends in marriage and divorce among American women. *Journal of Marriage and the Family, 49*, 3–14.

Norton, K. I., Olds, T. S., Olive, S., & Dank, S. (1996). Ken and Barbie at life size. *Sex Roles, 34*, 287–294.

Novack, L. L., & Novack, D. R. (1996). Being female in the eighties and nineties: Conflicts between new opportunities and traditional expectations among white, middle class, heterosexual college women. *Sex Roles, 35*, 57–77.

Oakley, A. (1974). *The sociology of housework.* New York: Pantheon.

Oakley, A. (1992). Social support in pregnancy: Methodology and findings of a 1-year follow-up study. *Journal of Reproductive and Infant Psychology, 10*, 219–231.

Öberg, P. (2003). Images versus experience of the aging body. In C. A. Faircloth (Ed.), *Aging bodies: Images and everyday experiences* (pp. 103–139). New York: AltaMira Press.

O'Connell, A. N., & Russo, N. F. (Eds.). (1980). Models for achievement: Eminent women in psychology. *Psychology of Women Quarterly, 5*, 6–10.

O'Dea, M. (1993). *Gender exploitation and violence: The market in women, girls and sex in Nepal.* Nepal: UNICEF.

O'Farrell, B., & Harlan, S. L. (1982). Craftworkers and clerks: The effect of male co-worker hostility on women's satisfaction with nontraditional jobs. *Social Problems, 29*, 252–265.

Ofosu, H. B., Lafreniere, K. D., & Senn, C. Y. (1998). Body image perception among women of African descent: A normative context? *Feminism & Psychology, 8*, 303–323.

Oliver, M. B., & Hyde, J. S. (1993). Gender differences in sexuality: A meta-analysis. *Psychological Bulletin, 114*, 29–51.

The Onion. (2004, September). *Female athletes making great strides in attractiveness.* Volume 40, Issue 37. Retrieved September 16, 2004 from: http://www.theonion.com/

Oransky, M., & Marecek, J. (2002). *Doing boy.* Unpublished manuscript, Swarthmore College.

Oropesa, R. S. (1996). Normative beliefs about marriage and cohabitation: A comparison of non-Latino Whites, Mexican Americans, and Puerto Ricans. *Journal of Marriage and the Family, 58*, 49–62.

O'Sullivan, L. F., Graber, J. A., & Brooks-Gunn, J. (2001). Adolescent gender development. In J. Worell (Ed.). *Encyclopedia of women and gender* (pp. 55–67). San Diego, CA: Academic Press.

Ottati, V., & Lee, Y. (1995). Accuracy: A neglected component of stereotype research. In Y. Lee, L. J. Jussim, & C. R. McCauley (Eds.), *Stereotype accuracy: Toward appreciating group differences* (pp. 29–63). Washington DC: American Psychological Association.

Owen, P. R., & Laurel-Seller, E. (2000). Weight and shape ideals: Thin is dangerously in. *Journal of Applied Social Psychology, 30*, 979–990.

Owen, S. A., & Caudill, S. A. (1996). Contraception and clinical science. In R. L. Parrott & C. M. Condit (Eds.), *Evaluating women's health messages* (pp. 81–94). Thousand Oaks, CA: Sage.

Owens, L. K., Hughes, T. L. & Owens-Nicholson, D. (2003). The effects of sexual orientation on body image and attitudes about eating and weight. *Journal of Lesbian Studies, 7*, 15–33.

Oyserman, D., Mowbray, C. T., Mears, P. A., & Firminger, K. B. (2000). Parenting among mothers with serious mental illness. *American Journal of Orthopsychiatry, 70*, 296–315.

Padavic, I. (1991). Attractions of male blue-collar jobs for Black and White women: Economic need, exposure, and attitudes. *Social Science Quarterly, 72*, 33–49.

Palace, E. M. (1999). Response expectancy and sexual dysfunction in women. In I. Kirsch (Ed.), *How expectancies shape experience* (pp. 173–196). Washington, DC: American Psychological Association.

Palmore, E. (2001). The ageism survey: First findings. *Gerontologist, 41*, 572–575.

Paludi, M. A., & Bauer, W. D. (1983). Goldberg revisited: What's in an author's name? *Sex Roles, 9*, 387–390.

Paludi, M. A., & Strayer, L. A. (1985). What's in an author's name? Differential evaluations of performance as a function of author's name. *Sex Roles, 10*, 353–361.

Papanek, H. (1973). Men, women, and work: Reflections on the two-person career. *American Journal of Sociology, 78*, 852–870.

Parks, C. W., Woodson, K. M., Cutts, R. N., & Flarity-White, L. (2000–2001). The multicultural feminist treatment of gay and bisexual male adult survivors of male sexual victimization experiences. *Family Violence and Sexual Assault Bulletin,16*, 23–28.

Parlee, M. B. (1975). Review essay: Psychology. *Signs, 1*, 119–138.

Parlee, M. B. (1981). Appropriate control groups in feminist research. *Psychology of Women Quarterly, 5*, 637–644.

Parlee, M. B. (1985). Psychology of women in the 80s: Promising problems. *International Journal of Women's Studies, 8*, 193–204.

Parrot, A., & Bechhofer, L. (Eds.). (1991). *Acquaintance rape: The hidden crime.* New York: Wiley.

Parsons, T., & Bales, R. F. (1955). *Family, socialization, and interaction process.* Glencoe, IL: Free Press.

Pauwels, A. (1998). *Women changing language.* New York: Addison-Wesley Longman.

Pearlman, S. F. (1993). Late mid-life astonishment: Disruptions to identity and self-esteeem. *Women and Therapy, 14*, 1–12.

Peiss, K. L. (1998) *Hope in a jar: The making of America's beauty culture.* New York: Metropolitan Books, Henry Holt and Company.

Peplau, L. A., & Cochran, S. D. (1980). *Sex differences in values concerning love relationships.* Paper presented at American Psychological Association, cited in L. A. Peplau, & S. L. Gordon, (1983). The intimate relationships of lesbians and gay men. In E. R. Allgeier & N. B. McCormick (Eds.), *Changing boundaries: Gender roles and sexual behavior* (pp. 226–244). Palo Alto, CA: Mayfield.

Peplau, L. A., & Cochran, S. D. (1990). A relationship perspective on homosexuality. In D. P. McWhirter, S. A. Sanders, & J. M. Reinisch (Eds.), *Homosexuality/ heterosexuality: The Kinsey scales and current research* (pp. 226–244). New York: Oxford University Press.

Peplau, L. A., & Conrad, E. (1989). Beyond nonsexist research: The perils of feminist methods in psychology. *Psychology of Women Quarterly, 13,* 379–400.

Peplau, L. A., & Garnets, P. D. (2000). A new paradigm for understanding women's sexuality and sexual orientation. *Journal of Social Issues, 56,* 329–350.

Peplau, L. A., & Gordon, S. L. (1985). Women and men in love: Gender differences in close heterosexual relationships. In V. E. O'Leary, R. K. Unger, & B. S. Wallston (Eds.), *Women, gender, and social psychology* (pp. 257–292). Hillsdale, NJ: Erlbaum

Peplau, L. A., & Spalding, L. R. (2000). The close relationships of lesbians, gay men, and bisexuals. In C. Hendrick & S. S. Hendrick (Eds.), *Close relationships: A sourcebook* (pp. 111–124). Thousand Oaks, CA: Sage.

Perrone, K. M., Zanardelli, G., Worthington, E. L., & Chartrand, J. M. (2002). Role model influences on the career decidedness of college students. *College Student Journal, 36,* 109–112.

Perry, M. G. (1999). Animated gerontophobia: Ageism, sexism, and the Disney villainess. In S. M. Deats & L. T. Lender (Eds.), *Aging and identity: A humanities perspective* (pp. 201–212). Westport, CT: Praeger.

Perun, P. J., & Bielby, D. D. (1981). Towards a model of female occupational behavior: A human development approach. *Psychology of Women Quarterly, 6,* 234–252.

Phares, V., & Compas, B. E. (1993). Fathers and developmental psychotherapy. *Current Directions in Psychological Science, 2,* 162.

Phillips, L. (1998). The girls report: What we know and need to know about growing up female. New York: National Council for Research on Women.

Phillips, S. D., & Imhoff, A. R. (1997). Women and career development: A decade of research. *Annual Review of Psychology, 48,* 31–59.

Phoenix, A., Woollett, A., & Lloyd, E. (Eds.). (1991). *Motherhood: Meanings, practices, and ideologies.* London: Sage.

Pickup, E. (2001). *Ending violence against women: A challenge for development and humanitarian work.* Oxford, England: Oxfam.

Pierce, R. L., & Kite, M. E. (1999). Creating expectations in adolescent girls. In S. N. Davis, M. Crawford, & J. Sebrechts (Eds.), *Coming into her own: Educational success in girls and women* (pp. 175–192). San Francisco: Jossey-Bass.

Pillemer, K., & Finkelhor, D. (1988). The prevalence of elder abuse: A random sample survey. *The Gerontologist, 23,* 33–56.

Pingitore, R., Dugoni, B. L., Tindale, R. S., & Spring, B. (1994). Bias against overweight job applicants in a simulated employment interview. *Journal of Applied Psychology, 79,* 909–917.

Pinhas, L., Toner, B. B., Ali, A., Garfinkel, P. E., & Stuckless, N. (1999). The effects of the ideal of female beauty on mood and body satisfaction. *International Journal of Eating Disorders, 25,* 223–226.

Piotrkowski, C. S. (1998). Gender harassment, job satisfaction, and distress among employed white and minority women. *Journal of Occupational Health Psychology, 3,* 33–43.

Pipher, M. (1994). *Reviving Ophelia: Saving the selves of adolescent girls.* New York: Putnam.

Piran, N. (1999). *The feminist frame scale.* Paper presented at the annual meeting of the American Psychological Association as part of a symposium entitled: Measuring process and outcomes in short-and long-term feminist therapy, Boston.

Piran, N. (2001). Re-inhabiting the body from the inside-out: Girls transform their school environment. In D. Tolman & M. Brydon-Miller (Eds.). *From subjects to subjectivities: A handbook of interpretive and participatory methods* (pp. 218–238). New York: New York University Press.

Plant, E. A., Hyde, J. S., Keltner, D., & Devine, P. G. (2000). The gender stereotyping of emotions. *Psychology of Women Quarterly, 24,* 81–92.

Plous, S., & Neptune, D. (1997). Racial and gender biases in magazine advertising: A content analysis study. *Psychology of Women Quarterly, 21,* 627–644.

Polakow, V. (1993). *Lives on the edge: Single mothers and their children in the other America.* Chicago: University of Chicago Press.

Pollitt, K. (1998). "Fetal rights": A new assault on feminism. In R. Weitz (Ed.), *The politics of women's bodies: Sexuality, appearance, and behavior* (pp. 278–287). New York: Oxford University Press.

Pomerleau, A., Bloduc, D., Malcuit, G., & Cossette, L. (1990). Pink or blue: Environmental gender stereotypes in the first two years of life. *Sex Roles, 22,* 359–367.

Ponse, B. (1978). *Identities in the lesbian world.* Westport, CT: Greenwood Press.

Pope, K. (2001). Sex between therapist and client. In J. Worell (Ed.), *Encyclopedia of women and gender* (pp. 955–962). New York: Academic Press.

Pope, K., & Vetter, V. (1991). Prior therapist-patient sexual involvement among patients seen by psychologists. *Psychotherapy, 28,* 429–438.

Popenoe, D. (1987). Beyond the nuclear family: A statistical portrait of the changing family in Sweden. *Journal of Marriage and the Family, 49,* 173–183.

Popenoe, D., & Whitehead, B. D. (1999). *The state of our unions: The social health of marriage in America.* New Brunswick, NJ: National Marriage Project of Rutgers University.

Popp, D., Donovan, R. A., Crawford, M., Marsh, K. L., & Peele, M. (2003). Gender, race, and speech style stereotypes. *Sex Roles, 48,* 317–325.

Posovac, H. D., Posovac, S. S., & Posavac, E. J. (1998). Exposure to media images of female attractiveness and concern with body weight among young women. *Sex Roles, 38,* 187–201.

Potts, M. K., Burnam, M. A., & Wells, K. B. (1991). Gender differences in depression detection: A comparison of clinician diagnosis and standardized assessment. *Psychological Assessment, 3,* 609–615.

Poudel, P., & Carryer, J. (2000). Girl trafficking, HIV/AIDS, and the position of women in Nepal. *Gender and Development, 8,* 74–79.

Pough, G. D. (2003). Do the ladies run this . . .?: Some thoughts on hip-hop feminism. In R. C. Dicker & A. Piepmeier (Eds.), *Catching a wave: Reclaiming feminism for the 21st century* (pp. 232–243). Boston: Northeastern University Press.

Pour-El, M. B. (1974). Mathematician. In R. B. Kundsin (Ed.), *Women and success: The anatomy of achievement* (pp. 36–37). New York: William Morrow.

Powell, B. (2003). Strip clubs lure business clients. *Toronto Star,* February 23, p. A07.

Powlishta, K. K., Sen, M. G., Serbin, L. A., Poulin-Dubois, D., & Eichstedt, J. A. (2001). From infancy through middle childhood: The role of cognitive and social factors in becoming gendered. In R. K. Unger (Ed.), *Handbook of the Psychology of Women and Gender* (pp. 116–132). New York: Wiley.

President's Council on Physical Fitness and Sport. (1997, May). *Physical activity and sport in the lives of girls: Physical and mental health dimensions from an interdisciplinary approach.* Washington, DC: Author.

Press '1' if you're steamed. (2002, July 7). *The New York Times,* p. 8.

Price, S. J., & McKenry, P. C. (1988). *Divorce.* Beverly Hills, CA: Sage.

Public Interest Directorate of the American Psychological Association. (1987). Follow-up report to oral presentation of December 2, 1987. Psychological sequelae of abortion.

Purdy, L. M. (1992). Another look at contract pregnancy. In H. B. Holmes (Ed.), *Issues in reproductive technology* (pp. 303–320). New York: Garland.

Puri, J. (1997). Reading romance novels in postcolonial India. *Gender & Society, 11,* 434–452.

Quadagno, J. (1999). *Aging and the life course.* Boston: McGraw-Hill.

Quinn, D. M., & Spencer, S. J. (2001). The interference of stereotype threat with women's generation of math problem-solving strategies. *Journal of Social Issues, 57,* 55–72.

Quirouette, C. C., & Pushkar, D. (1999). Views of future aging among middle-aged, university-educated women. *Canadian Journal of Aging, 18,* 236–258.

Raag, T., & Rackliff, C. L. (1998). Preschoolers' awareness of social expectations of gender relationships to toy choices. *Sex Roles, 38,* 685–700.

Radlove, S. (1983). Sexual response and gender roles. In E. R. Allgeier & N. B. McCormick (Eds.), *Changing boundaries: Gender roles and sexual behavior* (pp. 87–105). Palo Alto, CA: Mayfield.

Radway, J. A. (1984). *Reading the romance: Women, patriarchy, and popular literature.* Chapel Hill, NC: University of North Carolina Press.

Raffaelli, M., & Ontai, L. L. (2001). "She's 16 years old and there's boys calling over to the house": An exploratory study of sexual socialization in Latino families. *Culture, Health and Sexuality, 3,* 295–310.

Raffaelli, M., & Ontai, L. L. (2004). Gender socialization in Latino/a families: Results from two retrospective studies. *Sex Roles, 50,* 287–299.

Ragsdale, J. D. (1996). Gender, satisfaction level and the use of relational maintenance strategies in marriage. *Communication Monographs, 63,* 354–369.

Raitt, F., & Zeedyk, S. (2000). *The implicit relation of psychology and law: Women and syndrome evidence.* New York: Routledge.

Ralston, P. A. (1997). Midlife and older black women. In J. M. Coyle (Ed.), *Handbook on women and aging* (pp. 273–289). Westport, CT: Greenwood Press.

Ramirez-Valles, J., Zimmerman, M. A., & Juarez, L. (2002). Gender differences of neighborhood and social control processes: A study of the timing of first intercourse among low-achieving, urban, African American youth. *Youth and Society, 33,* 418–441.

Randolph, S. M. (1995). African American children in single-mother families. In B. J. Dickerson (Ed.), *African American single mothers* (pp. 117–145). Thousand Oaks, CA: Sage.

Raymond, J. G. (1993). *Women as wombs: Reproductive technologies and the battle over women's freedom.* New York: HarperCollins.

Reame, N. K. (2001). Menstruation. In J. Worell (Ed.). *Encyclopedia of women and gender* (pp. 739–742). San Diego, CA: Academic Press.

Reed, M. D. (1994). Pornography addiction and compulsive sexual behavior. In D. Zillmann & J. Bryant (Eds.), *Media, children, and the family: Social scientific, psychodynamic, and clinical perspectives* (pp. 249–269). Hillsdale, NJ: Erlbaum.

Regan, P. C. (1996). Sexual outcasts: The perceived impact of body weight and gender on sexuality. *Journal of Applied Social Psychology, 26,* 1803–1815.

Regan, P. C., Levin, L., Sprecher, S., Christopher, F. S., & Cate, R. (2000). Partner preferences: What characteristics do men and women desire in their short-term sexual and long-term romantic partners? *Journal of Psychology and Human Sexuality, 12,* 1–21.

Regan, P. C., Medina, R., & Joshi, A. (2001). Partner preferences among homosexual men and women: What is desirable in a sex partner is not necessarily desirable in a romantic partner. *Social Behavior and Personality, 29,* 625–633.

Reid, P. T. (1993). Poor women in psychological research: Shut up and shut out. *Psychology of Women Quarterly, 17,* 133–150.

Reid, P. T., & Kelly, E. (1994). Research on women of color: From ignorance to awareness. *Psychology of Women Quarterly, 18,* 477–486.

Reid, P. T., & Trotter, K. H. (1993). Children's self-presentations with infants: Gender and ethnic comparisons. *Sex Roles, 29,* 171–181.

Reitz, R. R. (1999). Batterers' experiences of being violent: A phenomenological study. *Psychology of Women Quarterly, 23,* 143–166.

Rejeski, W. J., & Thompson, A. (1993). Historical and conceptual roots of exercise psychology. In P. Seraganian (Ed.), *Exercise psychology: The influence of physical exercise on psychological processes* (pp. 3–35). New York: Wiley.

Remer, P. & Rostosky, S. (2001a). Gender role consciousness raising for male clients. *The Feminist Psychologist, Spring,* 29–30.

Remer, P. & Rostosky, S. (2001b). Building feminist therapeutic relationships with male clients. *The Feminist Psychologist, Summer, 22,* 25.

Rheingold, H. L., & Cook, K. V. (1975). The contents of boys' and girls' rooms as an index of parents' behavior. *Child Development, 46,* 459–463.

Rhoades, J. M. (1989). Social support and the transition to the maternal role. In P. N. Stern (Ed.), *Pregnancy and parenting* (pp. 131–142). New York: Hemisphere.

Rice, J. (1994). Reconsidering research on divorce, family life cycle, and the meaning of family. *Psychology of Women Quarterly, 18,* 559–584.

Rich, A. (1976). *Of woman born: Motherhood as experience and institution.* New York: Norton.

Rich, A. (1980). Compulsory heterosexuality and lesbian existence. *Signs, 5,* 631–660.

Rich, F. (2001, May 20). Naked capitalists. *The New York Times.* Sunday late edition, Section 6, p. 51.

Richman, E. L., & Shaffer, D. R. (2000). "If you let me play sports": How might sports participation influence the self-esteem of adolescent females? *Psychology of Women Quarterly, 24,* 189–199.

Rideout, V., Foehr, U., Roberts, D., & Brodie, M. (1999). *Kids & media @ the new millennium.* Menlo Park, CA: Kaiser Family Foundation Report.

Ridgeway, C. (1992). *Gender, interaction, and inequality.* New York: Spring-Verlag.

Rintala, D. H., Howland, C. A., Nosek, M. A., Bennett, J. L., Young, M. E., Foley, C. C., et al. (1997). Dating issues for women with physical disabilities. *Sexuality and Disability, 15,* 219–242.

Ripa, Y. (1990). *Women and madness: The incarceration of women in nineteenth-century France.* Minneapolis: University of Minnesota Press.

Risman, B. J. (1998). *Gender vertigo.* New Haven, CT: Yale University Press.

Risman, B. J., & Johnson-Sumerford, D. (1998). Doing it fairly: A study of postgender marriages. *Journal of Marriage and the Family, 60,* 23–40.

Roberts, A. R. (1996). Police responses to battered women: Past, present, and future. In A. R. Roberts (Ed.), *Helping battered women* (pp. 85–95). New York: Oxford University Press.

Roberts, D. E. (1998). The future of reproductive choice for poor women and women of color. In R. Weitz (Ed.), *The politics of women's bodies: Sexuality, appearance, and behavior* (pp. 270–277). New York: Oxford University Press.

Roberts, T. A., Goldenberg, J. L., Power, C., & Pyszczynski, T. (2002). "Feminine protection": The effects of menstruation on attitudes toward women. *Psychology of Women Quarterly, 26,* 131–139.

Robinson, D. A., & Worell, J. (2002). Issues in clinical assessment with women. In J. Butcher (Ed.), *Clinical personality assessment: Practical approaches* (2nd ed.) (pp. 190–207). New York: Oxford University Press.

Rodin, J., Silberstein, L., & Striegel-Moore, R. (1984). Women and weight: A normative discontent. *Nebraska Symposium on Motivation, 32,* 267–307.

Rohner, R. P., & Veneziano, R. A. (2001). The importance of father love: History and contemporary evidence. *Review of General Psychology, 5,* 382–405.

Rosario, M., Meyer-Bahlburg, H. F. L., Hunter, J., & Exner, T. M. (1996). The psychosexual development of urban lesbian, gay, and bisexual youths. *The Journal of Sex Research, 33,* 113–126.

Roscoe, W. (1996). How to become a berdache: Toward a unified analysis of gender diversity. In G. Herdt (Ed.), *Third sex, third gender: Beyond sexual dimorphism in culture and history* (pp. 329–372). New York: Zone Books.

Rose, S., & Frieze, I. H. (1989). Young singles' scripts for a first date. *Gender & Society, 3,* 258–268.

Rosell, M. C. & Hartman, S. L. (2001). Self-presentation of beliefs about gender discrimination and feminism. *Sex Roles, 44,* 647–659.

Rosenberg, R. (1982). *Beyond separate spheres: Intellectual roots of modern feminism.* New Haven, CT: Yale University Press.

Rosenblum, K. E., & Travis, T. M. C. (1996). *The meaning of difference: American constructions of race, sex and gender, social class, and sexual orientation.* New York: McGraw-Hill.

Rosenbluth, S. C., & Steil, J. M. (1995). Predictors of intimacy for women in heterosexual and homosexual couples. *Journal of Social and Personal Relationships, 12,* 163–175.

Rosenbluth, S. C., Steil, J. M., & Whitcomb, J. H. (1998). Marital equality: What does it mean? *Journal of Family Issues, 19,* 227–244.

Rosenfeld, P., Newell, C. E., & Le, S. (1998). Equal opportunity climate of women and minorities in the Navy: Results from the Navy Equal Opportunity/Sexual Harassment (NEOSH) Survey. *Military Psychology, 10,* 69–85.

Rosenfield, S. (2000). Gender and dimensions of the self: Implications for internalizing and externalizing behavior. In E. Frank (Ed.), *Gender and its effects on psychopathology.* Washington, DC: American Psychiatric Publishing.

Rosenthal, N. B. (1984). Consciousness raising: From revolution to reevaluation. *Psychology of Women Quarterly, 8,* 309–326.

Rosenthal, R., & Jacobson, L. (1968). *Pygmalion in the classroom.* New York: Holt, Rinehart, and Winston.

Rosenwasser, S. M., & Patterson, W. (1984–1985). Nontraditional males: Men with primary childcare/household responsibilities. *Psychology and Human Development, 1,* 101–111.

Rosser, P. (1992). *The SAT gender gap: ETS responds: A research update.* Washington, DC: Center for Women Policy Studies.

Rosser, P. (with the staff of the National Center for Fair and Open Testing). (1987). *Sex bias in college admissions tests: Why women lose out* (2nd ed.). Cambridge, MA: National Center for Fair and Open Testing.

Rothblum, E. D. (2000). Sexual orientation and sex in women's lives: Conceptual and methodological issues. *Journal of Social Issues, 56,* 193–204.

Rothblum, E., Brand, P. A., Miller, C. T., & Oetjen, H. J. A. (1990). The relationship between obesity, employment discrimination, and employment-related victimization. *Journal of Vocational Behavior, 37,* 251–266.

Rouselle, R. (2001). "If it is a girl, cast it out": Infanticide/exposure in ancient Greece. *Journal of Psychohistory, 28,* 303–333.

Rousso, H. (1988). Daughters with disabilities: Defective women or minority women? In M. Fine & A. Asch (Eds.), *Women with disabilities: Essays in psychology, culture, and politics* (pp. 139–171). Philadelphia: Temple University Press.

Roy, A. (1998). Images of domesticity and motherhood in Indian television commercials: A critical study. *Journal of Popular Culture, 32,* 117–134.

Rubin, G. (1984). Thinking sex: Notes for a radical theory of the politics of sexuality. In C. S. Vance (Ed.), *Pleasure and danger: Exploring female sexuality* (pp. 267–319). Boston: Routledge & Kegan Paul.

Ruble, D. N., Fleming, A. S., Hackel, L. S., & Stangor, C. (1988). Changes in the marital relationship during the transition to first time motherhood: Effects of violated expectations concerning division of household labor. *Journal of Personality and Social Psychology, 85,* 78–87.

Rudman, L. A., & Borgida, E. (1995). The afterglow of construct accessibility: The behavioral consequences of priming men to view women as sexual objects. *Journal of Experimental Social Psychology, 31,* 493–517.

Rudman, L. A., & Glick, P. (1999). Feminized management and backlash against agentic women: The hidden costs to women of a kinder, gentler image of middle managers. *Journal of Personality and Social Psychology, 77,* 1004–1010.

Ruscher, J. B. (2001). *Prejudiced communication: A social psychological perspective.* New York: Guilford.

Ruscher, J. B., & Duval, L. L. (1998). Multiple communicators with unique target information transmit less stereotypical impressions. *Journal of Personality and Social Psychology, 74,* 329–344.

Russell, D. (1995). *Women, madness, & medicine.* Cambridge, England: Polity Press.

Russell, D. E. H. (1993). *Against pornography: The evidence of harm.* Berkeley, CA: Russell Publications.

Russett, C. E. (1989). *Sexual science: The Victorian construction of womanhood.* Cambridge, MA: Harvard University Press.

Russo, N. F. (1979). Overview: Sex roles, fertility, and the motherhood mandate. *Psychology of Women Quarterly, 4,* 7–15.

Russo, N. F. (2000). Understanding emotional responses after abortion. In J. C. Chrisler, C. Golden, & P. D. Rozee (Eds.), *Lectures on the psychology of women* (pp. 113–128). Boston, MA: McGraw-Hill.

Russo, N. F., & Dumont, B. A. (1997). A history of Division 35 (Psychology of Women): Origins, issues, activities, future. In D. A. Dewsbury (Ed.), *Unification through division: Histories of the divisions of the American Psychological Association, Vol. 2.* Washington, DC: American Psychological Association.

Rust, P. C. (1993). Neutralizing the political threat of the marginal woman: Lesbians' beliefs about bisexual women. *Journal of Sex Research, 30,* 214–228.

Rust, P. C. (2000). Bisexuality: A contemporary paradox for women. *Journal of Social Issues, 56,* 205–222.

Ruth, S. (1990). *Issues in feminism.* Mountain View, CA: Mayfield.

Sadker, M., & Sadker, D. (1994). *Failing at fairness: How America's schools cheat girls.* New York: Scribner.

Safir, M. P., Rosenmann, A., & Kloner, O. (2003). Tomboyism, sexual orientation, and adult gender roles among Israeli women. *Sex Roles, 48,* 401–410.

Sakalli, N. (2002). Application of the attribution-value model of prejudice to homosexuality. *Journal of Social Psychology, 142,* 264–271.

Salgado de Snyder, V. N., Acevedo, A., Diaz-Perez, M., & Saldivar-Garduno, A. (2000). Understanding the sexuality of Mexican-born women and their risk for HIV/AIDS. *Psychology of Women Quarterly, 24,* 100–109.

Salmon, P. (2001). Effects of physical exercise on anxiety, depression, and sensitivity to stress: A unifying theory. *Clinical Psychology Review, 21*, 33–61.

Sampselle, C. M., Harris, V., Harlow, S. D., & Sowers, M. (2002). Midlife development and menopause in African American and Caucasian women. *Health Care for Women International, 23*, 351–363.

Sanchez, L., & Thomson, E. (1997). Becoming mothers and fathers: Parenthood, gender, and the division of labor. *Gender & Society, 11*, 747–772.

Sapiro, V. (1994). Women *in American society: An introduction to women's studies* (3rd ed.). Mountain View, CA: Mayfield.

Sarantakos, S. (1991). Cohabitation revisited: Paths of change among cohabiting and noncohabiting couples. *Australian Journal of Marriage and Family, 12*, 144–155.

Scanzoni, L., & Scanzoni, J. (1976). *Men, women, and change: A sociology of marriage and the family.* New York: McGraw-Hill.

Scarborough, E., & Furumoto, L. (1987). *Untold lives: The first generation of American women psychologists.* New York: Columbia University Press.

Scarr, S. (1998). American child care today. *American Psychologist, 53*, 95–108.

Scarr, S., Phillips, D., & McCartney, K. (1990). Facts, fantasies and the future of child care in the United States. *Psychological Science, 1*, 26–35.

Schafer, A. T., & Gray, M. W. (1981). Sex and mathematics. *Science, 211*, 231.

Schippers, M. (2003). Rocking the gender order. In R. C. Dicker & A. Piepmeier (Eds.), *Catching a wave: Reclaiming feminism for the 21st century* (pp. 279–293). Boston: Northeastern University Press.

Schlesinger, B. (1982). Lasting marriages in the 1980's. *Conciliation Courts Review, 20*, 43–49.

Schoen, R., & Wooldredge, J. (1989). Marriage choices in North Carolina and Virginia, 1969–71 and 1979–81. *Journal of Marriage and Family, 51*, 465–481.

Schultz, M. R. (1975). The semantic derogation of women. In B. Thorne & N. Henley (Eds.), *Language and sex: Difference and dominance* (pp. 64–73). Rowley, MA: Newbury House.

Schwartz, I. (1993). Affective reactions of American and Swedish women to their first premarital coitus: A cross-cultural comparison. *The Journal of Sex Research, 30*, 18–26.

Schwartz, M. D. (1989). Asking the right questions: Battered wives are not all passive. *Sociological Viewpoints, 5*, 46–61.

Schwartz, P. (1994). *Peer marriage.* New York: Free Press.

Scott, B. A. (2003). Women and pornography: What we don't know can hurt us. In J. Chrisler, C. Golden, and P. Rozee (Eds.) *Lectures on the Psychology of Women, 2nd ed.* (pp. 292–309). New York: McGraw-Hill.

Scott, B. A., Fenlon, M. A., Stevens, J., & Vaske, A. (2002). *Words speak louder than pictures: How beauty ads impact women.* Paper presented at the annual meeting of the American Psychological Association, Chicago, IL.

Scott, J. P. (1997). Family relationships of midlife and older women. In J. M. Coyle (Ed.), *Handbook on women and aging* (pp. 367–384). Westport, CT: Greenwood Press.

Sears, D. O. (1986). College sophomores in the laboratory: Influences of a narrow data base on social psychology's view of human nature. *Journal of Personality and Social Psychology, 51*, 515–530.

Segar, M., Jayaratne, T., Hanlon, J., & Richardson, C. R. (2002). Fitting fitness into women's lives: Effects of a gender-tailored physical activity intervention. *Women's Health Issues, 12*, 338–347.

Senn, C. Y. (1993). Women's multiple perspectives and experiences with pornography. *Psychology of Women Quarterly, 17*, 319–341.

Seto, M. C., Maric, A., & Barbaree, H. E. (2001). The role of pornography in the etiology of sexual aggression. *Aggression and Violence Behavior, 6*, 35–53.

Shachar, S. A., & Gilbert, L. A. (1983). Working lesbians: Role conflicts and coping strategies. *Psychology of Women Quarterly, 7*, 244–256.

Shackelford, T. K., Buss, D. M., & Weekes-Shackelford, V. A. (2003). Wife killings committed in the context of a lovers triangle. *Basic and Applied Social Psychology, 25*, 137–143.

Shapiro, A. F., Gottman, J. M., & Carrere, S. (2000). The baby and the marriage: Identifying factors that buffer against decline in marital satisfaction after the first baby arrives. *Journal of Family Psychology, 14*, 59–70.

Shepard, M. F, Falk, D. R., & Elliott, B. A. (2002). Enhancing coordinated community responses to reduce recidivism in cases of domestic violence. *Journal of Interpersonal Violence, 17*, 551–569.

Sherif, C. W. (1979). Bias in psychology. In J. A. Sherman & E. T. Beck (Eds.), *The prisms of sex: Essays in the sociology of knowledge* (pp. 93–133). Madison: University of Wisconsin Press.

Sherif, C. W. (1983). Carolyn Wood Sherif (autobiography). In A. O'Connell & N. F. Russo (Eds.), *Models of achievement* (pp. 279–293). New York: Columbia University Press.

Sherman, J. A., & Fennema, E. (1978). Distribution of spatial visualization and mathematical problem solving scores: A test of Stafford's X-linked hypothesis. *Psychology of Women Quarterly, 3*, 157–167.

Sherman, P. J., & Spence, J. T. (1997). A comparison of two cohorts of college students in responses to the male-female relations questionnaire. *Psychology of Women Quarterly, 21*, 265–278.

Sherman, S. R. (1997). Images of middle-aged and older women: Historical, cultural, and personal. In J. M. Coyle, (Ed.) *Handbook on women and aging* (pp. 14–28). Westport, CT: Greenwood Press.

Shields, S. A. (1975). Functionalism, Darwinism, and the psychology of women: A study in social myth. *American Psychologist, 30,* 739–754.

Shields, S. A. (1982). The variability hypothesis: The history of a biological model of sex difference in intelligence. *Signs, 7,* 769–797.

Shields, S. A., (2002). *Speaking from the heart: Gender and the social meaning of emotion.* Cambridge, MA: Cambridge University Press.

Shih, M., Pittinsky, T. L., & Ambady, N. (1999). Stereotype susceptibility: Identity salience and shifts in quantitative performance. *Psychological Science, 10,* 80–83.

Showalter, E. (1986). *The female malady: Women, madness, and English culture, 1830–1980.* New York: Pantheon.

Shulman, J. L., & Horne, S.G. (2003). The use of self-pleasure: Masturbation and body image among African American and European American women. *Psychology of Women Quarterly, 27,* 262–269.

Shumaker, S. A. (2004). Conjugated equine estrogens and incidence of probable dementia and mild cognitive impairment in postmenopausal women: Women's health initiative memory study. *Journal of the American Medical Association, 291,* 2947–2958.

Shuster, R. (1987). Sexuality as a continuum: The bisexual identity. In Boston Lesbian Psychologies Collective (Eds.), *Lesbian psychologies* (pp. 56–71). Urbana: University of Illinois Press.

Sidanius, J., & Pratto, F. (1999). *Social dominance: An intergroup theory of social hierarchy and oppression.* New York: Cambridge University Press.

Sieg, E. (2000). "So tell me what you want, what you really want . . .": New women on old footings? *Feminism & Psychology, 10,* 498–503.

Sigall, H., & Aronson, E. (1969). Liking for an evaluator as a function of her physical attractiveness and nature of the evaluations. *Journal of Experimental Social Psychology, 5,* 93–100.

Sigelman, C. K., Thomas, D. B., Sigelman, L., & Ribich, F. D. (1986). *Gender, physical attractiveness, and electibility: An experimental investigation of voter biases.*

Silbert, M. H., & Pines, A. M. (1984). Pornography and sexual abuse of women. *Sex Roles, 10,* 857–868.

Silveira, J. (1980). Generic masculine words and thinking. In C. Kramarae (Ed.), *The voices and words of women and men* (pp. 165–178). Oxford, England: Pergamon.

Silverman, J. G., Raj, A., Mucci, L. A., & Hathaway, J. E. (2001). Dating violence against adolescent girls and associated substance use, unhealthy weight control, sexual risk behavior, pregnancy, and suicidality. *Journal of the American Medical Association, 286,* 572–579.

Silverstein, B., Perdue, L., Peterson, B., & Kelly, E. (1986). The role of the mass media in promoting a thin standard of bodily attractiveness for women. *Sex Roles, 14,* 519–532.

Silverstein, L. B. (1991). Transforming the debate about child care and maternal employment. *American Psychologist, 46,* 1025–1032.

Silverstein, L. B. (1996). Fathering is a feminist issue. *Psychology of Women Quarterly, 20,* 3–37.

Silverstein, L. B. (2002). Fathers and families. In J. P. McHale & W. S. Grolnick (Eds.), *Retrospect and prospect in the psychological study of families* (pp. 35–64). Mahwah, NJ: Erlbaum.

Silverstein, L. B., & Auerbach, C. F. (1999). Deconstructing the essential father. *American Psychologist, 54,* 397–407.

Simes, M. R., & Berg, D. H. (2001). Surreptitious learning: Menarche and menstrual product advertising. *Health Care for Women International, 22,* 455–469.

Simmons, R. G., & Blyth, D. A. (1987). *Moving into adolescence: The impact of pubertal change and school context.* New York: Aldine De Gruyter.

Simon, B. L. (1987). *Never-married women.* Philadelphia: Temple University Press.

Simpson, G. (1996). Factors influencing the choice of law as a career by black women. *Journal of Career Development, 22,* 197–209.

Sinclair, A. H., Berta, P., Palmer, M. S., Hawkins, J. R., Griffiths, B. L., Smith, M. J., et al. (1990). A gene from the human sex-determining region encodes a protein with homology to a conserved DNA binding motif. *Nature, 346,* 240–244.

Singh, D., & Young, R. K. (1995). Body weight, waist-to-hip ratio, breasts, and hips: Role in judgments of female attractiveness and desirability for relationship. *Ethology and Sociobiology, 16,* 483–507.

Skodol, A. E., & Bender, D. S. (2003). Why are women diagnosed borderline more than men? *Psychiatric Quarterly, 74,* 349–360.

Sleek, S. (1994, August). APA amicus brief affects outcome of Va. court case. *American Psychological Association Monitor, 8.*

Sluzki, C. (2003). Censorship looming. *American Journal of Orthopsychiatry, 73,* 131–132.

Smith, E. A. (1989). A biosocial model of adolescent sexual behavior. In G. R. Adams, R. Montemayor, & T. P. Gullotta (Eds.), *Advances in adolescent development* (pp. 143–167). Newbury Park, CA: Sage.

Smith, J. (1991). Conceiving selves: A case study of changing identities during the transition to motherhood. *Journal of Language and Social Psychology, 10,* 225–243.

Smith, M. (1997). Psychology's undervaluation of single motherhood. *Feminism & Psychology, 7,* 529–532.

Smith, P. H., Smith, J. B., & Earp, J. A. (1999). Beyond the measurement trap: A reconstructed conceptualization and measurement of woman battering. *Psychology of Women Quarterly, 23,* 177–193.

Smith-Rosenberg, C. (1975). The female world of love and ritual: Relations between women in nineteenth-century America. *Signs, 1,* 1–30.

Smolak, L., & Striegel-Moore, R. (2001). Body image concerns. In J. Worell (Ed.), *Encyclopedia of sex and gender* (pp. 201–210). New York: Academic Press.

Snyder, M., Tanke, E. D., & Berscheid, E. (1977). Social perception and interpersonal behavior: On the self-fulfilling nature of social stereotypes. *Journal of Personality and Social Psychology, 35,* 656–666.

Sokolovsky, J. (1997). Culture, aging and context. In J. Sokolovsky (Ed.), *The cultural context of aging: Worldwide perspectives,* 2nd ed. (pp. 1–15). Westport, CT: Bergin & Garvey.

Somer, E., & Saadon, M. (1999). Therapist-client sex: Clients' retrospective reports. *Professional Psychology: Research and Practice, 30,* 504–509.

Sommer, B., Avis, N., Meyer, P., Ory, M., Madden, T., Kagawa-Singer, M., et al. (1999). Attitudes toward menopause and aging across ethnic/racial groups. *Psychosomatic Medicine, 61,* 868–875.

Sommers, E. K., & Check, J. V. (1987). An empirical investigation of the role of pornography in the verbal and physical abuse of women. *Violence and Victims, 2,* 189–209.

Sommers-Flanagan, R., Sommers-Flanagan, J., & Davis, B. (1993). What's happening on music television? A gender-role content analysis. *Sex Roles, 28,* 745–753.

Spence, J. T., & Buckner, C. E. (2000). Instrumental and expressive traits, trait stereotypes, and sexist attitudes. *Psychology of Women Quarterly, 24,* 44–62.

Spencer, S. J., Steele, C. M., & Quinn, D. M. (1999). Stereotype threat and women's math performance. *Journal of Experimental Social Psychology, 35,* 4–28.

Spender, D. (1980). *Man made language.* London: Routledge and Kegan Paul.

Spitzer, B. L., Henderson, K. A., & Zivian, M. T. (1999). Gender differences in population versus media body sizes: A comparison over four decades. *Sex Roles, 40,* 545–565.

Sprecher, S., Barbee, A., & Schwartz, P. (1995). "Was it good for you, too?": Gender differences in first sexual intercourse experiences. *The Journal of Sex Research, 32,* 3–15.

Sprecher, S., & Regan, P. C. (2000). Sexuality in relational context. In C. Hendrick & S. S. Hendrick (Eds.), *Close relationships: A sourcebook* (pp. 217–228). Thousand Oaks, CA: Sage Publications, Inc.

Sprock, J., Blashfield, R. K., & Smith, B. (1990). Gender weighting of *DSM-III-R* personality disorder criteria. *American Journal of Psychiatry, 147,* 586–590.

Sprock, J. & Yoder, C. Y. (1997). Women and depression: An update on the report of the APA task force. *Sex Roles, 36,* 269–303.

Srebnik, D. S., & Saltzberg, E. A. (1994). Feminist cognitive-behavioral therapy for negative body image. *Women & Therapy, 15,* 117–133.

Stangor, C. (1995). Content and application inaccuracy in social stereotyping. In Y. Lee, L. J. Jussim, & C. R. McCauley (Eds.), *Stereotype accuracy: Toward appreciating group differences* (pp. 275–293). Washington DC: American Psychological Association.

Stanley, J. P. (1977). Paradigmatic woman: The prostitute. In D. L. Shores & C. P. Hines (Eds.), *Papers in language variation* (pp. 303–321). University of Alabama: University of Alabama Press.

Stapleton, K. (2001). Constructing a feminist identity: Discourse and the community of practice. *Feminism and Psychology, 11,* 459–491.

Statham, A., Miller, E. M., & Mauksch, H. O. (Eds.). (1988). *The worth of women's work: A qualitative synthesis.* Albany, NY: State University of New York Press.

Steele, J., James, J. B., & Barnett, R. C. (2002). Learning in a man's world: Examining the perceptions of undergraduate women in male-dominated academic areas. *Psychology of Women Quarterly, 26,* 46–50.

Steiger, J. (1981). The influence of the feminist subculture in changing sex-role attitudes. *Sex Roles, 7,* 627–634.

Steil, J. M. (1994). Supermoms and second shifts: Marital inequality in the 90's. In J. Freeman (Ed.), *Women: A feminist perspective* (5th ed., pp. 149–161). Mountain View, CA: Mayfield.

Steil, J. M. (1997). *Marital equality: Its relationship to the well-being of husbands and wives.* Thousand Oaks, CA: Sage.

Steil, J. M. (2000). Contemporary marriage: Still an unequal partnership. In C. Hendrick & S. S. Hendrick (Eds.), *Close relationships: A sourcebook* (pp. 125–138). Thousand Oaks, CA: Sage.

Steil, J. M. (2001). Family forms and member well-being: A research agenda for the decade of behavior. *Psychology of Women Quarterly, 25,* 344–363.

Steil, J. M., McGann, V. L., & Kahn, A. S. (2001). Entitlement. In J. Worell (Ed.), *Encyclopedia of women and gender* (pp. 403–410). San Diego, CA: Academic Press.

Steil, J. M., & Turetsky, B. A. (1987a). Marital influence levels and symptomatology among wives. In F. Crosby (Ed.), *Spouse, parent, worker: On gender and multiple roles* (pp. 74–90). New Haven, CT: Yale University Press.

Steil, J. M., & Turetsky, B. A. (1987b). Is equal better? The relationship between marital equality and psychological symptomatology. In S. Oskamp (Ed.), *Family processes and problems: Social psychological aspects* (pp. 73–97). Beverly Hills, CA: Sage.

Steil, J. M., & Weltman, K. (1991). Marital inequality: The importance of resources, personal attributes, and social norms on career valuing and the allocation of domestic responsibilities. *Sex Roles, 24,* 161–179.

Stein, M. B., & Kennedy, C. (2001). Major depressive and post-traumatic stress disorder comorbidity in female victims of intimate partner violence. *Journal of Affective Disorders, 66,* 133–138.

Stein, N. (1995). Sexual harassment in schools: The public performance of gendered violence. *Harvard Educational Review, 65,* 145–162.

Steinberg, L., & Silverberg, S. B. (1987). Influences on marital satisfaction during the middle stages of the family life cycle. *Journal of Marriage and the Family, 49,* 751–760.

Steinem, G. (1980). Erotica and pornography: A clear and present difference. In L. Lederer (Ed.) *Take Back the Night* (pp. 35–39). New York: William Morrow.

Steinem, G. (1983). *Outrageous acts and everyday rebellions.* New York: New American Library.

Sterk, H. M. (1996). Contemporary birthing practices. In R. L. Parrott & C. M. Condit (Eds.), Evaluating women's health messages (pp. 124–134). Thousand Oaks, CA: Sage.

Stern, S. (2002). Sexual selves on the world wide web: Adolescent girls' home pages as sites for sexual self-expression. In J. D. Brown, J. R. Steele, & K. Walsh-Childers (Eds.), *Sexual teens, sexual media: Investigating media's influence on adolescent sexuality* (pp. 265–287). Mahwah, NJ: Erlbaum.

Stevens, D., Kiger, G., & Riley, P. J. (2001). Working hard and hardly working: Domestic labor and marital satisfaction among dual-earner couples. *Journal of Marriage and Family, 63,* 514–526.

Stewart, A. J., Copeland, A. P., Chester, N. L., Malley, J. E., & Barenbaum, N. B. (1997). *Separating together: How divorce transforms families.* New York: Guilford.

Stewart, A. J., & Gold-Steinberg, S. (1990). Midlife women's political consciousness: Case studies of psychosocial development and political commitment. *Psychology of Women Quarterly, 14,* 543–566.

Stewart, S., Stinnett, H., & Rosenfeld, L. B. (2000). Sex differences in desired characteristics of short-term and long-term relationship partners. *Journal of Social and Personal Relationships, 17,* 843–853.

Stice, E., Presnell, K., & Bearman, S. K. (2001). Relation of early menarche to depression, eating disorders, substance abuse, and comorbid psychopathology among adolescent girls. *Developmental Psychology, 37,* 608–619.

Stice, E., & Shaw, H. E. (1994). Adverse effects of the media portrayed thin-ideal on women and linkages to bulimic symptomatology. *Journal of Social and Clinical Psychology, 13,* 288–308.

Stice, E., Spangler, D., & Agras, W. S. (2001). Exposure to media-portrayed thin-ideal images adversely affects vulnerable girls: A longitudinal experiment. *Journal of Social and Clinical Psychology, 20,* 270–288.

Stice, E., & Whitenton, K. (2002). Risk factors for body dissatisfaction in adolescent girls: a longitudinal investigation. *Developmental Psychology, 38,* 669–678.

Stoebe, M., Stroebe, W., & Schut, H. (2001). Gender differences in adjustment to bereavement: An empirical and theoretical review. *Review of General Psychology, 5,* 62–83.

Stone, L., & McKee, N. P. (2000). Gendered futures: Student visions of career and family on a college campus. *Anthropology and Education Quarterly, 31,* 67–89.

Storrs, D., & Kleinke, C. L. (1990). Evaluation of high and equal status male touchers. *Journal of Nonverbal Behavior, 14,* 87–95.

Straus, M. A. (1999). The controversy over domestic violence by women: A methodological, theoretical, and sociology of science analysis. In X. B. Arriaga & S. Oskamp (Eds.), *Violence in intimate relationships* (pp. 12–44). Thousand Oaks, CA: Sage.

Streeter, S. A., & McBurney, D. H. (2003). Waist-hip ratio and attractiveness: New evidence and a critique of a "critical test." *Evolution and Human Behavior, 24,* 88–98.

Stricker, L., Rock, D., & Burton, N. (1992). *Sex differences in SAT predictions of college grades.* New York: The College Board.

Striegel-Moore, R. H., Goldman, S. L., Garvin, V., & Rodin, J. (1996). Within-subjects design: Pregnancy changes both body and mind. In F. E. Donelson (Ed.), *Women's experiences: A psychological perspective* (pp. 430–437). Mountain View, CA: Mayfield.

Strommen, E. F. (1993). "You're a what?": Family member reactions to the disclosure of homosexuality. In L. D. Garnets & D. C. Kimmel (Eds.), *Psychological perspectives on lesbian and gay male experiences* (pp. 248–266). New York: Columbia University Press.

Strossen, N. (1995). *Defending pornography: Free speech, sex, and the fight for women's rights.* New York: Scribner.

Stryker, S. (1998). The transgender issue. *GLQ—A Journal of Lesbian and Gay Studies, 4,* 145–158.

Sugarman, D. B., & Hotaling, G. T. (1989). Dating violence: Prevalence, context, and risk markers. In M. A. Pirog-Good & J. E. Stets (Eds.), *Violence in dating relationships* (pp. 3–32). New York: Praeger.

Suzuki, M. F. (1995). Women and television: Portrayal of women in the mass media. In K. Fujimura-Fanselow & A. Kameda (Eds.), *Japanese women: New feminist perspectives on the past, present and future* (pp. 75–90). New York: Feminist Press.

Swim, J. K., Aikin, K. J., Hall, W. S., & Hunter, B. A. (1995). Sexism and racism: Old-fashioned and modern prejudices. *Journal of Personality and Social Psychology, 68,* 199–214.

Swim, J. K., Hyers, L. L., Cohen, L. L., & Ferguson, M. J. (2001). Everyday sexism: Evidence for its incidence, nature and psychological impact from three daily diary studies. *Journal of Social Issues, 57,* 31–54.

Szasz, T. (1970). *The manufacture of madness: A comparative study of the inquisition and the mental health movement.* New York: Harper & Row.

Szasz, T. (Ed.). (1973). *The age of madness; the history of involuntary mental hospitalization, presented in selected texts.* Garden City, NY: Anchor Books.

Tang, S., & Zuo, J. (2000). Dating attitudes and behaviors of American and Chinese students. *Social Science Journal, 37,* 67–78.

Tashakkori, A. (1993). Gender, ethnicity, and the structure of self-esteem: An attitude theory approach. *Journal of Social Psychology, 133,* 479–488.

Tasker, F. (1999). Children in lesbian-led families: A review. *Clinical Child Psychology and Psychiatry, 4,* 153–166.

Tasker, F. L., & Golombok, S. (1997). *Growing up in a lesbian family.* New York: Guilford.

Tavris, C. (1992). *The mismeasure of woman: Why women are not the better sex, the inferior sex, or the opposite sex.* New York: Simon & Schuster.

Taylor, J., Gilligan, C., & Sullivan, A. (1995). *Between voice and silence: Women and girls, race and relationship.* Cambridge, MA: Harvard University Press.

Taylor, R. L. (1997). Who's parenting? Trends and patterns. In T. Arrendell (Ed.), *Contemporary parenting: Challenges and issues. Understanding families* (vol. 9, pp. 68–91). Thousand Oaks, CA: Sage.

Taylor, S. E., & Langer, E. J. (1977). Pregnancy: A social stigma? *Sex Roles, 3,* 27–35.

Teachman, J. D., & Polenko, K. A. (1990). Cohabitation and marital stability in the United States. *Social Forces, 69,* 207–220.

Teitelbaum, P. (1989). Feminist theory and standardized testing. In A. M. Jaggar & S. Bordo (Eds.), *Gender/body/knowledge* (pp. 324–335). New Brunswick, NJ: Rutgers University Press.

Tenenbaum, H. R., & Leaper, C. (2002). Are parents' gender schema related to their children's gender-related cognitions? A meta-analysis. *Developmental Psychology, 38,* 615–630.

Tevlin, H. E., & Leiblum, S. R. (1983). Sex-role stereotypes and female sexual dysfunction. In V. Franks & E. D. Rothblum (Eds.), *Stereotyping of women: Its effects on mental health* (pp. 129–148). New York: Springer.

Tewksbury, R. (1994). Gender construction and the female impersonator: The process of transforming "he" to "she." *Deviant Behavior, 15,* 27–43.

Thibault, J. W., & Kelley, H. H. (1959). *The social psychology of groups.* New York: Wiley.

Thoits, P. A. (1987). Negotiating roles. In F. J. Crosby (Ed.), *Spouse, parent, worker: On gender and multiple roles* (pp. 11–22). New Haven: Yale University Press.

Thompson, T. L., & Zerbinos, E. (1995). Gender roles in animated cartoons: Has the picture changed in twenty years? *Sex Roles, 32,* 651–673.

Thorne, B. (1993). *Gender play: Girls and boys in school.* New Brunswick, NJ: Rutgers University Press.

Thorne, B., & Luria, Z. (1986). Sexuality and gender in children's daily worlds. *Social Problems, 33,* 176–190.

Thornhill, R. & Palmer, C. T. (2000). *A natural history of rape: Biological bases of sexual coercion.* Cambridge, MA: MIT Press.

Thurer, S. L. (1983). Deinstitutionalization and women: Where the buck stops. *Hospital and Community Psychiatry, 34,* 1162–1163.

Tichenor, V. J. (1999). Status and income as gendered resources: The case of marital power. *Journal of Marriage and the Family, 61,* 638–650.

Tiedemann, J. (2000). Parents' gender stereotypes and teachers' beliefs as predictors of children's concept of their mathematical ability in elementary school. *Journal of Educational Psychology, 92,* 144–151.

Tiedens, L. Z., Ellsworth, P. C., & Mesquita, B. (2000). Stereotypes about sentiments and status: Expectations about high-and low-status group members. *Personality & Social Psychology Bulletin, 26,* 560–574.

Tiefer, L. (1989, August). Feminist transformations of sexology. In M. Crawford (Chair), *Feminist psychological science: Frameworks, strengths, visions, and a few examples.* Symposium conducted at the meeting of the American Psychological Association, New Orleans, LA.

Tiefer, L. (1995). *Sex is not a natural act & other essays.* San Francisco: Westview.

Tiefer, L. (2000). Agreeing to disagree: Multiple views on gender laws and transsex. *Feminism & Psychology, 10,* 36–40.

Tighe, C. A. (2001). "Working at disability": A qualitative study of the meaning of health and disability for women with physical impairments. *Disability and Society, 16,* 511–529.

Timmerman, G. (2003). Sexual harassment of adolescents perpetrated by teachers and by peers: An exploration of the dynamics of power, culture, and gender in secondary schools. *Sex Roles, 48,* 231–244.

Tjaden, P., & Thoennes, N. (1998*). Stalking in American: Findings from the national violence against women survey.* Denver, CO: Center for Policy Research.

Tolman, D. L., & Brown, L. M. (2001). Adolescent girls' voices: Resonating resistance in body and soul. In R. K. Unger (Ed.), *Handbook of the psychology of women and gender* (pp. 133–155). New York: Wiley.

Tong, R. P. (1998). *Feminist thought* (2nd ed.). Boulder, CO: Westview.

Tougas, F., Brown, R., Beaton, A. M., & Joly, S. (1995). Neosexism: Plus la change, plus c'est pareil. *Personality and Social Psychology Bulletin, 21,* 842–849.

Travis, C. B., & Compton, J. D. (2001). Feminism and health in the decade of behavior. *Psychology of Women Quarterly, 25,* 312–323.

Treadway, C. R., Kane, F. J., Jarrahi-Zadeh, A., & Lipton, M. A. (1969). A psycho-endocrine study of pregnancy and puerperium. *American Journal of Psychiatry, 125,* 1380–1386.

Trent, K., & South, S. J. (1989). Structural determinants of the divorce rate: A cross-societal analysis. *Journal of Marriage and the Family, 51,* 391–404.

Trost, J. (1996). Family studies in Sweden. *Marriage & Family Review, 23,* 723–743.

Tsui, L. (1998). The effects of gender, education, and personal skills self-confidence on income in business management. *Sex Roles, 38,* 363–373.

Turk, J. L., & Bell, N. W. (1972). Measuring power in families. *Journal of Marriage and the Family, 34,* 215–223.

Twenge, J. M. (1997). Attitudes toward women, 1970–1995: A meta-analysis. *Psychology of Women Quarterly, 21,* 35–51.

Ulrich, M., & Weatherall, A. (2000). Motherhood and infertility: Viewing motherhood through the lens of infertility. *Feminism and Psychology, 10,* 323–336.

Udry, J. R., Talbert, L., Morris, N. M. (1986). Biosocial foundations for adolescent female sexuality. *Demography, 23,* 217–230.

UNESCO. (2000). *EFA 2000—Literacy assessment: Progress in literacy.* Retrieved September 29, 2004 from http://www.accu.or.jp/litdbase/efa/progress/htm

Unger, R. K. (1979a). *Female and male: Psychological perspectives.* New York: Harper & Row.

Unger, R. K. (1979b). Toward a redefinition of sex and gender. *American Psychologist, 34,* 1085–1094.

Unger, R. K. (1983). Through the looking glass: No Wonderland yet! (The reciprocal relationship between methodology and models of reality.) *Psychology of Women Quarterly, 8,* 9–32.

Unger, R. K. (1990). Imperfect reflections of reality: Psychology and the construction of gender. In R. Hare-Mustin & J. Marecek (Eds.), *Making a difference: Representations of gender in psychology* (pp. 102–149). New Haven, CT: Yale University Press.

Unger, R. K. (1998). *Resisting gender: Twenty-five years of feminist psychology.* London: Sage.

Unger, R. K. (2001). Women as subjects, actors, and agents in the history of psychology. In R. K. Unger (Ed.), *Handbook of the psychology of women and gender* (pp. 3–16). New York: Wiley.

Unger, R. K. (Ed.) (2001). *Handbook of the psychology of women and gender.* New York: Wiley.

Unger, R. K., & Crawford, M. (1989). Methods and values in decisions about gender differences (Review of Alice H. Eagly, Sex differences in social behavior: A social role interpretation.) *Contemporary Psychology, 34,* 122–123.

UNIFEM. (1998). *Trade in human misery: Trafficking in girls and women.* New Delhi: Author.

United Nations. (1995). The Beijing Declaration and Platform for Action. gopher://gopher.undp.org:70/00/unconfs/women/off/a—20.en

United Nations. (2000). *The world's women 2000: Trends and statistics.* New York: Author.

United Nations Children's Fund. (2000, May). Domestic violence against women and girls. *Innocenti Digest* (No. 6.) Florence, Italy: Innocenti Research Centre.

U.S. Department of Labor. (2002). *Highlights of women's earnings in 2001* (Report 960) Washington, DC: U.S. Department of Labor, Bureau of Labor Statistics.

U.S. Department of Justice, Office of Justice Programs. (2000). *Bureau of Justice Statistics: Intimate partner violence.* Washington, DC: Author.

U.S. General Accounting Office (2002). *Prescription drugs: FDA oversight of direct-to-consumer advertising has limitations.* Retrieved May, 2004, from General Accounting Office Web site: http://www.gao.gov/new.items/d03177.pdf

U.S. Merit Systems Protection Board. (1981). *Sexual harassment in the federal workplace: Is it a problem?* Washington, DC: Office of Merit Systems Review and Studies/Government Printing Office.

U.S. Merit Systems Protection Board. (1987). *Sexual harassment in the federal workplace: An update.* Washington, DC: Office of Merit Systems Review and Studies/Government Printing Office.

U.S. Merit Systems Protection Board. (1995). *Sexual harassment in the federal workplace: Trends, progress, continuing challenges.* Washington, DC: U.S. Government Printing Office.

U.S. v. Commonwealth of Virginia, U.S. 1941 (1994).

Ussher, J. M. (1989). *The psychology of the female body.* London: Routledge.

Ussher, J. M. (1992). *Women's madness: Misogyny or mental illness?* Amherst: University of Massachusetts Press.

Ussher, J. M., & Mooney-Somers, J. (2000). Negotiating desire and sexual subjectivity: Narratives of young lesbian avengers. *Sexualities, 3,* 183–200.

Valentine, J. C., Blankenship, V., Cooper, H., & Sullins, E. S. (2001). Interpersonal expectancy effects and the preference for consistency. *Representative Research in Social Psychology, 25,* 26–33.

Valian, V. (1998). *Why so slow? The advancement of women.* Cambridge, MA: MIT Press.

Vallois, T. (1998). La Salpêtrière. *Paris Kiosque, 5.* Retreived December, 2003, from magazine's Web site: www.paris.org/Kiosque/

Vance, C. S. (1984). Pleasure and danger: Toward a politics of sexuality. In C. S. Vance (Ed.), *Pleasure and danger: Exploring female sexuality* (pp. 1–27). Boston: Routledge and Kegan Paul.

Vance, E. B., & Wagner, N. N. (1976). Written descriptions of orgasm: A study of sex differences. *Archives of Sexual Behavior, 5,* 87–98.

Vander-Ven, T. M., Cullen, F. T., Carrozza, M. A., & Wright, J. P. (2001). Home alone: The impact of maternal employment on delinquency. *Social Problems, 48,* 236–257.

Vanek, J. (1984). Housewives as workers. In P. Voydanoff (Ed.), *Work and family: Changing roles of men and women* (pp. 89–103). Palo Alto, CA: Mayfield.

Vartanian, L. R., Giant, C. L., & Passino, R. M. (2001). "Ally McBeal vs. Arnold Schwarzenegger": Comparing mass media, interpersonal feedback and gender as predictors of satisfaction with body thinness and muscularity. *Social Behavior and Personality, 29*, 711–723.

Vasquez, M. J. T. (1994). Latinas. In L. Comas-Díaz & B. Greene (Eds), *Women of color: Integrating ethnic and gender identities in psychotherapy* (pp. 114–138). New York: Guilford.

Vedovato, S., & Vaughter, R. (1980). Psychology of women courses changing sexist and sex-typed attitudes. *Psychology of Women Quarterly, 4*, 587–590.

Veroff, J., Wilcox, S., & Atkinson, J. W. (1953). The achievement motive in high school and college age women. *Journal of Abnormal and Social Psychology, 43*, 108–119.

Vigorito, A. J., & Curry, T. J. (1998). Marketing masculinity: Gender identity and popular magazines. *Sex Roles, 38*, 135–152.

Vinton, L. (2001). Violence against older women. In C. M. Renzetti, J. L. Edleson, & R. K. Bergen (Eds.), *Sourcebook on violence against women* (pp. 179–192). Thousand Oaks, CA: Sage.

Vobejda, B. (1994, June 16). Abortion rate slowing in U.S., study concludes. *The Washington Post*, p. A13.

von Baeyer, C. L., Sherk, D. L., & Zanna, M. P. (1981). Impression management in the job interview: When the female applicant meets the male (chauvinist) interviewer. *Personality and Social Psychology Bulletin, 7*, 45–51.

Von Hippel, W., Sekaquaptewa, D., & Vargas, P. (1995). On the role of encoding processes in stereotype maintenance. In M. P. Zanna (Ed.), *Advances in Experimental Social Psychology Vol. 27* (pp. 177–254). New York: Academic Press.

Vosk, S. (2004, April 11). Man fatally shoots former wife, then self, police say. *Boston Sunday Globe*, p. B2.

Wade, T. J. (2000). Evolutionary theory and self-perception: Sex differences in body esteem, predictors of self-perceived physical and sexual attractiveness, and self-esteem. *International Journal of Psychology, 35*, 36–45.

Waite, L. J., & Joyner, K. (2001). Emotional satisfaction and physical pleasure in sexual unions: Time horizon, sexual behavior, and sexual exclusivity. *Journal of Marriage and the Family, 63*, 247–264.

Wajcman, J. (1998). *Managing like a man: Women and men in corporate management.* Cambridge, England: Polity Press.

Waldo, C. R., Berdahl, J. L., & Fitzgerald, L. F. (1998). Are men sexually harassed? If so, by whom? *Law and Human Behavior, 22*, 59–79.

Walker, L., Timmerman, G. M., Kim, M., & Sterling, B. (2002). Relationships between body image and depressive symptoms during postpartum in ethnically diverse, low income women. *Women and Health, 36*, 101–121.

Walker, L. E. A. (2000). *The battered woman syndrome* (2nd ed.). New York: Springer.

Walker, L. E. A. (2001). Battering in adult relations. In J. Worrell (Ed.), *Encyclopedia of women and gender* (pp. 169–188). San Diego, CA: Academic Press.

Walker, N. A. (Ed.) (1998). *Women's magazines 1940–1960: Gender roles and the popular press.* Boston: Bedford/St. Martin's.

Wallace, A. (2001, Winter). *FDA approval of mifepristone immediately targeted.* Retrieved October 1, 2004, from http://www.now.org/nnt/winter-2001/mifepristone.html

Wallace, J. E. (2001). The benefits of mentoring for female lawyers. *Journal of Vocational Behavior, 58*, 366–391.

Wallston, B. S., & Grady, K. E. (1985). Integrating the feminist critique and the crisis in social psychology: Another look at research methods. In V. E. O'Leary, R. K. Unger, & B. S. Wallston (Eds.), *Women, gender and social psychology* (pp. 7–34). Hillsdale, NJ: Erlbaum.

Walter, J. L., & LaFreniere, P. J. (2000). A naturalistic study of affective expression, gender competence, and sociometric status in preschoolers. *Early Education & Development, 1*, 109–122.

Walzer, S. (1998). *Thinking about the baby.* Philadelphia: Temple University Press.

Wang, P. (2000). *Aching for beauty: Footbinding in China.* Minneapolis, MN: University of Minnesota Press.

Warren, M. P. (1983). Physical and biological aspects of puberty. In J. Brooks-Gunn & A. C. Petersen (Eds.), *Girls at puberty* (pp. 3–28). New York: Plenum.

Warshaw, C. (2001). Women and violence. In N. L. Stotland & D. E. Stewart (Eds.), *Psychological aspects of women's health care*, 2nd ed. (pp. 477–548). Washington, DC: American Psychiatric Press.

Waszak, C., Severy, L. J., Kafafi, L., & Badawi, I. (2001). Fertility behavior and psychological stress: The mediating influence of gender norm beliefs among Egyptian women. *Psychology of Women Quarterly, 25*, 197–208.

Watson, M. S., Trasciatti, M. A., & King, C. P. (1996). Our bodies, our risk. In R. L. Parrott & C. M. Condit (Eds.), *Evaluating women's health messages* (pp. 95–108). Thousand Oaks, CA: Sage.

Watts, B. (1996). Legal issues. In M. A. Paludi (Ed.), *Sexual harassment on college campuses: Abusing the ivory power* (pp. 9–24). Albany: State University of New York Press.

Waxman-Fiduccia, B. F. (1999). Sexual imagery of physically disabled women: Erotic? Perverse? Sexist? *Sexuality and Disability, 17*, 277–282.

Weatherall, A., & Walton, M. (1999). The metaphorical construction of sexual experience in a speech community of New Zealand university students. *British Journal of Social Psychology, 38*, 479–498.

Weber, J. C. (1996). Social class as a correlate of gender identity among lesbian women. *Sex Roles, 35*, 271–280.

Weber, L. (1998). A conceptual framework for understanding race, class, gender, and sexuality. *Psychology of Women Quarterly, 22*, 13–32.

Weber, L., & Higginbotham, E. (1997). Black and white professional-managerial women's perceptions of racism and sexism in the workplace. In E. Higginbotham & M. Romero (Eds.), *Women and work: Exploring race, ethnicity, and class* (vol. 6, pp. 153–175). Thousand Oaks, CA: Sage.

Weissman, M. M., Bland, R. C., Canino, G. J., Faravelli, C., Greenwald, S., Hwu, H. G., et al. (1996). Cross-national epidemiology of major depression and bipolar disorder. *Journal of the American Medical Association, 276,* 293–299.

Weisstein, N. (1968). *Kinder, Kirche, Kuche as scientific law: Psychology constructs the female.* Boston: New England Free Press.

Weitz, R., & Gordon, L. (1993). Images of black women among Anglo students. *Sex Roles, 28,* 19–34.

Weitzman, L. J. (1979). *Sex role socialization.* Palo Alto, CA: Mayfield.

Wells, J. D., Hobfoll, S. E., & Lavin, J. (1997). Resource loss, resource gain, and communal coping during pregnancy among women with multiple roles. *Psychology of Women Quarterly, 21,* 645–662.

Welter, B. (1966). The cult of True Womanhood: 1820–1860. *American Quarterly, 18,* 151–174.

Werner, P. D., & LaRussa, G. W. (1985). Persistence and change in sex-role stereotypes. *Sex Roles, 12,* 1089–1100.

Wertz, D. C. (1992). How parents of affected children view selective abortion. In H. B. Holmes (Ed.), *Issues in reproductive technology* (pp. 161–189). New York: Garland.

West, C. M. (2004). Mammy, jezebel, and sapphire: Developing an "oppositional gaze" toward the images of black women. In J. C. Chrisler, C. Golden, & P. D. Rozee (Eds.), *Lectures on the Psychology of Women Third Edition* (pp. 236–252). Boston: McGraw-Hill.

West, C., & Zimmerman, D.H. (1987). Doing gender. *Gender & Society, 1,* 125–151.

Whitam, F., Diamond, M., & Martin, J. (1993). Homosexual orientation in twins: A report on 61 pairs and three triplet sets. *Archives of Sexual Behavior, 22,* 187–206.

Whitam, F. L., Daskalos, C., Sobolewski, C. G., & Padilla, P. (1998). The emergence of lesbian sexuality and identity cross-culturally: Brazil, Peru, the Philippines, and the United States. *Archives of Sexual Behavior, 27,* 31–56.

Whitbourne, S. (1986). *The me I know: A study of adult identity.* New York: Springer-Verlag.

White, J. W., Bondurant, B., & Donat, P. L. N. (2004). Violence against women. In M. Crawford & R. Unger, *Women and gender: A feminist psychology* (pp. 439–475). New York: McGraw-Hill.

White, J. W., Bondurant, B., & Travis, C. B. (2000). Social constructions of sexuality. In C. B. Travis & J. W. White (Eds.), *Sexuality, society and feminism: Psychological perspectives on women* (pp. 11–33). Washington, DC: American Psychological Association.

White, J. W., Donat, P. L. N., & Bondurant, B. (2001). A developmental examination of violence against girls and women. In R. K. Unger (Ed.), *Handbook of the psychology of women and gender* (pp. 343–357). New York: Wiley.

White, J. W., & Koss, M. P. (1993). Adolescent sexual aggression within heterosexual relationships: Prevalence,

characteristics, and causes. In H. E. Barbarbee, W. L. Marshall, & D. R. Laws (Eds.), *The juvenile sexual offender* (pp. 182–202). New York: Guilford.

White, J. W., & Kowalski, R. M. (1998). Violence against women: An integrative perspective. In R. G. Geen & E. Donnerstein (Eds.), *Perspectives on human aggression.* New York: Academic Press.

Whitman, T. L., Borkowski, J. G., Keogh, D. A., & Weed, K. (2001). *Interwoven lives: Adolescent mothers and their children.* Mahwah, NJ: Erlbaum.

Widiger, T. A. (1998). Invited essay: Sex biases in the diagnosis of personality disorders. *Journal of Personality Disorders, 12,* 95–118.

Widiger, T. A., & Anderson, K. G. (2003). Personality and depression in women. *Journal of Affective Disorders, 74,* 59–66.

Wiederman, M. W. (2002). Women's body image self-consciousness during physical intimacy with a partner. *The Journal of Sex Research, 37,* 60–68.

Wiest, W. M. (1977). Semantic differential profiles of orgasm and other experiences among men and women. *Sex Roles, 3,* 399–403.

Wilkinson, S. (1997a). Feminist psychology. In D. Fox & I. Prilleltensky (Eds.), *Critical psychology: An introduction* (pp. 247–264). London: Sage.

Wilkinson, S. (1997b). Still seeking transformation: Feminist challenges to psychology. In L. Stanley (Ed.), *Knowing feminisms: On academic borders, territories and tribes* (pp. 97–108). Thousand Oaks, CA: Sage.

Wilkinson, S., & Kitzinger, C. (Eds.). (1993). *Heterosexuality: A Feminism and Psychology reader.* London: Sage.

Williams, C. L. (1992). The glass escalator: Hidden advantages for men in the "female" professions. *Social Problems, 39,* 253–267.

Williams, J. E., & Best, D. L. (1990). *Measuring sex stereotypes: A multination study.* Newbury Park, CA: Sage.

Williams, L. S. (1992). Biology or society? Parenthood motivation in a sample of Canadian women seeking in vitro fertilization. In H. B. Holmes (Ed.), *Issues in reproductive technology* (pp. 261–274). New York: Garland.

Williams, N. (1990). *The Mexican American family: Tradition and change.* New York: General Hall.

Williams, P. J. (1997). My best white friend: Cinderella revisited. In M. Crawford & R. Unger (Eds.), *In our own words: Readings on the psychology of women and gender* (pp. 291–295). New York: McGraw-Hill.

Williams, S. S., Kimble, D. L., Covell, N. H., Weiss, L. H., Newton, K. J., Fisher, J. D., et al. (1992). College students use implicit personality theory instead of safer sex. *Journal of Applied Social Psychology, 22,* 921–933.

Williams, W. L. (1987). Women, men, and others: Beyond ethnocentrism in gender theory. *American Behavioral Scientist, 31,* 135–141.

Wilson, A. (1996). How we find ourselves: Identity development and two-spirit people. *Harvard Educational Review, 66,* 303–317.

Wilson, M. I., & Daly, M. (1995). Male sexual proprietariness and violence against wives. *Current Directions in Psychological Science, 5,* 2–7.

Winston, A. (Ed.). (2003). *Defining difference: Race and racism in the history of psychology.* Washington DC: American Psychological Association.

Witkin, H. A., Mednick, S. A., Schulsinger, F., Bakkestrom, E., Christiansen, K. O., Goodenough, D. R. et al. (1976). Criminality in XXY and XYY men. *Science, 193,* 547–555.

Wizemann, T. M., & Pardue, M. (Eds.). (2001). *Exploring the biological contribution to human health: Does sex matter?* Washington, DC: National Academy Press.

Wolf, N. (1991). *The beauty myth: How images of beauty are used against women.* New York: William Morrow.

Wollstonecraft, M. (1792). *Vindication of the rights of woman.* Middlesex, England: Penguin Books, 1983.

Woloshin, S., Schwartz, L. M., Tremmel, J., & Welch, H. G. (2001). Direct-to-consumer advertisements for prescription drugs: What are Americans being sold? *The Lancet, 358,* 1141–1146.

Women's Health Initiative Steering Committee (2004). Effects of conjugated equine estrogen in postmenopausal women with hysterectomy: The women's health initiative randomized controlled trial. *Journal of the American Medical Association, 291,* 1701–1712.

Women's Task Force of the Michigan Department of Mental Health (1984). Women and their physicians: The evidence. *Women & Therapy, 3,* 121–127.

Wood, G. (2002). *Art nouveau and the erotic.* New York: Harry N. Abrams.

Wooldredge, J., & Thistlewaite, A. (2002). Reconsidering domestic violence recidivism: Conditioned effects of legal controls by individual and aggregate levels of stake in conformity. *Journal of Quantitative Criminology, 18,* 45–70.

Wooley, H. T. (1910). Psychological literature: A review of the recent literature on the psychology of sex. *Psychological Bulletin, 7,* 335–342.

Woolf, V. (1929). *A room of one's own.* London: Harcourt Brace Jovanovich.

Worell, J. (1988). Women's satisfaction in close relationships. *Clinical Psychology Review, 8,* 477–498.

Worell, J. (1996). Opening doors to feminist research. *Psychology of Women Quarterly, 20,* 469–485.

Worell, J. (2001). Feminist interventions: Accountability beyond symptom reduction. *Psychology of Women Quarterly, 25,* 335–343.

Worell, J., & Johnson, D. (2001). Therapy with women: Feminist frameworks. In R. K. Unger (Ed.), *Handbook of the psychology of women and gender* (pp. 317–329). New York: Wiley.

Worell, J., & Remer, P. (2003). *Feminist perspectives in therapy: Empowering diverse women* (2nd ed.). New York: Wiley.

Wurtele, S. K. (2002). School-based child sexual abuse prevention. In P. A. Schewe (Ed.), *Preventing violence in relationships: Interventions across the life span* (pp. 9–25). Washington, DC: American Psychological Association.

Wyatt, G. E., & Riederle, M. H. (1994). Reconceptualizing issues that affect women's sexual decision-making and sexual functioning. *Psychology of Women Quarterly, 18,* 611–626.

Wylie, P. (1942). *A generation of vipers.* New York: Ferris.

Xu, X., & Lai, S. C. (2002). Resources, gender ideologies, and marital power: The case of Taiwan. *Journal of Family Issues, 23,* 209–245.

Yoder, J. D. (2002). Context matters: Understanding tokenism processes and their impact on women's work. *Psychology of Women Quarterly, 26,* 1–8.

Yoder, J. D., Adams, J., Grove, S., & Priest, R. F. (1985). To teach is to learn: Overcoming tokenism with mentors. *Psychology of Women Quarterly, 9,* 119–132.

Yoder, J. D., & Kahn, A. S. (1992). Toward a feminist understanding of women and power. *Psychology of Women Quarterly, 16,* 381–388.

Yoder, J. D., Schleicher, T. L., & McDonald, T. W. (1998). Empowering token women leaders: The importance of organizationally legitimated credibility. *Psychology of Women Quarterly, 22,* 209–222.

Yoder, J. D., & Sinnett, L. M. (1985). Is it all in the numbers? A case study of tokenism. *Psychology of Women Quarterly, 9,* 413–418.

Young, D. R., Gittelsohn, J., Charleston, J., Felix-Aaron, K., & Appel, L. J. (2001). Motivations for exercise and weight loss among African-American women: Focus group results and their contribution towards program development. *Ethnicity and Health, 6,* 227–245.

Young, I. M. (1998). Breasted experience: The look and the feeling. In R. Weitz (Ed.), *The politics of women's bodies: Sexuality, appearance, and behavior* (pp. 125–136). New York: Oxford University Press.

Youngblut, J. M., Singer, L. T., Madigan, E. A., Swegart, L. A., & Rodgers, W. L. (1997). Mother, child, and family factors related to employment of single mothers with LBW preschoolers. *Psychology of Women Quarterly, 21,* 247–263.

Zampano. (2003, November 6). Move over beauty queens, Italy seeks Miss Digital. *Milan Reuters.*

Zanna, M. P., & Pack, S. J. (1975). On the self-fulfilling nature of apparent sex differences in behavior. *Journal of Experimental Social Psychology, 11,* 583–591.

Zeedyk, M. S., & Raitt, F. E. (1997). Psychological theory in law: Legitimating the male norm. *Feminism & Psychology, 7,* 539–546.

Zelnik, M., Kanter, J. F., & Ford, K. (1981). *Sex and pregnancy in adolescence.* Beverly Hills, CA: Sage.

Zernike, K. (1999, March 21). MIT women win a fight against bias. *The Boston Globe,* pp. F1, F4.

Zheng, Y. (2004). Hair-coloring product use and risk of non-Hodgkin's lymphoma: A population-based case-control study in Connecticut. *American Journal of Epidemiology, 159,* 148–154.

Zimmerman, D. H., & West, C. (1975). Sex roles, interruptions, and silences in conversation. In B. Thorne & N. Henley (Eds.), *Language and sex: difference and dominance* (pp. 105–129). Rowley, MA: Newbury House.

Zucker, A. N., Ostrove, J. M., & Stewart, A. J. (2002). College-educated women's personality development in adulthood: Perceptions and age differences. *Psychology and Aging, 17*, 236–244.

Zucker, K. (2001). Biological influences on psychosexual differentiation. In R. K. Unger (Ed.), *Handbook of the psychology of women and gender* (pp. 101–115), New York: Wiley.

Zuckerman, M., & Kieffer, S. C. (1994). Race differences in faceism: Does facial prominence imply dominance? *Journal of Personality and Social Psychology, 66*, 86–92.

Photo Credits

Page 29: © IT'S PAT, Julia Sweeney, 1994, © Touchstone Pictures/Courtesy of Everett Collection; **31:** © New Line/The Kobal Collection/Lorey Sebastian; **34:** (both) © Annie Leibovitz/Contact Press Images; **38:** © Javier Pierini/Getty Images; **39:** © Jack Star/PhotoLink/Getty Images; **65:** © Time Life Pictures/Mansell/Time Life Pictures/Getty Images; **66:** © Bettmann/Corbis; **67:** (left) © Hunter Martin, (right) © Kirby Lee/WireImage.com; **69:** (top) © Michael Newman/Photo Edit, (bottom) © Bill Aron/Photo Edit **70:** © Contographer ®/Corbis; **72:** © Hel/Petit/Prestige/Newsmakers/Getty Images; **89:** © Joel Gordon; **96:** Courtesy of Jean Kilbourne; **116:** Women's College Coalition; **120** (left) © Pace Gregory/CORBIS SYGMA, (right) © Dave Hogan/Getty Images; **124:** © Digital Vision; **144:** Courtesy of Jessica Lord; **148:** (both) www.mattkailey.com; **156:** © Nick Cardillicchio; **160:** © Fox Searchlight/The Kobal Collection/Bill Matlock; **165:** (both) © Jessie Walker; **166:** © Kathy Sloane; **169:** © Elizabeth Crews; **180:** © Digital Vision; **182:** (top) Courtesy of Michelle Kaufman; **203:** (left) © Hulton Archive/Keystone/Getty Images, (right) © Hulton Archive/Getty Images; **204:** © CORBIS SYGMA; **208:** (both) © Andrew Eccles/jbg photos **209:** Courtesy of Hooters; **211:** (both) The McGraw-Hill Companies, Inc./Lars Niki, photographer; **212:** © Thinkstock; **214:** Brooke Pleasanton; **226:** © Michael Neveux (left), © John C. Anderson/Bettmann/CORBIS (right); **229:** © Andrew Eccles/JBGPHOTO.COM; **273:** © Robbie Jack/CORBIS; **327:** © Annie Leibovitz/Contact Press Images; **329:** © Suzanne Arms/The Image Works; **333:** *The Crowning,* from the **Birth Project,** © Judy Chicago 1984, Needlework and painting on 80-mesh canvas, 40½″ × 61″. Needlework by Frannie Yablonsky. Collection of The Albuquerque Museum, Albuquerque, NM. Photo: © Through the Flower Archives; **347:** © Shelburne/PhotoLink/Getty Images; **350:** © Mel Curtis/Getty Images; **359:** © Richard Freeda/AP/Wide World Photos; **364:** © Sigrid Estrada; **371:** © Courtesy of Janice D. Yoder, Ph. D.; **385:** © PhotoLink/Getty Images; **413:** © Kelly Corigan/Courtesy of Random House Inc.; **415:** © Royalty-Free/CORBIS **420:** © Ryan McVay/Getty Images; **435:** D. Robert Franz and Lorri Franz; **437:** Courtesy of Paula Caplan, Ph. D.; **443:** © Stone/Getty Images; **449:** © Art Resource, NY; **451:** © The Granger Collection; **454:** © Judy Olausen; **460:** Courtesy of Luise Eichenbaum; **461:** © Carolyn Djanogly/IMAGE Magazine; **463:** © Royalty-Free/CORBIS; **471:** © Anat Givon/AP/Wide World Photos; **473:** © The Granger Collection

Text Credits

Chapter 2

Pp. 29–30 Excerpt from John & Sussman, "Initiative Taking as a Determinant of Role Reciprocal Organization," in *Representations: Social Constructions of Gender,* edited by Rhoda Unger. Copyright © 1989 Baywood Publishing Company, Inc. Reprint permission obtained via the Copyright Clearance Center.

Chapter 8

P. 245 Excerpt from *Song of Love,* by Rachel Elliott, 1984, 3 paragraphs from pp. 116–118. Copyright © 1984 Rachel Elliott. Used by permission of the publisher, Harlequin Enterprises II BV.

Chapter 9

P. 275 Excerpt from *Fantasy Lover,* by Sally Heywood, 1989, p. 187. Copyright © 1988 Sally Heywood. Used by permission of the publisher, Harlequin Enterprises II BV.

Chapter 10

P. 346 Excerpts from Gillian Darley's essay in *Balancing Acts: On Being a Mother,* by Katherine Gieve, pp. 124, 127–128. Reprinted by permission of PFD on behalf of Gillian Darley. Copyright © 1989 by Gillian Darley. **Pp. 346–347** Excerpts from *Balancing Acts: On Being a Mother,* by Katherine Gieve, pp. 41, 45, 51. Reprinted by permission of Katherine Gieve. **Pp. 346–347** Excerpts from Jean Radford's essay in *Balancing Acts: On Being a Mother,* by Katherine Gieve, pp. 138–139, 140, 143–144. Reprinted by permission of Jean Radford. **Pp. 346–347** Excerpts from Elizabeth Peretz, p. 159, Jennifer Uglow, p. 114, Hillary Land, p. 77, Victoria Hardie, pp. 53–54 in *Balancing Acts: On Being a Mother,* by Katherine Gieve.

Chapter 13

P. 436 DSM-IV-TR Definition of Mental Disorder. Reprinted with permission from the *Diagnostic and Statistical Manual of Mental Disorders.* Copyright 2000, American Psychiatric Association.

Name Index

Subject Index